CONFLICT AND TRANSFORMATION

In this important compendium, one of the leading scholars of EU law and its legal framework, reflects on his previous writings in the context of current challenges the European project is facing. More than a simple restatement, it offers an important theoretical comment at this defining time for EU law. The author offers a welcome counterbalance to what some perceive to be a surfeit of optimism when assessing the EU and its development. In so doing, Professor Joerges identifies three flaws in the current European ideology. Firstly, he points to the intellectual weakness of the 'integration through law' ideology. Secondly, he sets out the systematic neglect of 'the economic' and its political dynamics. Finally, he addresses the complacency with respect to Europe's darker legacies. This is an important critical (and candid) assessment of Europe at its half century.

International Studies in the Theory of Private Law: Volume 15

International Studies in the Theory of Private Law

This series of books, edited by a distinguished international team of legal scholars, aims to investigate the normative and theoretical foundations of the law governing relations between citizens. The context for such investigations of private law systems is set by important modern tendencies in systems of governance. The advent of the regulatory state marks the withdrawal of the state from direct control and management of social and economic activity, and the adoption instead of procedural regulation and co-regulatory strategies that promote the use of private law techniques of ordering and self-regulation in social and economic interactions between citizens. The tendency known as globalisation and the corresponding increases in cross-border trade produce the responses of transnational regulation of commerce and private governance regimes, and these new systems of governance challenge the hegemony of traditional national private law systems. Furthermore, these tendencies towards transnational governance regimes compel an interaction between different national legal traditions, with their differences in culture and philosophy as well as their differences based upon variations in market systems, which provokes questions not only about competing policy frameworks but also about the nature and adequacy of different kinds of legal reasoning.

The series encompasses a diverse range of theoretical approaches in the examination of these issues including approaches using socio-legal methods, economics, critical theory, systems theory, regulation theory, and moral and political theory. With the aim of stimulating an international discussion of these issues, volumes will be published in Germany, France, and the United Kingdom in one of the three languages.

Volumes published with Hart Publishing, Oxford

1. David Campbell, Hugh Collins und John Wightman (eds), *Implicit Dimensions of Contract: Discrete, Relational and Network Contracts* (2003)
2. Christian Joerges, Inger-Johanne Sand and Gunther Teubner (eds), *Transnational Governance and Constitutionalism* (2004)
3. Oren Perez, *Ecological Sensitivity and Global Legal Pluralism: Rethinking the Trade and Environment Debate* (2004)
4. Harm Schepel, *The Constitution of Private Governance* (2004)
5. Nili Cohen and Ewan McKendrick, *Comparative Remedies for Breach of Contract* (2005)

6. Marc Amstutz and Gunther Teubner (eds), *Networks: Legal Issues of Multilateral Co-operation* (2010)
7. Gunther Teubner (edited and with an Introduction by Hugh Collins), *Networks as Connected Contracts* (2010)
8. Christian Joerges and Josef Falke (eds), *Karl Polanyi, Globalisation and the Potential of Law in Transnational Markets* (2011)
9. Poul F Kjaer, Gunther Teubner and Alberto Febbrajo (eds), *The Financial Crisis in Constitutional Perspective: The Dark Side of Functional Differentiation* (2011)
10. Jean Braucher, John Kidwell and William C Whitford (eds), *Revisiting the Contracts Scholarship of Stewart Macaulay: On the Empirical and the Lyrical* (2013)
11. Thomas Dietz, *Global Order Beyond Law: How Information and Communication Technologies Facilitate Relational Contracting in International Trade* (2014)
12. Anna Beckers, *Enforcing Corporate Social Responsibility Codes: On Global Self-Regulation and National Private Law* (2015)
13. Nahel Asfour, *Wrongful Enrichment: A Study in Comparative Law and Culture* (2017)
14. Pablo Marcello Baquero, *Networks of Collaborative Contracts for Innovation* (2020)
15. Christian Joerges, *Conflict and Transformation: Essays on European Law and Policy* (2022)

Volumes published in German by Nomos Verlagsgesellschaft, Baden-Baden

1. Peer Zumbansen, *Ordnungsmuster im modern Wohlfahrtsstaat: Lernerfahrungen zwischen Staat, Geseelschaft und Vertrag* (2000)
2. Dan Wielsch, *Freiheit und Funktion: Zur Struktur- und Theoriegeschichte des Rechts der Wirtschaftsgesellschaft* (2001)
3. Marc Amstutz, *Evolutorisches Wirtschaftsrecht: Vorstudien zum Recht und seiner Methode in den Diskurskollisionen der Marktgesellschaft* (2001)
4. Christian Joerges and Gunther Teubner, Gunther (eds), *Rechtsverfassungsrecht: Recht-Fertigungen zwischen Sozialtheorie und Privatrechtsdogmatik* (2003)
5. Gunther Teubner, *Netzwerk als Vertragsverbund: Virtuelle Unternehmen, Franchising, Just in Time in sozialwissenschaftlicher und juristischer Sicht* (2004)
6. Daniel Dédeyan, *Macht durch Zeichen: Rechtsprobleme der Kennzeichnung und Zertifikation* (2004)
7. Dietrich Claus Becker, *Von Namen und Nummern: Kollisionen unverträglicher Rechtsmassen im Interent* (2005)
8. Vagias Karavas, *Digitale Grundrechte: Elemente einer Verfassung des Informationsflusses im Intenet* (2007)
9. Peter Korth, *Dritthaftung von Ratingagenturen* (2009)

10. Cordula Heldt, *Baukooperation und Franchising als multilaterale Sonderverbindung. Vertragsnetzwerke – Parallelschuldverhältnisse – Personengesellschaften* (2010)
11. Jan Lüsing, *Die Pflichten aus culpa in contrahendo und positiver Vertragsverletzung* (§ 241 II BGB): *Über den hybriden Charakter der Schutzpflichten und zur Selbstbindung ohne Vertrag* (2010)
12. Moritz Renner, *Zwingendes transnationales Recht: Elemente einer Wirtschaftsverfassung jenseits des Staates* (2011)
13. Christoph Lüscher, *Zur Konzeptualisierung von Verbrauchervertragsrecht unter besonderer Berücksichtigung des schweizerischen und europäischen Verbrauchervertragsrechts. Eine Untersuchung im Schnittfeld von Vertragsrecht, Systemtheorie und Ökonomie* (2011)
14. Daniel Klösel, *Compliance-Richtlinien. Zum Funktionswandel des Zivilrechts im Gewährleistungsstaat* (2012)
15. Chunyi Qi, *Rechtstransfer in Chinas Produktionsregime? Zur Kontrolle der Allgemeinen Geschäftsbedingungen im deutschen und chinesischen Recht* (2013)

Conflict and Transformation

Essays on European Law and Policy

Christian Joerges

• HART •
OXFORD • LONDON • NEW YORK • NEW DELHI • SYDNEY

HART PUBLISHING
Bloomsbury Publishing Plc
Kemp House, Chawley Park, Cumnor Hill, Oxford, OX2 9PH, UK
1385 Broadway, New York, NY 10018, USA
29 Earlsfort Terrace, Dublin 2, Ireland

HART PUBLISHING, the Hart/Stag logo, BLOOMSBURY and the Diana logo are trademarks of Bloomsbury Publishing Plc

First published in Great Britain 2022

A catalogue record for this book is available from the British Library.

Library of Congress Cataloging-in-Publication data

Names: Joerges, Christian, author.

Title: Conflict and transformation : essays on European law and policy / Christian Joerges.

Description: Oxford ; New York : Hart, 2022. |
Series: International studies in the theory of private law ; volume 15 |
Includes bibliographical references and index.

Identifiers: LCCN 2022022131 (print) | LCCN 2022022132 (ebook) |
ISBN 9781509926954 (hardback) | ISBN 9781509960019 (paperback) |
ISBN 9781509926978 (pdf) | ISBN 9781509926961 (Epub)

Subjects: LCSH: Law—Germany. | Law–European Union countries.

Classification: LCC KK143 .J64 2022 (print) | LCC KK143 (ebook) |
DDC 349.43—dc23/eng/20220630

LC record available at https://lccn.loc.gov/2022022131

LC ebook record available at https://lccn.loc.gov/2022022132

ISBN: HB: 978-1-50992-695-4
ePDF: 978-1-50992-697-8
ePub: 978-1-50992-696-1

Typeset by Compuscript Ltd, Shannon

Preface

WE ARE NOT masters of the theories to which we find ourselves in thrall and to which we commit ourselves. Anyone reading this volume who has spent time enough in the *Bundesrepublik* (Federal Republic of Germany) will recognise the happenings that accompanied and influenced the works gathered here. With the benefit of hindsight, I understand the importance of the dates: 1962 marked the start of my legal studies in Frankfurt am Main; only one year later, and just a couple of kilometres distant from the University, the Auschwitz trial began and was to change German post-war identity, though in ways that were not at first apparent. For the year 1966, right after my first state exam, I found myself at Georgetown University Law School in Washington, DC; there I saw my American co-students intensifying their protests against the Vietnam War. Upon my return to Frankfurt in the autumn of 1967, I found myself confronted with a student body that was busy making Frankfurt the vanguard of the student protest movement. The Frankfurt Law Faculty became a core forum in debates on the relationship between law and the social sciences, as well as on the best way to reform the legal education system. In 1970 I completed my doctorate, writing on the so-called 'American Conflicts Revolution'. In 1974, I was appointed Professor for 'the Law of the International Economy and Labour Relations' at the University of Bremen. In 1982, the Centre for European Legal Policy was established. Subsequently. I was a visiting (1987–92) and then a full-time (1997–2007) Professor at the European University Institute in Florence, returning then to Bremen. During the years 2013–18, I was also Senior Professor for Law and Society at the Hertie School for Governance, Berlin.

Each station along the way of my career was specific to my generation, and as such an unearned opportunity; but to take advantage was likewise to be burdened by the legacies of German history and its jurisprudence. My path was nevertheless eased by colleagues at home and abroad, by academic assistants and support staff, by numerous inspiring students and PhD researchers. There are simply too many to mention. Here I must make an exception for one, Rudolf Wiethölter.[1] His arrival at the Frankfurt law faculty marked an awakening; he inspired and supported my work during and far beyond my studies and doctorate.

Christian Joerges
Bremen
March 2022

[1] See the portrait by D Simon, '... ein gewisser Wiethölter: Fünf akademische Bilderbogen zum Selbstbemalen', (1989) 22 *Kritische Justiz* 131, available at www.jstor.org/stable/23998211.

Contents

Preface vii

Introduction: Agenda and Structure of the Volume 1

PART I
LEGAL AND POLITICAL SCIENCE

1. *Introduction: The Contest of Disciplines in the Study of European Integration* 11
2. *Taking the Law Seriously: On Political Science and the Role of Law in the Process of European Integration* 13
3. *'Where the Law Runs Out': The Overburdening of Law and Constitutional Adjudication by the Financial Crisis and Europe's New Modes of Economic Governance* 34
4. *Conclusion – Part I* 46

PART II
INTEGRATION AND PRIVATE LAW

5. *Introduction: Tensions and Affinities Between Private Law and European Market Integration* 49
6. *The Science of Private Law and the Nation State* 52
7. *The Impact of European Integration on Private Law: Reductionist Perceptions, True Conflicts and a New Constitutional Perspective* 65
8. *Private Law in Europe's Political Economy after the Financial Crisis* 100
9. *Conclusion – Part II* 123

PART III
SOCIAL REGULATION AND THE TURN TO GOVERNANCE

10. *Introduction: The Integration Project in the Risk Society* 129

11. *Scientific Expertise in Social Regulation and the European Court of Justice: Legal Frameworks for De-nationalised Governance Structures* 132

12. *From Intergovernmental Bargaining to Deliberative Political Processes: The Constitutionalisation of Comitology* 161

13. *Integration through De-legalisation?* 193

14. *Conclusion – Part III* 217

PART IV
THE EUROPEAN SOCIAL MODEL: A NEW TYPE OF 'SOCIAL MARKET ECONOMY'

15. *Introduction: Problems with 'Social Europe'* 221

16. *Informal Politics, Formalised Law and the 'Social Deficit' of European Integration: Reflections after the Judgments of the ECJ in* Viking and Laval 225

17. *Will the Welfare State Survive European Integration? On the Exhaustion of the Legal Conceptualisations of the Integration Project from the Foundational Period and the Search for a New Paradigm* 247

18. *How is a Closer Union Conceivable under Conditions of Ever More Socio-Economic and Political Diversity? Constitutionalising Europe's* Unitas in Pluralitate 266

19. *Conclusion – Part IV* 280

PART V
THE CONTEST ON THE ECONOMIC CONSTITUTION

20. *Introduction: 'The Economic' in European Legal Scholarship* 285

21. *The Market without the State? The 'Economic Constitution' of the European Community and the Rebirth of Regulatory Politics* 287

22. *What is Left of the European Economic Constitution? A Melancholic Eulogy* 322

23. *Europe's Economic Constitution in Crisis and the Emergence of a New Constitutional Constellation* 354

24. *Conclusion – Part V* 394

PART VI
CONFLICTS LAW AS EUROPE'S CONSTITUTIONAL FORM

25. *Introduction: Semantics and Concepts* 399

26. *United in Diversity as Europe's Vocation and Conflicts Law as Europe's Constitutional Form* 401

27. *The Idea of a Three-Dimensional Conflicts Law as Constitutional Form* 446

28. *A Conflicts-Law Response to the Precarious Legitimacy of Transnational Trade Governance* 487

29. *Conclusion – Part VI* 515

PART VII
VERGANGENHEITSCHULD (GUILT ABOUT THE PAST) AND THE DUTY TO REMEMBER

30. *'Darker Legacies of Law in Europe' – Problems with a Research Project* 521

31. *Continuities and Discontinuities in German Legal Thought* 523

32. *Europe a* Großraum*? Shifting Legal Conceptualisations of the Integration Project* 534

33. *Working through 'Bitter Experiences' towards a Purified European Identity? A Critique of the Disregard for History in European Constitutional Theory and Practice* 559

34. *Conclusion – Part VII* 581

Epilogue: Europe's Crisis and Vocation 583
Index 591

*Introduction**
Agenda and Structure of the Volume

I.

THIS VOLUME CONTAINS essays on the European project written over a period of three decades. The volume is systematically organised and also addresses contemporary challenges. It seeks to reconceptualise the premises and structures that mould European law, that is, the underlying political and socio-economic modelling that has shaped the integration project and its law. This reconstructive endeavour is initially a backward-looking one: what are the visions and contentions that determined how the project was equipped and how it developed in practice? The many discrepancies between vision and realisation cannot be ignored. The historical conclusions drawn here inform a current challenge of future design: What are the potential (re) forms that might lead us out of contemporary crises? Systematic purpose and contemporary challenge are closely connected with one another. No new EU future is conceivable without a proper reckoning and revision of the premises and doctrines that have made themselves felt in the course of the integration process.

As the Preface to this volume makes clear, my efforts are rooted in my biography. Personal experience has formed my interest in the integration project, and explains my hopes and disappointments. This is necessarily specific to my generation and cannot claim any general application. However, the essays in this volume are, I hope, also far more than a collection of personal hobbies and orientations.

Frankfurt aM

This is true first, and above all, for the themes tackled in Part VII of this book, entitled '*Vergangenheitsschuld* (Guilt about the Past) and the Duty to Remember'. This issue has recently gained a frightening, contemporary/ new significance. Our socio-political regression is unexpectedly severe, yet is

* Translated by Michelle Everson, Birkbeck College, University of London.

not really surprising. Anyone beginning their legal studies in Frankfurt aM in 1962 had grown up in a physical environment dominated by ruins. But they/we had all had also lived through an economic miracle (the *Wirtschaftswunder*) and knew that success in study would equal lifelong employment in a secure civil service position. At the same time, we beginners were quick to learn that Hermann Hesse had been overly optimistic: not every beginning is blessed by wonder and magic. Nevertheless, the boring nature of our university life and the regained normality of the political life of the Bonn Republic were confronted just one year after the beginning of our studies with the Auschwitz trial. The Law Faculty mostly ignored events in the Gallus quarter of town. But the trial touched us students just as it changed the identity of the Bonn Republic. My generation, a generation who could not trust their fathers, lent this change a loud and imposing voice half a decade later. The trial in Frankfurt left its indelible traces in German history. It prompted overdue confrontation with the sins of the past, which led in its turn to a collapse of trust in the doctrines and traditions that had shaped German law and the education of its jurists. On my graduation in 1966, I was fortunate to receive a grant to study at Georgetown Law School in Washington, DC. In Frankfurt, the student movement was slowly gaining in momentum. In Washington, by related token, political life was determined by the course of the Vietnam War. A goodly proportion of my fellow students/colleagues enthusiastically engaged with the issue. Around a third of Georgetown students were also Jewish, and reacted to the election of Hans-Georg Kiesinger as Chancellor of the Federal Republic on 1 December 1966 with a mixture of incomprehension and fury. To each cause a reaction: my discomfort with the legal culture of my homeland grew. In my studies I learned much about common law traditions and the relationship between law and politics. The historical context was rich, but the theory was not demanding. Return to Frankfurt in the Autumn of 1967, however, brought further disjunction and challenge. The University was in uproar, but this was not identical with the political-moral protest being driven forward by my American classmates. Even at the highpoints of the student protests, Frankfurt retained a very specific character. Passions were not only expressed in student revolt, but also spilled over into theoretical conflicts. In the eye of the storm of all philosophical and social-political debates stood Jürgen Habermas. My mentor, Rudolf Wiethölter, stood alongside him, developing his 'political' legal theory and playing a major part in the construction of the most interesting Legal Faculty in the *Bundesrepublik*. I have been in thrall to these two themes ever since: on the one hand, critical confrontation with German legal tradition; on the other, the theoretical construction of law.[1]

[1] Dealt with in each essay, but most pertinently in chs 2, 31 and 32 of this volume.

Frankfurt–Bremen–Europe

Democratisation of state and society via legal reform, legal reform by means of educational reform, and an educational reform which seeks to find as wide as possible an audience for a theoretically enlightened legal reform by building bridges between theory and practice – any person committed to such ideas had to seek their academic luck and career in those universities that were struggling to develop a 'one-phase' approach to full legal qualification (integration of academic and practice elements). The most committed law faculty within this movement was at Bremen University, one amongst several reasons why it became known as a 'leftwing cadre-training-school'. Research across all the disciplines and factions of the Faculty resolutely pursued socio-political reform opportunities. However, there were so very few common points of reference with established academic thinking and dominant practice in legal education that, following many a gruelling debate, the critics of one-phase legal education were able to bring the experiment to an early end and to ensure a return to their normality. Bremen nevertheless remained true to its critical mission.

A further avenue opened up for me by virtue of the founding of the 'Centre for European Legal Politics' by the Bremen Senate, loyal to its (European) Hansa traditions, in the year 1982.[2] The Institute was named in accordance with a positive, normative programme: in German, 'legal policy' (*Rechtspolitik*) is an oxymoron, as well as an immediate provocation: even in its early phase, Europe was crystal clear that the integration project was to be understood to be a 'legal project.'[3] The mission to characterise this Community as a beacon for societal reform appeared futile at best. And indeed, it would be very easy to view the re-founding of the old reform project not simply as conceptually inherent, but also as hopelessly utopian. Nevertheless this project made sense even in 1982. Socially democratic by tradition and conviction, the small city state was early to recognise the simple fact that socio-political reforms could no longer be pursued at national state level. Even though prior to and post-1982 so-called negative integration impacts were dominant and the positive reform potential of the European Economic Community remained marginal,[4] all hope now resided in Europe. For all of its problems, a feature of the integration project had already

[2] Zentrum Für Europäische Rechtspolitik – Konzepte, Projekte, Personen, ZERP Diskussionspapier 1/1982, Bremen 1982 und Eröffnungsveranstaltung des ZERP am 21./22. April 1983 – Reden und Beiträge –, ZERP-DP 7/83,with commentaries by von Claus-Dieter Ehlermann, Norbert Reich, Ernst Steindorff.

[3] W Hallstein, *Der unvollendete Bundesstaat* (Düsseldorf, Wien: Econ, 1969) 38: Die EWG 'ist in dreifacher Hinsicht ein Phänomen des Rechts: Sie ist Schöpfung des Rechts, sie ist Rechtsquelle und sie ist Rechtsordnung.' ['The EEC is three times a legal phenomenon: it is a creator of law, a source of law and a legal order.'].

[4] Perceptive: J Pinder, 'Positive Integration and Negative Integration: Some Problems of Economic Union in the EEC' (1968) 24 *The World Today* 88.

become apparent: European initiatives were often modern and innovative.[5] The EEC did not want to and could not limit its self-presentation to one of an exclusively economically liberal undertaking. The early work of the Centre was dedicated to seizing upon European impetuses and taking them further.[6]

Bremen–Florence–Berlin

The foundation of the Centre in Bremen, and the hopes bound up with it, was meant to reflect Europe's rejection of its bellicose past following the end of the Second World War; it also reflected the commercial tradition and openness of the *Hansestadt*. The courage and confidence with which the famous founding fathers – Monnet, Schumann, Spaak, de Gaspari, Adenauer – set about the integration task deserve every respect and a far deeper degree of recognition than is typically granted to them in commemorative speeches. Jurists who share in this worldview cannot avoid the task of clarifying their visions of the functions of law, the challenges faced by judicial and administrative institutions, and even the legitimacy of supranational European law and governance. This task should be a highly demanding one. All efforts to codify in law the process of overcoming the dubious legacy of the national state are also necessarily confronted with the question of how to preserve the achievements of democratic constitutional states. Contributions from the early years of the integration process clearly articulated this tension.[7] The young European law discipline dedicated much

[5] V Gessner and A Höland, 'Konsultation und Anstiftung vor Ort – ein neuer Typus von Gemeinschaftspolitik' in Ch Joerges and K Sieveking (eds), *Europäische Integration, Nationalstaat und regionale Politikkompetenzen, ZERP-Diskussionspapier 2/87*, Bremen 1987.

[6] For example: N Reich, *Förderung und Schutz diffuser Interessen* (Baden-Baden: Nomos, 1987) (vol 1 of the ZERP-Schriftenreihe); C Joerges, J Falke, H-W Micklitz and G Brüggemeier, *Die Sicherheit von Konsumgütern und die Entwicklung der Europäischen Gemeinschaft* (Baden-Baden: Nomos, 1988) (vol 2 of the ZERP-Schriftenreihe); English translation published in the EUI Series of Law Working Papers, available at http://hdl.handle.net/1814/73; electronic reprint in (2010) 6(2) *Hanse Law Review*, available at http://hanselawreview.eu/vol-6-no-2-dezember-2010/); K Sieveking, *Erstattung von Rentenversicherungsbeiträgen an Ausländer* (Baden-Baden: Nomos, 1988) (vol 3 of the ZERP Schriftenreihe); N Reich, *Die Europäisierung des Arzneimittelmarktes – Chancen und Risiken* (Baden-Baden: Nomos, 1988) (vol 4 of the ZERP-Schriftenreihe). This represented the socio-political heritage of the Frankfurt/Bremen years. In addition, Bremen sought to advance upon the socio-methodological discussion. This followed on after a first 'Workshop zu Konzepten des postinterventionistischen Rechts' in 1984 (proceedings edited under this title by G Brüggemeier and C Joerges as vol 4 of the *Materialien des Zentrums für Europäische Rechtspolitik* (Bremen: 1984); and one year later with the Symposium 'Critical Legal Thought: An American-German Debate' (the conference volume, edited by C Joerges and DM Trubek was published in 1988 as vol 7 of the ZERP-Schriftenreihe; 2011 saw publication of an electronic reprint (C Joerges, DM Trubek and P Zumbansen (eds), 'Critical Legal Thought: An American-German Debate – Republication (with a new Introduction) Twenty-Five Years Later' (2011) 12 *German Law Journal* 1.

[7] For example, H Bülck, 'Zur Systematik der Europäischen Wirtschaftsgemeinschaften' (1959) 6 *Berichte der Deutschen Gesellschaft für Völkerrecht* 66. Constitutional and democratic doubts are comprehensively discussed by B Davies, *Resisting the European Court of Justice: West Germany's Confrontation with European Law, 1949–1979* (Cambridge: CUP 2012).

effort to explaining attempts to overcome conflict and tension.[8] It is unsurprising, however, that these efforts faltered, being characterised by compromises that privileged the pursuit of integration above the maintenance or establishment of democratic processes of opinion formation and decision-making. Law was thus ascribed a leadership role and stabilisation functions more usually exercised by political processes and the democratically legitimated governments of consolidated democracies. And in all of this, the source of the dilemma was repeatedly obscured and ignored. European law, but also European science as a whole,[9] was characterised by its belief in the process of European integration as a self-legitimising goal, and by its evaluation of the past and current steps taken to drive it forward as a success story. This intellectual strategy was always a questionable one. In view of the all-encompassing and overwhelming crises with which Europe is now confronted, it is now a hopeless one.

My contributions, the more recent, the more clearly, react to this dilemma with the thesis that Europe must base its Constitution upon 'the law of collisions'. *Unitas in pluralitate*: unity in diversity is the colloquial formulation of this concept and was taken up in the 2004 Draft Constitutional Treaty.[10] It demands recognition for both 'economy and society'. The two are inseparable.

This demand is a second leitmotif within contributions to this volume. Certainly, integration was given its decisive impulse by the effort to build an economic community. But this should never be seen as justification for the predetermination of European politics by economic rationality criteria, or for the substitution of an economic constitution, designed along ordo-liberal lines, for democratically legitimated decision-making processes. The notion of an economic community is inherently modest and is no longer appropriate to the growth in the daily significance of the European project. The refoundation of the economic communities as a European Union within the Maastricht Treaty of 1 November 1993 was a better reflection of the European reality – albeit that Maastricht failed to give the Union any sustainable conceptual form. Orientation was instead given by a conception that integration is a naturally evolutionary process, arguing that it need only ensure its conformity with market-driven conditions in order to be successful. Such a conception is nevertheless to be countered with the argument that the economy is a political happening – the 'economy is a polity'.[11] This opposition is not new. What is new, however, is the

[8] See, references in C Joerges, 'Recht, Wirtschaft und Politik im Prozess der Konstitutionalisierung Europas' in M Jachtenfuchs and B Kohler-Koch (eds), *Europäische Integration*, 2nd edn (Opladen: Leske + Budrich 2003) 183 (reproduced in pt I, ch 2 of this volume).

[9] On the concept and the search for self-reflection, see GF Schuppert, I Pernice and U Haltern (eds), *Europawissenschaft* (Baden-Baden: Nomos, 2005).

[10] Art 8-I.

[11] Ch Joerges, B Stråth and P Wagner, *The Economy as Polity: The Political Constitution of Contemporary Capitalism* (London: UCL Press, 2005).

renaissance of the political sociologist, Karl Polayni, which gave it an intellectual backbone.

A third theme has gained frightening relevance over the past few years. But the problem is not new. It is the very success of the integration process that has led to an ever-increasing disjunction between the significance of European competences on the one hand, and the degree of legitimacy that can be ascribed to European decision-making processes on the other, with the result that the doctrinal coherence of the European legal order is a mere fiction. Law has no choice but must cope with ever more extensive legalisation of decision-making processes.[12] This is getting harder and harder to sustain. Over the last decade, the justiciability of responses to financial and sovereign debt crises has led to the development of a politics of emergency powers. Ernst-Wolfgang Böckenförde was the first to diagnose this problem.[13] All disciplines within European academic thought have a tendency to designate extra-legal European 'crisis law' as a new normality.[14] The Hertie School of Governance, my final academic home, lies bang in the middle of the *Bundesrepublik*, as well as in its politics. The intellectual battle between a European Germany and a German Europe finds its natural home here. There are only three lawyers on the Faculty of the Hertie School and (legal) students numbers are rarely better. This suited the interdisciplinary nature of my studies. At the same time, being in Berlin opened a window to many political circles and debates. This is reflected in my works on crisis within the integration project.[15]

II.

The structure of this volume reflects the unfolding of my thoughts in this introduction. The beginning is provided by my engagement with political and legal analyses of the role of law in the integration process (Part I of this book).

[12] See for more details, pt IV, ch 17 and pt V, ch 23 of this volume. On the integration project in general, M Everson and Ch Joerges, 'Reconfiguring the Politics–Law Relationship in the Integration Project through Conflicts–Law Constitutionalism' (2012) 18 *ELJ* 644.

[13] 'Does necessity abide by no laws? The design failures of the EU and the indispensability of a new political decision' *Neue Züricher Zeitung*, 21 June 2010; reprinted in idem, *Wissenschaft, Politik, Verfassungsgericht* (Frankfurt aM: Suhrkamp, 2010) 299 (300).

[14] B de Witte, 'Euro Crisis Responses and the EU Legal Order' (2015) 11 *European Constitutional Law Review* 434; Th Beukers, B de Witte and C Kilpatrick (eds), *Constitutional Change through Euro-Crisis Law* (Cambridge: CUP 2017) viii–ix; Ph Genschel and M Jachtenfuchs, 'Alles ganz normal! Eine institutionelle Analyse der Euro-Krise' (2013) 20 *Zeitschrift für Internationale Beziehungen* 5; for critique of these positions, see pt V, chs 23 and 24 of this volume.

[15] See pt I, ch 3 and pt V ch 23 in this volume and, eg, C Joerges, 'Integration through law and the crisis of law in Europe's emergency', in D Chalmers, M Jachtenfuchs and C Joerges (eds), *The End of the Eurocrats' Dream. Adjusting to European Diversity* (Cambridge: CUP, 2016) 199; C Joerges, 'Three Transformations of Europe and the Search for a Way Out of its Crisis', in C Joerges and C Glinski (eds), *The European Crisis and the Transformation of Transnational Governance. Authoritarian Managerialism versus Democratic Governance*, (Oxford: Hart Publishing, 2014) 25.

This engagement concerns the 'facticity of normativity', and contains its own critique of the tendency of contemporary political science to restrict itself to analytical pronouncements and causal explanations.

Around about the millennium, the question of the Europeanisation of private law became an important topic of European academic study, both in Germany and the Netherlands (Part II of this book). If this material is tackled first, it is done so in order to underline the parallels between a narrowly focused politics of market integration and the core institutions of 'classical' private law. The primary aim is one of demonstrating that the institution of private law is only misunderstood or overburdened by the suggestion that it might act as blueprint for the integration process. The debate about private law is so much more interesting the more legal science harmonisation efforts are rebutted with the argument that they ride roughshod both over the 'social embeddedness' of private legal institutions and developments[16] and over the expectations of a private law professor.

The integration project failed to meet expectations that Europe post-1989 would experience 'a return of bourgeois society and its law'.[17] Institutional frameworks (regulation) are a necessary condition for the functioning of modern markets, and particularly so for their transnational integration. A major focus for market integration politics has been the modernisation of foodstuffs regulation, as well as the establishment or deepening of labour, consumer and environmental protections. Giandomenico Majone applied the term 'social regulation' to these developments. The core of the integration project should be understood as the creation of a 'regulatory state'; this state, however, would have no competence or legitimacy to peruse redistributive politics.[18] 'Social regulation' is counterpoint to 'the private legal society'. It forms the object of Part III of this book.

The 'regulatory state' differs fundamentally from the social/welfare states developed in post-war Europe and from the German 'social market economy'.[19] Where Majone felt a redistributive state would be impossible to achieve in practice and should in any case be deemed a political-normative error, many others have repeatedly argued in favour of a 'European social model'. These proposals and controversies are dealt with by each of the contributions that make up Part IV. The first criticises European Court of Justice jurisprudence that ranks

[16] For an exemplary illustration of this trend, the Habilitation by ChU Schmid, *Die Instrumentalisierung des Privatrechts durch die Europäische Union* (Baden-Baden: Nomos, 2010), as well as the follow-up studies by the same author on leasehold law in Europe, eg, ChU Schmid and J Dinse, 'The European Dimension of Residential Tenancy Law' [2013] *European Review of Contract Law* 201.

[17] See the title of a study by E-J Mestmäcker in the (1991) 10 *Rechtshistorischen Journal* 177.

[18] G Majone, *Regulating Europe* (London–New York: Routledge 1996).

[19] G Majone, 'The European Community: An "Independent Fourth Branch of Government"?' in G Brüggemeier (ed), *Verfassungen für ein ziviles Europa* (Baden-Baden: Nomos, 1994) 23.

European economic freedoms above national labour law, similarly regretting such developments since they act to retard social reform perspectives in the enlargement states. The second contribution takes up this theme. It makes a distinction between domestic and intra-state justice, pursuing and enlarging upon this volume's argument in favour of a conceptualisation of the integration project within the conflicts law idiom, which takes socio-economic divergence in the EU seriously, and seeks cooperative solutions, also to social problems.

The Europeanisation of the Economic Constitution that is discussed in Part V was always a core part of ordo-liberal legal and constitutional theory, albeit that barely anyone outside Germany paid it any attention. This changed following conclusion of the Maastricht Treaty and its Economic and Monetary Union. This Union is often understood to be a realisation of ordo-liberal visions, and is likewise often criticised as an expression of hegemonic German leadership ambitions. Chapters 22 and 23 argue that the Maastricht Treaty is not in fact a product of ordo-liberal visions. At the same time, however, Economic and Monetary Union is criticised for its normative and constitutional deficits. It is a precarious (economic, social and political) constellation.

Part VI documents the development of a theory of European constitutionalism founded within conflicts law. This conception has attracted some attention within legal science. With a few notable exceptions, the notion finds little understanding or resonance amongst political scientists. This distinction, however, has little to do with the notion *per se*: the idea that Europe must learn to live with and transform its differences into a productive potential has gained ever stronger and more widespread support.[20] A core of my argument is that this potential includes support for democratic decision-making processes.

Part VII builds a bridge between the 'darker legacies' of law in Europe and contemporary populist-anti-democratic movements. As an epilogue more closely explains, they are to be understood as a reaction to the overwhelming numbers of crisis phenomena to which the European Union is now exposed. The fact that the integration project was established as a counter-movement to the failures of a European past is sadly no guarantee that its mission and practical mechanisms can overcome crisis; rather, unrest confirms the urgent need for political–social reform.

[20] Reference is made here to D Leuffen, B Rittberger and F Schimmelfennig, *Explaining Variation in the European Union* (Basingstoke: Palgrave Macmillan 2012); F Chevenal and F Schimmelfennig, 'The Case for Demoicracy in the European Union' (2013) 51 *Journal of Common Market Studies* 334.

Part I

Legal and Political Science

1

*Introduction: The Contest of Disciplines in the Study of European Integration**

THE PRESENT COLLECTION is not just a mere reprint. On the contrary, it pursues re-constructive ambitions that are concerned with the conceptual history of essential recent stages of the integration process together with methodological reflections on these developments. The time span covered ranges from the Treaty of Maastricht, which was meant to 'complement' the construction of the European internal market by the Economic and Monetary Union in 1992, to the financial crisis that has dominated Europe's political agenda since 2008, and which is still far from being overcome. Both of these events concern first and foremost 'the economic' in a specific understanding. The catchword of the 'economy as a polity', first used in a collection of essays co-edited with a historian and a political theorist in 2005,[1] is a programmatic announcement: 'the economic' must not be understood as an autonomous sphere of self-regulating markets that follows its own inherent economic logic. The economy and its markets are, instead, always 'socially embedded'. This notion draws on Karl Polanyi's economic sociology.[2] It refers hence to a conceptual background that underlines the 'social embeddedness' of law. This is why the 'law of economic integration', as it is presented in this volume, has to consider so many fields, ranging from private law to risk regulation, labour relations and, last but not least, political and new economic governance. The essays in this volume focus on 'the law of European integration' in an understanding that departs not only from the 'integration through law' paradigm, but also from the instrumentalist analyses prevailing in political science. Ever since the so-called 'formative period'[3] of the integration process, legal scholarship has sought to present, in more or less sophisticated ways, the law as 'the object and

* Translated by Michelle Everson, Birkbeck College, University of London.

[1] C Joerges, B Stråth and P Wagner (eds), *The Economy as Polity: The Political Constitution of Contemporary Capitalism* (London: UCL Press, 2005).

[2] See the brief explanation by F Block, 'Towards a New Understanding of Economic Modernity', ibid, 3.

[3] This term was coined by JHH Weiler, 'The Transformation of Europe' (1991) 100 *Yale Law Journal* 2403.

the agent' of this process.[4] Only in the 1990s did students of European law start to explore the law 'in its context'.[5] In the same decade, political scientists, especially from the United States, started to pay intense attention to the European project and became aware of the importance of law therein. This constellation generated mutual curiosity between the two disciplines. This did not, however, as the first essay pleading with us to 'take the law seriously' argues (chapter 2), lead to a constructive synthesis. Legal research remained committed to its inherited techniques, whereas political science continued to cultivate an instrumentalist understanding of law and legal ordering – and both failed to pay tribute to the '*proprium*' of law, that is, the 'facticity of the normative'.

The second essay (chapter 3) is concerned with the present state of this controversy. Its messages are gloomier than those submitted in the first essay. The confident promotion of the law as 'object and agent' of the integration project and the ordoliberal vision of a 'European Economic Constitution' that would, in democratically unconvincing terms, consummate European ambitions, is by now confronted with an overburdening of law.

The analyses submitted in both essays reflect upon the relationship between the two disciplines. They plead for interdisciplinarity – and point to failings or insufficiencies of pertinent efforts. Both disciplines – legal as well as political science – have, to a large degree, lost their standing as the guides of the integration project. Their leadership has given way to economic expertise and 'the rule of economics'.[6]

The two essays within Part I of this volume relate to three decades of the development of the integration project. Their re-constructive analyses, and substantive and methodological arguments, are unfolded gradually throughout the volume – and this also holds true for a constructive counter-vision: the idea of 'conflicts law as the constitutional form' of the European polity.

[4] R Dehousse and JHH Weiler, 'The legal dimension' in W Wallace (ed), *The Dynamics of European Integration* (London: Pinter, 1990) 242, 243.

[5] The works of F Snyder were pioneering, in particular his 'The Effectiveness of European Community Law: Institutions, Processes, Tools and Techniques' (1993) 56 *MLR* 19.

[6] D Rodrik, *Economics Rules: The Rights and Wrongs of the Dismal Science* (New York: WW Norton, 2015).

2

*Taking the Law Seriously: On Political Science and the Role of Law in the Process of European Integration**

I. LEGAL SCIENCE AND POLITICAL SCIENCE

'INTEGRATION THROUGH LAW' was the title of a transatlantic project launched in the early 1980s by Mauro Capelletti, Monica Seccombe and Joseph Weiler at the European University Institute in Florence.[1] The formings of the American federation and of the European Community were to be compared and the experiences of both systems, with their respective legal frameworks and techniques, to be evaluated. For Europe, the title was of programmatic significance, albeit allowing for different readings of its meaning.

Firstly, the formula 'Integration Through Law' may be understood functionally: a statement regarding a particular strategy of integration policy and its strength. Social scientists might regard this interpretation as provocative, in so far as it appears to demonstrate a naïve or uncompromising understanding of law. The formula does not exhibit any of the contingencies of law-making and of the effectiveness of legal systems. It rather presents law as an autonomous world governed exclusively by legal doctrines and techniques of interpretation or of the effectiveness of legal systems, which, in contrast, present law as an autonomous world governed exclusively by legal doctrines and techniques of interpretation.

A second understanding proves to be more interesting. Here the formula 'integration through law' refers to the special contribution that law has made in the construction of the European Community. In this view, the quality of Community law as a 'constitutional charter' of the participating states is different from international legal orders: different from international law, which is based upon agreements between sovereign states and/or generally recognised legal principles; different from public international law, which leaves

* Published in (1996) 2 *European Law Journal* 105; pp 106–19 omitted from this reprint.

[1] M Cappelletti, M Seccombe and JHH Weiler (eds), *Integration Through Law* (Berlin: Walter de Gruyter, 1986).

the unilateral definition and defence of public or governmental interests to each individual state jurisdiction; and different from private international law, which – at least theoretically – regularly applies foreign laws, but bases such legal implants on domestic sources and, in principle, limits them to private law. This particular role of Community law may be re-constructed, in the language of political science, as a statement about the specific density of juridification on the European level, which needs to be distinguished from the contingencies of consensual cooperation among sovereign states, on the one hand, and international organisations or regimes, on the other.

Such parallelisms between legal conceptualisations and re-constructions informed by political science lead – as far as the recognition of the particular role of law in European integration is concerned – to a number of questions that relate to a third interpretation of the 'integration through law' formula: How – and within which limits – can legal science justify the validity of a supranational European legal order? How can the development of supranational law be explained, under which conditions can compliance with the law be expected and its effectiveness be ensured? We will explore these questions more fully below. They will require concrete analyses of the dynamic developments of integration policy and European law. The theoretical argument, which they are to submit, may, at the outset, be presented in an abstract way: The validity claims of European Law cannot be justified legalistically; they depend on its 'normative quality'. A further demand follows from here: political science ought to recognise these 'normative properties' of law – its integrity and its legitimacy – as a pre-condition of the effectiveness of Community law; it needs to integrate this normative dimension of law into its theoretical re-constructions.

A. Cleavages and Linkages

Introducing 'integration through law' as a subject of equal relevance for law and for the political sciences is not self-evident and should not be seen to imply the removal of disciplinary boundaries. In fact, there are good reasons for the different treatment of law in those sciences concerned with the study of European integration. Such differences are tied up with the definition of research questions, the methodologies, and the structure of theories in each discipline.

Legal science, almost by definition, deals only with the results of the juridification of social conditions – authoritative decisions about political processes – and thus concentrates on the results of such transformation processes, on what could be simply called the 'law as such'. Operations of the legal system are then perceived as reactions to legal issues as they present themselves in concrete conflicts; the decisions to be taken are then to be found upon the basis of given texts through hermeneutic determination of meaning, the formation of principles, rules, and dogmatics.

Social scientists take a different view on the legal system. They are more interested in the law's programmatic structure and its patterns of rationality. They refuse to believe in the determined power of purely legal arguments. Their research is not concerned with the *application* of rules but with the *implementation* of programmes. They view, with some suspicion, not just the routines of legal argument, but also the 'normative property' of law in general. The normative dimensions of their analyses may be detected in the premises of a theory that we approach, whereas the actual scientific operations are usually presented as being free of normative debate.

What we present here are, of course, only simplifications. The legal approach to European integration does not end with the treatment of purely legal issues. There is continuous basic research in which normative perspectives are identified and the conditions for their implementation deliberated.[2] There have also been repeated attempts to build bridges to the social sciences,[3] as well as novel attempts towards a 'contextual' Community law, which do consider the social scientific analysis of the evolution and working of the law in their normative discourse.[4] Quite correspondingly, political science recently demonstrates an increasing interest in law as a research object. This new departure is tied to the renewal of social scientific research on European integration in general, beginning to utilise practically the entire field of International Relations Theory and Comparative Politics and linking up with basic social scientific paradigms and discourses.

Consequently, the present treatment of the role of law in the process of integration, which is addressed to both social scientists and to lawyers, has to take account of the diversity of legal approaches. At the same time, it must consider the theoretical spectrum on offer in the field of political science. A systematical analysis would thus have to re-construct competing approaches of either discipline, and would then be able to make certain structural affinities visible: between an understanding of the Community based upon classical international law,[5] and 'realist' international relations analysis viewing the Community as intergovernmental cooperation; between the legal category of the Community as an 'association of functional integration' [*Zweckverband*

[2] See C Joerges, 'Markt ohne Staat? Die Wirtschaftsverfassung der Gemeinschaft und die regulative Politik' in R Wildenmann (ed), *Staatswerdung Europas? Optionen für eine polische Union* (Baden-Baden: Nomos, 1991) 225; English translation in pt V, ch 21 of this volume.

[3] P Behrens, 'Integrationstheorie – Internationale wirtschaftliche Integration als Gegenstand politischer, ökonomischer und juristischer Forschung' (1981) 45 *Rabels Zeitschrift für ausländisches und internationales Privatrecht* 8.

[4] F Snyder (ed), *European Community Law*, 2 vols (Aldershot: Dartmouth, 1993); *idem*, 'The Effectiveness of European Community Law: Institutions, Processes, Tools and Techniques' (1993) 56 *Modern Law Review* 19.

[5] See H Bülck, 'Zur Systematik der Europäischen Wirtschaftsgemeinschaften' (1959) 3 *Berichte der Deutschen Gesellschaft für Völkerrecht* 66.

funktionelller Integration][6] and neofunctionalism and regime theories;[7] between neoliberal conceptualisations of the Community as a supranational economic 'constitutional' order [*Wirtschaftsverfassung*][8] and neoclassical economic theory,[9] as well as institutional and social choice approaches. It would have to examine the potential for integrating the insights and research findings of other disciplines at a more pragmatic level than is foreseen by each of the competing legal schools of thought. The presentation of structural affinities among legal approaches and political science theories would help to convince political scientists that they must not take legal arguments at face value, but that they should instead become aware of their theoretical foundations.

* * *

Sections I.B and II.A and II.B (pp 106–19, text accompanying notes 14–63 in the European Law Journal*) offer a detailed analysis of the Maastricht judgment of the German Constitutional Court. They are omitted here; the analysis is taken up in section III of this essay and in 'What is Left' in Part V, chapter 22, section II.*

* * *

B. The Perception of Law in Political Science: An Eclectic Sketch

What seems so obvious to lawyers is hard to fit into the paradigms of social sciences. Lawyers are trained to produce normative arguments; they act under the assumption that these arguments matter. Social scientists seek to explain what really happens; they search for objectivity in their explanations. The schisms resulting from these differences are to be taken seriously. But they can become counterproductive. I shall not try to defend and substantiate this contention by engaging in the debates between intergovernmentalism, neo-functionalism and new institutionalism. The following observations will rather be confined to analyses explicitly addressing the legal system, and will only be concerned with their perception of legal discourses.

[6] HP Ipsen, *Europäisches Gemeinschaftsrecht* (Tübingen: JCB Mohr, 1972) 176.

[7] Th Gehring, 'Der Beitrag von Institutionen zur Europäischen Gemeinschaft' in G Brüggemeier (ed), *Verfassungen für ein ziviles Europa* (Baden-Baden: Nomos, 1994) 73.

[8] See P Behrens, 'Die Wirtschaftsverfassung der Europäischen Gemeinschaft' in G Brüggemeier (ed), *Verfassungen für ein ziviles Europa* (Baden-Baden: Nomos, 1994) 73; E-J Mestmäcker, 'On the Legitimacy of European Law' (1994) 58 *Rabels Zeitschrift für ausländisches und internationales Privatrecht* 615; E-U Petersmann, 'Grundprobleme der Wirtschaftsverfassung der EG' (1994) 48 *Außenwirtschaft* 389.

[9] See ME Streit and W Mussler, 'The Economic Constitution of the European Community – From "Rome" to "Maastricht"' (1995) 1 *European Law Journal* 5.

1. *Implementation of European Law*

Social scientists interested in legal programmes and specifically legal configurations specialise as a matter of course in the effects of the law. Namely, this is the field of implementation analysis, which has found an inexhaustible research terrain in the European legal system. Implementation studies usually result in a de-mystification of the law. Unlike lawyers, implementation analysts cannot be satisfied with the mere 'application' of legal rules. By contrast, it is shown that the political intent of legal rules is always accomplished in an imperfect way, that even within the legal system unpredictable factors influence and disturb the execution of programmes and that all this is related to imperfections, compromise formulas or unresolved problems of the legislative programme. The legal system itself can learn from all this how to improve its own instruments. In so far as this does not suffice, new demands for additional solutions need to be directed to the political system.

Pioneering work on the implementation of European law has followed the pattern of national implementation research and then turned to the particularities of the institutions of the EC: the dependency of European law on its implementation by the Member States, the weakness of European administrative competences and the scarcity of the Commission's resources, the limits of the controlling power of the European Court of Justice and its dependency on Member State courts. All of these observations point to the most significant characteristic of the European implementation process: the fact that the transposition of political-legal programmes is not sanctioned by a supranational authority. It is for this reason that what deserves attention is not so much non-implementation but rather the effectiveness of European law and the choice of law as an instrument of integration. This observation is hardly contested. It has led lawyers to understand why the Commission gives high priority to the implementation of Community law but is then satisfied with a purely formal transposition of directives, and why the Court of Justice is meticulously concerned to maintain its strictly legal line of reasoning. By the same token, political scientists can hardly avoid considering the impact of these institutional structures. Assuming that the European actors themselves are quite aware of the fragility of their institutional framework: Should one only look for strategic manoeuvres, or can these actors be expected to develop an interest in the integrity of the law on the acceptance of which they depend? Would it not simply be reasonable for the European Court of Justice to try to 'convince' its interlocutors in the Member States of the appropriateness and impartiality of its judgments?

2. *Neo-Functionalist Explanations*

Neo-functionalism once entertained close ties with legal integration theories, most notably with Hans Peter Ipsen's 'special purpose' (*Zweckverband*) concept of Community institutions.[10] These links have recently been renewed and refined by Burley and Mattli in their analysis of the role of the Court. Lawyers must feel uncomfortable with their messages: the integrative force of the law is not attributable to itself but to the circumstance that the institutional framework of the EC enhanced the development of a network of supranational and national actors whose interests in the European legal structures can be explained by pure utilitarianism. The self-reflective, 'unpolitical' reasoning of supranationalism is said to have united the courts, lawyers and practitioners specialising in European law in a neo-functionalist interest group *par excellence*. 'From this perspective, law functions both as a mask and as a shield. It hides and protects the promotion of one particular set of objectives against contending objectives in the purely political sphere.'[11] This explanation suggests even strategic consequences: the legal community may feel encouraged to stick to a strictly legal type of reasoning in order to maintain and extend its influence.

Why then did the *BVerfG* retract from the community of Community lawyers? Was Germany's Constitutional Court concerned with its own institutional power? Even if it was, how does the presentation of arguments and their critique fit into the 'mask and shield' metaphor? The explanatory dilemma of neo-functionalism apparently results from the fact that a utilitarian approach fails to understand the transformation of interest configurations into institutional and normative substance. It undervalues the legal system's normative obstinacy. This objection does not mean that social scientists would have to engage in a *lege artis* type of intra-legal discourse, but it does mean that their own explanations of the process of institution-building and rule-formation must be conceptualised in such a way that normative discourse maintains significance.

3. *Rationality Choice*

Theories of this kind are on offer. They range from institutional economics and public choice models,[12] regime theory and game theory,[13] to the aggregation of the conditions and perspectives of integration in political science and state-theoretical models[14] and in the guideposts of European policy.[15] In the context of

[10] See HP Ipsen, *Europäisches Gemeinschaftsrecht* (Tübingen: JCB Mohr, 1972) 176 ff and the comments in Behrens, n 3 above, 8.

[11] Ipsen, n 10 above, 72.

[12] R Vaubel and TD Willett (eds), *The Political Economy of International Organisations: A Public Choice Approach* (Boulder, CO: Westview Press, 1991); E-U Petersmann, 'Constitutionalism, Constitutional Law and European Integration' (1991) *Außenwirtschaft* 247.

[13] B Kohler-Koch, 'Zur Empirie und Theorie internationaler Regime' in B Kohler-Koch (ed), *Regime in den internationalen Politik*' (Baden-Baden: Nomos, 1989) 17; O Keck, 'Der neue Institutionalismus in der Theorie der Internationalen Politik' (1991) 32 *Politische Vierteljahresschrift* 635.

[14] P Schmitter, 'Representation and the Future Euro-Polity' (1992) 3 *Staatswissenschaften und Staatspraxis* 398.

[15] H Schneider, Rückblick für die Zukunft. Kozeptionelle Weichenstellungen für die europäische Einigung (Bonn: Europa Union Verlag, 1986).

his theoretical work on international relations, Michael Zürn[16] has elaborated a point of relevance for the linkage of legal and social sciences: if it is necessary, within the framework of an explanatory theory, to abstract from 'real' actional circumstances and the true motivations of actors, the theory must equally avoid systematic reductionism. At least on the part of the law, the transposition of an intra-theoretically sound re-construction of social action into politico-strategic recommendations may be refuted as 'social scientific imperialism'.

This objection may be illustrated using the example of Geoffrey Garret's explanation of the EC's institutional system combining a rational choice approach with game theory: Garret attributes the success of the Court's jurisprudence to the fact that it has its counterpart in the rationally reconstructible interests of the most important actors. The neo-functionalist critique contends that this explanation does not account for national governments' opposition to the EC's constitutionalisation.[17] Garret's approach, however, seems better equipped to cope with the emergence of European institutions, including the delegation of decision-making competences to the European Court of Justice, just because it reckons with uncertainties about interest-configurations and the inevitability of normative commitments.[18] And yet, it must be added that the normative meaning of the constitutionalisation of Europe points beyond interest configurations and the realisation of the Internal Market. For the Member States, the Community 'regime' generally has the effect of limiting their sovereign rights, binding the realisation of their interests to generally valid and directly binding principles of law and exposing their actions to a control of their compatibility with these general principles. At its core the supranationality of European law means nothing less than the stabilisation of normatively sensible principles with the aid of positively valid law. All of these provisos reiterate contentions already made. They presuppose that ideas and deliberation are even more important than Garret is ready to concede. Moreover, they suggest that it is the specific function of Law to further and to structure such deliberative processes. The first contention could be backed by constructivist approaches to the study of international relations and comparative politics.[19] The second

[16] M Zürn, Interessen und Institutionen in der internationalen Politik (Opaden: Westdeutscher Verlag, 1992) 26.

[17] A-M Burley and W Mattli, 'Europe before the Court: A Political Theory of Legal Integration' (1993) 47 *International Organisation* 51.

[18] G Garrett, 'International Cooperation and Institutional Choice: The European Community's Internal Market' (1992) 46 *International Organisation* 533; see also G Garret and BR Weingast, 'Ideas, Interests and Institutions: Constructing the ECS Internal Market' in J Goldskin and RO Keohane (eds), *Ideas and Foreign Policy. Beliefs, Institutions and Political Change* (Ithaca, NY: Cornell University Press, 1993) 173.

[19] See eg A Hurrel, 'International Society and the Study of Regimes. A Reflective Approach' in V Rittberger and P Mayer (eds), *Regime Theory and International Relations* (Oxford: Clarendon, 1993) 49; T Schaber, *Die internationale Verrechtlichung der Menschenrechte. Eine reflexive instiiutionentheoretische Analyse des UN-Menschenrechtsregimes* (PhD Thesis, Mannheim 1994) 81 et

is more difficult to sustain. To be sure, social scientists as well as lawyers know that foregoing hierarchical structures does not exclude the generation of normative institutions.[20] And yet, even if policy-making in the European system could be most adequately portrayed as a dynamic and evolutionary process in which consensus-building through argumentation plays a prominent role, it remains far from clear whether the legal system can really claim to structure these processes. The critical testing-ground for such queries is now to be examined.

III. THE EUROPEANISATION OF ECONOMIC LAW

The 1957 EEC Treaty initiated the process of European integration by opening up the borders. In this context, the project of economic integration and the realisation of a 'Common Market' certainly constituted a political programme. Yet its repercussions on the domestic conditions and the political sovereignty of the European nation-states remained undefined. Meanwhile the ambivalent results of the erosion of economic management potential of nation-states are becoming politically apparent and occupy a central space in the political science and legal discussion about the European Constitution. This, if nothing else, requires an analysis of the role of law in the process of European integration, to look at the significance, in particular, of economic law. Yet again, thematical limitations and a structuring of the argument are necessary at the outset. Firstly, the following initial discussion of the *BVerfG*'s statements on the constitutional value of economic integration should complete the critique of the judgment [section III.A]. This section will also serve to provide an alternative introduction to the search for a common starting-point to the political science analysis of European regulatory policy-making and legal analysis of the Europeanisation of economic law [sections III.B and III.C].

A. Constitutional States without Markets?

In the constitutional critique of the Maastricht Treaty, it was repeatedly asserted that the [German] Federal Republic would lose its quality as a state and become part of a European federation. This thesis was based not only on the loss of national monetary sovereignty, but also on the transfer of further regulatory

seq; H Müller, 'Internationale Beziehungen als kommunikatives Handeln. Zur Kritik der utilitaristischen Handlungstheorien' (1994) 1 *Zeitschrift für Internationale Beziehungen* 15; similar affinities are, however, less visible in the literature on European integration.

[20] M Zürn, n 16 above, 153; GF Schuppert, 'Zur Staatswerdung Europas. Überlegungen zu Bedingungsfaktoren und Perspektiven der europäischen Verfassungsentwicklung' (1994) 5 *Staatswissenschaften und Staatspraxis* 66.

competences to the EC.[21] The plaintiffs' arguments regarding the effects that the loss of economic regulatory powers would necessarily have on the constitutional state's ability to shape living conditions for its citizens did not impress the *BVerfG*. Their response was simple: European state-building does not occur if and because those competences, which have actually been transferred to the Community, are primarily and only of economic significance. Much more thorough was the *BVerfG* in its treatment of the agreements on Monetary Union. According to the overall conception of its argument, the *BVerfG* also had to examine in this respect whether the projected European monetary system was in line with the German Constitution. Yet the Basic Law did not explicitly determine German monetary policy. Article 88 merely envisaged the creation of a central bank, the independence of which was later guaranteed in the Federal Bank Law of 1957. Since then the constitutional debate has concerned the transfer of a monetary policy that is not constrained by explicit legal rules to a politically independent institution that is compatible with general constitutional principles.[22] The *BVerfG* sums up the discussion only very briefly: the 'modification of the democracy principle', with which monetary policy is being protected against short-term interests and pressures, has been proven to be successful and seems 'acceptable'.[23] The *Bundesbank*'s 'external relations' were re-organised by the new Article 88 (2), inserted into the Federal Bank Law by the Law of 21 December 1992. It stipulates that the *Bundesbank*'s tasks may be transferred to a European Central Bank that is 'independent and which serves the primary objective of price stability'. Tensions between supranational and domestic law result firstly from the fact that the institutionalisation of monetary policy is more insulated against democratically legitimised decision processes in the Treaty on the EMU than it is in the Basic Law. This increase in the autonomy of monetary policy-making is not addressed by the *BVerfG*. Any independent European monetary policy also lacks the backing that developed with decades of social and scientific consensus – the 'pre-legal pre-conditions', therefore, which formed the basis in the Federal Republic for the institutional independence of the *Bundesbank* and the orientation of its monetary policy. In contrast to its approach to the democratic deficit, the Court refrained from specifying the conditions for the workability of Monetary Union. Instead, it declared the

[21] See D Murswiek, 'Maastricht und der pouvoir constituant. Zur Bedeutung der verfassungsgebende Gewalt im Prozess der europäischen Integration' (1993) 32 *Der Staat* 187; E Steindorff, '*Quo vadis* Europa? Freiheiten, Regulierung und soziale Grundrechte nach den enveiterten Zielen der EG-Verfassung' in Forschungsinstitut fur Wirtschaft (ed), *Weiterentwicklung der Europäischen Gemeinschaften und der Marktwirtschaft* (Köln–Berlin–Bonn–Munich: Carl Heymanns, 1992) 13. Both authors referring to *Manfred Brunner and Others v The European Union Treaty* (Cases 2 BvR 2134/92 & 2159/92, BVerfGE 89, 155) [1994] 1 CMLR 57.

[22] See KH Ladeur, 'Die Autonomie der Bundesbank – ein Beispiel für die institutionelle Verarbeitung von Ungewissheitsbedingungen' (1993) 4 *Staatswissenschaften und Staatspraxis* 46.

[23] *Manfred Brunner* (n 21) para C I 2 b b1.

relationship between Monetary and Economic Union contingent and politically determinable.[24] Precisely in this way politics has indirectly become involved: the *Bundestag* has the right to examine, before entering the third stage of Monetary Union, the fulfilment of the Treaty criteria on price stability and convergence – and the exercise of the *Bundestag*'s right to supervision is bound to the agreed-upon objectives.[25] Furthermore, if Monetary Union 'could not develop continuously in line with the agreed stability mandate' then the Treaty conception assumed by the German ratification law would be abandoned.[26] Economic integration as a non-state and unpolitical process and Monetary Union as a project condemned to succeed and only legitimised by success – this argumentation is, at the least, in need of further interpretation: Did the Court endorse the *ordo*- and neo-liberal theory of the economic constitution, which always conceptualised supranational economic law as being independent of and unaffected by politics?[27] Hardly so. The *BVerfG* knew about the ardent critique by German *Ordnungstheorie* of the steady growth of European industrial policy and the incompatibility of the new Treaty provisions with the neo-liberal reading of Europe's economic constitution.[28] Did the Court subscribe to Ipsen's view of the Community as an 'association of functional integration', which remains limited to questions of 'technical realisation' and therefore sufficiently legitimated through expertise?[29] Did it implicitly confirm the neo-functionalist view of economic integration as 'low politics'? This reading would be compatible with neither the 'Herderian' [constitutions are tied to the people] nor the 'Kantian' strands [constitutions rest upon 'a continuous free debate between opposing social forces, interests and ideas'[30]] of the Court's argument.

B. Regulative Functions and Normative Qualities of Economic Law

All of these questions were not considered by the *BVerfG*. Yet confronting them is unavoidable if the Court's assertions are to be judged and the difficulties of the law in the process of integration are to be understood. In the following, the primary aim will be to delineate the domestic juridification of the economic system in such a way as to convey why normative structures can (and should) maintain their intrinsic value also in the process of Europeanisation of the economy.

[24] ibid para C II 2 f.
[25] ibid para C II d d2 (3).
[26] ibid para C II 2 e.
[27] See Behrens, n 8 above; Mestmäcker, n 8 above.
[28] See the thorough analysis of W Sauter, 'The Relationship between Industrial and Competition Policy under the Economic Constitution of the European Union, with a Case Study on Telecommunications' (PhD Thesis EUI Florence 1996) ch I.
[29] Ipsen, n 10 above, 176; and *idem*, 'Zur Exekutiv-Rechtsetzung in der Europäischen Gemeinschaft' in P Badura and R Scholz (eds), *Wege und Verfahren des Verfassungslebens. Festschrift für Peter Lerche* (Munich: Beck, 1993) 425.
[30] para C I 2 b b1.

1. *Functions of Economic Law*

The *BVerfG*'s careless treatment of the transfer of competences of economic regulation is – in view of the regulatory density and functions of domestic economic law – difficult to comprehend. Even if, by way of a functional delimitation of 'economic' law, one simply looked at those legal fields intended to institutionalise markets and provide for their functioning, there would be no end in sight. Apart from corporation law, intellectual property rights, competition law and general private law, on the one hand, and the law of public economic administration, on the other, would have to be considered. In addition, one would also need to examine the whole of product safety regulation, which covers the marketing of any product and thus both constitutes and regulates markets. Finally, in responding to the question of what else concerns 'the economy', one encounters labour and social law, environmental law and safety at work regulation. Thus, more than marginal matters are at stake when the European Union assumes 'competences and tasks' in the construction of an economic community. By contrast, we are faced with a project with highly complex regulatory techniques and extremely charged normative politics. In the normal scientific systematisation and in the doctrinal treatment of legal materials, these problem horizons are not always visible. Yet when economic lawyers consider the regulative functions of their fields, they resort to conceptualisations in which economists and social scientists can discover well-known theory patterns: the *ordo*-liberal tradition and its neo-classical successors; institutional economics and price-theoretical models; borrowings from social scientific normativism in the tradition of Durkheim and Parsons; transpositions of autopoetic systems theory and the theory of communicative action. All these conceptualisations must also regard institutional aspects, the regulatory and implementation conditions of legal programmes. Social scientific research on implementation and the political science debate on regulation have advanced and formed reflections on the methodology of economic regulation. Accordingly, lawyers have reduced their expectations as to the effectiveness of legislation. They know that not only the formulation, but also the transposition of economic law is being influenced by well-organised actors; they have come to realise the significance of case law and the specific quality of jurisprudence. Yet this does not fully encompass the normative terrain of the law. Economic legislation, its dogmatic application and the methodology of juridical decision-making may be confronted and penetrated with theoretically defined criteria, such as the efficiency demands of economic analysts. By contrast, one may insist on the realisation of distributive concerns and/or paternalistic motives. Any change in the law encounters institutions and rules which have developed through political and social conflict and through which historical experience and cultural traditions persist. All this – the conflict about theoretical concepts, the need for pragmatic compromises, the experience with proven practices, the recourse to normative traditions and their further development – is part of 'positively valid' economic law.

2. *Integration as Intervention and Disintegration*

Changing economic law with a view to market integration therefore comes up against a complex web of active rules and common practices. That is why integration policy can only proceed selectively – and it must have a two-sided effect: the Europeanisation of economic regulation with the objective of integration is, from the perspective of domestic legal orders, an intervention with disintegrative consequences.[31] Initially, this is true for the laws directly concerning the institutionalisation and the functioning of markets for goods and services. These laws are themselves legally, economically, and socially interdependent. Integration challenges these interdependencies in a specific way. The 1957 EC Treaty had geared economic integration completely towards market-oriented economic regulation. In the framework of harmonisation policy under Article 100, it was legally only possible to introduce legislation on social responsibility in the economy if this was done in the name of equal competitive conditions and with the aim of ensuring the functioning of the Common Market. Practically and politically, such measures are in any case ambivalent. Their realisation means that economies with low productivity sacrifice the competitive advantages of a low level of environmental and social regulation. Their non-realisation means that states with high levels of social protection are coming under pressure as a result of the opening of their markets; furthermore, this would indicate that international regulative gaps could not be filled by European law. The more integration proceeds through market-constitutive regulation, the more these repercussions will become apparent. Market integration does affect the constitutional state more fundamentally than appears from the *BverfG*'s judgment. The *BverfG*'s reasoning presupposes either a purely formal understanding of sovereignty, which ousts all the modern regulatory functions of the welfare state or, what amounts to the same result, a legally binding commitment of supranationalism to the concept of a minimal state.[32]

C. Regulatory Patterns of Europeanised Economic Regulation

For a long time, the Community only cautiously advanced the construction of a Common Market. Comparing the rules and decision procedures of the EEC Treaty to the substance and the law-making procedures in national economic law, this seems all but surprising. Certainly, the EEC Treaty was meant to guarantee

[31] M Everson, 'Laws in Conflict. A Rationally Integrated European Insurance Market?' (PhD Thesis EUI Florence 1993); C Joerges, 'Economic Law, the Nation-State and the Maastricht Treaty' in R Dehousse (ed), *Europe after Maastricht: an Ever Closer Union?* (Munich: CH Beck, 1994) 32.

[32] Wissenschaftlicher Beirat beim Bundesministerium für Wirtschaft, *Ordnungspolitische Orientierung für die politische Union* (Bonn: Bundesministerium für Wirtschaft, 1994) 11.

the four basic freedoms: the mobility of goods, services, capital and labour. But even though the Court of Justice deduced directly applicable civil rights and legal rules from these stipulations, European law hardly interfered with the networks of economic regulation. The Treaty's guarantee of the freedom of trade in goods was limited by all the objectives named in Article 36. Those who wanted to exercise the freedom of services were obliged to respect professional regulations and other rules concerning the quality of their performance. The title on the mobility of capital did in any case respect the sensibilities of monetary policy; this freedom was not 'directly applicable'.[33] Institutional limitations played their part. The Community could, within the limits of its enumerated competences, pass directives in accordance with Article 100 or it could act upon the basis of Article 235: the unanimity principle ensured that each Member State remained in a position to defend its regulatory system or its economic interests using its veto power. European competition policy continued a piecemeal existence, even though its rules were directly applicable and were implemented by the Commission itself – *vis-à-vis* protectionist national regulatory patterns this power proved to be helpless.

1. *The Single Market Programme*

This might explain why the continuous growth of European economic regulation was carefully documented, but – apart from the ordo- or neo-liberal legal theory – was rarely seen as a constitutionally relevant process. Only as it became possible in the 1980s to overcome the blockages of the integration process and to initiate a conceptually renewed Internal Market programme did the perception of 'Europe' change. The Internal Market initiative was presented as a project to enhance the competitiveness of the European economy through an efficiency-oriented deregulation strategy. The legislative core of this strategy was the retreat from the 'traditional' policy of harmonisation. In principle, the doctrine of mutual recognition of essential regulation was supposed to make the passing of detailed ('positive') Community regulations unnecessary. Essential regulatory objectives were to be brought into the form of easy-to-agree-upon general principles; the further concretisations of such essential requirements were to be removed from the European political system and their implementation transferred to the Commission, who would cooperate with non-governmental organisations and rely on the European committee system. The move to qualified-majority voting for all measures relating to the Internal Market (Article 100a) was the most visible institutional innovation. This transformation of the EC system not only kept policy-makers in suspense, but also caused commotion in the legal and social sciences. The move to majority voting affected precisely that legal-political

[33] Case 203/80 *Casati* [1981] ECR 2595.

balance between legal supranationalism and intergovernmental bargaining that Joseph Weiler had identified as the hidden stability condition of the EC system.[34] Did supranational law – as did Münchhausen when caught in the swamp – pull itself away from its ties to the nation-state? In fact, the new legislative policy turned out to be the 'implementation' of a principle that the European Court of Justice had previously developed from primary Community law. A German barrier to the marketing of French liquor had been declared incompatible with the principle of the free movement of goods in the *Cassis de Dijon* judgment.[35] The Federal Government's argument in that case that the higher alcohol content required by German law was to protect German citizens against alcoholism was refuted. This judgment was convincing. But it is also true that the Court of Justice had quite cautiously formulated the principle of mutual recognition and its competence regarding the control of national legislation. It remained for the Commission to read into the decision of the Court of Justice a new guiding principle of harmonisation policy and to expand on this in the White Paper on the Internal Market.[36] Yet this did not suffice either. The Internal Market initiative received its binding legal form only in the 1987 Single European Act that was negotiated by the national governments themselves. Did this herald the end of 'integration through law'? Is the broad acceptance of the Internal Market initiative due to a programmatic orientation that followed an efficiency and deregulation rhetoric which steered clear of controversial redistributive and other social welfare policy objectives?[37] Did the design of a new programme and the negotiating skills of the Commission President bring together European business interests, thus utilising an ultimately neo-functional logic?[38] Or should the change in the integration process be attributed to the interests and power of the three most important Member States?[39] Political science analyses of the conditions and consequences of the Internal Market programme always – at least implicitly or negatively – also contain judgments about the functions of law. It would certainly be rewarding to trace in more detail these perceptions (and misperceptions). In this context, the thesis must suffice that, particularly

[34] JHH Weiler, 'The Community System: The Dual Character of Supranationalism' (1981) 1 *Yearbook of European Law* 261.

[35] Case 120/78, Cassis de Dijon [1979] ECR 649; see also Case C-362/88 GB-INNO-BM [1988] ECR 1-667; and Case C-126/91 Yves Rocher [1993] ECR 3187.

[36] See Commission of the EC, Mitteilung der Kommission iiber die Auswirkungen des Urteils des Europäischen Gerichtshofes vom 20. Februar 1979 in der Rechtssache 120/78 (*Cassis de Dijon*), OJ 1980 C 256 1980, 2–3; and Commission of the EC, Weißbuch der Kommission an den Europäischen Rat zur Vollendung des Binnenmarktes, COM (85)310 final of 14 June 1985; KJ Alter and S Meunier-Aitsahalia, 'Judicial Politics in the European Community. European Integration and the Path-Breaking *Cassis de Dijon* Decision' (1994) 26 *Comparative Political Studies* 555.

[37] G Majone, 'Ideas, Interests and Institutions: Explaining the Revival of Policy Analysis in the 1980s' (Typescript EUI Florence 1995).

[38] W Sandholtz and J Zysman, '1992, Recasting the European Bargain' (1989) 42 *World Politics* 96.

[39] A Moravcsik, 'Negotiating the Single European Act: National Interests and Conventional State Craft in the European Community' (1991) 45 *International Organisation* 25.

in the implementation process of the Internal Market programme, the law has maintained its role as an independent and resistant factor. Evidence for this thesis is found in the results – equally surprising for both critics and supporters of the Internal Market programme – of its implementation. Internal Market policies have not removed the 'juridification' of the Western European economies. They have created a large number of arrangements which demonstrate notable patterns: a tendency towards high-level regulation; the development of new forms of cooperation; a restructuring of regulatory functions for the nation-state.[40]

(1) Market Integration and Legislative Activism

In each case in which Community law addresses the institutional framework and the legal fine-tuning of markets, this takes place in an extraordinary manner. The most striking examples are to be found in product regulations which aim at consumer and health protection, but which also seize some concerns of labour and environmental protection. In this context Article l00a (3) and the right 'to go it alone' given to those Member States willing to regulate[41] entail that an opening of markets can only be achieved at the price of modernising and improving the quality of respective regulation.[42] But it also became clear in the economic regulation of the markets for goods and services that a single market requires the establishment of sophisticated regulatory frameworks, such as a partial harmonisation of supervisory rights, arrangements for the coordination of practice of national supervisory authorities, provisions enabling Member States to protect their public interests.[43] The harmonisation of private law demonstrates that European law tends to cumulate and improve protective measures found in domestic legal systems whenever the functioning of markets actually demands genuine legal harmonisation.[44] Such legislative policy cannot identify itself as simply functional. It remains tied to the legal systems of the Member States and must respect the standards of justice which have won recognition in them.

[40] See more extensively Joerges, n 2 above, 234 ff; and *idem*, n 31 above, 105; for comprehensive analyses of product regulation, where the emergent structures are particularly visible, see H-W Micklitz, *Internationales Produksicherheitsrecht. Zur Begründung einer Rechtsverfassung für den Handel mit risikobehafteten Produkten* (Baden-Baden: Nomos, 1995) 136–47, 159–241; S Weatherill, 'Shaping Responsibility in the Legal Order of the 'European Community' in H-W Micklitz, T Roethe and S Weatherill, *Federalism and Responsibility. A Study on Product Safety Law and Practice in the European Community* (The Hague-Boston–London: Graham & Trotmad Martinus Nijhoff, 1995) 153.

[41] Article l00a Para 4, Article 118 Para 3, Article 130t.

[42] C Joerges, 'Rationalisierungsprozesse im Recht der Produktsicherheit: Öffentliches Recht und Haftungsrecht unter dem Einfluss der Europäischen Integration' (1995) 14 *Jahrbuch für Umwelt- und Technikrecht* 151.

[43] N Reich, 'Competition Between Legal Orders: A New Paradigm of EC Law? (1992) 29 *CMLRev* 869.

[44] C Joerges and G Brüggemeier, 'Europäisierung des Vertragsrechts und Haftungsrechts' in P-Ch Müller-Graff (ed), *Gemeinsames Privatrecht in der Europäischen Gemeinschaft* (Baden-Baden: Nomos, 1993) 252.

(2) Supremacy of European Law and Horizontal Cooperation

Since the EC does not itself wield the resources for the generation of standards and since it also lacks the administrative competence to enforce legally-binding decisions in the Member States, it must seek to counterbalance these deficits. It is for this reason that the Commission cooperates with European standardisation organisations in the definition of product safety regulation and supports the coordination of national certification authorities. Furthermore, the Community operates through a dense network of committees with the participation of administrative experts from the Member States, as well as independent scientists and representatives of economic and social interest organisations. This opening is supported by moves towards a procedural juridification which is based upon demands for transparency, promotes the consideration of scientific knowledge, gives in to claims for participation and extends the possibilities for judicial protection.[45] The dependence of the Community on national administration therefore demands some form of horizontal coordination. The intensity of judicial control over administrative acts and over the European 'fourth branch of government' will increase. In this way, the practical weakness of 'comitology' may become its normative strength: without the law, cooperative solutions to regulatory tasks will not be successfully mastered; and with the law, they can only succeed in the long term if they develop a legal constitution corresponding to the conflict potential of regulative politics. The dependence of the Community is still stronger in its efforts to harmonise private economic law through European directives. Following their adoption and transposition into domestic law, directives are primarily a matter for national courts. Through the procedures of Article 177, the Court of Justice comes to deal with Community legislation only after national courts have been involved. It would undermine the Court's own effectiveness if, in its interpretations of the meaning and content of Community, it was to go beyond the social ties of private and economic law – ties which national courts have established within their legal systems.[46]

(3) Market Integration and Regulatory Autonomy of the Member States

The validity claims of so-called secondary Community law – its supremacy and its pre-emptive effect – are not only limited where primary law gives Member States rights to 'go it alone', but are typically also circumscribed in the directives

[45] See Case C-212/91 *Angelopharm* (1994) 5 Europäische Zeitschrifr für Wirtschaftsrecht 213, more generally European Parliament, Bericht des Institutionellen Ausschusses über die Transparenz in der Gemeinschaft of 21 March 1994, PE 207.463 final.

[46] See Joerges and Brüggemeier, n 44 above, 281; and C Joerges, 'The Europeanisation of Private Law as a Rationalisation Process and as a Contest of Legal Disciplines – An Analysis of the Directive on Unfair Terms in Consumer Contracts' (1995) 3 *European Review of Private Law* 175, at 189.

themselves and interpreted quite cautiously by the Court.[47] Neither does the Court of Justice use its supervisory powers under primary law simply with a view to enforcing de-regulatory programmes or towards a European neo-liberal economic constitution. It is true that the case law of the European Court of Justice on Article 30 in the follow-up to the *Cassis de Dijon* case also evaluated national regulations according to their compatibility with the functional requirements of a market economy. But it is also true that 'legitimate' regulatory interests motivated by consumer, social or environmental protection were addressed very cautiously[48] and that the European Court of Justice has shown particular reserve when addressing issues that concern the national *ordre public*, that is, subjects that open up the debate over political-ethical traditions.[49] In the latter two groups of cases, the Court has now initiated an explicit withdrawal of its supervisory claims and has, at the same time, formalised this self-correction: only product regulation is now to fall under the *Cassis* terms of reference, while all 'modalities of purchase' may be regulated by Member States autonomously.[50]

In addition to Article 30, the European Court of Justice has used Articles 85 and 5 to gain access to state measures endorsing anti-competitive practices.[51] The German *Monopolkommission* has sought to read into that jurisprudence a move towards a general control of state measures'.[52] Yet once again, in 1993, the Court of Justice refused the request for a substantial examination of regulatory arrangements between state authorities and the 'economic circles concerned'. Instead, a kind of European 'act of state' doctrine was announced: EC law merely controls whether Member States take the formal responsibility for such regulatory techniques; it does not examine their regulatory rationale.[53] This renewed self-restraint should not be interpreted as the renunciation of regulatory competence,[54] nor can it be explained simply as the result of the Court's workload. The Court always had to react to the tension between the validity claims of Community law geared towards the realisation of trade liberalisation, on the one hand, and the regulatory

[47] A Furrer, Die Sperrwirkung des sekundären Gemeinschaftsrechts auf die nationalen Rechtsordnungen (Baden-Baden: Nomos, 1994) 43, 165.

[48] W Wils, 'The Search for the Rule in Article 30 EEC: Much Ado About Nothing? (1993) 18 *ELR* 413.

[49] DR Phelan, 'Right to Life of the Unborn *v* Promotion of Trade in Services: the European Court of Justice and the Normative Shaping of the European Union' (1992) 55 *MLR* 676.

[50] Cases 267 and 268/91 Keck and Mithouard [I9931 Europäische Zeitschriftt für Wirtschaftsrecht 770; Cases C-69 and 258/ 93 Punto Casa [1994] 5 Europäische Zeitschrift für Wirtschaftsrecht 434.

[51] Particularly Case 136/86 *BNIC v Aubert* [1987] ECR 4789 and Case 276/86 *Van Eycke* [I989] ECR I- 4789.

[52] Monopolkommission, *Achtes Hauptgutachten der Monopolkomrnission* 1988/1989, Bt-Drucksache 1117582 of 16 July 1990, 401.

[53] See Case C-185/91 Bundesanstalt für den Güterverkehr v Reiff [1993] 4 Europäische Zeitschrift für Wirtschafsrecht 769 and, as a recent example, Cases C-401 and 402/92 t'Heukske [1994] 5 Europäische Zeitschrift für Wirtschaftsrecht 435.

[54] N Reich, 'The 'November Revolution' of the European Court of Justice: Keck, Meng and Audi Revisited' (1994) 31 *CMLR* 473.

concerns of the Member States, on the other. The latest judgments respond negatively that these questions may not be decided according to a higher regulatory rationality of Community law; they may be understood as imposing demands for justifications at either level, the European as well as the national – and may thus be interpreted as a search for compatibility.[55]

2. *Rationalisation Processes*

All of these developments have also been observed, explained and interpreted by social scientists. This is true, first of all, for the legislative activism of the Community and its emphasis on market-related economic law and product-related regulation. This is indeed a process of 'market-building',[56] and the stringent level of regulation, particularly of products – which also concerns safety at work via machinery-safety – mirrors the configurations of interests in that process.[57]

The move to horizontal forms of cooperation in the 'production and implementation of European standards can be equally well explained. In the related growth of 'comitology', directed by the bureaucracy and supported by experts, Bach[58] has identified, very much in line with Ipsen,[59] the emergence of a new type of regime to which he attributes a technical-bureaucratic character removed from the domestic context. More open to the legitimacy problems of this regulatory practice is Majone's[60] perspective of a European 'fourth branch of government'. Majone[61] attributes to the whole range of Community activities in social regulation a role of politics that compensates market failure and deficits of 'soft' international cooperation. By insulating social policy and defining narrowly its mandate, he hopes to ensure its political accountability.[62] According to the normative vision of supranationalism suggested above, the law

[55] See Joerges, n 31 above, 59–62.

[56] W Streeck, 'From Market-Making to State-Building? Reflections on the Political Economy of European Social Policy' in S Leibfried and P Pierson (eds), *European Social Policy. Between Fragmentation and Integration* (Washington, DC: Brookings, 1995) 399.

[57] FW Scharpf, 'Autonomieschonend und gemeinschaftsverträglich: Zur Logik einer europäischen Mehrebenenpolitik' in *idem*, *Optionen des Foderalismus in Deutschland und Europa* (Frankfurt aM: Campus, 1994) 131 [English translation: 'Community and Autonomy: Multilevel Policy-making in the European Union' in *idem*, *Community and Autonomy. Institutions, Policies and Legitimacy in Multilevel Europe* (Frankfurt aM: Campus, 2021) 67].

[58] M Bach, 'Transnationale Integration und institutionelle Differenzierung. Tendenzen der europäischen Staatswerdung' (1993) 14 *Zeitschrift fur Rechtssoziologie* 223.

[59] Ipsen, n 6 above.

[60] G Majone, 'The European Community. An "Independent Fourth Branch of Government"?' in G Brüggemeier (ed), *Verfassungen für ein ziviles Europa* (Baden-Baden: Nomos, 1994) 23.

[61] G Majone, 'The European Community Between Social Policy and Social Regulation' (1993) 31 *JCMS* 156; and *idem*, 'Deregulation or Re-regulation? Policymaking in the European Community Since the Single European Act', EUI Working Paper SPS No 93/9 (1993).

[62] G Majone, 'Independence vs Accountability? Non-Majoritarian Institutions and Democratic Governance in Europe', EUI Working Paper SPS No 94/3 (1994); see the analysis of M Everson, 'Independent Agencies: Hierarchy Beaters?' (1995) 1 *European Law Journal* 180.

should strive for more complex responses. European legislation would have to be continuously exposed to demands for justification which cannot be dissolved by functional arguments. European comitology would have to be embedded into constitutional provisions ensuring the legitimacy of decision-making. European and national courts would refuse to pass the survival of normative ties of the economy on to the processes of regulatory competition and would engage in a cooperative search for rules ensuring the compatibility and coexistence of supranational commitments and national regulatory concerns. Wishful thinking? That depends on what can be discovered about the functioning of European governance and the ingenuity of institution-building.

3. *The Law of Denationalised Governance: Some Tentative Deliberations*

The logic of the reasoning presented so far may be understood as a defence of the European project against both the critics of European market-building and the advocates of a dichotomy of political autonomy (vested in the nation-state) and private rights (vested in Europe's economic constitution). That reading, however, would be too simplistic. The regulatory patterns of the European economy we have referred to certainly document the dependence of market integration on a dense network of rules and institutions, their constant adaptation and the indispensability of regulatory activities. There is an abundance of law and, one must even concede, its regulatory structures are quite sophisticated. And yet, if the normative quality of law is to be ensured through democratic institutions and a deliberative style of politics, the Europeanisation process exhibits highly ambivalent features. The processes of policy formation, and even the managing institutions which have emerged in the shadow of the harmonisation of legislation through 'discovery procedures of practice', were not foreseen by the European Treaties and are difficult to fit into the legal design of both supranationalism and national constitutionalism. Suffice it here to point again to the role of non-governmental organisations at both the European and the national level, the entrustment of expert networks with consulting functions, the importance of inter-administrative cooperation, and, last but not least, the comitology syndrome.

Just as lawyers begin to take these non-provided-for legal developments seriously,[63] political scientists are overcoming the schisms between neo-functionalist and intergovernmentalist paradigms. The integration process is conceptualised as a multi-level game with strong institutional interdependence between the different levels of political institutions.[64] Nation-states, regional political

[63] See most recently JHH Weiler, U Haltern and FC Mayer, 'European Democracy and Its Critique' (1995) 18 *West European Politics* 24.

[64] FW Scharpf, 'Die Politikverflechtungsfalle: Europäische Integration und deutscher Föderalismus im Vergleich' (1985) 26 *Politische Vierteljahresschrift* 323 [English translation: 'The Joint-decision Trap: Lessons from German Federalism and European Integration (1988)' in *idem*, *Community*

entities and European institutions seem no longer capable of designing and implementing policies without taking the other levels of European governance into account. One important implication of multi-level governance is the turn to cooperative modes of coordination between the supranational and the international level, between governmental and non-state actors. Constructivist accounts tend to attach far-reaching hopes to these developments. It seems plausible that consensus-building through persuasion, arguing and deliberation should be an indispensable element of problem-solving within non-hierarchical governance structures. The so to speak self-enforcing power of arguing will, however, remain dependent upon the issues at stake and their contexts. The most promising candidate for a positive performance is product regulation, because of the compelling need to reach consensus and its many in-built guarantees for reasonableness.[65] European process regulation, social policy[66] and re-distributive politics face more difficult problems: the uneven development among the European economies, the resultant differences among national preferences in the fields of labour, social or environmental law, the lack of a European system of fiscal equalisation in order to compensate for the raising of regulatory standards.[67] This is not to refute constructivist expectations and hopes. It is only to bring the Law back in: without the support of legal supranationalism, and the constraints it is to impose on the formation of consensual problem-solving, credible commitments to deliberative politics are hardly conceivable.

CONCLUSION

The analysis of the *BVerfG*'s Maastricht judgment has demonstrated that the judicial controversy over the qualification of the EC system as either a legal

and Autonomy, n 57 above, 21]; *idem*, 'Mehrebenenpolitik im vollendeten Binnenmarkt', MPIFG Discussion Paper 94/4; E Grande, 'Forschungspolitik in der PolitikverRechtungs- Falle?' (1995) 36 *Politische Jahresschrift* 460. For recent general accounts, see S Hix, 'Approaches to the Study of the European Community: The Challenge to Comparative Politics' (1994) 17 *West European Politics* 1; M Jachtenfuchs, 'Theoretical Perspectives on European Governance' (1995) 1 *European Law Journal* 115; M Zürn, 'The Study of European Integration in Political Science' (Typescript, Bremen, 1995); S Pierson and P Leibfried, 'The Dynamics of Social Policy Integration' in *eidem* (eds), n 56 above, 432; M Jachtenfuchs and B Kohler-Koch, 'Regieren im dynamischen Mehrebenensystem' in *eidem* (eds), *Europäische Integration* (Opladen: Leske+Budrich, 1996) 15.

[65] Joerges, n 42 above.

[66] See, W Streeck, 'Politikverflechtung und Entscheidungslücke: Zum Verhältnis von zwischenstaatlichen Beziehungen und sozialen Interessen im europäischen Binnenmarkt' in R Scheettkat, K Bentele and B Reissert (eds) *Reformfähigkeit von Industriegesellschaften: Festschrift für Fritz W Scharpf* (Frankfurt aM: Campus, 1995) 101; *idem*, 'From Market-Making to State-Building? Reflections on the Political Economy of European Social Policy' in S Leibfried and P Pierson (eds), *Prospects for Social Europe: The European Community's Social Dimension in Comparative Perspective* (Washington, DC: Brookings Institution, 1995) 389.

[67] On the related economic reasoning, see H-W Sinn, 'Wieviel Brüssel braucht Europa? Subsidiarität, Zentralisierung und Fiskalwettbewerb im Lichte der ökonomischen Theorie' (1994) 5 *Staatswissenschaften und Staatspraxis* 171.

Community or a mere 'association of states' is essentially about the compatibility of the European supranational legal constitution with democracy constituted in the nation-state. Yet it was only the discussion of economic integration that brought to light the difficulties of a coexistence of these two legal orders. The resort to supranational sovereign rights – this was the convincing dictum of the *BVerfG* – requires specific legitimation, a type of legitimation which cannot be achieved through the kind of legal operations on which the European Court of Justice has built its architecture of supranationalism. European economic integration directly affects individuals and social actors all over Europe. By granting these actors European rights, the Court itself has paved the way for the emergence of a European civil society. By adapting their institutional structures into new forms of governance, the legal system has started to respond to the need for a 'juridification' of the European economy. There is a potential for the development of supranationalism into a constitutional charter which protects not just economic liberties but equally the political autonomy of European citizens. It furthermore protects and constrains the autonomy of constitutional states, and ensures the social responsibility of denationalised governance structures. These challenges should concern lawyers and political scientists alike. Legal science is dependent on economic and political science analyses in its search for institutional solutions; but political science ought also to be interested in the potential of the law to pre-structure intergovernmental bargaining and to tie the conflicts over economic and social consequences of market integration to principles and rules.

3

*'Where the Law Runs Out': The Overburdening of Law and Constitutional Adjudication by the Financial Crisis and Europe's New Modes of Economic Governance**

With Economic and Monetary Union (EMU), the Treaty of Maastricht has institutionalised a complex conflict constellation: the Treaty confirmed the autonomy of socio-economically and politically heterogeneous states in the spheres of fiscal, economic, labour and social policy, but subjected them to a uniform monetary regime administered by a Central Bank (European Central Bank, ECB) of unmatched autonomy. As even Friedrich A von Hayek has underlined, a stable currency is a pre-condition of a market economy which the market cannot generate autonomously, a task hence within the genuine responsibility of a state.[1] The paradox, then, is that the ECB, however, has to administer the monetary policy of a state which does not exist.[2] Conceptually speaking, the Maastricht Treaty has produced a hybrid, an odd compromise of German and French preferences, with Germany defending its stability philosophy in substantive principles and statutory norms and ceding to French preferences in the procedural norms of the General ECB Council. For nearly a decade, EMU operated reasonably well and was widely perceived as a success story. Tensions made themselves felt, but seemed manageable. This changed dramatically after the economic crisis began to unfold in 2008. Since then, we have witnessed a turbo-speed establishment of new modes of transnational economic governance and a resort to unheard of regulatory techniques.

* Published in in S Garben, I Govaere and P Nemitz (eds), *Critical Reflections on Constitutional Democracy in the European Union* (Oxford: Hart Publishing, 2019) 168–78.

[1] FA von Hayek, *The Constitution of Liberty* (Chicago, IL: University of Chicago Press, 2011) 452: money is 'a kind of loose joint in the otherwise self-steering mechanism of the market'.

[2] H Enderlein, 'The Euro as a Showcase for Exploratory Governance. Why There are no Simple Answers' in Hertie School of Governance (ed), *The Governance Report 2015. The Eurozone Crisis: Lessons Learned for Europe's Future* (Oxford: OUP, 2015) 29.

Detailed descriptions are available,[3] but cannot, and need not, be reproduced here. Our focus is on the judicial responses to the conflict constellation inherent in the construction of EMU, which can best be characterised as 'diagonal', as I have submitted repeatedly.[4]

This notion requires an explanatory remark. Monetary policy has become an exclusive competence of the Union (Article 3(1)c TFEU). With this provision, the Union claims supremacy in the policy area conferred to it, a conferral which did not include economic and fiscal policies. The exercise of these reserved powers can generate external effects and lead to 'horizontal' conflicts. As experienced immediately after the establishment of the EMU, monetary policy and the national policies could, indeed, come into conflict. This, however, is not a vertical conflict for which supremacy would provide a response. Both the Union and the Member States are certainly interested in the functioning of their economies. But the powers needed to accomplish this objective are attributed to two distinct levels of governance. The type of conflict resolution foreseen in Article 119 TFEU is 'the adoption of an economic policy which is based on the close coordination of member states' economic policies' as substantiated in Article 121 TFEU. As is plainly visible from the legal texts, this instrument was a *lex imperfecta*, an order devoid of meaningful sanctions. The 'stability community' of the EMU existed only on paper. Neither the Treaty of Maastricht provided for mechanisms to enforce its ideational basis, nor did the successive Stability and Growth Pact of 1997 complement the Treaty accordingly. The functioning of the new regime was dependent on good economic luck and constant political bargaining. Is it nevertheless possible to call this 'muddling-through' arrangement a legal framework of constitutional quality? This query leads to the crux of the matter alluded to in the title. The discrepancies between the premises and expectations upon which the design of legal and constitutional provisions relied and later real-world developments are anything but unusual. The *problématique* of EMU, however, *is* unusual. No authority has been entrusted with powers which would ensure that the policies pursued at the European and national levels of governance would be coordinated effectively in compliance with legally valid criteria. Again, the failure to provide such a framework is neither wilful nor accidental. The economic and fiscal policies of Member States reflect the specifics of their economies and societal conditions. Their markets, to take up Karl Polanyi's famous insight, will always be 'socially embedded'.[5] This multifaceted heterogeneity with its multiple causes could not and did not dissolve under the impact

[3] Most comprehensively, perhaps, T Beukers, B de Witte and C Kilpatrick (eds), *Constitutional Change through Euro-Crisis Law* (Cambridge: CUP, 2017).

[4] See, eg, C Joerges, 'Integration Through Law and the Crisis of Law in Europe's Emergency', in D Chalmers, M Jachtenfuchs and C Joerges (eds), *The End of the Eurocrats' Dream. Adjusting to European Diversity* (Cambridge: CUP, 2016) 312.

[5] K Polanyi, *The Great Transformation: The Political and Economic Origins of Our Time* [1944], first Beacon paperback edn (Boston, MA: 1957) most famously at 57.

of the common currency. The uniformity of European monetary policy was, instead, to become ever more dysfunctional.[6] What we have observed, instead, namely, the resort to intergovernmental bargaining, soft supervision, and tentative coordination is, hence, unsurprising – and simultaneously an irritating aberration from the commitment of the integration project to the rule of law.[7]

It took its time but it was bound to happen: the conflicts inherent in the construction of EMU were reframed as legal problems and adjudicated, most famously in the controversy over the ECB's Outright Monetary Transaction (OMT) programme. The legal controversy had, of course, a not yet legalised background. Mario Draghi's 'Whatever it takes' announcement,[8]

> has come to be seen as the turning point of the eurozone crisis. In the aftermath, markets immediately calmed. Yields for the most vulnerable borrowers came down. There was no more talk of a eurozone breakup. It is an explanation with deep appeal. The ECB had held the key to stability all along. Draghi, finally, was the one to turn it.[9]

What the historian Adam Tooze tells us in the passage cited is also common knowledge in the community of European lawyers. His further reporting is not so well known. At the time of the announcement, the ECB and Draghi had no ready-made script or strategy. And the elaboration of the programme did by no means occur with the ECB acting in full autonomy:

> As usual, the inflation hawks at the Bundesbank were aghast at the idea of ECB bond buying. But for Merkel it was the better of two bad options ... With backing from both Merkel and Schäuble the die was cast. The ECB formalised its new role as a conditional lender of last resort, under the title of Outright Monetary Transactions (OMT). But this was a strictly conditional promise. The ECB would go into action only if the country in question had agreed on an austerity and aid program approved by the ESM.[10]

[6] Outside legal discourses the awareness of the broad 'varieties of capitalism' is widespread. Only a handful of lawyers have taken this issue seriously enough, among them Gunther Teubner, whose seminal 'Legal Irritants: Good Faith in British Law or How Unifying Law Ends Up in New Differences' (1998) 61 *Modern Law Review* 11 was republished in the classic of P Hall and D Soskice (eds), *Varieties of Capitalism: The Institutional Foundations of Comparative Advantage* (Oxford: OUP, 2001). For a recent exemplary analysis, see J Hien and C Joerges (eds), *Responses of European Economic Cultures to Europe's Crisis Politics: The Example of German-Italian Discrepancies* (Florence: European University Institute, 2018), e-book available at: hdl.handle.net/1814/59884.

[7] Somewhat paradoxically, according to a widespread rumour and complaint, EMU has established some ordoliberal iron cage (suffice it here to cite the non-academic yet prestigious example of *The Economist* of 9 May 2015); for an extensive discussion, see J Hien and C Joerges, 'Dead Man Walking? Current European Interest in the Ordoliberal Tradition' (2018) 24 *European Law Journal* 142.

[8] 'Within our mandate, the ECB is ready to do whatever it takes to preserve the euro. And believe me, it will be enough.' *Verbatim* at: www.ecb.europa.eu/press/key/date/2012/html/sp120726.en.html.

[9] A Tooze, *Crashed: How a Decade of Financial Crises Changed the World* (New York: Viking, 2018) 484.

[10] ibid, 487; his more general comment at 374, 'Europe entered an emergency regime defined not by a single sovereign author, but by the absence of any such authority', citing J White, 'Emergency Europe' (2015) 63 *Political Studies* 300.

Can we expect the German Constitutional Court to move from barking to biting under these conditions to falsify Joseph Weiler's irony?[11] It seems after all not so surprising that Karlsruhe submitted 'its first reference ever' to the Court of Justice (CJEU).[12] In due course, Advocate General Cruz Villalón made his views known.[13] The CJEU handed down its judgment on 16 June 2015.[14] Karlsruhe responded on 21 June 2016.[15] Both Courts are repeat players. *Gauweiler* has been prepared by *Pringle*[16] and was complemented by *Weiss*.[17] There is also much continuity with the German plaintiffs and their legal counsel.[18] The Advocates General change, but their views remain the same.[19]

My focus will be on the OMT controversy, which attracted the highest attention and addressed the constitutional issues most directly and clearly. Most remarkably, in my view, two of the justices from Karlsruhe submitted dissenting opinions in which they pleaded for inadmissibility of the constitutional complaint (*Verfassungsbeschwerde*). This is a technical term with no equivalent elsewhere. This alternative was a road not taken by the majority and treated with benign neglect in the heated debates on the controversy. I will, in the following, summarise briefly the questions submitted by Karlsruhe to Luxembourg (1), report more extensively on the dissenting opinion by Judge Gertrude Lübbe-Wolff (2), then turn to the discretionary powers claimed by the ECB (3) and the marginalisation of judicial control (4), look at the responses to these developments in various branches of European studies (5) and conclude with further reflections on my title.

[11] See JHH Weiler, 'The "Lisbon Urteil" and the Fast Food Culture' (2009) 20 *European Journal of International Law* 505.

[12] BVerfG, 2 BvR 2728/13 vom 14.1.2014, paras 1–105, available at: www.bverfg.de/entscheidungen/rs20140114_2bvr272813en.html.

[13] Opinion in Case C-62/14 *Peter Gauweiler and others v Deutscher Bundestag*, delivered on 14 January 2015.

[14] Case C-62/14 *Peter Gauweiler and others v Deutscher Bundestag*, Judgment (Grand Chamber) of 16 June 2015, EU:C:2015:400.

[15] Judgment of 21 June 2016–2 BvR 2728/13, 2 BvR 2729/13, 2 BvR 2730/13, 2 BvR 2731/13, 2 BvE 13/13.

[16] Case 370/12 *Pringle v Ireland*, Judgment (Grand Chamber) of 27 November 2012, EU:C:2012:756.

[17] Case C-493/1 *Heinrich Weiss and Others*, Judgment of the Court (Grand Chamber) of 11 December 2018, EU:C:2018:1000, responding to the Order of 18 July 2017–2 BvR 859/15 of the FCC, BVerfG, Order of the Second Senate of 18 July 2017–2 BvR 859/15 paras 1–137, available at: www.bverfg.de/e/rs20170718_2bvr085915en.html:www.bundesverfassungsgericht.de.

[18] Most persistently, Peter Gauweiler, Member of the *Bundestag* for the Christlich Soziale Union and his legal advisor, Professor Dr Dietrich Murswiek, once a legal advisor of 'The Greens' and also of *Die Linke*; both entertain instructive webpages, which give information about their political and advisory activities and cooperation; see: archiv.peter-gauweiler.de/esm_pressemitteilungen.html and www.dietrich-murswiek.de/praxis.html.

[19] AG Kokott, *Pringle*; AG Cruz Villalón, *OMT, Gauweiler*; AG Wathelet, *Weiss*.

AD 1: KARLSRUHE'S QUERIES

The context of the proceedings in Karlsruhe was delicate.[20] What could the judges have had in mind when submitting their 'first reference ever'? Speculations aside, the questions they submitted were straightforward: Did the Governing Council of the ECB with its announcement of the OMT programme act within Europe's monetary policy mandate? Did the ECB by its explicit reference and approval of the conditions of the financial assistance programmes of the European Financial Stability Facility (EFSF) and/or the European Stability Mechanism (ESM) overstep its monetary policy competence and interfere with the powers of the Member States in the sphere of economic policy? Was the OMT programme compatible with the prohibition of monetary financing (Article 123 TFEU)? The *BVerfG*, furthermore, wondered how the support granted could be compatible with the budgetary autonomy and responsibility of Member States, which it held to be 'constituent for the design of the monetary union' (as evidenced by Article 125 TFEU).[21] How daring are these queries? The German court's position seemed supported not only by the TFEU, but also by the traditional views on the role and limits of central banks as lenders-of-last resort, commented a renowned economist from Princeton.[22]

AD 2: JUSTICE LÜBBE-WOLFF'S DISSENT

The dissenters did not take sides on this controversy. They moved to another institutional level and questioned the power of the German court to adjudicate: they opted for inadmissibility of the constitutional complaint. Judge Lübbe-Wolff has submitted a host of reasons.[23] Here is a selection:

a. The order goes 'beyond the limits of judicial competence under the principles of democracy and separation of powers' (3).
b. 'The more far-reaching, the weightier, the more irreversible – legally and factually – the possible consequences of a judicial decision, the more judicial restraint is appropriate' (7).
c. 'Where for reasons of law the judges' courage must dwindle when it comes to the substance, they ought not to go into the substance at all' (27).
d. 'The democratic legitimacy which the decision of a national court may draw from the relevant standards of national law (if any) will not, or not without substantial detriment, extend beyond the national area' (28).

[20] See nn 9–11 above.
[21] BVerfG, judgment of 14.01.2014, n 12 above, para 41; see also para 71.
[22] A Mody, 'Did the German Court do Europe a Favor?', Bruegel Working Paper 2014/09, available at: aei.pitt.edu/52709/1/Did_the_German_court_do_Europe_a_favour%2D_(English).pdf, 4.
[23] The following numbers go to the paragraphs of her dissent.

This latter point is particularly interesting. What Lübbe-Wolff criticises here has been thoroughly neglected in the judgment on the rescue package for Greece, where the Court defended the budgetary power of the German *Bundestag* while, by the same token, not caring at all for the rights of the Greek Parliament.[24] She furthermore emphasised that the complaint could not insist on a specific action of the German Government and Parliament. 'With regard to the question of whether there exists a qualified *ultra vires* act, the Federal Government and the *Bundestag* must have a margin of appreciation and discretion, which the citizen needs to accept' (15). Note that this is not the type of discretion which is the key concept of the *Gauweiler* judgment[25] to which I now turn.

AD 3: THE ECB'S DISCRETIONARY POWERS

The legally and literally decisive argument in *Gauweiler* is about the competence of the ECB. 'The primary objective of EU monetary policy, price stability, and support for the general economic policies in the Union, form the principal criterion for defining monetary policy (Articles 127(1) TFEU and 282(2) TFEU).'[26]

What the ECB claims here is the competence to decide what monetary policy 'is'. This kind of autonomy is at odds with what has been so far a *communis opinio* among the protagonists of independent, non-majoritarian institutions, namely, that they are not the masters of their mandate. Paul Tucker has recently re-constructed the rationale of the conventional wisdom with utmost care.[27] The CJEU, however, has legalised the position of the ECB without any substantial *caveats*. The *Kronberger Kreis*, by now the most prominent ordo-liberal forum in Germany, has questioned the validity of this move,[28] indicating, however, that we may have to live with such imperfections.[29]

[24] See C Joerges, 'Der Berg kreißte – gebar er eine Maus? Europa vor dem Bundesverfassungsgericht' (2012) 65 *WSI-Mitteilungen* 560; M Everson, 'An Exercise in Legal Honesty: Rewriting the Court of Justice and the Bundesverfassungsgericht' (2015) 21 *ELJ* 474, 497.

[25] *Gauweiler* judgment, n 14 above.

[26] ibid, para 127.

[27] P Tucker, Unelected Power: The Quest for Legitimacy in Central Banking and the Regulatory State (Princeton, NJ: Princeton University Press, 2018).

[28] Kronberger Kreis (LP Feld, C Fuest, J Haucap, H Schweitzer, V Wieland, BU Wigger), 'Dismantling the Boundaries of the ECB's Monetary Policy Mandate: The CJEU's OMT Judgment and its Consequences' (Berlin: Stiftung Marktwirtschaft, 2016) available at: www.stiftung-marktwirtschaft.de/fileadmin/user_upload/KK-Studien/KK_61_OMT-Judgement_2016.pdf.

[29] On p 17, we read 'by extending the ECB's mandate so far as to encompass any "rectification" of disruptions in the monetary policy transmission mechanism, the court's judicial review practically becomes an illusion'. On p 36, we learn 'If the German Federal Constitutional Court is required to rule on the substance of the case, then a substantial divergence from the CJEU's OMT judgement seems inescapable. In order to respect its duty to perform the ultra vires control in a Europe-friendly manner, and in order to minimise damage to the EU as a community of law, the Federal Constitutional Court may, however, wish to contain the conflict as far as possible. An option may be to uphold the CJEU's judgment in effect, but base this finding on a different reasoning.' Reconciling the irreconcilable is part of 'operative strategies' of Ordo-liberalism (see fn 68).

In view of such ambivalences, it seems instructive to recall how European law used to assess discretionary powers. The '*Meroni*-doctrine', with its distinction of 'wide discretionary powers' and 'clearly defined executive powers', comes to the mind of European lawyers when they encounter our notion.[30] *Meroni* is as old as it is outdated, they would tend to add. But is it really? Joana Mendes, in her recent subtle re-construction of the relationship between discretion, law and judicial review, has documented how the *Meroni* dichotomy survived in the distinction between 'discretionary power involving policy choices and discretion stemming from technical assessments'.[31] Is this a sound refinement? It is, at least, a bridge to the reasoning of the Court. 'Monetary policy', so the Advocate General opined, is 'a highly technical terrain in which it is necessary to have an expertise and experience which, according to the Treaties, devolves solely upon the ECB'.[32] The two points are connected here. First, in the case of monetary policy, it is the technical side of the dichotomy which justifies discretion and requires judicial caution. Second, and somewhat surprisingly, this expertise is declared to be uncontroversial or sacrosanct. It must not be contested, not be exposed to scrutiny by other bodies because the Treaty has assigned it to the ECB. Both points are as bold as they are unconvincing. Monetary policy is a very complex matter, but by no means a merely technical one. Here, as in so many other instances, Joana Mendes correctly notes, 'technical assessments and policy choices are inextricably intertwined'.[33]

The whole weight of this assignment of discretionary powers becomes apparent only in the light of the institutional framework of EMU. The German court had not only defended another concept of monetary policy, namely, that submitted by the President of the German *Bundesbank*, Jens Weidmann, it had also asked, or rather insinuated, whether the ECB, by its explicit reference and approval of the conditions of the financial assistance programmes of the EFSF and/or the ESM, had overstepped its monetary policy competence and interfered with the powers of the Member States in the sphere of economic policy. It had suggested that the OMT programme was incompatible with the prohibition of monetary financing (Article 123 TFEU). The *Bundesverfassungsgericht*, furthermore, had wondered how the support granted could be compatible with the budgetary autonomy and responsibility of Member States, which it held to be 'constituent for the design of the monetary union', as evidenced by Article 125 TFEU.[34]

[30] Case C-9/56 *Meroni* v *High Authority*, EU:C:1958:7 (*Meroni*).

[31] J Mendes, 'Bounded Discretion in EU Law: A Limited Judicial Paradigm in a Changing EU' (2017) 8 *Modern Law Review* 443.

[32] Opinion of AG Cruz Villalón in Case C-62/14 *Gauweiler*, n 13 above, para 111.

[33] n 31 above, 471.

[34] BVerfG, 2 BvR 2728/13 vom 14.1.2014, paras 1–105, available at: www.bverfg.de/entscheidungen/rs20140114_2bvr272813en.html.

The argument of the Court of Justice on the epistemic nature of monetary policy and the supremacy of the expertise of the ECB is a response to the entire range of these queries. The whole construction is such that the conferral of *de facto* unlimited discretionary powers to the ECB becomes but a stringent implication of the design of EMU.

This design, so the Court stresses, is, in one respect, incomplete. Economic and fiscal policy remained a reserve of the Member States, but the substance of monetary policy, which becomes the exclusive competence of the EU, was not positively defined. What is nevertheless clear under Articles 127(1) TFEU and 282(2) TFEU is the objective of monetary policy, namely, the defence of price stability and hence the mandate of the ECB to pursue this objective with the help of the instruments described in Chapter IV of the Protocol on the European System of Central Banks (ESCB) and the ECB.[35] In the parlance of Niklas Luhmann's sociology of law,[36] the Court moves here into realms of 'purposive' programming, a move which liberates it from the disciplining power of traditional 'conditional' legal programming. This liberating move does not do away with the importance of precedential case law. In its reference, the German court had cited the passage of the *Pringle* judgment in which the Court of Justice had qualified the financial aid under the ESM Treaty as a matter of economic policy.[37] Again, through the resort to purposive programming, this constraint is overcome:

> When the ESM buys up bonds on secondary markets, it is 'economic policy'. When the ECB does the same, and makes these purchases conditional on compliance with the ESM's 'macroeconomic adjustment' demands, it is 'monetary policy'.[38]

It is hence the difference between the objectives of the respective operations which is decisive. This is precisely the magic charm of purposive programming.

The ESCB/ECB are entitled to define the objectives and to determine the means in full autonomy. This cannot be otherwise, once it has been held that the conduct of monetary policy 'requires an expertise and experience which, according to the Treaties, devolves solely upon the ECB'.[39] Governance in the eurozone, we have to realise, is a technocratic exercise. By definition, this type of *praxis* can be exposed neither to quests for democratic legitimacy, nor to the constraints of the rule of law. What does this entail? The American law and political science scholar Alec Stone Sweet has characterised the foundational

[35] *Gauweiler* judgment, n 13 above, paras 42–45.

[36] See, eg, N Luhmann, *Recht und Automation in der öffentlichen Verwaltung* (Berlin: Duncker & Humblot, 1966) 36 ff.

[37] *Pringle* judgment, n 16 above, para 64.

[38] H Schepel, 'The Bank, the Bond, and the Bail-out: On the Legal Construction of Market Discipline in the Eurozone' (2017) 44 *Journal of Law & Society* 79, 96.

[39] Opinion of AG Cruz Villalón in Case C-62/14 *Gauweiler*, n 13 above, para 111.

jurisprudence a 'juridical *coup d'état*, a fundamental transformation in the normative foundations of a legal system through the constitutional law-making of a court'.[40] *Pringle* and *Gauweiler* present another example. Stone Sweet was sure to be empirically correct about the foundational jurisprudence but refrained from a definite normative assessment. Was this the type of 'constitutional moment' which Bruce Ackerman has identified in the constitutional history of the United States? Is it conceivable that the present transformation will 'deserve recognition', or is this an unconstitutional amendment of the European legal order?

I will return to this point in my final remark. For the present, I am just concerned with the disquieting theoretical poverty of this revolutionary jurisprudence. One core assumption upon which it builds is plainly wrong. Technical expertise cannot be neatly separated from, or insulated against, normative assessments and policy choices.[41] A second weakness is not so plainly visible. It is the distinction between monetary policy and fiscal policy, which the Treaty has firmly institutionalised and which the OMT litigation sought to clarify. This legal architecture has a long history, which Isabel Feichtner, when she was still an assistant professor at the House of Finance at Goethe University, has re-constructed in an eye-opening essay.[42] We have learned to treat money as a commodity on which the state raises taxes. Tax revenues are sound finance; the alternative is to print money, a temptation that governments have to withstand in order to avoid inflation. This is why we need politically independent monetary authorities. In order to defend us against inflation, these authorities must discipline governments and their fiscal policy. This is the narrative which we have internalised in our nation-states and on which the EMU relies. But this is also why we have established, in the eurozone, a governance regime which does not content itself with the adjustment of interest rates and the use of other conventional monetary policy instruments. An irresistible logic is at work here. The ECB cannot restrain itself to a focus on price stability and leave financial stability operations to national governments. The Bank's concerns for financial stability are unlimited in their scope. They reach out into the whole range of economic and social policies with requests for structural reforms and adjustments.[43] The fundamental error, Feichtner argues, is to treat money as an external factor and to conceal its construction by the state. Money should be understood as credit, be regarded as credit; the transfers of such credit only work if a state that guarantees their enforceability exists. She refers to sophisticated literature defending

[40] A Stone Sweet, 'The Juridical Coup d'État and the Problem of Authority' (2007) 8 *German Law Journal* 915, 924 ff.

[41] Mendes, n 31 above.

[42] I Feichtner, 'Public Law's Rationalization of the Legal Architecture of Money: What might Legal Analysis of Money Become?' (2016) 17 *German Law Journal* 875.

[43] ibid, 895.

this re-conceptualisation. This, however, is beyond my horizon. What I can see and what I feel is clearly visible in the destruction of the separation of fiscal and monetary policy by Europe's crisis politics and the jurisprudence of the CJEU. To repeat, 'When the ESM buys up bonds on secondary markets, it is "economic policy"' – this is the *Pringle* judgment. When the ECB does the same, and makes these purchases conditional on compliance with the ESM's 'macroeconomic adjustment' demands, this is 'monetary policy'. It all depends, hence, on who does it for what purpose.

AD 4: A JUDICIAL *COUP D'ETAT*?

However sophisticated this reasoning may seem, the practice, which it legalises, is anything but legitimate. Our crisis politics has created a sharp asymmetry between the north and the south of Europe; it has, to cite Habermas, divided Europe because of its palpable, indeed glaring, social injustice.[44] The harsh critique of the famous philosopher is widely noted but does not impress European integration studies. What I find amazing and telling are the affinities between all of its pertinent branches, law, economics and political science: a tacit consensus not to take normative concerns about the integrity of law too seriously.

This seems most amazing in my own discipline. The *Pringle* judgment has hardly irritated anybody. The decision in *Gauweiler* is praised as a thoughtful and non-polemical examination of the somehow cheeky German reference. What is true for the jurisprudence of the CJEU is *cum grano salis* also true for the enormous body of the so-called crisis law. I cite from the introductory chapter to a pertinent volume of the EUI in Florence:

> After over half a decade of legal measures and prolific commentary on those measures, it is helpful to stand back and take stock. We will consider whether euro-crisis law … has by now mainly become simply the macro-economic law of the EU.[45]

The considerations end with a principled discharge, constrained by a few *caveats*.

Economists have replaced us lawyers as the prime advisers in European politics. Their views are dominated by functionalist reason. Even a statement such as 'The first victim of the crisis is democracy' pronounced by my Berlin

[44] J Habermas, 'Democracy in Europe: Why the Development of the EU into a Transnational Democracy is Necessary and How it is Possible' (2015) 21 *ELJ* 546, 550 (a crisis politics of 'palpable, indeed glaring social injustice').

[45] T Beukers, C Kilpatrick and B de Witte, 'Constitutional Change Through Euro-Crisis Law: Taking Stock, New Perspectives and Looking Ahead' in T Beukers, B de Witte and C Kilpatrick (eds), *Constitutional Change through Euro-Crisis Law* (Cambridge: CUP, 2017).

colleague Henrik Enderlein, is not meant to question that commitment.[46] One of the leading German authorities in the field of monetary policy is the Director of the Max Planck Institute for Public Goods, Martin Hellwig, who seems to believe that the law has nothing useful to contribute to the *praxis* of monetary policy.[47] The German Constitutional Court – and then likewise its economic experts – are ignorant. 'Economists are the ones who assess economic situations, whether there is an extraordinary crisis or not, how actors have to act to improve or protect welfare and how the economic order looks like.'[48]

And what about political science, a discipline brought to post-war Germany to teach us, especially us lawyers, democracy? Political scientists explain events, identify independent and dependent variables, and analyse changes within the framework of their integration theories. These attitudes did not fundamentally change after the crisis.[49] 'Business as usual' – this diagnosis of my Berlin colleague Markus Jachtenfuchs dates from 2013.[50] Business is even improving because we are witnessing a takeover of a 'core state function' by European institutions. Not only neo-functionalists, but inter-governmentalists, too, are delighted; they observe a takeover by some new 'deliberative' intergovernmentalism – more Europe hence – and this is, by definition, progress.[51]

AD 5: TINA (THERE IS NO ALTERNATIVE)?

Is it too cheap to submit critical comments without, at the same time, offering a 'solution'? Is the TINA mantra of Chancellor Merkel justified? Is her 'market conforming democracy',[52] what is left of the '*soziale Rechtsstaat*' of the Basic Law? Do we have to live with the replacement of political ownership of democratically-legitimated governments by austerity-driven 'structural reforms'? It is important to remain aware of the tragic choices at stake. They have been explained with admirable clarity in the comments on the *Gauweiler* reference

[46] H Enderlein, 'Das erste Opfer der Krise ist die Demokratie: Wirtschaftspolitik und ihre Legitimation in der Finanzmarktkrise 2008-2013' in H Buchstein (ed), *Die Versprechen der Demokratie* (Baden-Baden: Nomos, 2013) 45.

[47] M Hellwig, 'Finanzstabilität, Transparenz und Verantwortlichkeit: Stellungnahme für das Bundesverfassungsgericht' (2017) 50 *Credit and Capital Markets/Kredit und Kapital* 421.

[48] F Traut, 'Banking Crisis Interventions in Germany and Italy: The Unpleasant Case of the New European Bank Resolution Framework' in J Hien and C Joerges (eds), *Responses of European Economic Cultures to Europe's Crisis Politics: the Example of German-Italian Discrepancies*, European University Institute, Robert Schuman Centre for Advanced Studies, San Domenico di Fiesole 2018, 108–19; available at http://cadmus.eui.eu/handle/1814/59884.

[49] C Kreuder-Sonnen, 'Beyond Integration Theory: The (Anti-)Constitutional Dimension of European Crisis Governance' (2016) 54 *Journal of Common Market Studies* 1350.

[50] P Genschel and M Jachtenfuchs, 'Alles ganz normal! Eine institutionelle Analyse der Euro-Krise' (2013) 20 *Zeitschrift für Internationale Beziehungen* 75, 83.

[51] U Puetter, The European Council and the Council: New Intergovernmentalism and Institutional Change (Oxford: OUP, 2014).

[52] See Tooze, n 9 above, 438 with references.

of the Federal Constitutional Court (FCC) by Ashoka Mody. The economist explains:

> The legal and economic question of interest is whether the OMT tried to bypass the intent of the Treaty by creating a de-facto fiscal union (a liability or transfer union in *Bundesbank* terminology). If so, without their explicit authorisation, countries had become fiscally responsible for the mistakes of other member countries.[53]

To substantiate this query, Mody continues 'Can such a fiscal union be implicitly located in the ECB without the political willingness to transparently achieve that elusive goal?'[54] The economist as true teacher of law? Mody acknowledges the constraints under which law and politics operate. He warns us to subject fundamental constitutional principles to a functionalist logic of problem-solving strategies which operate under the highest uncertainties. Lübbe-Wolff's dissent is valuable because she refuses to cover unresolved problems with a thin veneer of legality. Could we expect more? Gerhard Anschütz has been criticised for empowering implicitly non-legitimated actors with decision-making powers.[55] Somewhat ironically, the non-existence of a transnational authority with comprehensive powers can turn into an asset: Europe cannot be governed by some central command-and control regime. It is destined to operate through cooperative problem-solving. Is it conceivable that the courts would impose some conditionality upon institutional and political actors? Constitutional courts would then be courageous enough to act as instigators and supervisors of deliberative political processes.

[53] Mody, n 22 above, 6.
[54] ibid, 4.
[55] See n 1 above.

4

Conclusion – Part I

I. OUTLOOK

THE ISSUES DISCUSSED in the essay of 1996 (chapter 2), with its plea 'to take the law seriously' and its implications, are taken up and pursued further in this volume and elsewhere in a variety of ways. I would emphasise here the re-construction of the integration process,[1] the contest over the European economic constitution in general[2] and German Ordoliberalism in particular.[3] The idea and project of a 'horizontal constitutionalism', which relies on the deliberative quality of cooperative problem-solving, is taken up first in Part III in the context of the European establishment and institutionalisation of 'social regulation' (the protection of consumers, the environment and safety-at-work policies) in the European Internal Market, and thereafter, in Part VI, more systematically in the concept of 'conflicts law as Europe's constitutional form'. The critique of the benign neglect of 'the economic' in European legal scholarship, on the one hand, and the normative complacency of political science, on the other, which is the subtext of both essays in the present Part, is repeated and updated in the critique of the readiness of both disciplines to accept the transformation of Europe's constitutional constellation, after more than a decade of crisis politics, as Europe's 'new normalcy'.

II. RELATED PUBLICATIONS

C Joerges and C Kreuder-Sonnen, 'European Studies and the European Crisis: Legal and Political Science between Critique and Complacency' (2017) 23 *ELJ* 118.

M Everson and C Joerges, 'Who is the Guardian for Constitutionalism in Europe after the Financial Crisis?' in S Kröger (ed), *Political Representation in the European Union: Still democratic in times of crisis?* (London: Routledge, 2014) 400.

[1] M Everson and C Joerges, 'Facticity as validity: the misplaced revolutionary praxis of Europe' in E Christodoulidis, R. Dukes and Goldoni (eds), *Research Handbook on Critical Legal Theory* (Cheltenham: Edward Elgar, 2020) 407'; and C Joerges, 'Integration Through Law and the Crisis of Law in Europe's Emergency' in C Joerges, D Chalmers and M Jachtenfuchs (eds), *The End of the Eurocrats' Dream. Adjusting to European Diversity* (Cambridge: CUP, 2016) 299.

[2] See pt V.

[3] See J Hien and C Joerges (eds), *Ordoliberalism, Law and the Rule of Economics* (Oxford: Hart Publishing, 2017).

Part II

Integration and Private Law

5

Introduction: Tensions and Affinities Between Private Law and European Market Integration

PRIVATE LAW WAS a latecomer to Europe's integration politics. Only after a tentative if not timid beginning, with an essay by the first Commission President,[1] did a few scholars from private international law (conflict of laws) and comparative law start to pay some attention to the new field. This disregard was unsurprising. The new law of European integration, with its rigid doctrines, its commitment to legal approximation and the establishment of a supranational order, had moved far beyond the methods and tools of those scholars' disciplines and was perceived as an essentially technocratic enterprise.[2] The newcomer took up residence in the public law departments as a neighbour of administrative law (*Verwaltungsrecht*) and constitutional law (*Staatsrecht*). Even there, the new neighbour looked somewhat out of place.[3]

The hesitancy of private law scholars to engage with the emerging new body of law had both methodological and pragmatic reasons. Private international law, its doctrinal complexities notwithstanding, was defended as the valid tool in response to legal diversity. Ernst Steindorff, one of the most creative proponents of European economic law, simply questioned the need for a Europeanisation of private law. Lawyers and courts, he opined, were diligent enough to cope with the diversity of Europe's private law systems.[4] Such reservations were to be followed by more principled objections against the threat to the systematic coherence of private law by new European prescriptions.

[1] W Hallstein, 'Angleichung des Privat- und Prozeßrechts in der europäischen Wirtschaftsgemeinschaft' (1964) 28 *RabelsZeitschrift für ausländisches und internationales Privatrecht* 211.

[2] With good reason, in light of the self-understanding of the leading representative of the new discipline; see HP Ipsen, *Europäisches Gemeinschaftsrecht* (Tübingen: Mohr Siebeck, 1972) 176 ff, and the comments on Ipsen in pt V, ch 20, section I.2.b.

[3] H Bülck, 'Zur Systematik der Europäischen Wirtschaftsgemeinschaft' (1949) 3 *Berichte der Deutschen Gesellschaft für Völkerrecht* 66.

[4] See his comments on the report of O Remien on the conference 'Alternativen zur legislatorischen Rechtsvereinheitlichung' (1992) 36 *Rabels Zeitschrift für ausländisches und internationales Privatrecht* 304. For the later development of his views, see E Steindorff, *EG-Vertrag und Privatrecht* (Baden-Baden: Nomos, 1996); he criticises jurisprudential tendencies to infer prescriptions for private law from the European Treaty and to subject it to the logic of market building.

The European initiatives started with a consumer protection directive. This was followed by more comprehensive codification endeavours, promoted under the guardianship of the European Commission and welcomed by a steadily increasing number of private law scholars, in particular by the 'Study Group on a European Civil Code' led by Christian von Bar.[5] Having been initially perceived by so many private law scholars as a threat to the coherence of their discipline, the ordoliberal school of thought was now understood as a chance to advance their project of a European 'private law society'. Such ordoliberal perspective will be discussed in many contributions to this volume, most intensively in Part V on the economic constitution. The argument, in a nutshell, is that the conceptualisation of the economic freedoms as basic rights that Europe's market citizens could invoke against their nation-states, in tandem with the commitment to a 'system of undistorted competition', seemed to be perfectly in line the with ordoliberal vision of a transnational economic constitution. This vision was not in need of some political endorsement via democratic will formation. It could rely on an institutional configuration, which entrusted the judiciary with the institutionalisation of open markets and the European Commission with their protection against a distortion of competitive ordering.

The three contributions to this Part re-construct the stages of these developments. The first (chapter 6) argues that the post-formalist and social dimensions of contemporary private law have created obstacles to its Europeanisation, which cannot be overcome within the integration-through-law paradigm. The 'substantive logic' of these developments is briefly summarised and then contrasted with the 'logic of the integration process'. The ordoliberal response to this tension is conceptually coherent but normatively unconvincing. The essence of the concept is a strengthening of the commitments of private law to the economic rationality of market processes. It is precisely this kind of reorientation, however, that would be irreconcilable with the post-formalist accomplishments of the post-war welfare state that have strengthened the social embeddedness of private law significantly, and which cannot be replaced at the European level due to the lack of pertinent legislative powers.

The second contribution (chapter 7) explores the potentially available and actual responses to this constellation in three fields of exemplary importance, namely, product liability law, company law, and the tensions between private law and the social objectives of services of general interest. It builds, in the theoretical re-construction of these constellations, upon analyses of the integration project as a 'multi-level-system of governance', as advocated widely in political science.[6] These analyses suggest that Europeanisation should not search for substantive uniformity but should instead seek to mediate between the commitment to European integration, on the one hand, and respect for national autonomy,

[5] See M Schmidt-Kessel, 'Study Group on a European Civil Code', available at http://hwb-eup2009.mpipriv.de/index.php/Study_Group_on_a_European_Civil_Code.

[6] See ch 7, section III.A, with pertinent references.

on the other.[7] The legal equivalent to such perspectives is the understanding of European law as a 'new type of conflicts law', a notion that is substantiated in the discussion of the three above-mentioned fields, and elaborated in many further contributions to this volume, most systematically in Part VI.

Under the impact of the financial and state debt crises during the last two decades, the chances of the perspectives advocated in chapter 7 have been impaired significantly. The insistence of Europe's crisis politics on ever more 'competitiveness' expected from 'structural reforms' is deeply at odds with the social dimensions and functions of private law in constitutional democracies. This welfare-state legacy of private law provides potential for its resistance against/to the imposition of a one-dimensional, socially insensitive market rationality, discussed in chapter 8.

[7] As most prominently explained by FW Scharpf, 'Community and Autonomy: Multilevel Policy-Making in the European Union' (1994) 1 *Journal of European Public Policy* 219.

6

*The Science of Private Law and the Nation State**

Preliminary Remark

THIS ESSAY ORIGINATED as a contribution to a much more comprehensive project portraying the history of legal science in the 'Bonn Republic' orchestrated by Dieter Simon, who edited it under the title *Rechtswissenschaften in der Bonner Republik* (Frankfurt aM: Suhrkamp 1994). It was written during my period as Fellow at the Institute for Advanced Study Berlin in 1991/92. At that time private law scholars had become aware of European law only because of the European initiatives in the field of consumer protection policy. This disregard was to last until the end of the century. Tensions between the European consumer protection legislation and the national systems of private law were nevertheless apparent from early on. The introduction to the essay deals with this unruly relationship. The then following two sections deal with private law developments in the 'Bonn Republic'. Only the final section addresses the Europeanisation *problématique*.

Introduction

The two concepts mentioned in the title of this essay have a tense relationship. It was in the 'nation state' that Europe's societies found their sovereignty, fought out their internal economic and social conflicts, and organised their legal systems. The links forged between private law and the nation state called into question private law's pre-positive self-justifications: both those in classical natural law and in modern rational law, the links to a common European legal culture and, finally, even the trust in the scientific nature of the private-law

* Published in F Snyder (ed), *The Europeanization of Law. The Legal Effects of European Integration* (Oxford: Hart Publishing, 2000) 47–82; only pp 47–49 and 74–82 are reproduced here. The original German version, 'Die Wissenschaft vom Privatrecht und der Nationalstaat' in D Simon (ed), *Rechtswissenschaften in der Bonner Republik*, Frankfurt aM: Suhrkamp, 1994, 311–63) was translated by IL Fraser, EUI Florence. The full text of the essay is also available in both languages at https://cadmus.eui.eu/handle/1814/140.

systems constructed.[1] 'Called into question' is intended to mean that the non-positive self-justifications of private-law principles and laws proved to be precarious without the new reference point of the positivity of all law, conveyed through the nation state, which brought an end to the history of the influence of those remnants of tradition.

The tension between the nation state form of law and its suprapositive, universalist content and validity claims puts all disciplines of legal science, both dogmatic and non-dogmatic branches, on the spot. Not just private lawyers, but also private international lawyers and comparative lawyers, legal historians, theorists and sociologists know that the particularism of the positive law in force cannot be laid solely at the door of the nation state. Yet the nation state offers a rich reference point for the history of private law. Its suitability as a classificatory and reference concept stems from the fact that the universal dependency relationships of cultural, economic, social and political history come into view.[2]

Although German private law found its formal unity in the nation state, its codification could not, in contrast with the French,[3] be constructed as an act of giving law to itself. Furthermore, German private law could not be portrayed in the same way as American common law,[4] as an institutionalised sub-system of a democratic constitutional state. German private law's codification was the product of a legal culture that had, through the historical legal school, separated itself from Enlightenment natural law and the constitutional developments of the 'West',[5] in order to justify the autonomy of private law by the scientific nature of its reconstruction.[6] In this tradition, universalist approaches were still very much at work. Of course, the trinity of the organic formation of law, the legal profession and legal science itself refers, in the theory of the *Volksgeist*, merely to a national culture. But this legal culture saw itself as a part of a European tradition, and the freedom-guaranteeing quality of private law was taken for granted.

[1] See R Stichweh, 'Selbstorganisation und die Entstehung nationaler Rechtssysteme (17.–19. Jahrhundert)' (1990) 9 *Rechtshistorisches Journal* 254, at 264 ff.

[2] See, more generally, H Plessner, *Die verspätete Nation* (1935) (Frankfurt aM: Suhrcamp, 1974); N Elias, *Studien über die Deutschen*, 4th edn (Frankfurt aM: Suhrcamp, 1990) 159; RM Lepsius, 'Nation und Nationalismus in Deutschland', in *idem*, *Interessen, Ideen und Institutionen* (Opladen: Westdeutscher Verlag, 1988) 232; J Habermas, 'Staatsbürgerschaft und nationale Identität' (St Gallen: Erker, 1991) 6 ff, reprinted in *idem*, *Faktizität und Geltung* (Frankfurt aM: Suhrkamp, 1992) 632, at 635 ff [English trans J Habermas, 'Citizenship and National Identity' in J Habermas, *Between Facts and Norms. Contributions to a Discourse Theory of Law and Democracy*, (Cambridge, MA: MIT Press, 1998) Appendix II, 491–516].

[3] See JH Merryman, *The Civil Law Tradition*, 2nd edn (Stanford, CA: Stanford University Press, 1985) 26 ff; I Maus, *Zur Aufklärung der Demokratietheorie* (Frankfurt aM: Suhrkamp, 1992) 203 ff.

[4] See Ph Selznick, *The Moral Commonwealth. Social Theory and the Promise of Community*, Berkeley, CA: University of California Press, 1992) 448 ff.

[5] See D Grimm, 'Der Staat in der kontinentaleuropäischen Tradition' in *idem*, *Recht und Staat in der bürgerlichen Gesellschaft* (Frankfurt aM: Suhrkamp, 1987) 53, at 69 ff.

[6] On these qualities of the BGB as an achievement of scientific codification, see HH Jakobs, *Wissenschaft und Gesetzgebung im bürgerlichen Recht nach der Rechtsquellenlehre des 19. Jahrhunderts* (Paderborn-München-Wien-Zürich: Schöningh, 1983) 134 ff.

This remained so in the era of legal formalism. However, this private-law tradition was not conceptually prepared to respond to such modern phenomena as the modern State's assumption of welfarist functions, the intervention of public authorities into the spheres of private law (the 'publicisation' of private law), or the instrumentalisation of law for external economic purposes in the interest of national economic polity. Responding to these developments were new conceptions and methodologies, such as those of the later Jhering, of Interest Jurisprudence and of Free Law, all of which created a new realism and strove for a new 'social' justice at the price of their formerly universalist claims.[7]

The difficulties of private law with the German nation state and its anti-formalist commitments to social justice continued and deepened in the brief Weimar period. Even in the retrospective view of contemporary legal historians, the problematic of the new Republic's interventionist legislative practice is one-dimensionally described as endangering the universalist traditions of private law.[8] But this conceptual difficulty is not the only burden placed upon post-war West German private legal science. Its most pressing task was to deal with the racist re-definition of the ethno-cultural *Volksnation* of National Socialism, which had been substantively and methodologically underpinned in the contemporary science of private law by theoretically quite ambitious 'legal innovations'. After the war, the legacy of the Nazi era had to be overcome in two ways: first, the links between private-law theories and the ideologies of National Socialism had to be recognised so that private law could be freed from the influence of *völkisch* legal thinking, thereby enabling its older traditions to regenerate. Secondly, it was also important to deal simultaneously with the unresolved tensions between those traditions and the interventionist, welfarist side of the nation state.

The way this dual-track programme came about and the doctrinal tendencies that subsequently emerged will be dealt with in the first part of this article (Section I, not reproduced). It goes almost without saying that even after the move away from the state of the *Volksnation*, the conflict between the regulatory aspect of the nation state and the traditions of private law still remained on the agenda. In the Federal Republic's reform period, the debates on the need for a renewal of the codification and on the reasonableness of the new statutes record the difficulty of the concept of a 'nation of citizens' (*Staatsbürgernation*). The disputes surrounding the new Republic's legislative activism in private law and the insistence of doctrinal thinking on its inherited authority were basically concerned with the new Polity's legislative calling (Section II, not reproduced). The history of the Federal Republic, from its inception, is one of the deliberate

[7] See R Dubischar, *Einführung in die Rechtstheorie* (Darmstadt: Wissenschaftliche Buchgesellschaft, 1983) 46 ff.

[8] See KW Nörr, *Zwischen den Mühlsteinen. Eine Privatrechtsgeschichte der Weimarer Republik* (Tübingen: Mohr, 1988) 13 ff, 242 ff, and the criticism by S Simitis, 'Stolpersteine der Privatrechtsgeschichte' (1989) 8 *Rechtshistorisches Journal* 3.

ceding of state sovereignty claims to European institutions. After 1989, the continuously accelerating process of European integration has not only left its traces in private law, but has also added a new dimension to the debates about universalism and particularism in private law because the Europeanisation of private law must be reconciled with the renewal of the nation state as a democratic constitutional policy (Section III).

The presentation of the material in this paper is, therefore, to be read systematically and historically. It is systematic to the extent that the *Volksnation*, the *Staatsbürgernation* and the 'erosion' of the nation state denote three aspects of nation-statehood,[9] which were always operating simultaneously in the history of the Federal Republic, constituting a continuing problem for positive private law. It involves a historical reconstruction because various aspects of nation-statehood came rhythmically on to the law's agenda, at intervals of some 20 years, with an urgency determined in each case by the times.

* * *

Sections I and II (original pp 50–73) deal with the development of German private law in the Federal Republic. They are omitted from this reprint. The full text is available as Working Paper EUI Law at http://hdl.handle.net/1814/140. The present reprint continues with Section III (original pp 74–82).

* * *

SECTION III. BEYOND THE NATION STATE: EUROPEAN INTEGRATION AND PRIVATE LAW

The Europeanisation of private law is a current process but it concerns not just the present and future of private law because the readiness, in principle, to abandon national statehood in favour of European unification was present throughout the whole history of the Federal Republic. It found expression in the constitution itself, in generally accepted political orientations and in the political culture. All this is more than comprehensible given the historical experience with the German nation state. However, the sacrifice of national statehood in favour of European institutions also always meant a loss: not just an erosion of a 'sovereignty' that was, in any case, imperfect, but also a limitation on the validity claims of the new democratic institutions. Alongside this dilemmatic mediation between the internal democratisation of the nation state and its political domestication in external relationships, the decision in favour of integration was associated with realistic insights into economic dependencies and economic

[9] These concepts are taken from RM Lepsius, n 2 above; see also *idem*, *Der europäische Nationalstaat: Erbe und Zukunft*, ibid, 256.

policy necessities; the decision in favour of Europe came from a response to the internationalisation of the economy and a decision in favour of opening up the national economy.[10]

If, accordingly, the option in favour of European unification can be explained from the Federal Republic's initial position, it nonetheless involved original and continuing problems of national statehood that had long been known. With the merciless clarity typical of him, Max Weber formulated these problems in his Freiburg inaugural address – a year before the proclamation of the BGB:

> And the nation State is for us not an indefinite something that one feels one can place all the higher the more its essence is shrouded in mystical gloom, but the worldly power organisation of the nation, and in this nation State is raison d'état for us, the ultimate value criterion on economic considerations too. It does not mean to us, as a strange misunderstanding believes: 'state assistance' instead of 'self-help', national regulation of economic life instead of the free play of economic forces, but we want, through this slogan, to raise the demand that for questions of German national economic policy – including the question whether and how far the State should interfere in economic life or whether and when it ought instead to set the nation's economic forces free to develop themselves and tear down restraints on them – in the individual case the last and decisive vote ought to go to the economic and political power interests of our nation, and its bearer, the German nation State.[11]

A nasty pronouncement, as Weber later admitted.[12] But the speech's content cannot be deduced from its national tone alone. Weber was carrying on a debate with the economic wisdom of his time. He was turning against the ethico-normative position of the historical school of national economics and holding his value judgement theory up against it. The economy was treated by Weber – as even the passage cited shows – as an *international* phenomenon, and recognition of this internationality was, for him, beyond question. But economic *policy* decisions, his economic theoretical message stated, are to be counted as value judgements and justified accordingly. Weber's option for the 'power interests of our nation and its bearer, the German nation State' as a criterion of national economic policies was a plea in favour of the de-moralisation of politics, for a political realism that, on the one hand, did not wish to believe in the reconciliation between 'cosmopolitanism and the nation State'[13] but, at the same time, also turned away from ethno-cultural exaltations of the national idea.[14]

[10] Very early see A Müller-Armack, *Zur Diagnose unserer wirtschaftlichen Lage* (Bielefeld: Küster, 1947).

[11] 'Der Nationalstaat und die Volkswirtschaftspolitik' in Max Weber, *Gesammelte Politische Schriften*, 3rd edn (edited by J Winckelmann) (Tübingen: Mohr Siebeck, 1971) 1, 14 ff.

[12] See the references in WJ Mommsen, *Max Weber und die deutsche Politik 1890–1920*, 2nd edn (Tübingen: Mohr Siebeck, 1974) 40; W Schluchter, *Religion und Lebensführung*, vol 1 (Frankfurt aM: Suhrkamp, 1988) 33.

[13] See F Meinecke, *Weltbürgertum und Nationalstaat. Studien zur Genesis des deutschen Nationalstaates* (Munich-Berlin: R Oldenbourg, 1908).

[14] See WJ Mommsen, n 12 above, 53 ff.

Those who take their distance from Weber's value criterion must, nonetheless, take his diagnosis seriously. This diagnosis says that the economy is internationalising, but for the solving of the economic and social problems of society only the organisational and political unity of the nation state is available; that the internationalisation of the economy is to be recognised, but also to be understood as a problem for policy. This diagnosis, however, fits the Federal Republic's initial situation just as much as its present-day position.[15] It also concerns private law. The internationalisation of the economy calls for corresponding legal institutions. The building up of such institutions is a political and institutional challenge to the democratic constitutional state, which cannot evade the responsibility for economic and social problems, and is committed to rule-of-law, and democratic procedures for solving problems.

Private law is completely predestined by its core institutions and universalistic principles to be the bearer of the internationalisation process of economy and the law, but the legitimacy of those 'post-formal' contents that constitute the regulatory and justicial content of modern private law are, to date, owed to nation-state institutions. If internationalised private law is to replace national law, then it has to take over its regulatory functions, show its own legitimacy, and harmonise its validity claims with the constitutional state's political constraints on action. All this, of course, amounts to abstract descriptions of the need for, and problems of, 'post-national' private law. Nonetheless, these problems must not be removed from the agenda of private law; they are of profound importance in all of its subdisciplines.

1. Denationalisation of Private Law Scholarship

In the early history of the Federal Republic, the freeing of private law from its nation-state setting, like all other basic problems of the discipline, was discussed in the context of the so-called renaissance of natural law.[16] But it was also and especially an important theme of the disciplines that, as it were, by definition treated private law 'internationally': private international law and comparative law.[17]

In private international law (PIL), the continuation of the Savigny tradition as enriched by Ernst Rabel was taken as a matter of course and an obligation.[18] This meant, as far as the understanding of private law went, the conservation

[15] See FW Scharpf, 'Die Handlungsfähigkeit des Staates am Ende des zwanzigsten Jahrhunderts' (1991) 32 *Politische Vierteljahresschrift* 621.

[16] See Section I above, before 1.

[17] Another international discipline is legal theory, in which in part (also) German contributions can now be understood only in the context of an internationalised debate in which, admittedly, relations to positive private law and legal theory evaporate, except where legal theory sees itself from the outset as 'sociology of law'.

[18] See M Martinek in D Simon, n * above, 529 ff.

of classical, formalist conceptions which were all the easier to maintain in practical terms because PIL had, for a long time, exempted the 'strictly positive' laws of the nation state, economic law and public law from the scope of its internationalistic, universalistic principles. It was not until the comparison with the fundamental-rights content of private-law principles mediated through linkages with 'social values' and the 'materialisation' of private law that there came a new fundamental debate in which the nation state displayed itself in all its aspects.[19] The multifaceted debate involved the omnipresence of 'binding' rules in private law, which led to a reversal of the relationship between 'regular' and 'special' linkages; the particularity of national arrangements which, while they took 'social values' into account, could not, nonetheless, lay claim to any universal bindingness, and could no longer be reconciled with 'blind' references; the insight that belonging to a legal system justified qualitative expectations of legal decisions, and that such expectations need not necessarily be confined to the nationality of positive law mediated through citizenship, compelled 'loosenings' of the citizenship principle;[20] and in all this, it also emerged that the sovereign nation state pursuing its 'power interests' 'unilaterally' over and above PIL continued to exist only as a dogmatic fiction, but had become helpless in practical regulatory terms, and normatively unattractive.

While PIL had to take a lesson from private law, the neighbouring discipline of comparative law broadcast messages of a different nature. Following his renewal of the 'third school in international private law',[21] Konrad Zweigert, very early on, introduced legal comparison, too, as a source of knowledge of substantive private law.[22] This programme yielded fruit not just in legal comparison itself[23] but in private law, too, including domestic private law. Zweigert had still confined his plea for the incorporation of foreign legal conceptions to the 'world-wide' subjects 'with a cosmopolitan function or a tendency to universalism'.[24] But he also saw that his 'method' had to strengthen the tendency inherent in Interest Jurisprudence to relate the law's rules functionally to regulatory problems, that a science of private law using comparative law has to relativise the meaning of establishing the 'will' of national legislators, and the relative value of dogmatic systematics.[25]

[19] See M Martinek, in D Simon, idem, 529 ff, 588 ff, as well as, on the connection between substantive law and conflict of laws, E Mazza-Teubner, 'Die Wiederkehr der "comitas". Zu den Wandlungen des Politikbegriffs im amerikanischen und deutschen Kollisionsrecht', Diss jur Bremen, 1992.

[20] See R Pitschas, 'Verfassungsrechtliche Vorgaben für das Statsangehörigkeitsprinzip des Internationalen Privatrechts' in E Jayme and H-P Mansell (eds), *Nation und Staat im Internationalen Privatrecht* (Heidelberg: CF Müller, 1990) 93.

[21] K Zweigert, 'Die dritte Schule im Internationalen Privatrecht' in HP Ipsen (ed), *Festschrift für Leo Raape* (Hamburg: Rechts-und Staatswissenschaftlicher Verlag, 1984) 35.

[22] 'Rechtsvergleichung als universale Interpretationsmethode' (1949/50) 15 *Rabels Zeitschrift für ausländisches und internationales Privatrecht* 5.

[23] For more details, see M Martinek in D Simon, n * above, 529 ff.

[24] K Zweigert, n 21 above, 12.

[25] See, also, K Zweigert, 'Die Rechtsvergleichung im Dienste der europäischen Rechtsvereinheitlichung' (1951) 16 *Rabels Zeitschrift für ausländisches und internationales Privatrecht* 387.

All this was immediately presented by Ernst von Caemmerer in his eminent paper on 'Enrichment and Delict'(*Bereicherung und unerlaubte Handlung*) in the *Festschrift* for Ernst Rabel.[26] In the future, incorporative comparative law ought to develop as the most innovative element specifically both in specific legal fields[27] and in more general methodological orientations.[28] But it has not just inspired comparative law excursus in whole legions of dissertations and habilitation theses on questions of substantive private law, but has also contributed to letting private-law theoretical approaches of all kinds developed elsewhere – realistic, legal-sociological, social-critical and economic – infiltrate German private-law science. It, thereby, promoted a form of internationalisation of private-law science that respects the cultural and socio-political particularism in positive law but, at the same time, brings universalistic elements to bear in objective and methodological terms. The internationalisation process is clearest in the economic analysis of law. The tendencies emerging here are scarcely less numerous than their American inspirers.[29] They share their various premises without wishing to suggest that 'non-national' solutions to problems can, on this ground, be converted into positive law. What applies to the internal

[26] H Dölle, M Rheinsteins and Konrad Zweigert (eds), *Festschrift für Ernst Rabel*, vol I: *Rechtsvergleichung und Internationales Privatrecht* (Tübingen: JCB Mohr, 1954), 553.

[27] See representatively, E Steindorff on 'Abstrakte und konkrete Schadensberechnung' ['Calculation of Damages'], *Archiv für die civilistische Praxis* 158 (1960) 431, at 434 ff.; on manufacturer liability, S Simitis, 'Soll die Haftung des Produzenten gegenüber dem Verbraucher durch Gesetz, kann sie durch richterliche Rechtsfortbildung geregelt werden?' *Gutachten zum 47. Deutschen Juristentag*, vol I (Munich: CH Beck, 1968) C 1; on the function of liability law HL Weyers, *Unfallschäden. Praxis und Ziele von Haftpflicht- und Vorsorgesystemen* (Frankfurt aM: Athenäum, 1971).

[28] Josef Esser's brilliant *magnum opus* (*Grundsatz und Norm in der richterlichen Rechtsfortbildung des Privatrechts*, Tübingen: JCB Mohr, 1956) was hard to make use of, so that its effect is hard to estimate. In his substance and intention, it was a path breaker and a promoter of this development. In the early postwar years, Esser had distanced himself from the romantic and organicist conceptions of law and society, as well as free-law irrationalism and against the eternity claims of natural-law systems, defending instead the 'indispensability of a rationally established, clear, positive constitution', where 'not an ounce of justice is sacrificed to any sort of political ideology' (see his article on Julius von Kirchmann: 'Hundert Jahre Anklagezustand über die Jurisprudenz' (1947) 2 *Deutsche Rechts-Zeitschrift* 315, reprinted in J Esser, *Wege der Rechtsgewinnung* (Tübingen: JCB Mohr, 1990), 265, 271, and Esser's *Einführung in die Grundbegriffe des Rechts und des Staates* (Wien: Springer, 1949) 17. This was not meant as a restoration of formalism, and was certainly not intended to deliver the law over to the sovereign, as *Grundsatz und Norm* went on penetratingly to show; here, Esser polemicises against 'legal theoretical solipsism' and the 'statist' attitude of nation-state legal political concepts (337), but also turns against the abstractness of Rabel's autonomism (340 ff); if legal principles and ideas of justice can lay claim to supranational validity, this is because justice, given 'equalizing common factors, including economic ones' also 'requires equal decisions in principle and therefore equivalent institutions, even with different legal systematics and legal structure' (378 ff).

[29] See HD Assmann, C Kirchner and E Schanze, *Ökonomische Analyse des Rechts* (Kronberg/Ts: Athenäum, 1978) and M Adams, *Ökonomische Analyse der Gefährdungs- und Verschuldenshaftung* (Heidelberg: von Decker, 1985); P Behrens, *Die ökonomischen Grundlagen des Rechts* (Tübingen: Mohr Siebeck, 1986); HB Schäfer and C Ott, *Lehrbuch der ökonomischen Analyse des Zivilrechts* (Berlin-Heidelberg-New York: Springer, 1986); W-R Walz, 'Ökonomische und rechtliche Überlegungen zur Verkehrsfähigkeit von Gegenständen' in C Ott and HB Schäfer (eds), *Allokationseffizienz in der Rechtsordnung* (Berlin: Springer, 1989) 93.

differentiation of the economic analysis of law, also emerges in this school's attitude towards competing tendencies which, in turn, establish themselves as trans-national networks. Thus, it seems that legal science is about to follow[30] internationalisation processes which both legal theory and its neighbour disciplines in the social sciences have already undergone.

2. The Europeanisation of the 'Private-law Society' (*Privatrechtsgesellschaft*)

From the comparative-law or conflict-of-laws viewpoint there is no objective reason to relate hopes of internationalisation and universality to the participatory states in the European integration project. This is essentially true also of *Ordo*liberalism. It is not to the historical organisational forms of the nation state, the German or any other, that legal dignity as such attaches itself: the guarantee of the parallel course of law and the economy required by regulatory theory is the key problem in the internationalisation of the economy. Even the early writings of *Ordo*liberal theoreticians, dealing with questions of international trade and the world economy, treat the internationalisation of the economy as a regulatory task centring round the question of how an institutional legal framework ought to appear when it compels the competition between economies and commercial policy to obey the guiding mechanism of the price system.[31]

The hopes for a reform of the world economy inspired by *ordo*liberal ideas rooted in the Second World War and pursued thereafter were quickly downcast.[32] It was accordingly only consistent for the *ordo*liberal school to promote specifically European unification endeavours[33] with interest from the outset and through all stages. Here, despite all the resistance to a political sacrifice of nation statehood, and precisely because of the restriction of the 1957 Rome Treaties to opening up the economies, the prospect seemed to be the opening of a Europe-wide private-law society. This prospect could certainly not be derived from the Treaties without interpretative efforts. However, it took shape, to the extent that, under the leadership of the European Court of Justice, the freedoms guaranteed in the EEC Treaty were recognised as directly applying private rights, the ban on discrimination enforced against state measures and the Treaty provisions on competition policy made applicable as legal rules, thus establishing

[30] A development long evident eg in tort law and liability law; for contract law, see eg J Köndgen, *Selbstbindung ohne Vertrag* (Tübingen: Mohr Siebeck, 1981); HC von der Crome, *Rahmenverträge* (Zürich: Habilitation Thesis, 1993).

[31] W Eucken, *Grundsätze der Wirtschaftspolitik* (Bern-Tübingen: Francke + Mohr, 1952) 167 ff; W Röpke, *Internationale Ordnung – now*, 2nd edn (Erlenbach-Zürich: Rentach, 1954) 101 ff; for a systematic summary, see H Willgerodt, 'Staatliche Souveränität und die Ordnung der Weltwirtschaft' (1989) 40 *Ordo* 40, 401, 408 ff and E-J Mestmäcker, 'Wirtschaftsrecht' (1990) 54 *Rabels Zeitschrift für ausländisches und internationales Privatrecht* 409, 415 ff.

[32] See G Ambrosius and WH Hubbard, *Sozial- und Wirtschaftsgeschichte Europas im 20. Jahrhundert* (Munich: CH Beck, 1986) 269 ff.

[33] ibid, 274 ff.

the primacy of the supranational legal order of the EEC Treaty.[34] Private law had [been] ignored [by] the EEC Treaty. This did not, however, prevent treating the economic system brought into effect through the treaty as a 'private-law system',[35] ascribing the treaty's reticence regarding private law to the circumstance that the Community Member States were in any case [...] legal systems that coincided in their essentials.[36] Additionally, approximation of laws pursuant to Treaty Article 100 opened up access to private law based functionally on the objective of creating the Common Market: since the integration aim of the supranational constitution of a 'Community economy' seemed clearly defined, how the opportunities opened by the EEC Treaty were to be understood and dealt with could also be indicated.[37] Admittedly, the more recent developments in the integration process and the revision of *ordo*liberal theory as initiated by FA von Hayek brought rethinking here too.

3. The Europeanisation of Private Law

For a long time, *Ordo*liberalism stood alone in its interest in the fundamental importance of European integration within national private-law science.[38] This benevolent neglect slowly changed as the European Community began to convert its consumer policy programmes for the years 1971 and 1975[39] into specific directives in private law[40] and brought its 10-years' work on product liability to a conclusion[41] – slowly, because this first generation of directives was still content to lay down minimum standards entirely capable of consensus, thus leaving national law largely intact. The intensivation of internal market policy following the Commission's 1985 White Paper[42] and the 1987 Single European

[34] See E-J Mestmäcker, 'Offene Märkte im System unverfälschten Wettbewerbs in der europäischen Wirtschaftsgemeinschaft' in E-J Mestmäcker and H Sauermann (eds), *Wirtschaftsordnung und Staatsverfassung – Festschrift für Franz Böhm zum 80. Geburtstag* (Tübingen: Mohr Siebeck, 1965) 345.

[35] See W Hallstein, 'Wirtschaftliche Integration als Faktor politischer Einigung' in F Greiß and FW Meyer (eds), *Wirtschaft, Gesellschaft und Kultur – Festgabe für Alfred Müller-Armack* (Berlin: Duncker & Humblot, 1961) 267, 275.

[36] See the testimony of Franz Böhm, as reported by E-J Mestmäcker, 'Über die Rolle der Politik in der Marktwirtschaft – dargestellt anhand eines unveröffentlichten Briefes von Franz Böhm' (1978) 29 *Ordo* 3, 11.

[37] See the – cautious – statements by W Hallstein, 'Angleichung des Privat- und Prozeßrechts in der europäischen Wirtschaftsgemeinschaft' (1964) 26 *Rabels Zeitschrift für ausländisches und internationales Privatrecht* 211; much more incisively later, IE Schwartz, '30 Jahre EG-Rechtsangleichung' in E-J Mestmäcker (ed), *Eine Ordnungspolitik für Europa: Festschrift Hans von der Groeben* (Baden-Baden: Nomos, 1987) 333, 335.

[38] On the international-law disciplines, see M Martinek in D Simon, n * above, 529 ff, 567 ff, 577 ff.

[39] OJ C 92/1975, 1; C 133/1981, 1.

[40] Doorstep selling: OJ L 372/ 1985, 31; Consumer credit: OJ L 42/1987, 47; Package travel: OJ L 158/1990, 59; Unfair terms in consumer contracts: OJ L 95/1993, 29.

[41] OJ L 210/1985, 29.

[42] COM85 (310) final 14.6.1985.

Act radically changed this situation. Unexpectedly, the science of private law was again confronted – 20 years after the beginning of its internal and not yet formally concluded codification debate – with legislative interventions in private law.

This debate determines the present[43] and will, whatever happens to the Community following the Maastricht Treaty, intensify still further. Accordingly, it does not belong in a historical article. All the same, the history of private law is rich in suggestions for this debate. The integration process forces renewed grappling with the universalisability of private-law principles and rules, with the meaningfulness of legislative activities – but also with the erosion of the nation state and its political institutions.

Europe's integration means, however, that the legal quality of the Community developing may be assessed, and that the democratically constituted nation states can no longer decide autonomously as to the law and their policies. There is a manifest, undisputed difference between the national constitutional structures and the Community's institutional system.[44] It is worth questioning the significance of this observation: the articles on the effects of integration and private law, on the replacement of private-law law-making processes of national political institutions and cultural traditions, confirm how thoroughly the science of private law is entangled with the history of its patterns of perceptions and interpretations.

If the rational core of European integration consists in its bringing about the preconditions for the achievement of a supranational private-law society, then it is, at least in principle, clear how the process of integration is to be understood and utilised from the regulatory-theory viewpoint.[45] Only the forms of realisation of the supranational private-law society remain to be considered. A European codification of the market-oriented core materials of civil law has been advocated for years by Wilfried Tilmann on the basis of his conceptualisations of the functions of commercial and private law inspired by regulatory and systems theory.[46] A compelling alternative has been formulated by Fritz Rittner:[47] differences between the private-law systems were consciously accepted

[43] The rich literature and the current state of debate are documented by P-C Müller-Graff (ed), *Gemeinsames Privatrecht in der Europäischen Gemeinschaft* (Baden-Baden: Nomos, 1993); for an analysis taking up the theoretical perspectives of this essay, see C Joerges, 'The Impact of European Integration on Private Law: Reductionist Perceptions, True Conflicts and a New Constitutionalist Perspective' (1997) 3 *ELJ* 378, reprinted in ch 7 of this volume.

[44] For a current diagnosis, see D Thürer, 'Der Verfassungsstaat als Glied einer europäischen Gemeinschaft', *Veröffentlichungen der Vereinigung Deutscher Staatsrechtslehrer* 50 (1991) 97 ff, 109 ff, 122 ff.

[45] E-J Mestmäcker, 'Die Wiederkehr der bürgerlichen Gesellschaft und ihres Rechts' (1991) 10 *Rechtshistorisches Journal* 177.

[46] *Wirtschaftsrecht* (Berlin-Heidelberg-New York-Tokyo: Springer, 1986) 237 ff; Mestmäcker prefers this way because he sees harmonisation of private law as an opportunity to promote the development of private law in the states of Eastern and South-Eastern Europe, ibid 192.

[47] 'Die wirtschaftliche Ordnung der EG und das Privatrecht' (1990) 45 *JuristenZeitung* 838.

by the EEC Treaties. Dealing with them is to be entrusted not to the Community legislature but to the decisions of the market citizens themselves. The opening of the markets and the obligation on the States to recognise their legal systems mutually was supposed to include the freedom of market citizens to choose the regulation which suited them. Indirectly, then, a private law meeting the wishes of private persons was to come to prevail. From this viewpoint, the debates about the EC's democratic deficit concern a pseudo-problem: the constitutionality and freedom of the legal system(s) in the Community legitimate the effects of integration on private law, because their form does not concern matters concerning national citizens, but concerns only matters concerning market citizens.

In practice, neither of the alternatives has consistently been implemented to date. The Community's decisional procedures have, instead, meant that the European legislature, when coming up against legal obstacles to the achievement of the internal market, often enough imposes not the abolition of binding rules but their unification at a 'high level of protection' through majority decision. The law of the European internal market is constitutive altogether, not just of freedoms but also of protective rules and claims.[48] Private lawyers discussing these easily explicable findings[49] rightly complain that the 'pointillist' operations[50] of Community law inside the national legal systems have, as a consequence, system breakdowns, contradictory evaluations and forced coordination, so that Community law simultaneously acts innovatively and destructively, integratively and disintegratively.[51] The science of private law will learn to deal with these difficulties just as it did with the 'fragmentary and periodic character'[52] of domestic legislation. But even if it shows this willingness, the follow-up question remains on the agenda: how is the legitimacy that national private law owes to the reciprocally informed and controlling influences of legislation, adjudication and practice, science and the public, to be guaranteed in the process of Europeanisation of private law?

This question concerns the future constitution of the European polity. The fact that this question concerns not just the public-law disciplines but also the science of private law is a lesson from German history. But what does private law have to do with the nation state's claims to power as diagnosed by Max Weber?

[48] N Reich, 'Binnenmarkt als Rechtsbegriff' (1991) 2 *Europäische Zeitschrift für Wirtschaftsrecht* 203.

[49] See E Steindorff, 'Freedoms, Regulation and Fundamental Social Rights After the Expanded Goals of the EC Constitution' in H-W Micklitz and St Weatherill, *European Economic Law* (Aldershot: Ashgate, 1997) 71 ff; JHH Weiler, 'The Transformation of Europe' (1991) 100 *Yale LJ* 2403, 2456 ff.

[50] H Kötz, 'Gemeineuropäisches Zivilrecht' in H Bernstein, U Drobnig and H Kötz (eds), *Festschrift für Konrad Zweigert zum 70. Geburtstag* (Tübingen: Mohr Siebeck, 1981) 481, 483.

[51] P Hommelhoff, 'Zivilrecht unter dem Einfluss europäischer Rechtsangleichung' (1992) 192 *Archiv für die civilistische Praxis* 71.

[52] See J Esser, 'Gesetzesrationalität im Kodifikationszeitalter und heute' in H-J Vogel and J Esser (eds), *100 Jahre deutsche Justizbehörde: Vom Reichjustizamt zum Bundesministerium der Justiz* (Tübingen: Mohr Siebeck, 1977) 13, 18.

There is little doubt as to the innocence of private law as such. It is equally indubitable that the rules of private law are interwoven with all those institutions and regulatory measures whereby the nation state keeps its own economy operational and ensures the social integration of its society. The constitution of a European republic could not leave these questions out. A purely rule-of-law organisational form that does not simultaneously both enable and legitimate solidarity-based action cannot domesticate the Weberian power State – another lesson from history.

7

The Impact of European Integration on Private Law: Reductionist Perceptions, True Conflicts and a New Constitutional Perspective[*]

I. INTRODUCTION

THROUGHOUT EUROPE, EVER more attention is being focused on the impact of the integration process upon our systems of private law. This extraordinary growth in academic work exploring new and theoretically fascinating private legal aspects, contrasts strikingly, however, with the so far seemingly marginal impact of European legislation on what is commonly understood to represent the core of private law. Equally, the jurisprudence of the European Court of Justice (ECJ) has to date left only subtle and sometimes hardly visible traces within national private legal systems.

This essay will not even attempt to give an overview of all the relevant legal events, nor a comprehensive account of the academic comments upon them.[1] Instead, it concerns itself with the elaboration of a specific theoretical, namely, 'constitutionalist' perspective which makes use of the analytical tools and normative perspectives which more general studies on the Europeanisation of

[*] Published in (1997) 3 *ELJ* 378–406.

[1] For a brief summary of relevant legislative acts and the jurisprudence of the ECJ, see W Kilian, *Europäisches Wirtschaftsrecht* (Munich: CH Beck, 1996), at 317–324, including a rich bibliography; for a less topical but very useful overview, see also E Hondius, 'Towards a European Civil Code. General Introduction' in AS Hartkamp et al (eds), *Towards a European Civil Code* (Leiden: Nijhoff, 1994) 1; P-C Müller-Graff, 'Directives as a Means of Private Law Unification', ibid, 77; among the more recent initiatives the proposal of the European Parliament and Council for a Directive on the sale of consumer goods and associated guarantees, OJ C 307/1996, 8 with the first editorial comment on a private law issue in (1997) 34 *Common Market Law Rev* 207 stands out; see the preparatory Greenbook on consumer guarantees, COM(93) 509 final of 15 November 1993; E Hondius, 'Kaufen ohne Risiko: Der Europäische Richtlinienentwurf zum Verbraucherkauf und zur Verbrauchergarantie' (1997) 5 *Zeitschrift für Europäisches Privatrecht* 130; P Schlechtriem, 'Verbraucherkaufverträge – ein neuer Richtlinienentwurf' (1997) 52 *Juristen Zeitung* 441; extremely critical, W Kircher, 'Zum Vorschlag für eine Richtlinie über den Verbrauchsgüterkauf und Garantien' (1997) 30 *Zeitschrift für Rechtspolitik* 290.

regulatory policies have evolved, and then applies them to the field of private law.[2] This approach, however, entails well-known risks. Cross-references must at times remain sketchy and thus difficult to understand; practical suggestions based on the analytical concepts and normative considerations employed often remain quite abstract. To point to such risks, however, is to assert that they be worth taking. These, then, are the steps I would like to suggest.

In a first section, a series of current controversial perceptions, policy or other prescriptive statements on the Europeanisation process will be summarised and grouped in three categories. A subsequent evaluation of the three groups, however, lends support to one of the major contentions of this essay: namely, that any analysis neglecting the 'constitutionalist' dimensions of the Europeanisation process is reductionist and therefore inadequate, and that this holds true for the most widely held views on the Europeanisation of private law, albeit for very different reasons. The first category comprises all those private law scholars who simply equate 'Europeanisation' with the substitution of national private law by European-wide applicable rules and principles; the second, a significant school (at least in Germany), interprets the supremacy of European law as establishing the primacy of Europe's 'economic law' over all 'politicised' national law. The third grouping comprises those various positions which defend 'national' private law on the basis of its supposedly superior normative quality.

Analytical and Normative Alternatives

All of these approaches draw upon their own specific theoretical, methodological, historical and empirical assumptions. For reasons of limited space, I will not describe these various background agendas in any detail; I will, however, also try to avoid 'falsifying' them. Instead, I attempt to follow a more straightforward and constructive approach, based upon an analytical conceptualisation of the EU as a 'multi-level system of governance', which is borrowed from political science. The normative perspectives of this approach are inspired by legal theories of deliberative democracy and by the on-going search for a new European constitutionalism. This programme can and should be read as an alternative to current conceptualisations which lay emphasis upon the non-legal basis of our private laws, or upon their underlying 'national' specificity, '*Volksgeist*' or '*moralité*'. Instead, it focuses upon the problem of legitimacy within private law and private governance, as perceived by constitutionalist legal theories.

Implications

A drama in three acts. The third section attempts to illustrate the implications of an application of this normative theory and analytical approach to three

[2] I will build quite heavily on my previous work, cited where necessary in the text.

concrete examples. Based upon an examination of the manner in which the judiciary deals with current controversies, the examples all seek to demonstrate the current need: first, to cope with the detection of elusive 'universal' legal principles; secondly, to adapt to the emergence of transnational legal structures; and thirdly, to deal with the disintegration of formerly more consolidated national legal systems.

II. REDUCTIONIST PERCEPTIONS AND THE CONSTITUTIONAL DIMENSIONS OF THE EUROPEANISATION PROCESS

As indicated, this section deals with current positions and controversies. It does not seek to present a comprehensive overview, but instead aims to introduce a specific interpretational framework which will be more fully elaborated in the following sections. This framework is specifically designed to enable the identification and exploration of the 'constitutional' dimensions of the Europeanisation process. A discussion of these issues, or so it is suggested, is indispensable to the development of an adequate and true understanding of the fundamental importance of the changes which private law is currently undergoing by virtue of the impact of European integration.

A. Neglecting European Law

To many observers, the suggestion that the process of European integration has affected the constitutional dimensions and importance of private law may seem exaggerated, counter-intuitive or purely academic. To date, most 'European' private law commentators have begun with the understandable assumption that private law is by definition a simple matter of 'traditional core areas' such as 'contracts, torts, property, inheritance or family law'.[3] If such definitions are accepted, one might declare the importance of 'European law private law' to be marginal, or alternatively question the relevance of private law to the process of European integration.

And indeed, not only the Community legislator, but also the notoriously activist ECJ have proven to be extremely cautious in their approach to the traditional realms of private law.[4] It is only in the field of consumer protection that

[3] M Reimann, 'American Private Law and European Legal Unification – Can the United States be a Model?' (1996) 3 *Maastricht Journal of European and Comparative Law* 217, at 219; see, also, H Collins, 'European Private Law and the Cultural Identity of States' (1995) 3 *European Review of Private Law* 353, at 354.

[4] See the observations in D Caruso, 'The Missing View of the Cathedral: The Private Law Paradigm of European Legal Integration' (1997) 3 *ELJ* 3. A telling example is provided by the ECJ's reluctance to invoke the four freedoms of European primary law as a yardstick against which rules and principles of private law are to be measured and justified. For recent accounts of this, especially in

the Community has an impressive record;[5] and such activity might in fact be read as confirmation that Europe has only marginal importance in the 'core areas' of private law.[6]

But is the fact that the 'core areas' of private law have rarely been directly touched by Europe at all significant? Even if one refuses to take Community activities in the field of consumer protection seriously, one cannot deny that they do affect the realm of private ordering, the legal meaning of autonomy and liability, and the balance between self-responsibility and paternalism. In all these respects consumer protection measures form part of the *institutional frameworks* of markets. They (co-) determine what it means to be a 'market citizen'. Once one begins to pay attention to these, the 'regulatory' functions of European legislation, their fundamental impact upon private law is immediately recognisable. The entire institutional framework of the European economy has been affected by Community legislation and its implementation. European integration has, as Majone puts it,[7] contributed to the transformation of the 'positive' (Keynesian, welfare) state with its emphasis upon re-distributive policies and the discretionary management of aggregate demand, into the much leaner 'regulatory' state with its alternative focus upon the promotion of privatisation, liberalisation, welfare reform, deregulation strategies; all the while tailoring its 'juridification' of economy and social forces to these objectives. These new strategies have deeply affected the basic orientation of our legal systems as well as individual legal fields. One need here only to point to such areas as competition law; company law; insurance law; banking and capital market law; intellectual property rights and the broad areas of social regulation (product safety law, safety at work law, environmental law).

Private lawyers may still insist that all of these developments occur outside their own premises. What they can no longer convincingly deny, however, is that it is 'Europe', and no longer national legislation or the Member States, which determines the extent of the 'private' and the mode of its regulation. Equally, however, my discomfort with such reductionist perceptions is based upon one

Germany intense debate, see E Steindorff, *EG-Vertrag und Privatrecht* (Baden-Baden: Nomos, 1996), 277 ff; P v Wilmowsky, 'EG-Freiheiten und Vertragsrecht' (1996) 51 *JuristenZeitung* 590; N Reich, 'A European Constitution for Citizens: Reflections on the Rethinking of Union and Community Law' (1997) 3 *ELJ* 131.

[5] References throughout the text.

[6] In Germany, consumer protection measures through *special* legislation have been regarded as threatening the systematic unity and coherence of private law and, probably to the surprise of common law lawyers, been criticised as a legislative usurpation of law-making powers; for a historical account of the German debate on '*Sondergestzgebungs*', see C Joerges, 'Die Wissenschaft vom Privatrecht und der Nationalstaat' in D Simon (ed), *Rechtswissenschaft in der Bonner Republik* (Frankfurt aM: Suhrkamp, 1994) 311, at 345–351, with references [reprinted in part in ch 6 of this volume].

[7] G Majone, 'From the Positive to the Regulatory State: Causes and Consequences of Changes in the Mode of Governance' (1997) 17 *Journal of Public Policy* 139; see, also, G Majone, *Regulating Europe* (Abingdon: Routledge, 1996) at 265–301.

further observation. Whereas the 'traditional core areas' of private law may have retained their familiar grammar, the institutional frameworks of the private economy and all concomitant regulatory activities have been 'Europeanised'; a fact which has radically altered the overall legal (and normative) environment in which private law operates. Even where private law appears to have preserved its 'national' characteristics, the Europeanisation process has replaced its former institutional environment. It is this discrepancy between the apparent survival of private law institutions and the erosion and renewal of their social function which the analysis of the EU as multi-level system of governance is able to capture.[8]

B. Claiming Supremacy for Europe's 'Economic' Constitution

Whereas the European Community's economic and social regulatory frameworks form part of a limited supranational – albeit non-statal – autonomous legal order, national private law remains embedded in the comprehensive – albeit diverse – legal orders of constitutional nation-states. This discrepancy implies a paradox, if not a normative *scandalum*. European law, through the supremacy both of the economic freedoms guaranteed by primary law and of the many regulatory provisions found in its secondary legislation, has established legal frameworks which not only regulate the operation of markets and the activities of 'market citizens' but also claim primacy over and independence from the legal systems of national states within which citizens are supposed to 'govern' themselves through the exercise of their constitutionally guaranteed (political) rights. Nowhere has this problem been more explicitly dealt with than in the German ordoliberal tradition with its interpretation of the European (formerly: Economic) Community as an economic legal order of constitutional validity.

Summarising this position briefly:[9] the integration of the Member States and the consequential renunciation of sovereignty set the scene for the creation of a 'Law' which would dictate the substantive process and the substantive results of integration. This 'Law' is at its core '*economic*' constitutional law since integration should be based on open markets and should aim for the creation of one common market; at the same time this 'Law' is economic '*constitutional*' law as it envisages that the opening up of markets should follow through the competitive process and that this common market should take the form of a system of undistorted competition. The foundations of this interpretation were laid during the construction phase of the EEC and were further refined during

[8] See Section III A below.

[9] For more comprehensive analyses, see C Joerges, 'Economic Law, the Nation-State and the Maastricht Treaty' in R Dehousse (ed), *Europe after Maastricht: an Ever Closer Union?* (Munich: CH Beck, 1994) 29; and idem, 'The Market without a State? States without Markets? Two Essays on the Law of the European Economy', EUI Working Paper Law 1/96, Florence 1996 [first essay reprinted in ch 21 of this volume].

the debates of the late 1970s.[10] That this theory did not accurately portray the construction phase of the EEC and the historical 'will' of the Member States that can be deduced from it was well known by its supporters.[11] But nevertheless the fact that the agreement made among the founder states resulted in the growth of a Treaty dominated by very strong anti-interventionist policies, and thus favoured the establishment of a liberal economic regime, has been interpreted – most notably, by Müller-Armack – as 'the cunning of reason' (*List der Vernunft*).[12]

The interpretation of the EEC Treaty as an economic constitution committed to the advancement of market integration and the achieving of the principles of a market economy then gave a theoretical evaluation of this 'cunning of reason'. This brought two results: on the one hand, the Community, through its interpretation as an order constituted by law and committed to economic freedoms, acquires a legitimacy that protected it against all attacks motivated by democracy theory or constitutional policy. On the other, the restriction of Community powers developed an effect of blocking social policy moves illegitimate from the point of view of neoliberal order theory.[13]

Leaving aside the emergence of so many European regulatory frameworks, and just considering the status of economic freedoms as guaranteed by primary law, the ambivalent implications of the ordoliberal doctrine in general and the quasi-constitutional importance of 'private' law become even more apparent.[14] By granting the Union's 'market citizens' (*Marktbürgern*) freedoms/rights which they can assert against their 'own' state, European law is disempowering the constitutional state's (political) citizens.[15] Students of American law will note the affinity of Germany's ordoliberalism with the famous *Lochner* decision of 1905[16] and more topical authors such as Richard Epstein.[17] Private law in this

[10] See J Scherer, Die Wirtschaftsverfassung der Europäischen Gemeinschaft (Baden-Baden: Nomos, 1970); DW Rahmsdorf, Ordnungspolitischer Dissens und europäische Integration (Kehl: Engel, 1982).

[11] H von der Groeben, 'Zur Wirtschaftsordnung der Europäischen Gemeinschaft' (1981) in idem, *Die Europäische Gemeinschaft und die Herausforderungen unserer Zeit. Aufsätze und Reden 1967–1987* (Baden-Baden: Nomos, 1987) 201.

[12] A Müller-Armack, 'Die Wirtschaftsordnung des Gemeinsamen Marktes' in idem, Wirtschaftsordnung und Wirtschaftspolitik. Studien und Konzepte zur Sozialen Marktwirtschaft und zur Europäischen Integration (Freiburg: Rombach, 1964) 401.

[13] E-J Mestmäcker, 'Politische und normativ-funktionale Legitimation der Europäischen Gemeinschaften' in idem, *Recht und ökonomisches Gesetz* (Baden-Baden: Nomos, 1972) 82; for updated versions of this argument see, idem, 'Zur Wirschaftverfassung der Europäischen Union' in RH Haase *et al* (eds), *Ordnung und Freiheit. Festschrift für Hans Willgerodt zum 70. Geburtstag* (Tübingen: Mohr/Siebeck, 1996) 263; idem, 'On the Legitimacy of European Law' (1994) 58 *Rabels Zeitschrift für ausländisches und internationales Privatrecht* 615; for a recent restatement in terms of economic theory, see K Mayer and J Scheinpflug, *Privatrechtsgesellschaft und die Europäische Union* (Tübingen: Mohr/Siebeck, 1996).

[14] See E-J Mestmäcker, 'Die Wiederkehr bürgerlichen Gesellschaft und ihres Rechts' (1991) 10 *Rechtshistorisches Journal* 177.

[15] See JHH Weiler, 'The Reformation of European Constitutionalism' (1997) 35 *JCMS* 97, 115.

[16] *Lochner v New York*, 198 US 45 (1905).

[17] RA Epstein, *Simple Rules for a Complex World* (Cambridge MA: Harvard UP, 1995).

perspective *is* constitutional law. European integration has constitutionalised a transnational 'private-law society' with supremacy over national states.[18]

German ordo[liberalism] and Anglo-Saxon neoliberalism mark clear theoretical positions. This does not, however, prejudice many pragmatic issues such as the usefulness of a European code,[19] the possible replacement of choice-of-law rules by a unified substantive body of rules, the workability or not of the concept of regulatory competition. Their in-built reservation about the intrusion of political processes into the pre-political realm of private ordering under the rule of law, however, is not a mere transpositive fantasy. The EU as a 'Market Without a State' and the Member States of the Union as (constitutional) 'States Without a Market';[20] this is a normatively well-elaborated conception with powerful practical backing.

The dichotomy between an unpolitical European private law society and its 'political' counterpart is, in one sense, highly artificial and may be argued to be a misleading construct. As has already been pointed out, the EU has never even tried to rely exclusively upon private law or privately organised governance structures in its integration policies and market building activities. However, in the minds of those who pursue the *normative* project of establishing a European 'private law society' this point is easily dismissed as a 'positive' argument, best to be treated with benign neglect or even turned into a critique of the EU's practices. Furthermore, however, supporters of the ordoliberal conception of an economic constitution also possess a trump card. Opponents of this tradition who believe that constitutional states should through their political processes actively endorse and delimit the realm of private governance are, in the European setting, logically called upon to conceptualise equivalent constitutional structures for a pluralist rather than unitary European polity: a notoriously difficult task. To phrase this point slightly differently, the real (and negative) strength of ordoliberalism derives from the difficulties which its opponents have in designing and substantiating the constitutional structures which could legitimately determine the social functions of private law in the European polity.

C. Defending the Normative Quality of (National) Private Law

Do we private lawyers really have to tackle such issues? They seem very distant from current controversies; are we witnessing a gradual convergence of private

[18] See, again, Mestmäcker, 'On the Legitimacy ...', n 13 above, and, in a historical perspective, O Lepsius, *Verwaltungsrecht unter dem Common Law* (Tübingen: Mohr/Siebeck, 1997) 51 ff.

[19] But see Mestmäcker, n 14 above, at 192 (arguing that the harmonisation of private law would be helpful for the new democracies of Eastern Europe); W Tilmann, 'Eine Privatrechtskodifikation für die Europäische Gemeinschaft' in P-C Müller-Graff (ed), *Gemeinsames Privatrecht in der Europäischen Gemeinschaft* (Baden-Baden: Nomos, 1993) 485.

[20] See the analyses in Joerges, 'The Market without a State?' n 9 above.

law systems in Europe or will the trenches especially between common law and civil law jurisdictions prove so deep as to render convergence impossible?[21] Should we seek unity at all, and would we not be better placed defending the values of diversity?[22] If we believe in the need for a Europeanised private law, should we become heirs of Thibaut and opt for a European code, soft in the beginning and hard at a later stage,[23] or should we instead follow in von Savigny's footsteps and trust in the continued vigour of what may be a common legal heritage?[24] Alternatively, should we revive the spirit of Ernst Rabel and breathe life into a dusty *ius commune* heritage?[25] How are we to defend nascent European private law against a new parochialism, and promote the cause of international uniformity?[26] What will be the appropriate role for private international law, and how might it be used to ensure the interests of private actors in transnational cooperation be furthered?[27]

These are all distinct issues; and yet, they do have constitutional dimensions and can be rephrased within the interpretative framework previously outlined. The contrasts and missing links between this new constitutionalist perspective on the legitimacy and validity of European private law and current academic controversies on the desirability of Europeanisation processes, can probably be best identified by closely analysing the objections against private law

[21] See P Legrand, 'European Legal Systems are not Converging' (1966) 45 *International and Comparative Law Quarterly* 52; idem, 'Uniformity, Legal Traditions, and Law's Limits' (1996–97) *Juridisk Tisdskrift* 306.

[22] See P Legrand, 'Against a European Civil Code' (1997) 60 *MLR* 44.

[23] O Lando, 'Teaching a European Code of Contracts' in B de Witte and C Forder (eds), *The Common Law of Europe and the Future of Legal Education/Le droit commun d'Europe et l'avenir de l'enseignement juridique* (Alphen a/d Rijn: Kluwer, 1992) 223ff, O Lando, 'Principles of European Contract Law: An Alternative to or a Precursor of European Legislation' (1992) 56 *Rabels Zeitschrift für ausländisches und internationales Privatrecht* 261ff; O Lando and H Beale (eds), *Principles of European Contract Law. Part I: Performance, Non-Performance and Remedies* (The Hague: Martinus Nijhoff, 1995).

[24] R Zimmermann, 'Das Römisch-Kanonische Ius commune als Grundlage europäischer Rechtseinheit' (1992) 47 *JuristenZeitung* 8; idem,'Der Europäische Charakter des englischen Rechts-Historische Verbindungen zwischen civil law und common law' (1993) 1 *Zeitschrift für Europäisches Privatrecht* 4; idem, 'Civil Code and Civil Law. The "Europeanization" of Private Law Within the European Community and the Re-emergence of a European Legal Science' (1994/95) 1 *Columbia Journal of European Law* 63; see R Schulze, 'European Legal History – A New Field of Research in Germany' (1992) 13 *Journal of Legal History* 270.

[25] H Kötz and A Flessner, *Europäisches Vertragsrecht* (Tübingen: Mohr/Siebeck, 1996).

[26] See, as an early example from the work of MJ Bonell, 'Das autonome Recht des Welthandels – rechtsdogmatische und rechtspolitische Aspekte' (1978) 42 *Rabels Zeitschrift für ausländisches und internationales Privatrecht* 485, and idem, 'The Unidroit Principles – A Modern Approach to Contract Law' in H-L Weyers (ed), *Europäisches Vertragsrecht* (Baden-Baden: Nomos, 1997) 9.

[27] See, from an expanive debate, J Basedow, 'Europäisches Internationales Privatrecht' (1966) 19 *Neue Juristische Wochenschrift* 1921; idem, 'Der kollisionsrechtliche Gehalt der Produktfreiheiten im europäischen Binnenmarkt: *favor offerentis*' (1995) 49 *Rabels Zeitschrift für ausländisches und internationales Privatrecht* 1; W-H Roth, 'Die Freiheiten des EG-Vertrages und das nationale Privatrecht – Zur Entwicklung internationaler Sachnormen für europäische Sachverhalte' (1994) 2 *Zeitschrift für Europäisches Privatrecht* 5; HJ Sonnenberger, 'Europarecht und Internationales Privatrecht' (1996) 95 *Zeitschrift für vergleichende Rechtswissenschaft* 3.

harmonisation. These objections may all be identified as variations upon one dominant theme: disintegration. And indeed, any European legal innovation claiming to become part of 'the law of the land' can be called an intervention with disintegrating effects.[28] Such effects have been identified at different levels. Whilst German critics of European harmonisation measures have often pointed to the disintegration of systematic interdependencies within the whole body of private law,[29] common law lawyers are more commonly struck by the challenge posed by integration to the linkages between private law and cultural identity.[30] Importantly, the differences between such concerns should not be simply interpreted as reflecting widely held views on the 'typical' preoccupations of civil law and common law lawyers. The divergence may instead seem less extreme upon precise inquiry into the underlying meaning of legal systematics, the subtle ties between legal doctrines and social practices, and the equal need to determine the meaning of new principles and rules in the context of the whole of the legal system which is to implement them.[31] References to the specifics of legal systems may, however, take the form of quasi epistemological objections to the replacement of old law through the adoption of new law with identical meaning and/or be presented as a defence of the values of legal diversity. The most profound and eloquent proponent of this form of scepticism is Pierre Legrand whose critical stance is readily apparent in his philippics against any convergence expectations[32] and even more explicit in his rejection of the idea of a European code.[33] Legrand's assertions as to the characteristics of civil law and common law systems and the 'typical views' of academics may all be questioned by pointing to this and that development or the listing of typical views.[34]

[28] See Joerges, 'Economic Law …', n 9 above, at 32–35 (pointing to the conceptual bases of legal regulation); M Everson, 'Laws in Conflict. A Rationally Integrated European Insurance Market?' PhD Thesis, EUI Florence 1993, esp ch 5 (emphasising the socio-economic embeddedness and functions of regulatory traditions); K Dyson, 'Cultural Issues and the Single European Market: Barriers to Trade and Shifting Attitudes' (1993) 64 *Political Quarterly* 84.

[29] H Kötz, 'Gemeineuropäisches Zivilrecht' in H Bernstein, U Drobnig and H Kötz (eds), *Festschrift für Konrad Zweigert zum 70. Geburstag* (Tübingen: Mohr/Siebeck, 1981) 481, at 483; P Hommelhoff, 'Zivilrecht unter dem Einfluß europäischer Rechtsangleichung' (1992) 192 *Archiv für die civilistische Praxis*71.

[30] H Collins, 'European Private Law and the Cultural Identity of States' (1995) 3 *European Review of Private Law* 353.

[31] See P Schlechtriem, 'Good Faith in German Law and in International Uniform Laws' (Rome: Centro di Studi e Ricerche di Diritto Comparato e Straniero, 1997) 6.

[32] See n 21 above.

[33] Legrand, 'Against a European Civil Code', n 22 above.

[34] I simply fail to see in what sense the differences between German and French adjudication in its highest courts or the styles of the German Constitutional Court and the ECJ might be less significant than the differences with eg their American counterparts; similarly, I suggest that the formation of theoretical positions in legal science – including that of Legrand – has long become transnational – even though any detailed elaboration of such positions and their transformation into rules, principles and doctrines may require much fine-tuning. See, for a short elaboration, C Joerges, 'Introduction' in idem (ed), *Franchising and the Law: Theoretical and Comparative Approaches in Europe and the United States* (Baden-Baden: Nomos, 1991) at 9.

Even his references to 'deeply-embedded world-views within societies'[35] could be taken as indicating that transnational legal discourses need to include such transpositive elements of practical philosophy. Legrand, however, accumulates all these complexities to render his '*rien ne va*' message plausible: the 'fundamental differentiation between the civil law and common law', he argues, is one of 'two *moralités*'[36] which are not simply competing but unable to communicate about their differences in a meaningful search for better or commonly acceptable solutions. 'What point, then, a unitary text of reference in the absence of a unitary rationality and morality …'[37]

This post-modern point cannot be falsified; it nevertheless seems inconclusive. Even if there is no universal rationality, the drafters of European legal texts do daily arrive at understandings which they consider to be meaningful; the same holding true for the implementation of complicated legal texts by European committees consisting of the representatives of many diverse scientific and legal communities.[38] There seems in reality to be a far greater potential for intercultural discourse than post-modern accounts would suggest. What Legrand pre-supposes is, in my view, far more unlikely than an understanding among lawyers from common law and civil law countries that 'national' traditions continue to convey 'deep-seated convictions' on the social order, 'world-views', *Vorverständnisse*, *mentalités* and *moralités*. It is one thing, however, to insist on the importance of such terms; it is quite another to term them 'cultural'[39] and assert their ongoing structuring force. At the end of this century our '*mentalités*' have long been informed by and exposed to many influences from very divergent 'cultural' origins. The convergence/non-convergence dichotomy, then, seems misleading because it rests upon the organicist premise that our societies continue to (re)-produce coherent legal cultures including some distinctive idiosyncrasies. What if we can no longer reckon with this type of commonly shared background life-world, but instead with a fragmentation or pluralisation of cultures within our legally unitary societies? The real issue, then, would be whether we can in our political democracies and legal institutions build on the

[35] Legrand, 'Against a European Civil Code', n 22 above, at 48.

[36] Ibid, at 47.

[37] Ibid, at 60.

[38] See C Joerges and J Neyer, 'From Intergovernmental Bargaining to Deliberative Political Processes: The Constitutionalisation of Comitology' (1997) 3 *ELJ* 273 [reprinted in ch 12 of this volume]. More familiar examples include the interpretation of international conventions, the ECJ's quest for '*richtlinienkonforme Auslegung*' and the follow-up of its jursprudence on state liability; see W van Gerven, 'Bridging the Unbridgeable: Community and National Tort Laws after *Frankovich* and *Brasserie*' in H-W Micklitz and N Reich (eds), *Public Interest Litigation before European Courts* (Baden-Baden: Nomos, 1997) 57 [also in (1996) 45 *International and Comparative Law Quarterly* 507].

[39] Suffice it to point here to the example of the somewhat long-winded, yet convincing re-construction of German formalism by W Ewald, 'Comparative Jurisprudence (I): "What was it Like to Try a Rat?"' (1995) 143 *U Pennsylvania Law Rev* 1889, at 2045ff and 2119–21.

power of reason to deal reasonably with cultural diversity – and this seems to me the more attractive alternative, at least in normative terms.[40]

III. MULTI-LEVEL GOVERNANCE STRUCTURES AND DELIBERATIVE POLITICAL PROCESSES

As the preceding section illustrated, the dichotomies which have to date characterised the debate on European integration may all be argued to suffer from very similar positive (or factual) and/or normative shortcomings. While a positive critique highlights the role of explicit or implicit assumptions about the Europeanisation process, a normative critique draws more upon the constitutional dimensions both of private law systems in general and of the integration process in particular. Both aspects will now be specified. The positive or analytical side of the argument draws upon political science approaches to European integration; the normative argument refers to deliberative theories of democracy.

A. Analytical Tools: The Multi-level Governance Approach to European Integration

Up until quite recently political scientists commonly began their analyses of the problems of European integration by relating their own research to two specific and competing schools of thought; namely, intergovernmentalism, on the one hand,[41] and neo-functionalism,[42] on the other. However, this routine has now altered to a degree which suggests that this once well-established dichotomy has been overcome. A major challenge comes from a new school of thought, upon which the following observations are based, and which portrays the EU as a 'multi-level system of governance'. This analysis highlights the erosion of nation-states, denies, however, their transformation into a new European super state. The concept of governance used is flexible enough both firmly to capture certain *sui generis* characteristics of the emerging European polity such as its lack of internal hierarchy and its reliance upon 'Law', and to leave open the question of exactly where the European system lies on a scale between the

[40] See G Teubner, 'Legal Irritants: Good Faith in British Law. Or How Unifying Law Ends up in New Cleavages' [(1998) 61 *MLR* 11], with all relevant references.

[41] See A Moravcsik, 'Preferences and Power in the European Community: A Liberal Intergovernmentalist Approach' (1993) 31 *JCMS* 473; idem, 'Why the European Community Strengthens the State. Domestic Politics and International Cooperation', Harvard University, *Center for European Studies, Working Paper* 1994, No 52.

[42] For a classic elaboration see EB Haas, *Beyond the Nation State. Functionalism and International Organisation* (Stanford CA: Stanford UP, 1964).

traditional nation-state and looser forms of international cooperation. Equally importantly, however, this approach also conceptualises 'integration' as a contingent political process and is therefore better equipped than functionalism to deal with the interests and strategies engaged in and pursued by institutional as well as non-governmental actors at both national and supranational levels. Rather than elaborate on this extremely brief sketch,[43] however, my use of aspects of the multi-level analysis in the context of private law might be better explained in the light of the compatibility of 'multi-levelism' with three 'positive' aspects of the Europeanisation process; trends characteristic of the overall European legal system and particularly important for private law.

First, the multi-level approach appears to be perfectly compatible with certain specific and oft-noted features of the present situation; the conservation of the core elements of national private law systems; the imposition by the EC of a patchwork of substantive consumer protection rules which are designed to further market-building processes; the substitution of national by European frameworks of economic and social regulation; and finally, the openness of the European legal system to international cooperation both in its regulatory activities and in its efforts to facilitate private law relations. Secondly, however, this approach also has the advantage of being able to conceptualise 'governance' independent from or beyond our formalised nation-state and Community legal structures, and likewise seems compatible with what we 'know' about the erosion of national sovereignty on the one hand and the growth of regulatory powers at the European level on the other. Thirdly, however, and most important for my purposes, this analytical framework also allows the interdependence of legal integration with disintegration to be articulated and characterised as a dual and simultaneous development; the building up of frameworks for economic and social regulation in so many institutional variants is certainly an important element of Europe's market-building strategies. This integrationist move, however, likewise cuts the ties between national markets and their traditional institutional environment.

The qualitative impact of this restructuring on private law is only indirect; it is nevertheless of fundamental importance. It suffices to rephrase three points. First, the freedoms granted to Union citizens strengthen their autonomy. Secondly, the dismantling of so many of the regulatory frameworks which have governed important sectors of the economy, together with the privatisation of formerly state-owned enterprises, necessarily widens the private realm. Third, new European regulatory policies, especially in the area of social regulation,

[43] The literature is abundant; important contributions include FW Scharpf, 'Community and Autonomy: Multilevel Policy-Making in the European Union' (1994) 1 *Journal of European Public Policy* 219; M Jachtenfuchs, 'Theoretical Perspectives on European Governance' (1995) 1 *ELJ* 115; M Jachtenfuchs and B Kohler-Koch, 'Regieren im dynamischen Mehrebenensystem' in eidem (eds), *Europäische Integration* (Opladen: Leske + Budrich, 1996) 15; G Marks, L Hooghe and K Blank, 'European Integration from the 1980s: State-centric v Multi-level Governance' (1996) 34 *JCMS* 343.

cannot simply be qualified as 'less rigid' than their national counterparts;[44] instead, they tend to strengthen the role of non-governmental actors and likewise rely on the expertise and management capacities of private enterprises.[45] Private law scholars have only just begun to explore the far-reaching implications of this transformation. However, if legal systems increasingly rely on the assumption or redefinition of regulatory tasks by non-governmental organisations and private actors, the normative goal of law is likely to shift, directing a greater deal of its energies towards ensuring the 'social responsibility' of new structures of private governance. In short, the end of the era of interventionist (public law) regulation may likewise usher in an unexpected *renaissance* in private law.[46] In any case, analytical examinations of these processes must bear in mind such potential.

B. Normative Suggestions: Borrowings from and Amendments to Deliberative Democratic Theory

Interdisciplinary excursions, though useful, entail many risks, including the potential fallacy of misplaced equations. One need not be an avid supporter of the autopoietic understanding of social systems to recognise that the simple transplantation of analytical integration theory into the various normative *weltanschauung* of legal disciplines entails dangers of its own. 'Multi-level governance' is not a legal concept. Its relevance to legal discourse can only be indirect or suggestive and also needs to be backed by a thorough exploration of its potential convergence with distinctive (and self-contained) legal reconstructions of the social world. Likewise, a related risk stems from the divergent manner in which legal and political sciences use normative premises and articulate their prescriptive perspectives. The multi-level governance approach to Europe entails normative implications and aspirations which are immediately relevant within the political sciences, but which cannot and must not be conclusive in the matter of the elaboration of a constitutional charter for the European Union. While the bridge made here between multi-level analysis and certain established normative concerns, is itself founded upon a well-elaborated body of thought which has

[44] For a comprehensive recent analysis of European social regulation, see V Eichener, *Entscheidungsprzesse in der regulative Politik der Politischen Union* (Habilitation, University of Bochum, 1997) [later published as V Eichener, *Das Entscheidungssystem der Europäischen Union: Institutionelle Analyse und demokratietheoretische Bewertung* (Opladen: Leske + Budrich, 2000)].

[45] See C Joerges, 'Rationalisierungsprozesse im Recht der Produktsicherheit: Öffentliches Recht und Haftungsrecht unter dem Einfluß der europäischen Integration' (1994) 27 *Jahrbuch des Umwelt- und Technikrechts* 141.

[46] It is again important to note that the EC acts as a promoter of developments that have broad bases and precursors in national systems; see G Teubner, 'The "State" of Private Networks: The Emerging Legal Regime of Polycorporatism in Germany' (1993) 2 *Brigham Young University Law Rev* 553; J Black, 'Constitutionalising Self-Regulation' (1996) 59 *MLR* 24.

historically inspired both (normative) political theory and legal constitutionalism, one must nevertheless continue to be aware of the in-built assumptions inherent to individual contributions. Most refer to integrated unitary societies whereas the process of Europeanisation demands additional reflection upon two further queries; namely the imposition of 'external restraints' on the political autonomy of constitutional states on the one hand, and the emergence of transnational governance structures on the other.

1. *Deliberative Supranationalism and National Constitutionalism*

One intuitively appealing analytical feature of the multi-level governance approach is its portrayal of the EU as a non-state and non-hierarchical system, and here it shares many of (though not all) the characteristics of a 'richer' understanding of 'supranationalism' which goes beyond the legal logic of direct effect and instead attempts to respect the normative logic of constitutionalism by resorting to the concept of 'deliberation'.[47] The explicitly normative term 'deliberative supranationalism' thus not only accepts the open-endedness or contingency of the integration process, but also bases itself on two intuitions: on the one hand, it builds upon legal theories which ground the law's validity upon the institutions of the traditional constitutional state and the disciplining of internal political controversies through them;[48] on the other, however, it also takes the notion of 'deliberation' further, no longer grounding supranationalism in formal international law or in technocratic or ordoliberal traditions, but in the establishment of external and taming deliberative political processes between states (institutional actors) and societies.

Explaining this argument further: the legitimacy of governance within constitutional states is flawed in so far as it remains inevitably one-sided and parochial or selfish: built on inclusionary principles 'national' constitutions famously remain exclusionary. The taming of the nation-state through

[47] This reading of suprantionalism I have advocated in various contexts; for private law, see C Joerges and G Brüggemeier, 'Europäisierung des Vertrags- und Haftungsrechts' in P-C Müller-Graff (ed), *Gemeinsames Privatrecht in der Europäischen Gemeinschaft* (Baden-Baden: Nomos, 1993) 233, at 278–286; for social regulation, see C Joerges, 'Scientific Expertise in Social Regulation and the European Court of Justice: Legal Frameworks for Denationalised Governance Structures' in C Joerges, K-H Ladeur and E Vos (eds), *Integrating Scientific Expertise into Legal Decision-Making* (Baden-Baden: Nomos, 1997) 295, at 300–319.

[48] For a recent elaboration, see O Gerstenberg, *Bürgerrechte und deliberative Demokratie* (Frankfurt aM: Suhrkamp, 1997); important American references include Michelman, 'Law's Republic' (1988) 97 *Yale Law Journal* 1493; C Sunstein, 'Legal Interferences with Private Preferences' (1986) 53 *U of Chicago Law Rev* 1129–1147; idem, *After the Rights Revolution* (Cambridge MA: Harvard UP, 1990); a German author may mention the vicinity to the work of Jürgen Habermas; see FI Michelman and J Habermas, 'Between Facts and Norms: Contributions to a Discourse Theory of Law and Democracy' (1996) 93 *Journal of Philosophy* 307. For contributions dealing more specifically with issues of regulation, see M Seidenfeld, 'A Civic Republican Justification of the Bureaucratic State' (1992) 105 *Harvard Law Rev* 1511; RH Pildes and C Sunstein, 'Reinventing the Regulatory State' (1995) 62 *UChicLR* 1.

democratic constitutions has its limits. If and because democracies presuppose and represent collective identities, they have very few mechanisms ensuring that 'foreign' identities and their interests be taken into account within their decision-making processes. The legitimacy of supranational institutions can be designed as a cure to these 'deficiencies' – as a correction of 'nation-state failures' as it were. It seems easy to detect such elements in European law and to base its claim to supranational validity on exactly that normative quality. Thus, the non-discrimination guarantee of Article 6 can be read as aiming at compensating for the particularism and exclusionary nature of 'national' basic rights; similarly, the prohibition of protectionist policies by Article 30 can be read as meaning that European nation-states must not try to resolve their economic and social problems at the cost of their neighbours.[49] The constitutionalisation of such principles is in line with the inclusionary ideals embodied in democratic constitutions, and legal supranationalism can thus be understood as complementing common features of national constitutionalist traditions.

Equally, however, it is further submitted that they entail a normatively attractive response to so many critics of the European project and that they can be elaborated into a supranational version of the deliberative reading of pluralism. Assuming that 'we the peoples' of Europe do not wish to build a Federal State which would be entrusted with the whole range of tasks which were once assigned to constitutional nation-states; and given that we are nevertheless to live with an opening of the borders of our formerly national economies, we are bound to strive towards an unprecedented polity. We must conceptualise supranational constitutionalism as an alternative to the model of the constitutional nation-state which respects that state's constitutional legitimacy but at the same time clarifies and sanctions the commitments arising from its interdependence with equally democratically legitimised states and with the supranational prerogatives that an institutionalisation of this interdependence requires. The legitimacy of supranational constraints imposed upon the sovereignty of constitutional states can in principle be easily understood. Extra-territorial effects of national policies may be intended; indeed, they are real and unavoidable in an economically and socially interdependent community. This raises the question of how a constitutional state can legitimise the burden it unilaterally imposes upon its neighbours? 'No taxation without representation' – this principle can claim universal validity; the very idea of democratic constitutionalism requires that constitutional states apply this principle against themselves. A supranational constitutional charter therefore does not need to represent a new 'state'. Nor does supranationalism require that democracies concede a right to vote to non-nationals. What it does require is that the interests and concerns of non-nationals should be considered even within the national polity. In this sense,

[49] See JHH Weiler, 'Fin-de-Siècle Europe' in R Dehousse (ed), *Europe After Maastricht: An Ever Closer Union?* (Munich: CH Beck, 1994) 203.

supranationalism does convey *political* rights and not just economic freedoms to Community citizens. Supranationalism is therefore to be understood as a fundamentally *democratic* concept. 'Supremacy' of European law can and should be read as giving voice to 'foreign' concerns and imposing corresponding constraints upon Member States. What supremacy requires, then, is the identification of rules and principles ensuring the co-existence of different constituencies and the compatibility of these constituencies' objectives with the common concerns they share. Community law should lay down a legal framework which structures political deliberation about exactly these issues. It is a constitutional mandate of the ECJ to protect such legal structures and principles and to resolve controversies surrounding their contents.

2. *Transnational Governance?*

One of the problems which this particular reasoning does not resolve, however, is that of the on-going transformation of the 'Community of Constitutional States' into a real and visible 'European polity', characterised by the emergence of an 'institutionalised surplus' of transnational interests and powers out of the process of the constitutionalisation of interaction between its decentral units. This *de facto* process is legalised under European law and constrained by Treaty rules. Its legitimacy, however, is altogether another matter. Once again, one could point for justification to the specific limits of the nation-state in an era of internationalisation and globalisation, namely its lack of capacity and inability to fulfil so many governmental tasks which embody constitutionalised welfare state promises.[50] A closer look, however, reveals the normative (and factual!) limits of such purely functional arguments. An important constitutional divide in the ongoing debate on Europe's future polity can be portrayed with the help of two analyses which both build upon the experiences of constitutional nation-states: the first, by now well-elaborated, being Majone's plea for the establishment of non-majoritarian transnational institutions capable of, and confined to, the credible implementation of non-distributive regulatory objectives;[51] the second, far less visible at the supranational level,[52] being Cohen/Rogers'[53] and more recently Cohen/Sabels'[54] proposal that current shortcomings in traditional constitutional institutions might be compensated for by the

[50] See FW Scharpf, 'Democratic Policy in Europe' (1996) 2 *ELJ* 136.

[51] See references in n 7 above; as an interesting German legal precursor, see HP Ipsen, *Europäisches Gemeinschaftsrecht* (Tübingen: JCB Mohr, 1972) at 176 ff (for further references and a short analysis, Joerges, 'Economic Law', n 9 above, at 38–41); Majone has acknowledged this *Geistesverwandtschaft* in 'The European Community. An "Independent Fourth Branch of Government"?' in G Brüggemeier (ed), *Verfassungen für ein ziviles Europa* (Baden-Baden: Nomos, 1993) 23.

[52] But see V Eichener, n 44 above, Chapters 5 and 6.

[53] J Cohen and J Rogers, 'Secondary Associations and Democratic Governance' (1992) 20 *Politics and Society* 393.

[54] J Cohen and C Sabel, 'Directly-Deliberative Polyarchy' (1997) 3 *ELJ* 313.

development of new forms of democratic governance; importantly, this latter approach also suggests that the search for new but equivalent forms of direct democratic governance should be extended into transnational arenas.

This problem cannot and need not be discussed here in its entirety. Both Majone's plea for non-majoritarian institutions and Cohen/Sabels' thoughts on the legitimisation of democratic governance outside established constitutional structures are complex and carefully tailored to the specific demands of individual policy fields; with Majone's constitutional perspectives being closer to, but by no means identical with, the neoliberal equation of private with (transnational) constitutional law. Accordingly, the following considerations will be restricted in their scope: first, to general observations on the relevance of constitutionalism to private law; and secondly, to the constitutional specifics of the integration process.

3. *Private Law Constitutionalism*

An enormously complex detour, leading nowhere and with no possible application in the field of private law scholarship? In answer, let me first repeat what Europe has done and continues to do to national legal systems. It inserts new individual freedoms into them and so strengthens the realm of private autonomy. It is disintegrative, alienating markets from their traditional institutional environments. It imposes new duties upon traders and assigns inalienable minimum rights to consumers. It establishes transnational regulatory frameworks to which national institutions of private law must adapt themselves.

Such (selective) interventions into national legal systems not only determine the social space which is allocated to markets and to private ordering, but also sets its limits and restricts the techniques which might be used to identify and correct market failures. In other words, European interventions are concerned with exactly those asymmetries in private relationships which legal systems have traditionally affirmed or sought to cure. In the perspective of national legal systems, the fundamental importance of issues of asymmetry thus seems obvious. There may of course be doubt as to whether they will formally be accepted to be of 'constitutional' relevance, with the exact use of this term depending upon the national legal system in question. Thus, on the one hand, private law's function in the common law tradition as a stronghold of individual liberty and societal autonomy,[55] is so obvious as to render further comment superfluous: the defence of this realm in the US against both the external threat of state intervention and the internal danger of self-destruction through the abuse of liberties being *the* classic constitutional issues.[56] As far as civil law traditions and especially Germany are concerned, however, the famous rigidity of the

[55] See O Lepsius, n 18 above, at 31 ff, 37 ff.
[56] Ibid, at 51 ff.

formal state/society divide may confuse matters, with pertinent debates often being fought out within 'isolated' fields of substantive law or legal methodology and thus often making no explicit mention of their constitutional context. Nonetheless, when seen in the perspective of deliberative theories of liberal democracy, the constitutional dimension of issues such as the delineation of the realm of private autonomy and the protection of basic and inalienable rights is simply irrefutable.[57]

4. *Constitutionalising Law-making Outside Constitutional States*

It is one thing to identify the constitutional dimensions of private law within the organisational structures of nation-states; it is quite another to spell out their normative meaning within the integration process. This task represents the core problem of this essay. It may accordingly be useful to rephrase it in two ways. First, the search for a constitutionalist perspective on the Europeanisation process can be understood as a response to the ongoing 'contest' among those individual legal disciplines which are seeking recognition for their specific values and methodologies in an effort to guide the process of Europeanisation:[58] it is an alternative to the organisation of transnational legal relations on the basis of private international law;[59] to a reliance upon the *longue durée* effects of a 'common' European legal heritage (either on its own or in tandem with a comparative foundation for denationalised private law);[60] and, last but certainly not least, to orthodox (formalist) readings of European supranationalism.

Secondly, the search for a constitutionalist perspective for private law is inspired by analyses of European *regulation*. To simply transfer regulatory concepts into private law with its independent focus upon the guaranteeing of spheres of autonomy would certainly be implausible. On the other hand, however, one must likewise take care not to remain bogged down in out-dated and 'pre-Community' versions of the public/private distinction. The regulatory

[57] See O Gerstenberg, 'Private Ordering, Public Intervention and Social Pluralism', Typescript Bremen (Centre for European Law and Politics) 1997.

[58] See the 'Concluding Remarks', Section V below.

[59] That discipline remains perplexed with many issues which Community law has long settled. (1) the protection of basic rights requires exceptional private international law provisions whereas primary and secondary Community law promote transnational principles of justice as a matter of course. (2) Legal systems of private law are recognised as being equivalent as a matter of principle; the application of mandatory foreign rules, however, remains 'one-sided' under PIL even where Community law requires mutual recognition. (3) PIL is not in a position to organise transnational continuous cooperation and refuses, at least in the dominating Continental schools of thought, to assign legal validity to 'interests' societies pursue at an international level, whereas the establishment of transnational regulatory frameworks and the constant accommodation of regulatory concerns and economic interests is a dominant feature and daily business of Community law and its implementation.

[60] See recently for this combination, R Zimmermann, 'Savigny's Legacy. Legal History, Comparative Law and the Emergence of a European Legal Science' (1996) 112 *The Law Quarterly Review* 576.

state's intrusion into the economic sphere by means of all manner of mandatory, paternalistic or distributive legal provisions and the recognition of fundamental rights even within private relationships, are simple facts, omnipresent in all our systems of private law. European integration did not invent but merely promoted and shaped these developments; the originality of European challenges stems instead from the transnational origins and effects of regulation, and it seems useful to consider its typical patterns separately.

(i) 'Positive' Integration and its Disintegrative Implications

As already indicated, and paradoxically enough, a plausible response to normative queries about the European 'impact' appears to be most easily formulated where Community intervention is relatively stringent; for example, in the case of the establishment of regulatory frameworks of transnational governance which are designed to deal with market failures and the externalities of one-sided national regulations, and which are implemented through networks of European committees. But even if this perspective is acknowledged, two further implications must still be considered. The first concerns the replacement and restructuring of formerly national governance structures by new regulatory regimes. Within each and every Member State institutional responses to market failures or otherly-perceived problems are the outcome of specific historical experiences and political compromises which contribute to their social acceptance and thus to their 'functioning'.[61] Such contextual responses cannot be simply replaced and substituted by some isolated legislative fiat. Furthermore, 'traditional' regulatory schemes tend to carry with them promises of social (distributive) justice which may not compensate for their inefficiency but which likewise cannot be simply revoked. The present debate on the universality principle in telecommunications provides a telling example.[62] A second series of problems equally underlies the chorus of disapproval about the many disruptions which Europe has provoked in systematic legal methodology.[63] Even though such complaints are at times purely formalistic exercises in legal logic, they nevertheless often relate to concerns about justice, especially where an institutional innovation threatens the normative coherence of a legal system or fosters new inequalities. European impacts of this kind cannot be predicted or addressed in advance. Instead, their remedy is fully dependent on the development and

[61] See Joerges, 'Economic Law …', n 9 above, at 30 f, 60 f. Closer analysis of most regulatory traditions will reveal such dependencies; for the inevitability of historical compromise and its pivotal role in shaping institutional, regulatory structures, see M Everson on insurance regulation, 'The German Federal Supervisory Authority for Insurance' in G Majone (ed), *Regulating Europe* (Abingdon: Routledge, 1996) 202.

[62] See W Sauter, 'The Evolution of Universal Service Obligations in the Liberalization of the European Telecommunications Sector' (1996) 7 *Utilities Law Rev* 75.

[63] See the references in n 29 above.

maintenance of sensitive cooperation between European and national judiciaries; on the one hand, requiring a decentralised fine-tuning of the impact of European law on national legal systems by national courts; and on the other, being equally dependent upon the underlying readiness of the European legal system to respect normative concerns within the Member States even at the price of a loss in overall uniformity. Rephrasing once more; just as the incompleteness and imperfection of the European polity requires the recognition of spheres of regulatory autonomy, even those European frameworks and regulatory legal objectives which have prior and overwhelming consent may not pre-empt the autonomous search for justice through private law at decentralised levels.[64]

(ii) Transnational Governance Structures and Transnational Legal Principles

The Europeanisation of regulatory policies (which, please note, has just been called a relatively easy issue), establishes transnational structures of governance which require and tend to develop a logic of their own. It is by definition impossible to conceive of the responses developed to new regulatory issues within the networks of European governance as mere 'harmonisation' or a 'compromise' between pre-existing national positions. European regulatory networks are by necessity transformed into genuine governance structures of the European polity. The constitutional issues are not identical, but share important characteristics with the problem of legitimising regulatory policy-making within constitutional states. A whole series of legal fields might be identified, ranging from standardisation and highly controversial risk regulation or environmental protection, to more mundane private law issues such as the control of standardised contract terms in which 'law-finding' has been more or less openly delegated to 'discovery processes' existing outside constitutionally foreseen procedures.[65] Once again, we are faced with the divide or choice already noted;[66] should we simply place our (democratic) faith in non-majoritarian institutions (including courts), or alternatively insist upon the establishment of direct ties with civil society? With their concept of 'directly-deliberative polyarchy',[67] Joshua Cohen and Charles Sabel have recently presented us with a systematic normative account which both demonstrates the increasing need to supplement traditional forms of democracy and insists upon the efficacy of directly democratic forms of governance. Translated to the transnational level, this suggestion would be encouraging of a search for legitimate *fora* of democratic governance to complement the form of

[64] See Section III A below.

[65] For an early version of this observation in the field of private law, see C Joerges, *Verbraucherschutz als Rechtsproblem* (Heidelberg: Recht und Wirtschaft, 1981) at 111 ff; idem, 'Quality Regulation in Consumer Goods Markets: Theoretical Problems and Practical Examples' in T Daintith and G Teubner (eds), *Contract and Organisation* (Berlin: Walter de Gruyter, 1986) 142.

[66] See Section II B 2 above.

[67] See n 54 above.

deliberative cooperative problem-solving just described. This step is less spectacular than it may at first sight appear. Both common and civil law jurisdictions have long agreed that the legislature would be hopelessly overburdened by the task of handing down proper principles and rules of private law. Why should that be any different in a transnational arena? The real difficulties may instead derive from that insight.[68] Is it at all possible to conceive of and conceptualise a transnational legal discourse at the EU level with the same degree of sensitivity as long-established and embedded national legal systems and thus sufficiently open to the claims of diverse social actors and the plurality of demands for justice? However, even given the fact that diversity and plurality will necessarily be even greater in the context of a non-unitary polity, the potential ability of the European legal system to detect and define uniform standards should not simply be ruled out; and for the time being, it would seem to be important to set about establishing institutional safeguards which will ensure the proper delineation of the spheres of transnational private law and the legitimacy of its contents.[69]

(iii) 'Negative' Integration, its Innovative Potential and Normative Risks

According to a long-accepted distinction established by economists[70] and then adopted by legal scholars[71] and political scientists,[72] the abolition of trade barriers and implementation of the freedoms guaranteed by the Treaty are characterised as 'negative' integration whereas the use of the term 'positive' integration is restricted to the adoption of common policies and laws. The dichotomy is misleading not only for positive[73] but equally for theoretical reasons. Where formerly regulated spheres have been replaced by market regimes, this shift implies a 'positive' reorganising initiative which cannot be based upon some pre-conceived conception of a European 'economic constitution', but must be justified as a deliberate widening of the spheres of private autonomy. Both the structure of the relevant Treaty Articles, as well as the jurisprudence of the ECJ, are nonetheless incompatible with this view.[74]

[68] See F Kübler, 'Ideologieverdacht und universale Diskursverpflichtung' in E Schmidt and H-L Weyers (eds), *Liber Amicorum Josef Esser: Zum 85. Geburstag am 12. März 1995* (Karlsruhe: CF Müller, 1995) 91, at 105.

[69] See Section III B below.

[70] J Tinbergen, *International Econonomic Integration*, 2nd edn (Amsterdam: North-Holland, 1965). For a recent quasi authoritative definition, see J Pelkmans, *European Integration: Methods and Economic Analysis* (Harlow: Longman, 1997) 6.

[71] N Reich, *Europäisches Verbraucherschutzrecht* 3rd ed. (Baden-Baden: Nomos, 1996) 48ff.

[72] Scharpf, 'Negative and Positive Integration in the Political Economy of European Welfare States' in G Marks, FW Scharpf, P Schmitter and W Streeck (eds), *Governance in the European Union* (London: Sage, 1996) 15.

[73] See Section II A above and the references in n 44 above.

[74] See A Furrer, *Die Sperrwirkung des Gemeinschaftsrechts auf die nationlen Rechtsordnungen* (Baden-Baden: Nomos, 1994), at 161 ff; M Poiares Maduro, 'Reforming the Market or the State? Article 30 and the European Constitution: Economic Freedom and Political Rights' (1997) 3 *ELJ* 55.

IV. TRUE CONFLICTS: THREE EXEMPLARY PATTERNS

Recapping briefly on the argument presented so far: the current debate on the impact of European integration upon private law suffers from reductionist perceptions and an overemphasis on misleading dichotomies. The inappropriateness of such views may be attributed to an insufficient and contradictory perception of the European system as a horizontally structured association of legal systems which are on the one hand, autonomous and representative of unitary polities, but which are also on the other hand, subordinate elements in a European hierarchy which not only claims supremacy for its legal acts but which is also seeking to establish legal unity. In stark contrast to such oversimplified perceptions, the multi-level governance analysis allows us to reconstruct the European system in a more complex, but at the same time far more realistic manner. Such a reconstruction, however, likewise demands the evolution of new normative perspectives; perspectives which are not now readily available to us, being largely absent not only from the orthodox reading of supranationalism in European law, but also from private international and comparative law. The complex and contingent nature of both the current and future state of private law within the EU appears to be decisive, determining that lawyers should *not* at the outset attempt to develop or promote comprehensive and systematic responses to the integration challenge. European integration forces us to re-evaluate the societal links of our legal systems in general, and to reconsider the normative tasks of private law in particular. Since this is an extraordinarily complex task and because future European evolution is contingent in so many ways, the design of new ready-made systems does not seem feasible, and it would instead appear to be more constructive to restrict oneself to the analysis of patterns of exemplary importance and to generalise only in relation to methodological considerations. This, at any rate, is all this concluding section will seek to do.

In accordance with the patterns identified by the constitutionalist interpretation of the integration process,[75] three particular configurations will be explored; each being a case of exemplary importance. The term 'true conflict' merely indicates that the investigation is based on the analytical tools and normative perspectives already outlined; it is not meant to suggest that European integration creates conflicts which are not open to 'legal' resolution.

A. Europeanised Regulatory Politics and National Standards of Justice: The Case of Franchising

European regulatory initiatives never address the legal-institutional environment of a social field in its entirety, but always only concern one particular

[75] Section II B 4 above.

aspect. Their innovative potential and their disintegrative effects in fact derive from this selectivity.[76] European competition law and policy is a case in point. The Treaty rules have been used to substitute national by European regulation, to replace out-dated regulatory patterns with more competitive structures, and to control national and further European industrial policies. Of particular interest to the private lawyer are all those changes which have affected the realm of national contract law.

1. Pronuptia

Examples abound, the *Pronuptia* saga being amongst the most famous. A mirror in prose of the multi-level governance approach to the European system, it clearly highlights the new type of conflict between 'Europeanised' elements and national enclaves which the EU system inevitably generates.

Dealing briefly with the facts, this saga began[77] with a franchising agreement on the distribution of wedding and evening dresses, signed on 16 December 1974 between a French Company, *Pronuptia de Paris SA*, and one Ms Schillgalis. Under the terms of elaborate and supplementary contracts, concluded between herself and Pronuptia de Paris GmbH in November 1975 and January 1980, Ms Schillgalis, as franchisee, was required to remit a fee to the company amounting to 10 per cent of her annual turnover. This, however, she failed to do, justifying her refusal with the argument that the franchisor had not complied with certain agreed-upon commitments. In December 1981, *Pronuptia GmbH* went to court, obtaining a judgment from the *Landgericht* Frankfurt[78] which dismissed nearly all of Ms Schillgalis' claims and ordered her to pay 160.000 DM. Ms Schillgalis promptly appealed to the *Oberlandesgericht* in Frankfurt. To the delight of the franchisee, European competition law was now to intervene, with the *Oberlandesgericht*[79] determining that one clause in the agreement was not compatible with Article 85(1) EC and that the entire contract would thus be void under Article 85(2) EC. Importantly, the relevant clause concerned the franchisee's territorial protection; with the contractual prohibition on the sale of Ms Schillgalis' garments outside the Hamburg region – an assignment common in franchising contracts and specifically designed to protect the interests of the franchisee – falling foul of the Judges. Equally, however, German law interestingly took a back seat. Neither were the Civil Code's (§ 139 BGB) and Unfair Contract Terms Act's (§ 6 AGBG) relevant, complex and extremely sensitive rules on contractual voidability in cases of invalid clauses, to play a part in the case. Nor was the law on unjust enrichment (§ 812 BGB I 1, 2nd alternative) to

[76] See Section I C above.

[77] Legal annotations on the various chapters of the story are too numerous to be mentioned; the following narrative relies on W Skaupy, 'Der Pronuptia-Prozeß 1974–1995' (1996) 51 *Betriebs-Berater* 1899.

[78] LG Frankfurt 3/8 0.49/81 – not reported.

[79] WuW/E OLG 2946.

be invoked to create a *quasi* contractual or non-contractual basis for the remuneration of *Pronuptia*.

Instead, in our saga, European competition law was to play the principal role for many years to come. Pronuptia subsequently appealed to the German Federal High Court (FHC). Refusing initial judgment, this Court instead requested a preliminary ruling from the ECJ in 1984.[80] And accordingly, the ECJ was allowed to hand down its famous *Pronuptia* judgment in January 1986;[81] a judgment which subsequently guided the Commission in its drafting and adoption of Regulation 4087/88 'on the application of Article 85 (3) of the Treaty to categories of franchising agreements'.[82]

All of this led to new contract law chapters in our saga. The FHC having jurisdiction only on points of law, received the ECJ's interpretation of Article 85 EC and referred the case back to the *Oberlandesgericht* in Frankfurt who in turn took the European prohibition of resale price maintenance and of territorial restrictions literally, and held the franchising contract to be void in December 1992. *Pronuptia* promptly re-appealed to the FHC, who reversed the lower Court's decision in February 1994 and instructed it to reconsider the consequences of the invalidity of the anti-competitive clauses in the agreement. This led finally to an *Oberlandesgericht* judgment in September 1994, which gave *Pronuptia* the same sum awarded by the *Landgericht* in 1981. Though Ms Schillgalis gave proof of her staying-power, appealing again to the FHC, that Court declared the story to be over on procedural grounds (§ 554 b ZPO), denying its doctrinal importance and refusing to deal with it a second time.[83]

A tortuous, multi-faceted and paradox-laden story. The following discussion concentrates upon the differentiation between competition policy implications dealt with under European law and issues of contractual fairness addressed by German law.

2. *Diagonal Conflicts*

The EC has a clear mandate to develop and implement a European competition policy. Ms Schillgalis and the Community authorities had taken offence at *Pronuptia*'s disregard for firmly established rules and doctrines of European competition law, namely the prohibition of resale price maintenance and of territorial restrictions. The wisdom of an application of these rules to the franchising agreement at hand might be questioned, and indeed it can be argued that the ECJ did not treat the specific problems of franchising contracts seriously. Nevertheless, and undoubtedly so, the rules in the books provided a

[80] See OJ C 1984/191, 11.
[81] Case 161/84 Pronuptia de Paris GmbH v Irmgard Schillgalis [1986] ECR 353.
[82] OJ L 359/1988, 46.
[83] Case III ZR 241/94, order of 28 September 1995, not reported.

basis for the ECJ's involvement in an assessment of franchising. Its somewhat solemn affirmation of European principles paid tribute to the apparent need for legal continuity in the administration of European competition policy, and this doctrinal umbrella then shielded a shift of paradigmatic importance in the ECJ's reasoning; to wit, a turn to an efficiency-oriented assessment of vertical restraints.

It is exactly this long expected and much celebrated innovation which has accentuated the tensions caused by the Europeanisation process. How does the competition policy driven approach to franchising as a means of efficiently organising distribution interact with a private legal logic which seeks to assess the fairness of such arrangements under contract law? From the perspective of antitrust's new economic rational, any protection of the franchisee's interests through mandatory rules of contract law will seem to be misguided in principle.[84] All legal orders must deal with substantive conflicts of this kind. Within the European system, however, these tensions have an additional 'constitutional' dimension. European competition law claims 'supremacy' over national law. The 'uniform application' and 'full effectiveness' of its 'positive' measures may not be hindered by national law:[85] national competition law, to be sure. But what about other legal fields? The EC cannot simply claim jurisdiction in contract law matters. Equally, however, its Member States may not be allowed to camouflage their disrespect for European law through resort to some other legal label. In short, they may not continue to administer their national contract law as if they had retained full autonomy over its institutional environment.

Official documents tend to avoid the issue.[86] Although 'a block exemption regulation may deal with certain provisions of the protection of franchisees, it only deals with such provisions from the point of view of the competition rules', the drafter of the European regulation explains.[87] And he goes on: '[A]s no harmonisation [of contract laws and social laws] has been judged necessary at Community level, national laws continue to apply. The only limitation to such application is that such legislation should not conflict with the principles of competition law.'[88]

But how can this circle be squared? Before advocating a specific response, however, it may prove useful to consider three dimensions of the conflict and the implications of conceivable solutions.

[84] See the discussion in AW Dnes, 'The Economic Analysis of Franchising and its Regulation', in C Joerges (ed), *Franchising and the Law*, n 34 above, 133.

[85] Case 14/68 *Walt Wilhelm* [1968] ECR 1.

[86] Even the recent 'Green Paper on Vertical Restraints in EU Competition Policy' [COM (96) 721, www.europa.eu.int/en/comm/dg04entente/en/96712/en.htm] does not even mention contract law but discusses only cooperative arrangement within competition policy (Ch III, Parts IV and V).

[87] J-E de Cockborne, 'Franchising and European Community Competition Law' in C Joerges (ed), *Franchising and the Law*, n 34 above, 312.

[88] Ibid, at 313.

A broad interpretation of the supremacy doctrine and/or a wide-ranging acceptance of the pre-emptive effects of European competition law would imply that the 'substantive' conflicts between economic liberties and protective policies have been solved in favour of the former, thereby confirming the neoliberal reading of Europe's 'economic constitution' and, implicitly, through the 'pre-emption' of autonomous national contract law policies contributing to their convergence within in the EU.

An explicit rejection of such far-reaching consequences leads logically to fundamentally different conflicts. European competition law, even if conceived of as a hierarchical system, would be confronted with a broad range of legal doctrines and practices which would multifariously affect its regulatory functions. No longer would European competition policy be a simple matter of the streamlined implementation of its own regulatory objectives. Instead, it would in each individual case be fully dependent upon the cooperation of national jurisdictions.

In many fields, the search for legal formulae acceptable throughout the Community, may be fittingly characterised as a process of regulatory competition, during which governmental and non-governmental actors promote the adoption of regulatory policies which serve their particular economic interests and/or are in line with certain general normative concerns.[89] In legal science terms, such a reconstruction of the process of 'harmonisation', and in particular its highlighting of the simultaneous presence within it of economic and normative interests, might be identified as a modernised version of the late Brainerd Currie's 'governmental interest analysis', reminding us that the supporters of a specific legal solution tend in an international context to identify with what they perceive to be the 'real' concerns of their home jurisdictions. Fortunately enough for private law, both the type of conflict which it is called upon to resolve, and the formalised processes of adjudication in which it evolves, effectively shield it from any explicit or blatant political involvement. Nevertheless, an effective resolution of existing 'diagonal conflicts' between European competition policy and national contract law systems will need to be based on something more than formal comparative research or (horizontal) conflict of laws rules.

3. *Compatibility versus Supremacy*

But what exactly might form the normative leitmotif for the resolution of conflicts within the EU's multi-level system of governance? If we start from the assumption that the Europeanisation of competition policy is a sound and

[89] See, for an institutional economics perspective, L Gerken, 'Institutional Competition: An Orientative Framework' in idem (ed), *Competition Among Institutions* (London: Macmillan, 1995) 1, and for a political science analysis, A Héritier, S Mingers, C Knill and M Becka, *Die Veränderung von Staatlichkeit in Europa* (Opladen: Leske + Budrich, 1994) at 1–5, 12–19 and 386–395; A Héritier, 'The Accommodation of Diversity in European Policy-making and its Outcomes: Regulatory Policy as a Patchwork' (1996) 3 *JEPP* 149.

legitimate project, the defence of national autonomy in contract law must be limited. Again, however, the quest for a conflict-mediating mechanism can seek inspiration from other fields of integration policy, and most notably from the very rich jurisprudence on the compatibility of national regulatory policies with Article 30. Interestingly enough, the ECJ has on numerous occasions been able here to find answers which respect both the Community's market-building objectives and national concerns.[90] It is, however, per definition impossible to isolate a single doctrinal formula from which such solutions might be formally 'deduced'. They need instead to be detected. In the specific example of franchising, it seems conceivable that national courts base their assessment of the fairness of such relational contracts upon a materialised understanding of the autonomy of semi-independent entrepreneurs. Though a full explanation of this point would require too lengthy an [exposition],[91] its major characteristics may once again be underlined; the process of conflict resolution must mediate between Europeanised policies and national autonomy; it will and must not lead to uniformity in Europe's contract law, but needs, instead, to be based upon conceptual reorientation and inventiveness.

B. Transdisciplinary Elements in the Europeanisation Process

A second dimension of the Europeanisation process identified above,[92] is the emergence of transnational, non-hierarchical governance structures unforeseen in any national constitution or the European legal system. The development of such governance structures is closely linked with the numerous European market-building projects and the regulatory problems which they must resolve. Unsurprisingly, the logic of market building has rarely if ever affected private law directly; the one possible exception to this rule being European consumer protection measures, which, somewhat unconvincingly, have been presented as being motivated by market integration objectives.[93]

Private law thus appears to retain its (relative) autonomy. It therefore seems all the more remarkable that the absence of specific Community projects notwithstanding, integration has nonetheless likewise triggered an adaptation process in private legal fields. As numerous examples demonstrate, European law presents legal entrepreneurs with new opportunities.[94] These actors pursue all manner and kinds of interest, and the legal reactions they provoke cannot be expected

[90] See Section II B 4 iii (text accompanying n 74 above).

[91] See the deliberations in C Joerges, 'Contract and Status in Franchising Law' in idem (ed), *Franchising ...*, n 34 above, especially at 64–66.

[92] Section II B 4 ii above.

[93] See, extensively, Joerges and Brüggemeier, 'Europäisierung des Vertrags- und Haftungsrechts', n 47 above.

[94] See the rich analyses by N Reich, 'Public Interest Litigation before European Jurisdictions' and H-W Micklitz, 'The Interest in Public Interest Litigation' in eidem (eds), *Public Interest Litigation ...*, n 38, at 3–20, 21–38, respectively.

to amount to any systematic body of law; lacking formal guidance, their strategies are structured only to the degree that the actions of national courts are very loosely coordinated with those of the ECJ. It is nevertheless justified, albeit in a primarily negative sense, to regard such legal events as elements within new transnational governance structures, since the legal developments referred to here all arise out of the interdependence of the national polities which make up the EU. They confirm the emergence of new legal structures if and insofar as they transcend the conceptual boundaries of our conventional legal techniques.

The following two examples have this in common: they could and would have been decided under the rules of private international law had not practising lawyers been ingenious and the national courts been ready to take European law seriously. Instead, the ECJ was given an opportunity to examine and delineate the impact of European law. This impact prove to be limited yet important. Though the replacement of national law by a unitary European regime was never at issue, a new type of legal pluralism nonetheless emerged within the European system.

1. GB-Inno-BM: *A Supranational Economic Constitution Structuring the Rights of Market Citizens?*

The ECJ's 1990 decision in *GB-Inno-BM*[95] is often cited, not only as providing support for the contention that market freedoms take precedence over national economic regulation, but also as being proof of the existence and validity of a normative EU commitment to consumers.[96] The ECJ held that Luxembourg's prohibition upon the distribution of leaflets from a Belgian supermarket within the Grand Duchy was incompatible with Article 30 EC; Luxembourg considered the Belgian firm's leaflets, advertising price reductions with reference to both the limited duration of the campaign and the prices previously charged, to be an act of unfair competition. Both a market-oriented and consumerist interpretation may draw comfort from the Court's reasoning. On the one hand, the ECJ explained that 'national rules of the type at issue … may not be justified by reasons of consumer protection';[97] on the other, the Court likewise stressed that 'free movement of goods concerns not only traders but also individuals', and further that '[the] freedom of consumers is compromised if they are deprived of access to advertising available in the country where purchases are made'.[98]

[95] Case 362/88 GB-INNO – BM v Confédération du commerce luxembourgeois [1990] ECR I-667; see, also, Case C-126/91 Schutzverband gegen das Unwesen in der Wirtschaft v Yves Rocher [1993] ECR I-2361 and Case C-305/92 Verband sozialer Wettbewerb v Estée Lauder [1994] ECR I-317. One is, as a matter of course, expected to point to Cases 267 and 268/91 Keck and Mithouard [1993] ECR I-6097 limiting the scope of Article 30; in the reading of the case law submitted in Section II B 4 iii above, the ECJ appears to have acted much more cautiously than many of its supporters and critics suggest.

[96] See Reich, 'A European Constitution …', n 4 above, at 143 with references.

[97] Case C-362/88, n 95 above, at 689, para 19.

[98] Ibid, at 686, para 8.

Importantly, however, this simultaneous confirmation of two principles, namely the free movement of goods under Article 30 *and* the legal enforceability of the ancillary opportunities which this freedom confers upon individuals, was likewise complemented and prompted by a series of additional considerations which could not and cannot simply be transformed into rules with Europe-wide application. Indeed, the ECJ's reasoning was subtle in the extreme, and two considerations accordingly deserve particular mention. First, among all the Member States of the EU, only Luxembourg and Germany were found to prohibit this form of promotional material;[99] and even these two countries were shown to have played their part in the Council adoption of two Resolutions on consumer policy,[100] both of which contained an explicit 'consumer right' to adequate information.[101] Secondly, the competitors in the case were also neighbours.[102] Luxembourg citizens habitually cross-border shop, and could thus safely be assumed to have been able to understand and assess Belgian marketing campaigns. Taken together, these considerations militated in favour of the interests of the Belgian trader and the freedoms of Luxembourg consumers. The recognised principles of free movement and consumer opportunity were therefore not promoted as generally applicable absolutes, but were instead accepted both in view of 'real' European events and in the light of the particular local environment in which they were to have force.

Qualifying considerations of this sort transcend the conceptual frameworks of our more traditional legal disciplines. The logic of private international law would demand that a clear and generalisable choice be made between the application of Luxembourg's more stringent legislation and the more liberal Belgian law; both the alternative as such and the likely decision in favour of the law of Luxembourg, however, do not do justice to the embeddedness of the controversy in an integrated region and an integrating Community. Even European law, at least in its more orthodox reading, does not foresee the fine-tuning activities in which the ECJ engages.

This, then, seems to be the message of *GB-Inno-BM*: the ECJ is not prepared simply to impose a Community-wide regime in an area not covered by Community legislation; it is, however, ready to remind both governmental and non-governmental actors of what it means to live in a 'legal' Community.

2. Alpine Investments: *Supervising Regulatory Policies Softly*

The ECJ's reluctance to act as the final arbiter on competing regulatory philosophies on the one hand, and its tolerance towards the fragmentation of the EU's legal system on the other, is even more explicitly demonstrated by the much

[99] Ibid, at 687, para 12.
[100] OJ C 92/1975, 1; OJ C 13/1981, 1.
[101] Case C-362/88, n 95 above, at 687 f, paras 14–16.
[102] Ibid, at 686, para 8.

discussed judgment in *Alpine Investments* decided in March 1995.[103] Alpine, a Dutch company, was active in the market for commodities futures. A Dutch Finance Ministry rule imposed a blanket prohibition on the marketing of these investments through the 'cold calling' of potential customers and a motion of Alpine to obtain an exemption was rejected.

In its appeal, Alpine argued that the Dutch general prohibition was incompatible with the freedom of services guaranteed by Article 59 in so far it applied to potential investors in other Member States such as Belgium which do not prohibit cold calling. The ECJ rejected that contention. Again one is struck by the unconventional nature of the ECJ's reasoning. From the viewpoint of private international law, the ECJ's approval of the Dutch prohibition can be read as an extraterritorial application of Dutch law, which is all the more remarkable as the ECJ endorsed a 'governmental interest' analysis, arguing that it be legitimate for the Dutch legislator to adopt regulations with a view to 'inspiring confidence in investors' and that 'maintaining the good reputation of the national financial sector may therefore constitute an imperative reason of public interest capable of justifying restrictions on the freedom to provide financial services'.[104] But could we expect a Belgian court, if asked for protection by a [Belgian] customer, to apply Dutch law? This the ECJ did not suggest explicitly. If Community law restricts quasi *ex officio* the liberties of service providers, does this amount to the judicial imposition of a Community-wide regulatory regime? All the ECJ suggested was that in view of the 'speculative nature and complexity of commodities futures contracts',[105] regulatory measures are justified and those imposed by the Dutch authorities do not seem disproportionate to the objectives they seek to achieve.[106]

Strictly 'private' [Belgian] law and Dutch regulatory philosophies, so we can safely conclude, may coexist. Belgian courts, however, should feel encouraged to resort to 'foreign' mandatory policies in order to protect their own citizens. Dutch providers of inherently risky financial services must at any rate comply with the orders of their authorities, even when they are asked not to exploit the regulatory gaps in their neighbour's legal systems. This again is a 'fill-gap' rule hindering any race to the regulatory bottom. This form of judicial supervision neither negates in principle nor systematically resolves the regulatory problems of financial services in an integrating market; and yet the ECJ assumes an active protective role, determining which form of justificatory reasoning the proponents or opponents of regulatory intervention may bring forward.

[103] Case C-384/93 Alpine Investments BV v Minister van Financiën [1995] ECR I-1141.

[104] Ibid, at 1179, paras 42 and 44.

[105] Ibid, at 1179, para 42.

[106] Ibid, at 1179, paras 45–46. See A Furrer, 'European Law without Peak and Centre?' [in O Gerstenberg and C Joerges (eds), *Private Governance, Democratic Constitutionalism and Supranationalism* (Luxembourg: European Commission, 1998) 167], pointing out that the ECJ did by no means require the UK to adapt her regulatory provisions to the Dutch model.

3. *Setting Standards of Justice Through Legislation and Primary Law?*

One cannot simply demand that the judiciary pro-actively construct a coherent transnational legal framework. What can be expected, however, is normative coherence, or at least a degree of sensitivity where the constitutional elements of private law are at stake. This tension between the need for normative certainty and the inevitable factual uncertainty about the effects of judicial actions can be observed in the interpretation of both secondary and primary law. The first of the examples cited here is hardly spectacular, the second, a *cause célèbre*.

(i) Doorstep-selling and Bank Guarantees

Back in 1985, the Community, then still acting under Article 100 EC's unanimity requirement, adopted a directive on doorstep selling[107] introducing a cooling-off period of one week for consumers who had been persuaded to contract at home. At this time, no one could possibly have predicted that this simple and limited legal act [would] one day be used, for good normative reasons, to put into question a deep-seated doctrinal tradition embedded in the German Civil Code's (BGB) provisions on guarantees. This opportunity nevertheless arose thanks to the attentiveness of one German lawyer and the readiness of the Federal High Court (FHC) to refer a controversy which had even annoyed the German Judiciary, to a European forum.

Under §§ 765 ff BGB, guarantees, which must always be confirmed in written form, require no consideration, creating one-sided obligations. As a matter of course, the German legislator implemented the 1985 Directive.[108] However, in translation the term 'mutual obligation' had become '*entgeltlicheLeistung*' – or contract with financial consideration – thus raising a presumption that the implementing legislation only be applicable to synallagmatic contracts but not to unilateral engagements. Had the German legislature failed in its European duties; should bank guarantees signed outside the bank's premises, nonetheless be covered? No, explained the 9th Senate of the *Bundesgerichtshof* three times.[109] But their colleagues in the 11th senate had their doubts. What was and is at issue? An intra-German controversy on legal formalism and the specifics of statutory interpretation? A defence of the autonomy of German law against European interventions in general? A confirmation and clarification of the

[107] Council Directive of 20-12-1985 to protect the consumer in respect of contracts negotiated away from business premises (85/577/EEC), OJ L 372/1985, 31.

[108] Gesetz über den Widerruf von Haustürgeschäften und ähnlichen Geschäften of 16 January 1986, BGBl. I 122.

[109] Judgment of 24 January 1991, IX ZR 174/90 (1991) 44 *Neue Juristische Wochenschrift* 975; Judgment of 28 May 1991, IX ZR 260/90 (1991) 44 *Neue Juristische Wochenschrift* 2905; Judgment of 12 Janaury 1993, IX ZR 90/92 (1993) 46 *Neue Juristische Wochenschrift* 1261.

principle that directives must not claim direct ('horizontal') effects? These questions have attracted enormous academic attention.[110]

Is European law in a position to decide all of these issues? Should not the controversy among the two Senates of the FHC be decided upon by the 'Great Senate' as provided for in § 132 *Gerichtsverfassungsgesetz*? The justices of the 11th Senate preferred not to challenge their colleagues' legal wisdom directly but chose instead to invoke the superior authority of European law. They argued, first,[111] that Germany's implementing legislation must respect the original Directive to the point of reproducing its paternalistic objectives. Having only then become aware that the scope of the European Directive was not itself that clear, they secondly determined that its interpretation should therefore be left to the ECJ.[112]

Whilst the issues just named may be discussed in purely formal methodological terms, it nonetheless entails a matter of substantive justice. The cooling-off period prescribed by European law is designed to promote 'reasonableness' within contracting; it reflects a 'civic' or materialised understanding of the concept of private autonomy. Does the general acceptance of this principle, however, require its uniform application throughout the Community, even in borderline cases? Would it be more appropriate for the European legal system to restrict its control of Germany's implementing legislation in line with the standards laid down by the *Francovich*, *Brasserie* and *Factortame* jurisprudence?[113] As is the case with all European consumer protection legislation, the doorstep-selling directive expressly allows for more stringent national standards. The ECJ has the means to interpret and enforce minimum standards of justice. Should this power be used even in borderline cases? Or should the ECJ trust in the self-correcting mechanisms available under German law to the Federal High Court's Great Senate?

(ii) European Rights

The impact of guaranteed Treaty freedoms upon private law is a widely-discussed issue, especially in Germany.[114] This debate has a famous traditional and topical background in national law. It vitally concerns the relation between private

[110] See, for particularly careful reconstructions of the whole debate, T Pfeiffer, 'Ein zweiter Anlauf des deutschen Bürgschaftsrechts zum EuGH' (1996) 49 *Neue Juristische Wochenschrift* 3297; C Baldus and R Becker, 'Haustürgeschäfte und richtlinienkonforme Auslegung' (1997) 5 *Zeitschrift für Europäisches Privatrecht* 874.

[111] Judgment of 26 September 1995, XI ZR 199/94 (1996) 49 *Neue Juristische Wochenschrift* 55.

[112] Order of 11 January 1996, IX ZR 56/95 (1996) 49 *Neue Juristische Wochenschrift* 930.

[113] Cases C-60/90 and C-9/90 *Francovich & Bonifaci* [1991] ECR I-5357; Cases 46/93 and 48/93 *Brasserie du pêcheur* [1996] ECR I-01029.

[114] See, with many further references, Reich, 'A European Constitution …' n 4 above; Basedow, 'Der kollisionsrechtliche Gehalt der Produktfreiheiten …' n 27 above, at 18-19; Roth, 'Die Freiheiten …' n 27 above; and Steindorff, *EG-Vertrag …*, n 4 above, at 277-202.

and public (constitutional) law, or the inevitable tensions between the role of the autonomous market citizen and that of the sovereign political citizen.[115] At the European level, the (German) core of the debate relates once again to the theory of an 'economic constitution' or European 'private law society'.[116] To assert that European freedoms 'trump' national restrictions of 'natural' liberties is to regard these possibly separable and individual rights as a comprehensive legal body, and to assign to this body of law constitutional validity and supremacy over national law.

Bosman[117] clearly presents us with a whole series of complex and interesting issues;[118] in the present context, however, it would seem most important to focus upon the ECJ's conceptualisation of European subjective rights, and the main queries in the preceding analysis all converge upon this issue. Are the freedoms guaranteed by the Treaty merely private economic freedoms, or should they have a broader 'political' dimension? An answer to this question is implicit in the ECJ's insistence upon the 'applicability' of Article 48 in the 'private' sphere. The free movement of workers guaranteed by this provision, so the Court explains, 'not only applies to the action of public authorities but extends also to rules of any other nature aimed at regulating gainful employment in a collective manner';[119] it must accordingly not be understood as a mere 'negative' right protecting the individual against public authorities, but instead possesses a comprehensive validity. The acknowledgement that basic European rights have such effects has manifold implications. It obviously implies that controversies concerning the exact contents of a subjective right are to be resolved within 'civil society' where they conflict with other legally recognised freedoms.[120] An acceptance of this task is, however, commensurate with a promise to provide legal yardsticks for 'private' governance structures.[121] Once these implications are acknowledged, extremely complex issues arise. Should the legal control of private governance structures by European law be exercised uniformly throughout the Community or can Europe's legal pluralism be maintained? Is the pluralist option open where the governance structures established by non-governmental actors are truly international?

[115] See Gerstenberg, 'Private Ordering, Public Intervention and Social Pluralism', Typescript Bremen 1996, and, in a historical perspective, Joerges, 'Die Wissenschaft vom Privatrecht ...' n 6 above, at 334ff.

[116] See Section II B above and, for an effort to bridge the channel intellectually, M Everson, 'The Legacy of the Market Citizen' in J Shaw and G More (eds), *New Legal Dynamics of European Union* (London: Clarendon Press, 1995) at 82-90.

[117] Case C-415/93 Union royale belge des sociétés de football association ASBL et al v Jean-Marie Bosman [1995] ECR I-4921.

[118] See S Weatherill, 'European Football Law', [*Collected Courses of the 7th Session of the Academy of European Law* (The Hague: Kluwer Law International, 1999) 339] with many references.

[119] Case C-415/93, n 117 above, at 5065–66, para 82.

[120] Ibid, at 5065, paras 79–80.

[121] See Section III A above (text accompanying n 46).

These questions merely repeat, in a rephrased form, the queries which arise in relation to the legal structuring of Europe's overall multi-level system of governance.[122] Again one may not expect unequivocal answers from the ECJ. My reading of this case, however, is that the ECJ wisely refrained from giving Mr Bosman's right a narrow and definite meaning precisely because it could not predict the practical consequences of such a decision; instead it contented itself with the establishment of a principle which will need to be taken into account [in] any future re-organisation of football.[123] This judicial self-restraint allowed the ECJ to evade the all too delicate issues of pluralist constitutional values and the uniformity of private transnational governance structures. Its interpretation of Article 48 respects the autonomy of Member States, allowing them to weigh the pros and cons of individual freedoms against the organisational freedoms of associations. To impose a duty to reform it was necessary only to explain the incompatibility of the current practices of the football associations with Article 48. European law cannot and will not prescribe a specific regime but should seek instead to civilise reform processes.

V. CONCLUDING REMARKS

There is no real conclusion but rather a suggestion. In prior analyses of the impact of European integration on private law, I tried first to organise legal materials with the help of a dichotomy between the (functionalist) logic of market-building on the one hand and the (normative) logic of private law development on the other;[124] I then related the efforts of the various legal disciplines to win support for their specific values and techniques to Immanuel Kant's famous treatise on the contest amongst university faculties about their proper ranking, suggesting that the logic of market-building will further rationalisation processes in the sense of Max Weber.[125] This essay does not reject those analyses, but seeks instead to develop them further. It seems possible to understand the efforts of the legal disciplines (legal history, private international law, comparative law, European law) to cope with the Europeanisation process as representations of specific rationalities, each combining reconstructions of the European 'reality' with the promotion of normative perspectives. The present effort is above all an analytical alternative. The reference to the 'multi-level governance' approach in political science implies a critique of the (un-coordinated) horizontalism in private international law, of the hierarchical

[122] See Section IV B 2 (discussing *Alpine Investments*).

[123] Case C-415/93, n 117, especially at 5064, para 77 and 5072, para 110.

[124] Joerges and Brüggemeier, n 47 above.

[125] 'The Europeanisation of Private Law as a Rationalisation Process and as a Contest of Legal Disciplines – an Analysis of the Directive on Unfair Terms in Consumer Contracts' (1995) 3 *European Review of Private Law* 175 (Kant's 'Streit der Fakultäten' dates from 1798).

understanding of supranationalism in European law, of the neglect of social diversity in comparative law. 'Deliberative supranationalism' is a normative perspective which responds to the specific structures of the European legal systems. But it does not represent a ready made substantive super system of rules and principles; it is instead meant to operate as a regulative idea providing guidance in the normative evaluation of the conflicts over interests and values the integration process is bound to produce and must resolve.

8

*Private Law in Europe's Political Economy after the Financial Crisis**

I. INTRODUCTORY REMARKS AND THE STRUCTURING OF THE ARGUMENT

PRIVATE LAW HAD a late arrival in European studies. Its mention by the first President of the Commission was cautious, even somewhat timid.[1] Our discipline entered the European legal edifice with some none too impressive directives through the backdoor of consumer policy only in the 1980s, via activities in a sub-discipline which was, at the time, still perceived as a poor and unwelcome relation in the private law family. This inconspicuous beginning was to be followed by a more spectacular career when the integration process unfolded unheard-of dynamics starting from the mid-1980s. The new activities, in particular in the realm of social regulation (consumer protection, safety at work, and environmental protection), did not reach into the core areas of private law. But they did affect the interdependences of private law with such mandatory legal requirements. After the proclamation of an 'ever closer Union' in the Maastricht Treaty of 1992 had fostered new debates on the constitutional architecture and the quest for a 'Constitutional Treaty', it seemed but logical to complement these endeavours with the project of a European civil code. The conceptual background of all these new horizons and initiatives remained, however, indebted to the accomplishments of the foundational period of the integration process and its legendary 'integration through law' agenda.[2]

By now, we have become aware of the flaws of this legacy. The deepening of the integration project has become a much more complex and conflictual process than was once assumed. To carry some coals to Newcastle, the Treaty

* Published in M Ruffert (ed), European Economy and People's Mobility. Project Conference of the Jean Monnet Centre of Excellence Jena (Tübingen: Mohr Siebeck, 2016) 101–25.

[1] W Hallstein, 'Angleichungdes Privat- und Prozeßrechts in der Europäischen Wirtschaftsgemeinschaft' (1964) 28 *Rabels Zeitschrift für auslndisches und internationales Privatrecht* 211.

[2] C Joerges, 'The Impact of European Integration on Private Law: Reductionist Perceptions, True Conflicts and a New Constitutional Perspective' (1997) 3 *ELJ* 378 (reprinted in ch 7 of this volume); and idem, 'On the Legitimacy of Europeanising Private Law: Considerations on a Law of Justi(ce)-fication (*justumfacere*) for the EU Multi-level System' in A Hartkamp *et al* (eds), *Towards a European Civil Code*, 3rd edn (The Hague: Kluwer Law International, 2004) 159.

of Rome and the establishment of the European Economic Community could build upon the principled acceptance of, and allegiance to, democratic constitutionalism in the original six Member States, an allegiance which implied their commitment to the welfare state.[3] The understanding of this background and basis as a common legacy of the integration project is not discredited by the social poverty of the Rome Treaty. That Treaty's grand accomplishment was a rejection of economic nationalism and a transformation of the precarious state of the nature of international relations into a legal ordering of inter-state relations. The focus of the EEC Treaty on the opening of the national economies and the restriction of their political ambitions [was] not perceived as a threat to social values and achievements. It could, instead, be understood as a confirmation of nation-state powers in the realm of welfare policies. This understanding enjoyed wide support and received strong theoretical backing in John Gerard Ruggie's notion of 'embedded liberalism'.[4] The same holds true for the commitment to democracy. To be sure, '"democracy" was not part of the DNA of European Integration',[5] but this 'deficit' mirrored the foundation of the project on an international treaty. International law could neither establish a democracy nor do away with it. And private law? It experienced fundamental transformations after the era of 'classical liberalism' and the establishment of constitutional democracies. It received a social imprint through methodological innovations, judicial activism and democratically-legitimated legislative innovations.[6]

These observations should suffice to elucidate the tensions and conflicts which the integration project was bound to experience once it gained momentum. It seems, in particular, obvious that the steady strengthening of European regulatory activities would be accompanied by debates about the legitimacy of European rule and its democratic credentials. It was, against the background of the common, if manifold, legacy of the welfare state, equally unavoidable that these discussions would include the quest for a European social model and address the tensions between European market-building and the social policies pursued within the Member States. The systems of private law had all experienced moves towards a materialisation of their formalist heritage and an inclusion of regulatory functions into their objectives. The background pattern of these ensuing queries and difficulties is recurrent. The Member States of the

[3] T Judt, *Postwar:A History of Europe since 1945* (New York: Penguin Press, 2005), 791 ff; idem, *Ill Fares the Land* (New York: Penguin Press, 2010), 127 ff.

[4] See, most notably, the 'Ohlin Report': International Labour Organisation, 'Social Aspects of European Economic Co-operation. Report by a Group of Experts' (1956) 74 *International Labour Review* 99; JG Ruggie, 'International Regimes, Transactions, and Change: Embedded Liberalism in the Postwar Economic Order' (1982) 36 *International Organization* 379.

[5] JHH Weiler, 'Europe in Crisis – on "Political Messianism", "Legitimacy" and the "Rule of Law"' (2012) *Singapore Journal of Legal Studies* 248, at 268.

[6] C Joerges, 'The Science of Private Law and the Nation-State' in F Snyder (ed), *The Europeanization of Law. The Legal Effects of European Integration* (Oxford–Portland: Hart Publishing, 2000), 47 (excerpts reprinted in ch 6 of this volume).

Union underwent democratically-legitimated developments which often had much in common but nonetheless mirrored the diversity of their socio-economic and political backgrounds. This diversity constituted the conceptual and political challenge to the integration project which the following sections are going to address. Our discussion will distinguish between the early years – the so-called 'formative period' of the integration process, the dynamic developments that followed the adoption of the Single European Act in 1985 and the programmatic of the White Paper on the completion of the internal market,[7] and, last but not least, the unfortunate turning-point of 1992 with the establishment of Economic and Monetary Union. We will argue that the responses of the European integration policy to the challenges posed by Europe's diversity were, throughout these developments, ill-conceived, and, finally, dramatically wrong in 1992. We will also submit in a separate section (Section III) that all this was by no means unavoidable and '*alternativlos*'.

II. THREE NARRATIVES ON PRIVATE LAW AND EUROPEAN INTEGRATION

The re-construction of the encounters of private law with the integration project can be read as an illustration of path dependencies which led to a lock-in: a foreclosure of constructive alternatives. The conceptual framing of this relationship occurred in the early years of the EEC, long before private law arrived on the agenda of integration politics.

A. 'One Size Fits All': The Messages of the Integration Through Law Project

Re-constructions of the formative period in general and of the early jurisprudence of the ECJ tend to be characterised by unconditioned praise and admiration. 'Integration through law' became a trademark of the European project.[8] Law, we were taught and believed, was to be understood as both the 'agent and the object of integration'.[9] The Treaties were conceptualised as Europe's 'constitutional charter', which the doctrines of direct effect, supremacy, and pre-emption brought to bear in a powerful way. With the benefit of hindsight, the weaknesses of the doctrinal edifice seem readily apparent. Why

[7] Completing the Internal Market: White Paper from the Commission to the European Council (Milan, 28–29 June 1985), COM(85) 310, June 1985.

[8] M Cappelletti, M Seccombe and JHH Weiler, *Integration Through Law: Europe and the American Federal Experience*, vols 1–5 (Berlin: Walter de Gruyter, 1986–2013).

[9] R Dehousse and JHH Weiler 'The Legal Dimension' in W Wallace (ed), *The Dynamics of European Integration* (London, New York: Pinter, 1990) 242, at 243.

should the harmonisation of legal systems lead to a *justice* surplus? Why should the Member States of a Community with socio-economically diverse configurations and divergent political orientations strive for uniformity of their legal regimes and their implementation? How could the primacy of any provision of European law over national law, including provisions of constitutional validity, become the common core of the ordering of the EEC? Why can the most influential of all European law scholars still conclude that '*Van Gend en Loos* is Europe, with all its complexities'?[10] One illuminating explanation remains that *quasi*-irreversible decisions of crucial importance were taken far away from the political arenas[11] and their far-reaching implications became visible only much later.[12]

A touch of *Realpolitik* can be added. The cornerstones of the doctrinal edifice of integration through law, such as the understanding of the economic freedoms as fundamental rights which could be invoked by Europe's market citizens against their national sovereigns, were fully in line with powerful economic interests. It does not matter that the authors of the foundational doctrinal edifice never talked about the economy and its ordering. Out of necessity, Treaty provisions which affected the economy and opened new opportunities to economic agents were to become extraordinarily important.

Here lies the basis of the *de facto* alliance between integration through law, on the one hand, and the 'economic constitutionalism' of Germany's ordo-liberal school, on the other. Ordo-liberalism dominated the private law departments of the young Federal Republic of Germany. This school of thought had a well-elaborated programme for the ordering of the economy 'through law'. This ordering was to be accomplished both through legal rules that institutionalised free markets and through the supervision of their functioning in a system of undistorted competition by the judiciary and independent antitrust authorities. The autonomy of the economy, and the legal protection of that autonomy and its supervision through non-political bodies were understood as the constitutive elements of a *Wirtschaftsverfassung* (economic constitution) that was compatible with democratic constitutionalism and which deserved to be protected against any discretionary political interventions.[13]

[10] JHH Weiler, 'Van Gend en Loos: The Individual and the "Rule of Law" as Subject and Object and the Dilemma of European Legitimacy' (2014) 12 *International Journal of Constitutional Law* 94, at 103.

[11] E Stein, 'Lawyers, Judges, and the Making of a Transnational Constitution' (1981) 75 *American Journal of International Law* 1.

[12] M Rasmussen, 'Revolutionizing European law: A History of the *Van Gend en Loos* Judgment' (2014) 12 *International Journal of Constitutional Law* 136, at 143.

[13] For a concise summary, see F Böhm, 'Privatrechtsgesellschaft und Marktwirtschaft' (1966) 17 *ORDO: Jahrbuch für die Ordnung von Wirtschaft und Gesellschaft* 75; abbreviated English version: F Böhm, 'Rule of Law in a Market Economy' in AT Peacock and H Willgerodt (eds), *Germany's Social Market Economy: Origins and Evolution* (New York: St. Martin's Press/London: Macmillan, 1989) 46. For a seminal elaboration, see E-J Mestmäcker, 'Power, Law and Economic Constitution' (1973) 11 *The German Economic Review* 177.

It is easy to understand why the proponents of ordo-liberalism embraced the agenda of the 'integration through law' project. European law seemed to be perfectly in line with ordo-liberal notions, not only substantively, but also because of its institutional configuration, which entrusted the judiciary with the institutionalisation of open markets and the European Commission with their protection against distortions of their competitive ordering.[14] In what way did all this affect private law? With respect to the dominating 'integration through law' agenda, we can underline its full complacency; with respect to the ordo-liberal school, we can note that the conceptualisation of the EEC as an economic constitution offered a coherent framing of private law, albeit one that remained an abstract utopia of which hardly anybody outside the Federal Republic took notice.

B. The Institutionalisation of Market Rationality after 1985

The Single European Act (SEA) of 1985 and the Internal Market Programme were a shift of paradigmatic dimensions. M Rainer Lepsius has characterised this re-orientation of the integration project as an institutionalisation of a specific rationality-pattern which was to guide the entire spectrum of European policies.[15] In a very similar vein, Marija Bartl discerned the establishment of an 'internal market rationality' as a specific pattern of political action, which 'transformed the very concept of justice underpinning private law, the concept of the person or subject of law, the (re-) distributive pattern of private law as well as the normative basis on which private law stands'.[16] 'Instrumentalisation' is the notion that Christoph Schmid has used to capture the objectives and normative specifics of the Europeanisation of private law.[17] These analyses of the normative contents of European private law must not be equated with the institutionalist explanatory suggestions of the Cologne School of political science and economic sociology,[18] but they do converge in the diagnosis of a 'neo-liberal tilt' of the integration project.

[14] See, in more detail, C Joerges, 'Integration through Law and the Crisis of Law in Europe's Emergency' in D Chalmers, M Jachtenfuchs and C Joerges (eds), *The End of the Eurocrats' Dream: Adjusting to European Diversity* (Cambridge: CUP, 2016), 299.

[15] MR Lepsius, 'Max Weber und das Programm einer Institutionenpolitik' (1995) 5 *Berliner Journal für Soziologie* 327.

[16] M Bartl, 'The Way we do Europe: Subsidiarity and the Substantive Democratic Deficit' (2015) 21 *ELJ* 23; eadem, 'Internal Market Rationality and the Direction of the Union: Resuscitating the Market at the Object of the Political' (2015) 21 *ELJ* 572.

[17] CU Schmid, Die Instrumentalisierung des Privatrechts durch die Europäische Union: Privatrecht und Privatrechtskonzeptionen in der Entwicklung der Europäischen Integrationsverfassung (Baden-Baden: Nomos, 2010); idem, 'The Instrumentalisation Thesis in a Nutshell' in C Joerges and T Ralli (eds), 'European Constitutionalism without Private Law: Private Law without Democracy' (Oslo: Arena Report 3/11; Recon Report 14, 2011), 17.

[18] M Höpner and A Schäfer, *Die Politische Ökonomie der europäischen Integration* (Frankfurt aM: Campus, 2008). See, also, FW Scharpf, *Governing in Europe Effective and Democratic?* (Oxford: OUP, 1999).

This second stage of the encounter between private law and European integration was characterised by tensions and conflicts between the new emphasis on economic rationality and the intensification of European market-building, on the one hand, and the plethora of regulatory objectives pursued by the Member States, on the other. In its seminal judgment in *Cassis de Dijon*[19] the ECJ had defined the concerns which European law accepts as legitimate exhaustively. There is a striking parallel between this holding and the infamous *Lochner* case of 1905[20] in which the American Supreme Court restricted the New York legislature to specific police powers, which were defined as relating to the safety, health, morals, and the general welfare of the public. The much-praised *Cassis*, just like the infamous *Lochner*, was a judgment which asserted the primacy of economic principles over democratic processes.[21] The convergence between jurists and social scientists has its *fundamentum in re*. But this is not the whole story. Neither Lepsius' diagnosis of the institutionalisation of new economic rationality criteria, nor the strength of 'negative', as opposed to 'positive', integration, which the authors from Cologne have meticulously documented in their analyses, mirror the life of the law comprehensively and adequately. This life is much less stringent and coherent than the presentation by observers who rely on sociological categories or the analyses of the political economy would have us believe.[22] Practicing and academic lawyers cannot avoid the discussion of the normative claims raised by litigants, and will, in their evaluations, consider the factual specifics of the particular cases. The life of the law is more messy than the analyses that social scientists deliver.

This, however, is still not the whole story. What lawyers seek to accomplish is a re-construction of the conflict constellations that they encounter in terms of their own discipline, its specific perceptions of societal conditions. Franz Wieacker famously characterised these perceptions as the 'social models' upon which the law relies in its understanding of the social functions of law and the law's normative assumptions.[23] Jürgen Habermas and many others have built on this example.[24] In my own re-construction of the encounters between private

[19] Case 120/78, *Cassis de Dijon* [1979] ECR 649.

[20] *Lochner v New York*, 198 US 45 (1905).

[21] In prior publications, I have neglected this analogy and argued that the judgment in *Cassis* can be read as a wise mitigation between French interests and German concerns (eg, C Joerges, 'Rethinking European Law's Supremacy: A Plea for a Supranational Conflict of Laws' in B Kohler-Koch and B Rittberger (eds), *Debating the Democratic Legitimacy of the European Union* (Lanham, MD: Rowman & Littlefield, 2007) 311. By now, I appreciate the critique of my all-too-positive interpretation by D Chalmers, 'A Comment on Joerges' in Kohler-Koch and Rittberger (eds), this note above, 329; see also AJ Menéndez, 'United they Diverge? From Conflict of Laws to Constitutional Theory? On Christian Joerges' Theory' (*RECON Online Working Paper* 2011/06, Oslo 2006).

[22] C Möllers, 'Krisenzurechnung und Legitimationsproblematik in der Europäischen Union' (2015) 43 *Leviathan* 339.

[23] F Wieacker, Das Sozialmodell der klassischen Privatrechtsgesetzbücher und die Entwicklung der modernen Gesellschaft (Karlsruhe: CF Müller, 1953).

[24] For example, see J Habermas, *Faktizität und Geltung* (Frankfurt aM: Suhrkamp, 1992; idem, *Between Facts and Norms* (Cambridge, MA: The MIT Press, 1999); and idem, 'Paradigms of Law'

law and European integration, I have contrasted the 'logic of private law' with the 'logic of integration', suggesting that these logics differ categorically,[25] with the former being committed to the enhancement of domestic social justice, while the latter has to mitigate between these concerns and the interests of the Community (Union), the details of which cannot and need not concern us in the present context. What has to be underlined is the discrepancy between this re-construction of the relationship between private law and the prevailing narratives.

III. ALTERNATIVE VISIONS

The tensions between market rationality and democratic legitimacy have hence to be understood as a twofold problem with empirical and normative dimensions. We will address first the empirical dimension in terms of economic sociology, before turning to legal conceptualisations of the normative *problématique*.

A. The Economy as Polity

Markets are anything but mechanically-functioning entities. They are social institutions. This is a core message of Karl Polanyi's seminal *Great Transformation*, which has experienced a remarkable renaissance recently[26] and been elaborated upon significantly.[27] Upon this basis, one conceptualises 'the economy as a polity' and the policy implications which Polanyi underlined are definitely noteworthy:[28]

> [G]overnments will find it possible to ... tolerate willingly that other nations shape their domestic institutions according to their inclinations, thus transcending the pernicious nineteenth century dogma of the necessary uniformity of domestic regimes

in M Rosenfeld and A Arato (eds), *Habermas on Law and Democracy* (Berkeley, CA: University of California Press, 1998) 13. See, also, F Kübler, *Über die praktischen Aufgaben zeitgemäßer Privatrechtstheorie* (Karlsruhe: CF Müller, 1975).

[25] See, for example, Joerges, 'Rethinking European Law's Supremacy: A Plea for a Supranational Conflict of Laws', n 21 above; Joerges, 'On the Legitimacy of Europeanising Private Law', n 2 above; C Joerges and G Brüggemeier, 'Europäisierung des Vertrags- und Haftungsrechts' in P-C Müller-Graff (ed), *Gemeinsames Privatrecht in der Europäischen Gemeinschaft* (Baden-Baden: Nomos 1993, 2nd edn 1999), 301.

[26] K Polanyi, *The Great Transformation: The Political and Economic Origins of our Time* (Boston, MA: Beacon Press, 2001 [1944]), edition with Foreword by J Stiglitz and Introduction by F Block. Tellingly, Germany's leading economic sociologist observes: 'We are all Polanyians now'; see J Beckert, 'The Great Transformation of Embeddedness: Karl Polanyi and the New Economic Sociology', *MPIfG Discussion Paper* 07/1, Cologne, 2007, 7.

[27] See, eg, F Block, 'Karl Polanyi and the Writing of "The Great Transformation"' (2003) 32 *Theory and Society* 275; Ruggie, n 4 above; and E Esposito, *The Future of Futures* (Cheltenham: Edward Elgar, 2011) 63.

[28] C Joerges, B Stråth and P Wagner, The Economy as a Polity: The Political Constitution of Contemporary Capitalism (London: UCL Press, 2005).

> within the orbit of world economy. Out of the ruins of the Old World, cornerstones of the New can be seen to emerge: economic collaboration of governments and the liberty to organize national life at will.[29]

With this remark, Polanyi anticipated the insights and messages of the studies on the varieties of capitalism which were initiated by Peter Hall and David Soskice in 2001[30] and taken up and substantiated further in the debates on the financial crisis.[31] All these analyses confirm and underline that the operation of market economies is not uniform because their institutional configurations vary significantly. The main reference and starting-point is 'the way in which firms resolve the coordination problems they face' in five spheres: industrial relations; vocational training and education; corporate governance; inter-firm relations; and employees.[32] In these perspectives, Hall and Soskice developed their by now famous distinction between the (Anglo-Saxon) liberal market economies and the northern European coordinated market economies. They refuse to evaluate the performance of these economies in normative terms, and they do not specify the legal anchoring of the institutions that they have identified. But it is obvious that juridification is a pre-condition for the functioning of both varieties: two implications of normative significance seem equally obvious: a transformation of one variety into another is hard to achieve, and selective insertion of elements of one variety into the fabric of the other can have disintegrative effects.[33]

It is difficult to understand why this, by now, very considerable body of literature has attracted little attention within legal disciplines. Outstanding exceptions include Duncan Kennedy and Gunther Teubner, whose pertinent writings are all the more important in the present context where they are concerned with the Europeanisation of private law.[34] Teubner's work deserves to be cited at some length:

> Contrary to all expectations, the globalisation of markets and the computerisation of the economy have not led to a world-wide convergence of economic institutions.

[29] Polanyi, n 26 above, 253 f.

[30] P Hall and D Soskice, Varieties of Capitalism: The Institutional Foundations of Comparative Advantage (Oxford: OUP, 2001).

[31] M Höpner and A Schäfer, 'A New Phase of European Integration: Organised Capitalisms in Post-Ricardian Europe' (2010) 33 *West European Politics* 344; W Streeck, 'E Pluribus Unum? Varieties and Commonalities of Capitalism', *MPIfG Discussion Paper* 10/12, Cologne, 2010; T Iversen and D Soskice, 'A Structural-Institutional Explanation of the Eurozone Crisis' in Ph Manow, B Palier and H Schwander (eds), *Welfare Democracies and Party Politics: Explaining Electoral Dynamics in Times of Changing Welfare Capitalism* (Oxford Scholarship Online, Oxford, 2018), ch 1; PA Hall, 'Varieties of Capitalism and the Euro Crisis' (2014) 37 *West European Politics* 1223; FW Scharpf, 'After the Crash: A Perspective on Multilevel European Democracy' (2015) 21 *ELJ* 384; and P Manow, *Social Protection, Capitalist Production – The Bismarckian Welfare State in the German Political Economy 1880–2010* (Oxford: OUP, 2000).

[32] Hall and Soskice, n 30 above, 6–8.

[33] A Hassel, 'Adjustments in the Eurozone: Varieties of Capitalism and the Crisis in Southern Europe', *LEQS Paper* No 76/2014; eadem, 'The German Model in Transition' in B Unger (ed), *The German Model; Seen by its Neighbours* (Düsseldorf: Hans-Böckler-Stiftung, 2015) 105.

[34] D Kennedy, 'Political Ideology and Comparative Law' in M Bussani and U Mattei (eds), *The Cambridge Companion to Comparative Law* (Cambridge: CUP, 2012) 35. In particular, see

> Despite all undeniable tendencies to minimise transaction costs, selective mechanisms of the market, processes of re-litigation and regulatory competition, institutional differences have not been wiped out. On the contrary, globalisation and indeed European harmonisation have produced new institutional divergences. One of the most remarkable developments of the last thirty years is that divergences between economic institutions – corporate finance, corporate governance, industrial relations, education and training, inter-company relations, contracting networks, standard setting and dispute resolution – have increased in advanced societies and not decreased, despite the liberalisation of the world markets and the establishment of a common market in Europe.[35]

In this passage, the legal theorist and sociologist prevails over the lawyer. But the translation of the analysis into the world of law follows:

> Production regimes are the institutional environment of economic action. They organise the production of goods and services through markets and market-related institutions and determine the framework of incentives and constraints. Production regimes are the 'rules of the game' which govern economic action. Their idiosyncrasies which equally irritate legal harmonisers and evolutionary economists are explained by the fact that single institutions are not isolated from each other but interact as interdependent elements of a stable system. Financial arrangements and corporate governance are strongly influenced by industrial relations, education and training, contracting networks, inter-company relations, standard setting and dispute resolution and vice versa. They constitute an interlocking system which tends to be self-perpetuating. Fed by strategies of rational collective actors, economic institutions interact with each other and produce specific stable configurations which in their turn enable institutional advantages to be formed in the international competition of production regimes. 'Varieties of Capitalism' are thereby explained by the intra-systemic dynamics of production regimes.
>
> Regimes differ widely from economy to economy, even within the European context. As can be expected, the strongest divide exists between continental European production regimes (Austria, Benelux, Germany, Norway, Sweden, Switzerland) on the one hand and their Anglo-Saxon counterparts (Great Britain, USA, Ireland, Canada, Australia, New Zealand) on the other. Each production regime reacts against external influences as an interlocking system. Thus, they develop a considerable stability in relation to efficiency-driven evolutionary pressures, a remarkable resilience towards changing demands of various markets, a continual resistance against institutional transfers, in short: a considerable historical continuity.[36]

G Teubner, 'Legal Irritants: Good Faith in British Law or How Unifying Law Ends up in New Differences' (1998) 61 *MLR* 11; idem, 'Idiosyncratic Production Regimes: Co-evolution of Economic and Legal Institutions in the Varieties of Capitalism' in J Ziman (ed), *The Evolution of Cultural Entities: Proceedings of the British Academy* (Oxford: OUP, 2002), 161; [and more recently, idem, 'Transnational Economic Constitutionalism in the Varieties of Capitalism' (2020) 1 *Global Perspectives* 13412].

[35] Teubner, 'Idiosyncratic Production Regimes', n 34 above, text accompanying fnn 9–10.

[36] Ibid, text accompanying fnn 25–27.

B. Legal Responses

A number of normative implications for the legal conceptualisation of European integration seem obvious. The diversity of preferences and orientations within the EU is the product of historical experiences, political contestation, societal learning, and continuous decision-making. They cannot be treated as an obstacle to integration which has to be overcome either in judicial proceedings or in intergovernmental-bargaining processes. The 'integration through law' agenda with its one-size-fits-all philosophy is not only sociologically, but also normatively, flawed because of its disregard of the normative infrastructure of the economy. We need to understand the normative fabric of our economic orders as a 'social *acquis*' which is, of course, subject to changes but nonetheless deserves to be protected against illegitimate intrusions.

This understanding and similar insights have informed a variety of endeavours to overcome the 'integration through law' orthodoxy. Only two shall be sketched out here.

1. *Conflicts-law Constitutionalism*

In my own work, I have sought a way to reconcile the democratic deficits of the European project with its democratic commitments by a detour which departs from a critique of the democratic potential of nation states: under the impact of Europeanisation and globalisation, contemporary societies experience an ever stronger chasm between decision-makers and those who are impacted upon by the decision-making. This chasm is a *normative challenge to democratic orders*. Increasingly, constitutional states are unable to guarantee the inclusion of all of those persons who are impacted upon by their policies and politics within their internal decision-making processes. The democratic notion of self-legislation, however, which postulates that the addressees of a law should be able to understand themselves as its authors, demands 'the inclusion of the other'. The conflicts-law approach builds upon these observations and arguments. As a consequence of their manifold degree of inter-dependence, the Member States of the European Union are no longer in a position to guarantee the democratic legitimacy of their policies. A European law that concerns itself with the amelioration of such external effects, ie, which seeks to compensate for the failings of the national democracies, may induce its legitimacy from this compensatory function. With this, European law can, at last, free itself from the critique of its legitimacy, which has accompanied it ever since its birth. Instead of requesting the Union to cure its democracy deficit, we should understand and develop the potential of European law to compensate the structural democracy deficits of the European nation states. Three challenging tasks, which are of particular importance for the evaluation of Europe's crisis management, follow these premises: the first concerns the definition and delineation of the undemocratic external effect of national decision-making, and the definition and delineation of their compensation by European law.[37] The second concerns the normative quality of cooperative arrangements and procedures. The third concerns the handling of 'true' conflict constellations, in which a positive solution cannot be achieved, and both the law and politics must learn to live with the resultant 'undecidability'.[38]

The normatively strongest case for the conflicts-law approach [is] 'diagonal' conflicts, ie, constellations in which the resolution of a problem cannot be achieved with the powers conferred, but needs to engage competences which have been reserved to the Member States. The pattern of pertinent conflicts and tensions was recurring over and over again: the European market-building agenda intruded into spaces which the Member States had exempted from market governance on the grounds of competences which they had not conclusively or only partly conferred to the European level. In such 'diagonal' conflict constellations, European law cannot plausibly claim 'supremacy' or resort to the doctrine of 'pre-emption'. The two levels of governance could, instead, be expected to coordinate their agendas cooperatively. In many instances, the ECJ has indeed found innovative responses to such complex conflict constellations solutions. These responses had to depart from the one-size-fits-all philosophy and to resort, instead, to a development of procedural frames within which the EU and the concerned jurisdictions could accommodate their concerns and interests.[39]

2. *'A Dialogue of Mutual Responsiveness'*

'Mutual responsiveness' is the key concept of a new approach to the problem of 'social legitimacy in the internal market'. This approach has many affinities with

[37] In view of the critique of this point (see Section III.A.2 below), a prestigious endorsement deserves to be noted: 'Nation-states … encumber each other with the external effects of decisions that impinge on third parties who had no say in the decision-making process. Hence, states cannot escape the need for regulation and coordination in the expanding horizon of a world society that is increasingly self-programming, even at the cultural level …' (J Habermas, 'Does the Constitutionalization of International Law still have a Chance?' in idem, *The Divided West* (Cambridge: Polity Press, 2007) 113, at 176.

[38] J Lenoble, 'Law and Undecidability: A New Vision of the Proceduralization of Law' (1995-1996) 17 *Cardozo LRev* 1935.

[39] Joerges, 'On the Legitimacy of Europeanising Private Law', n 2 above; and C Joerges and CU Schmid, 'Towards Proceduralization of Private Law in the European Multi-Level System' in Hartkamp *et al* (eds), *Towards a European Civil Code. Fourth Revised and Expanded Edition* (The Hague: Kluwer Law International, 2010), 277, at 291 ff. Famous examples include: Case C-67/96, *Albany International BV v Stichting Bedrijfspensioenfonds Textiel industrie* [1999] ECR I-5751; Case C-280/00, *Altmark Trans GmbH v Regierungspräsidium Magdeburg und Nahverkehrsgesellschaft Altmark GmbH* [2003] ECR I-07747; Case C-212/97, *Centros Ltd v Erhvervs-og Selskabsstyrelsen* [1999] ECR I-1459; most recently Case C-573/12, *Ålands Vindkraft AB v Energimyndigheten*, judgment of 1 July 2014 (Grand Chamber), ECLI:EU:C:2014:2037.

conflicts-law constitutionalism, but is, by the same token, a critical innovation – a very promising one in my view.[40]

Jotte Mulder starts his deliberations with reflections on the 'argument from external effects' – a point of departure in the re-conceptualisation of 'European law as a new type of conflicts law'. He focuses in his discussion on the objection Alexander Somek summarised in a 'fundamental question' in which he wonders 'what might be done to prevent the argument from transnational effects from slipping into a freewheeling rampage of economic due process?'.[41] Mulder apparently approves of Somek, with the latter's equation of the two versions of the argument which Miguel Maduro and I had delivered at about the same time.[42] To rephrase, the argument questions the democratic legitimacy of national decision-making which affects 'third parties who had no say in the decision-making process'.[43] In Somek's understanding, the proponents of the argument advocate a correction of this nation-state failure through a European version of the American notion of 'economic due process': an imposition of free movement rules which is meant to give voice to the outsiders. My own understanding of the argument was different, however. With my use of the 'democracy failure' argument, I sought both to justify European compensatory interventions *and to define their conditions and limitations.* They must use European law to foster democratic will formation. It is, of course, up to the author to ensure the clarity of his messages. Mine were obviously not clear enough. But my critique of the Opinion that AG Maduro delivered in the *Viking* case,[44] my critique of his Opinion in the *Temelin* litigation,[45] and, last but not least, my critique of his plea for interventions into core competencies of the Member States by some

[40] J Mulder, 'Social Legitimacy in the Internal Market – A Dialogue of Mutual Responsiveness', PhD thesis Florence: European University Institute, 2016 [(Oxford: Hart Publishing, 2018)].

[41] A Somek, 'The Argument from Transnational Effects I: Representing Outsiders through Freedom of Movement' (2010) 16 *ELJ* 315, at 332.

[42] C Joerges and J Neyer, 'From Intergovernmental Bargaining to Deliberative Political Processes: The Constitutionalisation of Comitology' (1997) 3 *ELJ* 273 (reprinted in ch 12 of this volume), building on C Joerges, 'Die Beurteilung der Sicherheit technischer Konsumgüter und der Gesundheitsrisiken von Lebensmitteln der Praxis des europäischen Ausschußwesens ("Komitologie")', *ZERP-Diskussionspapier* 1/95, Bremen, 1995; MP Maduro, 'Reforming the Market or the State? Article 30 and the European Constitution: Economic Freedom and Political Rights' (1997) 3 *ELJ* 55; and idem, *We the Court: The European Court of Justice and the European Economic Constitution* (Oxford: Hart Publishing, 1998).

[43] J Habermas, 'Does the Constitutionalization of International Law still have a Chance?' in idem, *The Divided West* (Cambridge: Polity Press, 2007) 113, at 176.

[44] Opinion delivered on 23 May 2007, Case C-438/05, *The International Transport Workers' Federation and The Finnish Seamen's Union v Viking Line ABP and OÜ Viking Line Eesti*; see the critique in C Joerges and F Rödl, 'Informal Politics, Formalised Law and the "Social Deficit" of European Integration: Reflections after the Judgments of the ECJ in *Viking* and *Laval*' (2009) 15 *ELJ* 1 (reprinted in ch 16 of this volume).

[45] Opinion of AG Poiares Maduro delivered on 22 April 2009, Case C-115/08, *Oberösterreich v ČEZ as* [2009] ECR I-10265; and the critique in C Joerges, 'The Timeliness of Direct Democracy in the EU – and the Contest over Atomic Energy in Conflicts-law Perspectives' in J Busch *et al* (eds), *International Constitutional Law in Legal Education. Proceedings of the Erasmus Intensive Programme NICLAS 2010-2012* (Vienna: Facultas, 2014) 89.

administrative supranationalism,[46] my critique of economic constitutionalism,[47] all militate against a 'representation of outsiders through free movement'. Fortunately enough, Mulder is primarily interested in a constructive response to Somek's query. And his search is, in my view, very successful. Two conceptual arguments seem particularly important here.

The first concern is his re-conceptualisation of the argument from external effects, which he reads as an 'argument from containment':

> [T]he argument from containment conceptualises the intentions of the EU internal market not necessarily as 'pro trade' but as a means to engage in a dialogue with Member States on how their national systems can and need to be adjusted in order to accommodate the out of nation state interests that are to be made part of national processes of governing or governance structures.[48]

The notion of 'deliberative supranationalism' through which Jürgen Neyer and I sought to capture the potential of the European committee system to arrive at reason-based responses to regulatory diversity relied on very similar intuitions. Mulder's re-conceptualisation is more ambitious. It engages not just the administrative machinery, with its support by expertise and observers in social society, but the legal systems of the Union in their entirety, with a judiciary engaged in learning and mitigating conflicts.[49]

This re-conceptualisation of the 'argument from external effects' is linked with a re-conceptualisation of the so-called 'social deficit' of the integration project. This deficit is widely defined by the EU's lack of powers in fields which are of constitutive importance for core welfare-state functions.[50] It follows that 'the social' remains a province of constitutional democracies which needs to be defended against de-regulatory dismantling by the EU. Again, Mulder's approach is much more comprehensive. Departing from a very thoughtful review of the main works of the varieties of capitalism studies and intensive discussion of Karl Polanyi's economic sociology and the Polanyian account of the social embeddedness of 'the economic',[51] Mulder arrives at a definition

[46] See MP Maduro, 'A New Governance for the European Union and the Euro: Democracy and Justice', *EUI RSCAS PP*, 2012/11, Global Governance Programme, Europe and the World.available at http://hdl.handle.net/1814/24295; and the critique in C Joerges, 'Three Transformations of Europe and the Search for a Way out of its Crisis' in idem and C Glinski (eds), *The European Crisis and the Transformation of Transnational Governance: Authoritarian Managerialism versus Democratic Governance* (Oxford: Hart Publishing, 2014), 25, at 35 ff.

[47] See, for example, C Joerges, 'What is Left of the European Economic Constitution? A Melancholic Eulogy' (2005) 30 *ELR* 461 (reprinted in ch 22 of this volume).

[48] Mulder, n 40 above, Chapter II, text accompanying fnn 7 and 20 [et seq].

[49] Quite similar for an exemplary case, see C Joerges, 'Interactive Adjudication in the Europeanisation Process? A Demanding Perspective and a Modest Example' (2000) 8 *European Review of Private Law* 1.

[50] See, eg, FW Scharpf, 'The Asymmetry of European Integration, or Why the EU cannot be a "Social Market Economy"' (2010) 8 *Socio-Economic Review* 211.

[51] n 40 above, Chapter II.

of the integration *problématique* which corresponds, in many ways, to my understanding of 'united in diversity as Europe's vocation':[52] the diversity of European economies and societies can be economically and socially beneficial. The 'integration through law' agenda with its 'one-size-fits-all' philosophy risks, if carried through with the rigour that we are witnessing in Europe's management of the financial crisis, the destruction of the various *acquis sociales* within the Union. Mulder moves far beyond these affinities in two important respects: (1) Implicit in his understanding of the integration problem is a new conceptualisation of 'the social' and the legitimacy of European internal market law and market governance. Europe has to meet the integration challenge through 'a reconciliation of local domestic social values within supranational market objectives [which] requires a form of explicit responsiveness to the social context that is being adjudicated'.[53] (2) What this type of responsiveness requires and how it can be accomplished is then spelled out in three 'normative standards', namely, 'the interplay of principles of substantive efficiency, margins of discretion and good governance in free movement adjudication'. This 'interplay' is not a simply discretionary exercise. The standards both structure *and* discipline the evaluation of a highly specific conflicts constellation. There is, at the same time, much realism in Mulder's formula. This realism has a solid basis in the operation of the judiciary, which is bound to seek normative recognition. Mulder does not claim that litigation and adjudication will generate a 'system'. What he does claim and then convincingly documents is the re-constructive potential and validity of the normative standards which guide his analyses.

These extensive analyses are impressively subtle and mostly convincing. Mulder distances himself from the rigidities in the critique of the case law of the ECJ by the Max-Planck scholars of Cologne who underline the contribution of this jurisprudence to a neo-liberal agenda of 'negative' integration and market-building.[54] A further specific: his, so to speak, horizontal conceptualisation of social legitimacy in the internal market renders the category of 'diagonal conflicts', which are of high importance in the conflicts approach (Section III.B.1 above), superfluous. This is a stringent conclusion within the scope of Mulder's analyses. The category remains indispensable for an adequate analysis of the failings of Europe's institutional configuration in the financial crisis, to which we now turn.

[52] See C Joerges, 'United in Diversity as Europe's Vocation and Conflicts Law as Europe's Constitutional Form' in R Nickel and A Greppi (eds), *The Changing Role of Law in the Age of Supra- and Transnational Governance* (Baden-Baden: Nomos, 2014), 125, available also at: http://papers.ssrn.com/sol3/papers.cfm?abstract_id=1723249.

[53] Mulder, n 40 above, Chapter I.

[54] Ibid, in particular, 35–62; see Section II.B for references.

IV. THE SECOND TRANSFORMATION OF EUROPE AND ITS IMPACT ON PRIVATE LAW

It is, by now, high time to substantiate the assumption that the financial crisis will have an impact on the Europeanisation of private law. Our analysis will undertake three analytically distinguishable but interrelated, steps. The first will be a summary account of the transformations of the European constitutional constellation,[55] which the responses to the European crisis have brought about: How does the move to the new modes of economic governance affect the social functions of private law? (Section IV.A) The second will be concerned with indirect or ideational changes: How will the quest for increased competitiveness and the so-called structural reforms impact upon pertinent fields of private law? (Section IV.B). The third will deal with the effectiveness of the new European governance. If there is a kernel of truth in the messages of the varieties of capitalism studies, it seems hardly likely that the 'second transformation of Europe' which we are witnessing at present will accomplish a beneficial convergence of the European economies under a renewed legal framework (Section IV.C). Somewhat more comforting pronouncements will be reserved for the epilogue (Section V).

A. Crisis 'Law'

It is essential, for my argument, to understand the transformation of the European order after the crisis. 'Constitutional Change through Euro Crisis Law' is the title of a grand project at the EUI, which is going to document comprehensively the developments that we are witnessing at all levels of governance throughout the entire Union.[56] My account, in contrast, will be anything but comprehensive. It will, instead, content itself with a discussion of the European Monetary Union (EMU) as established by the Maastricht Treaty and the subsequent Stability and Growth Pact (SGP) of 1997, and will focus on its use of quotation marks in the notion of 'law'.

This focus is an announcement of my thesis: in my understanding, the Maastricht Treaty is the all-important and decisive turning-point of the integration project, one which has replaced the 'integration through law' agenda by modes of emergency governance beyond the rule of law.

This harsh critique may be counter-intuitive. The Maastricht Treaty was perceived by the mainstream of European legal studies as a continuation and a deepening of what had been accomplished so far, a move hence towards 'an ever

[55] As to the first transformation, see JHH Weiler, 'The Transformation of Europe' (2000) 100 *Yale Law Journal* 2403, at 2431 ff.

[56] http://eurocrisislaw.eui.eu.

closer union'. But both the opening of new policy-fields and the crowning of the completion of the internal market by monetary union met with very considerable reserves on the part of leading scholars committed to the Freiburg School.[57]

With the benefit of hindsight, the Treaty of Maastricht is very widely characterised as a turning-point of the greatest importance in the integration project, albeit a problematical one. In particular, it has become obvious that the EMU did by no means lead to a strong convergence of economic policies. The thesis that the pressure to harmonise, stemming from integration, would become stronger and even irresistible under a common currency, which may have had its *fundamentum in re* in the smaller and more homogeneous Community of the 1960s and 1970s, has been falsified.[58] The EMU, as it was established in Maastricht, can no longer be defended as a command of economic reason but is more adequately understood as a political project, assuring Germany's neighbours that the country would be faithful to its European commitments.[59] Conceptually speaking, the Maastricht compromise produced a hybrid, an odd mixture of ordo-liberalism and *planification*, with Germany defending its stability philosophy in substantive principles and statutory norms and ceding to French preferences in the procedural norms of the General ECB Council. Legally speaking, the hybrid should – in the parlance of the conflicts approach – be characterised as a diagonal conflict constellation. This notion requires an explanatory remark, however.

Monetary policy has become an exclusive competence of the Union (Article 3(1) c TFEU). With this provision, the Union claims supremacy in the policy area conferred on it, a conferral which did not include economic and fiscal policies. The exercise of these policies can have external effects and lead to 'horizontal' conflicts. As experienced immediately after the establishment of the EMU, monetary policy and national policies could still come into conflict. This, however, is not a vertical conflict for which supremacy would provide a response. It is a 'diagonal conflict': both the Union and the Member States are certainly interested in the functioning of their economies. But the powers needed to accomplish this objective are attributed to two distinct levels of governance. The type of conflict resolution foreseen in Article 119 TFEU is 'the adoption of an economic policy which is based upon the close coordination of Member States' economic policies' as substantiated in Article 121 TFEU. As is plainly visible from the legal texts and substantiated by meticulous analyses,[60] this

[57] ME Streit and W Mussler, 'The Economic Constitution of the European Community: From "Rome" to "Maastricht"' (1995) 1 *ELJ* 5; instructive were the reservations against entering into the third stage of the EMU in K Biedenkopf, *Der Weg zum Euro. Stationen einer verpassten Chance* (Berlin: Hertie School of Governance, 2012) 78.

[58] Mestmäcker, n 13 above.

[59] K Dyson, States, Debts and Power. Saints and Sinners in European History and Integration (Oxford: OUP, 2014) 609 ff.

[60] B Braams, *Koordinierung als Kompetenzkategorie* (Tübingen: Mohr Siebeck, 2013).

instrument was legally imperfect. The 'stability community' of the EMU existed only on paper. It was a fictitious order which could not be implemented. The Treaty of Maastricht did not provide for mechanisms to enforce its ideational background, neither did the successive SGP of 1997 complement the Treaty accordingly. The functioning of the whole new regime was dependent on good economic luck and constant political bargaining.

If the Maastricht EMU and the SGP are, legally speaking, too soft, why not fix the construct through strong rules? This question, which is so often answered in the affirmative, brings us to the gist of the matter both in practical and in constitutional terms. As to the first aspect, it is illuminating to consider the insights of the non-legal disciplines cited in Section I. Not only does the diversity of socio-economic conditions even within the Eurozone generate a variety of interests, but the differences in the institutional configurations and economic cultures and in the social norms practised also explain why European command and control governance cannot accomplish its objectives. The normative and constitutional implications of this conflict constellation are of fundamental importance. There is nothing unusual or inherently problematical with compromises, incoherencies or hybrids embodied in, or generated by, the creation of legal acts. What is specific about the European example and what distinguishes the European order from constitutional democracies is the lack of a political infrastructure and an institutional framework in which democratic political contestation could occur and legitimate a completion or improvement of the imperfect edifice to be accomplished. The Maastricht arrangement, we have to conclude, sadly represented an ill-defined political compromise, rather than the sustainable accomplishment of constitutional validity and strength.

The fragility of the Maastricht arrangement was a birth defect that remained latent until the economic crisis began to unfold in 2008. Since then, we have witnessed a turbo-speed establishment of new modes of EU economic governance and regulatory mechanisms. Unfortunately, I cannot go into the details here. Instead, I focus on three particularly intriguing features of the new modes and mechanisms of economic governance.

The first: the supervision and control of macro-economic imbalances, which the two 'six-pack' Regulations 1176/2011 and 1174/2011 mandate,[61] disregard the principle of enumerated powers and, by the same token, the democratic legitimacy of national institutions, in particular the budgetary powers of the parliaments of the 'states receiving assistance'. The second: in its departure from the one-size-fits-all philosophy that orients European integration in general and monetary policy in particular, European crisis management nonetheless fails to achieve a variation, which might be founded in democratically-legitimated choice; quite to the contrary, the individualised scrutiny of all Member States

[61] Texts in F Losada and AJ Menéndez (eds), *The Key Legal Texts of the European Crises. Treaties, Regulations, Directives, Case Law* (Oslo: ARENA Centre for European Studies, 2014) 443 ff and 449 ff.

is geared to the objective of budgetary balances and seeks to impose the functionally seemingly necessary accompanying discipline; the 'receiving states' cannot but respond to pertinent requests through austerity measures: reductions of wage levels and of social entitlements. The third: the machinery of the new regime, with its individualised measures which are oriented only by necessarily indeterminate general clauses, is regulatory in its nature, establishing transnational executive machinery outside both the realm of democratic politics *and* the form of accountability which the rule of law used to guarantee; core concepts used by new economic governance cannot be defined with any precision, either by lawyers or by economists, and are, therefore, not justiciable; rule-of-law and legal protection requirements are being suspended. This type of de-legalisation is accompanied by assessments of Member State performance which cannot be but highly discretionary.

It seems both remarkable and irritating that similar concerns can be discerned in the Opinion in the OMT [Outright Monetary Transactions] Case C-62/14, which the Advocate General of the CJEU delivered on 14 January 2015:[62]

> The Treaties are silent … when it comes to defining the exclusive competence of the Union in relation to monetary policy.[63]
>
> The division that EU law makes between those policies is a requirement imposed by the structure of the Treaties and by the horizontal and vertical distribution of powers within the Union, but in economic terms it may be stated that any monetary policy measure is ultimately encompassed by the broader category of general economic policy.[64]

It follows that the delineation which the text of the Treaty expects us to make when characterising measures as monetary, rather than economic, policy has to rely on 'the objectives ascribed to that policy'.[65] In contrast to facts, which can be ascertained when a decision is being taken, it is usually uncertain and controversial whether such objectives can be realised at all, and, if they can, then how.[66]

The assertion that the Maastricht EMU should not be called an accomplishment of constitutional validity is anathema to the community of European law scholars. I conclude from the [second] passage just cited that it has, albeit only implicitly, the blessing of an Advocate General. His insistence that

[62] AG Pedro Cruz Villalón, Opinion in Case C-62/14, *Peter Gauweiler and others and Fraktion Die Linke im Deutschen Bundestag v Deutscher Bundestag*, delivered on 14 January 2015.

[63] Ibid, para 127.

[64] Ibid, para 129.

[65] Ibid, para 127.

[66] The CJEU endorsed the reasoning of its AG in its judgment of 16 June 2015 (Case C-62/14, *Peter Gauweiler and others*, and *Fraktion Die Linke im Deutschen Bundestag v Deutscher Bundestag*). Just like the AG, the Court underlines that the 'Treaty contains no precise definition of monetary policy but defines both the objectives of monetary policy and the instruments which are available to the ESCB' (para 41). What the ECB decides to undertake is legal as long as 'it does not appear that that analysis of the economic situation of the euro area as at the date of the announcement of the programme in question is vitiated by a manifest error of assessment' (para 74).

'the Union today is governed by a set of principles relating both to its objectives and to its boundaries, which overall represent its "constitutional framework"'[67] is incompatible with the Advocate General's analysis of the actual contents of this framework. It is true, but not comforting, that national constitutions, too, operate with vague formulas and ill-defined competences. What distinguishes 'the European order from that of constitutional democracies ... is the lack of a political infrastructure and institutional framework in which democratic political contestation could continue and legitimate a completion or improvement of what had been agreed'.[68]

Compliance with the Maastricht EMU and the SGP, so we have argued, was never an option, because Maastricht has generated a truly unruly conflict constellation. This assertion implies that we should be cautious when rejecting the responses to this unruliness as simply wilful and malicious. Ernst-Wolfgang Böckenförde, a renowned constitutionalist and former judge of the German Constitutional Court, was the first to characterise the crisis of the EMU as a state of emergency.[69]

B. The Impact on Private Law

Does Europe's crisis law affect private law at all without direct interference? It does affect both of the traditions to which we have referred above (Section II) in fundamental, albeit different, ways.

It was an essential of Franz Böhm's notion of a 'private law society' that societal ordering was brought about by de-centralised decision-making guided by market prices, 'supervised' by, and embedded in, the competitive *ordo*. To cite again Gunther Teubner:

> This autonomous order of social-steering and coordinating instruments is transformed into a genuine constitution of the economy as soon as it is stabilized by legal rules .... It is decisive that these legal norms cannot be conceived apart from the social order; rather, one must grasp the economic constitution as an inseparable relation between legal order and social ordering.[70]

Crisis law has left us with a different kind of economy. It has lost trust in de-centralised and autonomous decision-making, but seeks to supervise the economy and society in their entirety: it replaces the economic *ordo* by discretionary interventions. Mestmäcker's vision of a return to the civil society

[67] AG Cruz Villalón, n 63 above, para 215.

[68] C Joerges, 'The Legitimacy Problématique of Economic Governance in the EU' in Hertie School of Governance, *The Governance Report 2015* (Oxford: OUP, 2015) 69, at 80.

[69] E-W Böckenförde, 'Kennt die europäische Not kein Gebot? Die Webfehler der EU und die Notwendigkeit einer neuen politischen Entscheidung' *Neue Zürcher Zeitung* 21 June 2010.

[70] Teubner, *Transnational Economic Constitutionalism*, n 34 above, texts accompanying fnn 16–17.

(*bürgerliche Gesellschaft*) and its law, submitted impressively and passionately in 1991, has become an abstract utopia.[71]

The damaging of the 'social' tradition is even more dramatic. It occurs partly clandestinely, partly directly. Simon Deakin has identified the less apparent impact in an analysis of the famous judgments in *Laval* and *Viking* which the ECJ handed down in 2007 – in the immediate aftermath of the financial crisis.[72] There is, Deakin underlines, no direct link discernible either to the financial crisis or to the sovereign debt crisis. What is apparent, however, is that the developments in the constitutional architecture of the EU have helped to legitimise a specific way of thinking about the relationship between the legal system and the process of economic integration. What Deakin submitted somewhat hesitantly some years ago seems, by now, quite obvious to the leading protagonists of European consumer protection law.[73] As Marija Bartl summarises it: the protection of the consumer against the hardships of the market mechanism has given way to a market citizen who is supposed to promote and execute the functioning of the market mechanism.[74]

A thorough and comprehensive study of exemplary importance is under way at the Centre of European Law and Politics in Bremen (ZERP) under the Directorship of Christoph Schmid. This project is concerned with tenancy law and housing, a 'false commodity' in the parlance of Karl Polanyi.[75] The economic, political and social complexity is obvious. Housing, be it as a tenant or owner, is embedded in an enormously broad spectrum of policies beyond contract law: the regulation of credit, tax law, energy policy, urban policies, etc, etc. It is completely unsurprising that the impact of the financial crisis on housing in the EU was anything but uniform. Equally important for my argument: this dense regulatory network has been generated in a multitude of nationally specific economic, political and social processes. The outcome represents a social *acquis*. Uniformity is not feasible, nor would its imposition be legitimate.

[71] E-J Mestmäcker, 'Die Wiederkehr der bürgerlichen Gesellschaft und ihres Rechts' (1991) 10 *Rechtshistorisches Journal* 177.

[72] S Deakin, 'The Lisbon Treaty, the *Viking* and *Laval* Judgments, and the Financial Crisis: In Search of New Foundations for Europe's "Social Market Economy"' in N Bruun, K Lörcher and I Schömann (eds), *The Lisbon Treaty and Social Europe* (Oxford: Hart Publishing, 2012) 19. Case C-438/05, International Transport Workers' Federation, Finnish Seamen's Union v Viking Line ABP, OÜ Viking Line Eesti [2007] ECR I-10779; Case C-341/05, Laval un Partneri Ltd v Svenska Byggnadsarbetareförbundet [2007] ECR I-11767; somewhat later and even more problematic Case C-346/06, *Rechtsanwalt Dr Dirk Rüffert v Land Niedersachsen* [2008] ECR I-01989.

[73] H-W Micklitz, 'The Expulsion of the Concept of Protection from the Consumer Law and the Return of Social Elements in the Civil Law: A Bittersweet Polemic' Florence: *EUI Working Paper LAW* 2012/03; H-W Micklitz and N Reich, 'The Court and Sleeping Beauty: The Revival of the Unfair Contract Terms Directive' (2014) 51 *CMLR* 771.

[74] Bartl, n 16 above; and eadem, 'Internal Market Rationality and the Direction of the Union: Resuscitating the Market at the Object of the Political' (2015) 21 *ELJ* 572.

[75] M Glasman, *Unnecessary Suffering: Managing Market Utopia* (London: Verso Books, 1996) 5 ff.

C. The Resistance and Validity of Economic Cultures

As mentioned, the varieties of capitalism school tend to avoid any normative ranking. Nevertheless, inherent to their analyses is an implicit defence of the institutional configurations that they investigate. Economic historian Werner Abelshauser is much more explicit in this respect, and his notion of 'economic cultures' reflects this normative concern.[76] Lawyers simply cannot treat their object with normative complacency. Gunther Teubner, whom I have cited above at some length, has recently submitted a re-statement of his analysis. Departing again from the 'resilience of collective mentalities and particularities of production cultures', he now underlines more stringently the interdependence of the institutional elements of production regimes – enterprise financing, managerial education, contractual relationships between enterprises, inter-organisational networks, standardisation processes, and inter-enterprise conflict regulation – and their self-regulatory potential,[77] and proceeds to a refinement of his theory of 'societal constitutionalism'. I am neither prepared nor able to engage in passing in a discussion of this concept. I simply note that my understanding of the institutional infrastructures of the economy as a social *acquis* – of 'the economy as a polity' – seeks to retain links with state constitutions and their democratic legitimacy.[78] Against this background, the intergovernmental and executive authoritarian destructive intrusion into the institutional infrastructures of economy and society seems deeply problematical.

V. CONTESTATION THROUGH PRIVATE LAW? A SPECULATIVE EPILOGUE

We have continuously looked at our topic from the point of view of the long-term developments of the integration-project as a whole and will conclude at this level of abstraction and generality. Our comments on the relationship between private law and market integration were certainly critical with respect to the expectation of, and the quest for, an ever more comprehensive system of private law in an ever closer EU. To underline it again: this critical distancing is anything but euro-sceptic. It is, instead, meant to substantiate the alternative vision of the fortunate motto of the ill-fated Draft Constitutional Treaty submitted in 2003. The motto was 'united in diversity'.

Let me submit a restatement of this paradoxical formula in three steps: first, with the help of an American observer, then with a further reference to the insights and assertions of economic historians and the varieties of capitalism

[76] W Abelshauser, 'Ricardo neu gedacht: Komparative institutionelle Vorteile von Wirtschaftskulturen' in idem, DA Gilgen and A Leutzsch (eds), *Kulturen der Weltwirtschaft* (Göttingen: Vadenhoeck & Ruprecht, 2012) 29.

[77] Teubner, *Transnational Economic Constitutionalism*, n 34 above, texts accompanying fnn 11–12.

[78] I Maus, Menschenrechte, Demokratie und Frieden. Perspektiven globaler Organisation (Berlin Suhrkamp. 2015), 157 ff.

studies, which will, in a concluding step, be linked to the law's responses to Europe's emergency.

Dani Rodrik, a political economist from the Kennedy School, who only occasionally comments on European issues, has, in a by now famous book on globalisation,[79] submitted a 'trilemma thesis'. Rodrik asserts the impossibility of the simultaneous pursuit of economic globalisation, democratic politics and national determination (autonomy), highlighting that only two goals can be paired: either economic globalisation and democratic politics, or democracy and national autonomy. In one of his comments on Europe's crisis,[80] he has underlined that the EU furnishes a dramatic illustration of his trilemma thesis. The EU could transnationalise democracy through federalisation and thereby defend the advantages of the common market. Federalisation would imply that it would, at the same time, be forced to establish common European politics to legitimise the necessary assumption of fiscal and social policy. Is this a plea for a comprehensive body of European law, for 'more Europe' and the further substitution of national law by European law? Rodrik's diagnosis is *de facto* deeply pessimistic, because the federal option is, in his view, but an abstract utopia. A political democratic union would have to be accomplished and defined not through the various new modes of economic governance and 'crisis law'; it would have to emerge from democratic processes. The same holds true for the institutional configurations of the economy. All this would have to happen very soon, but is, *hélas*, simply inconceivable under the current political, social and economic pressures in the foreseeable future.

In my reading, Rodrik's trilemma thesis is but a drastic sharpening of the prevailing views. If Rodrik is right, Europe is indeed 'entrapped', to use a qualification coined by Claus Offe.[81] But how realistic is this pessimism, which leaves little or no space for a politically realistic but also normatively attractive non-federalised Union. According to the political economists and economic historians referred to in Section III.C, there is prominent support for the assumption that the 'united-in-diversity vision' is economically and socially sound. In particular, Werner Abelshauser, in a recent *unitas in pluralitate* manifesto,[82] has not only underlined the resistance of the varieties of capitalism against economic 'integration by command' but added that this resistance is anything but deplorable. Institutional diversity, he argues, is an asset. Diversity is economically beneficial, rather than detrimental. There is considerable and prominent support for this view.[83]

[79] D Rodrik, The Globalization Paradox. Democracy and the Future of the World Economy (New York–London: WW Norton, 2011).

[80] Idem, 'The Future of European Democracy' in L v Middelaar and PV Parijs (eds), *After the Storm: How to save democracy in Europe* (Tielt: Lannoo Publishers, 2015) 53.

[81] C Offe, 'Europe Entrapped. Does the EU have the Political Capacity to Overcome its Current Crisis?' (2013) 19 *ELJ* 595; and idem, *Europe Entrapped* (Oxford: Polity Press, 2015).

[82] W Abelhauser, 'Europa in Vielfalt einigen. Eine Denkschrift' (2014), available at www.homes.uni-bielefeld.de/wabelsha/Denkschrift.pdf, last accessed 14 January 2015.

[83] G Majone, 'The Deeper Euro-Crisis or: The Collapse of the EU Political Culture of Total Optimism', *EUI Working Paper LAW* 2015/10, 2015; Manow, n 31 above.

The implications for private law are considerable. We have argued that the moves towards ever more so-called market rationality and the quest for 'competitiveness' are deeply at odds with the social functions of private law in constitutional democracies. If there is a kernel of truth is the findings just referred to, then our normative claims are anything but an abstract utopia. We have also pointed to the dichotomy of 'normalisation' and 'contestation' as responses to the authoritarian imposition of Europe's new modes of governance and the dismantling of the legacy of the post-war accomplishments of European welfare states. 'Contestation' which, in particular by the 'states requiring financial assistance', has, to date, made little impression on the organisers of Europe's crisis politics. Their authority is nevertheless limited. It is simply inconceivable that the entire body of the law which constitutes the infrastructure of the EU can be subjected to the 'structural reforms' envisioned and requested so emphatically, in particular by the members of the Executive Board of the ECB.[84] The pretence of knowledge, which characterises Europe's monetary policy, may well encounter the limits of its 'power fantasies' in the ordering functions of private law.

[84] Y Mersch, 'On European Unity: Economic and Institutional Challenges Facing Europe', Speech at the European Economics & Financial Centre, London, 25 June 2015, available at www.ecb.europa.eu/press/key/date/2015/html/sp150625.en.html.

9

Conclusion – Part II

I. OUTLOOK: A LAW OF LAW-PRODUCTION FOR THE EUROPEANISATION OF PRIVATE LAW

LET US PROCEED on the – albeit overly optimistic – assumption that the impact of Europe's crisis politics can be contained and private law will prove to be resilient enough to preserve essential elements of its post-formalist substantive and methodological accomplishments. This would not be the 'solution' to the *problématique* of its Europeanisation. It would mean that we could continue the pre-crisis debates. These were dominated by two opposing modes of wishful thinking. The mainstream of European legal scholarship favoured, albeit in different nuances, the search for greater uniformity, preferably through the adoption of a European code.[1] Their opponents sought to defend the social accomplishments of the national private-law systems, be it through the defence of the nation State competences or through a move towards a European law with a transnational social imprint.[2] Our exemplary discussions in this Part and countless further cases provide theoretical and pragmatic arguments against both perspectives. The theoretical objections can be based on Karl Polanyi's economic sociology and his insights into the 'social embeddedness' of markets and legal relations.[3] We return to Polanyi throughout this volume.[4] Suffice it to underline here the topicality of his insights by a reference to the recent controversy between Jürgen Habermas and Wolfgang Streeck. In this debate, both the sociologist and the philosopher refer in instructive passages to law. Streeck notes in a footnote:

> [W]hat I would suggest to call the acquises démocratiques of the national demoi in Europe … importantly comprises a wide range of political-economic institutions

[1] See ch 5, text accompanying n 5. For a comprehensive account, see CU Schmid, Die Instrumentalisierung des Privatrechts durch die Europäische Union: Privatrecht und Privatrechtskonzeptionen in der Entwicklung Der Europäischen Integrationsverfassung (Baden-Baden: Nomos, 2010).

[2] Markedly the 'Study Group on Social Justice in European Private Law' in its 'manifesto' on 'Social Justice in European Contract Law' (2004) 10 *ELJ* 653; for a recent comprehensive endeavour, see H-W Micklitz, *The Politics of Justice in European Private Law: Social Justice, Access Justice, Societal Justice* (Cambridge: CUP, 2018).

[3] K Polanyi, *The Great Transformation: The Political and Economic Origins of our Time [1944]*, first Beacon paperback edn (Boston, MA: Beacon Press, 1957).

[4] See chs 18, 23, 28.

> that provide for democratic corrections of market outcomes – for democracy as social democracy.[5]

These remarks document an awareness of the 'co-originality' of societal conditions and their normative ordering. Streeck conceptualises the social embeddedness of legal relations as a normatively loaded facticity, of institutionalised practices that deserve social and legal recognition. What I characterise as a quasi Habermasian dimension of Streeck's argument seems in no way to be to the philosopher's liking. Habermas' response to Streeck is vigorous:[6]

> 'Can we transfer the well-founded legal protection of cultural identities without further ado, eg, on systems of labour relations or social policy regimes', he wonders and submits: 'an ensemble of socio-economic practices' does not deserve to be protected like a 'natural reserve'.[7]

The contest between the two master thinkers mirrors the controversies of the European project and its democratic potential. Streeck cannot imagine how the level of democracy achieved in the nation states could be realised in a transnational setting. Habermas proclaims the erosion of the democratic potential of national governance and tries to explain how a transnational democracy might be realised.[8] Not all of this is fully beyond the horizons of legal scholarship. Suffice it here to recall some queries from the debate on a European code of private law.[9]

Can we imagine how the *Code civil* in which the *grande nation* gave expression to its revolutionary achievements, the German *Bürgerliches Gesetzbuch* (Civil Code) that, in the name of German *Rechtswissenschaft*, made an important piece of German legal unification possible, the Anglo-Saxon common law that has produced an evolutionary legitimised autonomous law, and other private law traditions might find a way to merge? Even if the various traditions sometimes make nostalgic declarations of reservations against unification, the point is a deeper one. The private-law systems have to mitigate between economic efficiency and social justice. Their various responses are deeply entwined in the economic and political circumstances of the polities which they order and to which they owe their legitimacy.

[5] W Streeck, *How Will Capitalism End?* (London: Verso Books, 2016) 198, fn 20.

[6] J Habermas, 'Der Demos der Demokratie' (2015) 43 *Leviathan* 145, 154; see also J Habermas, 'Demokratie oder Kapitalismus. Vom Elend der nationalstaatlichen Fragmentierung in einer kapitalistisch integrierten Weltgesellschaft' (2013) 58 *Blätter für deutsche und internationale Politik* 59.

[7] The original reads: 'Ich sehe nicht, wie sich ein kultureller Naturschutz für ein jeweils bestehendes Ensemble von sozioökonomischer Praktiken begründen ließe'. Habermas, 'Der Demos der Demokratie' (n 7).

[8] See J Habermas, 'Democracy in Europe: Why the Development of the EU into a Transnational Democracy is Necessary and How it is Possible' (2015) 21 *ELJ* 546.

[9] On the following see C Joerges, 'On the Legitimacy of Europeanising Europe's Private Law' (2002) 2 *Global Jurist Topics*, available at www.bepress.com/gj/topics/vol2/iss2/art1.

The decisive question then becomes: Does the European polity really 'need' a unitary legal system? And if Europeanisation levels out the differences in private-law systems, will that leave their social state dimension behind? Would private law thereby lose the legitimacy it has gained in the constitutional state? The German case is of exemplary importance here. The basic law has legalised both the commitment to democracy in the eternity clause of Article 79(3) of the Basic Law and the openness for European integration in Article 23. Does the Basic Law assume that we could reconcile such apparently irreconcilable commitments?

At the core argument of this volume there is: 'Yes, we can'; *tertium datur*. 'United in diversity', the fortunate motto of the unfortunate Draft Constitutional Treaty of 2004,[10] is not an empty phrase but a potential that can be realised through a 'new type of conflicts law'. Chapter 7 documents that this perspective is present in the practice of European law. The argument is pursued throughout many contributions reprinted in this volume, most systematically in Part VI.

II. RELATED PUBLICATIONS

C Joerges, 'Interactive Adjudication in the Europeanisation Process? A Demanding Perspective and a Modest Example' (2000) 8 *European Review of Private Law* 1.

C Joerges and CU Schmid, 'Towards Proceduralization of Private Law in the European Multi-Level System' in AS Hartkamp et al (eds), *Towards a European Civil Code*, 4th edn (The Hague: Wolters Kluwer, 2011) 277.

[10] Art I-8; for the full text, see [2004] OJ C310/1 (16 December 2004).

Part III

Social Regulation and the Turn to Governance

10

Introduction: The Integration Project in the Risk Society

EUROPE IS EXPERIENCING a societal – both economic and social – transformation of fundamental significance, Ulrich Beck submitted in his seminal monograph published in 1986.[1] 'Risk society', his key concept, was to make a furore worldwide. The concept hit the integration project in various sensitive contexts. These are discussed in the four contributions to Part III of this volume.

The first, on 'Scientific Expertise in Social Regulation and the European Court of Justice' (chapter 11) deals with the importance of the risk phenomenon for our understanding of the functioning of markets and their legal oversight. European integration had been launched as an economic project that trusted in the autonomy of markets and the beneficial effects of their functioning. Ulrich Beck addressed facets of markets that were not visible in conventional conceptualisations of markets and consumer sovereignty. The sensitivity for risks and their valuation had, however, attained a steadily growing importance not only for the decisions of consumers, but likewise for the design of products, production processes and marketing strategies. In such contexts, Europe's 'market citizens' can no longer trust their intuitions. It is a great accomplishment of the integration politics for which the Community has been properly characterised as a policy instigator,[2] that it realised the need to take action and to do so through the establishment of sophisticated machinery – superior to the measures in place at national level. It is both noteworthy and praiseworthy that the Community did not simply turn to state interventionism but recognised the merits of self-regulation, upon which the German standardisation system, in particular, relied, but focused on the detection of the weaknesses of this system – and their correction.[3]

[1] U Beck, Risikogesellschaft – Auf dem Weg in eine andere Moderne (Frankfurt aM: Suhrkamp, 1986); translation *Risk Society: Towards a New Modernity* (London–New York: Sage, 1992).

[2] V Gessner and A Höland, 'Konsultation und Anstiftung vor Ort – ein neuer Typus von Gemeinschaftspolitik' in C Joerges and K Sieveking (eds), *Europäische Integration, Nationalstaat und regionale Politikkompetenzen* (1987) 2 *ZERP-Diskussionspapier* Bremen 1987.

[3] An important example can be found in the regulation of product safety and the risks of foodstuffs, analysed in the study of C Joerges, J Falke, H-W Micklitz and G Brüggemeier, *Die Sicherheit von Konsumgütern und die Entwicklung der Europäischen Gemeinschaft* (Baden-Baden: Nomos, 1988);

These issues are taken up in the following contribution on the 'Constitutionalisation of Comitology' (chapter 12). This certainly somewhat opaque-looking system was entrusted with regulating the risks inherent in the production of foodstuffs – the economically most important sector of the European economy. The two core theses developed in this essay are a(?)/ the backbone of the conceptual and pragmatic messages of the whole volume. The first: the debate on the legitimacy of European rule (its democratic deficit should turn from the European to the national level). Nation states, so the argument goes, are, in view of the economic and social interdependence of European societies, not in a position to deliver democratically-legitimated laws and regulations, because their decisions and action will have external effects and those affected cannot be involved in the political will formation of nation states. The second line of arguments follows from these insights: it is the prime vocation of the European politics to correct the democracy deficits of national politics. Given that Europe will generate a European state or federation in the foreseeable future, it has to operate through cooperative arrangements and practices that rely on the organisation of deliberative processes ('deliberative supranationalism'). This idea has attracted attention and provoked critique. To list just three responses: (i) 'How can you know it is deliberation when you see it? – You can't!'[4] (ii) Deliberation will not be strong enough to overcome conflicts with distributional implications.[5] (iii) Deliberative supranationalism, as it is organised, will further technocratic modes of policy-making.[6]

Our argument in the essay is, in an important respect, obsolete: the system we have analysed and defended could not cope with the enormous growth and complication of regulatory tasks generated by the deepening of socio-economic differences in the Western Member States and the Eastern enlargement of the EU. It shifted to bureaucratic routines,[7] and was, in large part, replaced by an

translation published in the Working Paper Series of the EUI (available at http://hdl.handle.net/1814/73) and reprinted in (2010) 6 *Hanse Law Review* 107, available at http://hanselawreview.eu/vol-6-no-2-dezember-2010.

[4] See T Gehring, 'Communicative Rationality in European Governance? Interests and Communicative Action in Functionally Differentiated Single Market Regulation' in EO Eriksen, C Joerges and J Neyer (eds), *European Governance, Deliberation and the Quest for Democratization*, 2003ARENA Report, 2003/02, available at http://hdl.handle.net/1814/2519.

[5] FW Scharpf, 'Introduction. The problem-solving capacity of multi-level governance' (1997) 4 *Journal of European Public Policy* 520; for an exemplary analysis, see H Deters, *The EU's Green Dynamism Deadlock and Change in Energy and Environmental Policy* (London–New York: ECPR Press, 2018) in particular 106 ff.

[6] R Schmalz-Bruns, 'Deliberativer Supranationalismus. Demokratisches Regieren jenseits des Nationalstaats' (1999) 6 *Zeitschrift für Internationale Beziehunge* 185.

[7] See C Joerges and J Neyer, Deliberativer Supranationalismus in der Krise' in O Fluegel-Martinsen et al (eds), *Deliberative Kritik – Kritik der Deliberation. Festschrift für Rainer Schmalz-Bruns* (Wiesbaden: Springer, 2014) 353; A Pilniok and E Estermann, 'Strukturwandel im Verwaltungsverbund? Eine Analyse des neuen Rechtsrahmens der unionalen Komitologieausschüsse' (2012) 103 *Verwaltungsarchiv* 379; M Weimer, *Risk Regulation in the Internal Market* (Oxford: OUP, 2019) 60 ff, 237 ff.

'agencification' of regulatory politics – as comprehensively analysed by the Maastricht-based 'TARN' project.[8]

Two core theorems, however, remained valid and are explored further in subsequent chapters. One is the argument on the structural democracy deficits of nation-state governance. The other is the conclusion that Europe must learn to operationalise the 'united in diversity' motto of the Draft Constitutional Treaty,[9] a request to which the idea of 'conflicts law as Europe's constitutional form' seeks to respond.[10]

The European Commission and influential strands of European legal and political science tried another direction: they advocated a turn from the cumbersome 'Community method' in European rule-making to 'new modes of governance'. This move was initiated by Romano Prodi, the President of the Commission at the time, and was spelled out in a very widely noticed White Paper.[11] The paper announced an innovative agenda. It proposed a renewed division of labour and cooperation between political actors and civil society, and democratic forms of partnership between the layers of the European multi-level system. The paper's plea for novel forms of governance was meant to overcome the rigid restrictions imposed by the principle of enumerated powers, which was ever more clearly at odds with Europe's regulatory needs, and it promised that these new 'good governance' activities would be committed to the principles of '*openness, participation, accountability, effectiveness and coherence*'.[12] The paper avoided any explicit approval of the 'Open Method of Co-ordination' with its socially progressive agenda, as proclaimed by the Lisbon European Council in 2000.[13]

The turn to governance generated enormous research efforts and the production of many more than 3,000 publications.[14] The evaluation in the fourth contribution (chapter 13) is sceptical. Its reservations are in line with the more recent characterisation of governance as an empty signifier[15] and the objections against its democratic legitimacy.[16] The core of the argument is pragmatic. The hopes invested in the new modes of soft governance did not bear fruit. The 'deformalisation' of governance favours the interests of the more powerful actors. The weakening of the discipline of the rule of law is much too high a price to pay for the new flexibility.

[8] See the project report available at www.bipr.eu/documents/Frosini-TARN-20190515.pdf.

[9] Art I-8, Draft European Constitutional Treaty [2004] OJ C 310/1.

[10] See ch 13, section IV.3 and, more extensively, pt VI, chs 27 and 28.

[11] *European Governance. A White Paper*, COM(2001) 428 final of 25 July 2001, [2001] OJ C287/5.

[12] Original emphasis (ibid at 10).

[13] See the presidency conclusions of 23–24 March 2000, available at www.europarl.europa.eu/summits/lis1_en.htm.

[14] See the bibliography of the CONNEX project at www.connex-network.org/govlit.

[15] C Offe, 'Governance – An "Empty Signifier"' (2008) 16 *Constellations* 550.

[16] H Hazenberg, 'Is Governance Democratic?' (2015) 18 *Critical Review of International Social and Political Philosophy* 285.

11

*Scientific Expertise in Social Regulation and the European Court of Justice: Legal Frameworks for De-nationalised Governance Structures**

1. AN ANALYTIC FRAMEWORK

THE EUROPEAN COURT of Justice (ECJ) 'cannot shy away from technical questions'. This observation of Advocate General Walter van Gerven in his opinion in the *TU München* case[1] is certainly valid. The ECJ has, indeed, in many contexts, been forced to take a stand on issues involving the legal assessment of non-legal evidence in general[2] and scientific expertise in particular.[3] It is one thing, however, to acknowledge that the ECJ's involvement in such issues has proved to be unavoidable, and quite another to assess its performance in dealing with this challenge. The involvement of courts and administrative bodies poses multi-faceted problems. To these, the European legal system adds further genuine difficulties stemming from its specific institutional features and the constraints that they imply. It is, of course, possible and instructive to contrast the performance of the European legal system with international debates on the legal regulation of scientifically controversial issues, or to compare the attitudes of national courts or administrative bodies and their

* Published in C Joerges, K-H Ladeur and Ellen Vos (eds), *Integrating Scientific Expertise into Regulatory Decision-Making. National Traditions and European Innovations* (Schriftenreihe des Zentrums für Europäische Rechtspolitik, Band 23) (Baden-Baden: Nomos, 1997) 295–324.

[1] Case C-269/90 *Hauptzollamt München-Mitte v Technische Universität München* [1991] ECR I-5469 at I-5483.

[2] Ellen Vos' celex research for a few keywords ('scientific committees'; 'scientific'; 'technical'; 'risk and health'; 'risk and safety') has brought to light more than 60 cases which were directly in point.

[3] It is common to differentiate between these two categories of knowledge (see, eg, CM Radaelli, 'The Role of Knowledge in the Policy Process' (1995) 2 *JEPP* 159, although resorting to non-scientific expertise, such as economic analyses, as used in so many fields of economic regulation, poses similar problems; furthermore, an insulation of scientifically-based decision-making criteria from other policy concerns, such as the economic consequences of standard-setting in the field of social regulation here under consideration, is to be understood as a deliberate choice which pre-supposes a specific institutional setting and needs to be based upon an adequate design of such an institutional framework.

experiences with traditional and modern regulatory approaches.[4] But any such comparison will have to reflect carefully upon its own yardsticks.[5]

References to expertise occur in many fields and angles of modern legal systems; the categories of knowledge required vary, as does the intensity of its impact on decision-making. The Community system, however, is not comprehensive in two important respects. Its own need for expertise typically arises in the context of European regulatory activities, ie, in the field of economic regulation and competition policy on the one hand and in the various areas of social regulation on the other. It is in this latter field of social regulation that resorting to 'scientific expertise' plays a highly prominent role. Outside the field of agricultural policy, where the protection of health and consumers has always been treated as an integral element of 'market'-building,[6] the intense involvement of the Community in social regulation has taken place in conjunction with its efforts to complete and manage the Internal Market. As a result of these linkages with primarily economic objectives, the European system must implement its social regulation at a complex crossroads of often merely functional Community and residual Member State competencies. Equally important, the Community remains dependent upon the cooperation of national courts, administrative bodies, and non-governmental actors in the implementation of its policies. Last, but not least, judicial review at European level is usually prompted by preliminary proceedings under Article 177, which do not, however, foresee a comprehensive or definite resolution of the regulatory issues concerned.

This background to the jurisprudence of the ECJ will not be addressed comprehensively in this chapter, nor will it be traced through a detailed description of legislative developments. It will rather be presented, first, by a general observation on the attractiveness of scientifically-endorsed decision-making criteria for the European legal system; second, by an outline of regulatory patterns that have emerged in the Europeanised fields of social regulation; and third, by a hypothesis concerning the constitutional importance of these developments and the challenges they present to the ECJ. These observations and assumptions will then serve as guides through the ECJ's jurisprudence. Because of its dependence on partly trans-legal and non-positivist premises, it goes without saying that this kind of interpretation cannot claim any definite or exclusive validity. But it is submitted that any meaningful interpretation of the ECJ's

[4] See R Rausch, *Die Kontrolle von Tatsachenfeststellungen und -würdigungen durch den Gerichtshof der europäischen Gemeinschaften. Zu gerichtlichen Nachprüfung von Kommissionsentscheidungen im Vergleich zum deutschen und französischen Recht* (Berlin: Duncker & Humblot, 1994); S Schlacke, *Risikoentscheidungen im europäischen Lebensmittelrecht. Eine Untersuchung am Beispiel des gemeinschaftlichen Zusatzstoffrechts unter besonderer Berücksichtigung des europäi-schen Ausschußwesens ('Komitologie')*, Dissertation (Baden-Baden: Nomos, 1998); on machinery safety, see A Bücker, *Von der Gefahrenabwehr zur Risikovorsorge und Risikomanagement im Arbeitsschutzrecht* (Berlin: Ducker & Humblot, 1997).

[5] See, generally, R Dehousse, 'Comparing National and EC Law: The Problem of the Level of Analysis' (1994) 42 *AJCL* 761.

[6] See 2.2.1 below.

case-law needs to resort to the kind of framework employed here. It is only through its refinement and improvement that one can (and should!) search for an interpretation of greater explanatory strength and more thorough normative plausibility.

1.1. The Territorial Boundaries of Legal Systems and the Trans-legal Status of Scientific Knowledge

The resort of legal systems to scientific expertise is inextricably linked with modern technological developments and the social responses they provoke. Along with improvements in scientific knowledge which enable us to detect the sources of 'dangers', to identify the likely implications of activities, and thus to transform 'dangers' into 'risks',[7] legal systems have come under pressure to integrate this knowledge and to devise regulatory schemes which allow for its use. This story need not be retold here.[8] But there is one aspect of particular importance in the Community context which should be stressed.

Recourse to scientific expertise in regulatory decision-making gains authoritative validity only through its attribution to some specific legal system which endorses the bindingness of scientific findings, ensures the enforcement of expert assessments, and takes responsibility for prohibiting activities and/or accepting risks. The reach of legal systems, be they nationally or supranationally organised, remains limited to their territorial boundaries. From the viewpoint of the scientific community, this segmentation seems contrary to the standards of science – there is no such thing as German physics or European mathematics. To be sure, cultural and political traditions have shaped the practices of engineering, for instance, or the schools of thought in medicine and other disciplines. It is equally true that one has to differentiate between the scientific level of risk analysis and the practices of risk-management which involve political and policy questions such as the acceptability of risks and regulatory responses to them.[9] And yet, the standards of science as well as the techniques of risk assessment claim universal validity. Where scientists cannot agree, they nonetheless continue to interpret their controversies as a scientific exercise and entrust the scientific community with the competence to assess their claims. The integration of scientific expertise into legal systems may therefore be seen as a paradox. By resorting to scientific expertise, legal systems subject themselves to 'external' validity criteria. By the same token, through a reliance on scientific assessments, they overcome their built-in parochialism; the legal system becomes entitled to a recognition of its position beyond its own borders.

[7] See N Luhmann, *Soziologie des Risikos* (Berlin-NewYork: Walter de Gruyter, 1991) 9 ff.

[8] See, more generally, W Köck, 'Die rechtliche Bewältigung technischer Risiken' (1993) 26 *Kritische Justiz* 125.

[9] See AW Gouldner, 'Cosmopolitans and Locals: Towards an Analysis of Latent Social Roles' (1957) 2 *Administrative Science Quarterly*, Part 1, 281 and Part 2 (1958), 444.

These interfaces between science-based evaluations and legal decision-making lend themselves to prudent and strategic exploitation in the Community context. On the one hand, Community law may, wherever it manages to promote science-based standards of validity, ensure its own authority without the usual entanglements in complex controversies over competencies, conflicting economic interests and highly sensitive issues of political accountability. Member States, on the other hand, when pointing to scientific expertise as providing support for their regulatory concerns, can hardly be accused of promoting one-sidedly some parochial or projectionist interest.

1.2. 'Negative Integration', the Europeanisation of Social Regulation and the Emergence of Regulatory Networks

The resort to science cannot occur in a legal vacuum. It pre-supposes legal provisions and regulatory frameworks to facilitate the recourse to expertise and expert assessments. The Community has thus had to devise and build up an adequate environment in order to exploit the integrating functions of scientific expertise.

Article 30 EC, as interpreted by the ECJ, has been the main source of inspiration in primary law. This provision is to be read in conjunction with Article 36 EC and the explicit recognition of enumerated regulatory concerns therein. The Court's jurisprudence on Article 30 EC has been praised and criticised for its 'de-regulatory' implications. A closer look, however, reveals that these observations are inadequate in that they fail to substantiate the criteria upon which the ECJ based its controls. What the Court did was to impose standards of regulatory reasonableness on Member States, albeit in a way which severely restricts regulatory discretion and forces Member States to provide scientific bases for protective policies they wish to pursue.[10]

Because of these in-built limitations of control over regulatory policies that can be exercised under Article 30, this provision has proven to be a far from perfect tool for overcoming barriers to trade. In order to realise its objective of completing the Internal Market, the Community was bound to pursue a strategy which de-legitimised national regulatory policies, while at the same time ensuring that 'reasonable' regulatory concerns were taken care of within sophisticated European regulatory frameworks. Product regulation provides the most telling example.[11] The Community never tried to simply guarantee the free circulation of goods. It also sought to ensure their acceptability – and was therefore forced to replace not only mandatory national legislation but even non-mandatory

[10] See 2.1. below.

[11] See C Joerges, 'Paradoxes of Deregulatory Strategies at Community Level: The Example of Product Safety Policy' in G Majone (ed), *Deregulation or Reregulation?: Regulatory reform in Europe and in the United States* (London: Pinter; New York: St Martin's Press, 1990) 176.

product standards. It did so by promoting innovative regulatory schemes at European level, which have now reached the point of almost comprehensively covering the whole range of technical goods and other products.

The market rationale for re-regulation at European level does not apply to 'process regulation'. The interest configurations in pertinent fields seem to render it unlikely that economically less advanced Member States might accept costly regulatory standards which would deprive them of their competitive advantages towards jurisdictions with stricter standards.[12] The analytical distinction between product- and process-oriented regulation proves to be less clear, however, if one considers the outcome of European policies. As the Community's safety at work legislation in particular demonstrates, the 'technical' and 'political' interdependence of product and process regulation can be such that they are dealt with as one sole package. Even in areas of environmental legislation which clearly have no impact on the quality of products, the European policy process has not resulted in a 'race to the bottom'. In the case of air quality regulation, Héritier and her collaborators[13] have detected a theoretically unpredicted form of 'regulatory competition'; namely, efforts on the part of the most important Member States to impose their own regulatory approaches on the whole of the Community. Their political moves have been motivated by economic advantages stemming from such regulatory victories, but have not been directed towards environmental deregulation.

The processes of re-regulating Europe have taken place despite the well-known constraints under which the Community's system is to operate. The Community does not dispose of the coercive power that the modern state once monopolised. Adoption of legislative acts still depends upon the consent of at least a qualified majority of the Member States. Compliance with regulations and even the rulings of the ECJ depends upon the obedience of national institutions. Most noteworthy in our present context are the scarcity of administrative resources and the lack of genuine administrative powers. These constraints have influenced both the design of European regulatory techniques and the strategies of implementation:[14]

- At all stages of the process of planning new initiatives and in the implementation of Community policies, the Commission ensures the cooperation of national actors;

[12] See, for an elaboration of this argument, FW Scharpf, 'Negative and Positive Integration in the Political Economy of European Welfare States' in G Marks, FW Scharpf, PC Schmitter and W Streeck (eds), *Governance in the European Union* (London: Sage, 1996) 15.

[13] A Héritier, S Mingers, C Knill and M Becka, *Die Veränderung von Staatlichkeit in Europa. Ein regulativer Wettbewerb: Deutschland, Großbritannien, Frankreich* (Opladen: Leske & Budrich, 1994).

[14] See, more extensively, C Joerges, 'Rationalisierungsprozesse im Recht der Produktsicherheit: Öffentliches Recht und Haftungsrecht unter dem Einfluß der Europäischen Integration' (1994) 27 *Jahrbuch des Umwelt- und Technikrechts* 141; idem, 'Die Beurteilung der Sicherheit technischer Konsumgüter und der Gesundheit von Lebensmitteln in der Praxis des europäischen Ausschußwesens ("Komitologie")', *ZERP-Diskussionspapier* 1/95.

- Increasingly, the Community encourages and requests not only mutual recognition of decisions taken by national bodies but a continuous cooperation among national administrations. This includes the assignment of specific tasks, and thus amounts to a division of labour among Member States;
- When preparing decisions on the acceptable level of risk and during the whole process of implementation, the Community establishes scientific committees or otherwise guarantees scientific advice; when concretising the essential safety requirements of directives adopted under the New Approach to Technical Harmonisation and Standards, the Commission relies on the expertise of European standardisation organisations.

1.3. De-nationalised Governance Structures and the European Legitimacy Problem

Interest formation and decision-making in the kinds of networks described above fit neither into the institutional structures foreseen within national constitutional States nor into those of the European Community. It seems equally impossible to explain the emergence and the functioning of these networks within the neo-functionalist or intergovernmentalist paradigms of integration research. They may be most adequately conceptualised as multi-level games with a strong interdependence of national and supranational institutions, as well as national and transnational non-governmental actors.[15] Positive characterisations in legal terms are extremely difficult because they cannot build upon any elaborated model of political governance and legal institutions. Lawyers do, of course, observe all the elements of Europeanised regulatory networks, the continuous presence of Commission officials and representatives of national governments, the involvement of national and supranational non-governmental organisations in the processes of policy formation and implementation, the dependence of Community law on its support by national administrative bodies, and the compliance of courts. It is equally apparent that decision-making within European networks is not restricted to purely technical issues but regularly affects economic interests and often normatively and politically sensitive concerns. Because of these implications, the 'functioning' of regulatory networks will, in the last resort, be dependent upon their legitimacy.

This delicate category cannot be neglected. But for the reasons just outlined, it seems futile to address it directly upon the basis of some abstract preconceived

[15] See FW Scharpf, 'Community and Autonomy: Multi-level Policy-making in the European Union' (1994) 1 *JEPP* 219; E Grande, 'Das Paradox der Schwäche. Forschungspolitik und die Einflußlogik europäischer Politikverflechtung' in M Jachtenfuchs and B Kohler Koch (eds), *Europäische Integration* (Wiesbaden: VS Verlag für Sozialwissenschaften, 1996) 373. For recent general accounts, see S Hix, 'Approaches to the Study of the European Community: The Challenge to Comparative Politics' (1994) 17 *West European Politics* 1; M Jachtenfuchs, 'Theoretical Perspectives on European Governance' (1995) 1 *ELJ* 115.

normative model of social regulation in Europe. It seems equally unlikely that legislators and courts will come up with perfect and comprehensive solutions. What one is entitled to expect, however, is a sensitivity in principle, especially on the part of the ECJ, for the legitimacy of its rulings, which can be interpreted as a background agenda of the specific issues and contexts the Court is to address.

2. THE JURISPRUDENCE OF THE EUROPEAN COURT OF JUSTICE

If international governance structures for social regulation are to emerge, scientific expertise can be expected to fulfil a prominent role in processing information and delivering commonly acceptable criteria for the assessment of risks. If one must attribute practical importance to these new governance structures, the acceptance of their decisional output by both the Community and the Member States must be ascertainable. The problem with this contention is, however, that it can only be validated indirectly. The search for de-nationalised legal structures must therefore take some detours. The following review of the jurisprudence of the ECJ will first turn to European primary law, which at first sight is only concerned with the imposition of restraints on unilateral national legislation. It will then examine controversies over regulatory competencies and inter-institutional conflicts. The primary focus of these analyses will be the resort to scientific expertise as a means to overcome the territorial boundaries of legal systems. Special attention will be paid, however, to the limits of such a strategy, which can be attributed either to the normative sensitivity of the ECJ or to its awareness of the practical need to supplement the validation of science-based decision-making with transnational frameworks for risk management (2.1. and 2.2. below). This more indirect confirmation of the ECJ's readiness to accept and to promote de-nationalised governance structures will be followed by an examination of those judgments which have more directly addressed the legal issues of European social regulation. These cases are few in number and their review will demonstrate that the law of de-nationalised governance is still at an infant stage. But it will become apparent that the ECJ has, despite its limited capacity to structure Europe's regulatory practice, at least started to pronounce principles and rules which provide some guidance for future developments.

2.1. Regulatory Competencies and Scientific Expertise

Among the constitutional issues to be confronted in the Europeanisation of social regulation, controversies over the Community's competencies can be expected to play, and indeed have played, a prominent role. 'Social regulation' is a type of policy that the original Treaty on the European Economic Community had not foreseen. Its prominence at Community level is a consequence of the market-building efforts which have ranked high on the European agenda since 1985 and the adoption of the Single European Act. It was this policy that prompted re-regulatory activities especially in the field of product, safety-at-work and environmental legislation and that led to the emergence of European regulatory networks.[16] Precisely because the adoption and implementation of the new regulatory policies have occurred very much as an unpredicted discovery process, constitutional issues only gradually became apparent and have been left unresolved or even unexplored in many respects. This somewhat complacent attitude seems to a certain degree understandable. Insistence on the elaboration and clarification of constitutional issues prior to the adoption of new policies can have quite destructive implications when it leads to the conclusion that a socially desirable activity cannot be pursued for want of pertinent constitutional mandates.

The many-faceted delineation of Community and Member State competencies serves well to illustrate these general observations. Prior to the shift to majority voting in 1987, the Community objective of achieving a Common Market was restricted substantively by the explicit recognition of residuary national competencies in Article 36 and institutionally by the unanimity requirement for Community directives replacing national legislation. The consent of Member States to Community measures reduced the likelihood of controversies over the scope of 'functional' competencies derived from Article 100. That situation changed with majority voting and the Community's mandate to pursue a 'high level' of health, safety, environmental and consumer protection.

2.1.1. *Article 30 and the Disciplining of the Member States*

The most obvious example demonstrating how scientific universalism can be used to overcome the particularism of legal systems is offered by the extremely rich jurisprudence on Articles 30 and 36. This potential emerged from the well-known structuring of the meaning of these provisions by the ECJ. According to the famous holding in *Dassonville*, the prohibition by Article 30 of measures having an effect equivalent to quantitative restrictions covers 'all trading rules enacted by Member States which are capable of hindering, directly or indirectly, actually or potentially, intra-Community trade'.[17] This broad interpretation of the notion of equivalent effect leaves Article 36 unaffected. However, the regulatory objective which this Article exempts from the principle enshrined in Article 30, made the *Dassonville* formula a potential threat, especially to areas such as consumer and environmental protection. In its famous *Cassis de Dijon* decision, the ECJ found a way to uphold the potential for supervision of

[16] See 1.2. above, and, more extensively, C Joerges, 'Markt ohne Staat?, Die Wirtschaftsverfassung der Gemeinschaft und die Regulative Politik' in R Wildenmann (ed), *Staatswerdung Europas. Optionen für eine Europäische Union* (Baden-Baden: Nomos, 1991) 225 with further references; English translation: *EUI Working Paper Law 1996/02*, reprinted in pt V, ch 21.

[17] Case 8/74 *Procureur du Roi v Dassonville* [1974] ECR 837.

Member States opened up by *Dassonville* while at the same time tempering the anxieties of Member States about the Community's incursion into their regulatory concerns. The Court explained that essential public interests related, for example, to the protection of public health, consumer protection and environmental policy[18] were not to be qualified as measures of equivalent effect.[19]

The many subtleties of the Court's jurisprudence – the changing scope of its supervision of Member States,[20] its deregulatory effects and their impact on the protection of consumers, the instrumentalisation of Article 30 as a means to promote Community legislation – need concern us here only in two respects. First, to what degree did the Court substitute legal criteria with scientific assessments, thereby overcoming the territorial boundaries of legal competencies? And second, in so far as the Member States were required to respect scientific expertise, how did the ECJ determine and delineate the validity of scientific assessments?

2.1.2. *The Imposition of Science-based Criteria on National Legislatures*

Cassis de Dijon has become famous for promoting a principle that the ECJ did not endorse; namely, the duty of Member States to open up their borders to products lawfully marketed elsewhere in the Community.[21] The message of the *Dassonville/Cassis de Dijon* jurisprudence was more modest, but nonetheless daring. The ECJ's distinction between legitimate and illegitimate regulatory concerns imposed a conceptual framework on the Member States within which they had to substantiate their regulatory interests. Furthermore, and even more importantly, the ECJ requested Member States to take only such action which is 'proportionate to the aim in view'.[22] In order to become an effective supervisory tool, the principle of proportionality needed to be concretised further. At that point, science came into view. This occurred with three variations, with foodstuffs law providing the most elaborated example.

Member States must not only state their views as to the risks for public health, but 'the risk must be measured, not according to the yardstick of general conjecture but on the bases of relevant scientific research'.[23] This is by no means

[18] Case 302/86 *Commission v Denmark (Danish Bottles)* [1988] ECR 4607.

[19] Case 120/78 *Cassis de Dijon* [1979] ECR 649.

[20] See Cases C-267/91 and C-268/91 *Keck and Mithouard* [1993] ECR I-6097; and now Case C-391/92 *Commission v Greece* [1995] ECR I-1621.

[21] See, notably, the Communication from the Commission concerning the consequences of the judgment given by the Court of Justice on 20 February 1979 in Case 120/78 ('Cassis de Dijon'), OJ 1980 C 256, 2.

[22] The principle of proportionality is an import into Community law from German constitutional law (see M Zuleeg, 'Deutsches und europäisches Verwaltungsrecht – Wechselseitige Einwirkungen' (1994) 53 *Veröffentlichungen der Vereinigung Deutscher Staatrechtslehrer* 153, at 171–172 with further references). The principle has been cited as underlying the last sentence of Article 36 since Case 174/82 *Officier van Justitie v Sandoz* [1983] ECR 2445; Case 247/84 *Motte* [1985] ECR 3887; and Case 304/84 *Muller* [1986] ECR 1511.

[23] See, as a recent example, Case C-17/93 *Van der Veldt* [1994] ECR I-3537 at 3560.

a trivial requirement. It restricts legislative discretion and imposes standards on decision-making processes within the Member States. Once it had been established that legislation must be backed by relevant scientific evidence, it became unavoidable to decide upon the properties of such evidence. This delicate issue came up again and again when importers of foodstuffs, in response to being summoned by national authorities because of a violation of domestic law, invoked the *Cassis de Dijon* principle. When assessing the validity of national legislation, the Court asked Member States to respect 'the findings of international scientific research, and in particular of the work of the Community's Scientific Committee for Food,[24] the Codex Alimentarius Committee of the Food and Agriculture Organization of the United Nations (FAO) and the World Health Organization (WHO)'.[25]

The authority attributed to the international and European expert community need not be unconditional. In a judgment concerning residues in foodstuffs,[26] the ECJ introduced the concept of '*per se*' dangerous substances. The prohibition of such substances does not require the establishment of a 'danger', but may form a more general policy designed to prevent their presence.[27] 'The authorities of the importing Member State are, however, obliged to review the prescribed maximum level if it appears to them that the reasons which led to its establishment have changed, for example, as a result of the discovery of a new use for such and such a pesticide.'[28]

A second retraction concerns objective differences among the Member States such as 'climatic conditions, the normal diet of the population and their state of health'.[29] The most prominent example is provided by the beer case, where Germany, in defence of its *Reinheitsgebot*, argued that it was particularly desirable to prohibit the use of any additive in the manufacture of this product because 'more beer is consumed by Germans than any other foodstuff'.[30] This argument was not taken seriously by the ECJ.[31] It has, however, been accepted in a series of other decisions, such as *Melkunie*.[32] There the Court approved the Dutch *Melkbesluit*, prohibiting micro-organisms beyond a threshold number

[24] See, as to its tasks and composition, the pertinent Commission decisions in OJ 1974 L 136, 1 and OJ 1986 L 163, 40.

[25] See, eg, Case 178/84 *Commission* v *Germany (Reinheitsgebot)* [1987] ECR 1227 at 1274.

[26] Case 94/83 *Albert Heijn BV* [1984] ECR 3263.

[27] Ibid, at 3279–80.

[28] Ibid, at 3280.

[29] Ibid, at 3280.

[30] Case 178/84 *Reinheitsgebot*, n 25 above, report for the hearing at 1236.

[31] See 2.1.4. below, for one of the Court's reasons, namely, the lack of consistency in Germany's legislation. The Court also referred to the requirement of Case 304/84 *Muller*, n 22 above, that Member States are to provide a procedure for traders to apply for the authorisation of additives contained in foreign products but prohibited in the importing state, see 2.1.4. below. In my reading, the Court's reasoning reflects its own uncertainty about Germany's insistence on the degree of uncertainty in the assessment of the risks involved; see p 1274 and the opinion of Advocate General Sir Gordon Slynn at 1257–1260.

[32] Case 97/83 *Melkunie* [1984] ECR 2367.

in pasteurised milk in view of the Dutch habit of keeping 'such products for a period of time in less suitable conditions than those in the distributor's plant'.[33] Giving in to the national conditions argument implies a partitioning of the Internal Market. It should be noted that the Court supported this concession by pointing to a broad acceptance of the Dutch standards on daily intake both in other Member States and outside the Community.[34] The *Melkunie* judgment can therefore be read as giving priority to a high level of protection not adopted by the Community but reflecting a broadly accepted tendency.

2.1.3. Scientific Uncertainties

Both the distinction between ordinary and *per se* dangerous substances in the *Albert Heijn* case and the consideration of local conditions in the *Melkunie* judgment overlap with a second differentiation of fundamental importance.[35] As the Court has consistently held since *Eyssen*,[36] Member States cannot be reproached for discriminating arbitrarily or disguisedly restricting trade between Member States within the meaning of Article 36 when protective measures seem reasonable in view of 'difficulties and uncertainties' of risk assessments equally encountered by other countries or international organisations. As this reasoning indicates, the existence of uncertainties by no means entitles Member States to adopt whatever policy they may feel to be appropriate. Although the Court has repeatedly stated that, in the absence of harmonisation, it is up to the Member States to decide how to react to 'uncertainties at the present stage of research',[37] its reasoning in all pertinent cases[38] is concerned with restrictions of the competencies of Member States to decide autonomously upon their regulatory policies. Where they are in principle entitled to require the explicit approval of plant production products, they must not 'unnecessarily require technical or chemical or laboratory tests when the same analyses have already been carried out in another Member State and their results are available to those authorities or may at their request be placed at their disposal'.[39] They are entitled to request the authorisation of additives to foodstuffs, the more so since limiting the use of additives is 'in accordance with a joint approach adopted by the Member States'.[40] They are not required when deciding upon authorisation to attribute

[33] At 2386 para 19.

[34] See the Opinion of Advocate General VerLoren van Themaat at 2395.

[35] On the following, cf the comprehensive analysis of S Schlacke, 'Foodstuffs Law and the Precautionary Principle: Normative Bases, Secondary Law and Institutional Tendencies' in Joerges, Ladeur, and Vos (n * above, 169.

[36] Case 53/80 *Kaasfabriek Eyssen (Nisin)* [1981] ECR 409 at 422 f.

[37] See, for instance, Case 174/82 *Sandoz*, n 22 above, at 2445, para 16, citing as a precedent Case 272/80 *Biologische Producten* [1981] ECR 3277, although the formula is not to be found there.

[38] Including Case 304/84 *Muller*, n 22 above, although the references to the international scientific community in that case are quite unspecific (see, especially, at 1529).

[39] Case 272/80 *Biologische Producten*, n 37 above, at 3292.

[40] Case 247/84 *Motte*, n 22 above, at 3904.

binding force to the opinions of the Community's Scientific Committee. But they must refer an importer's application 'to a committee of experts in order to obtain an opinion on the harmfulness of the additive, the degree of the human organism's tolerance of it and the necessity, value and suitability of its use'.[41] If it is then established by the authorities of the importing Member State that there is a 'real need' for that additive, 'they may not … refuse authorisation solely on the ground that it is contained in the imported foodstuff'.[42]

2.1.4. Legislative Coherence

One facet of the Court's interpretation of the proportionality principle deserves particular mention. As the Court has consistently held, national regulations must be 'appropriate' to meet the legislature's ends. This ends–means rationality is a well-defined concept in political sociology. Its plausibility as a yardstick for the functioning of legal systems seems, however, highly questionable. Two cases may serve to illustrate this point.

In its decision on the compatibility with Article 30 of a French requirement for the construction of woodworking machines,[43] the Court explained that France must only prescribe a specific level of protection but must not impede the importation of products solely on the ground that they are manufactured using an alternative technique.[44] The Court added that the safety design of machines is to be seen as an element of a regulatory 'concept', which may give priority either to the construction or to the training of workers using machines. It then left France with the freedom to pursue its own safety philosophy. The famous judgment on the German *Reinheitsgebot*[45] is a second case in point. The Court there attached particular importance to the fact that Germany permitted the use of the additive in question in virtually all beverages with the exception of beer. To interpret the proportionality principle as prohibiting a general ban for beer is to require Germany to adopt a regulatory approach which is in line with that of the Community.[46] The Community now favours 'horizontal' regulations, which deal with additives as such and no longer prescribe the composition of particular foodstuffs. Within this approach it is perfectly reasonable to provide for procedures which enable traders to apply for an authorisation.[47] At the same time, this regulatory technique does not preclude Member States from pursuing

[41] At 3906.

[42] At 3905; see Case 174/82 *Sandoz*, n 22 above, at 2445.

[43] Case 188/84 *Woodworking Machines* [1986] ECR 419.

[44] Para 16.

[45] Case 178/84 *Reinheitsgebot*, n 25 above.

[46] Namely, the shift away from regulating the composition of specific foodstuffs in favour of horizontal legislation following the Commission's adoption of the 'New Approach' in the foodstuffs sector; see the Commission's Communication COM (85) 603 final of 8 November 1985.

[47] See Case 178/84 *Reinheitsgebot*, n 25 above, at 1274 and Case 304/84 *Muller*, n 22 above (again the Court cites a precedent which does not really contain the position the Court is attributing to it.)

policies aiming at a high level of protection. But such policies are to adhere to a regulatory scheme which ensures some consistency in risk policies.

It does not seem easy to reconcile the holdings on French woodworking machines and German beer. As both cases show, it is one thing to require Member States to take account of the findings of scientific institutions and quite another to ensure the equivalence of regulatory philosophies. We will have to return later to these limits of the Court's interference with the regulatory autonomy of Member States.[48] One interim conclusion can, however, be drawn at this point. The ECJ's references to the normative importance of scientific evidence can be attributed neither exclusively to the Community nor to national legal systems. Both the Community and the Member States play important roles in authorising risk policies. But the interaction between them is infiltrated by trends and actors outside their boundaries. Policy trends promoted by states inside and outside the Community, standards of scientific expertise formulated by international organisations, or even the prevailing view within the international scientific community may enjoy normative validity. Member States are requested to design their legislation in a way that enables integration of scientific findings and they are bound to give credit to scientific analyses undertaken beyond their territories.

2.1.5. Instrumentalising the Commission's Powers under Article 100a (4)

The legal relevance of transnational science and infranational policy communities has been confirmed by the Court's handling of the only controversy to date that has been fought out under Article 100a (4).[49] The history of this controversy is complicated but sufficiently well-known. At issue was the compatibility of the German prohibition of pentachlorophenol (PCP), which was stricter than the pertinent Community Directive 91/173/EEC adopted by qualified majority on 21 March 1991 against Germany's vote.[50] The Commission had explicitly endorsed Germany's position – and France complained. This is how the controversy over Germany's legislation muted into a legal controversy between the Commission and France. The ECJ used the opportunity to teach the Commission a lesson and to upgrade its position at the same time.

The Court achieved this result by first attributing a constitutive importance[51] to the supervision of unilateral action taken by Member States under Article 100a (4) to which it could therefore apply the requirements of Article 190. By doing so, the Court shifted the burden of providing good reasons for Germany's

[48] See 2.2.2. and 3.2. below.

[49] Case C-41/93 *France v Commission* [1994] ECR I-1829; see also Case C-314/99 *Kingdom of the Netherlands v Commission of the European Communities* [2002] ECR I-05521 (hereinafter after '*PCP* judgment').

[50] See OJ 1991 L 85, 34.

[51] See, on this point, Advocate General Tesauro, Case C-41/79, n 49 above at, 1836.

legislation to the Commission.[52] This then led the Commission to consult a scientist of international standing, Professor Rappe from the University of Umea, Sweden. In its decision of 14 September 1994,[53] the Commission was able to explain in detail why it considered Germany's position to be justified and announced that it would re-examine the adequacy of the Community Directive on the basis of further research it had commissioned. It is important to note that Sweden, at the time of the proceedings, had not yet joined the Community. This aspect of the controversy only underlines what is already obvious: the validity of scientific findings cannot depend on the boundary of the legal system which integrates these findings into its laws.

2.2. The Defence of Community Competencies

The ECJ is famous (in the sense of *fameux*) for rarely questioning the Community's own competencies *vis-à-vis* the Member States. Significantly enough, conflicts over the Community's regulatory competencies have come up in a field where the Community is acting on the basis of majority decisions, namely in the field of agricultural policy. Majority voting at Community level tends to favour 'positive' integration, ie, the adoption of measures which aim at the imposition of a regulatory framework on the functioning of the Internal Market. The questioning of the Community's competence then typically serves as a means to restore the veto power which the unanimity rule once implied. The ECJ's tendency to defend the Community's regulatory powers thus supports 'market building through positive regulation'. This is typically achieved by adherence to the stricter standards at Community level. Where uniform standards cannot be realised, a favouring of high standards may at least pave the way for future legislation.

2.2.1. Article 43, EC Protectionism and the Politicisation of Social Regulation

Real world conflicts, however, are usually more complex. They do not simply involve the dichotomy between the free market and social regulation, but simultaneously concern more trivial policy objectives. A case of exemplary importance may suffice to illustrate this point.[54]

Through Directive 85/649/EEC of 31 December 1985,[55] adopted by a qualified majority upon the basis of Article 43, the EC prohibited the use of hormones in livestock farming. The effect of this policy was to prevent the import of American products into the Community. The legal controversy within the Community over

[52] See Case C-41/93 *France v Commission*, n 49 above, at I-1849/1850.
[53] OJ 1994 L 316, 43.
[54] Case 68/86 *United Kingdom v Council* [1988] ECR 855.
[55] OJ 1985 L 382, 228.

the policy did not address this trade issue directly. It was rather concerned with the regulatory contents of Community law. Even the questioning of Community competencies played but a minor role. The argument brought forward by the United Kingdom was that, in view of its health objectives, Directive 85/649/EEC should have been based upon Article 100. That provision requires unanimity. It would thus have enabled the United Kingdom to veto the Community prohibition. The Court response to this challenge was unambiguous: 'Efforts to achieve the objectives of the common agricultural policy ... cannot disregard requirements relating to the public interest such as the protection of consumers or the protection of health and life of humans and animals ...'[56] The all-encompassing 'nature' of the Treaty provisions on agricultural policy thus served as a means to justify a 'positive' measure and to refute the questioning of its legal basis.[57]

A further complaint by the United Kingdom related to the failure of the statement of reasons in the Directive to take into consideration a scientific report which had been prepared in accordance with Article 8 of Directive 81/602/EEC on the prohibition of 'certain substances having a hormonal action and of any substances having a thyrostatic action'.[58] Again, the Court rejected that complaint somewhat bluntly: the said Article 'imposed an obligation on the Commission only. ... Consequently, the Council was not under an obligation to refer to those antecedents.'[59] This answer is unsatisfactory because the complainants had based their argument upon the principle of proportionality which the Court imported into Community law and explicitly interpreted as requiring national legislation to take scientific findings into account.[60]

This inconsistency appears less surprising, and at the same time more interesting, if one considers the sensitivity of the issues involved. The scientific report on the risks of hormone use, commissioned in accordance with Directive 81/602/EEC, had led the Commission to re-consider the strict prohibition of Community law.[61] Its announcement of a policy change then met with strong opposition from both the Economic and Social Committee (ECOSOC)[62]

[56] Case 68/86 *United Kingdom v Council*, n 54 above, at 896 (para 12).

[57] This reasoning was repeated in Case C-331/88 *Fedesa and Others* [1990] ECR I-4023 at I-4065.

[58] OJ 1981 L 222, 32.

[59] Case 68/86 *United Kingdom v Council*, n 54 above, at 900 (para 35).

[60] See 2.1.2. above; in the follow-up case *Fedesa and Others* (n 57 above), the competence issue was similarly overlaid by arguments on the justification and reasonableness of Community law. In its response to the complaint that the Community had infringed 'legitimate expectations of traders' that hormones 'would not be prohibited in the absence of any objectively based doubt', the Court repeated the arguments it uses when dealing with national legislation (see 2.1.2. above); 'it need merely be stated that, faced with divergent appraisals by the national authorities of the Member States ... the Council remained within the limits of its discretionary power in deciding to adopt the solution of prohibiting the hormones in question, and respond in that way to the concerns expressed by the European Parliament, the Economic and Social Committee and by several consumer organisations' (at I-4061/62, para 9).

[61] See the Report of the Hearing at 856.

[62] OJ 1985 C 44, 14.

and the European Parliament.[63] Following the European Parliament's resolution, the Commission cancelled further meetings of the scientific group entrusted with the examination of reports the Commission had received. Political opposition to the Commission's readiness to reconsider the Community's hormones policy was thus translated into giving reference to the 'interests of consumers in general (since it could be seen that meat from animals treated with hormones is widely rejected)'.[64] This type of consumer protection cannot, and need not be, supported by scientific evidence. Once its legitimacy as an objective of agricultural policy in general and the hormones directive in particular is accepted, there is 'really no reason to examine the health problem … and so the fact that in the preamble to the contested directive the Council did not go into the partial findings of the scientific group … certainly cannot be regarded as a failure to state reasons'.[65]

This is a serious observation with ironic legal consequences. European opposition to the use of hormones in livestock farming creates a broad collision of interest groups and public anxieties. Only the latter, however, is classified as a problem of social acceptability by experts of risk assessment. The ironic consequence of the Court's reasoning was that it excluded those political actors who could claim to represent the European public from articulating that concern. It is even more ironic that, had the Court given in to the arguments brought forward against the use of Article 43, it would actually have rendered those political actors helpless. Assuming the ECJ has given thought to all this, its judgment can be understood as supporting the political alliance between the majority of Member States and Europe's political institutions against the veto powers of the United Kingdom implied in the unanimity rule of Article 100. Nevertheless, the disregard of scientific evidence that the Commission had been prepared to bring to bear can hardly be heralded as a triumph of legitimate political authority over the neglect of public anxieties by insulated technocrats. The institutional mechanism actually endorsed by the Court was the bargaining process within the Council. Intergovernmental bargaining should not be equated with deliberative political processes on the social acceptability of technological developments.

2.2.2. *The Scope of Secondary Law and Incomplete Harmonisation*

Once the Community has, through harmonisation, 'occupied' a field of secondary legislation, the supremacy of European law in tandem with the principle of pre-emption are said in principle to exclude Member States from taking unilateral measures. Doctrinal statements of the said principles tend to convey

[63] OJ 1985 C 288, 158.
[64] Thus Advocate General Lenz in Case 68/86, n 54 above, at 882.
[65] Ibid.

simplistic messages.[66] One problem that the ECJ needs to address when determining the impact of Community legislation is the delimitation of harmonised and non-harmonised fields; ie, the delimitation of Community from national competencies. The definition of medicinal products provides a particularly interesting example.

In three cases dealing with Directive 65/65/EEC concerning proprietary medicinal products[67] the Court was faced with complaints alleging that Member States had unjustly classified products as medicines, thereby preventing their unauthorised marketing. *Van Bennekom*[68] concerned vitamins which the importer into the Netherlands regarded as foodstuffs;[69] in *Upjohn v Farzoo*[70] the parties litigated over the classification of a hair-restoring product as a cosmetic or medicinal product; Case C-290/90[71] involved a French eye lotion which Germany treated as a medicine. In all of these cases, the Court voted in favour of the stricter law. These holdings are remarkable because the Court's directions in terms of defining the concepts of medicinal products were not sufficient to achieve the Community's free-trade objective. In *Van Bennekom*, the Court construed Directive 65/65/EEC as covering products presented to and used by consumers as medicines; but it then referred to the uncertainties in assessing vitamin consumption and underlined the authority of Member States to determine for themselves to what risks they were prepared to expose consumers.[72] In *Upjohn*, the Court's broad interpretation of Directive 65/65/EEC was supported by all the intervening Member States; but at least in theory market integration could equally have been achieved under the Community legislation on cosmetics.[73] In the case on eye lotions, the Court again underlined the competence of national authorities to determine whether a particular product constitutes a medicinal product and then pointed to the conformity of Germany's practice with the views of the Council of Europe's European Pharmacopoeia Commission.[74]

What all of these cases demonstrate is the inherent weakness of harmonisation policies which remain restricted to the adoption of common rules but fail to provide for the unification of their application.[75] Even the Court's insistence on its prerogatives in interpreting integration. All the Court is able to do under such circumstances is to invoke the authority of scientific expertise as a yardstick for

[66] See A Furrer, Die Sperrwirkung des sekundären Gemeinschaftsrechts auf die nationalen Rechtsordnungen (Baden-Baden: Nomos, 1994).
[67] OJ (English Special Edition) 1965-1966, 20.
[68] Case 227/82 *Leendert van Bennekom* [1983] ECR 3883.
[69] See Case 174/82 *Sandoz*, n 22 above, at 2445.
[70] Case C-112/89 *Upjohn* v *Farzoo and Kortmann* [1991] ECR I-1703.
[71] Case C-290/90 *Commission v Germany* [1992] ECR I-3317.
[72] Case 227/82 *van Bennekom*, n 68 above, at 3901, 3902, 3905.
[73] See para 26 of the Opinion delivered by Advocate General Lenz.
[74] Case C-290/90 *Commission v Germany*, n 71 above, at I-3347.
[75] See 3.2. below.

the assessment of both the reasonableness of national practices and the justification for Community intervention.[76]

2.2.3. *Inter-institutional Conflicts*

More recently, controversies concerning the proper bases for Community legislation have often been initiated by the European Parliament,[77] understandably so, if and because the legal bases for Community legislation determine the rights of the European Parliament in the legislative process. This type of institutional conflict between the European Parliament and the Council is not directly concerned with the mediating role of scientific expertise. This holds equally true for the Parliament's crusade against the delegation of regulatory tasks to the Commission under Article 145 and the comitology procedure,[78] or its ongoing efforts to reduce the scope of Council regulations based on Article 43.[79] These conflicts are truly constitutional in that they concern rights of participation in legislative procedures and the potential role of the European Parliament in the implementation of Community legislation.

The relation of these institutional controversies to the role of science in Community law is only indirect but still illuminating enough. Involvement of the European Parliament in the Community's legislative or administrative activities weakens the autonomy of the compound of Community and national administrations. At the same time, it challenges the functioning of the networks of experts managing risk regulation in Europe. One has, of course, to ask further whether the involvement of Parliament actually leads to a 'constructive' politicisation of risk assessments. One must wonder whether the Parliament's protest against its exclusion from the implementation of legislation adopted under the procedures of Articles 189b or 189c is already backed by a convincing concept of parliamentary control of the Community's executive law-making.

Before exploring these issues further, a second interim conclusion may be drawn. The controversies over the Community's competencies offer only very limited opportunities for questioning or defending the reasonableness of the Community's regulatory policies. Legal guarantees promoting such objectives have to be detected elsewhere. In the end, it will turn out that scientific expertise and its transnational status are to fulfil important functions in the juridification process.

[76] See Advocate General van Gerven's Opinion in Case C-290/90 *Commission* v *Germany*, n 71 above, at I-3335: 'If the Commission wishes to contest the data furnished by the Member State, it must do so on the basis of equally reliable data.'

[77] See, for a recent summary of the Court's jurisprudence, J Falke and C Joerges, 'Rechtliche Möglichkeiten und Probleme bei der Verfolgung und Sicherung nationaler und EG-weiter Umweltschutzziele im Rahmen der europäischen Normung' (Gutachten erstellt im Auftrag des Büros für Technikfolgen-Abschätzung des Deutschen Bundestages; unpublished ms) (Bremen: Centre for European Law and Politics, 1995).

[78] See HA Crams, 'Komitologie im Gesetzgebungsprozess der Europäischen Union und die Einbeziehung des Europäischen Parlaments' (1995) 28 *Kritische Justiz* 112.

[79] See Case C-156/93 *European Parliament v Commission* [1995] ECR I-2019.

2.3. The Community's Commitments in the Exercise of its Law-making Functions

The Community's commitments in the exercise of its powers stem from many sources. It makes some, albeit limited, sense to organise these sources in analogy to conventional hierarchy models of legal systems. Constitutional elements of the European legal system which rank high in their validity claims, such as human rights and the principle of proportionality, have only been introduced by the ECJ. Community primary law itself has undergone changes which are of fundamental importance in the present context. The jurisprudence of the ECJ spells out principles in practically marginal cases, which may turn out to be significant for the whole of Community law. And most importantly, the dynamics of the integration process further the emergence of unforeseen practices which then require normative ingenuity. All of these preliminary remarks serve to underline the infant state of European law and the need to exercise great caution in its interpretation.

2.3.1. Recent Developments in Primary Law

It still makes sense to start with provisions of the Treaty in pertinent policy fields. Thus Article 130r (3) explicitly requires that available scientific and technical data be taken into account in the Community's environmental policy. Article 130 (2) introduced the principle of 'precaution', which by its very nature presupposes that public authorities be open to scientific evaluations of risks to the environment; one may conclude that this principle should *a fortiori* be applicable to the protection of human health. The legal obligations that follow from these provisions still seem to be insufficiently explored.

Just because the ECJ has so far had very limited opportunities to consider the legal implications of these new provisions for the Community itself, a case should be mentioned[80] which primarily concerned the pre-emptive effects of Directives 74/442/EEC and 84/631/EEC concerning waste,[81] and the compatibility with Articles 30 and 36 of a Wallonian regulation prohibiting the import of waste. This issue concerned the tensions between two Community objectives; namely, the prohibition of discriminatory restrictions of trade on the one hand and the principle contained in Article 130r (2) that impairments to the environment should be remedied at their origin. The Court's readiness to give priority to environmental policy relates first of all to the Community itself. But it indirectly affects Member States because they are bound to adopt the Community's environmental policy in order to ensure the effectiveness of their legislation.[82]

[80] Case C-2/90 *Commission v Belgium* [1992] ECR I-4431.

[81] Directive 75/442/EEC on waste, OJ 1975 L 194, 47 and Directive 84/631/EEC on the supervision and control within the European Community of the transfrontier shipment of hazardous waste, OJ 1984 L 326, 31, as amended by Directive 87/112 EEC, OJ 1987 L 48, 31.

[82] See Case C-2/90, n 80 above, para 34.

The Court's holding does not concern the integration of scientific expertise into the legal system. But it is a further illustration of the merging of two levels of governance; the Community system determines the design of national environmental policies and in that sense deploys a rationalising effect.[83]

Because of their tendency to alienate legal systems from their cultural background and historical ties, rationalisation processes not only improve the conditions for a 'de-nationalised' discussion of regulatory issues but also pave the way for resorting to scientific expertise as a regulatory tool. This interdependence can be illustrated by the recent *Angelopharm* judgment.[84] The proceeding started with the German producer of Sedaterm, a substance designed to prevent genetically-conditioned hair loss, opposing the prohibition of the marketing of his product which had been based on a German *Verordnung* implementing a Commission directive.[85] The complainant argued that Sedaterm was not injurious to human health and the *Verwaltungsgericht* Hamburg, having commissioned an expert's opinion from Professor Braun, was prepared to invalidate the German prohibition. However it felt unable to do so because the *Verordnung* was implementing Community law.

The ECJ, to which the case was referred, did not answer that question directly but addressed a logical precondition for the validity of the Sedaterm prohibition – namely, the validity of the Commission directive that Germany had so faithfully implemented. The yardstick against which the ECJ then measured Community law is difficult to decipher. Having considered the not so ambiguous wording of the Cosmetics Directive which vests the Commission with the power to issue implementing directives,[86] the Court stated: 'The drafting and adaptation of Community rules governing cosmetic products are founded on scientific and technical assessments which must themselves be based on the results of the latest international research …'[87] To adopt this standard amounts to unauthorising two Community institutions; neither the Commission nor the 'Committee on the Adaptation to Technical Progress of the Directives on the Removal of Technical Barriers to Trade in the Cosmetic Products Sector which consists exclusively of representatives of the Member States is in a position to carry out the type of assessment', which 'in the nature of things and apart from any provision laid down to that effect' requires the assistance of 'experts on scientific and technical issues delegated by the Member States'.[88]

[83] See 2.1.3. above.

[84] Case C-212/91 *Angelopharm GmbH v Freie und Hansestadt Hamburg* [1994] ECR I-171.

[85] Twelfth Commission Directive 90/121/EEC of 20 February 1990 (OJ 1990 L 71, 40).

[86] Article 8(2) reads: 'The amendments necessary for adopting Annexes II to VII to technical progress shall be adopted in accordance with the same procedure [laid down in Article 10] after consultation of the Scientific Committee for Cosmetology at the initiative of the Commission or a Member State.'

[87] Case C-212/91, n 84 above, at I-210.

[88] At I-211 (para 33).

'The nature of things' is by its very nature a meta-positive principle. It is designed to promote the adequacy of regulatory policies by ensuring that they take the 'latest international research' into account. This type of guarantee is neither dependent upon an interference with individual rights; nor is it to be inferred from the requirements of Article 190 or shifting the burden of proof to this or that actor. All of these well-established legal techniques had been considered in the opinion of Advocate General Jacobs.[89] The Court was equally free to refer to its jurisprudence on the concept of medicinal products and, following the precedent of *Upjohn v Farzoo*,[90] to classify Sedaterm as a medical product and then leave its assessment to the German authorities. The very fact that these alternatives were not chosen constitutes the importance of the Court's step towards a further rationalisation of regulatory policies in *Angelopharm*. To be sure, the conditions which are to trigger off the obligation to consult science need to be specified further, and rules governing the selection of experts and the structuring of their deliberations will have to be developed. Follow-up problems of this kind are, however, inevitable wherever a re-conceptualisation of legal approaches is initiated.[91]

2.3.2. *Towards Differentiated Standards of Judicial Review under Article 190*

One obvious candidate for the further juridification of the Community's regulatory practices, which has already been addressed in the context of controversies on Community competencies,[92] is the statement-of-reasons requirement of Article 190. This provision seems to have the potential to structure legal reactions according to the complexities of European legislation and decision-making. Significantly enough, the initiators of pertinent proceedings tend to invoke Article 190 as an additional basis for their dissatisfaction with the Community's regulatory practices. This holds true for both the efforts of the European Parliament to defend or broaden its rights of participation[93] and for complaints concerning the proper basis of Community measures.[94]

The Court has adopted a differentiating approach. The Council tends to be treated as a regular legislator, enjoying wide margins of discretion.[95] The Commission, however, has been controlled more strictly. As has already been observed,[96] the readiness of the Court to rigidly interpret the statement-of-reasons

[89] At I-190/192.

[90] Case C-112/89, n 70 above; see 2.2.2. above.

[91] It should be pointed out that the Community can build upon its well-established practices of nominating members of its scientific committees and their procedures.

[92] See 2.2.1. above.

[93] See 2.2.3. above.

[94] See 2.2.2. above.

[95] See, for instance, Case C-331/88 *Fedesa and Others*, n 57 above, at I-4063.

[96] See 2.1.4. above.

requirement where controversial assessments of risks are at stake indirectly imposes equivalent obligations on national legislators, who are thereby placed on the same footing as the Community executive.

A further step has been taken in relation to decisions concerning individual rights of direct action. The statement of reasons required by Article 190 'must disclose in a clear and unequivocal fashion the reasoning followed by the Community authority ... in such a way as to make the persons concerned aware of the reasons for the measure and thus enable them to defend their rights and to enable the court to exercise its supervisory jurisdiction'. This is the Court's own restatement of its prior jurisprudence in *Hauptzollamt München-Mitte v Technische Universität München*.[97] It sounds somewhat illuminating.[98] And yet in the *TU München* case, the rejected formula led the Court to annul the decision in question.

The importance of this decision results from its concurrent recognition of basic procedural rights: where Community institutions have the power to carry out complex technical appraisals, respect for the rights of individuals is to be ensured by the 'duty of the competent Community institutions to examine carefully and impartially all the relevant aspects of the individual case, the rights of the persons concerned to make their views known and to have an adequately reasoned decision'.[99]

2.3.3. Testing Regulatory Reasonableness and the Principle of Proportionality

It seems fair to assume that the obligations imposed by the Community on Member States in the exercise of their legislative competencies must equally be respected by itself. Such equations will of course have to cautiously consider whether the Court's jurisprudence contains normative elements of general application or must be understood as a means to overcome legal barriers to market integration. Any conclusion based on the ECJ's resort to scientific expertise in the supervision of national legislation under Articles 30 and 36 will have to be prepared to differentiate between the need to establish a Community-wide reference framework for the assessment of regulatory policies and the use of the principle of proportionality as a normative yardstick of general validity for the balancing of regulatory concerns and private rights. Such caution is prompted by the interpretation of the Community's powers as originating from transfers of competencies originally vested with nation-states. The 'transferor' is supposed to respect the position obtained by the 'transferee'. Accordingly, one must not readily infer from the obligation of Member States to take Community

[97] Case C-269/90, n 1 above, at I-5499.
[98] See the Opinion of Advocate General Jacobs at I-5492/93.
[99] At I-5499 (para 14); on the further procedural and organisational implications, see 2.3.4. below.

objectives into account when pursuing their own regulatory concerns that an equivalent restriction holds in relation to the Community's own legislative discretion.

The Court has been very reluctant indeed to question the wisdom of any measures approved by the Council. Thus, in *Fedesa and Others*, the Court limited its review of the discretionary power conferred on the Council in the implementation of the Common Agricultural Policy to 'examine whether the measure in question is vitiated by a manifest error or misuse of powers, or whether the authority in question has manifestly exceeded the limits of its discretion'.[100] This broad discretion is to shrink where measures are taken by the Commission acting alone or with one of its committees. In the above-mentioned *TU München* case, the Court's quest for a substantiated statement of reasons implies that Community institutions are to base their decisions on a careful and impartial examination of all the aspects of the case.[101] Similarly, the Court's questioning of the capacity of the Commission and its Regulatory Committee to assess the risk of Sedaterm[102] restricts its discretionary power quite drastically. Last but not least, the Commission's (newly acquired) powers under the procedure of Article 100a (4) are severely limited by the Court's request for a qualified examination of national measures.[103]

All of these requirements do not merely concern the Commission and its Advisory, Administrative and Regulatory Committees. They relate to the legal system as such, and even challenge the authority of the ECJ. The Court's twofold objective of promoting the technical and scientific sophistication of regulatory decision-making while at the same time preserving its own supervisory powers and ensuring the protection of individual rights necessitates the development of a new body of rules and principles capable of bridging the gap between law and science. This is, however, by no means an unprecedented challenge.

2.3.4. Proceduralisation of Legal Controls

The search for legal guarantees for the substantive adequacy of regulatory decisions and their fairness to individuals concerned has only been taken on occasionally and in quite different settings. One group of cases which has not yet been referred to is the judicial review of refusals of the Commission to recruit applicants on grounds of physical unfitness. Such decisions are taken on the basis of Staff Regulations which foresee an appraisal of the candidate's health by a medical committee. Review of such appraisals is limited to questions of the committee's constitution and its proper proceedings. But the Court has made it clear that judicial restraint is dependent upon the appropriateness

[100] Case C-331/88 *Fedesa and Others*, n 57 above, at I-4061; see 2.2.1. above.
[101] Case C-269/90, n 1 above, at I-5499 (para 14).
[102] See 2.3.1. above.
[103] See 2.1.4. above.

of the complaints procedure as well as the objectivity of the committee's investigations.[104]

Much more directly in point is once again the Court's case-law on the decisional practices concerning the importation of Community Customs Tariff duties on scientific and other materials under Council Regulation 1789/75.[105] According to the procedure laid down in Regulation 2784/79,[106] the Commission is to consult Member States and, if necessary, a group of experts comprising representatives of Member States. As to the practices of this group, Advocate General Jacobs observed that its composition of officials from the Ministries of Finance or Trade may render it 'unduly sensitive to the interests of manufacturers in their respective countries'.[107] Indeed, the group's refusal to accept the request of the *TU München* for the free importation of a microscope from Japan on the ground that an instrument of equivalent scientific value was available in the Community coincided all too obviously with the views of Philips Nederland BV submitted at each stage of the proceedings. This striking coincidence then led the Court to point out that the expert committee on which the Commission is to rely must be 'composed of persons possessing the necessary knowledge in the various fields concerned';[108] furthermore, 'the person concerned should be able, during the actual proceedings before the Commission, to put his own case and properly make his views known on the relevant circumstances, and, where necessary, on the documents taken into account by the Community institutions'.[109]

Even easy cases can make good law. Integration of experts into the Community's regulatory decisions amounts to a delegation of legal responsibilities which needs to be compensated by adequate procedural safeguards. This message of the *TU München* case was even more clearly articulated in a different field of Community law, namely, the Court's jurisprudence on the compatibility of self-regulatory practices with the competition rules of the Treaty and the duties of Member States under Article 5.[110] The most interesting case in the present context concerns a German self-regulatory commission of experts from the transport sector entrusted by the Ministry of Transport with the task of fixing freight rates.[111] The Court accepted this type of supervised self-regulation, assuming, however, that

- the commission was bound to respect the public interest in providing encompassing services;
- its composition corresponded to all the interests involved;

[104] Case 156/80 *Morbelli* [1981] ECR 1357 at para 19; Case 265/83 *Suss* v *Commission* [1984] ECR 4029 at para 11; see, more recently, Case T-10/93 *A v Commission* [1994] ECR II-179 (refusal to accept a HIV-positive candidate).

[105] OJ 1975 L 184, 1; amended by Regulation 1027/79, OJ 1979 L 134, 1.

[106] OJ 1979 L 318, 32.

[107] Case C-269/90, n 1 above, at I-5490.

[108] Ibid at I-5550 (para 22).

[109] Ibid at I-5501 (para 25).

[110] On the following, see, for a more detailed analysis, Falke and Joerges, n 77 above, at 147 ff.

[111] Case C-185/91 *Bundesanstalt für den Güterfernverkehr v Reiff* [1993] ECR I-5801.

- the expert members did not pursue the interests of their undertakings; and
- the Ministry was represented at commission meetings and in a position to eventually reject commission proposals.

Apart from second-guessing whether the ECJ actually applied the principles it pronounced to the case at hand, one must ask whether the restraints imposed on economic self-regulation are exclusively designed to structure vertical relations between the Community and Member States. The better reasons militate in favour of a broader interpretation. Not only do Member States need to respect the regulatory objectives of free competition, but the Community itself needs to balance its twofold commitment to a system of undistorted competition *and* regulatory objectives explicitly laid down in the Treaty. The criteria developed by the Court for its supervision of economic self-regulation at national level provide guidance for exactly that task. They are particularly suited to structuring the participation of non-governmental bodies, such as the European standardisation organisations, in concretising legislatively defined essential safety requirements.

Administrative law in bits and pieces, one may conclude. But it seems possible to fit the puzzling and scattered evidence into a quite coherent picture. The Commission is bound to resort to scientific advice where the 'nature of things' so requires. The expertise it is supposed to take into account must be objective, impartial and of high calibre. All of these requirements have an impact on the composition of expert committees and on the procedures of risk assessments and management. Interested persons and institutions must have access to files and be in a position to state their views. Compliance with all of these criteria is subject to judicial review. The picture, however, is still incomplete. One of its most troublesome facets should now be further examined.

3. GOVERNANCE BEYOND THE STATE: SOME TENTATIVE DELIBERATIONS

The normative problematic of the legal developments we have described so far can only be fully understood when analysed within the broader framework of Europe's institutional structures and the regulatory challenges posed by the integration process. This concluding section will therefore return to the theses and queries submitted at the beginning of the paper.[112] It will first summarise the findings on the ECJ's resort to the authority of science as a means of both overcoming the territorial boundaries of legal systems and improving the quality of regulatory decision-making. It will then point to the practical limits of these judicial strategies and finally address the core normative problem of the emerging European governance structures.

[112] See 1.3. above.

3.1. The Autonomy of Science and the Authority of Expert Communities

As has become apparent when considering the jurisprudence of the ECJ on the compatibility of national regulations with Community law, the Court's quest for 'objectivity' and 'proportionality' amounts to an assignment of regulatory authority to scientific communities.[113] We have then observed how the Court tends to subject Community institutions to equivalent obligations. Even when reviewing decisions taken by the Council, the ECJ has examined their compatibility with the majority view among national authorities.[114] Both the *PCP* and the *Angelopharm* judgments strengthened this tendency considerably. When interpreted as laying down a principle of general validity, the holding in *PCP* requires the Community to base its control of national policies on scientific evidence of international standing.[115] Similarly, the judgment in *Angelopharm* forces the Commission, and implicitly the Community legislator, to seek scientific advice wherever the 'nature of things' so requires.[116]

The meta-legal authority of science can equally be identified as a basis for the ECJ's jurisprudence on the inter-state recognition of scientific appraisals and the opening up of national authorisation procedures to foreign applications. These obligations are supported by Article 5 of the Treaty and are designed to implement the Community concept of mutual recognition, which, in turn, is to overcome the traditional conceptual limits of international administrative law. But the kind of obligation the ECJ has brought to bear refers once again to non-legal authorities. This becomes particularly clear when the Court accepts national regulatory autonomy in situations of scientific uncertainties and, at the same time, restricts that autonomy by invoking the state of international research.[117] It becomes equally apparent when national authorities are requested to make use of scientific analyses carried out in other Member States in their authorisation procedures.[118]

One must certainly not assume that the ECJ is so naïve as to believe in an unquestionable validity of expertise or in a clear demarcation line between 'certainty' and 'uncertainty' in science-based assessments. The scientific authority to which the Court refers is none other than a social construct. But the Court has not only indicated which scientific institutions and communities can claim authority, it has also addressed the needs and constraints of transforming scientific findings into risk-management policies. Pertinent case-law is abundant.

[113] See 2.1.1. and 2.1.4. above.

[114] See Case C-331/88 *Fedesa and Others*, n 57 above, at I-4061.

[115] See 2.1.4. above.

[116] See 2.3.1. above.

[117] See 2.1.1. above, and as an additional example Case 54/85 *Mirepoix* [1986] ECR 1067 at 1079: 'National authorities are obliged to review the prohibition of a pesticide ... if it appears to them that the reasons which led to the adoption of such measures have changed, for example, as a result of the discovery of a new use for a particular pesticide, or as a result of further information becoming available through scientific research.'

[118] Case 272/80 *Biologische Producten*, n 37 above, at 3292; see 2.1.2. above.

The Court has been forced to consider linguistic problems and communication difficulties of German administrators;[119] the appropriateness of a Belgian nomination of the director of a water-purifying company as the competent authority to issue permits;[120] the Greek certificates for pasteurised butter;[121] and countless similar issues.[122]

3.2. Practical Difficulties

The Court's entanglement in such a morass follows a compelling logic. Once the authority of science in risk assessments is established, the guidelines of risk-management practices must equally adhere to non-national standards. This logic, however, comes at a price. Cases on the compatibility of national risk-management practices are responses of the legal system to highly specific constellations. Judicial review is, of course, meant to resolve such matters. It may even detect and pronounce principles of general validity. But it is not capable of coherently building up the kind of infrastructures transnational risk-management practices require. Similar difficulties have been identified in the case-law on Directive 65/65/EEC.[123] Any European prerogative in determining the meaning of legal concepts, such as 'medicinal products', remains an insufficient means of achieving the free-trade objective, unless the Community ensures that the indispensable determination of normative requirements is supported by a Europeanisation of implementation practices. The infrastructures which such backing pre-supposes cannot be imposed through Community legislation. It is even less conceivable that they be created through judicial review.

Where the judicial branch pronounces principles which tend to overburden the infrastructures of the legal system, financial support and legislative action become indispensable. And indeed, as has already been pointed out,[124] Community legislation and many accompanying measures are responding to these needs. Suffice it here to point again to the omnipresence of expert committees in the preparation and implementation of Community legislation; the strengthening of the position of scientific committees within the Community's comitology, even prior to the *Angelopharm* judgment; and the furthering of cooperation among national administrative bodies and with non-governmental

[119] Case 247/81 *Commission v Germany* [1984] ECR 1111.

[120] Cases 372-374/85 *Ministère publique v Traen* [1987] ECR 2141.

[121] Case C-205/89 *Commission v Greece* [1991] ECR I-1361.

[122] Cf, for instance, Case C-132/80 *United Foods et al v Belgium* [1981] ECR 995 (health inspection of fish); Case 124/81 *Commission v United Kingdom* [1983] ECR 203 (licence systems of milk inspection); Case 42/82R *Commission v France* [1982] 841 (customs clearance of Italian wine); Case C-426/92 *Germany v Deutsches Milch-Kontor GmbH* [1994] ECR I-2757 (detection of fraudulent practices).

[123] See 2.2.2. above.

[124] See 1.2. above.

organisations. It is by no means clear to what degree the normative logic of the ECJ's jurisprudence, the Community's legislative initiatives as well as the many efforts to ensure the cooperation of national administrative bodies and non-governmental organisations have already established, or are likely to achieve, the building up of efficient infrastructures for de-nationalised European practices of risk assessment and management. One should at any rate be prepared to reckon with one latent difficulty: the need to ensure the legitimacy of regulatory decisions affecting the interests of enterprises and citizens all over Europe. The practical importance of this problem may be difficult to specify. There is nevertheless every reason to consider the potential of European law to ensure the normative quality of decision-making that European citizens have learned to appreciate within the boundaries of their constitutional States.

3.3. The Accountability of De-nationalised Governance Structures

Assuming that 'we the peoples' of Europe do not want to build up a Federal State which would be entrusted with the tasks of social regulation; assuming further that Europeans are nevertheless interested in benefiting from an opening up of their formerly national economies; assuming, last but not least, that the Europeanisation of markets requires institutional structures which ensure both the effectiveness and the legitimacy of risk assessments, then we are bound to strive for institutional solutions which transcend the boundaries of our constitutional states without replacing these states with a Europeanised equivalent. Social regulation thus provides a case of exemplary importance for the normative dilemmas of regulatory politics in transnational contexts: all the Member States and (the greater part of) their societies are interested in principle in the exchange of products and services; none, however, seems ready to waive the type of protection provided by the regulation of risks or to simply leave the level of protection to processes of regulatory competition. Even more important, each individual society asks for protection against risks originating beyond its own polity. And yet, the building up of European political institutions and administrative authorities entrusted with supranational competencies for all the sensitive issues of social regulation seems neither normatively desirable nor practically conceivable.

For the time being, institutional models which would resolve all of these difficulties are not readily available. What does seem possible at this stage is to summarise guidelines which should be taken into account in the development of institutional responses:

- De-nationalised governance structures are to be conceived as complementing national and supranational institutions. Their social acceptability and legitimacy will depend upon the concomitant institutionalisation of economic freedoms and public responsibilities;

- Risk assessment and management policies within European networks should reflect the concerns of European societies; they must mediate between the functional needs of efficient decision-making, its public transparency and accessibility for administrative and non-governmental actors;
- The legal system must continue its search for guarantees of regulatory reasonableness, procedural safeguards and the protection of rights. This search should be complemented by the institutionalisation of political accountability. Such institutional innovations would have to correspond to the emerging structures of governance beyond intergovernmentalism and below orthodox supranationalism. One conceivable step might be the entrustment of parliamentary committees, composed of both European Parliament members and national delegates, with the task of regularly reviewing the experiences of Community and national officials, of organising hearings to which experts and non-governmental organisations would be invited, and of initiating legislative action at European and national level.

These are but tentative suggestions. And yet, the underlying normative vision should have become sufficiently clear. In the absence of a uniform European society and a European state, the structures of social regulation in Europe must resolve the tensions arising from the openness of markets, on the one hand, and the need to respond to 'legitimate' regulatory concerns, on the other. The search to comply with, and mediate between, these two objectives needs to build upon their respective normative merits: societies granting freedoms or imposing regulatory burdens must consider the adverse extraterritorial effects of their policies. This obligation amounts to the granting of voice to 'foreign' citizens and their representatives. European law can be interpreted as ensuring exactly such rights. In this vision, the quest for 'regulatory reasonableness' of national measures reflects the respect for concerns which are not represented in internal policy processes. Legal constraints imposed by European law to ensure the openness not only of markets but also of regulatory decision-making are by no means undemocratic; the building up of de-nationalised governance structures should therefore aim at the strengthening of deliberative processes dealing with the interests and concerns of those who are affected by, but not represented in, decision-making processes.

12

*From Intergovernmental Bargaining to Deliberative Political Processes: The Constitutionalisation of Comitology**

I. INTRODUCTION

WHILST THE REMARKABLE recent explosion of legal and political science research on the Community's committees in general, and Comitology in particular,[1] has uncovered a broad range of practical, legal and theoretical issues, it has yet to lead to any consolidated consensus between the two disciplines. This study attempts to find a path through such

* Co-Author Jürgen Neyer. The study was first published in (1997) 3 *ELJ* 273–299. It originated from a project on Comitology, located in Bremen at the Centre for European Law Politics, and sponsored by the Volkswagen-Stiftung. The authors are indebted to A Bücker, M Everson, J Falke, FW Scharpf, S Schlacke and E Vos for their help and advice. Readers should also note, C Joerges and J Neyer, 'Transforming Strategic Interaction into Deliberative Problem-solving: European Comitology in the Foodstuffs Sector' (1997) 4 *Journal of European Public Policy*, with a greater emphasis on political science methodology.

[1] See, for the relevant literature, citations in C Joerges, 'Die Beurteilung der Sicherheit technischer Konsumgüter und der Gesundheitsrisiken von Lebensmitteln der Praxis des europäischen Ausschußwesens ("Komitologie")', *ZERP-Diskussionspapier* 1/95, 78–89, and in RH Pedler and GF Schaefer (eds), *Shaping European Law and Policy: The Role of Committees and Comitology in the Political Process*, (Maastricht: European Institute of Public Administration, 1996) 38, at 195–198; more recent publications include: FU Pappi and W Schnorpfeil, 'Das Ausschußwesen der Europäischen Kommission: Grundstrukturen und Kommunikationsmöglichkeiten für Verbände' in T König, E Rieger and H Schmitt (eds), *Das europäische Mehrebenensystem* (Frankfurt aM: Campus, 1996) 135; W Wessels, 'Capturing Transformation Processes: On the Fusion of Administrations in Europe' (Manuscript, Bonn/Cologne, 1996); J Neyer, 'Administrative Supranationalität in der Verwaltung des Binnenmarktes:and Zur Legitimität der Komitologie' (1997) 20 *Integration* 24; M Bach, 'Verwaltungs- und Expertenstäbe im multibürokratischen Entscheidungsprozeß der EU' (1992) 21 *Zeitschrift für Soziologie* 16; V Eichener, *Entscheidungsprozesse in der regulativen Politik der Europäischen Union* (Opladen: Leske + Budrich, 2000); M Everson, 'The Oversight of Delegated Legislation within the European Union: An Administrative Law of Bits and Pieces' (Manuscript, EUI Florence, 1997); S Schlacke, *Risikoentscheidungen im europäischen Lebensmittelrecht: Eine Untersuchung am Beispiel des europäischen Zusatzstoffrechts unter besonderer Berücksichtigung des europäischen Ausschußwesens ('Komitologie')* (Baden-Baden: Nomos, 1988); E Vos, *Institutional Frameworks of Community Health and Safety Regulation: Committees, Agencies and Private Bodies* (Oxford: Hart Publishing, 1999).

complex issues by deploying a dual strategy; choosing a relatively narrow field of enquiry, namely the regulation of risks to health in the foodstuffs sector, and then interpreting it from a variety of perspectives. The field is chosen for two reasons: first, the foodstuffs sector is at a cross-roads with market-building interests now being confronted by the establishment of a Europeanised regulatory machinery; and secondly, the completion of the foodstuffs market ranked so highly on the Community agenda that the legislative framework was completed before other areas were tackled. Thus, this framework is now primarily concerned with implementation rather than new legislation. Equally, the committee system works particularly well and with enormous intensity.

Our enquiry into the committee system in section II of this article is related to the theoretical and interdisciplinary objectives pursued in sections III and IV. We seek to identify practices within the decision-making process which challenge the analytical and normative assumptions upon which the majority of integration research rests. The entrenched nature of these assumptions is demonstrated by the parallel and independent discussion of Comitology within legal discourse and political science. We are particularly interested in exploring certain deep-rooted schisms between these two disciplines. Lawyers, on the one hand, tend to restrict themselves to normative arguments and expect political scientists simply to provide them with information about the 'real world'; political scientists, on the other, tend to confine themselves to explanatory and analytical arguments – where they do look at legal institutions they tend to perceive them either as constraints or opportunities. These disciplinary demarcation lines often appear counterproductive. We not only hope to substantiate this claim by documenting a number of serious shortcomings in the two disciplines' analyses of Comitology, but also, and perhaps more importantly, we attempt to establish a trans-disciplinary discourse.

The more ambitious section of our contribution (section IV) suggests that Comitology is characterised by an institutional innovation which will necessitate a re-definition of our existing normative understanding of the European polity, and similarly challenges the analytical assumptions of current integration research. Methodologically speaking, we claim that the schisms between and the shortcomings in mono-disciplinary analyses of the European polity can and should be overcome through a constitutionalist interpretation of 'supranationalism'. It is, however, important immediately to emphasise that although the concept of deliberative supranationalism presented here is a regulative idea, and not an existing legal framework or a factual given, it nonetheless entails far more than a purely normative fantasy. Deliberately conceived as a means to surmount the incoherence and impasse in the current legal debate on European integration, it claims the status of a 'legal theory of the integration process';[2]

[2] For a description of this term, see C Joerges, 'European Economic Law, the Nation-State and the Maastricht Treaty' in R Dehousse (ed), *Europe After Maastricht: An Ever Closer Union?*

but it at the same time also attempts to give concrete form to the normative arguments and institutions envisaged by the constructivist strand in political science. At the theoretical level, deliberative supranationalism seeks to overcome the age-old dichotomy between *Sein* (being) and *Sollen* (ought), but equally has the very practical goal of bridging the gap between legal and political theories of European integration through the application of the model which constitutionalism provides for the disciplining of political processes and the legitimacy of governance within the nation-state.

II. A DESCRIPTION OF 'COMITOLOGY' AND SOME QUERIES

The story of the apparently irresistible rise of the general committee system, and Comitology in particular, need be recounted only very briefly here.[3] The intensity of the 'Europeanisation' of agricultural policies in the 1960s determined that this sector would lead the way in developing the 'archetypal' forms of committee: the 'management' and 'regulatory' committees,[4] which were subsequently to be complemented by a richer typology.

The expansion of the committee system, and its subsequent refinement, was accelerated by the adoption of the Internal Market Programme in 1985 and the Single European Act (hereinafter, SEA) of 1987. The new legislative strategy, announced and agreed upon in these documents, was meant to achieve broad harmonisation objectives through relatively few European legislative acts. Both the Commission and the drafters of the SEA foresaw that this policy would only enhance the existing need for regulatory techniques to ensure that broadly defined legislative objectives and principles could be continually concretised and adapted to new economic and technological developments. Therefore, the amendment to Article 145 by the SEA provided, in the third indent, that the Council shall 'confer on the Commission in the acts which the Council adopts, powers for the implementation of the rules which the Council lays down'.[5]

The formulation of the amendment entailed a political compromise, but it soon became clear that the Council was by no means willing to leave to the Commission the new implementing powers for programmes which so often touched upon economically important interests and politically sensitive issues.

(Munich: CH Beck, 1994) 29, at 36-41; and idem, 'Rechtswissenschaftliche Integrationstheorien' in B Kohler-Koch and W Woyke (eds), *Lexikon der Politik – Band 5. Die Europäische Union* (Munich: CH Beck, 1996) 229.

[3] See references in n 1 above, and for a particularly careful review of available data, J Falke, 'Comitology and other Committees: A Preliminary Empirical Assessment' in Pedler and Schaefer, n 1 above, 117.

[4] See C Bertram, 'Decision-Making in the EEC: The Management Committee Procedure' (1967-68) 5 *CMLR* 346.

[5] This provision continues: 'The Council may impose certain requirements in respect of the exercise of these powers. The Council may also reserve the right, in specific cases, to exercise directly implementing powers itself.'

In the Comitology Decision of 13 July 1987,[6] the Council, rather than definitely conferring implementing powers in accordance with Article 145 (3), restricted itself to defining the procedural alternatives for such a delegation. The Council's political message was crystal clear: Member States are not willing to loosen their intergovernmental grip on the implementation process in favour of supranational institutions. In more constructive terms, the Comitology decision rejects the idea of a supranational central implementation machinery headed by the Commission, and thus indirectly forces national governments into a cooperative venture.

A. The Comitology System in the Foodstuffs Sector

The perfectioning of the legislative frameworks and the sophistication of the committee system were to occur in tandem. The entire development precisely mirrored the general trends in market integration policies.[7] It was the legendary *Cassis de Dijon* ruling and the subsequent adoption of the new harmonisation policy in 1985, with its switch to a 'horizontal' approach,[8] which triggered the successful growth of European legislation to a 720-page volume.[9]

Foodstuffs clearly presented illuminating regulatory challenges. Not only were sophisticated institutional frameworks and more or less stringent regulatory standards to remain intact in the best interest of the functioning of real-world foodstuffs markets; but legislation was also to be informed of the fact that foodstuffs regulation needs to address particularly interesting traditional and modern issues such as: information-related market failure, agency problems in the selection of regulators, conflicting expert opinion on the risks attributable to foodstuffs and/or nutrition habits, the growing importance of new concerns about animal welfare and the environmental dimensions of food production, as well as the impact of cultural traditions on production and consumption. Clearly, problems of this complexity could not be dealt with uniformly and definitely via legislative fiat at European level but instead continued to require unceasing regulatory activity to ensure that the costs and benefits of regulatory measures would be identified and balanced, and that regulators would remain

[6] Council Decision 87/373/EEC of 13.07.1987, laying down the procedures for the exercise of implementing powers conferred on the Commission, OJ L 197/1987, 33.

[7] See R Streinz, 'Gesundheitsschutz und Verbraucherinformation im Lebensmittelrecht der Europäischen Gemeinschaften' in R Damm and D Hart (eds), *Rechtliche Regulierung von Gesundheitsrisiken* (Baden-Baden: Nomos, 1993) 151–185.

[8] COM(85)603 final 8 November 1985.

[9] See European Commission, Foodstuffs. Co-ordinated instruments (Position Paper on 30.4.1994, Luxembourg: Office for Official Publications of the European Communities, 1994); see, for a recent overview, R Hankin, 'The Role of Scientific Advice in the Elaboration and Implementation of the Community's Foodstuffs Legislation' in C Joerges, K-H Ladeur and E Vos (eds), *Integrating Scientific Expertise into Regulatory Decision-Making: National Traditions and European Innovations* (Baden-Baden: Nomos, 1997) 141.

well-versed in the ever-growing knowledge basis for regulatory action, and so would be in a position to respond to new public concerns. Indeed, the 'scientification' of foodstuffs' regulation, taken together with its 'politicisation', has exerted such pressure on traditional foodstuffs' law that innovations would have occurred at the national level even without any European market-building and harmonisation efforts.

When the institutions of the EC embarked on their venture of market-building, they had only a limited number of options available. The policy did not depart from the point of *whether* foodstuffs should be regulated at all, but rather from the pragmatic issue of *how* the EC was to overcome the obstacles presented by legal divergence, ossifying regulatory policies and the completion of the project in a short time-span.[10] It is no surprise that the committee system flourished, but its development and internal differentiation are of exemplary importance since they represent the sophisticated model of 'regulation through committees' which, since its very inception, was understood to be the European alternative to centralised regulation through agencies on the one hand, and regulatory competition or mutual recognition on the other.[11]

- The Standing Committee on Foodstuffs (StCF) is of paramount importance. This committee was set up in 1969[12] as a regulatory committee (variant IIIb of the Comitology decision).[13] Currently, there are some 35 directives and regulations which refer to this committee. Josef Falke identifies 117 different groups of tasks the StCF is expected to cope with.[14] Functionally speaking, the StCF is the joint political organ of the Member States designed to support and control the Commission.
- The Scientific Committee for Food (SCF) was established back in 1974[15] and was reorganised in 1995.[16] This committee draws upon the – by definition transnational and objective – world of science. Accordingly, committee members are supposed not to represent national interests but the state of their disciplines. However, it is worth noting that a scarcity of scientific resources at the European level is compensated for not only by the committee's ability to form working groups and invite further experts, but also by Directive 93/5 on assistance to the Commission and cooperation by the Member States in

[10] Hankin, n 9 above.

[11] See R Dehousse et al, 'Europe After 1992: New Regulatory Strategies', *EUI Working Paper Law 92/31* (1992); C Joerges, 'Product Safety in the European Community: Market Integration, Social Regulation and Legal Structures' in F Snyder (ed), *European Community Law. Vol II* (Hanover NH: Dartmouth, 1993) 297. For much more detailed descriptions of the committees operating in the foodstuffs sector, see Schlacke, n 1 above (Ch 1 D and E), and Vos, n 1 above (Ch IV).

[12] Council Decision 69/414/EEC of 13 November 1969, OJ L 291/19969, 9.

[13] Council Resolution of 13 November, OJ C 148/19969, 1.

[14] Falke, n 3 above, at 127.

[15] OJ L 136/1974, 1.

[16] Commission Decision 95/273/EEC, OJ L 167/1995, 22.

the scientific examination of questions relating to food;[17] a measure fostering cooperation with the relevant national bodies.

- The Advisory Committee on Foodstuffs (ACF) was established in 1975.[18] This committee represents the economic and social interests at the European level. The Commission seeks its advice only when preparing new legislation. The ACF is not represented in the implementation process.

B. The Performance of the Comitology System: A Series of Queries and Some Findings

An empirical assessment of the performance of the Comitology system might draw on a wide range of information including the readily available legal acts and official documents already outlined, as well as less accessible data such as: the working practices and formal procedures of committees,[19] the frequency of their meetings, the establishment of expert groups and the access of interested parties, the role of the Commission and the official status of experts from Member States, the numbers of people participating in committee meetings, and the budgeted cost in ECU for a legislative act.[20] In the following, however, we also draw upon our own research into the attitudes and perceptions of committee members, in order to allow for an analysis of committee performance which is sensitive to the very novel forms of interest group formation and political decision-making process which have sprung up under the umbrella of the Comitology system. Ultimately, however, we likewise conclude that any meaningful assessment of such data will depend fully upon the evolution of new normative yardsticks; traditional legal and political science analyses being unable adequately to address such new phenomena.

The 'Nature' of Risk Regulation

Judgments on the social acceptability of risks associated with the consumption of food require a balancing of benefits and costs which cannot be meaningfully performed without the help of experts but which, at the same time, must also pay due regard to normative, political and occasionally ethical considerations. For present purposes, it is sufficient to note that to date[21] no constitutional state

[17] OJ L 52/1993, 18.

[18] By Commission Decision 75/420/EEC, OJ L 182/1975, 35.

[19] The 'rules of procedure' of the Standing Committee for Foodstuffs as of 11.05.1993, III/3939/93 have been published by DG III.

[20] Falke, n 3 above, at 133–138.

[21] For recent summaries in sociology and political science upon which our argument is based, see G Bechmann, 'Risiko und gesellschaftlicher Umgang mit Unsicherheit' (1994) 19 *Österreichische Zeitschrift für Soziologie* 8; KS Shrader-Frechette, *Risk and Rationality: Philosophical Foundations for Populist Reforms* (Oakland, CA: University of California Press, 1991).

has delegated risk assessments entirely and exclusively to expert bodies.[22] The normative, ethical, cultural and political dimensions of risk calculation will make themselves felt at Community level: not only do they militate against the delegation of risk assessments to bodies of experts; but they also render it highly unlikely that one single body will be able to come up with uniform decisions which are socially acceptable within the entire internal market. The institutional implications of these considerations are far-reaching. If and because risk assessments must also include normative-political considerations, there the committee system needs equally to mediate between 'universal' (European-wide agreed upon) criteria and 'national' concerns. Thus, it must not be replaced by a central authority which would be politically unaccountable for its risk assessments.

Economic Implications: Distributional Concerns and Industrial Policy

The control of risks imposes costs on competent authorities and a high level of protection increases costs to industry and consumers. The economic implications of such decisions are by no means uniform throughout the internal market, thereby complicating still further the balancing of the costs and benefits of European decisions. The difficulties inherent in the economic equation remain a further barrier to attaining uniformity. Beyond the costs of risk regulation, further economic consequences need to be envisaged. The raising of standards and the development of sophisticated regulatory schemes which ensure the safety of foodstuffs, inevitably work in favour of those Member States with technically highly-developed industries as they may now more easily penetrate 'foreign' markets. We suggest that both types of economic implications need to be distinguished. The advantages or disadvantages of risk assessments for specific industries will give rise to 'national concerns' which can be classified as industrial policy considerations. Administrative costs and, more importantly, the costs for producers, traders and consumers which higher safety standards may entail are to be classified as 'distributional' because they affect the economic interests of these actors. Contrary to the re-distributional objectives of 'traditional' welfare policies, however, the distributional consequences of stringent safety regulation for products are widely dispersed; consumers are not classes with, either in principle or theory, identical economic interests.

Interest Formation and Decision-making Processes in the European Polity

Both of the above issues indicate deep-seated tensions between the dual supranational and intergovernmentalist structure of the EC on the one hand, and its

[22] For summary of the underlying considerations, see W Köck, 'Risikovorsorge als Staatsaufgabe' (1966) 121 *Archiv für öffentliches Recht* 1; RH Pildes and CR Sunstein, 'Reinventing the Regulatory State' (1995) 62 *University of Chicago L Rev* 1, at 46–72.

problem-solving tasks on the other.[23] The committee system needs to be understood as an institutional response to that tension. In the gap between the EC structure and its tasks, Comitology has proved a forum for the development of novel and mediating forms of interest-formation and decision-making. Any attempt to provide for its analytical conceptualisation and normative evaluation, may therefore be confronted with institutional innovations which fit neither into the analytical models of functionalism and intergovernmentalism, nor into the normative concepts of corresponding legal theories. This is why research on Comitology should be prepared to encounter 'under-theorised' phenomena and scrutinise interactions both inside and beyond the formalised institutional structures, decision-making processes and practices of the committee system.

Findings

Within the framework of the above-named project,[24] 45 expert interviews have already been conducted, some 100 questionnaires[25] have been sent out and hundreds of documents have been studied. The findings, presented in detail in the Table included within this article,[26] may be summarised as follows, and to a large degree substantiate what might in any case have been expected:

- the boundaries of the committee system cannot be equated with its formal structures; both the representatives of Member States and the Commission itself exploit many sources of information and are open to receive advice from 'outside'. This may explain why the ACF has never been invited to comment upon implementation issues;
- the agenda of committees is dominated by the Commission. Its room for manoeuvre is by no means substantially constrained by the shadow of majority voting which the Council included in its legislative acts.[27] However, the Commission pursues long-term strategies aiming at consensual rather than conflictual decision-making. Points which are bound to arise in the foreseeable future are handled at an early stage and when they can still be quite openly discussed. Where serious objections against proposals are raised,

[23] See, more extensively, Joerges, n 11 above; and idem, 'Markt ohne Staat? Die Wirtschaftsverfassung der Gemeinschaft und die regulative Politik' in R Wildenmann (ed), *Staatswerdung Europas? Optionen einer Europäischen Union* (Baden-Baden: Nomos, 1991) 225–268 (English translation: 'The Market without the State? States without Markets? Two Essays on the Law of the European Economy', *EUI Working Paper Law 1/1996* at 28-42).

[24] N * above.

[25] Only preliminary results are given; further quantative analysis will be conducted upon completion of all interviews.

[26] Ibid; for a systematic account, see A Bücker and S Schlacke, 'Die Entstehung einer politischen Verwaltung durch EG-Ausschüsse – Rechtstatsachen und Rechtsentwicklungen' in C Joerges and J Falke (eds), *Das Ausschußwesen der Europäischen Union. Praxis der Risikoregulierung im Binnenmarkt und ihre rechtliche Verfassung* (Baden-Baden: Nomos, 2000) 161.

[27] See n 13 above.

decisions will be postponed. Even delegations of Member States tend to use the StCF as a forum for an exchange of views on new and unsettled issues;

- the Commission's dominating role as an agenda setter appears not to be constrained by the SCF. The Commission feels entitled autonomously to determine the issues in which it seeks scientific advice.[28] However, both the Commission and the SCF respect the conditions which contribute to the high reputation of the SCF as an highly experienced body of experts. This may be explained by the institutional interests of both actors. An appeal to the authority and impartiality of science-based findings is obviously useful to the Commission where conflicts of interests among relevant parties impede consensus building but it also simultaneously strengthens the position of the SCF. It should already be noted here that institutional interests of this kind may help to ensure compliance with sound decisional criteria.[29]

'Quality' of Decision-making

Having detailed the workings of committees system, a question now arises of how such a system is best to be evaluated. Here, however, both the law and political science are faced with certain difficulties. When asked about the performance of the committee system, lawyers are tempted to refer simply to their distinction between legal and illegal acts. The Comitology issue, however, forecloses such an easy way out. European law may require an evaluation of decisional outputs;[30] more importantly, the state of the law is so uncertain that any legal discourse specifying potentially applicable rules and principles will have to rely on substantive argument. Political scientists trying to conceptualise decision-making practices may draw on a broad array of theories or approaches. In recent contributions on the EC dichotomies such as argument *vs.* bargaining,[31] instrumental rationality *vs.* communicative action[32] have been tried out; further theorems are on offer.[33] Although this piece will return to this point later,[34] it is sufficient to mention the two commonalties: both disciplines tend, at least implicitly, to conceptualise the committee system as a non-hierarchical

[28] This attitude, which the Commission's Legal Service shares, is not in accordance with the judgment of the ECJ Case 12/91 *Angelopharm* [1993] ECR 1-171 at 210; see Section III A below.

[29] See Section IV below.

[30] This is the case in Article 100a (4) and, more generally, where the right of Member States to take unilateral action is at stake.

[31] T Gehring, 'Regieren im internationalen System. Verhandlungen, Normen und internationale Regime' (1995) 36 *Politische Vierteljahresschrift* 197.

[32] T Risse-Kappen, 'Exploring the Nature of the Beast: International Relations Theory and Comparative Policy Analysis Meet the European Union' (1996) 34 *JCMS* 53.

[33] For a recent critical summary, see M Zürn and B Zangl, 'Argumentatives Verhandeln bei internationalen Verhandlungen. Moderate Anmerkungen zur post-realistischen Debatte' (1996) 3 *Zeitschrift für Internationale Beziehungen* 341.

[34] Section III B below.

form of governance. Lawyers are ready to accept, or at least feel compelled to ensure, unprovided-for structures for decision-making where these seem to further compliance with European objectives. Similarly, political scientists tend to acknowledge the 'reality' of argument as a prerequisite to and result of the functioning of the committee system. This shift from 'power to reason' implies that the performance of committees must not simply be assessed in terms of a 'high' or 'low' level of their regulatory output but rather be evaluated in terms of 'procedural' devices designed to ensure the reasonableness of decision-making practices.

The Need for a Normative Meta Theory

The convergent perceptions of the committee system in both disciplines remain troublesome.[35] Political scientists will ask whether and how one might operationalise dichotomies, such as argument and strategic action, in order to be in a position to assess interactions within the committee system or to identify the impact of rules concerning the presentation of arguments (the '*Darstellung von Entscheidungen*') on the decisions actually taken (the '*Herstellung von Entscheidungen*'). Lawyers would insist that the style of reasoning alone can never replace formalised legality and legitimacy requirements. Our response to these difficulties relies on a specific, albeit so far unfinished, version of supranational constitutionalism. We argue[36] that the committee system must be based upon, and controlled by, constitutional provisions favouring a 'deliberative' style of problem solving. Where these structures can be identified and established, the motives of decision-makers become irrelevant.

III. THE OBSERVATION OF COMITOLOGY BY LEGAL AND POLITICAL SCIENCE

Returning to the question of how Comitology might best be evaluated, legal and political science perceptions of Comitology will now be examined in greater, though by no means comprehensive, detail. It is noteworthy that whilst academic discussion on Comitology has now reached many quarters, legal science continues to hold the usual lead in terms of both the time and the space devoted to the subject. However, such legal debate remains unsatisfactory, since the law would appear to have difficulties in tackling the emergence of institutional structures which are not to be found in either national legal systems or

[35] We are especially indebted to Peter A Hall for confronting us with these problems; this is not to say that we have resolved them.
[36] See Section IV below.

the Treaties. Equally, political scientists have been caught somewhat unaware by developments not predicted either by intergovernmentalist or by functionalist approaches to integration. As becomes apparent in our analysis, the perceptions of the two disciplines thus share to a surprising degree common premises and difficulties.

A. Comitology and the Legal System: Institutional Conflicts and the Search for a European Administrative Law

When faced with new problems or developments, lawyers are bound to discriminate between legal and illegal events. The yardsticks they use are the legal structures as provided for in the Treaties or developed on that basis in the case law of the ECJ. The legal system should, therefore, not be expected to conceptualise a new phenomenon like Comitology in positive terms. It will rather respond to concrete conflicts as they are brought into legal arenas. The recognition and positive transformation of innovative developments into new legal concepts is likely to happen gradually and indirectly. The 'juridification' of the committee system follows such patterns. Two important arenas can and need to be distinguished.

The most visible legal debates on Comitology have been initiated by the interests and moves of institutional actors, which seem neither willing nor able to consider the whole range of legal issues which any meaningful debate on the committee system would have to address. Thus, the long-term interest expressed by the European Parliament (EP) in its initiatives was not motivated by the search for a comprehensive legal framework for the establishment and working of European committees; nor did the Council ever submit a futuristic concept explaining what it might mean to defend the administrative powers of Member States against centralist tendencies in the management of the Internal Market. Rather, the EP more or less continuously supported the Commission in its drive to strengthen the Community's administrative powers, whereas the Council defended the influence Member States are expected to exert through the committee system. These conflicts clearly concern the institutional frameworks of the European regulatory policies and mirror the well-known conflict between supranationalism and intergovernmentalism. The attention they have attracted seems, nevertheless, disproportional. The institutional debates should be viewed as just one part of the juridification process, because its less spectacular, more subtle and probably more important counterpart was the step-by-step development of principles and rules concerning the administrative powers and practices of European bodies. The supranationalism/intergovernmentalism divide can easily be re-detected in this second arena but the kind of issues that have been dealt with here address the problems of establishing a post-national and non-hierarchical system of governance much more directly.

'On the Road to Nowhere': Commission and EP vs Council and the Meroni *Doctrine*

Two phases in the institutional conflicts over the committee system can be distinguished. The first phase started decades before the adoption of the SEA: the committee system had become a distinguishing institutional mark, especially of the Common Agricultural Policy. Already during that period the EP took an intense and critical interest in this development. Parliament, however, had at that time no standing before the ECJ.[37] The first decisions of the ECJ, which endorsed in principle the legality of the management procedures practised by pertinent committees, took hardly any notice of the EP's institutional concerns.[38] A second phase began with the adoption of the SEA, which, although intended to increase the power of the Commission, was in fact undermined by the Council's 'Comitology Decision' of 13 July 1987,[39] in which the Member States indicated their intention not to loosen their control over the implementation process. Parliament sought relief, but failed to convince the Court to recognise its capacity to bring an action for annulment.[40]

The institutions entered a third phase and the EP was more successful in promoting its position through the institutional agreements. In 1988, Commission (acting through its President Jacques Delors) and Parliament (represented by its President Henry Plumb) agreed that the Commission would provide Parliament with all the essential information about Comitology committees (the Plumb Delors Agreement). After the TEU came into force, the new co-decision procedure under Article 189b provided a new basis for the Parliament's claims. Following a Commission initiative, all the relevant institutional actors signed a Draft Interinstitutional Agreement on Comitology between the EP, the Council and the Commission.[41] According to this *modus vivendi*,[42] any draft general implementing act submitted by the Commission would also be sent to the appropriate parliamentary committee.

The institutional conflict is multi-faceted but it is unlikely to generate a sophisticated institutional response to the many queries surrounding the Europeanisation of risk regulation policies. Implicitly, the EP is furthering through its initiatives a centralisation of administrative powers without, however, being able to demonstrate how it might effectively supervise the Commission and hold it politically accountable.[43] The counterproductive implications of the

[37] See KStC Bradley and E Vos (eds), *EU Committees: Social Regulation, Law and Politics* (Oxford–Portland: Hart Publishing, 1999) 71.

[38] The leading case is Case 25/70 *Einfuhr- und Vorratsstelle für Getreide und Futtermittel v Koester, Berodt & Co* [1970] ECR 1161; see, also, Case 5/77 *Tedeschi v Denkavit* [1977] ECR 1555.

[39] See n 6 above.

[40] Case 302/87 *European Parliament v Council* [1988] ECR 5615 at 5644.

[41] SEC (94) 645 final; see Falke, n 3 above, at 125–127.

[42] OJ C 43/1995, 40.

[43] This is not to say that a constructive role of the EP would be simply inconceivable. For an instructive analysis of the role of the EP in the BSE saga, see GR Chambers, 'The BSE Crisis and

EP's institutional strategy become more clearly visible when they are read in conjunction with the famous *Meroni* doctrine.

The *Meroni* principle prohibits the delegation of 'discretionary powers' which would amount to a transfer of responsibility replacing the choices of the delegator by those of the delegatee.[44] This doctrine is of such widespread recognition that it cannot only be invoked to question the legality of the whole new approach to harmonisation and standards;[45] but it has also forced Community legislation to camouflage continuously the real functions of standardisation bodies and even the new Medicines Agency.

The *Meroni* doctrine must be read together with the request to respect the 'institutional balance' between Community organs.[46] This principle is not very helpful in the search for an adequate legal framework for risk regulation because it does not address the specific problems of this type of regulatory activity. Fortunately, the ECJ refrained from concretising this principle into a rigid doctrine, suggesting instead that the Council should be free to specify the conditions under which the Commission might exercise 'executive powers' delegated to it.[47] Its function can be constructively interpreted as safeguarding pluralism in the European implementation process – although the ECJ has never explicitly acknowledged that the participation and cooperation of Member States may be required by this principle.[48]

Administrative Law of Bits and Pieces

The second approach to 'juridifying' Comitology can be understood as a reaction to its 'administrative' functions (as a rule-making executive[49]), by which the legal system undertakes some preliminary steps towards a European administrative law which should eventually lead to the adoption of an act on administrative procedures. It seems normatively highly plausible to insist upon a clarification of the boundaries of the delegation of 'essential' issues to the Comitology

the European Parliament' in Joerges and Vos (eds), *EU Committees* (n 37 above), 95–108; constructive effects seem to depend upon the ability of the EP to go into the depths of an issue and to thus identify problems of exemplary importance.

[44] Cases 9 and 10/56 *Meroni* [1958] ECR 9 and 51 at 43–44.

[45] The point has first been made by R Lauwaars, 'The "Model Directive" on Technical Harmonization' in R Bieber, R Dehousse, J Pinder and JHH Weiler (eds), *1992: One European Market? A Critical Analysis of the Commission's Internal Market Strategy* (Baden-Baden: Nomos, 1988) 151.

[46] See, for more comprehensive analyses, Schlacke, n 1 above (Ch G III), and Vos, n 1 above (Ch III.5), elaborated by E Vos and M Everson, 'European Agencies: What about the Institutional Balance?', *Maastricht Faculty of Law Working Paper No 4*, available at: https://ssrn.com/abstract=2467469.

[47] See Case 25/70, n 38 above.

[48] See Vos and Everson, n 46 above.

[49] See, for an explanation of this oxymoron, J Falke and G Winter, 'Management and Regulatory Committees in Executive Rule-Making' in G Winter (ed), *Sources and Categories of European Union Law: A Comparative and Reform Perspective* (Baden-Baden: Nomos, 1996) 583.

complex; to advocate greater transparency in the decision-making processes; and to search for institutional guarantees which would ensure the independence and plurality of scientific committees. It seems equally obvious that those affected by Comitology decisions must have access to judicial protection and that the standing of groups representing social interests needs to be enhanced.[50] However, equations of the decisional practices of the Comitology system with those of national administrations and/or of American agencies rest upon weak premises.[51] Advocates of a European act on administrative procedures seem to presuppose that Comitology will transform into one hierarchical system of European governance, but they may under-estimate the dependence of administrative law models on the organisational structure and the social conditions of nation-states or federations.[52]

The difficulties of the analogy can be substantiated with the help of the list of queries presented above.[53] We argue that risk regulation at European level is more complex than in the more integrated societies of national states for two reasons. First, its normative, ethical and cultural dimensions may be so diverse in Europe that they cannot be delegated to one single body with the competence to adopt uniform rules. Second, the economic costs and benefits of such decisions are felt unevenly across the internal market. Again, it would seem neither practically feasible nor normatively attractive to entrust one single body with the task of weighing the costs and benefits of social regulation in Europe. In other words, the resistance of Member States (and the Council) to participating in the implementation process and the reservation of some regulatory autonomy (‘*nationale Alleingänge*’) reflects legitimate concerns which cannot be adequately met by a transformation of the Comitology complex into a type of unified and centralised administrative body.

Bridging the Gap between Intergovernmentalist Bargaining and Centralised Rule-making

Examining the case law of the ECJ with the reservations which have just been raised in mind, against the agenda of the actors in the institutional debates on the one hand and analogies to the administrative law models of fully fledged federations or nation-states on the other, one is inclined to praise the ECJ for its cautious attitude and even detect elements in the judgments which begin to define the legal structures of multi-level governance in a way which mediates between the interests in the establishment of a functioning internal market on

[50] See, for a particularly careful recent exploration of these issues, Schlacke, *Risikoentscheidungen*, n 1 above, Ch G IV.

[51] See Joerges, ‘The Market without the State’, n 23 above, at 29–31.

[52] See, for a similar argument, C Harlow, ‘Codification of EC Administrative Procedures? Fitting the Foot to the Shoe or the Shoe to the Foot’ (1996) 2 *ELJ* 3.

[53] Section II B above; text accompanying nn 20 et seq.

the one hand and the concerns of national constituencies and the European public for the social responsibility of the internal market project on the other. Limitations of space prevent an extensive discussion of the legal issues;[54] it is sufficient to point to a number of indicators which support our interpretation.

One legal basis at the disposal of the ECJ to structure the Europeanisation of risk regulation stems from primary law, and in particular the use of Article 30.

As the ECJ has consistently held in its review of national legislation, Member States must not simply rely on Article 36 when defending a national regulation; where they are concerned about public health, 'the risk must be measured, not according to the yardstick of general conjecture, but on the basis of relevant scientific research'.[55] With this requirement, the Court restricts legislative discretion and imposes standards on decision-making processes within the Member States.

Once it had been established that legislation must be backed by relevant *scientific* evidence, it became unavoidable to decide upon the validity of such evidence. The ECJ has wrestled with this problem. Member States were asked to respect 'the findings of international scientific research, and, in particular, the work of the Community's Scientific Committee for Food, the Codex Alimentarius Committee of the Food and Agriculture Organisation of the UN (FAO) and the World Health Organization (WHO)'.[56] The expert committees to which the ECJ refers, however, often do not arrive at a uniform and globally applicable conclusion. Disagreements are taken as an indicator of the difficulties and uncertainties of risk assessments which enhance the discretionary power of legitimised decision-makers, without, however, giving them carte blanche.[57]

A more extensive body of case law concerns the constraints upon the discretion of decision-makers within European committees, and there are a few cases which have considered directly the decision-making procedures.

One important step taken by the ECJ is the judgment concerning the non-consultation of the Scientific Committee on Cosmetology. The Court stated: 'The drafting and adaptation of Community rules governing cosmetic products are founded on scientific and technical assessments which must themselves be based on the results of the latest international research …'[58] To adopt this requirement amounts to the de-authorisation of two Community institutions: neither the Commission nor the 'Committee on the Adaptation to Technical Progress of the Directives on the Removal of Technical Barriers to Trade in the

[54] See, more comprehensively, C Joerges, 'Scientific Expertise in Social Regulation and the European Court of Justice: Legal Frameworks for Denationalised Governance Structures' in C Joerges, K-H Ladeur and E Vos (eds), *Integrating Scientific Expertise into Regulatory Decision-Making* (Baden-Baden: Nomos, 1997) 295 (reprinted in ch 11 of this volume).

[55] See, as a recent example, Case 17/93 *Van der Veldt* [1994] ECR I-3537 at 3560.

[56] See, for example, Case 178/84 *Reinheitsgebot* [1987] ECR 1227 at 1274.

[57] See, for example, Case 272/80 *Biologische Producten* [1981] ECR 3277 at 3292, and Case 2047/84 *Léon Motte* [1985] 3887 at 3904.

[58] Case 12/91 *Angelopharm* [1993] ECR I-171 at 210.

Cosmetic Products Sector' which consists exclusively of representatives of the Member States, is in a position to carry out the type of assessment which 'in the nature of things and apart from any provision laid down to that effect' requires the assistance of 'experts on scientific and technical issues delegated by the Member States'.[59] Experts must not take over; but they must be heard!

One thought-provoking American observer predicts that the statement-of-reasons requirement of Article 190 will serve as the key to open the door of judicial control over the European regulatory process.[60] The ECJ seems to remain sceptical and cautious. The Court tends to treat the Council as a normal *legislature*, enjoying a very wide margin of discretion.[61] The discretion of the Commission, however, has been controlled more stringently. A further step has been taken in relation to decisions concerning individual rights of direct action. The statement of reasons required by Article 190 'must disclose in a clear and unequivocal fashion the reasoning followed by the Community authority … in such a way as to make the persons concerned aware of the reasons for the measure and thus enable them to defend their rights and to enable the Court to exercise its supervisory jurisdiction'. This is the Court's only statement of its prior jurisprudence in *Hauptzollamt München-Mitte v Technische Universität München*.[62] The importance of this ruling results from its concurrent recognition of basic procedural rights: where Community institutions have the power to carry out complex technical appraisals, respect for the rights of individuals is to be ensured by the 'duty of the competent Community institutions to examine carefully and impartially all the relevant aspects of the individual case, the rights of the persons concerned to make their views known and to have an adequately reasoned decision'.[63]

This does not suggest that the authority of the ECJ is backing our vision of a law of transnational governance, which would avoid the pitfalls both of intergovernmentalism and of building up a centralised technocratic governance structure. What we contend, however, is that the case law remains compatible with the normative vision we are trying to elaborate.

B. Comitology in the Perspectives of Political Science

Our interest in the analytical and prescriptive potential of political sciences is guided by our own research objectives. It is not our aim to present an analytical model and explain the functioning of Comitology; rather, we hope to demonstrate why both an adequate description and any normative assessment of

[59] Ibid, at 211 (para 33).

[60] M Shapiro, 'Codification of Administrative Law: The US and the Union' (1996) 2 *ELJ* 26, at 44–45.

[61] See Case C-331/88, *Fedesa and Others* [1990] ECR I-4023, at 4063.

[62] Case C-269/90 [1991] ECR I-5469, at 5499.

[63] Ibid, at 5499.

Comitology need to cope with the issues we have listed before turning to disciplinary analyses.[64] We suggest that our list can serve as a yardstick to assist the comparison and assessment of the problem-solving capacity of competing approaches. This implies that we look first for the analytical capacity to acknowledge the interaction of supranational and national, governmental and non-governmental actors; secondly, for the sensitivity to capture the economic, political and ethical facets of risk assessments and their social acceptability; and thirdly, for the potential to appreciate both the impact of institutions and of normative commitments of the actors involved.

The overview could only appear comprehensive if we were to confine it to studies which focused on the committee system. Our broader interdisciplinary interests in analyses of the normative structures of social action, the effects of law, the social acceptability of, and compliance with, regulatory policies, however, suggest a stronger epistemological orientation along the dividing lines between realism, utilitarianism and constructivism.

Intergovernmentalism and Agency Structures

It is one thing to acknowledge in studies on European integration that institutional patterns and legal actors matter, and quite another to come to grips with that impact. The high visibility of the legal frameworks under which actors operate in the EU, well-documented inter-administrative cooperative relations, the dense networks among a multiplicity of actors have not led intergovernmentalists and neo-realists to abandon their paradigms. These three factors merely require that the general assumptions of international anarchy and interaction patterns among states be relaxed and modified.

One such modification has recently been put forward by Pollack in his attempt to understand the role of supranational institutions on the basis of an enrichment of rational choice institutionalist theory by general insights into 'principal–agent' relationships.[65] From the Member States' perspective, the argument is that the delegation of competences by an act of Council to the Commission establishes an interest in policing the agent (the Commission). The ensuing conflicting institutional interests seem obvious; contrary to the Commission, which tends to promote the liberalisation of markets, individual Member States balance the collective aim of deepening the internal market with their specific interests in economic and social protection.

In order to bridge this conflict between the Commission and Member States, the latter have been keen to establish mechanisms ensuring compliance of the Commission with their objectives. The Comitology decision of the Council[66]

[64] See Section II B above, text accompanying nn 20 et seq.

[65] MA Pollack, 'Obedient Servant or Runaway Eurocracy? Delegation, Agency, and Agenda Setting in the European Community', *Harvard Working Paper No 95-10*, 1995).

[66] N 6 above.

can then be interpreted as representing the Council's concern with its control powers. The different procedures provided in the Comitology decision involve specific mixtures of autonomy of the Commission and control by the Member States which, in turn, have varying effects on the efficiency of the implementation process and influence the relation of group rationality as opposed to the protection of specific interests of one of the principals.

Intergovernmentalists advocate that the unequal distribution of power among Member States is an important variable in the explanation of interactions speaking. Generally, intergovernmentalism seems to assume that the powerful interest of domestic industries to achieve a specific regulatory outcome, with its attendant substantial economic costs or benefits, will induce these industries to provide their national administration with 'objective' arguments such as scientific evidence to defend their position.[67] Thus, on the one hand those countries with only marginal interests in achieving a specific result find themselves on the 'demand side' of expertise and will be more inclined to accept European suggestions which shape their regulatory preferences; on the other, those countries which host industries with a strong economic interest may rather be on the supply side and therefore more keen to convince, and capable of convincing, other parties of their point of view. The process of framing the way in which problems are defined and being dealt with may, therefore, often be rather asymmetrical.

Asymmetrical power resources do not diminish under the conditions of institutionalised interactions but are well presented in terms of a variety of capacities. In Comitology, power-play among Member States is not exercised through open threats but by setting the terms of discourse in which interaction is to be conducted. By emphasising the need to provide reasons, administrations without the requisite resources for elaborating their reasoning in 'reasonable terms' (terms which are backed by scientific evidence and refer to agreed upon standards) face serious difficulties in giving credence to their position. Because of the function of scientific discourse to serve as a filter for claims, it is very difficult for participants to maintain positions without being backed by generally acceptable arguments. Their arguments are easily de-legitimised by the terms of the discourse. The rather high level of consumer protection by which the decision of the StCF is most often characterised therefore reflects not only the reasonability of its deliberations, but also the 'silencing' of relatively powerless Member States. The silence on distributive concerns therefore mirrors the dominance of powerful Member States and a discourse which strongly works in favour of their interests.

[67] This argument has been supported by several interviews conducted with representatives from the Bund für Lebensmittelrecht und Lebensmittelkunde (BLL), 14.02.96, the Confederation of the Food and Drink Industries of the EU (CIAA), 26.04.96 and an official from the Bundesministerium für Gesundheit, Bonn, 28.02.96.

Political scientists have a great record in demystifying the normative world of legal discourse. Nevertheless it is legitimate to ask whether this search for realism is itself realistic. The modelling of the relations between the Member States and the Commission with the help of the principal–agent paradigm seems to add a greater degree of plausibility to the suggestion that the quality of reasoning, the authority of experts, and the commitments to legal rules and principles matter in a way rational utilitarianism is unable to conceptualise. If and because the interests of the many principles of the Commission are not uniform but nevertheless remain in favour of establishing a single market, it seems highly likely that the principals can be persuaded to engage in serious deliberations and accept their outcome. Even the advantages that economically strong Member States enjoy in articulating their positions do not necessarily denounce the 'quality' of the interaction within committees; Member States which do not yet have a defined position on specific issues may be well advised to take a free ride on the findings of their stronger neighbours and develop their preferences accordingly.

Functional Supranationalism

Pioneering studies of the committee system have underlined the importance of inter-administrative partnership[68] and the potential of the Commission to shape the transnational flow of information. The Commission can exert this power due to its superior information that enables it to determine the agenda of the whole system.[69] From a supranational perspective, it is not the Member States' interests which dominate European politics but rather European institutions which have the capacity to channel and influence Member State interaction in a way that is compatible with European interests.

Important factors strengthen the bargaining power of the Commission; in preparing its proposals the Commission manages to use the authority of the Scientific Committee for Foodstuffs (SCF), which is consulted whenever this seems appropriate to the Commission.[70] Although the ECJ has now insisted on the consultation of the scientific committees whenever 'the nature of things' so requires,[71] the Commission remains in a position to decide whether this

[68] Wessels, n 1 above; and idem, 'Verwaltung im EG-Mehrebenensystem: Auf dem Weg zur Megabürokratie?' in M Jachtenfuchs and B Kohler-Koch (eds), *Europäische Integration* (Opladen: Leske + Budrich, 1996) 165.

[69] M Bach, 'Vom Zweckverband zum technokratischen Regime: Politische Legitimation und institutionelle Verselbständigung in der Europäischen Gemeinschaft' in HA Winkler and H Kaelble (eds), *Nationalismus – Nationalitäten – Supranationalität* (Stuttgart: Klett-Cotta, 1993) 288.

[70] Not surprisingly, the Commission explicitly rejects demands for a more autonomous and self-conscious role of the SCF, which include the right of the SCF to give opinions without being asked (see Interview conducted with Commission's official at DG III, Brussels 22.02.96). The Commission's practice of instrumentalising the SCF is a fact which is heavily critiqued by a number of delegates; see Interview conducted with official from the Permanent Representation of Germany in Brussels, 26.04.96.

[71] See n 28 above.

condition is met.[72] As far as scientific evidence in Comitology is accepted to be the most valid currency for making convincing arguments, this is an important bargaining-chip which the Commission uses intelligently to support those arguments which suit its own goals. The second most important function of the Commission is to chair the negotiations about the adoption of its proposals and to set the agenda of the committee and the working groups. In combining different topics in one session, the Commission can not only encourage package-deals among the Member States and itself but also place a high demand on the technical expertise of Member States' delegations whose limited resources are not always able to meet the standard. It comes as no surprise to learn that overloaded agendas and the pressure of the Commission to proceed according to tight time-tables remain of central concern to the delegations. Member States in the StCF frequently express concern about the Commission's efforts to speed up negotiations. The period of time which is put at the disposal of national delegations to respond to the Commission's proposals and formulate their own interests and positions is sometimes reduced to a few weeks.[73] In general, this does not leave enough room for domestic consultations with all interested parties.[74] The Commission does not hesitate to take a vote on proposals where consensus is unattainable and voting is the only successful option within the tight time-limit. Consequently, a number of respondents to our questionnaire[75] argued that the whole process of negotiation is not only heavily influenced but even dominated by the Commission. Apart from one respondent, even delegates expressed concerns either about the Commission being too assertive in pushing for results or for using its competences too extensively.

The whole argument turns the insights of the principal–agent thesis on its head. It rests on the assumption that the Commission, and eventually its partners in national administrations, will be able to define and implement a

[72] For challenging the opinion of the Commission as to whether the conditions for asking the StCF have been met, Member States must apply to the European Court of Justice – a time-, energy- and money-consuming undertaking.

[73] The rules of procedure of the StCF require that all documents related to the sessions of the committee (eg, the notice convening the meeting, the agenda, the draft measures on which the committee's opinion is requested) must reach the offices of the permanent representatives of the Member States not later than 21 days before the date of the meeting (Art 3). In urgent cases, however, the chairman of the committee may shorten the time to 10 clear working days or even include an item on the agenda for a meeting in the course of that meeting (in cases of 'extreme urgency').

[74] This problem is obviously even more demanding for the German Länder which must consult one another before being able to reach common positions. It also highlights the difficulties Germany's federal structure faces in being compatible with the demands for decision-making under intense time pressure (cf, interviews conducted with officials at the Landesuntersuchungsamt für die amtliche Lebensmittelüberwachung, Bremen, 15.01.96, the Behörde für Arbeit, Gesundheit und Soziales der Freien Hansestadt Hamburg, 29.04.96, the Niedersächsisches Ministerium für Landwirtschaft und Forsten, Hannover, 3.05.96, a representative of the Bundesrat, Wiesbaden, 15.08.96 and the Ministerium für Umwelt, Raumordnung und Landwirtschaft des Landes Nordrhein-Westfalen, 4.06.96).

[75] One element of our empirical investigations has been to distribute a questionnaire among the delegates in the StCF. For some of the results, see the table at the end of the article.

common agenda. If one considers the difficulties of identifying risks, the problems of balancing the costs and benefits of regulatory decisions, the need to explore new issues and deal with the many uncertainties of risk management, the picture drawn of the Commission starts to look so simplistic that it becomes highly implausible. Not only is the Commission dependent upon cooperation; it also needs to bring about a type of consensus that stabilises its own prerogative. Is this possible without a 'sound' basis of decision-making and the reputation of acting as a 'fair' broker between conflicting interests and concerns?

Constructivism

Constructivist approaches conceptualise social norms as an important independent variable for explaining the behaviour of (national) actors.[76] Their argument builds upon two principles: first, people act towards objects, including other actors, upon the basis of the meanings that the objects have for them; and second, the meanings in terms of which action is organised arise out of interaction.[77] The identity of actors, therefore, is understood as being 'an inherently social definition of the actor grounded in the theories which actors collectively hold about themselves and one another and which constitute the structure of the social world'.[78] Consequently, the institutionalisation of interaction is not conceived of as being only a device for overcoming problems of interdependence and cooperation but also as a process of internalising new preferences and even identities. Institutionalisation therefore is not something occurring outside actors and only affecting their behaviour but is a cognitive process that involves a redefinition of the self and the other.

It seems important to note that negotiations among delegations may last for years with the same personnel attending. Delegates not only meet frequently during the sessions of the Standing Committee, but have very often also met one another before in the preparation of draft legislation and the negotiations about its adoption in the Council's working groups.[79] During the course of working together, delegates approximate not only national legal provisions but also different problem definitions and problem-solving philosophies. They slowly move from being representatives of the national interest to representatives of a Europeanised inter-administrative discourse in which mutual learning and understanding of each others' difficulties surrounding the implementation

[76] For an illuminating critic of rationalism, see A Wendt, 'Anarchy is What States Make of it: the Social Construction of Power Politics' (1993) 46 *International Organization* 391; and Risse-Kappen, n 32 above.

[77] Wendt, n 76 above, at 403.

[78] Ibid, at 398.

[79] On the following, see the findings of J Lewis, 'Constructing Interests: EU Membership, COREPER and the Constitutive Processes of National Preference Formation' (Manuscript Cologne/ Madison, WI, 1996).

of standards become of central importance. The emergence of shared feelings of inter-administrative partnership is crucial to understanding the course of the negotiation because the control which national governments have over delegates is generally rather weak. Sometimes, governments have not defined their preferences and therefore leave delegates a wide margin of discretion. In other instances, delegates use their unique informational status to influence their governments' perception of their own preferences, or even simply by-pass them.[80] It is not by accident that even the intergovernmental Committee of Permanent Representatives (COREPER) is commonly known in the German administration as the 'Committee of Permanent Traitors'.[81] And it is exactly for this reason that observers of international negotiations have always pointed to the double-edged character of the actions of delegates: they perform not only strategic bargaining with the aim of maximising particular utilities by trying to externalise costs and internalise benefits, but also deliberative problem-solving with a rather problem-oriented approach and the aim of finding solutions which maximise collective utilities.

Law

All three of the approaches outlined above help to identify specifics of the Comitology system, including its neglect of economic/distributive concerns. Intergovernmentalism adds to it the bargaining power of the highly-regulated Member States. Supranationalism points to the strength of the Commission in emphasising the goal of deepening the internal market. Constructivism explains the emergence of some sense of Europeanisation on the part of the delegates. In our comments we have always rephrased one single observation: although it seems simply realistic to insist on the importance of argument and discursive processes in the decision-making of committees, one should accept that it is impossible to measure the 'real weight' of an argument against the interests it furthers, to detect whether the reasons given for a decision reflect its real motivation. To accept this impossibility is not to devalue the quality of decision-making processes which are based upon arguments valid and acceptable in principle for all participants. On the contrary, scepticism as to the force or practical impact of reason in real-world processes is a good reason to establish institutions furthering the respect for good arguments and imposing pertinent constraints; this is why decision-making should become embedded into Law. This then leads to the final step of our argument; it is submitted that the constitutional commitments of the actors involved should 'govern' the operation of committees and ensure a deliberative style of policy-making. This is a complicated suggestion. It

[80] Interview conducted with official from the Bundesministerium für Gesundheit, Bonn, 28.02.96.
[81] Interview conducted with official from the Permanent Representation of Germany in Brussels, 26.04.96.

requires us to substantiate our normative perspectives on European governance in general and on risk regulation in particular.

IV. DELIBERATIVE SUPRANATIONALISM

The disciplinary analyses we have submitted converge in one important respect: they support a *sui generis* characterisation of the European polity. As our overview of the legal debate emphasised, the many unsettled legal problems with Comitology all confirm our observation that the committee system does not fit into the interpretation of the EC-system as either a supra-national legal order or a mere association of nation-states. Comitology, so we have asserted, must rather be interpreted as positively evidencing that transnational markets can be governed by institutions representing 'more than a regime and less than a federation'. Similarly, our search in current integration research for an analytic approach which is compatible with our empirical evidence confirms the emergence of governance structures which can no longer be attributed to either nation-states or a supranational state-like entity. These findings certainly lend support to our hypotheses at the outset of this contribution and they are very much in line with widely shared views on the *sui generis* character of the European Community.[82]

However, the insight that Comitology presents itself as Queen's evidence for the *de facto* emergence and the legal recognition of transnational governance structures should not be read as the conclusion but rather understood as the intellectual challenge of our story. If and because lawyers cannot content themselves with equating the factual with the normative; if and because political scientists are expected to be interested in the 'quality' of the emerging European polity, we have to come to terms with the normative ambivalence of our findings.

These, then, are the issues we need to consider. We will first identify and defend a general normative vision which responds to the normative ambivalence of our findings, this vision we term 'deliberative supranationalism' (*A below*); second, we will substantiate our general notion for the field under scrutiny, namely the regulation of product risks through the committee system (*B below*); third, we will concretise our concepts further with a view to developing a legal framework for the Europeanisation of risk policies (*C below*). Each step of the argument is normative in that it strives to identify criteria which should enable us to address, ensure and improve the 'quality' of non-hierarchical transnational governance. We attribute to our normative ideas the characteristics of regulative principles which are capable of guiding the assessments of decisional problems,

[82] See, for an elaboration of these perspectives, M Jachtenfuchs, 'Theoretical Perspectives on European Governance' (1995) 1 *ELJ* 115; M Jachtenfuchs and B Kohler-Koch, 'Regieren im dynamischen Mehrebenensystem' in idem (eds), *Europäische Integration* (Opladen: Leske + Budrich, 1996) 15.

the further elaboration of institutional frameworks and legal principles. At each of the three levels of our normative deliberations, and in our efforts to bridge the gap between normative ideas and actual policy-making and decision-taking, a crucial function will be ascribed to the 'law'. In this, sense our argument is trans-disciplinary and paraphrases a classical problem in our specific context: how do institutions affect social practices; how might institutions help to discipline politics? It goes without saying that we do not deal with that problem in general because we are exclusively concerned with the potential of legal commitments to structure regulatory practices within the EC.

A. Constitutionalism Beyond the Nation-State

In a recent summary of the discussion and her own vision of democratic legitimacy, Benhabib lists three tasks modern democratic societies have to face, namely securing legitimacy, economic welfare and 'a viable sense of collective identity'.[83] Any resolution of these tasks, so the proponents of the theory claim, depends upon the institutionalisation of a public sphere of opinion formation, and the recognition of basic rights – basically, on the institutional achievements of constitutional states. This is at least the common understanding of those legal theorists and constitutionalists who have transposed the deliberative model of democracy into the legal discourse thereby equating the legitimacy of modern law with its backing by democratic political institutions – and *vice versa*: no valid law outside democracy, no democracy without law.[84]

The nation-state foundations of such arguments are readily apparent. We therefore do not by any means suggest that the deliberative model of legitimate governance could be simply 'applied' at the EC level. The notion of deliberative supranationalism denotes a long-term project which needs to be elaborated in two dimensions. It should be read as compensating shortcomings ('failures') of constitutional nation-states and thus present a normative basis for supranational constitutional commitments; it should, however, also draw upon deliberative ideals in structuring supranationalism.

The kernel of our argument is:[85] the legitimacy of governance within constitutional states is flawed in so far as it remains inevitably one-sided and parochial

[83] S Benhabib, 'Toward a Deliberative Model of Democratic Legitimacy' in idem (ed), *Democracy and Difference: Contesting the Boundaries of the Political* (Princeton NJ: Princeton University Press, 1996) 67; for the impact of these ideas in Europe, see, for example, EO Erikson, 'Deliberative Democracy and the Politics of Pluralist Societies', *Arena Working Paper 6/94*, Oslo 1994.

[84] See, most recently, O Gerstenberg, *Bürgerrechte und deliberative Demokratie* (Frankfurt aM: Suhrkamp, 1997).

[85] Although we may have used a neologism, we believe that it will be possible to identify many parallels to our ideas. Especially, international relations scholars seem increasingly aware of the normative *problématique* of the core concepts of power and interest; what they term a 'domestification' of international politics refers to the sectorial and/or gradual transformation of international anarchy into a more civilised (rule bound) system. See JA Caporaso, 'The European Union and Forms of State: Westphalian, Regulatory or Post-Modern?' (1996) 34 *JCMS* 29.

or selfish. The taming of the nation-state through democratic constitutions has its limits. If and because democracies presuppose and represent collective identities, they have very few mechanisms ensuring that 'foreign' identities and their interests be taken into account within their decision-making processes. The legitimacy of supranational institutions can be designed as a cure to these deficiencies – as a correction of 'nation-state failures' as it were. It seems easy to detect such elements in European law and to base its claim to supranational validity on exactly these normative qualities. Thus, the non-discrimination guarantee of Article 6 can be read as aiming at compensating the particularism of national basic rights; similarly, the prohibition of protectionist policies by Article 30 can be read as meaning that European nation-states must not try to resolve their economic and social problems at the cost of their neighbours.[86] The constitutionalisation of such principles is in line with the ideals embodied in democratic constitutions, and legal supranationalism can thus be understood as complementing common features of national constitutionalist traditions.

We also submit that they entail a normatively attractive response to so many critics of the European project and that they can be elaborated into a supranational version of the deliberative reading of pluralism. Assuming that 'we the peoples' of Europe do not wish to build up a Federal State which would be entrusted with the whole range of tasks which were once assigned to constitutional nation-states; and given that we are nevertheless to live with an opening of the borders of our formerly national economies, we are bound to strive towards an unprecedented polity. We must conceptualise supranational constitutionalism as an alternative to the model of the constitutional nation-state which respects that state's constitutional legitimacy but at the same time clarifies and sanctions the commitments arising from its interdependence with equally democratically legitimised states and with the supranational prerogatives that an institutionalisation of this interdependence requires. The legitimacy of supranational constraints imposed upon the sovereignty of constitutional states can in principle be easily understood. Extra-territorial effects of national policies may be intended, indeed they are real and unavoidable in an economically and socially interdependent community. This raises the question of how can a constitutional state legitimise the burden it unilaterally imposes upon its neighbours? 'No taxation without representation' – this principle can claim universal validity; the very idea of democratic constitutionalism requires that constitutional states apply this principle against themselves. A supranational constitutional charter therefore does not need to represent a new 'state'. Nor does supranationalism require that democracies concede a right to vote to non-nationals. What it does require is that the interests and concerns of non-nationals should be considered even within the national polity. In this sense, supranationalism does convey *political* rights and not just economic freedoms to Community

[86] See JHH Weiler, 'Fin-de-Siècle Europe' in R Dehousse (ed), *Europe After Maastricht. An Ever Closer Union?* (Munich: CH Beck, 1994) 203.

citizens. Supranationalism is therefore to be understood as a fundamentally *democratic* concept. 'Supremacy' of European law can and should be read as giving voice to 'foreign' concerns and imposing corresponding constraints upon Member States. What supremacy requires, then, is the identification of rules and principles ensuring the co-existence of different constituencies and the compatibility of these constituencies' objectives with the common concerns they share. Community law is to lay down a legal framework which structures political deliberation about exactly these issues. It is a constitutional mandate of the ECJ to protect such legal structures and principles and to resolve controversies surrounding their contents.

B. Social Regulation, its Insulation in the EC and National Concerns

In the context of our enquiries into the legal framework for European social regulation, it is certainly important to take those elements of the *acquis communautaire* into account which function as a stable legal framework for the implementation process. These are two outstanding general problems: the insulation of risk assessment policies from national economic ('industrial policy') concerns,[87] and the need to delineate Community and national powers in the normative/political elements of risk regulation. A closely related issue concerns the transposition of general normative commitments into concrete decisional practices which a juridification of the practices within Comitology is to ensure.

The fields of product regulation belong to those core activities where the EC has been specifically active and successful. Following Majone, the focus of European policies on areas of social regulation and the insulation of regulatory activities from what he calls distributive concerns is not only an empirically and analytically adequate characterisation of the EC's political practice, but also a normatively sound orientation.[88] Majone's characterisation of the EC's regulatory activities strikes us as capturing perfectly well the EC's policy *agenda* at any rate in the field of *product* regulation. In that sense, we cannot but subscribe to his analysis. The famous rejection of traditional harmonisation strategies back in 1985 and the entirely new approach were indeed a deliberate response to the constant subversion of the Community's market-building objective by the unanimity requirement which prevented the adoption of comprehensive regulatory programmes and protected parochial orientations of each and every Member State towards the furthering of the economic well-being of its national constituency.

[87] For the terminology used, see Section II B above.

[88] G Majone, 'The European Community: An "Independent Fourth Branch of Government"?' in G Brüggemeier (ed), *Verfassungen für ein ziviles Europa* (Baden-Baden: Nomos, 1994) 23; see the analyses of Caparaso, n 86 above, 39–44; M Everson, 'Independent Agencies: Hierarchy Beaters?' (1995) 1 *ELJ* 180; Majone's argument is once more systematically and in full clarity presented in G Majone, *Regulating Europe* (Abingdon: Routledge, 1996) at 284–300.

However, as we have already pointed out,[89] we suggest a much more differentiated analysis. First, we would like to distinguish between 'industrial policy' objectives and the more diffuse impact of regulatory policies on the 'distribution of risks' and their costs. The political and normative prerequisites for insulating social regulation from these consequences are as diverse as their economic implications. Second, we believe that the political-normative and ethical dimensions of risk regulation in our fields militate both empirically and normatively in favour of institutional compromises between the strengthening of non-majoritarian institutions and the preservation of cooperative forms of governance allowing for flexibility towards national concerns. 'Double Pluralism' may be an adequate term to denote our normative intuition and its relation to the concept of deliberative supranationalism.

C. Insulation from Economic Implications

The price for European regulatory policies is to be paid for, at the end of the day, by industry and consumers. This burden, however, is by no means uniform throughout the Community. The economies of high standard countries are privileged by high standards of protection. There can be no doubt that industrial policy concerns connected with the adoption of specific regulatory strategies rank high on the agenda of national political actors and negotiators at European level. Is it practically conceivable, or at least normatively sound, to support a systematic disregard of these implications? Our answer to this question is specific. In order to explain our suggestions, we have to take up once again the distinction between 'industrial policies' and 'risk distribution'.

Contrary to our contention, the whole European single market programme and, similarly, the case law of the ECJ on Articles 30 and 36 since the decision in *Cassis de Dijon* can be and have been read as supporting and furthering the insulation of social regulation without any further distinction from all 'distributive' concerns. In our view, this jurisprudence requires a more subtle interpretation.[90] One should first note that the ECJ has never questioned, in principle, the regulatory autonomy of the Member States nor subjected them to some comprehensive deregulatory programme. What the Court did was to impose duties of justification on Member States pursuing regulatory policies which seem incompatible with the economic objective of establishing a single market. The Court took both principles enshrined in the Treaty's provisions seriously: the free trade and anti-protectionism objectives of Article 30 *and* the respect for the regulatory autonomy of constitutional states contained in Article 36. What political scientists rightly perceive as an 'insulation' of social regulation from 'distributive'

[89] Section II B above.

[90] On the following, see, more extensively, Joerges, 'Scientific Expertise …', n 54 above, and, for a similar interpretation, M Poiares Maduro, 'Reforming the Market or the State? Article 30 and the European Constitution: Economic Freedoms and Political Rights' (1997) 3 *ELJ* 55, at 73–79.

concerns must at the same time be appreciated as an effort of the legal system to mediate between two conceptually different concerns and to find rules which the specifically European regulatory pluralism requires. Our reading of the Court's jurisprudence as ensuring the compatibility of the commitments to establishing a common market and respecting the regulatory concerns of constitutional states is first of all a rejection of an interpretation of the ECJ's jurisprudence as a deregulatory agenda. This reading affects, however, the normative evaluation of 'distributional' concerns. It seems logical to infer from the ECJ's case law that no Member States can defend its own low regulatory standards against a higher level of protection realised in a European standard. The regulatory autonomy to expose its own citizens to higher risks than those agreed upon at a European level is indeed lost. Does this imply that the European Community should not care about the implication of its policies for national economies? To demonstrate the normative contents of this issue there is a recent example: the British Government must not claim the regulatory autonomy to expose European citizens to the risks inherent in its management of the disease of BSE. But would it be justified to impose all the costs of BSE on the British economy? To ask the Community to share the economic burden of BSE with the UK is to view BSE as an accident which does not find the UK Government (and its citizens) liable.

Any interpretation of the ECJ's jurisprudence should consider the limitation of the Court's oversight. It is one thing to search for rules ensuring the compatibility of the single market project with national regulatory concerns. It is quite another to impose an economic solidarity on European societies. When asked whether the Community is entitled to treat BSE as an accident and use its resources to compensate British farmers for their losses, would the ECJ interfere? Certainly not. This reluctance is our answer to the insulation issue: the legal rules and principles favouring the insulation of the Comitology committees from economic considerations are justified insofar as they disregard the prerogatives of Member States to determine for themselves the level of risk to which their citizens are exposed. The disregard of 'industrial policy' implications, however, can only be pragmatically justified with respect to the fact that such implications cannot be adequately dealt with in the implementation process.

Experts, Laymen and Public Concerns

Our second general observation on the nature of risk regulation concerns the political-normative elements of decision-making which cannot be reduced due to aggregated costs and benefits – an expert's judgment cannot claim a per se higher rationality than those of laymen.[91] In the EC context, this well-known problem exhibits specific facets which can be exposed by reflecting on the meaning of well-established legal principles.

[91] See the references in n 22 above.

The normative elements of risk assessments form part of the political agenda of constitutional states. They exemplify the importance of a public sphere of continuous deliberation – including the need to rationalise such deliberations through adequate institutional frameworks. Such considerations clearly militate against centralised decisional powers in the EC. On the other hand, once it is acknowledged that constitutional nation-states are not entitled or legitimised to treat their preferences and interests simply as 'given' (just like economic theories tend to treat the preferences of consumers), one must be ready to relativise the decisional autonomy of national societies, to accept supranational intervention even into the normative realm of risk assessment. Furthermore, there must be a continued awareness of the fact that even within constitutional states the risk problem has inspired many institutional innovations. To indicate just one aspect: the elaboration of sound standards is nowhere left to parliaments instructing administrative bodies and courts. The political arenas of risk regulation are more dispersed and often fragmented. Once the indispensability of delegating regulatory issues to representative but specialised arenas is recognised, Europeanisation processes can be perceived as a chance rather than a threat.[92] Not only do they enhance the opportunities for the generation of knowledge, they also entail chances for the broadening and deepening of debates among experts and the strengthening of non-professional associations.

The weighing of supranational prerogatives against national competences is a background agenda not only of the jurisprudence on Articles 30 and 36, but also on residual national competences under Article 100a (4), within safeguard procedures and the pre-emptive effects of secondary Community law. These issues are particularly sensitive after the introduction of majority voting; of course, even under the unanimity rule, tension between supranational powers and national concerns was frequently felt and resolved by the ECJ. However, with the growing involvement of the Community into regulatory policies in general and risk regulation in particular, the search for a European-wide coordination of risk management becomes ever more important. Both centralisation of decisional powers at European level and the defence of national competences would seem counter-productive. The committee system, which couples decision-making across territorial boundaries, which encourages European-wide coordination of policies without completely pre-empting national reactions, proves to be a sensible compromise – both politically and normatively. Until 1987, the legitimacy of EC decision-making rested upon the unanimous consent of governments. The reliance on governmental will was at the same time the starting point

[92] Eichener, n 1 above; he also refers to J Cohen and J Rodgers, 'Solidarity, Democracy, Association' in W Streeck (ed), *Staat und Verbände* (1994) 35 *Politische Vierteljahresschrift (Sonderheft 25)* 136 as a legitimising background theory. The equation of national and transnational conditions seems, however, premature; see Everson, n 1 above, and Gerstenberg, n 84 above, at 119–126.

of intergovernmentalism in political science. To be sure, even before the SEA of 1987, the ECJ's interpretation of EC law had identified (and to some degree cured), the deficiencies of these positions: Governments were to respect rights granted by the Treaty. They must not define their policies unilaterally, but must think about their compatibility with the rights and interests of other EC citizens. In other words, supranationalism not only requires the Community to respect a pluralism of regulatory concerns; it also requires that national regulators are exposed to transnational arenas scrutinising the validity of their arguments.

V. CONCLUSION: COMITOLOGY AS A SUPRANATIONAL POLITICAL FORUM

The establishment of non-hierarchical governance structures turns out to be an indispensable prerequisite of the functioning of the Common Market. This type of governance will depend upon persuasion, argument and discursive processes rather than on command, control and/or strategic action. Positive normative connotations with this assertion can be claimed in theory. Any equation of the legal and administrative practices we have described with a normatively attractive new model of governance would, however, still be premature. Two kind of issues need to be explored further before we can present affirmative or deconstructive conclusions. First, we have to develop and explain the normative yardsticks against which we want to measure the Comitology system. Second, we will have to operationalise more precisely the categories and concepts on which we rely with a view to assessing the practices we have identified in a more reliable way.

Notwithstanding these challenges, we feel able to assert that intrusions into national autonomy must be complemented by positive supranational decision-making. The questioning of national autonomy and the (supranational) judicial control of its limits implies that supranational decision-making cannot be left to the state of nature but requires its own legitimacy. Just as problem-solving within constitutional states is bound to respect individual rights and democratic procedures, supranational interactions aiming at mutually acceptable problem-solving must not be conceived as merely strategic games. It would be the task of the law to further this kind of orientation – for example through clear commitments represented primarily by the Commission to arrive at a common solution; the establishment of *fora* where the views of all concerned societies can be included; legal principles and rules civilising the decision-making process and providing an institutional context for practical reasoning – to ensure the potential of the system to manage tensions between output rationality (high standards), procedural transparency and fairness; to control the regulatory bargaining power of individual states; and to promote the generation and dissemination of knowledge.

Table Compilation of questionnaires from 14 delegates of 11 Member States in the Standing Committee for Foodstuffs*

MS identified according to voting weight under Art 148(2) EEC	**10 (I+II)**	**10**	**5**	**5**	**5**	**5**	**4**	**3**	**3 (I+II)**	**2**	**0 (I+II)**
Representation in other European food bodies	three	some	some	some	four	some	no	three	some	three	some
Delegate to StCF since	1986; 1992	1988	1985	1996	1994	1975	1994	1994	1995	1972	1993; 1995
Size of delegation	2–4	1	1–2	1–3	3	2	1–2	1–2	1–4	1–2	1–3
Do delegates also sit in Council?	yes	yes	yes	yes	yes	yes	no	no data?	no; yes	no data	no
Importance of economic considerations	secondary	difficult to answer	secondary	secondary	important but not explicit	important issue	not explicit	secondary	explicit but secondary	secondary	depends on context; not explicit
Importance of procedures	low	high	high	Medium	low	fairly high	low	low	low	low	low
Where is consensus actually reached	WGs	WGs	StCF, sometimes informal	WGs	StCF or WG	WGs	WGs	mainly in WGs	StCF and WGs	WG, informal	During meetings
Consultation with other delegations	sometimes	sometimes informal	rarely	yes, often	sometimes	rarely	only for information exchange	rarely	rarely, only with Nordic countries	sometimes	only with Nordic countries
Neutrality of the COM in the StCF	own interests	objective	own interests	own interests	neutral broker	looking for majorities	own interest	own interest	neutral, mediating	mediator with own interests	own interests
Consultation with own government?	never	if proposals substantially modified	if proposals substantially modified	only if necessary	sometimes	no data	once	if necessary	rarely; never	if necessary	rarely; never

(continued)

Table *(Continued)*

MS identified according to voting weight under Art 148(2) EEC	10 (I+II)	10	5	5	5	5	4	3	3 (I+II)	2	0 (I+II)
Ability to influence agenda	adequate	adequate	mostly present	Adequate	adequate	adequate	adequate	adequate	adequate	adequate	adequate
Independence and quality of SCF	satisfactory; good	good	intransparent	very good, high reputation	high reputation, and independence	too slow, only limited independence, intransparent	no negative experience	no comment	good work, no bad experience, independent	high reputation, quality, independence	high reputation, quality, independence
Should SCF have rights of initiative?	no opinion; no	yes, but careful	no data	Yes	no	no	no	yes	no; yes	yes	yes
Should Parliament participate in Comitology?	no need	yes	no, inefficient	No	no need	no need	no need	no opinion	no	no need	no need; no experience
Miscellaneous remarks	Commission too assertive	General satisfaction	General satisfaction	More access to SCF needed	Low, only IIIb is acceptable	Commission too dominant	Commission too dominant	high, but poor transparency	efficient, translation missing	high	No delegation of further competencies to Commission

* For reasons of confidentiality, we do not identify the responses of individual delegations with reference to nationality. Instead delegations are identified according to voting weight. Furthermore, all answers listed are our own interpretations of the responses given by delegates to a questionnaire which was distributed during the 2nd and 54th sessions of the Standing Committee of Foodstuffs. If two delegates from one country have responded, they are separated in the table (if necessary) with a semi-colon.

Abbreviations: StCF denotes Standing Committee for Foodstuffs; SCF denotes Scientific Committee for Foodstuffs; WG denotes Working Group.

13

*Integration through De-legalisation?**

INTRODUCTION: THE CHANGE TO GOVERNANCE AS A CHALLENGE TO THE RULE OF LAW AND THE STRUCTURING OF THE ARGUMENT

THIS ESSAY DEALS with the precarious tensions between the European Union's (EU's) commitment to the rule of law, on the one hand, and its regulatory practices on the other. These tensions became readily apparent with the proclamation of a change to governance in the European Commission's White Paper of 2001[1] and the intensive research activities in its aftermath.[2] Governance is not a genuinely legal concept. It is therefore unsurprising that pertinent analyses within political science hardly ever include reflections on the compatibility of governance practices with the rule of law and the idea of law-mediated legitimisation of the exercise of public power. Important strands within the legal literature have followed suit and are considering alternatives to the rule of law.[3]

This, it is submitted, is a big step too far and not really required, let alone justified by functional needs. This critique evolves in three steps. The first short step undertaken in Part 1 is a reminder of the intense debates in the 1980s on the failures of interventionist conceptions of law and the search for methodologies, such as 'proceduralisation' and 'reflexive law', which could then cope

* 'Integration Through De-Legalisation?' (2008) 33 *EL Rev* 219; original German version: 'Integration durch Entrechtlichung?' in GF Schuppert and M Zürn (eds), *Governance in einer sich wandelnden Welt* (Opladen: Westdeutscher Verlag, 2008) 213; translated by Iain F Fraser and PhD researcher Rory S Brown, EUI Florence.

[1] European Commission, 'European Governance: A White Paper', COM(2001) 428 final of 25.07.01, [2001] OJ C287, available at: http://europa.eu.int/comm/governance/index_en.htm; see, also, European Commission, 'Enhancing democracy in the European Union. Working Programme', SEC(2000) 1547, 7 final of 11.10.2000, available at: http://europa.eu.int/comm/governance/work/en.pdf.

[2] The CONNEX bibliography containing the relevant literature currently holds 3,345 records (see www.connex-network.org/govlit).

[3] G de Búrca and J Scott (eds), *New Governance, Law and Constitutionalism* (Oxford: Hart Publishing, 2006); DM Trubek and LG Trubek, 'New Governance and Legal Regulation: Complementarity, Rivalry, and Transformation' (2007) 13 *Columbia Journal of European Law* 529; CF Sabel and J Zeitlin, 'Learning from Difference: The New Architecture of Experimentalist Governance in the European Union', *EUROGOV Working Paper* No C-07-02, available at: www.connex-network.org/eurogov/pdf/egp-connex-C-07-02.pdf.network.org/eurogov.

with new post-interventionist practices. These practices already reflected, albeit under different headings, a turn to governance. 'Proceduralisation', as advocated by critical theory, and 'reflexive law', as promoted by systems theory, were responses to the failures of interventionism, steering fantasies and command and control regulation, which deserve to be revisited prior to a premature farewell to the rule of law. Both of these responses, however, have not yet reflected upon globalisation and Europeanisation processes. These processes require the development of denationalised governance arrangements and legal responses which are not dependent on a supranational statal entity. Part 2 provides an overview of old and not so old modes of European governance through which Europe has managed to adapt its regulatory machinery to transnational regulatory needs. It also documents the readiness for institutional innovations and those efforts aimed at keeping them in the shadow of the law which have become ever more difficult with the advent of the truly new modes of governance, in particular that of the Open Method of Coordination. The third step of the argument, undertaken in Part 3, suggests that further erosion of the rule of law can be avoided. Rather than softening the law, transforming its substance or abandoning it, we should strive for a re-conceptualisation of Europe's constitutional charter. We should learn to understand European law as a supranational conflict of laws which is striving to cope with Europe's diversity. The concluding section considers some practical implications of the conflict-of-laws approach.

PART 1: REMARKS ON THE RECENT CAREER OF THE CONCEPT AND A REMINDER OF OLDER METHODOLOGICAL DEBATES

Governance is not a legal concept. Its intellectual *Heimat* can be traced to international relations theory and practice.[4] Reflections by lawyers on practices characterised as governance will hence have to be interdisciplinary. The quest for interdisciplinarity is *en vogue*. Compliance with it, however, remains difficult. As far as the interaction between legal and political science is concerned, we have to remain aware of the fact that each of our disciplines subscribes to a logic of its own; political science preoccupies itself mainly with explanations, legal science primarily with the interpretation of authorised texts and the elaboration of dogmatics. We also have to bear in mind that the practices which the term refers to differ from the forms of administrative and governmental action presumed in the inherited legal concepts of administrative and constitutional law. The re-conceptualisation of 'foreign' concepts, in legal terms, can be sharpened through the lens of systems theory.[5] For its main interlocutor, the discourse

[4] JN Rosenau, 'Governance, Order, and Change in World Politics' in JN Rosenau and E-O Czempiel (eds), *Governance without Government: Order and Change in World Politics* (Cambridge: CUP, 1992) 1.

[5] See G Teubner, Netzwerk als Vertragsverbund. Virtuelle Unternehmen, Franchising, Just-in-time in sozialwissenschaftlicher und juristischer Sicht (Nomos: Baden-Baden, 2004) at 17 ff.

theory of law,[6] a fundamental question arises: will the law, if it adopts and consecrates those practices, have to redesign the understanding of validity which is characteristic of constitutional democracies? If it cannot retain these validity standards, are there any conceivable criteria that shape national and transnational practices in such a way that, to use yet another formula from Habermas, they '*deserve recognition*'?[7] Can we, using a term yet to be analysed, 'constitutionalise' modern *praxis*?

Legal science in Germany has reacted with quite understandable hesitancy towards the change to governance, so emphatically proclaimed by the Prodi Commission.[8] Since then the debate at national level has intensified considerably, at least in Germany. We are not reconstructing these efforts here because they still presuppose the existence and appropriateness of a comprehensive legal and political system. One theoretical and methodological feature of these efforts, however, deserves to be underlined. Pertinent contributions (see, notably, Trute *et al*, 2004; Schuppert, 2005; Franzius, 2006) seek to identify governance practices according to a normatively (constitutionally) accredited context and they are considered analytically, as compensations for the failure of traditional command and control regulatory policies;[9] their methodologies seek to provide normative guidance for the adoption of new governance practices.[10] Core theoretical and methodological assumptions of these debates are by no means specifically national. They concern the rule of law as such and, in particular, the idea of law-bound and law-legitimated rule (*Herrschaft*), the exercise of power over the governed through governance – and it is these *leitmotivs* which should be taken seriously also at European level.

[6] J Habermas, *Between Facts and Norms* (Cambridge MA: The MIT Press, 1998).

[7] J Habermas, 'Remarks on Legitimation through Human Rights' in P de Greiff and C Cronin (eds), *Global Justice and Transnational Politics* (Cambridge MA: The MIT Press, 2002) 197, at 198; emphasis in the original.

[8] This is common tendency of the contributions to C Joerges, Y Mény, and JHH Weiler (eds), 'Mountain or Molehill? A Critical Appraisal of the Commission White Paper on Governance' (European University Institute/Robert Schumann Centre and NYU School of Law-Jean Monnet Center, 2001), available at: www.jeanmonnetprogram.org/papers/01/012201.html.

[9] R Mayntz, 'Governance Theorie als fortentwickelte Steuerungstheorie' in GF Schuppert (ed), *Governance-Forschung. Vergewisserung über Stand und Entwicklungslinien* (Baden-Baden: Nomos, 2005) 11.

[10] 'Governance through Regulatory Structures' (*Regelungsstrukturen)*, the formula coined by GF Schuppert, 'Governance im Spiegel der Wissenschaftsdisziplinen' in idem (ed), *Governance-Forschung. Vergewisserung über Stand und Entwicklungslinien* (Baden-Baden: Nomos, 2005) 371–469, that has now become influential (see C Franzius, 'Governance und Regelungsstrukturen' (2006) 97 *Verwaltungsarchiv* 186–219, with references), postulates a connection between the legal problems of structure and methodology in a form that no doubt corresponds to the move towards proceduralisation of law addressed in Part 2 below. In Part 3, however, we shall be concerned with specific features of the European polity that have led to the adoption of governance practices in Europe; in order to cope with them legally, the patterns developed in the context of our national states must be recast. The most thorough inquiry I am aware of is by C Franzius, *Gewährleistungsrecht. Grundfragen eines europäischen Regelungsmodells öffentlicher Dienstleistungen* (Tübingen: Mohr Siebeck, 2008), esp at 564 ff.

I should like to recall a related commonality, namely the legal theory criticism made in the 1980s regarding political and legal interventionism and the ensuing search for concepts of a 'post-interventionist' law. The disappointment at the ineffectiveness of legal 'purposive programmes' (*Zweckprogramme*)[11] and the concerns about 'colonisation of the lifeworld' by social policy programmes along with their conversion to administrative law[12] were, at the time, developed simultaneously and in critical equidistance. A common feature was the perception that economic and social processes are embedded in a much more complex way in modern societies than is indicated by the dichotomies that pitted market and state, economy and intervention, law and economics in (quasi-) oppositional relations. What was sought was a new legal rationality to replace social state interventionism and its 'material' ('substantive') rationality of law, without retreating into classical legal formalism and having to endure the associated weaknesses in relation to forms of economic and social power.[13] The new rationality of law was intended additionally to unmask the myth that law could cope with social reality by 'applying' social theories. The 'proceduralisation' of the category of law[14] and the concept of 'reflexive' law[15] were the new antagonistically disposed torchbearers.[16] Both tendencies dealt with numerous dimensions of the practice of law; with shortcomings in implementation, alternatives to

[11] N Luhmann, *Rechtssoziologie, Band II* (Reinbek bei Hamburg: Rowohlt, 1972) at 227 ff.

[12] J Habermas, Theorie des kommunikativen Handelns. Band II. Zur Kritik der funktionalistischen Vernunft (Frankfurt aM: Suhrkamp, 1981) at 522 ff.

[13] The common reference point of all debates in Germany were the pertinent passages in M Weber, *Rechtssoziologie*, ed J Winckelmann, 2nd edn (Neuwied-Berlin: Luchterhand, 1967) 123–126 and 329–343. These categories proved to be of long-term and trans-national significance (see D Kennedy, 'The Disenchantment of Logically Formal Legal Rationality, or Max Weber's Sociology in the Genealogy of the Contemporary Mode of Western Legal Thought' (2004) 55 *Hastings Law Journal* 1031).

[14] Wiethölter developed the category of proceduralisation in his analysis of the litigation on the constitutionality of Germany's co-determination act; see R Wiethölter, 'Entwicklung des Rechtsbegriffs (am Beispiel des BVG-Urteils zum Mitbestimmungsgesetz und – allgemeiner – an Beispielen des sog. Sonderprivatrechts)' in V Gessner and G Winter (eds), *Rechtsformen der Verflechtung von Staat und Wirtschaft* (Opladen: Westdeutscher Verlag, 1982) 38; idem, 'Materialisierungen und Prozeduralisierungen von Recht' in G Brüggemeier and C Joerges (eds), *Workshop zu Konzepten des postinterventionistischen Rechts* (Zentrum für Europäische Rechtspolitik, Materialien 4, Bremen, 1984) 25 [see A Fischer-Lescano and G Teubner, 'Prozedurale Rechtstheorie: Wiethölter' in S Buckel, R Christensen and A Fischer-Lescano (eds), *Neue Theorien des Rechts* (Stuttgart: Lucius and Lucius, 2006) 79]. Habermas took up the notion systematically in his *Faktizität und Geltung* (Frankfurt aM: Suhrkamp, 1992) at 516–540 [*Between Facts and Norms* (cited in n 6 above), at 427–446].

[15] G Teubner, 'Substantive and Reflexive Elements in Modern Law' (1983) 17 *Law and Society Review* 239.

[16] 'Proceduralisation' is widely understood as a soft substitute of hard law. Such a loose use of the term is simply incompatible with its theoretical origins. For a helpful re-construction of this background, see JL Cohen, *Regulating Intimacy: A New Legal Paradigm* (Princeton NJ: Princeton UP, 2002) 151; and, for its transposition into the debate on European constitutionalism, M Everson and J Eisner, *The Making of a European Constitution: Judges and Law beyond Constitutional Power* (Abingdon–New York: Routledge-Cavendish, 2007) 214 ff.

hierarchical 'command and control' regulations, alternatives to strict judicial settlement of disputes, the pros and cons of 'soft' alternatives to 'hard' law – and with the core problem of the current governance debate: how can the law retain its legitimising functions once it is recognised that problem-solving will require the cooperation of politically accountable bodies with societal actors, whilst serving as a 'cognitive opening' of legal discourses so as to ensure that scientific expertise and practical societal knowledge can come to bear in legal decision-making?

Déjà vu? Perhaps more precisely: the 80s revisited! After the change to governance, all the above-mentioned questions need to be asked again or, at least, be kept on the agenda. Is one irritation merely replacing another; is one fashion enormously rich in facets being replaced by a new trend? Historians of law with inclinations towards conceptual history may be able to clarify that. However, I wish to content myself by stressing three continuities which, in my opinion, are of utmost importance in the transition to the 'European level of governance':

1. One typical feature of governance arrangements is the usage of expert knowledge, not just, say, scientific knowledge, as is necessary for risk policy, but all sorts of expert know-how that may serve to solve and manage problems. This is a very old phenomenon, widespread even in national states. Wolfgang Schluchter[17] described it in terms of Weber's distinction between *Amtsautorität* and *Sachautorität*, respectively; institutionally derived authority as opposed to authority based upon specific expertise.
2. If the administration cannot content itself with carrying out of tasks in the execution of norm-programmes, then the involvement of society as the provider of expert knowledge will be required. This is a facility which the administration does not possess. It then seems also appropriate to incorporate social actors in tasks aimed at executing public functions, not just because of their expert knowledge but in order to employ their management capacities.
3. Of crucial importance for the arguments below is a phenomenon known in the tradition of American *Critical Legal Studies* as the law's 'indeterminacy'[18] and 'fragmentation'.[19] From a systems theory viewpoint, Helmut Willke[20] coined the term 'complex conflict situations' (*komplexe*

[17] W Schluchter, Aspekte bürokratischer Herrschaft. Studien zur Interpretation der fortschreitenden Industriegesellschaft (Frankfurt aM: Suhrkamp, 1972/reprint 1985) 145-176.

[18] D Kennedy, 'Freedom and Constraint in Adjudication: A Critical Phenomenology' (1986) 36 *Journal of Legal Education* 518; M Koskenniemi, *From Apology to Utopia: The Structure of International Legal Argument* (Helsinki: Finnish Lawyers' Pub 1989; re-issue with a new Epilogue, Cambridge: CUP, 2005).

[19] M Koskenniemi, 'Constitutionalism as Mindset: Reflections on Kantian Themes about International Law and Globalization' (2006) 8 *Theoretical Inquiries in Law* 9.

[20] H Willke, Entzauberung des Staates. Überlegungen zu einer gesellschaftlichen Steuerungstheorie (Königstein/Ts: Athäneum, 1983) at 26; idem, Ironie des Staates (Frankfurt aM: Suhrkamp, 1992) at 177 ff.

> *Konfliktlagen*), to which the 'supervisory state ought to respond with "relational programmes" (*Relationierungsprogramme*)'.[21] His findings can also be described in more conventional terms. There are problems for which various competences have to be coordinated, and there may be conflicts among the objectives of political programmes in force, the solution to which is not pre-programmed anywhere.

This third aspect points to the unavoidability and difficulty of the proceduralisation of law. Coordination efforts of the type just mentioned are *de facto* brought about in 'discovery procedures of practice'.[22] What normative qualities do such responses have? Under what conditions do they 'deserve recognition'? Given that my focus is on Europe, I content myself with underlining affinities between the national and the post-national European constellation: even within national state legal systems, there is a need to decide between or to coordinate incompatible legal principles or conflicting objectives. The result of these cannot be pre-programmed in any substantive way. The outcomes of such processes must derive their legitimacy from the normative quality of the processes themselves. All of this brings the discourse theory of law into some embarrassment. Habermas took a seemingly traditionalist position in that respect:

> When faced with political decisions relevant to the whole of society, the State must be able to perceive, and if necessary assert, public interests as it has in the past. Even when it appears in the role of an intelligent advisor or supervisor who makes procedural law available, this kind of law-making must remain linked back to legislative programs in a transparent, comprehensible and controllable way.[23]

In the framework of the discourse theory of law this caveat is indispensable. Habermas highlights the necessity and difficulty of 'constitutionalising' decentralised production of law very clearly. The difficulty is two-fold: solutions to problems are dependent on *productive* performance by *social* actors, and therefore cannot be pre-programmed. The only procedural rules that can come into consideration have to extend to the consultation of governmental and non-governmental actors described brilliantly, if arcanely, in Wiethölter.[24] We shall return to this in the European context in Part 3.

[21] The resemblance of this to the Open Method of Coordination (discussed at the end of Part 2) and to its terminology are both striking. Relational programmes ought not to programme contents, and their supervision must be correspondingly reticent.

[22] On that notion, see C Joerges, 'Quality Regulation in Consumer Goods Markets: Theoretical Concepts and Practical Examples' in T Daintith and G Teubner (eds), *Contract and Organization* (Berlin: de Gruyter, 1986) 142.

[23] *Between Facts and Norms* (cited in n 6 above) at 441.

[24] R Wiethölter, 'Just-ifications of a Law of Society' in O Perez and G Teubner (eds), *Paradoxes and Inconsistencies in the Law* (Oxford: Hart Publishing, 2005) 65, available at: www.jura.uni-frankfurt.de/ifawz1/teubner/RW.html.

PART 2: NEW AND NOT SO NEW FORMS OF EUROPEAN GOVERNANCE: A CHRONOLOGY

Officially, unmistakeably and with far-reaching practical political ambitions, the change to governance in Europe was instigated under the aegis of the Prodi Commission.[25] Now, law and legal science cannot simply allow themselves to be impressed by a fine-sounding political agenda authorised from on high. In the White Paper on governance[26] itself, there are very clear traces of legal-technical opposition to the 'modernisation' of the traditional community method inspired by political and administrative science out of commitment to that method.[27] These communication difficulties very clearly reflect the differences between the disciplines involved, addressed above. The following section will be structured according to these differences. It will not commence with one of the definitions of governance that have by now been developed,[28] but will follow the development of European practice, and only then will it go on to ask whether this 'deserves recognition' (Part 3).

The law has taken a markedly pragmatic attitude towards the change to governance. Those who embraced the change at an initial stage were not economic or sociology think-tanks, but practitioners, officials and judges who considered themselves as being forced to operate in the shadow of and behind the back of the treaties. They soon did what has always typified the practice of law: the practice of normally going about things unspectacularly, but always remaining conscious of the need to clothe even far-reaching innovations in the conceptual garb of the established community method or at least present them as prosaic application of rules of adjudication. It was only in the course of implementing the 1985 internal market White Paper[29] that this reticence was gradually dropped. Options that had 'emerged' became approaches and regulatory models.

The gamut of forms of European governance that has been established over and above the traditional community method has increased considerably.

[25] B Kohler-Koch and B Rittberger, '"The Governance Turn" in European Studies' (2006) 44 *JCMS* 27.

[26] European Commission, 'European Governance: A White Paper', cited in n 1 above.

[27] C Joerges, 'The Commission's White Paper on Governance in the EU: A Symptom of Crisis?', Guest Editorial, (2002) 39 *CMLR* 441.

[28] This form of descriptive approximation admittedly does not provide some analytically satisfying concept of governance. However, the way legal practice introduces innovations and legal science reflects them is not subject to the methodological discipline of political science. The turn away from the 'community method' and the development of alternative forms of governance displays an exemplary course: (1) Practice 'discovers' an undeniable need and 'acts'. (2) The interested parties and the academic experts become aware of these irregularities and endeavour to link them back to established positions of law. (3) The more hopeless such efforts appear, the more prospects there are for theoretical and methodological innovations and even interdisciplinary approaches. See, very instructively, P Craig, *EU Administrative Law* (Oxford: OUP, 2006).

[29] 'Completing the Internal Market. White Paper from the Commission to the European Council', COM(85) 310 final of 14.06.85.

Lawyers are accustomed to seeking an overview to orient themselves through institutionalised forms of action, and are thus ignoring refined and subtle differentiations which are capable of distinguishing between five modes of governance.

A. Comitology

The European committee system is the oldest form of 'new' governance. It arose where complex European governance incorporating national actors first became indispensable, namely in agricultural policy.[30] In the course of the expansion and intensification of the Europeanisation process, the rise of the committee system became unstoppable. 'Comitology' is the technical legal term for those committees entrusted with the implementation of Community law framework provisions. Through these committees, made up of representatives of the Member States and experts appointed by them, the Commission organises a Community (ie, overarching and cooperative) administration of the internal market in such policy areas as food safety, safety of technical products and safety at work. The committee system has to compensate for the Community's lack of genuine administrative powers and guarantees. It ensures the accountability of the Commission-driven European administrative machinery to the Member States – not to the European Parliament, which for decades has striven for a strengthening of its institutional powers. By incorporating national bodies, however, it also promotes the acceptance of European rules in Member States. The committees perform the detailed work on reducing the functional and structural tensions of the internal market project. Even though, for the most part, the issues at stake seem purely technical, they may have important economic implications and politically sensitive dimensions. Thus comitology can be characterised as a mediator of functional requirements and normative concerns. The changing composition of the committees follows from the task of balancing differing sorts of technical knowledge and regulatory concerns and bringing them into some sort of synthesis. It also, however, reflects the multiplicity of interests and political differences that have to be reconciled in the implementation process. The committees often act like 'mini-councils'; they act as venues for mediation between market integration and Member States' concerns, and reliable indications suggest that their discussions take place objectively and deliberatively.[31]

[30] J Falke, 'Komitologie – Entwicklung, Rechtsgrundlagen und erste empirische Annäherung' in C Joerges and J Falke (eds), *Das Ausschusswesen der Europäischen Union. Praxis der Risikoregulierung im Binnenmarkt und ihre rechtliche Verfassung* (Baden-Baden: Nomos, 2000) 43.

[31] For more details, see C Joerges and J Neyer, 'From Intergovernmental Bargaining to Deliberative Political Processes: The Constitutionalisation of Comitology' (1997) 3 *ELJ* 273. Strikingly enough, the intense debate on comitology, and in particular the many critical voices, hardly ever touch upon the socio-economic implications of the system, even though their importance is obvious – and will become even more important with the accession of Eastern European states. This silence can be explained through an understanding of the internal market as a sphere without economic

B. The Principle of Mutual Recognition as a Governance Practice

Following the legendary *Cassis* decision of the Court of Justice,[32] the Commission, in a 1980 communication seeking to explain this judgment, presented the view that it should follow from the principle of mutual recognition developed by the Court of Justice that Europe could henceforth find the 'better law' through a competition of legal systems so that law-making had to take a correspondingly reticent stance.

However, such communication was wishful thinking that the practice of internal market policy neither could nor would follow. It could not because the assumption that processes arising from mutual observation by legal systems and the upholding of freedoms of European market citizens could be understood as a competitive discovery procedure was based on far too heroic premises. The pertinent Court of Justice jurisprudence was more sensitive and cautious, notwithstanding its constitutionalising ambitions. The Court of Justice assumed the role of a constitutional court. However, it undertook such role with prudent self-restraint and in a manner congruent with and inherent in the integration project. Member States were not confronted with 'positive' prescription but instead asked to present the justification for their regulatory concerns and urged to ensure their compatibility with Community objectives as far as possible.[33] Since this process of clarification, the debate on mutual recognition has become more intensive and more interesting.[34] The Court's caution need not be interpreted as some arrangement with the political power of the Member States. Its jurisprudence was – most of the time – normatively convincing, specifically in the area of internal market policy, because of questions of political sensitivity which political systems ought not simply leave to some invisible hand.

The Court of Justice's case law resulted, instead, in an opening of national legal systems to internal criticism in the area of fundamental freedoms. Such criticism was, however, able to apply viewpoints from other jurisdictions to support its arguments. National legislatures have to justify the reasonableness of their own laws before their own courts and before the Court of Justice. European law provides criteria for this – such as appropriateness and proportionality – and obliges Member States to take into account their neighbours' concerns. This proceduralisation of law does not imply that Europe's citizens

asymmetries of normative significance. It became apparent especially in the BSE crisis that this premise could be all too fictitious. Europe had to tolerate and to support compensatory measures which British farmers were unable to bear. Speaking in more positive terms, comitology operates on the premise that safety concerns should, in principle, be insulated from socio-economic concerns.

[32] Case C-120/78, *Rewe Zentrale v Bundesmonopolverwaltung für Branntwein (Cassis de Dijon)* [1979] ECR 649.

[33] M Poiares Maduro, *We the Court: The European Court of Justice and the European Economic Constitution* (Oxford: Hart Publishing, 1998) at 150 ff.

[34] V Mayer-Schönberger and A Somek (eds), 'Governing Regulatory Interaction. The Normative Question' (2006) 12 *ELJ* 431; K Nikolaïdes and SK Schmidt, 'Mutual Recognition as a New Mode of Governance' (2007) 14 *JEPP* 667.

are allowed to choose whatever law seems most favourable to their particular interests thus replacing legal policy debates about the proper law by a competition of legal systems.[35]

C. The 'New Approach' to Technical Harmonisation and Standards: 'Private Transnationalism'

The (success) story of the 'New Approach' has been re-constructed often enough.[36] It suffices here to recall only the following; efforts to remove non-tariff barriers to trade had placed the EEC in dilemmas because, being caught up in the paradigm of 'integration through law', it wanted to create the internal market by harmonising the relevant norms of Member States. This called for 'positive' legislative acts to an extent that would have outdone Sisyphus. The replacement of the old unanimity rule of Article 100 EEC by qualified majority decisions in 1987 (then Article 100a, now Article 95 EC), brought about little change. Again, transposing the mutual recognition obligation which resulted from the *Cassis* decision[37] proved tricky in practice in individual cases, and was basically inadequate for making broader changes. Typically, the formally private sets of standards which, particularly in Germany, fleshed out product safety requirements were no less integration-averse. Given the definition of these sub-legal product standards as non-mandatory, merely private obstacles to trade, the Community was impotent to act through harmonisation measures. The cunning in the New Approach was concealed in a package of interrelated measures: European law-making had a large burden taken away from it, essentially by henceforth contenting itself with laying down 'essential safety requirements'. Fleshing these out was delegated to experts from European and national standardisation organisations well used to dealing with each other. In practice, the inclusion of non-state actors meant 'a delegation' of legislative powers that obviously could not be admitted openly. The protagonists of the New Approach had to operate it with the fiction that the 'essential safety requirements' adequately programmed the work of the standardisation organisations.

D. Agencies: The Politicisation of Administrative Action

Independent agencies were the institutional core of Giandomenico Majone's ideas for steering the EU in the direction of a 'regulatory state'.[38] Majone's suggestions were never transposed one-to-one. While Europe took over the

[35] For the exemplary case of company law, see C Joerges, 'Europeanization as Process: Thoughts on the Europeanization of Private Law' (2005) 11 *European Public Law* 62, at 74–77.

[36] Brilliantly recently by H Schepel, *The Constitution of Private Governance: Product Standards in the Regulation of Integrating Markets* (Oxford: Hart Publishing, 2005) at 37 ff.

[37] Cited in n 32 above.

[38] G Majone, 'The Rise of the Regulatory State in Europe' (1994) 17 *West European Politics* 77.

terminology he had brought from the US, and also created – and continues to establish – an impressive number of institutions that were termed agencies, it is plainly visible that these new European agencies share only nomenclature with their American namesakes, the independent regulatory agencies. They are not self-sufficient administrative units, and have no law-making powers. They are concerned with licensing procedures, for instance for medicaments, or with general, informal tasks of gathering and disseminating information, which merely guide or accompany 'real' politics. The new European agencies, thus, as it were, fulfil the need for market-correcting, sector-specific regulations indirectly, or – in line with the European Commission's conceptual notions – merely as executive organs working under the Commission's political control. Correspondingly, it is assumed in many unofficial announcements that the agencies can do their jobs 'technocratically'. In fact, this conception accords with their semi-autonomous status. It is also entirely compatible with their function of assisting the stakeholders of internal market policy in articulating their interests. It is equally compatible with the position that the administration of the internal market has more to do with 'neutral' support for business activities than with laying down and implementing political and social programmes. However, the legal treatment of the agencies as mere auxiliary organs is nonetheless insufficient, if not indeed misleading. Despite their formal subordination and despite membership of representatives of national authorities on their management bodies, the agencies seem, thanks to their founding charters (Council Regulations and Directives), their organisational stability, the relative autonomy of their budgets (taking different shapes in individual cases), and their networking with national administrations, to be very well protected from direct, explicit political influences.[39] Admittedly, all these ties also imply that the agencies cannot develop their programmes but constitute a reorganised comitology, the powers of which are *de jure* confined to the form of the advisory committee. Their *de facto* functions in the decision-making process become a different matter as the Commission succeeds increasingly in its efforts to centralise expert advice in these bodies and to downgrade the role of national bodies.[40]

E. The Open Method of Coordination (OMC): 'Farewell to Law?'

The so-called OMC[41] cannot, as far as its record of success is concerned, be compared with the forms of governance mentioned so far. Nonetheless, since

[39] M Everson, 'Control of Executive Acts: The Procedural Solution. Proportionality, State of the Art Decision-Making and Relevant Interests' in D Curtin and AE Kellermann and S Blockmans (eds), *EU Constitution: The Best Way Forwards* (The Hague: Asser Press, 2005) 181.

[40] See, for an exemplary study, M Kritikos, *EU Policy-Making on GMOs: The False Promise of Proceduralism* (Basingstoke: Palgrave Macmillan, 2018); see also the remarks in Part 3 D on 'Prospects'.

[41] The quotation marks in the heading above are meant to serve as a reminder: R Voigt (ed), *Abschied vom Recht?* (Frankfurt aM: Suhrkamp, 1983).

the introduction of the new Title VIII on employment in the Amsterdam Treaty and after the Lisbon European Council's recommendation to apply the OMC in areas of social policy, it attracted great attention and became regarded as the new mode of governance *par excellence*.[42] The OMC's popularity is attributed to the fact that it appears to be helpful in areas where political actors feel considerable pressure to act but in which the treaty offers them no legislative powers, and anyway, little could be done using traditional Community methods. The primary cause of lawyers' conceptual and methodological headaches can be traced to the mode of action: the legal enforceability of legislative and administrative actions have been replaced in the coordination process by a procedure of multilateral supervision through which, on the basis of guidelines or benchmarks laid down by the European Council, the Council and the Commission, mutual systematic monitoring (multilateral surveillance) and assessment of the performance of the individual governments in the Council (peer review) take place. Public support for this policy coordination and comparison of best practices are intended to provide the necessary incentives to ensure success and performance which would inevitably lead to adaptation and change of national policies at Member State level.[43] No judicial protection is provided against this sort of political dominance, still less constitutional review thereof. Similar measures would, after all, appear downright dysfunctional if political action were to be exercised outside powers provided for in constitutional and European law, (be it) in social, educational policy, or harmonisation of civil law in Europe.

PART 3: A NEW TYPE OF SUPRANATIONAL CONFLICT OF LAWS AS EUROPE'S CONSTITUTIONAL FORM

The reasons adduced for the development of the paralegal practice of European governance are fairly well known from criticisms of interventionist law, which deserve to be taken seriously: we need to address complex conflict situations that cannot be dealt with centrally or hierarchically; at best, the law can provide a framework within which solutions to problems may be sought. Two features of the European system cause additional difficulties: Even where the nation state is not capable of programming solutions to problems and implementing its legislation through an administrative vertically stratified administration, nonetheless its integrative power, a requisite for consistent problem-solving, is stronger than that of the European multilevel system. In Europe, the law needs to adapt to

[42] See the references in n 3 above.

[43] For an instructive recent state-of-the-art report, see B Laffan and C Shaw, 'Classifying and Mapping OMCs in Different Policy Areas', *NewGov paper*, 02/D09, 2005, available at: www.eu-newgov.org/database/DELIV/D02D09_Classifying_and_Mapping_OMC.pdf. Political scientists seem to be more open to the method than lawyers, Anglo-Saxons less sceptical than German political scientists; see, quite typically, A Schäfer, *Die neue Unverbindlichkeit. Wirtschaftspolitische Koordinierung in Europa* (Frankfurt aM-New York: Campus, 2005) at 190 ff.

mediation between various levels of competence with legal ties that are weaker than in a federal system. European law also needs to accept the (relative) autonomy of its sub-units. The appropriate response to this difficulty is not to dissolve the law but, as we shall seek to show below, to re-conceptualise European law as a new type of supranational conflict of laws. Conflict-of-laws responses may require a cognitively open and more reflexive approach. The mere description of the practices of European governance here generates a trend that political scientists evidently find less irritating than do lawyers: the forms of governance that Europe uses were not provided for, or not 'that way' in the treaties. This retreat to extra-legal forms of action goes, in the case of the OMC, as far as governance with*out* the range of competences in the Treaty; and then it also tries to get by without law at all. Again, we will argue that this will amount to a case of throwing the baby out with the bathwater. It is conceivable within a conflict-of-laws model to provide for the integration of scientific and practical expertise without replacing the rule of law with some technocratic regime but with the aim of elaborating solutions on which politically accountable actors are able to agree at least provisionally.

A. *Unitas in Pluralitate*: First Order European Law of Conflict (Deliberative Supranationalism I)

The answer to the first difficulty stems from a proposal developed by Jürgen Neyer and the present author more than 10 years ago when we called for the introduction of 'Deliberative Supranationalism' in European law instead of the traditional or orthodox version[44] – an approach we continue to defend and develop.[45] Deliberative Supranationalism was developed on the example of a then theoretically neglected but a (relatively) venerable practice, namely comitology. Comitology, we found, in fact functioned far better than its opaque appearance might suggest. We did not assert that the deliberative processes we had observed in transnational bodies could, in themselves, be democratic or ensure the type of legitimacy constitutional democracies can provide; still less did we suggest a transnational functional bureaucracy as a mode of good European governance. We wanted instead to evade the usual debate about Europe's democratic deficit by inverting the usual perception of Europe's legitimacy dilemma. Rather than complaining that Europe did not fulfil/meet the standards of democratic constitutional states, we suggested that European law could be legitimated because of its potential to cure structural democracy failures of the national states.

[44] C Joerges and J Neyer, 'From Intergovernmental Bargaining to Deliberative Political Processes', cited in n 31 above.

[45] C Joerges and J Neyer, '"Deliberative Supranationalism" Revisited' (2016) 44 *JCMS* 779; see, also, C Joerges, 'Rethinking European Law's Supremacy: A Plea for a Supranational Conflict of Laws' in B Kohler-Koch and B Rittberger (eds), *Debating the Democratic Legitimacy of the European Union* (Lanham MD: Rowman & Littlefield, 2007) 311.

The central argument may date back to Rousseau[46] and is not as idiosyncratic as our terminology:

> The legitimacy of governance within constitutional states is flawed in so far as it remains inevitably one-sided and parochial or selfish. The taming of the national state through democratic constitutions has its limits. [If and, indeed, because] democracies presuppose and represent collective identities, they have very few mechanisms to ensure that 'foreign' identities and their interests are taken into account within their decision-making processes.[47]

If the legitimacy of supranational institutions can be designed so as to cure these deficiencies – as a correction of national state failures, as it were – they may then derive their legitimacy from this compensatory function. In a recent re-statement:

> We must conceptualise supranational constitutionalism as an alternative to the model of the constitutional national state which respects that state's constitutional legitimacy but, at the same time, clarifies and sanctions the commitments arising from its interdependence with equally democratically legitimised states and with the supranational prerogatives that an institutionalisation of this interdependence requires.[48]

That is of course not the way the supranational validity of European law was originally understood and justified.[49] Fortunately enough, however, the methodologically and theoretically bold and practically successful constitutionalising decision[50] can be rationalised in this way. The European 'federation' thus found a legal constitution that did not have to strive towards Europe's becoming a state but was able to derive its legitimacy from the fact that it compensates for the democratic deficits of the national states. This is precisely the point of Deliberative Supranationalism. Existing European law had, we argued, rendered valid principles and rules that deserve supranational recognition because they constitute a palpable community project. All one has to do is look: Community members cannot implement their interests or laws unconstrainedly, they are obliged to respect the European freedoms, are not allowed to discriminate, they can pursue only legitimate regulatory policies approved/blessed by the Community; they must, in relation to the objectives they wish to pursue through regulation, be in harmony with each other and they must reform their national systems in the most community-friendly way possible. This kind of law, we said, was not undemocratic but was compensating for the national state's democratic deficits. The legal form through which such objectives can be achieved can be found in the methodology of conflict of laws. Conflict of laws is an old discipline with

[46] R Grant and RA Keohane, 'Accountability and Abuses of Power in World Politics' (2005) 99 *American Political Science Review* 29.

[47] Joerges and Neyer, 'From Intergovernmental Bargaining to …' (cited in n 31 above) at 293.

[48] Joerges, '"Deliberative Political Processes" Revisited', n 45 above, at 790.

[49] See JHH Weiler, 'The Community System: The Dual Character of Supranationalism' (1981) 1 *Yearbook of European Law* 257.

[50] Case 26/62 *Van Gend en Loos v Nederlandse Administratie der Belastingen* [1963] ECR 1.

multi-faceted traditions. Its 'modern' era (which began in Germany in 1849[51]) is itself full of nationalist prejudices to the extent that in international situations, it seeks to pronounce one of the legal systems with which the case has an applicable relation. That tradition of conflict of laws (private international law; international administrative law) denies application of any foreign public law *a priori* and determines the scope of its own public law unilaterally. It is the paradigm example of 'methodological nationalism'.[52] However, thoughts pertaining to conflict of laws have one further instructive potential: it can be applied in any situation where legal principles differing in content and objectives come up against each other and have to be coordinated within a legal system or in its external relations. The views of those who use the conflict-of-laws terminology[53] are by no means uniform. However, they agree in their perception that legal responses to conflicting claims of democratically legitimised legal systems need to be conceptualised in conflict-of-laws terms and be based on a proceduralisation of the category of law. European law of conflict of laws has to be understood as a 'law of law-making'.[54] This conflict-of-laws viewpoint retains the supranationality of European law, but gives it a new meaning. It takes away from European law the practical and legitimatory expectations it cannot reasonably expect to fulfil. At the same time, it opens a window on the manifold vertical, horizontal, and diagonal[55] conflict situations in the European multilevel system. It promotes the insight that the Europeanisation process should aim to achieve flexible, varied solutions to conflicts rather than strive for the perfection of an ever more comprehensive body of law.[56]

[51] The date of the publication of vol VIII of FC von Savigny, *System des heutigen Römischen Rechts* (Berlin: Veit und Comp, 1849).

[52] M Zürn, 'The State in the Post-national Constellation – Societal Denationalization and Multi-Level Governance' (Oslo: *ARENA Working Paper No 35/1999*).

[53] R Wiethölter, 'Begriffs- oder Interessenjurisprudenz – falsche Fronten im IPR und Wirtschaftsverfassungsrecht: Bemerkungen zur selbstgerechten Kollisionsnorm' in H-J Musielak and K Schurig (eds), *Festschrift für Gerhard Kegel zum 75 Geburtstag* (Stuttgart: Kohlhammer, 1987) 213; G Teubner, 'Der Umgang mit den Rechtsparadoxien: Derrida, Luhmann, Wiethölter' in C Joerges and G Teubner (eds), *Rechtsverfassungsrecht. Recht-Fertigung zwischen Privatrechtsdogmatik und Gesellschaftstheorie* (Baden-Baden: Nomos, 2003) 22; A Fischer-Lesacano and G Teubner, *Regime-Kollisionen. Zur Fragmentierung des globalen Rechts* (Frankfurt aM: Suhrkamp, 2006); K-H Ladeur, 'Die Bedeutung eines Allgemeinen Verwaltungsrechts für ein Europäisches Verwaltungsrecht' in T Groß, C Möllers, H-C Röhl and H-H Trute (eds), *Grundannahmen des Allgemeinen Verwaltungsrechts* (Tübingen: Mohr Siebeck, 2008) 795.

[54] FI Michelman, *Brennan and Democracy* (Princeton NJ: Princeton UP, 1999) at 34; see also R Wiethölter, 'Just-ifications of a Law of Society', cited in n 23 above.

[55] These conflicts emanate from the allocation of powers needed for problem-solving and therefore objectively connected to different levels of government [see CU Schmid, 'Diagonal Competence Conflicts between European Competition Law and National Law. The example of book price fixing' (2000) 8 *ERPL* 155]. It follows from the principle of limited individual empowerment that the primacy rule can find no application here.

[56] This is readily compatible with the existence of European secondary law and does not in any way in principle call its legitimacy into question. There are important problem areas in which 'second order' laws of conflict are insufficient and the 'federation' has to develop supranational substantive law. This question cannot be dealt with systematically here.

All of this is not just wishful thinking. Europe has long had available a legal system that binds the Community to a legal policy which respects the political autonomy of Member States, and the Member States to one compatible with Community demands.[57] Member States may not discriminate and must take their neighbours' concerns into account. European citizens can bring actions through which their home country is compelled to justify its legislation. In the more familiar language of the *acquis communautaire*, the states of the Union may conceive and apply their interests and laws as they see fit; but they are obliged to comply with the European freedoms; they may not discriminate; they may pursue only regulatory objectives recognised in Community law; in pursuing such objectives they must comply with the proportionality principle.[58]

B. The Juridification of European Governance Practices through Second Order Conflict of Laws (Deliberative Supranationalism II)

The plausibility of a law of conflict of laws interpretation of European governance practices seems obvious in case of mutual recognition, and the proceduralised version of this principle can be reconstructed in socio-legal terms (as 'managed mutual recognition'[59]). The conflict-of-laws interpretation of European law need not be restricted to this example. It is equally illuminating in the case of other forms of governance, specifically, comitology. The comitology procedures were developed in the course of the 'completion' of the internal market in order to keep the internal market project compatible with concerns of 'social regulation' (safety at work, consumer and environmental protection). The pertinent new framework legislation to be 'implemented' *via* comitology committees typically employs general clause type formulas that do not seek to program this coordination in detail but leave the elaboration of individual solutions to the implementation process. Typically, the problem situations concerned are ones in which expert knowledge has to be taken into account. It is the involvement of Member States through their representatives on the regulatory committees combined with discussions by a plural expert community that should guarantee

[57] See FW Scharpf, 'Community and Autonomy. Multilevel Policy-making in the European Union' (1994) 1 *JEPP* 219.

[58] I have to refrain here from any systematic discussion of the kind of political order Europe's *supranational* conflict of laws must require. It may suffice to refer to the recent *renaissance* of the notion of 'Bund' [see C Schönberger, 'Die Europäische Union als Bund. Zugleich ein Beitrag zur Verabschiedung des Staatenbund-Bundesstaats-Schemas' (2004) 129 *Archiv des öffentlichen Rechts* 81] and also to JHH Weiler's 'The Community System', cited in n 49 above, characterising the 'Principle of Tolerance' as the Union's *normative proprium*. Accepting and living with diversity is exactly what a supranational conflict of laws seeks to promote.

[59] K Nikolaïdes, 'Globalization with Human Faces: Managed Mutual Recognition and the Free Movement of Professionals' in F Kostoris Padoa Schioppa (ed), *The Principle of Mutual Recognition in the European Integration Process* (Basingstoke: Palgrave Macmillan, 2005) 190.

both political legitimacy and the objective viability of the regulations developed. Safeguard clause procedures employed when new knowledge is acquired or a regulation proves unsatisfactory, strengthen their normative and procedural qualities. A conflict-of-laws interpretation of this form of governance is appropriate because the coordination efforts aim at a solution which is acceptable to a Union of relatively autonomous states that have to get by without any hierarchically ordered or at least uniformly structured administrative apparatus. Admittedly, a 'constitutionalisation' of this machinery ensuring that it 'deserves recognition' has to find answers to a series of further questions: the appointment and function of the expert circles to be included in the decision-making process; ties with parliamentary bodies on the one hand and with civil society on the other; reversibility of decisions taken in the light of new knowledge or changes in social preferences. Last, but not least, one has to remain aware that these coordination media are not the proper modality for ethical concerns, nor capable of facilitating decisions with major distributional implications. Because of the complexity of these requirements, the oft-heard quests for a European administrative procedures based on the US model are hardly convincing.[60] They risk catalysing the strengthening of the executive in the European polity. '*The EU can currently be understood as a decentralized, territorially differentiated, transnational negotiation system dominated by elites*' – this generalising description of the Union by Ulrich Beck and Edgar Grande[61] captures *cum grano salis* the Comitology system well. The adequate prescriptive response to that finding is a conflict-of-laws approach rather than juridification strategies based on administrative law models.

C. Interim Summary

Summarising, we conclude that the European multilevel system is dependent on a law that guarantees its functioning, without, however, transforming the EU into a state or a state-like federation, or even only a comprehensive and unified legal order. Neither can this state of the Union be substantially changed, nor would such a change seem desirable. To use the fortunate formulation of the otherwise unfortunate Constitutional Treaty, 'unity in diversity' should be 'the motto of the Union'.[62] We feel encouraged to read: it is not the removal of diversity but instead respect for it that should characterise Europe. As far as the multiplicity of its legal traditions is concerned, it should be the ethos of 'unity in diversity' that constitutes the *proprium* of post-national EU law. The conflict-of-laws understanding of EU law is an interpretive precept

[60] See J Corkin, 'A Manifesto for the European Court: Democracy. Decentred Governance and the Process-Perfecting Judicial Shadow', PhD Thesis, EUI, Florence, 2007.

[61] U Beck and E Grande, *Cosmopolitan Europe* (Cambridge: CUP, 2007) at 53 (italics in original).

[62] Art I-8 of the Treaty on a Constitution for Europe, [2004] OJ C310/1.

intended to take into account solely these specific features. This new conflict of laws aims to 'proceed through proceduralisation', but is supranational hard law. It is intended truly to constitute Europe and thus stands in the tradition of 'integration through law'.

The complexity of this law is conditioned by the complexity of European governance arrangements whereby decisions are neither delegated to supranational expert bodies nor entrusted to the European Commission and cannot be referred back to national parliamentary bodies either, or brought under the ultimate responsibility of the European Parliament. There is no in-built guarantee that this system will arrive at a transnational consensus where contested issues arise. This, however, should not be interpreted as a disadvantage. The difficulty in delivering consensual decisions has its *fundamentum in re*. It really does seem reasonable to take no irreversible steps but to continue to organise national and transnational discourses in which political actors and expert bodies are involved and both civil society and the general public can be heard. To put it slightly differently: the conflict-of-laws interpretation of Europe takes its stance on diversity seriously. It does not provide for some invisible hand and ensures that 'autonomy-sparing, community compatible'[63] solutions to conflicts are not merely thought up but also implemented. It can only confirm the existence in the EU of pre-conditions favouring a deliberative form of political communication bound by rules and principles, which not only promotes a system whereby arguments are accepted only when those concerned can follow them because they do not merely strategically reformulate particular interests, but which is also realistic because it admits this fragility of the system.[64]

The same holds true for Europe's old and new governance practices. Whether a constitutionalisation of these processes is possible is an open question. The only conceivable forms of response whereby these processes can legally be accepted as worthy of recognition are of a procedural nature, namely: transparency, pluralism, opening of consultancy and decision processes, incremental juridification strategies and reversibility guarantees, respect for ethical reserves, evaluations by national and supranational parliamentary bodies. All the law can do is to promote the deliberative quality of the essential interchanges entailed in European governance; it cannot guarantee the success of these processes.

[63] 'Autonomieschonend und gemeinschaftsverträglich' is the title of the original version of FW Scharpf, 'Community and Autonomy. Multi-Level Policy-Making in the European Union' (1994) 1 *JEPP* 219. The English title does not capture the gist of his message.

[64] Here again the conflict-of-laws approach remains obliged to the tradition of 'integration through law', at any rate in the version that JHH Weiler developed with his dualism of legal supranationality and political intergovernmentalism (n 47 above). Nothing in this construction guaranteed the stability of the balance of the two modes of integration that Weiler diagnosed in the formative phase of the integration process.

D. Prospects

In the year 2000, M Rainer Lepsius[65] re-constructed the *Wandelverfassung* (adaptable constitution)[66] of the integration project as a history of institutionalisation of various rationality criteria. The term can be used to describe the various functions allotted to law in the chequered history of integration, in which the following three periods can be distinguished:

1. Integration through law, in which the Court of Justice, in contemplative Luxembourg, unobtrusively and successfully managed to write a 'constitutional charter' that was to endure through political crises, no doubt owed its integrative power to the fact that this charter contented itself with rules and principles that did not seek to impose any detailed programmes on the integration project, whether an economic neo-liberal pattern or a technocratic managerialism such as that conceived by Ipsen in his thesis on the purpose of association.[67]
2. A decisively economic approach came about later, in connection with the Delors Commission's internal market project when Europe's competitiveness and economic efficiency squeezed out the law, seen as too cumbersome – but only nonetheless to initiate an unexpectedly intensive re-regulation of the internal market.
3. The change to governance, proclaimed by the Prodi Commission, can be seen not only as an attempt to respond to the practices developed in the shadow of the internal market policy, but also as compensation for their pragmatic and legitimatory weaknesses, and a means of developing new prospects for a democratically-reformed 'system of European governance'.

As in the previous periods, we have to draw a distinction between proclaiming a programme and implementing it. The question regarding what is 'really' happening is [discussed in] 3,345 publications to be found at the CONNEX website.[68] One cannot obtain an overall picture of all this, far less engage in some sort of sophisticated assessment. Cassandra warnings are out of place. However, anyone who takes the idea of law-mediated legitimacy seriously cannot refrain from articulating a number of concerns about the European move to governance:

1. Jürgen Neyer and the present author surprisingly discovered more than a decade ago,[69] during our studies on the foodstuffs sector (not the

[65] MR Lepsius, 'Die Europäische Union als rechtlich konstituierte Verhaltensstrukturierung' in H Dreier (ed), *Rechtssoziologie am Ende des 20. Jahrhunderts. Gedächtnissymposion für Edgar Michael Wenz* (Tübingen: Mohr Siebeck, 2000) 289.

[66] HP Ipsen, 'Europäische Verfassung – Nationale Verfassung' [1987] Europarecht 195, at 201.

[67] HP Ipsen, *Europäisches Gemeinschaftsrecht* (Tübingen: Mohr/Siebeck, 1972) at 197 ff; on this tradition, see M Kaufmann, *Europäische Integration und Demokratieprinzip* (Baden-Baden: Nomos, 1997) at 174 ff.

[68] See n 2 above.

[69] 'From Intergovernmental Bargaining to …', cited in n 31 above.

agricultural sector, especially not its veterinary compartments), that the comitology system was then operating sensibly. We had observed debates between competing schools of thought, serious discussions of public interests and strategies of risk management. We concluded that it was advisable to develop a legal framework that would stabilise these practices and correct the Kafkaesque features of comitology. Since then, much has happened. The Commission proposed new provisions in 2002,[70] which were taken into account in the Constitutional Treaty.[71] Quite recently, in July 2006, a Council Decision was adopted[72] which ushered in a reform. It strengthens Parliament's rights in areas which are subject to the co-decision procedure (Art 251 EC):[73] To that extent – but only to that extent – it removes one stumbling block in the regulatory Committee procedure, namely, the Commission's powers, the so-called *contre-filet* procedure. A comprehensive reform which could be called a proper constitutionalisation of comitology has not been accomplished. That would have required a reconsideration of what the Commission, Council and Parliament perceive as their institutional interests.

Is the new world of the agencies better? Until very recently, the most interesting example was the Food Safety Authority set up in 2002.[74] The fact that this agency is not empowered to take legal decisions (which would then be directly reviewable judicially) has already been noted. Its remit and its power are of a different nature. As stated in the 22nd Recital, it is supposed to strengthen 'the trust of consumers and trading partners'. How is this to come about? An instructive example is the design of the licensing procedure for genetically modified foodstuffs.[75] The agency here has to organise the best possible scientific assessment of permit applications. It organises bodies of knowledge that no decision-maker can overlook. Will it thereby be able to diminish the irritations of European consumers? The text of the Regulation itself does not back this up. Article 37(2) guarantees the independence of scientific advice from any external influence. By virtue of Article 37(1), members of the administrative board, the advisory board and the managing director are also independent. Their independence does not, however, serve to shield them in the same way as it shields science; it is supposed to oblige them to act 'in the public interest'. This is a concept that opens up the political dimensions of the foodstuffs market. It is no

[70] COM(2002) 719 final of 11 December 2002.

[71] See Arts 36–37 and the recommendations of the WG IX of the Conv (together with the Amato Report – CONV 424/02; http://european-convention.eu.int). K Bradley, 'Halfway House: The 2006 Comitology Reforms' (2008) 31 *West European Politics* 837.

[72] Council Resolution 2006/512/EC 17.7.2006, [2006] OJ L200/11; consolidated version in [2006] OJ C255/4.

[73] Art 5a ('Regulatory Committee Procedure with Scrutiny').

[74] Regulation 187/02, [2002] OJ L31/1.

[75] P Dabrowska-Klosinka, *EU Governance of GMOs* (Oxford: Hart Publishing, 2016) ch 4; Kritikos, EU Policy-Making on GMOs', n 40 above, esp ch 7.

coincidence that the composition of the administrative board (Article 25), advisory board (Article 27) and the regulations on scientific consultancy (Article 28) again show the triad we are familiar with from comitology procedures.

Article 37(1) of the Regulation not only guarantees the independence of those bodies but obliges them to act 'in the public interest'. In the institutionalisation of independence, of the public mandate and of the framework conditions of agency action, Everson observes fascinating prospects for a 'political administration' of the internal market in which the law can assert itself:

> Within a context of 'arguing' rather than 'bargaining', a political administration might identify the appropriate basis for regulatory self-restraint; the context specific primacy of competing public interests. In short, 'effective problem-solving' is a criterion that matches the Commission's desire to ensure the factual legitimacy of European regulatory bodies ... whilst deliberation augments the normative legitimacy functions of 'accountability', especially as regards the adequate representation of all civil society interests ... [T]he current genius of European law lies in the fact that, in view of the lack of conventional Constitution settlement, it has never been able simply to refer to outdated and inappropriate legal doctrines within its judgments, but has instead always been required to respond to the political complexities of the Union with its own evolving and functionally appropriate mechanisms and doctrines of control. Most importantly, European law has already begun to generate a series of procedural doctrines that seem to support the on-going process of adjustment between equally valid public interests in policy facilitation and restraint through political deliberation.[76]

The new agencies, and not the committee system, would then act as representatives of a transnational form of democracy:

> However, where, and to the degree that, the law of review is tailored to ensure that all relevant interests participate in decision-making, either through a widened basis for locus standi or through the 'deliberative' stipulation that all relevant interests are reviewed during decision-making, lack of representation within the plural polity presents a lesser problem.[77]

Are such perspectives compatible with the notion of the 'second order conflict of laws'? Their *problématique* can at least be restated in that framework: On the one hand, both socio-economic discrepancies within the Union and the likelihood of normative divergence militate against uniform decision-making which the food authority seeks to promote. It is, on the other hand, simply reasonable that risk-evaluation is coordinated so as to facilitate intra-Community trade. This is acceptable as long as the Comitology-like internal structure of the food authority prevents

[76] 'Control of Executive Acts', n 39 above, at 196–197.
[77] 'Control of Executive Acts', cited in n 39 above, at 198.

a take-over of decision-making powers by an autonomous executive and politically accountable actors can bring the views of their constituencies to bear. The more difficult issue concerns the socio-economic dimensions of safety standards. One can be sure that they have an impact on the evaluation of products. But it is difficult to see how such concerns can adequately be discussed in a procedure insulating the safety aspects from such potentially conflicting concerns,[78] albeit motivated by industrial policy preoccupations of Germany's former Chancellor[79] by establishing a Committee for Socio-Economic Analysis alongside a Risk Assessment Committee and a Member State Committee.

2. The OMC is a more radical alternative to Comitology than the new agencies. Here the de-formalisation of transnational governance has been perfected – even though one has to differentiate between the many OMCs now in place. Proponents of the method oscillate between two types of legitimation. One strand underlines the apparent need to take supranational action and legitimises open coordination by its potentially favourable output. Theoretically more ambitious are efforts to legitimise the OMC through its inherent normative qualities which are spelled out in the concept of democratic experimentalism.[80] Iterative benchmarking of national practices, the management of national states to agree upon guidelines and the mutual learning thereby stimulated are seen as genuinely democratic processes through which a problem-related *demos* articulates itself. These are fascinating and highly conditioned perspectives which provoke sceptical questions: how can transnational criteria that enable and legitimate a benchmarking of national experience, national history and national expectations be found? Why can we reliably expect that confrontation with the experience of others will change national perceptions and practices so as to lead to coordinated policies? And if indeed learning

[78] In this respect, the most recent of all agencies, entrusted with the regulation of chemicals, takes an exceptional step [Regulation (EC) No 1907/06 of the European Parliament and of the Council of 18 December 2006 concerning the Registration, Evaluation, Authorisation and Restriction of Chemicals (REACH), establishing a European Chemicals Agency, amending Directive 1999/45/EC and repealing Council Regulation (EEC) No 793/93 and Commission Regulation (EC) No 1488/94 as well as Council Directive 76/769/EEC and Commission Directives 91/155/EEC, 93/67/EEC, 93/105/EC and 2000/21/EC, [2006] OJ L396, 1-851(!)]. This regulation establishes a Committee for Socio-Economic Analysis side by side with a Risk Assessment Committee and a Member State Committee. The design of socio-economic analyses is regulated in detail in Annex XVI, Art 60(4), in the provision on how to deal with conflicts between socio-economic benefits, pros and the findings of the Committee for Risk Assessment. In such cases, authorisation may only be granted 'if it is shown that socio-economic benefits outweigh the risk to human health or the environment arising from the use of the substance and if there are no suitable alternative substances or technologies'; see the analysis by PF Kjaer, 'Rationality within REACH? On Functional Differentiation as the Structural Foundation of Legitimacy in European Chemicals Regulation' *EUI Working Papers (Law)* 18/2007, available at: http://cadmus.iue.it/dspace/handle/1814/6948.

[79] See the remarks in Kjaer, 'Rationality within REACH?', n 78 above, at 4 ff.

[80] Sabel and Zeitlin, 'Learning from Difference', n 3 above.

occurs in some quarters, how is its successful implementation conceivable if we are confronted not only with extremely complex fields of social policy but also with vested interests? There are no valid reasons which could be put forward against transnational exchanges of ideas among bureaucracies and expert communities. What seems risky, however, is the delegation of quasi-regulatory tasks to such networks. This sort of governance would be considered 'soft' to the extent that it is no longer dependent on binding law. But it might be considered 'strong' because its informality permits its evasion of risks of being tied down and controlled by the regular political process including the constraints of the rule of law.

3. The most successful mode of reconciling market-building objectives and regulatory concerns is still the New Approach to technical harmonisation and standards. Interestingly enough, this mode of governance not only has strong and quite ancient national roots but has also, from its inception, been predominantly privately constituted even before it was adopted at European level. This may seem downright paradoxical. A plausible explanation is that the juridification of this 'private transnationalism'[81] has assumed a much more intensive form than that of the traditionally public law areas now dominated by the new forms of governance. This, as Schepel has shown, holds true not only for European but also for international standardisation. Generally recognised and stable procedures which combine legal principles, professional standards and opportunities to participate, and which keep on leading to consensual solutions to problems, have matured. Significantly, European standardisation has taken on many of the features of comitology. Its non-unitary network structure ensures that national delegations each contribute their own views, *de facto* enabling learning processes. Administrations and the courts are sometimes actually and always latently present in standardisation questions. Committee members do not simply carry out instructions from governments, even though they act as their representatives. This 'private transnationalism' has been severed from national law but is not de-legalised. It feeds on expert knowledge but does not surrender to it. How could this happen?

> The paradox is, of course, that the mechanism through which this is achieved is, politics. Due process, transparency, openness, and balanced interest representation are norms for structuring meaningful social deliberation. They are not obviously the appropriate vehicles for revealing scientific 'truth' or for allowing room for the invisible hand.[82]

Law and politics both remain present. Admittedly, the political processes ordered by the law of private transnationalism are not directly achievable

[81] Schepel, *The Constitution of Private Governance*, cited in n 36 above.
[82] Ibid, at 223.

through public policy or public law. In other words, their juridification seemingly emanates 'from below'. This sort of 'law-making' takes account of the fact that the modern economy and its markets simply are not executing some economic *Gesetz* but need to address politically sensitive issues. How likely is it that the political processes within the economy and society will be socially responsible and that they will constitute themselves in such a way that will earn them recognition? A parallel with Comitology and the emerging law of the new agencies suggests itself: Comitology operates reasonably well thanks to the principles and rules it follows, and in the shadow of democratically legitimated institutions and their law. Similarly, the legitimacy that Schepel attributes to standardisation is based on the compatibility of its institutionalisation with the legal institutions that surround it, which are able to appreciate that they, on their own, cannot achieve what the standardisation process can. Is all this still accessible to the conflict-of-laws patterns of thought? The step to be taken is not too difficult. Conflict of laws deals with the acceptability of laws of 'foreign' jurisdictions. Once we recognise that our statal law cannot operate autonomously but is dependent upon the norm generation in non-statal spheres, we need to define the criteria for their recognition.[83] These criteria will primarily concern norm-generation processes. and their implementation will require the involvement of various legal areas such as antitrust and tort law.[84] There are avenues towards a legitimate juridification of transnational governance arrangements, even though the distances we have to cover make the task appear even more daunting.

[83] E Schanze, 'International Standards – Functions and Links to Law' in P Nobel (ed), *International Standards and the Law* (Bern: Stämpfli, 2005), 85, at 90 ff.

[84] Schepel, *The Constitution of Private Governance*, cited in n 36 above, at 285 ff and at 335 ff.

14

Conclusion – Part III

I. OUTLOOK: THE POLITICISATION OF MARKETS AND THE 'LURE OF TECHNOCRACY'

THE CONTRIBUTION ON the de-legalisation of the integration project (chapter 13) draws a sceptical summary on the outcomes of the far-reaching and ambitious reforms of European governance announced by President Romano Prodi in his speech of 15 February 2000, delivered in Strasbourg before the European Parliament,[1] and then substantiated in the Commission's White Paper on Governance of 27 July 2001.[2] The paper had been prepared thoroughly.[3] 'Governance', its key concept, was to designate a modernisation strategy, which would help to cure the evils afflicting the administrative and institutional *impasses* of the EU.[4] The Governance White Paper identified developments that are discussed throughout the contributions to Part III of this book. They all concern the problems of the 'risk society', which overburdened traditional legal and administrative programmes and routines because they required resort to non-legal knowledge, expertise in a multitude of disciplines, and the cooperation of governmental and non-governmental actors. These problems require responses that can never rely exclusively on expertise alone but will always have to address normative issues. These activities have an inherent political dimension that requires political legitimacy. Even within consolidated constitutional states, these issues are often highly controversial. Their adequate handling beyond the nation state is exacerbated by the lack of a democratically-legitimated actor with pertinent powers and resources. The essay on de-legalisation discusses responses that rely on expertise and/or the rationality of market processes. These strategies have their pragmatic reasons,

[1] Available at http://europa.eu.int/rapid/start/cgi/guesten.ksh?p_action.gettxt=gt&doc=SPEECH/00/41|0|AGED&lg=EN.

[2] 'European Governance: a White Paper', COM(2001) 428, [2001] OJ C297/1.

[3] Enhancing democracy in the European Union. Working Programme, SEC(200) 1547, 7 final of 11 October 2000, available at http://europa.eu.int/comm/governance/work/en.pdf; see also O De Schutter, N Lebessis and JB Paterson (eds), *Governance in the EU* (Luxemburg: Office for Official Publications of the EC, 2001).

[4] See, for a comprehensive account, the contributions to C Joerges, Y Mény and JHH Weiler (eds), *What Kind of Constitution for What Kind of Polity? Responses to Joschka Fischer* (Europäisches Hochschulinstitut, EUI Florence/Harvard Law School, 2000), available at https://cadmus.eui.eu/handle/1814/4110.

but remain nevertheless highly problematical.[5] The current coronavirus crisis provides a particularly dramatic illustration.

There is no easy, let alone comprehensive, solution to these complex problems. The first essay in this part (chapter 11) looks at the difficulties of the jurisprudence of the CJEU, which is, in part, unsatisfactory at times, however innovative and ground-breaking it may be. Of central importance for the whole volume is the analysis of the comitology system (chapter 12). This essay submits an alternative to purely pragmatic *ad hoc* solutions and technocratic concepts. The critique of 'de-legalisation' in chapter 13 builds on these suggestions and elaborates them further. This elaboration is most systematically continued in Part VI. The core of the argument and leitmotif is that the EU should, in principle, respect and live with the pluralist diversity of its democratically-legitimated traditions, and seek to address the implications of its economic and social interdependencies through deliberatively structured cooperative arrangements. The introduction to the chapter has outlined the challenges of such perspectives. Their outright rejection, as being purely utopian, risks damaging both the attractiveness and the potential of the European project.[6]

II. RELATED PUBLICATIONS

C Joerges, 'Paradoxes of deregulatory strategies at Community level: The example of Product Safety Policy' in G Majone (ed), *Deregulation or Reregulation? Regulatory reform in Europe and in the United States* (London: Pinter; New York: St Martin's Press, 1990) 176.

C Joerges and E Vos (eds), *EU Committees: Social Regulation, Law and Politics* (Oxford: Hart Publishing, 1999).

[5] Our concerns are widely shared. Suffice it here to point to the conceptual critique of C Offe, 'Governance – An "Empty Signifier"' (2008) 16 *Constellations* 550, and the normative reserves of H Hazenberg, 'Is Governance Democratic?' (2015) 18 *Critical Review of International Social and Political Philosophy* 285.

[6] See, in this context, J Habermas, 'The Lure of Technocracy. A Plea for European Solidarity' in J Habermas, *The Lure of Technocracy* (Cambridge: Polity, 2015) 3. This theme will be taken up in the discussion of Europe's crisis politics in pt V.

Part IV

The European Social Model: A New Type of 'Social Market Economy'

15

Introduction: Problems with 'Social Europe'

'THE SOCIAL' – SOCIAL or welfare state policies and commitments – can properly be called the poor relation of the integration project. The development of this *problématique* looks somewhat paradoxical. The Rome Treaty of 1957 in its Title III, Chapter 1 contained just six 'social provisions' (Articles 117–122); the only mandatory one established the principle of 'equal remuneration for equal work as between men and women workers'. What looks so meagre at first sight was anything but an anti-social programmatic. The Rome Treaty took the insight into account, that 'the social' is a highly sensitive field where policies had to be concerned not only with a democratic mandate, but also with social legitimacy. This was, in principle, undisputed. Post-war Europe, following the example of the UK, shared such commitments, documented convincingly in Alan S Milward's seminal monograph.[1] The silence about the 'Social' in the Rome Treaty was hence to be read as confirmation of the 'primacy' of national law and politics in this field, and the readiness to live with a plurality of national orientation. This re-construction is fully in line the views of an international relations scholar and political scientist, the emigrant John G Ruggie, and his theory of 'embedded liberalism'.[2] Ruggie praised the EEC for having accomplished a fortunate synthesis of openness and social justice.

The further development of the integration project does not deserve such benevolent assessments. This is essentially due to the two core objectives as they were defined and promoted under the 'integration through law' paradigm: one was the commitment to the opening of the borders between the formerly national economies. The other was the understanding of legal diversity as a barrier to free trade. The best way to promote both objectives side was legal harmonisation and the guarantee of a uniform understanding of such accomplishments through the recognition of the prerogative of the European Court of Justice in the interpretation of the content and reach of European legislation. These commands of economic integration have determined and curtailed

[1] AS Milward, *The European Rescue of the Nation-State* (London–New York: Routledge, 1992) (2nd edn, 2000).

[2] JG Ruggie, 'International Regimes, Transactions, and Change: Embedded Liberalism in the Postwar Economic Order' (1982) 36 *International Organization* 379.

the development of 'social Europe': social policies must respect the required primacy of economic rationality, and must not lead to a distortion of competition through discriminatory provisions. A moderation of social ambitions resulted from these orientations.

Legal scholarship and European politics turned a blind eye to the tensions created by the dynamics of integration. These dynamics were most intriguingly documented and explained in the works of the political scientist (and lawyer!) Fritz W Scharpf. He diagnosed the dominance of 'negative' over 'positive' integration, explained it stringently[3] and substantiated this analysis by his 'decoupling' theorem.[4] Scharpf was the first to underline to what degree the path taken by the integration project had been predicted in an essay of Friedrich A von Hayek on interstate federalism, published as early as 1939.

The validity of Scharpf's insights has been confirmed and deepened in many follow-up studies, in particular by the Max Planck Institute for the Study of Societies in Cologne.[5]

With dramatic stringencies, these analyses and predictions have been confirmed in a line of cases that became (in)famously known as the '*Laval* quartet'[6] – a holding of constitutional status, according to the jurisprudence of the European Court. The first contribution to this part of the book (chapter 16) criticises this jurisprudence. The arguments submitted build upon Scharpf's critique of the 'primacy' of negative integration and his 'decoupling' thesis. In the terminology of 'conflict law constitutionalism', the *Laval* quartet did not consider the tensions between European economic freedoms and national powers in the fields of labour and social policy to constitute a 'diagonal conflict'.[7] Such conflicts cannot be resolved by supremacy. The German Constitutional Court (FCC) has realised this, underlining that the national reserves are covered by the so-called

[3] FW Scharpf, *Regieren in Europa: effektiv und demokratisch?* (Frankfurt aM-New York: Campus, 1999) 47 ff. Scharpf's terms are older; they were previously used by J Pinder, 'Positive Integration and Negative Integration: Some Problems of Economic Union in the EEC' (1968) 24 *The World Today* 88. Scharpf himself had introduced them already in 1996; see his 'Negative and Positive Integration in the Political Economy of European Welfare States' in G Marks, FW Scharpf, PhC Schmitter and W Streeck (eds), *Governance in the European Union* (London: Sage, 1996) 15.

[4] FW Scharpf, 'The European Social Model: Coping with the Challenges of Diversity' (2002) 40 *JCMS* 645, at 646.

[5] See, eg, M Höpner and A Schäfer, *Die Politische Ökonomie der europäischen Integration* (Frankfurt aM: Campus, 2008).

[6] Case 341/05 *Laval unPartneri Ltd v Svenska Byggnadsarbetareförbundet, Svenska Byggnadsarbetareförbundetsavdelning 1, Byggettan und Svenska Elektrikerförbundet*, ECLI:EU:C:2007:809; Case C-438/05 *International Transport Workers' Federation und Finnish Seamen's Union v Viking Line ABP and OÜ Viking Line Eesti*, ECLI:EU:C:2007:772; Case C-346/06 *Rüffert v Land Niedersachsen*, ECLI:EU:C:2008:189; Case C-319/06 *Commission v Luxembourg*, ECLI:EU:C:2008:350.

[7] On this notion, see, in particular, the analysis of the tension between European monetary policy and national economic and fiscal policy analysed in ch 23 of this volume.

'eternity clause' of Article 79 (3) of the Basic Law.[8] The FCC, however, asserted that

> there are also no indications justifying the assumption that the Member States are deprived of the right, and the practical possibilities of action, to take conceptual decisions regarding social security systems and other measures of social policy and labour market policy in their democratic primary areas.[9]

A more interesting defence of the *Laval* quartet, submitted by Damjan Kukovec,[10] points to the implications of Eastern enlargement. The economic activities that were assessed in these cases, he argues, seek to profit from competitive advantages, thereby compensating the exposure of the East to the higher development of the old Member States. The risk, however, could be, so the final section of our contribution submits,[11] that the weakening of social protection in the West will provoke a 'race to the bottom', which would foreclose societal advances in Eastern Europe.

The issues of the *Laval* dispute are of very general importance. The second contribution unfolds this threefold *problématique*: (i) the Union lacks essential competence, which the development of a European *Sozialstaat* would require; (ii) the socio-economic diversity of Europe, which proves to be surprisingly resistant to imposed changes; and (iii) the establishment of a federation equivalent to the American or German model remains highly unlikely in the foreseeable future. Chapter 17 summarises the 'foundational' conceptual orientations that have led to the present impasses and re-orientations ventured in both legal and political science. It underscores what historians like Tony Judt have underlined[12] and the economic sociologist Karl Polanyi had, back in 1944, re-constructed, in highly topical alternatives. The social justice commitments of European welfare state, Judt submits, are of constitutive importance to Europe's democracies. The historical alternatives, which Polanyi has analysed in his 'Great Transformation' were the rise of Fascism and National Socialism.[13] At present, Europe's darkest legacies experience a revival in pertinent right-wing strands of populist movements. The alternative explored throughout the volume is to take the European

[8] See Bundesverfassungsgericht, Judgment of 30.06.2009, *BVerfGE* 123, 267, available at: http://www.bverfg.de/e/es20090630_2bve000208.html.

[9] Ibid, para 399.

[10] D Kukovec, 'Whose Social Europe? – The *Laval/Viking* Judgments and the Prosperity Gap' (Cambridge MA, Harvard Law School: *IGLP Working Paper Series* 2011; idem, 'Law and the Periphery' (2015) 21 *ELJ* 406.

[11] Ch 16, section III C.

[12] See, eg, his lecture of 19 October 2009, 'What is Living and What is Dead in Social Democracy?' *New York Review of Books*, 56:20, 17 December 2009.

[13] K Polanyi, *The Great Transformation: The Political and Economic Origins of our Time* [1944], 1st Beacon pbk edn (Boston, MA: Beacon Press, 1957).

'united in diversity' motto of the Draft Constitutional Treaty[14] seriously and institutionalise it through 'conflicts-law-constitutionalism'.

The implications of Europe's socio-economic diversity for the promotion of 'social Europe' are the core concern of chapter 18. At its core is the distinction between social justice both 'within' and 'between' the Member States of the Union. And it is precisely this distinction that is not taken into account in so much scholarly work and in so many political initiatives that seek to promote a 'Social Europe'.

[14] [2004] OJ C310/01, Art I.8.

16

Informal Politics, Formalised Law and the 'Social Deficit' of European Integration: Reflections after the Judgments of the ECJ in Viking *and* Laval*

INTRODUCTORY REMARKS

'SOCIAL EUROPE' HAS become an intensively discussed topic. The Maastricht Treaty, the Amsterdam Treaty, the Lisbon Council of 2000, together with the Convention on the Future of Europe, have constituted the basis of vital turning points within relevant debates. Today, however, with the Lisbon Reform Treaty awaiting ratification, public attention has shifted from treaty amendments and constitutional deliberations to the European Court of Justice (ECJ). With the two landmark decisions in *Viking*[1] and *Laval*,[2] most recently joined and complemented by *Rüffert* and *Luxembourg*,[3] the Court has reminded us that the hard law of negative integration can still be brought to bear where political processes have proven to be slow and cumbersome and the benefits of soft law mechanisms remain obscure.

'Social Europe', ie the ensemble of European social and labour law and policy and social rights, has become a wide and opaque field of such complexity that generalists in European law, let alone students of other sub-disciplines, tend to shy away from intervening in the dominating discourses. In our view,

* Co-author Florian Rödl, Bremen, Centre for Europen Law and Politics. Sincere thanks to Brian Bercusson for his extensive, critical and constructive comments on an earlier version of this contribution. The responsibility for remaining errors is ours. The essay was published in (2009) 15 *ELJ* 1.

[1] Case C-438/05, *International Transport Workers' Federation, Finnish Seamen's Union v Viking Line ABP, OÜ Viking Line Eesti*, judgment of 11 December 2007.

[2] Case C-341/05, *Laval un Partneri Ltd v Svenska Byggnadsarbetareförbundet, Svenska Byggnadsarbetareförbundet, avd. 1, Svenska Elektrikerförbundet*, judgment of 18 December 2007.

[3] Case C-346/06, *Rechtsanwalt Dr Dirk Rüffert v Land Niedersachsen*, judgment of 3 April 2008; Case C-319/06, *Commission v Luxembourg*, judgment of 19 June 2008. On *Rüffert*, see our remarks in n 80 below; we refrain from a discussion of the Luxembourg ruling, in which we cannot find any encouraging new signals.

this is unfortunate because the formation of the 'social' and the 'economic' are contemporaneous and the outcome of this dual process is of vital significance for the state of the European Constitution. Our essay will address these interdependencies. We will therefore start by developing a theoretical framework within which the project of 'social Europe' can be observed and assessed. In Section I, we will submit a reconstruction of what we call the 'social deficit' in the original design of the European Economic Community, arguing that a credible response to this deficit would be a pre-condition for the democratic legitimacy of the intensified integration project; alternatively, we will underline the need to link the rule of law with democracy and social justice.[4] Our second step will focus on the constitutional forms through which such linkages can be institutionalised. As we will argue in Section II, their realisation requires a re-conceptualisation of European law as a new type of supranational conflict of laws. This vision is contrasted in Section III, first with the steps towards Social Europe envisaged in the Draft Constitutional Treaty, and then with the principles established in *Viking* and *Laval*.

SECTION I: EUROPEAN INTEGRATION AND DEMOCRACY: A LEGACY OF UNRESOLVED TENSIONS

The project of European integration was launched not as an experiment in supranational democracy, but as a response to the Second World War and its devastating effects on the European economies. The opening of national economies and the establishment of a common market was intended to ensure lasting peace among former enemies. This integration strategy and its institutional design would mitigate the significant societal differences, concerns with Germany's '*Vergangenheitsschuld*' (*Guilt about the Past*) and anxieties of Germany's European neighbours.[5] This was accomplished through a primarily economic and technocratic integration strategy. That choice certainly did not come as a surprise. With hindsight, however, the implications of this choice, which were hardly foreseeable and certainly not a salient issue half a century ago, become apparent. This is true for both the queries on which our analysis will focus.

The first query may be referred to as a 'normative fact', namely, the exclusion of 'the social' dimension from the integrationist objectives, a design which Fritz W Scharpf famously characterised as the decoupling of the social and the

[4] The following argument is more extensively developed in C Joerges and F Rödl, 'The "Social Market Economy" as Europe's Social Model?' in L Magnusson and B Stråth (eds), *A European Social Citizenship? Pre-conditions for Future Policies in Historical Light* (Brussels: Lang, 2005) 125.

[5] Students of European law tend overly to focus their analyses upon the history of 'institutionalised Europe' rather than on the diverse histories of the Member States, their complex relations, and the legacies of inherited conflicts, as well as the generation of new ones.

economic sphere in the European project.[6] But why should this decoupling be problematical? We argue that this question is of fundamental constitutional significance. The exclusion of the social sphere from the integration project is a potential failure of constitutional significance for those who assume that the citizens of constitutional democracies are entitled to vote in favour of welfare policies. This is by no means a trivial premise, not even at national level.[7] The second query concerns the integration process. In the course of its intensifying and growing impact on the 'economy and society', a response to the 'social deficit' has become a political necessity.[8]

A. Europe's Equilibrium in the Formative Period of the Integration Process

Theories of legal integration can be regarded as efforts to provide a contextually (historically, socially and politically) adequate legal conceptualisation of the state of the European Community (now Union). Two such efforts aimed at capturing the 'nature of the beast' in its formative period stand out and remain important: Germany's ordoliberalism and Joseph Weiler's theory of supranationalism.

Ordoliberalism is not only an important theoretical tradition in Germany, but also a powerful contributor to German ideational politics. The ordoliberal school[9] re-constructed the legal essence of the European project as an 'economic constitution' which was not in need of an ideal like democratic legitimacy. The freedoms guaranteed in the EEC Treaty, the opening up of national economies and anti-discrimination rules, and the commitment to a system of undistorted competition were interpreted as a quasi-Schmittian 'decision' that supported an

[6] FW Scharpf, 'The European Social Model: Coping with the Challenges of Diversity' (2002) 40 *JCMS* 645.

[7] FA von Hayek was the most outspoken critic of this theory; the turn to welfare policies means taking *The Road to Serfdom* (London: Routledge, 1944). A legendary debate in the young German Federal Republic between Wolfgang Abendroth and Ernst Forsthoff concerned precisely that *problématique* [see A Fischer-Lescano and O Eberl, 'Der Kampf um ein soziales und demokratisches Recht. Zum 100. Geburtstag von Wolfgang Abendroth', (2006) 51 *Blätter für deutsche und internationale Politik*, 577] and these debates are still going on today [see the Special Issue on 'Social Democracy' in (2004) 17 *Canadian Journal of Law and Jurisprudence on Social Democracy* (Guest Editor: Colin Harvey)].

[8] For a recent analysis of this interdependence, see JP McCormick, Weber, Habermas, and Transformations of the European State. Constitutional, Social, and Supranational Democracy (Cambridge: CUP, 2007).

[9] European integration was, in its early years, by no means an uncontested project among the protagonists of ordoliberalism (see M Wegmann, *Früher Neoliberalismus und europäische Integration: Interdependenz der nationalen, supranationalen und internationalen Ordnung von Wirtschaft und Gesellschaft (1932-1965)* (Baden-Baden: Nomos, 2002) 297 ff, 351 ff. Her analyses fit well the enquiry into the politics of competition policy by Y Karagiannis, 'Preference Heterogeneity and Equilibrium Institutions: The Case of European Competition Policy', PhD Thesis, EUI, Florence, 2007, ch 7.

economic constitution, and which also conformed with the ordoliberal conceptions of the framework conditions for a market economic system. The fact that Europe had started out on its integrationist path as a mere economic community lent plausibility to ordoliberal arguments – and even required them: in the ordoliberal account, the Community acquired a legitimacy of its own by interpreting its pertinent provisions as prescribing a law-based order committed to guaranteeing economic freedoms and protecting competition by supranational institutions. This legitimacy was independent of the State's democratic constitutional institutions. By the same token, it imposed limits upon the Community: thus, discretionary economic policies seemed illegitimate and unlawful.[10] The ordoliberal European polity consists of a twofold structure: at supranational level, it is committed to economic rationality and a system of undistorted competition; while at national level, re-distributive (social) policies may be pursued and developed further.[11]

'Integration through law' is the legal paradigm commonly associated with the formative era of the European Community outside the German borders.[12] It is not by chance that generations of scholars have built upon it or tried to decipher its sociological basis.[13] The strength of the paradigm may well rest (in part) on assumptions that become apparent only when social and economic policies are viewed through its lenses. Then, we become aware of the *Wahlverwandtschaft* with German ordoliberalism, in that only the European market-building project was juridified through supranational law, whereas social policy at European level could, at best, be said to have been handled through intergovernmental bargaining processes.

Fritz Scharpf's decoupling theory is, at least on the surface, not intended to be a contribution to the debates on the constitutionalisation of Europe. However, it does build upon sociological assumptions with constitutional implications. This holds true in particular for the argument that the social integration of capitalist societies will require a balance between social and economic rationality. This is, of course, again a primarily empirical issue, but it is one with obvious implications for the legitimacy of the polity under scrutiny.[14] Since we can assume that 'welfarism' – notwithstanding its very diverse modes – is a common European

[10] Significant here is A Müller-Armack, 'Die Wirtschaftsordnung des Gemeinsamen Marktes' in idem, *Wirtschaftsordnung und Wirtschaftspolitik*, (Freiburg i.Br: Rombach, 1966) 401.

[11] Ordoliberalism has not attracted too much attention outside Germany. All the more important is the notable exception of M Foucault, *Naissance de la biopolitique. Cours au Collège de France* (Paris: Seuil-Gallimard, 2004), in particular the lectures of 7 February (at 105–134) and of 14 February 1979 (at 135–164).

[12] See, path-breaking, JHH Weiler, 'The Community System: the Dual Character of Supranationalism' (1981) 1 *Yearbook of European Law* 257.

[13] Most recently, A Vauchez, '"Integration-through-Law". Contribution to a Socio-history of EU Political Common Sense', *EUI Working Paper RSCAS* 2008/10.

[14] See the classical studies by J Habermas, *Legitimation Crisis* (Boston MA: Beacon Press, 1979); 'Towards a Reconstruction of Historical Materialism' in S Seidman (ed), *Jürgen Habermas on Society and Politics* (Boston MA: Beacon Press, 1989), 114; and McCormick, n 8 above, 176 ff.

heritage,[15] it will become imperative for European politics to address the social dimensions and implications of the integration project. Interestingly enough, German ordo-liberalism was well accustomed to this *problématique*. Its early proponents conceptualised it as the interdependence[16] of societal and economic 'orders' (*Ordnungen/Verfassungen*[17]).

To summarise: Europe was conceived according to principles of a dual polity. Its 'economic constitution' was non-political in the sense that it was not subject to political interventions. This was its constitutional-supranational *raison d'être*. Social policy was treated as a categorically-distinct subject. It belonged to the domain of political legislation, and, as such, had to remain national. The social embeddedness of the market could, and, indeed, should, be accomplished by the Member States in various ways – and, for a decade and a half, the balance appears to have been stable.[18]

B. The Completion of the Internal Market, the Erosion of the Economic Constitution and the Advent of Social Europe

The original equilibrium was not, however, to remain stable. One important reason for its instability was the progress of the integration project. The Delors Commission's 1985 *White Paper on Completion of the Internal Market*[19] is widely perceived not only as a turning point, but also as a breakthrough in the integration process. Jacques Delors' initiative provided the hope of overcoming a long phase of stagnation; the means to this end was the strengthening of Europe's

[15] See T Judt, *Postwar: A History of Europe Since 1945* (New York: Penguin, 2005), eg, at 777 ff.

[16] See, most famously, W Eucken, *Grundzüge der Wirtschaftspolitik* (Tübingen: Mohr/Siebeck, 1952; 6th edn 1990), 180 et seq); out of the rich literature on the interdependence theorem, see Wegmann, n 6 above, in particular at 369 ff.

[17] *Verfassung* has a double meaning in German. It can imply a legal constitution and a social structure or pattern. The notion of *Ordnung* (order), too, comprises this twofold meaning. This clarification is necessary to convey our idea of a constitutionalisation of the economy, of other societal spheres or parts of the legal system. Such constitutionalisation can either claim the dignity of constitutional law (eg, supremacy within the legal system) or be an integral part of the constitutional order (in this sense, Jürgen Habermas talks of the co-originality of private and public law; see his *Between Facts and Norms. Contributions to a Discourse Theory of Law and Democracy* (Cambridge MA: The MIT Press, 1998) at 84 ff.

[18] Reference is made here to JHH Weiler, who qualifies the years from '1958 to the middle of the 1970s' as Europe's foundational period (see *The Constitution of Europe: 'Do the New Clothes Have an Emperor?' and Other Essays on European Integration* (Cambridge: CUP, 1999), 16). His re-construction is compatible with the analysis of 'The National Configuration of the State in the Golden Age' by S Leibfried and M Zürn, 'Reconfiguring the National Constellation' in eidem (eds), *Transformation of the State* (Cambridge: CUP, 2005), 93 [= *European Review*, vol 13, Supplement S1, available at: http://0journals.cambridge.org] and J Ruggie, 'International Regimes, Transactions, and Change: Embedded Liberalism in the Postwar Economic Order' (1982) 36 *International Organization* 379.

[19] Commission of the EC, 'Commission White Paper to the European Council on Completion of the Internal Market', COM(85) 310 final of 14 June 1985.

competitiveness. Economic rationality, rather than 'law', was, from now on, to be understood as Europe's orienting maxim, its first commitment and its regulative idea. In this sense, it seems justified to characterise Delors' programme as a deliberate move towards an institutionalisation of economic rationality. This seems even more plausible when we consider two complementary institutional innovations accomplished through, and subsequent to, the Maastricht Treaty, namely, the Monetary Union and the Stability Pact. Europe resembled a market-embedded polity, governed by an economic constitution rather than by political rule.

This characterisation, however, soon proved to be too simplistic.[20] What had started out as an effort to strengthen Europe's competitiveness and to accomplish this objective through new (de-regulatory) strategies, soon led to the entanglement of the EU in ever increasing policy fields and the development of sophisticated regulatory machinery. It was, in particular, the concern of European legislation and the Commission with 'social regulation' (the health and safety of consumers and workers, and environmental protection) which served as irrefutable proof of this. The weight and dynamics of these policy fields had been thoroughly under-estimated by the proponents of the 'economic constitution'. Equally important and equally unsurprising was the fact that the integration process intensified with the completion of the Internal Market and affected ever increasing policy fields. This was significant not so much in terms of its factual weight, but in view of Europe's 'social deficit', in terms of the new efforts to strengthen Europe's presence in the spheres of labour and social policy.

These tendencies became mainstream during the preparation of the Maastricht Treaty, which was adopted in 1992. This is why this Amendment of the Treaty, officially presented as both intensification and a consolidation of the integration project, met with fierce criticism. The most outspoken critique came not from the political left, but from the proponents of the new economic philosophy, and, in particular, from Germany's ordoliberals.[21] And, indeed, the Maastricht Treaty of 1992 can be interpreted as a break from the ordoliberal economic constitution. Following the explicit recognition and strengthening of new policy competences, which was accomplished in Maastricht, it seemed simply no longer plausible to assign a constitutive function to the 'system of undistorted competition' because this competition policy had now been downgraded to one among many commitments. In addition, the expansion of competences in labour law by the Social Protocol and Agreement on Social Policy of the Treaty blurred the formerly distinct lines between Europe's

[20] See, on the following, in more detail, C Joerges, 'Economic Law, the Nation-State and the Maastricht Treaty' in R Dehousse (ed), *Europe after Maastricht: an Ever Closer Union?* (Munich: CH Beck, 1994), 29; and the re-construction in KW Nörr, *Die Republik der Wirtschaft. Teil II. Vom der sozial-liberalen Koalition bis zur Wiedervereinigung* (Tübingen: Mohr/Siebeck, 2007) 44–60. On the spill-over effects of market regulation even in the area of collective labour law, see B Bercusson, 'The Collective Labour Law of the European Union' (1995) 1 *ELJ* 157.

[21] See M Streit and W Mussler, 'The Economic Constitution of the European Community. From "Rome" to "Maastricht"' (1995) 1 *ELJ* 5.

(apolitical) economic constitution and the political responsibility assumed by Member States in relation to social and labour policies.

Up till now, a consensus on the interpretation of this new constellation has not emerged. Is this a result of contingent events and decisions? Has a deeper 'logic' been at work? Back in 1944, Karl Polanyi, in his seminal *Great Transformation*, had argued that markets will always be 'socially embedded'.[22] In Polanyian terms, both the initial decoupling of the economic from the social economic constitution in the design of the integration project and the later striving for competitiveness through the 'completion' of the internal market programme can be interpreted as disembedding moves. Such moves, he had insisted, will provoke countermoves directed at a re-embedding of the market. The European experience seems, in principle, reconcilable with his message.[23] It is important to underline, however, that Polanyi had refrained from predicting the intensity and direction of such countermoves. The message one can safely infer from his writings is that markets could not be understood simply as mechanisms that functioned perfectly and automatically to adjust supply and demand. This message, its indeterminacy notwithstanding, is important enough. As Fred Block, one of Polanyi's most important contemporary readers suggests:

> [t]he critical question is no longer the quantitative issue of how much state or how much market, but rather the qualitative issue of how and for what ends markets and states should be combined and the structures and practices that should exist in a civil society that will sustain a productive synergy of states and markets.[24]

It is exactly in this sense that we invoke the 'social embeddedness' theory. What happened in the implementation of the internal market programme, namely, the establishment of an ever greater sophisticated regulatory machinery entrusted with the management of the internal market, was simply not dictated by some functional necessity. This development can be better understood as having been facilitated and shaped by political countermoves which then also addressed Europe's social deficit more comprehensively until it became a prominent part of the European agenda.

SECTION II: CONFLICT OF LAWS AS CONSTITUTIONAL FORM

As stated in our introductory remarks, this section will outline an alternative to the prevailing understanding of Europe's constitutional perspectives.

[22] K Polanyi, *The Great Transformation: The Political and Economic Origins of our Time* [1944] (Boston MA: Bacon Press, 1992) esp at 45–58, 71–80.

[23] See JA Caporaso and S Tarrow, 'Polanyi in Brussels: Supranational Institutions and the Transnational Embedding of Markets' (2009) 63 *International Organization* 593.

[24] See F Block, 'Towards a New Understanding of Economic Modernity' in C Joerges, B Stråth and P Wagner (eds), *The Economy as a Polity: The Political Construction of Modern Capitalism – An Interdisciplinary Perspective* (London: UCL Press, 2005) 3; and, recently, J Beckert, 'The Great Transformation of Embeddedness: Karl Polanyi and the New Economic Sociology', *MPIfG Discussion Paper* 07/1, Cologne 2007.

We will start with a clarification of our intentions. We do not believe that lawyers are well equipped to decipher the historical, political and sociological determinants of the developments of law. Their vocation is, in our view, a more modest one, namely, to offer legal conceptualisations which are compatible with what we know about the law's context – and at the same time, seek to explain whether, or under what conditions, a deliberate adaptation to these contexts would be 'worthy of recognition'. Our conflict-of-laws approach is not intended to 'solve' the *problématique* of social Europe. What we seek to develop is a legal framework which adequately reflects Europe's post-national constellation and through which it seems possible to strive for a survival of Europe's social legacy.

Our idea of a new type of conflict of laws as Europe's proper constitutional form is less idiosyncratic in substance than its terminology may suggest. The core argument upon which it rests is in fact quite simple. Back in 1997, Jürgen Neyer and Christian Joerges submitted it under the heading of 'deliberative' (as opposed to 'orthodox') supranationalism:[25]

> The legitimacy of governance within constitutional states is flawed in so far as it remains inevitably one-sided and parochial or selfish. The taming of the nation-state through democratic constitutions has its limits. [If and, indeed, because] democracies pre-suppose and represent collective identities, they have very few mechanisms [through which] to ensure that 'foreign' identities and their interests are taken into account within their decision-making processes.[26]

If the legitimacy of supranational institutions can be designed to cure these deficiencies – as a correction of 'nation-state failures', as it were – they may then derive their legitimacy from this compensatory function. To quote a recent restatement:

> We must conceptualise supranational constitutionalism as an alternative to the model of the constitutional nation-state which respects that state's constitutional legitimacy, but, at the same time, clarifies and sanctions the commitments arising from its interdependence with equally democratically legitimised states and with the supranational prerogatives that an institutionalisation of this interdependence requires.[27]

This, of course, is not the way in which the supranational validity of European law was originally understood and justified. Fortunately enough, however, the methodologically and theoretically bold and practically successful ECJ decision in favour of a European legal constitution[28] can be rationalised in this way.

[25] C Joerges and J Neyer, 'From Intergovernmental Bargaining to Deliberative Political Processes' (1997) 3 *ELJ* 273.

[26] Ibid, at 293.

[27] C Joerges '"Deliberative Political Processes" Revisited: What Have we Learnt about the Legitimacy of Supranational Decision-Making?' (2006) 44 *JCMS* 779, at 790.

[28] Case 26/62 *Van Gend en Loos v Nederlandse Administratie der Belastingen* [1963] ECR 1.

The European 'federation' thus established a legal constitution that did not have to aim at Europe's becoming a state, but was able to derive its legitimacy from the fact that it compensates for the democratic deficits of the nation states. This is precisely the point of deliberative supranationalism. Existing European law had, according to the argument, validated principles and rules that meet with and deserve supranational recognition because they constitute a palpable community project: Community members cannot implement their interests or laws without restraint but are obliged to respect the European freedoms; they are not allowed to discriminate and can pursue only legitimate regulatory policies which have been approved by the Community; they must, in relation to the objectives that they wish to pursue through regulation, harmonise with each other, and they must reform their national systems in the most community-friendly way possible.

Why should this type of law be referred to as a new type of conflict of laws? This notion reminds us on the one hand of Europe's internal diversity, the fact that diversity is a cause of conflict of interests both, horizontally, among Member States and societal actors, and, vertically, between the different levels of governance and the institutional actors representing them.[29] It represents the effort to live with diversity rather than to strive for uniformity. European conflict of laws is 'new', even revolutionary, because conflict of laws has traditionally – in all its sub-disciplines: private international law, international administrative law, international labour law, etc – refused to acknowledge claims under foreign 'public' law; according to such tradition, each state not only determined the international scope of its own public law unilaterally, but was also solely responsible for its enforcement. Traditional conflict of laws is, therefore, a paradigm example of what Michael Zürn characterises as 'methodological nationalism'.[30] The 'new' European conflict of laws has, of course, to overcome this hostility. And the principles just cited do exactly that: they guide the search for responses to conflicting claims where no higher substantive law is readily available. To give voice to 'foreign' concerns means, in the EU, first of all, that Member States mutually 'recognise' their laws (that they are prepared to 'apply' foreign law), that they tolerate legal differences and refrain from insisting ruthlessly on their own *lex fori* and domestic interests. This European law of conflict of laws is 'deliberative' in that it does not content itself with appealing to the supremacy of European law; it is 'European' because it seeks to identify principles and rules that make different laws within the EU compatible with one another.[31]

[29] R Mayntz, 'The Architecture of Multi-level Governance of Economic Sectors', *MPIfG Discussion Paper* 07/13, Cologne, 2007 at 22–24.

[30] M Zürn, 'The State in the Post-national Constellation – Societal Denationalization and Multi-Level Governance', *ARENA Working Paper No 35/1999*, Oslo 1999.

[31] There is no space for detailed elaboration. Suffice it to mention two implications. One is methodological: European conflict of laws requires a proceduralisation of the category of law. It has to be understood as a 'law of law-making': FI Michelman, *Brennan and Democracy* (Princeton NJ: Princeton UP, 1999) 34; and in a similar vein, R Wiethölter, 'Just-ifications of a Law of Society'

The conflict-of-laws approach envisages a horizontal constitutionalism for the EU. It distances itself from both the orthodoxy of conflict of laws and orthodox supranationalism which promote top-down solutions to Europe's diversity. It seeks to accomplish what the Draft Constitutional Treaty had called the 'motto of the Union',[32] namely, the vision of 'united in diversity'.

Should this provide us with a new perspective for the cure of Europe's social deficit? This question will now be considered.

SECTION III: SOFT AND HARD RESPONSES TO THE QUEST FOR SOCIAL EUROPE

In a recent essay dealing with the state of the European Union following the signing of the reform treaty, Jürgen Habermas criticised the tendency of Germany's Social Democrats to respond to risks of economic globalisation through the means of the national welfare state. Would it not be preferable, he asked, to search for coordinated responses within the entire European economic space?[33] His question implicitly acknowledges the importance of Europe's social deficit. What answers are available? We are currently witnessing two seemingly contradictory but in fact complementary responses, namely, the resort to soft modes of governance on the one hand, and the turn to orthodox supranationalism on the other.

A. 'Social Market Economy', Social Rights and Soft Coordination

The first-mentioned alternative, which was the option pursued by the Draft Constitutional Treaty,[34] was supported by a great number of its proponents and can be found largely unchanged in the so-called reform treaty of Lisbon. 'Social Europe' was to be founded, in particular, on three cornerstones: the commitment to a 'competitive social market economy',[35] the recognition of 'social rights',[36] and new 'soft law' mechanisms for the coordination of social

in O Perez and G Teubner (eds), *Paradoxes and Inconsistencies in the Law* (Oxford: Hart Publishing, 2005) 65. The second concerns the need for a 'second order of conflict of laws'. This need stems from the 'turn to governance', which we witness not just at the European level but also with nation states. Just as nation states have long had to learn to deal with complex conflict situations, to integrate expertise in legal decision-making and to cooperate with non-governmental actors, the EU had to build up governance arrangements which complement its primary and secondary law; 'second order conflict of laws' seeks to constitutionalise this sphere primarily through a proceduralisation of law. See, in more detail, C Joerges, 'Integration through De-legalisation?' (2008) 33 *ELRev* 291.

[32] Article I-8 of the Draft Treaty on a Constitution for Europe (DCT), OJ C310/1, 16/12/2004.

[33] 'Erste Hilfe für Europa', *DIE ZEIT* no 49/2007.

[34] Unsurprisingly, the Lisbon Treaty, as signed on 13 December 2007, is moving along the same lines.

[35] Article 3 (3), DCT.

[36] See Title IV (Solidarity) in Part II (The Charter of Fundamental Rights of the Union) DCT.

and labour market policies.[37] Joschka Fischer and Domenique de Villepin, to whom the assignment of constitutional significance to the 'social market economy' is owed, thereby provided a political signal. However, they were hardly aware of the interdependence between the economic and the social constitution as illustrated in the theory of the 'social market economy'. The latter's legacy would have required what was not yet an imperative in the formative era of the European Economic Community, namely, a compensation for the decoupling of both spheres in the European Treaties.[38] Thus, all hope for a cure rested on new social rights and new coordination competences.[39] However, these expectations were never substantially justified.[40] This is why the Reform Treaty signed by the European governments in Lisbon will not markedly advance the agenda of social Europe.[41] In the present context, however, we cannot and indeed need not examine the intrinsic merits and failures of these options,[42] specifically because the recent jurisprudence of the ECJ has re-configured the agenda substantially. Following the ECJ judgments in *Viking* and *Laval*, one will have to ask what accomplishments could be achieved through the soft mechanisms of coordination in their confrontation with the 'hard law' of negative integration.

B. The ECJ Judgments in *Viking* and *Laval*

These two cases have attracted wide attention over the last years. The conflicts before the Court were directly related to the new socio-economic diversity in the Union following enlargement. In both cases, 'old' (high-wage) Member States defended the principle that their wage level must not be eroded by low-wage offers from new Member States. Furthermore, the latter States in both cases invoked the economic freedoms guaranteed by the Treaty and strategically used not least by companies in the old Member States, which seek to operate at home at the wage levels of their eastern neighbours. 'It is a bracing

[37] See, especially, Article I-14(4) DCT. For an instructive recent state-of-the-art report on the Open Method of Coordination, see B Laffan and C Shaw, 'Classifying and Mapping OMCs in Different Policy Areas' *NewGov Paper*, 02/D09, 2005, available at: www.eu-newgov.org/database/DELIV/D02D09_Classifying_and_Mapping_OMC.pdf.

[38] See, in more detail, C Joerges and F Rödl, 'The "Social Market Economy" as Europe's Social Model?' in L Magnusson and B Stråth (eds), *A European Social Citizenship? Pre-conditions for Future Policies in Historical Light* (Brussels: Lang, 2005) 125.

[39] See the contributions to G de Búrca and B de Witte (eds), *Social Rights in Europe* (Oxford: Hart Publishing, 2005); and G de Búrca and J Scott (eds), *Law and Governance in the EU and the US* (Oxford: Hart Publishing, 2006).

[40] See Joerges and Rödl, n 38 above.

[41] For a detailed analysis focusing on the lack of dynamically exercisable European competences to articulate the new social aims and rights at European level, see F Rödl, 'Labour Constitution' in A v Bogdandy and J Bast (eds), *Principles of European Constitutional Law* (Oxford: Hart Publishing, 2010) 605.

[42] For a critical discussion of the use of soft law in the field of social policy, see C Joerges, 'Integration through De-legislation?' (2008) 33 *EL Rev* 219.

reminder to EU lawyers of the power of political and economic context to influence legal doctrine', as observed by Brian Bercusson.[43] He also notes 'that the new Member States making submissions were unanimous on one side of the arguments on issues of fundamental legal doctrine (horizontal direct effect, discrimination, proportionality) and the old Member States virtually unanimous on the other'.

1. Viking: *Freedoms in Primary Law and Member State Labour Constitutions*

The plaintiffs in the *Viking* case[44] were a Finnish shipping company (Viking) and its Estonian subsidiary. Viking was a large ferry operator, running, among others, the ferry *Rosella* registered in Finland. Its crew was predominantly Finnish. A labour agreement negotiated by the Finnish Seamen's Union provided that the wages and conditions of employment were to accord with Finnish standards. But as the *Rosella* was not making sufficient profit at the time, Viking decided to re-flag the ferry in Estonia. The Finnish crew was to be replaced by Estonian seamen, as under Estonian labour law they were far less expensive.[45] This resulted in the Finnish Seamen's union threatening to go on strike. Both the Finnish and the Estonian unions were affiliates of the International Transport Workers' Federation (ITF). One of the ITF's prime policy targets included 'flags of convenience'. It was the ITF's aim to achieve collective agreements under the law in force at the very place where the ownership and control of a vessel was situated. In this way, it attempted to defend seafarers against low wage strategies from employers such as Viking, who replaced their seamen with labour from low-wage countries. In the case of Viking, ownership and control were situated in Finland; this meant that, according to the internal rules of the ITF, only Finnish unions were authorised to agree to wage settlements with Viking. As a result, the ITF had sent written correspondence to its member unions, advising them not to enter into collective negotiations with Viking, a suggestion that was also complied with by the Estonian union.

This was the reason for Viking's legal action against union activities, first in Helsinki and then, with reference to the ITF's having its headquarters in London, at the Court of Justice for England and Wales, Queen's Bench Division (Commercial Court) (United Kingdom) – this was a strategic practice known as *forum shopping*, which allowed the rules for European civil jurisdiction to

[43] 'The Trade Union Movement and the European Union: Judgment Day' (2007) 13 *ELJ* 279.

[44] Case C-438/05 (*Viking*). For a detailed analysis, see B Bercusson [n 43 above] and idem, 'Collective Action and Economic Freedoms: Assessment of the Opinions of the Advocates General in *Laval* and *Viking* and Six Alternative Solutions', European Trade Union Institute (ETUI-REHS), Brussels, 2007, available at: www.etui-rehs.org/research/publications.

[45] This implication of *Viking* was addressed not by the ECJ (see Case C-438/05, para 9), but in the findings of the Queen's Bench Division Commercial Court ([2005] EWHC 1222 (Comm), para 3) and repeated by the Court of Appeal ([2005] EWCA Civ 1299, para 1).

take effect (Article 6 no 1, Article 2(1), Article 60(1)(a) Brussels I-Regulation).[46] Viking argued *inter alia* that the threat of collective action by the Finnish union and the coordinating activities of the ITF were incompatible with Viking's right of establishment as guaranteed by Article 43 EC.

Two of the ECJ's arguments are of particular interest here. Pompously, it states: 'the right to take collective action, including the right to strike, must therefore be recognised as a fundamental right which forms an integral part of the general principles of Community law the observance of which the Court ensures.'[47] This benevolent confirmation of the right to strike explains the favourable reaction the judgment received, not least on part of the European trade unions.[48] The following argumentative step by the ECJ, however, is hardly worthy of any commendation, as here the Court fundamentally reconfigures the traditional balance between economic freedoms at the European level and social rights at the national level:

> It is sufficient to point out that, even if, in the areas which fall outside the scope of the Community's competence, the Member States are still free, in principle, to lay down the conditions governing the existence and exercise of the rights in question, the fact remains that, when exercising that competence, the Member States must nevertheless comply with Community law.[49]

At first glance, the Court here proposes a marginal step. All the ECJ seem to do is to bring to bear the framework which Community law has already developed in assessing the legitimacy of restrictions imposed by national law. However, in the present case, this move concerns a social autonomy, protected by fundamental rights, whose articulation does not lie within the competence of the Community, as it can be derived not least from Article 137(5) EC, which explicitly indicates that questions of 'pay, the right of association, the right to strike or the right to impose lock-outs' should continue to be regulated by the Member States.[50]

[46] According to English international civil procedure, the case fell under the Finnish rather than English jurisdiction. However, the doctrine of *forum non conveniens* cannot be invoked under Council Regulation 44/2001 on jurisdiction and the recognition and enforcement of judgments in civil and commercial matters (as amended), Article 2 and Article 6(1); see Case C-281/02 *Owusu* [2005] ECR I-1383.

[47] Case C-438/05 (*Viking*) para 44.

[48] Press statement by the European Trade Union Confederation, 11 December 2007, available at: www.etuc.org/a/4376 (4 February 2008). Whether an outright denial of a European fundamental right to strike was indeed a realistic menace can be doubted given the loss of public acceptance and political legitimation that would have resulted from such a 'finding' of the Court.

[49] Case C-438/05 (*Viking*) para 40.

[50] We are, of course, aware of the fact that Article 137(5) ECT does not prevent the Union from regulating on matters relating to pay, strikes and lock-outs on a treaty-base beyond Article 137(2) ECT. However, as has been underlined by AG Mengozzi, Article 137(5) must not be derogated by formalistic resort to some legal bases other than Article 137(2). See AG Mengozzi, Opinion delivered on 23 May 2007 – Case C-341/05 (*Laval*) Rz 57–58.

Moreover, the Court, with the same move, rejects the suggestion to infer from its ruling in *Albany*[51] that collective labour law including collective action must not be subjected to market freedoms. In *Albany*, the Court had exempted collective agreements from the scope of European competition rules. Its argument then was that certain restrictions of competition were inherent to collective agreements, and declaring them illegal would undermine the social functions of these agreements, which the Union's social objectives and commitments acknowledge.[52] While the Court's legal reasoning in *Albany* seemed methodologically questionable, its underlying constitutional rationale was perfectly sound: It follows from the decoupling of the social from the economic sphere in the integration project that European market rules should leave Member States' labour constitutions untouched. In *Viking*, however, the Court did not refer to this constitutional rationale; it took instead its own legal reasoning literally. The Court held that *Albany* should be read restrictively. While competition law would render collective action unlawful *per se*, such action is not inherently but only under specific conditions irreconcilable with the market freedoms; it must therefore, so the Court concluded, not be exempted from their scope.[53] Is this to say that subjecting collective action and collective labour law in general to market freedoms would erode the social objectives and commitments of the Union only partially? This implication seems to be acceptable to the ECJ.

The second argument brought forward by the ECJ concerns limits imposed by Community law on those fundamental rights guaranteed by national law in the area of their domestic labour and social constitutions. The remarkable scope of Article 43 EC, which has just been highlighted, appears to be qualified. The Court refers to a formula, well-known from the cases *Schmidberger*[54] and *Omega*,[55] according to which

> the protection of fundamental rights is a legitimate interest which, in principle, justifies a restriction of the obligations imposed by Community law, even under a fundamental freedom guaranteed by the Treaty.[56]

But the text continues:

> However, in Schmidberger and Omega, the Court held that the exercise of the fundamental rights at issue, that is, freedom of expression and freedom of assembly and respect for human dignity, respectively, does not fall outside the scope of the

[51] Case C-67/96; with Joined Cases C-115/97, C-116/97 and C-117/97 *Albany International BV v Stichting Bedrijfspensioenfonds Textielindustrie* [1999] ECR I-5751.

[52] *Albany* paras 52–60.

[53] *Viking* para 52.

[54] Case C-112/00 Eugen Schmidberger, Internationale Transporte und Planzuge v Republic of Austria [2003] ECR I-5659.

[55] Case C-36/02 *Omega Spielhallen- und Automatenaufstellungs-GmbH v Oberbrgermeisterin der Bundesstadt Bonn* [2004] ECR I-9609.

[56] Case C-438/05 (*Viking*) para 45.

provisions of the Treaty and considered that such exercise must be reconciled with the requirements relating to rights protected under the Treaty and in accordance with the principle of proportionality.[57]

With this asymmetrical (diagonal) interlinking of the freedoms of the European economic constitution with the fundamental rights of national labour constitutions, the very autonomy of Member States' labour and social constitutions is undermined, although it should have been protected by the principle of enumerated competences.

This remarkable move is accorded even greater effect by subjecting not only national labour legislation to European restraints but also directly the unions as actors entitled by such laws. Such extension of the idea of horizontal effect to trade unions represents not really a sharp turn but still a bold move in the Court's jurisprudence.[58] In its first relevant *dictum* on horizontal effect in 1974,[59] the Court had found that the obligations from the market freedoms should apply directly to non-state actors enacting collective regulations in the areas of work or provision of services.[60] The Court evidently wanted to prevent that Member States could, in order to adhere to their protectionist measures, defer to private actors by way of providing them with legal autonomy to regulate market affairs unilaterally, ie, the same way as the state did before. The factual constellation underlying this and the following rulings[61] of the Court on direct horizontal effect was always of the same type, namely, a legal entity (a corporation or organisation) was indeed provided with regulatory autonomy, and the enacted regulations applied to an individual who was not even a member of this legal entity endowed with participatory rights.

[57] Ibid para 46.

[58] The readiness to assign 'horizontal effect' not just to fundamental rights, but also to transnational market freedoms contrasts markedly with the origins and meaning of the '*Drittwirkungsdoktrin*' as developed by the German Constitutional Court in its seminal *Lüth* judgment (see *Bundesverfassungsgericht*, judgment of 15 January 1958, BVerfGE 7, 198). What may come as a self-evident analogy for some (eg, AG Maduro, Opinion delivered on 23 May 2007 – Case C-438/05 (*Viking*), para 39), represents actually a full turnaround: direct horizontal effect of fundamental rights constitutes the prevalence of the political constitution also in the economic and societal sphere (for thorough analyses, see T Henne (ed), *Das Lüth-Urteil aus rechtshistorischer Sicht* (Berlin: Berliner Wissenschafts-Verlag, 2005); direct horizontal effect of transnational market freedoms constitutes, in contrast, the predecence of an economic constitution over any other societal sphere. For a precise analysis of the Europeanisation of the *Drittwirkungs*-doctrine and of the tensions between the freedoms and the right to strike, see K Preedy, *Die Bindung Privater an die europäischen Grundfreiheiten. Zur sogenannten Drittwirkung im Europarecht* (Berlin: Duncker & Humblot, 2005), esp at 15 ff, 211ff.

[59] Case 36/74 *Walrave* [1974] ECR 1405.

[60] Ibid para 18.

[61] Case 13/76 *Donà* [1976] ECR 1333; Case C-415/93 *Bosman* [1995] ECR I-4921; Case C-309 /99 *Wouters* [2002] ECR I-1577. The exemption is Case C-281-98 *Angonese* [2000] ECR I-4139 : this judgment concerned a rule adopted by a private employer concerning a specific language certificate to be submitted by job applicants. But also in this case, the regulation was imposed unilaterally on individuals. Moreover, in this case the Court hampered the legal standards compared to a state or a state-like actor: only the prohibition to discriminate applies and justification of discriminative behaviour is eased.

These measures assessed by the Court in its earlier judgments are not equivalent to the collective actions organised by trade unions for various reasons. First, the right to collective action does not imply the power to regulate market affairs unilaterally. Quite to the contrary, collective action is meant to compensate the absence of such a unilateral regulatory autonomy. By the same token, the affected party, namely the employer, is not an individual who would be subject to such regulatory power, but acts as the counter power to trade unions at eye level. Second, the Court argues that the envisaged collective action measures were at least aiming at a collective agreement,[62] this is why the Court deems it justified to equate collective action measures with the agreement they seek to achieve. The riddle is, however, that if the trade unions' claims had been accepted by Viking and if they had been codified in a collective agreement, this agreement would not have violated Viking's freedom of establishment. Thus, if the content of an agreement would be legal under European law, why should the measures aiming at this very agreement be prohibited? Furthermore, the liability for a violation of market freedoms was not only imposed on the Finnish trade unions which were taking action against Viking, but extended to the ITF, ie, a supranational federation of trade unions. The only action undertaken by the ITF, however, was the sending of a letter to the Estonian trade union reminding it of its obligations under the ITF's decisions and statutes. If such a mere internal act is now classified as an impediment of market freedoms, nothing less than a total delimitation of the horizontal effect of market freedoms is looming.[63]

After this bombshell, the ECJ adopted a more conciliatory language, which it again refers to in the *Laval* case:

> According to Article 3(1)(c) and (j) EC, the activities of the Community are to include not only an 'internal market characterised by the abolition, as between Member States, of obstacles to the free movement of goods, persons, services and capital', but also 'a policy in the social sphere'. Article 2 EC states that the Community is to have as its task, *inter alia*, the promotion of 'a harmonious, balanced and sustainable development of economic activities' and 'a high level of employment and of social protection'.
>
> Since the Community has thus not only an economic but also a social purpose, the rights under the provisions of the Treaty on the free movement of goods, persons, services and capital must be balanced against the objectives pursued by social policy, which include, as is clear from the first paragraph of Article 136 EC, *inter alia*, improved living and working conditions, so as to make possible their harmonisation

[62] *Viking*, para 60.

[63] See *Viking*, paras 64–65. We would like to recall, in contrast, how cautiously Community law and policy have countered restrictions on the free movement of goods by non-state norms. See H Schepel, *The Constitution of Private Governance. Product Standards in the Regulation of Integrating Markets* (Oxford: Hart Publishing, 2005) 37 ff.

> while improvement is being maintained, proper social protection and dialogue between management and labour.[64]

What conclusion can be drawn from all this? In principle, the 'social purpose' would legitimise collective action that is aimed at 'protecting the jobs and conditions of employment'. The pre-conditions, however, are that the 'jobs or conditions of employment at issue ... are in fact jeopardised or under serious threat' and that actions taken 'do not go beyond what is necessary to attain that objective'.[65]

The Court leaves such evaluation to those national courts having jurisdiction – in this case ironically, an English court. Still the ECJ provides some indication that the actions of the Finnish union did not actually serve the general interest, generally accepted to restrict market freedoms, as Viking had offered not to discharge any Finnish employees.[66] Apparently, Viking had planned to gradually replace the expensive Finnish crew by a cheap Estonian workforce both through the non-renewal of fixed-term contracts and through transfers to other worksites. This concession would therefore only have meant that the process of re-flagging would not have been as cost-effective as originally intended. These vague indications provided and the direct subordination of unions to Treaty obligations by the ECJ limit in the end – after the European usurpation of Member States' labour constitutions and the direct obligation of unions to the European imperatives – the fundamental rights of the union to a right to protect contracts of employment as they stand.

In essence, the formulation of the ECJ results in a deprivation of the Finnish unions of their power, relativising their right to strike with the help of an entrepreneurial freedom of constitutional rank. However, it does not reform the Finnish social model in the name of a European economic constitution – such a move would be difficult to comprehend given the degrading of 'the system of undistorted competition' from an objective to a mere instrument by the Lisbon Treaty[67] – but in the name of an incomplete European social constitution and despite the explicit deferral to Member State competences in Article 137(5) EC.

2. *Laval: European Secondary Law and the Member States' Autonomy of Strike*

The plaintiff in the *Laval* case[68] was a company incorporated under Latvian law, whose registered office was in Riga. Laval's previous Swedish subsidiary (Bygg AB) – later both companies were only linked by identical share owners,

[64] Case C-438/05 (*Viking*) paras 78–79; this is in similar wording confirmed in *Laval* (Case C-341/05, paras 104–105).

[65] Case C-438/05 (*Viking*) paras 81, 84.

[66] Case C-438/05 (*Viking*) para 81.

[67] See Article 4 EG and Article 3(2) DCT on the one hand and Article 2 TEU on the other.

[68] Case C-341/05 (*Laval*).

managers and their brand name[69] – had been awarded the tender for a school building at the outskirts of Stockholm. In obtaining the tender, Bygg had benefited from its ability to post workers earning considerably lower wages from Latvia to Sweden. In May 2004, Laval posted several dozens of its workers to work at the Swedish building sites.

Concerning the applicability of the freedom to provide services (Article 49 EC) – a question of primary law – the ECJ followed its judgment in *Viking*.[70] However, *Laval* offers additional insights for secondary law, namely the 1996 Directive 96/71/EC concerning the posting of workers in the framework of the provision of services.[71] This Directive did not harmonise the substantial legal provisions concerning the employment of posted workers, but it required Member States to ensure that the working conditions of those workers posted to their territory, in a number of essential working conditions (Article 3(1)), complied with their own labour standards, provided by law or by collective bargaining agreements.[72]

Sweden implemented the Posted Workers Directive in 1999. The legislation included some legal minimum working conditions, for instance concerning working hours, but no provisions regarding minimum wages; it also introduced no system of internal universal applicability of collective bargaining agreements. The latter is, however, required by Article 3(1) of the Directive, in order to apply collectively bargained wage standards to the jobs of posted workers. Instead, Sweden intended to apply the special provision in Article 3(8)(2) of the Directive, according to which *de facto* generally binding wage standards can be equipped with international applicability.[73] However, the conferral of

[69] Ibid para 43.

[70] See the previous section, especially the text accompanying nn 43 et seq.

[71] Directive 96/71/EC concerning the posting of workers in the framework of the provision of services, OJ 1996, L18/1.

[72] The obligation to apply minimum working requirements to the jobs of posted workers, according to Article 3 (1) of the Directive 96/71/EC, has to be considered against the background of the case law of the ECJ which was established before the Directive came into effect (see Recital 12 of the Directive 96/71/EC). The case law stated that European law did not require (as did the Directive) but rather 'permitted' the application of domestic minimum working conditions to posted workers; this freedom has in fact been used, for example, by France and Germany (see W Eichhorst, *Europäische Sozialpolitik zwischen nationaler Autonomie und Marktfreiheit. Die Entsendung von Arbeitnehmern in der EU* (Frankfurt aM: Campus, 2000) 185 ff). For a systematic re-construction of the directive in a conflict of laws perspective, see F Rödl, 'Weltbürgerliches Kollisionsrecht', PhD Thesis, EUI, Florence, 2008, Part 2, B II.2.

[73] The Court simply ignores Swedish policy, see ECJ, Case 341/05 (*Laval*), paras 67 and 70. With this, the Court follows the Commission's account in its Communication COM(2003) 458 fin, where it declared it to be indispensable – without indicating any legal basis for its position – that such an intention be made explicitly within the legislative Act implementing the Directive (sub 4.1.2.1). But see the Swedish Government Bill 1998/99: 90, p 27, cited in the Judgment of the Swedish Labour Court, Judgment no 49/05, Case no A 268/04 on p 31 of the English translation (on file with authors): To require that foreign employers should *by law* apply Swedish collective bargaining agreements was considered by the Swedish Government to be discriminatory against foreign employers, as domestic employers are likewise exposed only to trade unions' claims. Hence, the extension of domestic agreements to posting employers and (posted) employees was considered a matter better left to the social actors concerned.

international applicability to collectively bargained internal standards should apparently again have been left to employers and employees to decide upon in collective agreements and not have been determined by state law – a choice which again underlines the strength of the unions in the Swedish social model. In this context, a so-called *lex Britannia* within the Swedish labour law is of particular importance. It states that collective agreements under foreign law do not generate an obligation to refrain from collective action and strike. This seems plausible as well: if the enforcement of domestic wages by trade unions is to be functionally equivalent to legal minimum working requirements – which was the intention of the Swedish legislator – then a foreign collective agreement cannot prevent collective action by the unions, as is equally the case for the application of minimum standards determined by state legislation.[74]

The Swedish building and public works union, supported by the electricians' trade union, was willing to bring to bear the transnational scope of its autonomy, guaranteed in Swedish law, against Laval with determination and intensity. Particularly effective was the blockade of the building sites, compelling Laval to give in.

The ECJ, however, declared illegal all demands and, accordingly, all associated activities of the Swedish unions. In its view, the *lex Britannia* was discriminatory. Discrimination consisted, according to the Court, in not differentiating between the case of a foreign employer having concluded a collective bargaining agreement under the law of his home state and the case of a domestic employer not being bound by any collective agreement under Swedish law; trade unions were entitled to strive for a collective agreement according in both cases.[75] We cannot see why the difference the Court underlines should matter. Both the domestic and the foreign are not bound by domestic collective agreements; but only a binding agreement can exclude the danger of transnational wage competition ('social dumping').

Moreover, the Court found that the Posted Workers Directive prohibits all union activities beyond those essential working conditions enumerated in Article 3(1) of the Directive, it prohibits union activities for essential working conditions that are better than those already legally provided[76] and it prohibits union activities for all wages outside of the lowest wage group.[77] It must be noted that the Posted Workers Directive, at least according to European public opinion, was enacted in order to prevent a wage-cost competition. The Court, however, interpreted the Directive as imposing a wide restriction on the right

[74] See the paradigmatic ECJ decision of 27 March 1990 in Case C-113/89 *Rush Portuguesa* [1990] ECR I-1417, para 18, according to which the permissibility of legally extending legal and wage minimum working conditions to posted workers does not depend on the fact that the posted workers fall under a collective agreement in their home states.

[75] *Viking*, para 116.

[76] Ibid para 99.

[77] Ibid para 70.

to strike. In so doing, the Court does not spend much energy on methodologically justified objections, such as – to cite just the most prominent one – Recital 22 of the Directive, which states that it is 'without prejudice to the law of the Member States concerning collective action to defend the interests of trades and professions'.

We wonder whether it was seriously considered, during the negotiations over the Directive, that it might restrict the unions' right to strike as protected by national constitutions. It is difficult to establish whether the Swedish delegates had realised that the Directive required quite a substantial modification of the Swedish system of collective labour relations, as, at least in the international context, legal provisions about the universal validity of collective agreements have to be introduced. Even if Sweden's capable officials had properly understood the complex regulations and, hence, envisaged their implications, could they not have relied on the fact that European interventions in Member States' collective action law would imply at least a careful and considerate examination of competences, given the negative competence norm in Article 137(5) EC, as cautiously pointed out by Advocate General Mengozzi?[78] Instead of encumbering the negotiations with Swedish concerns, could they not have counted on the fact that the ECJ also emphasised that the Posted Workers Directive did not aim to 'harmonise systems for establishing terms and conditions of employment in the Member States'?[79]

The statements of the ECJ interpret the supremacy claim of European law in a very broad way: Directive 96/71/EC is certainly an important regulation in labour law. However, it is only concerned with a conflict situation within the internal market and is not an element of a comprehensive European labour and social constitution, whereas the Sweden guarantee of the right to collective action has to be understood as an integral part of the Swedish social model.[80] Is the European Union, based upon a rather daring interpretation of a European Directive, authorised to insist that Sweden reconfigures the roles of unions and state competences, which constitute a part of the Swedish Constitution?[81]

[78] AG Mengozzi, Opinion delivered on 23 May 2007 in Case C-341/05 (*Laval*) paras 57–58. AG Mengozzi's argument does not seem convincing, however. For some, he explicitly negates the effects of Article 137(5) EC; even more surprising, he does not comprehensively justify the competence that he derives from Article 47(2) EC.

[79] Case C-341/05 (*Laval*) para 68.

[80] See Case C-341/05 (*Laval*) paras 10, 92.

[81] This article was written before the ECJ, on 3 April 2008, handed down its judgment in *Rüffert* (Case C-346/06). There, the Court confirmed its rigid interpretation of the Posted Workers Directive. Its new judgment does not directly affect the German system of industrial relations. Instead, it assaults and undermines the sensitive interplay established between the exercise of public authority and the autonomy of the social partners. It is worth noting that the German Constitutional Court had only recently – after years of debate and litigation – in a judgment of 11 July 2006 (1 BVL 4/00; available at the website of the Court at www.bverfg.de/entscheidungen) confirmed the constitutionality of provisions of the *Vergabegesetz* of the Land Berlin as being equivalent to those held to be illegal in *Rüffert*. The *Bundesverfassungsgericht* had considered the potential incompatibility of the *Vergabegesetz* with European law. It had concluded that there was need for it to examine that

C. *Viking*, *Laval* and the Vocation of the ECJ in Constitutional Politics

The references to conflict of laws in Section II above made no mention of a further query which was prominently raised by the American conflict-of-laws scholar Brainerd Currie back in the 1960s. This query concerned the judicial function in interstate constellations:

> The reason is that choice between the competing interests of coordinate states is a political function of a high order, which ought not, in a democracy, to be committed to the judiciary: ... the court is not equipped to perform such a function; and the Constitution specifically confers that function upon Congress.[82]

Currie was referring to the federal system of the US here. There are important differences to consider, before one applies his suggestions to the EU. One difference, or European peculiarity, was underlined at the beginning, namely, the sectoral decoupling of the social from the economic constitution – and the difficulties involved in the establishment of a single European *Sozialstaat*. The ECJ's argument implies that European economic freedoms, rhetorically tamed only by an unspecified 'social dimension' of the Union, trump the labour and social constitution (*Arbeits-* and *Sozialverfassung*) of a Member State. In view of the obstacles to the establishment of a comprehensive European welfare state, the respect for the common European legacy of *Sozialstaatlichkeit* seems to require both the acceptance of European diversity and judicial self-restraint whenever European economic freedoms come into conflict with national welfare state traditions. The ECJ is not a constitutional court with comprehensive competences. It is not legitimated to re-organise the interdependence of Europe's social and economic constitutions, let alone replace the variety of European social models with a uniform Hayekian *Rechtsstaat*. It should therefore refrain from 'weighing' the values of *Sozialstaatlichkeit* against the value of free market access. Its proper function, we have argued, is to develop supranational law which compensates for the 'democracy failures' of nation states. National welfare traditions do not – by definition – represent such failures. Against the background outlined above (Section I), the watering down of welfare state positions through supranational law cannot be accepted as a correction of the failures of national democracy but rather as a dismantling of modern democratic self-determination without offering any kind of replacement. The issue in the cases of *Laval* and *Viking* concerned the economic (ab)use of mere

statute because the ECJ would otherwise not know whether it was assessing valid or invalid national law (see para 52). In the context of its own assessment, the *Bundesverfassungsgericht* underlined, *inter alia*, that the *Vergabegesetz* was to be read in the light of the *Sozialstaatsprinzip* (social state principle) of Article 20(1) and the commitment to human dignity (Article 1(1) and Article 2(1) of the Basic Law). The German Court has hence institutionalised principles of social protection which the ECJ has overruled in the name of its own understanding of Europe's social commitments. One wonders whether the ECJ can be expected to discuss such discrepancies.

[82] B Currie, 'The Constitution and the Choice of Law: Governmental Interests and the Judicial Function' [1958] in idem, *Selected Essays* (Durham NC: Duke University Press, 1963) 188, at 272.

wage differences, which resulted in the unions reacting with national strategies in the *Laval* case and post-national strategies in the *Viking* case. The unions took action in order to counter the increased power of employers caused by the European economic freedoms. To argue that the right to collective action to national constellations is subject to a European right is not only to conceal the *de facto* decoupling of the social from the economic constitution, but also to *de jure* subordinate the former to the latter.

What does all this imply for Habermas' *monitum*? A definite evaluation of the impact of *Viking* and *Laval* is not yet possible. It is sufficiently clear, however, that this jurisprudence is a step towards the 'hard law' of negative integration. What about the possibilities for a correction of this step through 'social market economy', 'social rights' and the soft methods of coordination? We have expressed our scepticism clearly enough. This is why we have to ask whether it is really in the long-term interest of the new Member States to dismantle the welfarism of their western and northern European neighbours. What would be the implications for their own long-term competitive advantage and their chances for similar developments? Habermas may still be normatively right. The factual chances of his hopes materialising, however, have further diminished.

17

*Will the Welfare State Survive European Integration? On the Exhaustion of the Legal Conceptualisations of the Integration Project from the Foundational Period and the Search for a New Paradigm**

PROLOGUE: THE STATE OF THE UNION

EUROPE IS IN troubled waters. It has recently been called a 'faltering project' by none other than Jürgen Habermas,[1] probably the most famous public intellectual among its most ardent protagonists. Habermas is, of course, ranging and operating beyond mainstream European studies and legal academia. The mainstream views on, and perceptions of, the state of the Union are, needless to say, not uniform. This could be called an asset if the pluralism within our discipline were to be the outcome of an informed debate. However, to a significant degree, the plurality we experience and observe is the result of specialisation. It mirrors fragmentation rather than pluralism. Administrative law, private law, social and labour law, on the one hand, and the generalists in the European legal community and European constitutionalism, on the other hand, represent different communities and reach different audiences. This essay will seek to build bridges between these provinces. This effort is, somewhat ironically, undertaken by an author with a background in *Wirtschaftsrecht*, a term which is not even known outside the German tradition and loses both its most fascinating, and its most interesting, connotations when translated literally as 'economic law', and a discipline which the defenders of welfarism (*Sozialstaatlichkeit*) and promoters of social Europe tend to perceive as their

* Published in (2011) 1 *European Journal of Social Law* 4.

[1] J Habermas, *Europe: The Faltering Project* (Cambridge: Polity Press, 2009).

natural enemy,[2] whereas European constitutionalism tends to treat it with benign neglect.[3]

Both of these academic responses have their *fundamenta in re*, their reasons, which can be traced back to the original institutional design of the European (then Economic) Community, as it was understood in the legal conceptualisations during the foundational period (Section I). Our re-construction of three such attempts will be followed by observations on their development and their responses to the so-called transformations of Europe since the adoption of the Single European Act in 1987 (Section II). In our perception, the potential of all of these responses to cope with the current critical state of the Union is, by now, exhausted, a diagnosis which suggests the need for a paradigmatic renewal (Section III). Our plea for such a re-conceptualisation in the Epilogue of this essay takes up the 'united in diversity' motto of the Draft Constitutional Treaty.[4]

I. THE FOUNDATIONAL PERIOD

The analytical steps announced in our introductory remarks are an – admittedly – abstract and indirect step towards an answer to the query posed in the title of this essay, and the recourse to the foundational period of the integration project may be perceived as a cumbersome detour. It should become apparent, however, that this detour is a pre-condition for an understanding of our difficulties with Europe's present *impasses*.

The re-construction of the foundational period, which we are undertaking here, focuses on representative scholarly contributions. We do not seek to reveal 'the true story' of the integration project. What we do try to understand are the meta-positive assumptions upon which the legal conceptualisations of the integration project have relied, and from which they sought to derive normative guidance for their contributions to its operation. We will, then, necessarily, and deliberately so, have to proceed selectively, albeit not arbitrarily. Our re-construction will depart from, and be restricted to, three schools of thought of long-term significance. Their messages are in a nutshell: (1) 'Europe should be institutionalised as a technocratic regime and be restricted to that

[2] L Nogler and U Reifner, 'Social Contracts in the Light of the Common Frame of Reference for a Future EU Contract Law' in L Antoniolli and F Fiorentini (eds), *A Factual Assessment of the Draft Common Frame of Reference* (Munich: Sellier, 2010) 365 at 390 ff.

[3] This is not, of course, true for the ordoliberal protagonists of the theory of the 'economic constitution' (see Sections I.2 and III.2 below) and there are further exceptions to the rule, such as A v Bogdandy, 'A Bird's Eye View on the Science of European Law: Structures, Debates and Development Prospects of Basic Research on the Law of the European Union in a German Perspective' (2000) 6 *ELJ* 208.

[4] Article I-8 Draft European Constitutional Treaty (OJ C 310/1, 16/12/2004).

function'. (2) 'Europe's vocation is the establishment of an "economic constitution" which is to protect individual freedoms and to discipline the exercise of political power'; and (3) 'Europe has accomplished and should preserve an equilibrium between a supranational legal order and ongoing political bargaining'. Each of these three approaches can claim to conceptualise important elements of Europe's integration law, and each of them can provide normative reasons for its specific conceptualisation: the model of European rule which it defends and promotes. Even though the analytical assumptions and normative perspectives of these models differ very significantly, they have one crucial aspect in common which can be stated at best negatively: they did not conceive of the European Economic Community as a constitutional democracy in being, but sought to understand the Community as a legitimate mode of governance beyond nation-state confines and frames.

I.1. Europe as Technocratic Administration

An 'Executive Power',[5] an 'Executive Federalism',[6] 'Functional Constitutionalism',[7] a 'Transnational Administrative Power'[8] – ever since its inception – and in ever new variations – the integration project has been characterised as bureaucratic machinery, not only by lawyers but also by political scientists.[9] The path-breaking initiator of this tradition was Hans Peter Ipsen, the influential founding father of European Law as a new legal discipline in Germany.[10] The Nazi period had left him, to paraphrase Hans Ulrich Jessurun d'Oliveira, 'not totally flawless'.[11] His post-war work on the *Staatsrecht* of the young German democracy, however, documents very clear democratic commitments in general, and commitments to the *Sozialstaatlichkeit* of the new

[5] D Curtin, Executive Power of the European Union. Law, Practices and the Living Constitution (Oxford: OUP, 2009).

[6] R Schütze, 'From Rome to Lisbon: "Executive Federalism" in the (New) European Union' (2010) 47 *CML Rev* 1385.

[7] NT Isiksel, 'On Europe's Functional Constitutionalism. Towards a Constitutional Theory of Specialized International Regimes' (2012) 19 *Constellations* 102.

[8] PL Lindseth, Power and Legitimacy: Reconciling Europe and the Nation–state (Oxford: OUP, 2010).

[9] From S Puntscher-Riekmann, Die kommissarische Neuordnung Europas. Das Dispositiv der Integration (Vienna-New York: Springer, 1998), to J Trondal, An Emergent European Executive Order (Oxford: OUP, 2010).

[10] See HP Ipsen, 'Der deutsche Jurist und das Europäische Gemeinschaftsrecht' in *Verhandlungen des 43. Deutschen Juristentages* (Munich: CH Beck, 1964), vol 2, at 14 ff; idem, *Europäisches Gemeinschaftsrecht*, (Tübingen: Mohr/Siebeck, 1972) 176 ff; on Ipsen, see M Kaufmann, *Europäische Integration und Demokratieprinzip* (Baden-Baden: Nomos, 1997) 300 ff and 312 ff.

[11] HU Jessurun d'Oliveira, 'An Anecdote, a Footnote' in H-P Mansel et al (eds), *Festschrift für Erik Jayme*, (Munich: Sellier, European Law Publishers, 2004) 387. D'Oliveira, writing in 1968, referred to Hans Dölle, from 1954 onwards one of the Directors of the Max-Planck Institute für auländisches und internationals Privatrecht in Hamburg.

order in particular.[12] It is precisely his democratic commitments and his prior complicity with Germany's dark past[13] which may explain Ipsen's sensitivity for the precarious legitimacy of the European system and his search for a type of rule whose validity was not dependent on democratic legitimacy. With his understanding of the European Communities as '*Zweckverbände funktionaler Integration*' (organisations with functionally-defined objectives), Ipsen rejected both further-reaching federal ambitions *and* earlier interpretations of the Community as a mere international organisation. He characterised Community law as a *tertium* between federal or state law, on the one hand, and international law, on the other, an order constituted by its 'objective tasks' and adequately legitimated by the solution to them.[14]

I.2. Europe as Institutionalised Economic Rationality

Europe was launched as an economic project, and it is precisely this dimension which has been reiterated in powerful conceptualisations of its *Wesen* and vocation. Its most recent version, in Article 3 (3) TEU, the 'highly competitive social market economy' was formally introduced into Europe's constitutional parlance by a joint motion of Joschka Fischer and Domenique de Villepin in the course of the debates on the Constitutional Treaty.[15] Their initiative was meant to calm down the anxieties over what was perceived as a neo-liberal tilt in the constitutional project. The clause on the social market economy has fulfilled this function quite well in the general public, and in the constitutional discourses of both lawyers[16] and political scientists.[17]

[12] Suffice it here to point to HP Ipsen, 'Über das Grundgesetz' (1949), reprinted along with all of his later essays in idem, *Über das Grundgesetz* (Tübingen: Mohr/Siebeck, 1988) 1.

[13] See C Joerges, 'Europe a *Großraum*? Shifting Legal Conceptualisations of the Integration Project' in C Joerges and NS Ghaleigh (eds), *Darker Legacies of Law in Europe: The Shadow of National Socialism and Fascism over Europe and its Legal Traditions* (Oxford: Hart Publishing, 2003) 167, at 182–84 (note 92), reprinted in pt VII, ch 32 of this volume.

[14] See HP Ipsen, Verfassungsperspektiven der Europäischen Gemeinschaften (Berlin: Walter de Gruyter, 1970).

[15] See the references in C Joerges, 'What is Left of the European Economic Constitution? A Melancholic Eulogy' (2005) 30 *ELR* 461, at 486, reprinted in pt III, ch 22 of this volume.

[16] See, for example, FC Mayer, 'Die Rückkehr der Europäischen Verfassung? Ein Leitfaden zum Vertrag von Lissabon' (2008) 68 *Zeitschrift für öffentliches Recht und Völkerrecht* 1141, at 1165 ff; idem, 'Der EuGH und das soziale Europa' in *Internationale Politikanalyse* (Berlin: Friedrich-Ebert-Stiftung, 2009) 7, and the contributions to: U Neergaard, R Nielsen and L Roseberry (eds), *Integrating Welfare Functions into EU Law – From Rome to Lisbon* (Copenhagen: DJØF Publishing, 2009); most prominently the German Constitutional Court's judgment of 30 June 2008 on the Treaty of Lisbon. Bundesverfassungsgericht, file no: 2 BvE 2 / 08, 2 BvE 5 / 08, 2 BvR 1010 / 08, 2 BvR 1022 / 08, 2 BvR 1259 / 08 und 2 BvR 182 / 09, paras 195 et seq; the English translation at: www.bundesverfassungsgericht.de/entscheidungen/es20090630_2bve000208.en.html.

[17] See, for example, U Liebert, 'Reconciling Social with Market Europe? The EU under the Lisbon Treaty' in D Schiek, U Liebert and H Schneider (eds), *European Economic and Social Constitutionalism after the Treaty of Lisbon* (Cambridge: CUP, 2011), ch 2.

The appeal of the notion owes much to Germany's post-war success story with its '*sozialer Marktswirtschaft*'.[18] This notion, however, originally had fairly precise contours which neither Fischer nor de Villepin, let alone the drafters of the Treaty of Lisbon, was prepared to re-establish. As the renowned protagonist of the concept, Alfred Müller-Armack, explained repeatedly, the social market economy was to provide a 'third way' beyond economic liberalism, on the one hand, and beyond socialism, on the other. There was no conditioning of this model by requirements of 'competitiveness'; quite to the contrary, the governance of market mechanisms was subjected to demands of social justice.[19] To be sure, Müller-Armack and his political allies were keen to underline the compatibility of their social market economy with the economic *credo* of ordoliberalism, although the conceptualisation of this alliance was never entirely clear. However, the leading protagonists of the Freiburg School, the intellectual *Heimat* of Germany's post-war ordoliberalism in both economic and legal scholarship, namely, Walter Eucken and Franz Böhm, on their part, sought to come to terms with the dual commitments to their idea of an 'undistorted system of competition', on the one hand, and to the promise of social justice and security, on the other. This dual commitment required – in their view – the institutionalisation of specific, albeit inter-dependent, orders, namely, a legally-structured order of industrial relations and of social security ('*Arbeits- und Sozialverfassung*') along with the legally guaranteed economic *ordo*, the 'economic constitution' (*Wirtschaftsverfassung*). In this sense, the economic order which they envisaged was meant to be 'socially embedded'.

These perspectives remained theoretically somewhat vague. The 'really existing social market economy', however, proved to be remarkably robust, even though, or, maybe, precisely because, the economic *ordo* which the Freiburg School advocated so decidedly was never as coherently realised as their conceptual *Vordenker* would have liked to see it. Even its economic core institution – its *Wirtschaftsverfassung* – was by no means a theoretically-uncontested and legally-consolidated project. The strongest practical challenge to the Freiburg style of *Ordnungspolitik* was the *renaissance* of Germany's corporatist traditions already in the early years of the Bonn Republic. The Federal Republic was characterised by permanent tensions between *Theorie und Praxis*: striking discrepancies between the officious rhetoric of *Ordnungspolitik*, on the one hand, and the ongoing bargaining between the political system and the political

[18] See, on the following, P Manow, 'Modell Deutschland as an Interdenominational Compromise', *Minda De Gunzburg Centre for European Studies, Working Paper 003/2001*; A Ebner, 'The Intellectual Foundations of the Social Market Economy. Theory, Policy, and Implications for European Integration' (2006) 33 *Journal of Economic Studies* 206.

[19] See the references in C Joerges and F Rödl, '"Social Market Economy" as Europe's Social Model?' in L Magnusson and B Stråth (eds), *A European Social Citizenship? Preconditions for Future Policies in Historical Light. Preconditions for Future Policies from a Historical Perspective* (Brussels: Peter Lang, 2005) 125.

and economic actors, on the other – a German *Lebenslüge*, to be sure, albeit an economically successful and socially beneficial arrangement.[20]

The perception of this discrepancy will have influenced the (ordo-)liberal 'turn to Europe', which implied a retraction from their earlier, more global, political preference.[21] The European level of governance promised to ensure stronger barriers against Germany's corporatist traditions and its political opportunism in economic affairs than the institutional pillars of Germany's *Ordnungspolitik*.

I.3. Europe as Community

In his very first publication on European issues, Joseph Weiler presented a vision,[22] which he defended and substantiated further in his PhD thesis,[23] and later refined and complemented in his seminal narrative on the 'Transformation of Europe':[24] Europe, in its foundational period, so Weiler argued, had managed to establish an equilibrium between legal supranationalism and political intergovernmentalism. His portrayal of European integration was inspired by his teachers in international law, on the one hand, and by the work of Erik Stein, on the other, but it was, nonetheless, path-breaking and unique in both its doctrinal lucidity and its sensitivity for the European synthesis of 'the political' and the law.

Weiler's *œuvre* is a powerful critique of the type of national state which Weber's inaugural address describes.[25] Nowhere, however, did he talk about something akin to 'social Europe'. Even in the concluding passages on democracy in Europe and the legitimacy of the integration project of the 'Transformations of Europe', there is no mention of the possibility that democracy might pre-suppose social justice or that Europe's socially-defined legitimacy might erode through a destruction of welfare state traditions. And

[20] Well documented by W Abelshauser, Die Langen Fünfziger Jahre. Wirtschaft und Gesellschaft in Deutschland 1949–1966 (Düsseldorf: Schwann, 1987).

[21] The scepticism and resistance of leading ordoliberals has been re-constructed and explained in detail by M Wegmann, Früher Neoliberalismus und europaische Integration: Interdependenz der nationalen, supranationalen und internationalen Ordnung von Wirtschaft und Gesellschaft (1932–1965) (Baden-Baden: Nomos, 2002) 351 ff; for the importance of the political and social constitution for the project of economic integration, see ibid 359–366.

[22] JHH Weiler, 'The Community System: The Dual Character of Supranationalism' (1981) 1 *Yearbook of European Law* 257.

[23] Idem, *Il sistema comunitario europeo: struttura giuridica e processo politico* (Bologna: Il Mulino, 1985).

[24] Idem, 'The Transformation of Europe' (1990-91) 100 *Yale LJ* 2403.

[25] See the thorough analysis by D Gaus, 'Legitimate Political Rule without a State? An Analysis of Joseph HH Weiler's Justification of the Legitimacy of the European Union qua Non-statehood', *RECON Online Working Paper 2008/12*, Oslo 2008, available at: www.reconproject.eu/projectweb/portalproject/RECONWorkingPapers.html.

yet, even though Weiler's value-laden work is characterised by a profound distance from technocratic precepts and the economic rationalisation of the European Community, his visions seem surprisingly compatible with the benign neglect of the 'social deficit' of the European order in European legal studies during the foundational period. To be sure, Weiler's re-construction of Europe as a Janus-headed polity was not meant as a conceptualisation which would exclude Europe's engagement in social issues as a matter of (legal) principle. However, it is, nevertheless, true that, thanks to the *Realpolitik*-kernel of his analysis, 'social Europe' was an unlikely option, and one of very limited significance, anyway. It was highly unlikely simply because its advent was dependent on unanimous inter-governmental voting; it was, by the same token, of little concern as the later tensions between the integrationist objective and the legacy of European welfarism were still dormant.

II. ACCOMPLISHMENTS AND SHORTCOMINGS

As an interim summary, we can put on record an ambivalent legacy of the foundational period. On its bright side, we have both to note and to underline as the great and lasting accomplishment of Europe's foundational moment the turning away from the aggressive and bellicose past of Europe's nation states. However, we have to add two shortcomings. One concerns Europe's '*Vergangenheitsschuld*',[26] while the other concerns Europe's one-dimensional institutional design. Both of them are incommensurable in theory, but intertwined in practice.

II.1. Europe's 'Bitter Experiences'

Nobody has analysed both of these dimensions of the European project and their correlation more stringently and passionately than the historian Tony Judt. In the epilogue to his *magnum opus*, he concludes:

> The new Europe, bound together by the signs and symbols of its terrible past, is a remarkable accomplishment; but it remains forever mortgaged to that past. If Europeans are to maintain this vital link – if Europe's past is to continue to furnish Europe's present with admonitory meaning and moral purpose – then it will have to be taught afresh with each passing generation. The 'European Union' may be a response to history, but it can never be a substitute.[27]

[26] The term was coined by B Schlink; see his *Vergangenheitsschuld und gegenwärtiges Recht* (Frankfurt aM: Suhrkamp, 2002); *Guilt about the Past* (St Lucia AU: University of Queensland Press, 2009).

[27] T Judt, *Postwar. A History of Europe since 1945* (New York: Penguin, 2005) 831.

This is by now a widely shared insight.[28] But, notwithstanding this, neither the Holocaust, which Judt refers to as Europe's 'negative identity',[29] nor the fact that the Nazi regime had made the societies of the countries that it had conquered complicit in its persecution and in the annihilation of the European Jews, was understood as a European failure, and this remained outside the memory and the identity politics even in the Draft Constitutional Treaty of 2004.[30] Europe's perception of its past(s) remained one-dimensional. This is easy to understand, especially in the period after the war. But it meant that we missed the chance of deriving additional legitimacy for the integration process out of joint efforts to cope with the evils of the past.

The assumption that such a chance may have existed or could ever materialise may be all too utopian. The commitment to welfare state values, however, which Tony Judt emphasises equally strongly in his narrative on post-war Europe,[31] and again in a short monograph published shortly before he passed away on 6 August 2010,[32] can more easily be understood as a common legacy of democratic European traditions. However, in the institutional design of the integration project, this positive legacy is scarcely visible.

II.2. The Neglect of the Legacy of the Welfare State

The legal theories of the foundational period mirror the social poverty of the integration project faithfully. We have hence defined their second communality negatively. This is a troubling communality, because the institutionalisation of welfare commitments could be, and was in fact, widely understood as a 'second pillar' of Europe's democratic conversion, a societal shield providing protection against a rebirth of the social anxieties which nationalist movements had instrumentalised. Why is it, we are both inclined and entitled to ask, that it is precisely the welfare state traditions of European democracies that are not visible in the legal theories of European integration? Why does it need historians such as Alan Milward[33] and Tony Judt[34] to remind Europe's legal academia that

[28] See, for example, the contribution to Section 4 of M Pakier and B Stråth, *A European Memory. Contested Histories and Politics of Remembrance* (NewYork–Oxford: Berghahn Books, 2010) 163, in particular, CFS Banke, 'Remembering Europe's Heart of Darkness: Legacies of the Holocaust in Post-war European Societies' ibid at 163–174.

[29] T Judt, 'The Past is Another Country: Myth and Memory in Post-war Europe' in J-W Müller (ed), *Memory and Power in Post-war Europe. Studies in the Presence of the Past* (Cambridge: CUP, 2002) 157.

[30] See C Joerges, 'Working through "Bitter Experiences" towards Constitutionalisation: A Critique on the Disregard for History in European Constitutional Theory' in R Buchanan and P Zumbansen (eds), *Law in Transition. Human Rights, Development and Transitional Justice* (Oxford: Hart Publishing, 2014) 269.

[31] Judt, *Postwar*, n 27 above, at 791 ff.

[32] T Judt, *Ill Fares the Land* (New York: The Penguin Press, 2010) 127 ff.

[33] A Milward, *The Rescue of the European Nation-State*, 2nd edn (London: Routledge, 2000) at 21 ff.

[34] Judt, nn 31 and 32 above.

welfare traditions are what Europeans do have in common and it is this which distinguishes their collective memories from that of American citizens?

Why does it need political-scientists such as Fritz Scharpf[35] and Giandomenico Majone[36] to remind European constitutionalists, albeit from very different perspectives, of the structural asymmetries in their constitutional visions? Why is it that a scholar of the format and sensitivity of Joseph Weiler, in his seminal narrative on the 'Transformation of Europe',[37] fails to address the issue of 'social Europe', and, even in his comment on the Treaty of Maastricht, continues to present 'prosperity' as Europe's second value without ever relating it to social justice. What he offers, instead, is quite in line with his appeal to 'Community', a somewhat metaphorical uploading of the notion of 'prosperity' with a 'solidarity' dimension: a soft power, which he expects to control 'the demonic at the statal economic level'.[38] Is it by chance that, in European constitutionalism, it took primarily labour lawyers to remind us of the importance of 'the social' for democratic constitutionalism?[39]

On closer inspection, however, the omission of a 'social dimension' in the conceptualisation of the European project seems not so surprising an omission, let alone a downright failure. During the foundational period, welfare state policies and practices were, of course, controversial in many respects, but they were understood as *national* affairs. Only with hindsight have the implications and effects of this constellation become so clearly visible. Stefano Giubboni, who has re-constructed both the mindset of the 'founding fathers' and the political bargaining over the Treaty of Rome carefully, concludes that we have to understand this outcome not as a mere failure but as a 'historical compromise'.[40] The parties to this compromise are said to have trusted in the wisdom of eminent economists who expected very positive effects from an opening of national *Volkswirtschaften*;[41] they may also have trusted in the sustainability

[35] See, for example, FW Scharpf, 'The European Social Model: Coping with the Challenges of Diversity' (2002) 40 *JCMS* 645, at 645–646, and, recently, 'The Asymmetry of European Integration – Or Why the EU cannot be a Social Market Economy' (2010) 8 *Socio-Economic Review* 211.

[36] G Majone, *Europe as the Would-be World Power. The EU at Fifty* (Cambridge: CUP, 2010) 128 ff. Majone is well aware, however, of the foundational moment; see his classic *Regulating Europe* (London–New York: Routledge, 1996) 1: 'At the end of the period of reconstruction of the national economies shattered by the war income redistribution and discretionary macroeconomic management emerged as the top policy priorities of most Western European governments …'

[37] Weiler, n 24 above; see, in particular, 2476 ff.

[38] See idem, 'Fin-de-Siècle Europe' in R Dehousse (ed), *Europe After Maastricht: An Ever Closer Union?* (Munich: CH Beck, 1994) 203, at 208 ff.

[39] See B Bercusson, 'Social Policy at the Crossroads: European Labour Law after Maastricht' in Dehousse (ed), n 38 above, 149; S Giubboni, *Social Rights and Market Freedoms in the European Constitution. A Labour Law Perspective* (Cambridge: CUP, 2006); B Bercusson, S Deakin, P Koistinen, Y Kravaritou, U Mückenberger, A Supiot and B Veneziani, 'A Manifesto for Social Europe' (1997) 3 *ELJ* 189.

[40] Giubboni, n 39 above, at 7.

[41] See, most notably, the 'Ohlin Report' by the International Labour Organization: 'Social Aspects of European Economic Co-operation. Report by a Group of Experts' (1956) 74 *International Labour Review* 99.

of a constellation which eminent political scientists were to characterise as a politically and socially 'embedded liberalism'.[42] Such positive expectations seem to be completely compatible with stringent transnational regulation where such interventionism was held to be indispensable, ie, in agricultural policy. Legal scholarship, however, treated this socially extremely important and economically extremely costly domain as an 'exception' in the European edifice, which did not deserve, and did not, in fact, attract, closer academic scrutiny for a very long time to come.[43]

II.3. Historical Contingencies

The differences in the re-construction of the foundational constellation between the institutional generalists in European legal scholarship, on the one hand, and a later generation of labour law constitutionalists, on the other, are quite illuminating: Brian Bercusson, writing under the impression of the Treaty of Maastricht, put all his hopes on the 'outstanding importance' of what was accomplished therein.[44] Stefano Giubboni,[45] writing a decade later, complemented the projection of positive signals into the European development in his comments on the later Treaty amendments and on the (Draft) Constitutional Treaty;[46] in addition, he started to seek legally relevant backing for his views on the 'compromise' which he read into the Treaty of Rome:

> [T]he apparent flimsiness of the social provisions of the Treaty of Rome (and of the slightly less meagre ones of the Treaty of Paris) was in reality consistent with the intention, imbued with the embedded liberalism compromise, not only to preserve but hopefully to expand and strengthen the Member States' powers of economic intervention and social governance: ie, their ability to keep the promise of protection underlying the new social contract signed by their own citizens at the end of the war.[47]

The labour law jurisprudence of the ECJ since *Viking*[48] has not been in line with the implications which this reading suggests. This observation, however,

[42] JG Ruggie, 'International Regimes, Transactions and Change: Embedded Liberalism in the Postwar Economic Order' (1982) 36 *International Organization* 375; see J Steffek, *Embedded Liberalism and its Critics: Justifying Global Governance in the American Century* (New York: Palgrave Macmillan, 2006).

[43] Until F Snyder, *Law of the Common Agricultural Policy* (London: Sweet & Maxwell, 1985); for a comprehensive recent analysis, see K Zurek, *European Food Regulation after Enlargement: Facing the Challenges of Diversity* (Leiden: Brill, 2011) ch III.

[44] Giubboni, *Social Rights and Market Freedoms*, n 39 above, at 183.

[45] Giubboni, Diritti Sociali e Mercato. La Dimensione Sociale dell'Integrazione Europea (Bologna: Il Molino, 2003); (English version in n 39 above).

[46] Giubboni, *Social Rights*, n 39 above, at 94–150.

[47] Ibid, at 16.

[48] Case C-438/05, *International Transport Workers' Federation, Finnish Seamen's Union v Viking Line ABP, OÜ Viking Line Eesti*, judgment of 11 December 2007, [2007] ECR I-10779, more recently confirmed by the Court's Grand Chamber on 15 July 2010: Case C-271/08, *European Commission v Federal Republic of Germany*.

does not militate conclusively against it. Florian Rödl[49] has recently renewed the defence of 'Social Europe' by the re-construction of the foundational constellation as a legally significant 'compromise'. It seems, indeed, at least plausible to argue that the premises of the negotiators and their understanding of the EEC Treaty should be taken into account in the interpretation of Treaty provisions such as Article 153 (5) TFEU (ex-Article 137 (5)), which stipulates that 'the provisions of this Article shall not apply to pay, the right of association, the right to strike and the right to impose lock-out'.

To be sure, the Treaty of Rome had mentioned, in its Title III of Part Three, significant social fields, and Member States were, as Article 118 EEC Treaty confirms, expected to cooperate closely. It is also true that distributional and income policies were foreseen in an important part of the European Economy, namely, agriculture. Very different conclusions can be, and have been, drawn from these provisions. They can indeed, as Agustín José Menéndez[50] suggests, be read as strong elements of a federal structure foreshadowing the strengthening of the federalisation of Europe; they can also be understood, as Giandomenico Majone argues,[51] as confirming that the social-policy domain was 'considered to be outside the competence of the supranational institutions'.[52] Both of these readings are based upon the same historical evidence. Both of them need to base their claims upon re-constructions which are informed by non-historical theoretical premises. And it is precisely this recourse to trans-positive and non-legal premises which suggests that the argument from history is inconclusive.

What we can more safely assume is that the negotiators operated on the assumptions of some kind of vaguely presumed 'embedded liberalism' and the sustainability of the foundational constellation, so that the protagonists of welfare policies could live with the compromise which the negotiations had accomplished.

If such expectations proved to be wrong, legal reasoning must not assume that conclusive normative arguments can be derived from 'historical facts'; it must, instead, engage in conceptual deliberations and controversies. It must become aware of the non-historical normative and analytical issues underlying historical re-constructions such as those which we have just mentioned. These issues are complex and sensitive: Does democratic governance, as a matter of principle, require that the objectives of social justice can be pursued by the political system? If so, is it at all conceivable that welfare policies can be successfully

[49] F Rödl, 'Labour Constitution' in A v Bogdandy and J Bast (eds), *Principles of European Constitutional Law*, (Oxford: Hart Publishing, 2010), 605; for a very similar argument, see L Niglia, 'Form and Substance in European Constitutional Law: The "Social" Character of Indirect Effect' (2010) 16 *ELJ* 439.

[50] 'United they Diverge? From Conflicts to Constitutional Theory? Critical Remarks on Joerges' Theory of Conflicts of Law' in R Nickel and A Greppi (eds), *The Changing Role of Law in the Age of Supra- and Transnational Governance* (Baden-Baden: Nomos, 2014) 211.

[51] Majone, *Europe as the Would-be World Power*, n 36 above, at 131 ff.

[52] Ibid, at 132.

institutionalised at European level, or is it, in view of the diversity of socio-economic conditions, political traditions and preference, more promising to preserve their variety?

III. THE SENSITIVITY OF THEORY: THREE RETRACTIONS

The rejection of all the constitutional ambitions in the Treaty of Lisbon and the present *impasses* of the integration *praxis* are obvious and need not be documented here. What is less obvious is that the three theoretical traditions that we have sketched out in the first section of this essay have all succumbed to the siren song of mainstream constitutionalism. This seems all the more telling and remarkable as these three paradigms – technocratic rule, economic rationality, and the community vision – were not chosen at random. These three options represent quite comprehensively the evolutionary options among which the integration project can choose and does, in fact, keep oscillating. All of them have been continuously present and influential in the integration process ever since the foundational period. They had, of course, been prepared to adapt their constructs and visions to the dynamically moving target: they have been developing, even mutating, within their particular perspectives, be it in their responses to changing contexts, be it through mutual observation and political learning. We can neither try to document the continuities and innovations within each tradition, nor discuss the affinities and divergencies between them in any detail here. It is sufficient, for our argument, to characterise the crucial transformations within each of them – and to underline telling parallels in their diagnosis of the current *impasses*.

III.1. Technocracy without Efficiency? Majone's Sceptical Turn

The importance of the technocratic tradition in the *praxis* of the integration project can hardly be over-estimated. Its weight was bound to increase with the involvement of the European Community in ever more regulatory policies, which were to be organised at transnational levels without the backing of a consolidated democratic order. How else than through an 'objective' and expertise-based conceptualisation of its enormous tasks could the European Community hope to ensure the acceptance of its involvement in ever more problem-solving activities? By far the most interesting and influential work which renewed and refined the technocratic legacy is that of Giandomenico Majone.[53]

[53] Who confronted Europe's integration studies right upon his return to Europe with essays such as 'Regulating Europe: Problems and Prospects' (1989) 3 *Jahrbuch zur Staats- und Verwaltungswissenschaft* 159; 'Cross-national Resources of Regulatory Policymaking in Europe and the United States' (1991) 11 *Journal of Public Policy* 79, and has kept working on the perspectives outlined therein ever since (see, most recently, his *Europe as the Would-be World Power*, n 36 above.

It is unique not only in its clarity and coherence, but also in the precision and subtlety of its reflections on the options for an alternative to the democratic constitutionalism of the Member States of the European Union. Majone's famous conceptualisation of Europe as a 'Regulatory State'[54] which would operate essentially through non-majoritarian institutions was conceived as ensuring the credibility of commitments to, in principle, uncontested policy objectives. Welfare policies pose additional problems. The Union's failure to institutionalise a comprehensive social policy is explained by Majone by the 'reluctance of the member states to surrender control of a politically salient and popular area of public policy'; equally important is the factual difficulty and political impossibility of replacing the variety of European welfare state models and traditions with some integrated European scheme.[55] Not only does Majone respect the primacy of constitutional democracies, he is also, and with increasing urgency, underlining the fallacy of an ever more perfect and comprehensive subjection of the integration project to its 'operational code', the principle 'that integration has priority over all competing values',[56] and also the camouflage strategies which he calls 'integration by stealth'.[57] This is an alarming retraction from his earlier trust in the problem-solving potential of the European project. His warnings by no means reflect a change of theoretical premises. Majone continues to underline that Europe is not legitimated to pursue the type of distributional politics which welfare states have institutionalised.[58] He does not retract his plea for regulatory efficiency. His critical turn is, instead, motivated by the *inefficiencies* which he observes in the Union's operations. His quest for more modesty in Europe's ambitions ('*Geht's nicht eine Nummer kleiner?*')[59] summarises these observations. His adaption of the 'united in diversity' formula[60] is an implication of these insights to which we will return in the concluding section.

III.2. What is Left of the Economic Constitution? Ordoliberal Concerns

An institutionalisation of economic rationality is most widely perceived today, either affirmatively or critically, as Europe's main agenda.[61] This perception

[54] G Majone, 'The European Community as a Regulatory State' in *Collected Courses of the Academy of European Law* (The Hague-Boston MA–London: Martinus Nijhoff, 1996) 321.

[55] Majone, *Europe as the Would-be World Power*, n 36 above, at 144.

[56] Ibid, at 1.

[57] See his *Dilemmas of European Inregration: The Ambiguities and Pitfalls of Integration by Stealth* (Oxford: OUP, 2005).

[58] Majone, *Europe as the Would-be World Power*, n 36 above, 128 ff.

[59] Ibid, 170 ff.

[60] Ibid, 205 ff.

[61] See, on the one hand, the contributions on European economic law in von Bogdandy and Bast, n 49 above, by A Haltje, 'The Economic Constitution within the Internal Market', ibid, 589, and J Drexl, 'Competition Law as Part of the European Constitution', ibid, 659 (both authors are strongly indebted to the ordoliberal tradition); and M Höpner and A Schäfer, 'A New Phase of European Integration: Organized Capitalisms in Post-Ricardian Europe' (2010) 33 *West European Politics*

has gained prominence since the legendary White Paper on the Completion of the Internal Market.[62] At that stage of the integration process, the ordoliberal tradition had experienced a deep transformation. This mutation had started at national level with the move of Friedrich von Hayek from Chicago to Freiburg and his promotion of a renewed version of neo-liberalism situated between the Freiburg School's orthodoxy, on the one hand, and the Chicago School's normative complacency, on the other. Von Hayek's notion of 'competition as a discovery process' captures the essence of his messages best. They have led the second generation of ordoliberal scholars to re-define the objectives and the methods of national and European competition law. Attention shifted from the control of economic power to the protection of entrepreneurial freedom and the critique of anti-competitive regulation.

It seems worth noting that what happened in the 1980s at European level had not been predicted but was analysed with amazing precision a good number of years ago by Michel Foucault in the course of the lectures that he delivered at the *Collège de France*.[63] There, Foucault characterised the ordoliberal vision of the strong state, which is committed to the protection of the competitive ordering of the market, as a new type of *gouvernmentalité*, namely, the acceptance of market governance by the political system and the whole of society.[64] This is not, of course, to suggest uniformity in the legal re-conceptualisation of European market governance. There are, for example, remarkable affinities between the second generation of ordoliberals and the Chicago School when it comes to practical issues of competition law and policy, but they have never led to a real merger of the two schools. The heirs of Eucken and von Hayek did not subscribe to the Chicago understanding of 'output efficiency' and 'consumer welfare'; instead, they continued to define and defend the 'system of undistorted competition' as the core of Europe's 'economic constitution'.[65] They witnessed, however, a steady decline of the impact of their visions, which became clearly visible in the substantial broadening of European economic policies in the

344, on the other. Such theoretical controversies vary, of course, as strongly as Europe's varieties of capitalism.

[62] European Commission, 'White Paper to the European Council on Completion of the Internal Market', COM(85) 310 final, 14 June 1985.

[63] M Foucault, *Naissance de la biopolitique. Cours au Collège de France* (Paris: Seuil/Gallimard, 2004); in particular, the lecture of 7 February 1979, 105, and that of 14 February 1979, 135.

[64] Ibid: '[A]u lieu d'accepter une liberté du marché, définie par l'État et maintenue en quelque sorte sur surveillance étatique ... eh bien, disent les ordolibéraux, il faut entièrement retourner la formule et se donner la liberté du marché comme principe organisateur et régulateur de l'État ... Autrement dit, un État sous surveillance du marché plutôt qu'un marché sous surveillance de l'État', *Biopolitique* (note 7), Lecture 5, p 120.

[65] See E-J Mestmäcker, *Wirtschaft und Verfassung in der Europäischen Union. Beiträge zu Recht, Theorie und Politik der europäischen Integration* (Baden-Baden: Nomos, 2003), with a collection of essays written from 1965 to 2001 and his recent critique of E Posner in *A Legal Theory without Law Posner v Hayek on Economic Analysis of Law* (Tübingen: Mohr Siebeck, 2007), also available at: http://papers.ssrn.com/sol3/papers.cfm?abstract_id=1168422.

Treaty of Maastricht,[66] the so-called 'modernisation' of European competition law,[67] and the move towards a 'more economic approach'.[68] The weakening of their ideational power was symbolically confirmed when French Prime Minister Nicolas Sarkozy saw to it that the Union's commitment to 'a system ensuring that competition is not distorted' was not included in Article 3 TFEU (ex-Article 2 TEU) but moved back into Protocol 27 of the Treaty of Lisbon.[69]

III.3. Unity without Community? JHH Weiler's Constitutional Complacency

Joseph Weiler's early work can, in hindsight, be identified as truly path-breaking in that it synthesised, in a novel way, Europe's constitutive historical move towards a common peaceful future, the construction of a supranational legal alternative to the role of international law in the system, while remaining aware of the political embeddedness and dependency of these accomplishments. The great normative perspectives and the sensitive realism in his design of an equilibrium between 'legal supranationalism' and 'political inter-governmentalism', however, became gradually ever more apparent as Weiler sought to develop his construct and vision further in the light of European experiences, accomplishments and failures. In 'Transformation of Europe', he delivered an insightful diagnosis of the problematical implications of majority voting in terms of Europe's legitimacy.[70] He was among the first to realise the normative and political ambivalences of the completion of the Internal Market by the Delors Commission:

> [T]o regard the Community as a technological instrument is, in the first place, to under-estimate the profound political choice and cultural impact which the single market involves – a politics of efficiency, a culture of market.[71]

We can summarise the foregoing observations in a second interim conclusion: the *impasses* of the integration *praxis* are mirrored and foreshadowed by the exhaustion of the main theoretical perspectives which have accompanied and oriented legal reflections, theoretical conceptualisations and the prescriptive modelling of Europe's *finalité*. Where practice and theory concur so significantly

[66] See ME Streit and W Mussler, 'The Economic Constitution of the European Community. From "Rome" to "Maastricht"' (1995) 1 *ELJ* 5.

[67] H Schweitzer, 'Competition Law and Public Policy: Reconsidering an Uneasy Relationship: The Example of Art 81' (1 December 2007), *EUI Working Paper Law* 2007/30, available at SSRN: http://ssrn.com/abstract=1092883.

[68] See D Schmidtchen, M Albert and S Voigt (eds), *The More Economic Approach to European Competition Law* (Tübingen: Mohr Siebeck, 2007).

[69] Legally speaking, the removal looks insignificant, as, for example, Peter Behrens has underlined in his editorial 'Der Wettbewerb im *Vertrag von Lissabon*' (2008) 21 *Europaische Zeitschrift für Wirtschaftsrecht* 193; the letter of the law, however, is not the whole truth.

[70] Weiler, 'The Transformation of Europe', n 24 above, at 2461 ff.

[71] Idem, 'Fin-de-Siècle Europe', n 38 above, 215.

in their retractions, it seems high time to consider an alternative paradigm, which will be sketched out very briefly in the following concluding remarks.

EPILOGUE: DEFENDING SOCIAL EUROPE THROUGH CONFLICTS LAW

The brief monograph in which Tony Judt re-phrased his belief in the welfare tradition of Europe's democracies so emphatically[72] reads like a manifesto. This manifesto is not merely a moral and political plea for social justice in European societies; it also mirrors the bitter experiences with the reactions in the twentieth century to 'economic insecurity, physical insecurity, political insecurity' and Judt's diagnosis of *angst*: 'We have entered an age of insecurity,' he asserts, and we should remain aware of the enormous societal risks that such conditions entail. It would be grossly negligent, if not irresponsible, to take Judt's message of fear lightly. The mission of lawyers, however, is more mundane. We need to consider in what way we can conceptualise the legal dimension of European project against the background of our insights into not only its accomplishments, but also its deficit. The conflicts law approach is such an effort.

Its premises can be simply stated: the Member States of the European Union are no longer autonomous. They are, in many ways, inter-dependent, and hence depend upon cooperation. This cooperation, however, will not lead to the establishment of a strong federal entity in the foreseeable future. In view of the histories of European democracies, and their uneven potential and/or willingness to pursue objectives of distributional justice, to respond to economic and financial instabilities, and to cope with environmental challenges, it is highly unlikely that the Europeans will converge in their political perspectives, and, in view of the enormous complexity of their social systems and the diversity of their entitlements, it is inconceivable that they will institutionalise a pan-European welfare system.

'Social Europe' is such a delicate challenge because the sustainability of the whole European project seems to depend upon the construction and institutionalisation of a 'third way' between or beyond the defence of the nation state, on the one hand, and federalist ambitions, on the other.

If there is a kernel of truth in these premises, we should refrain from conceptualising and portraying European law as an ever growing and ever more comprehensive body of rules and principles of progressively richer normative qualities. What European law has, instead, to learn, especially when it comes to Europe's social dimension, is to live with its diversity and to take the fortunate motto of the otherwise unfortunate Draft Constitutional Treaty seriously.

[72] See n 32 above and also his lecture of 19 October 2009, 'What is Living and What is Dead in Social Democracy?' *New York Review of Books*, 56:20, 17 December 2009.

'United in Diversity'[73] is hence Europe's true vocation and, so we suggest, it is one that can be realised through a new type of conflicts law understood as Europe's constitutional form. This suggestion has its technical complexities. Its core analytical assumptions and normative messages, however, are transparent: the idea of a European conflicts law departs from the sociological observations already alluded to and spells out their normative implications. Under the impact of Europeanisation and globalisation, contemporary societies experience an ever stronger schism between decision-makers and those who are impacted upon by decision-making. This schism is a normative challenge to democratic orders. Increasingly, constitutional states are unable to guarantee the inclusion of all of those persons who are impacted upon by their policies and politics within their internal decision-making processes. The democratic notion of self-legislation, however, which postulates that the addressees of a law should be able to understand themselves as its authors, demands 'the inclusion of the other'. The conflicts law approach builds upon these observations and arguments. As a consequence of their manifold degree of inter-dependence, the Member States of the European Union are no longer in a position to guarantee the democratic legitimacy of their policies. A European law that concerns itself with the amelioration of such external effects, ie, which seeks to compensate for the failings of the national democracies, may induce its legitimacy from this compensatory function. With this, European law can, at last, free itself from the critique of its legitimacy which has accompanied it since its birth and which became ever more intriguing after the SEA of 1987 and the turn to majority voting. Instead of requesting the Union to cure its democracy deficit, we should understand and develop the potential of European law to compensate the structural democracy deficits of the European nation states.[74]

What difference does it make? This query requires and deserves, of course, detailed answers. The recent labour law jurisprudence of the ECJ[75] suggests itself as an acid test of the viability of the concept. The present author has discussed this jurisprudence so extensively elsewhere[76] that it should suffice here to emphasise two steps of a conflicts law approach to these cases, namely, first, the insistence of the approach on a characterisation of the potentially applicable laws, and, second, the suggestion that the functions of the ECJ be re-considered in the resolution of conflicts which Europe is bound to generate.

[73] Article I-8 Draft European Constitutional Treaty (OJ C 310/1, 16/12/2004).

[74] See, in more detail, C Joerges, 'Integration through Conflicts Law: On the Defence of the European Project by Means of Alternative Conceptualisation of Legal Constitutionalisation' in R Nickel (ed), *Conflict of Laws and Laws of Conflict in Europe and Beyond – Patterns of Supranational and Transnational Juridification* (Antwerp: Intersentia, 2010), 377; and 'Three-dimensional Conflicts Law as Constitutional Form' in C Joerges and E-U Petersmann (eds), *Constitutionalism, Multilevel Trade Governance and International Economic Law*, 2nd edn (Oxford: Hart Publishing, 2011) 413, also available at: www.reconproject.eu/projectweb/portalproject/RECONWorkingPapers.html.

[75] See n 48 above.

[76] See in particular C Joerges and F Rödl, 'Informal Politics, Formalised Law and the "Social Deficit" of European Integration: Reflections after the Judgments of the ECJ in *Viking* and *Laval*' (2009) 15 *ELJ* 1, reprinted in ch 16 of this volume.

(1) The most basic of all operations in cases with international dimensions is 'characterisation'. It is an operation which corresponds to the issue of competences in European law. The conflict with which we are confronted in cases such as *Viking* concerns economic freedoms, on the one hand, and collective labour law, on the other. Antoine Lyon-Caen, in a comment on the ECJ's judgments, has lucidly accentuated the diversity of both bodies of law:

> Dans les sociétés d'Europe de l'Ouest, le droit du travail s'est constitué par émancipation du droit du marché, dénommé moyennant les variations terminologiques qu'il importe de ne pas oublier: liberté du commerce ici, freedom of trade ailleurs … Ce n'est pas que des règles sur le travail n'existaient pas avant cette émancipation, mais elles relevaient d'avantage d'une police du travail, partie plus ou moins autonome d'une police du ou des marchés.[77]

It follows from this diversity that the economic freedoms cannot trump collective labour law. Both sets of provisions, which are potentially applicable to the case in question, have their specific legitimacy. But rather than pleading for the supremacy of the former and defending the latter as untouchable, we should ask how the two regimes can be coordinated. Such a coordinative effort is clearly visible in the Posting of Workers Directive;[78] it also seems obvious that Article 153 (5) TFEU (ex-Article 137 (5)), which stipulates that 'the provisions of this Article shall not apply to pay, the right of association, the right to strike and the right to impose lock-out', can, and indeed should, be read in this light. The reference of the Treaty to national orders should be understood not as a demand to replace labour law with market law; it should, instead, be understood as a principle of respect for labour law and a pragmatic implication of the insight into the enormous difficulties to overcome the diversity of national laws by a uniform European regime. Gerard Conway has framed and re-phrased the conflicts *problématique* in terms of the principle of enumerated powers:

> The application of *lex generalis* in *Viking* and *Laval* [ie, the ECJ's resort to the economic freedoms] seems clearly open to the criticism of denuding the principle of conferral of any significance, apart from the conceptual confusion as to the use of the term 'competence' in the judgments. Even the express exclusion of Union

[77] 'In West European societies labour law was constituted as an alternative to the law of the market. It developed terminological distinctions which one must not disregard: *liberté de commerce* here, freedom of trade there … To be sure, legislation relating to work had been in place prior to that emancipatory move, but pertinent rules were meant to control work in a way which was more or less akin to laws policing the market or markets in general' (translation by the author) – thus A Lyon-Caen, 'Droit communautaire du marché v.s. Europe sociale'. Contribution to the Symposium on '*The Impact of the Case Law of the ECJ upon the Labour Law of the Member States*', Berlin, 26 June 2008, organised by the Federal Ministry of Labour and Social Affairs, available at: www.bmas.de/portal/27028/2008__07__16__symposium__eugh__lyon-caen.html.

[78] Directive 96/71/EC concerning the posting of workers in the framework of the provision of services, OJ 1996, L18/1.

competence by the Member States, ie, a statement of negative competence, can be circumvented through the encompassing scope of the free movement principles.[79]

(2) The task of the European Court does not become less demanding or important in the perspectives of conflicts law. A supranational conflicts law which aims at the compensation of structural nation-state failures and which seeks to resolve conflicts generated by Europe's diversity is compatible with Europe's commitment to democracy. It assigns to the ECJ the role not of a constitutional court entrusted with the power to supervise the constitutional courts of the Member States and to replace national law by European constitutional law, but the distinct function of ensuring the viability of a union which needs to tolerate diversities. In the *Viking* case, this would have meant not only respecting Finnish law, but also respecting the efforts of trade unions to coordinate labour interests transnationally. The Court would then have not only confirmed its acceptance of the specifics of labour law, but also paid tribute to the political sensitivity of that field of law, which requires that national labour constitutions remain essentially the responsibility of democratically legitimated legislatures.[80]

Does all this mean that the established democracies of old Europe should be entitled to protect the interests of their labour force against the newcomers from the accession states? This question does not address the issue at stake here comprehensively enough. We need to ask whether it is really in the long-term interest of the new Member States to bring cheap labour to old Europe and to destroy the welfarist traditions of their western and northern European neighbours; we need to consider the implications of such moves for the long-term competitiveness of the accession states and their chances for similar developments. To cite Tony Judt once more: Why should we rush 'to tear down the dikes laboriously set in place by our predecessors? Are we so sure that there are no floods to come? … To abandon the labours of a century is to betray those who came before us as well as generations yet to come.' It would be misleading to represent the social democratic *acquis* as an ideal world or an ideal past. 'But among the options available to us in the present, it is better than anything else to hand.'[81]

[79] G Conway, 'Conflicts of Competence Norms in EU Law and the Legal Reasoning of the ECJ' (2010) 11 *German Law Journal* 966, at 993–994; idem, *The Limits of Legal Reasoning and European Court of Justice* (Cambridge: CUP, 2012).

[80] The ECJ quite solemnly recognised the 'right to take collective action, including the right to strike … as a fundamental right which forms an integral part of the general principles of Community law the observance of which the Court ensures' (Case C-438/05 (*Viking*) para 4); it has then, however, re-configured the traditional balance between economic freedoms at European level and social rights at national level when requiring that the Member States, when exercising their competence in the field of collective labour law, and the unions when exercising the social rights, must comply with Community law (Case C-438/05, para 40).

[81] N 72 above.

18

*How is a Closer Union Conceivable under Conditions of Ever More Socio-Economic and Political Diversity?**

Constitutionalising Europe's *Unitas in Pluralitate*

INTRODUCTION

THE RELATIONSHIP BETWEEN the title and the subtitle of this essay requires some explanatory remarks. The main title may imply an unfortunate dichotomy. In European studies, socio-economic, cultural and political diversity are widely perceived as an obstacle to integration, and hence as something which should be overcome on the road to an 'ever closer union'. This, however, is by no means the message of these pages. Quite to the contrary, we suggest that the Union would be well advised to live *with* diversity, that diversity can be a politically sound and economically beneficial alternative to the kind of convergence which the integration through law agenda of the formative period of the integration process and the crisis politics of the past decade have pursued so rigorously. But our thesis has a prominent precursor, albeit one which remained an unspecified proclamation. 'United in Diversity' was the fortunate motto of the ill-fated Draft Constitutional Treaty of 2004. The motto did not make it into the Treaty of Lisbon. This does not mean that it is outdated. The times Europe is going through are so hard that we cannot shy away from rethinking the project, from re-considering its foundations, from citing Germany's greatest poet in a translation through which the beauty of his language gets lost. To paraphrase Goethe: What holds Europe together 'at its innermost'? What could that be? Is our highest commitment to ensure

* Contribution to the conference 'Europe in Hard Times – What's to be Done?', 8–9 February 2018, Tallinn University, Estonia; published in (2018) 24 *ELJ* 257.

'the financial stability of the euro area as a whole ... and of the Union itself'?[1] Jan-Werner Müller[2] has recently recalled Ernst-Wolfgang Böckenförde's famous transferral of Goethe's query into the parlance of constitutionalism: secularised democracies, he submitted, live on normative resources, which they cannot generate themselves.[3] What if we bring this dictum to the peoples of Europe? A tentative and somewhat enigmatic answer will be submitted in the concluding remarks. The argumentations leading to that conclusion are more mundane. We will take four steps:

1. The first is an explication of Karl Polanyi's substantive understanding of 'the economic' (Section I);
2. Against this background Section II will proceed to a critique of 'one-size-fits-all' integration strategies;
3. Section III will criticise the efforts of Europe's crisis politics to impose convergence on the economies of the Union;
4. 'United in Diversity', the just-mentioned motto of the Constitutional Treaty of 2004, is read as an alternative vision, which Section IV will substantiate;
5. What could hold Europe together 'at its innermost'? The Epilogue will return to this query.

I. 'THE ECONOMIC' IN ECONOMIC SOCIOLOGY

'European economic law' is a discipline of huge proportions which explores meticulously every angle of the legal provisions which concern the European economy, the integration process, and governance arrangements which this process has generated. Why should there be a reason to re-consider these activities in the light of Polanyi's economic sociology? The surplus of such an exercise stems from conceptual deficiencies of the prevailing views in both law and economics and their understanding of markets or, rather, 'the economic'. The deficiency which has, in this author's view, to be cured is the insulation of economic processes from their embeddedness in society. This insulation is, to paraphrase another Polanyian notion, 'fictitious'. To be sure, it is by now common knowledge that the operation of markets pre-supposes the establishment of institutional frameworks; we are equally well aware of many micro-economic and macro-economic policies supporting or correcting the functioning of the economy. And yet, in the prevailing conceptualisations, the economy is portrayed

[1] Judgment of 27 November 2012 in *Pringle v Ireland*, C-370/12, EU:C:2012:756, para 5.

[2] *NZZ*, 26.8.2017, available at: www.nzz.ch/feuilleton/das-boeckenfoerde-diktum-was-haelt-demokratien-zusammen-ld.1312681.

[3] E-W Böckenförde, 'Die Entstehung des Staates als Vorgang der Säkularisation', in idem, *Staat, Gesellschaft, Freiheit. Studien zur Staatstheorie und zum Verfassungsrecht* (Frankfurt aM: Suhrkamp, 1975) 42.

as machinery, which is distinct from political and societal spheres, from *Staat und Gesellschaft*. In particular, markets are understood as autonomous, self-regulating entities. The contrast is striking: 'A self-regulating market,' so Polanyi has famously stated, 'could not exist for any length of time without annihilating the human and natural substance of society; it would have physically destroyed man and transformed his surroundings into a wilderness'.[4] I do not try to dig deeper but conclude with the summarising submission that the economy '*is*' a polity,[5] that its sustainability depends, to paraphrase Böckenförde, on social and moral resources which it cannot generate autonomously.

II. IMPLICATIONS AND OPTIONS

How should such an understanding of the economy as polity affect our views of European economic integration? I refrain from a systematic elaboration and take instead a shortcut. Karl Polanyi's *Great Transformation* is concerned with the emergence of 'market societies', where 'instead of the economy embedded in social relations, social relations are embedded in the economy'.[6] Writing at the end of the Great War, Polanyi had witnessed the destruction of liberal economic ordering by Fascism and Nazism. However, by now, at the end of the Second World War, the rebirth of alternative counter-movements was in sight and nurtured hopes in a better national and international future: alternatives to the Fascist transformation, namely, social counter-movements which would undermine the working of the market system. His somewhat enigmatic views are difficult to decipher. '*The Great Transformation* can legitimately be read either as an anti-capitalist manifesto or as a social democratic bedtime story.'[7] Be that as it may, my shortcut is a passage in which Polanyi considers that

> with the disappearance of the automatic mechanism of the gold standard, governments will find it possible to … tolerate willingly that other nations shape their domestic institutions according to their inclinations, thus transcending the pernicious nineteenth century dogma of the necessary uniformity of domestic regimes within the orbit of world economy. Out of the ruins of the Old World, cornerstones of the New can be seen to emerge: economic collaboration of governments and the liberty to organize national life at will.[8]

Was this just wishful thinking? The passage was written at a time when Keynes and the like-minded American economist and politician Harry Dexter White

[4] K Polanyi, *The Great Transformation: The Political and Economic Origins of our Time* (Boston MA: Beacon Press, 2001) (with Foreword by Joseph Stiglitz and Introduction by Fred Block), at 3.

[5] C Joerges, B Stråth and P Wagner, The Economy as Polity: The Political Constitution of Contemporary Capitalism (London: UCL Press, 2005).

[6] Polanyi, n 4 above, 57.

[7] G Dale, *Karl Polanyi: A Life on the Left* (New York: Columbia UP, 2016) 286.

[8] Polanyi, n 4 above, 253–254.

were working towards the post-war settlement of Bretton Woods. There were reasons to envisage a better future. Polanyi's considerations deserve attention for three additional and interrelated reasons. For one, he re-states his foundational argument that the capitalist market economy is not an evolutionary given but a political product – '*laissez-faire* was planned'[9] – which requires institutional backing and continuous political management. To put it slightly differently, 'the political' is inherent in 'the economic'; market economies 'are polities'.[10] A second insight of topical importance follows from this: capitalist market economies will exhibit varieties which mirror a variety of political preferences, historical experiences, and socio-economic configurations. This is what we can expect, and should respect, once our societies have gained the 'liberty to organise national life at will'. The third point is only alluded to in half a sentence. It is an implication of the new freedom. Polanyi predicts and advocates 'collaboration'; diversity, we can assume, is there to stay.

Let me postpone the discussion of this somewhat vague prospect and hope, and underline first its more substantiated basis and background. Since the 'varieties of capitalism' studies were initiated by Peter A Hall and David Soskice in 2011,[11] it has become common knowledge that the operation of market economies is anything but uniform. Their institutional configurations vary instead, significantly. The coordinated market economies of northern Europe and the Anglo-Saxon liberal market economies have become paradigmatic examples; mixed market economies haven been more recently identified in Southern Europe.[12] The discovery of Lucio Baccaro and others of 'Growth Models and Distributive Dynamics' has diversified the landscape further.[13] A cobbler like myself should stick to his last. What I find most noteworthy and what the varieties studies neglect is Polanyi's characterisation of economic ordering as a *political and societal process*.[14] This is a dimension which another forerunner of the varieties studies, namely, Walter Eucken, left aside when he conceded that the 'characteristics of national competitive orders … manifest differently, for

[9] Ibid, 'planning was not', at 147.

[10] For a very dense re-construction, see F Block, 'Towards a New Understanding of Economic Modernity' in C Joerges et al, n 5 above, 3.

[11] PA Hall and D Soskice, Varieties of Capitalism: The Institutional Foundations of Comparative Advantage (Oxford: OUP, 2001).

[12] A Hassel,'Adjustments in the Eurozone: Varieties of Capitalism and the Crisis in Southern Europe' *LESQ Working Paper 76/2014*; available at SSRN: https://ssrn.com/abstract=2426198. In much more detail and with many provisos, see G Dale, 'Double Movements and Pendular Forces: Polanyian Perspectives on the Neoliberal Age' (2012) 60 *Current Sociology* 3; idem, 'Social Democracy, Embeddedness and Decommodification: On the Conceptual Innovations and Intellectual Affiliations of Karl Polanyi' (2010) 15 *New Political Economy* 369.

[13] See L Baccaro and C Benassi, 'Throwing out the Ballast: Growth Models and the Liberalization of German Industrial Relations' (2017) 15 *Socio-Economic Review*, 85.

[14] Much later elaborated in K Polanyi, 'The Economy as Instituted Process' [1957] in M Granovetter and R Swedberg (eds), *The Sociology of Economic Life*, 2nd edn (Boulder CO–San Francisco CA–Oxford: Westview Press, 2001) 31.

example, in Germany, Belgium, or the United States'.[15] This political-process dimension, however, is a legal essential. We need to understand the normative fabric of our economic orders as an *acquis sociale*, which is, of course, subject to changes, but nonetheless deserves to be protected against illegitimate intrusions. A strong indicator of the importance of this point is the fierce controversy that it has provoked between Wolfgang Streeck and Jürgen Habermas. Streeck opts for a defence of the nation state and its institutions against a deepening of economic integration.[16] Habermas' critique is that this is a nostalgic option, a hideaway in the sovereign powerlessness of the overrun nation (*eine 'nostalgische Option für ei to F.W. ne Einigelung in der souveränen Ohnmacht der überrollten Nation'*).[17] I cite a recent re-statement of Streeck:

> [W]hat I would suggest to call the *acquises démocratiques* of the national *demoi* in Europe ... importantly comprises a wide range of political-economic institutions that provide for democratic corrections of market outcomes – for democracy as *social* democracy.[18]

I must admit that I find Streeck more Habermasian than Habermas himself. I read his defence of the national constellation as the plea to take deliberative democracy seriously. This plea is, of course, linked to sociological premises and political assessments. Streeck simply does not believe that a European social democracy is a conceivable option. But are we really entrapped in the dichotomy?

Back to Polanyi, however. The passage that I have cited is not about output legitimacy, let alone economic efficiency. Polanyi's appeal to the liberty of societies is, instead, concerned with ideational and cultural dimensions of 'the economic'. His argument takes seriously, or is at least open to, what the varieties of capitalism studies tend to neglect. Precisely for this reason his position seems so topical. Ideational, cultural, historical aspects are an indispensable element of an adequate understanding of 'the economic'. A whole new sub-discipline ('cultural political economy') focusing on this dimension is emerging.[19] This seems particularly

[15] W Eucken, 'What is a Competitive Order?' [1952] in T Biebricher and FS Vogelmann (eds), *The Birth of Austerity: German Ordoliberalism and Contemporary Neoliberalism* (London: Rowman and Littlefield, 2017) 99 at 100.

[16] W Streeck, 'Small-State Nostalgia? The Currency Union, Germany, and Europe: A Reply to Jürgen Habermas' (2014) 21 *Constellations* 213.

[17] J Habermas, 'Demokratie oder Kapitalismus. Vom Elend der nationalstaatlichen Fragmentierung in einer kapitalistisch integrierten Weltgesellschaft', *Blätter für deutsche und internationale Politik* (5/2013), 59 ('*Nostalgische Kleinstaaterei*' [Small-State Nostalgia] at 62).

[18] W Streeck, *How Will Capitalism End?* (London: Verso Books, 2016), 198, fn 20 [referring to FW Scharpf, 'Das Dilemma der supranationalen Demokratie in Europa' (2015) 43 *Leviathan* 11]; see, in a surprisingly similar vein, K-H Ladeur, '"Conflicts Law as Europe's Constitutional Form" ... and the Conflict of Social Norms as its Infrastructure' in C Joerges and C Glinski (eds), *The European Crisis and the Transformation of Transnational Governance: Conflicts-Law Constitutionalism and Authoritarian Managerialism* (Oxford: Hart Publishing, 2013) 383.

[19] See B Jessop and N-L Sum, *Towards a Cultural Political Economy: Putting Culture in its Place in Political Economy* (Cheltenham: Edward Elgar Publishing, 2013); B Jessop, 'Cultural Political Economy: Logics of Discovery, Epistemic Fallacies, the Complexity of Emergence, and the Potential of the Cultural Turn' (2010) 15 *New Political Economy* 445.

important in view of the deep diversities within the European space. The works of economic historians such as Werner Abelshauser and the path-breaking comparative law studies of Gunther Teubner share this view and add that 'cultures' tend to be remarkably resistant to imposed change.[20] Both underline that interventions into the respective social and institutional fabric of European economies can hardly be subtle and sufficiently fine-tuned to accomplish the desired re-orientation.[21]

III. THE STATE OF THE UNION AFTER A DECADE OF CRISIS POLITICS

The normative value of diversity does not inform us how this value might be established and preserved. Before entering into such uncharted waters and evaluating the risks of such an endeavour, we have to consider the state of the Union after a decade of crisis politics. The event from which we depart is the establishment of the EMU in the Maastricht Treaty. This is by no means to camouflage earlier unfortunate decisions and developments.[22] But it nevertheless seems obvious that the specific patterns of the crisis have been shaped by this Treaty.

III.1. An Ill-designed Treaty

This Treaty has produced a hybrid, an odd merger of ordoliberal principles and French endeavours to ensure some political governance of the economy. Germany was successful with the defence of its stability philosophy through substantive principles and statutory norms; France established a counterweight in the procedural norms of the General ECB Council.[23] Our focus here will be the tension between the conferral of exclusive powers in the – albeit undefined – field of monetary policy administered by a bank with unprecedented autonomy, and the reservation of economic and fiscal policies by the Member States. This dichotomy was not wilful or accidental but simply mirrored the concern of the Member States for 'the power of the purse'. The ensuing dilemmas were predictable. Already in 1992, the socio-economic diversity within the Union

[20] W Abelshauser, *Kulturkampf. Der deutsche Weg in die neue Wirtschaft und die amerikanische Herausforderung* (Berlin: Kadmos, 2003); W Abelshauser, D Gilgen, and A Leutzsch, 'Kultur, Wirtschaft, Kulturen der Weltwirtschaft' in W Abelshauser, D Gilgen and A Leutzsch (eds), *Kulturen der Weltwirtschaft* (Göttingen: Vandenhoek and Ruprecht, 2012) 9; G Teubner, 'Legal Irritants: Good Faith in British Law or How Unifying Law Ends up in New Differences' (1998) 61 *MLR* 11.

[21] A Hassel, 'Adjustments in the Eurozone', n 12 above.

[22] See G Majone, Rethinking the Union of Europe post-Crisis – Has Integration Gone too Far? (Cambridge: CUP, 2014) passim.

[23] In a similar vein, see S Fabbrini, 'The Euro Crisis and its Constitutional Implications' in S Champeau, C Closa, D Innerarity and M Poiares Maduro (eds), *The Future of Europe. Democracy, Legitimacy and Justice After the Euro Crisis* (London–New York: Rowman and Littlefield, 2015) 19.

and within the euro area was considerable, and it deepened continuously. The implications can be derived from the insights into the socio-economic, political and cultural variety sketched out in the previous section. European monetary policy is uniform, but it is confronted with an ever deeper variety of national configurations. 'One size fits none' – Henrik Enderlein's *barzelletta* captures this well.[24] The difficulties of macro-economic steering are exacerbated by the deeply engraved cultural diversities which render the euro area-wide communality of policy implementation illusory.

Hence, in a sense, the Maastricht regime embodied a kernel of wisdom. Article 119 TFEU provided for no more than 'the adoption of an economic policy which is based on the close coordination of Member States' economic policies', as substantiated in Article 121 TFEU. This instrument was a *lex imperfecta*. The same holds true for the Stability and Growth Pact of 1997. By the same token, however, this wisdom was not strong enough to prevent what was going to happen.

The tensions under the thin 'constitutional' veneer of the Maastricht Treaty remained latent for a couple of years. As we know, post-2007, the success of the early years of the EMU was only due to good economic luck and constant political bargaining. The real life of the constitutional compromise was a *praxis* of muddling. Under the conditions of the common currency, the socio-economic diversity within the euro area was deepening irresistibly. After the financial and the sovereign debt crises, this diversity was to become an explosive constellation. We have experienced highly differential growth and inflation rates, cyclical divergences. We have learned about the reasons and mechanisms of these disastrous developments. Under the EMU, responses to these problems were not available. The fundamental design failure and constitutional deficit of this regime is the lack of a political infrastructure and institutional framework in which democratic political contestation could continue and legitimate a completion or improvement of the imperfect edifice that had been established.[25]

III.2. Two Dead-end Alleys

My whole thesis depends on the explanation of this dilemmatic constellation. What went wrong? My message is anything but comforting: Europe had no chance! Let us consider the two options which the designers of the Treaty had

[24] H Enderlein, 'One Size Fits None' (2005) 16 *Central Banking* 24.

[25] The story of the European responses has been told often enough. Out of my own contributions see, eg, 'Europe's Economic Constitution in Crisis and the Emergence of a New Constitutional Constellation' (2014) 15 *German Law Journal* 985. The descriptions, analyses and discussions fill libraries; an analysis with an exceptional sensitivity for the normative, legal and political aspects of the 'rule of economics' is Klaus Tuori's 'The Eurosystem and the European Economic Constitution: A Constitutional Analysis of Common Central Banking Before and During the Crisis', PhD Thesis, Helsinki, 1017, available at: https://helda.helsinki.fi/handle/10138/200392.

in mind. One can be understood as a version of economic constitutionalism. It is characterised by the lack of a legitimated political authority. No such transnational political authority was needed if, and, if so, because financial markets can be expected to supervise the performance of the Member States. The famous no-bail-out clause of Article 125 of the Lisbon Treaty made it illegal for one Member to assume the debts of another. We were thus protected against moral hazard. Or were we? The weakest link in this chain of arguments is the reliance on financial markets. To be sure, von Hayek has tried to make us believe that markets are unique in their capacity to collect, process and coordinate knowledge which is dispersed in society.[26] But, as Lisa Herzog has objected with particular clarity,[27] the knowledge which markets can communicate is not the knowledge we need when we have to assess the performance of complex economic orders. Hayek's wonderful conceptualisation of 'competition as a discovery procedure'[28] will not deliver what we need to know. Such asymmetries, we have been assured will be compensated by highly professionalised ratings agencies which produce and offer such advice under competitive conditions. This, again, is all too wishful thinking. The famous three big ratings agencies embody expert knowledge but not the ethics of the classical professions. Can we expect expertise to accomplish what markets fail to do? This is a complex story in general. In the case of the ratings agencies, however, I can simply refer to Mario Draghi's famous defence of the OMT programme of the ECB on 26 July 2012.[29] The markets got it wrong, he argued; this is why the ECB had to step in.

Draghi's 'whatever it takes' announcement leads us to the second alternative: Are public authorities to step in where private organisations are not so reliable. Again, I hear von Hayek knocking at the door. He not only praised the performance of markets so impressively back in 1945; three decades later, he complemented his argument in his Nobel Prize Lecture on the 'Pretence of Knowledge'.[30] The lecture is thoroughly neglected in the debates on the performance of the ECB or European crisis politics. This is difficult to justify. Hayek's reserves against economic planning and steering deserve to be taken seriously. But this is again a matter which is too complex to be dealt with in passing. However, for my thesis, I can let this rest. The line of arguments that I have re-constructed upon the basis of Polanyi's economic sociology, the varieties of capitalism studies, and the insights into the importance of economic cultures are sufficiently instructive. It is, against this background, simply inconceivable

[26] FA von Hayek, 'The Use of Knowledge in Society' (1945) 35 *American Economic Review* 519.

[27] Out of the works of Lisa Herzog, see Lisa Herzog, 'Markets', in *Stanford Encyclopedia of Philosophy* 2013, 1; available at https://plato.stanford.edu/entries/markets.

[28] FA von Hayek, 'Competition as Discovery Procedure' (Wettbewerb als Entdeckungsverfahren, 1968), (2002) 5 *The Quarterly Journal of Austrian Economics* 9.

[29] *Verbatim* at: www.ecb.europa.eu/press/key/date/2012/html/sp120726.en.html.

[30] 'The Pretence of Knowledge', Nobel Memorial Lecture, 11 December 1974, (1989) 79 *The American Economic Review* 3, available at: http://pavroz.ru/files/hayekpretence.pdf.

that the ensemble of European economies will respond to the voices of public authorities in the same way; and it is even less likely that these authorities will be able to design and to implement sufficiently fine-tuned programmes targeted at the diversity of the constellation in the euro area.

III.3. Authoritarian Managerialism

It seems, against this background, but 'logical' that European crisis politics operated as it did, namely, *extra legem* and in an authoritarian managerial mode.[31] The first to underline this dilemma was the former constitutional judge Ernst-Wolfgang Böckenförde, tellingly a confessed Schmittian.[32] The treatment of law, Böckenförde explained in a comment published by the *Neue Züricher Zeitung* in June 2010,[33] was 'outrageous' (*abenteuerlich*). And, indeed, there is much to be irritated about. A particularly intriguing characteristic of Europe's new modes of economic governance is the form of its crisis management. This managerialism is problematical for three inter-dependent reasons. First, through the supervision and control of macro-economic imbalances, it disregards the principle of enumerated powers, and, by the same token, cannot respect the democratic legitimacy of national institutions, in particular, the budgetary powers of the parliaments of the states receiving assistance. Second, in its departure from the one-size-fits-all philosophy orienting European integration in general and monetary policy in particular, it nonetheless fails to achieve a variation which might be founded in democratically-legitimated choices; quite to the contrary, the individualised scrutiny of all Member States is geared to the objective of budgetary balances and seeks to impose the necessary accompanying discipline. Under the conditions of monetary unity, the Member States can only respond to pertinent requests through austerity measures: an 'internal devaluation' via reductions of wage levels and social entitlements.[34] Third, the machinery of the new regime, with its individualised measures which are oriented only by necessarily indeterminate general clauses, is regulatory in its nature, establishing a transnational executive machinery outside the realm of democratic politics and the form of accountability which the rule of law

[31] C Joerges and M Weimer, 'A Crisis of Executive Managerialism in the EU: No Alternative?' in G de Búrca, Claire Kilpatrick and J Scott (eds), *Liber Amicorum for David M Trubek* (Oxford: Hart Publishing, 2014), 295.

[32] On Böckenförde's indebtedness to Carl Schmitt, see the interview with D Gosewinkel, in idem (ed), *Wissenschaft, Politik, Verfassungsgericht. Aufsätze von Ernst-Wolfgang Böckenförde* (Frankfurt aM: Suhrkamp, 2010) 359.

[33] E-W Böckenförde, 'Kennt die europäische Not kein Gebot? Die Webfehler der EU und die Notwendigkeit einer neuen politischen Entscheidung' ['Does necessity not know rules? Design flaws of the EU and the necessity of a new political decision'], *Neue Züricher Zeitung* of 21 June 2010.

[34] See, eg, M Dawson and F de Witte, 'Constitutional Balance in the EU after the Euro-Crisis' (2013) 76 *MLR* 817, at 825–827, fnn 33–37.

used to guarantee. Core concepts used by new economic governance cannot be defined with any precision, either by lawyers or by economists, and are therefore not justiciable.[35] This implies that rule-of-law and legal protection requirements are being suspended.[36] This type of de-legalisation is accompanied by assessments of Member State performance, which cannot but operate in a highly discretionary manner.

The most drastic illustrations were provided by the Six-pack and the Two-pack Regulations, which seek to prevent and/or to correct excessive macroeconomic imbalances. As Fritz Scharpf has pointed out, the very logic of the excessive balance procedure 'dictates that it must operate without any pre-defined rule and that the Commission's *ad hoc* decisions must apply to individual Member States in unique circumstances rather than to the EMU states in general. Regardless of the comparative quality of its economic expertise, the Commission lacks legitimate authority to impose highly intrusive policy choices on Member States.'[37] Precisely, this is foreseen for an undefined range of policy areas in which the EU still lacks hard-law competences.

IV. 'UNITED IN DIVERSITY'

Critics are expected to explain what they have to offer. Such requests tend to have silencing effects. The discussion on the management of the crisis is dominated by economists and their expertise. A cobbler should stick to his last, goes a proverb in many languages. And indeed, among both lawyers[38] and political scientists,[39] the prevailing view is that we should learn to live with the 'new normalcy'. After all, the transformations which European crisis politics has brought about have been legalised by the European Court of Justice.[40]

This is a premature end. We simply cannot know how stable the new normalcy really is. What we know for sure, however, is that, the jurisprudence

[35] See D Adamski, 'National Power Games and Structural Failures in the European Macroeconomic Governance' (2012) 49 *CML Rev.* 1319; FW Scharpf, 'Monetary Union, Fiscal Crisis and the Disabling of Democratic Accountability' in W Streeck and A Schäfer (eds), *Politics in the Age of Austerity* (Cambridge: Polity, 2013), 108, at 139.

[36] See M Everson, 'The Fault of (European) Law in (Political and Social) Economic Crisis' (2013) 24 *Law and Critique* 107.

[37] See FW Scharpf, n 35 above, and idem, 'Monetary Union, Fiscal Crisis and the Pre-emption of Democracy' (2011) 9 *Zeitschrift für Staats- und Europawissenschaften/Journal for Comparative Government and European Policy* 163.

[38] See, prominently, T Beukers, C Kilpatrick and B de Witte, 'Constitutional Change through Euro-Crisis Law: Taking Stock, New Perspectives and Looking Ahead', in eidem (eds), *Constitutional Change through Euro-Crisis Law* (Cambridge: CUP, 2017) 1; for a critical review of the state of the debate, see D Curtin, '"Accountable Independence" of the European Central Bank: Seeing the Logics of Transparency' (2017) 23 *ELJ* 28.

[39] Eg, T Börzel, 'Researching the EU (Studies) into Demise' (2018) 25 *JEPP* 475.

[40] *Pringle*, n 1 above; judgment of 16 June 2015 in *Peter Gauweiler and others v Deutscher Bundestag*, C-62/14, EU:C:2015:400.

of the CJEU notwithstanding, the present state of the Union is threatening the legitimacy of the integration project. The implications are complex and far-reaching. It must suffice here to sketch out a series of intuitions about the socio-economic basis, the normative essentials and the constitutional form of an alternative approach. As announced in the first section, the argument departs from Polanyi's economic sociology and his quest for cooperation among political autonomous polities, then proceeds to the trilemma thesis of the Harvard political economist Dani Rodrik, and moves from there to the political philosophy of the EU recently submitted by Daniel Innerarity; it concludes with the thesis that conflicts law is the proper constitutional form of the EU.

1. The first step is very short. To cite the passage from the beginning again: 'Out of the ruins of the Old World, cornerstones of the New can be seen to emerge: economic collaboration of governments *and* the liberty to organize national life at will'.[41] Political autonomy should not get lost in integration but be preserved in cooperative arrangements.
2. Dani Rodrik has never cited Polanyi in his works on globalisation. But these works are infiltrated with Polanyian ideas, and Rodrik has acknowledged his indebtedness to Polanyi explicitly.[42] For our context, his most famous theorem seems particularly instructive. In his book, *The Globalization Paradox*,[43] Rodrik asserts the impossibility of simultaneous pursuit of economic globalisation, democratic politics and national determination (autonomy), highlighting a trilemma in which only two goals can be paired: economic globalisation and democratic politics, or democracy and national autonomy. For Rodrik, the EU furnishes dramatic illustration of his thesis. On the one hand, the EU could transnationalise democracy through federalisation and thereby defend the advantages of the common market; at the same time, however, it would be forced to establish a common European politics to legitimise its necessary assumption of fiscal and social policy, with negative consequences for national sovereignty. In the absence of such a denationalising will, the EU must give up the common currency and accept economic disintegration.[44] What is lacking here is Polanyi's 'Third Way': to wit, cooperation. This is the alternative referred to above.[45]

[41] K Polanyi, *The Great Transformation*, n 4 above, at 253–254 (emphasis in original).

[42] See http://rodrik.typepad.com/dani_rodriks_weblog/2017/03/a-foreword-to-kari-polanyi-levitt.html.

[43] D Rodrik, *The Globalization Paradox: Democracy and the Future of the World Economy* (New York–London: WW Norton, 2011).

[44] D Rodrik, 'The Future of European Democracy', in L v Middelaar and PV Parijs (eds), *After the Storm: How to save democracy in Europe* (Tielt: Lannoo Publishers, 2015) 53.

[45] See Section II. Rodrik's recent *Straight Talk on Trade: Ideas for a Sane World Economy* (Princeton NJ–Oxford: Princeton UP, 2017) has a chapter with an update on Europe (at 48–78); therein Rodrik repeats: 'If European democracies are to regain their health, economic integration and political integration cannot remain out of sync. Either political integration catches up with economic integration or economic integration needs to be scaled back' (at 76). There are, however signals of a

3. Fortunately enough, there is an elaborated philosophical underpinning for this vision, to be found in Daniel Innerarity's concept of 'inter-democracy'.[46] Two insights are particularly important for my argument. The first concerns Europe's heterogeneity, which excludes all 'one-size-fits-all' recipes. Instead:

    > If the EU is going to be more democratic, it will be so in the style of complex democracies. And that complexity is not only related to the diversity of its citizens but to the variety of issues about which it needs to decide, some of which may require proximity, but others that demand a certain distance.[47]

    'Inter-democracy' is his key concept: the democratisation of interdependencies must replace state-like or federal hierarchical models, he argues forcefully. And:

    > The states are increasingly more incapable of democratic action because they cannot include everyone affected by their decisions in the electoral process and, on the flip side, citizens cannot influence the behaviour of those who are making decisions in their name. This is the principal democratic deficit that the European Union should rectify. Extraterritorial effects and the burdens that one state imposes on others cannot be justified by recourse to domestic democratic procedures and require another type of legitimacy. That is why we can affirm that the fact that national actors keep outside interests in mind may improve the representation of *true* domestic interests, since they are no longer circumscribed by the state arena, either. In this sense, we might think that the EU helps strengthen the democratic authority of the member states, to the extent to which it can serve as a measure to manage externalities in an efficient fashion.[48]

4. The so-called principle of external effects has such ardent critics as Alexander Somek,[49] and such prominent defenders as Jürgen Habermas.[50] Jürgen Neyer and I first submitted it back in 1997 in an essay on European comitology.[51] The basic premise and intuition is very simple: it is a core premise of theories of democracy, most notably of Habermas' discourse theory of law and democracy that we, the citizens, must be able to understand

re-orientation. The in my view most promising of these is in line with his more general ideas about globalisation. Globalisation requirements must remain consistent with democratic delegation; they must 'enhance democratic deliberation domestically' (at 65). On such affinities with the conflicts-law approach, see, more systematically, F Bohnenberger and C Joerges, 'A Conflicts-Law Response to the Precarious Legitimacy of Transnational Trade Governance' in M Hirsch and A Lang (eds), *Research Handbook on the Sociology of International Law* (Cheltenham: Edward Elgar, 2020), 37, reprinted in pt VI, ch 28 of this volume.

[46] D Innerarity, *Democracy in Europe: A Political Philosophy of the EU* (London: Palgrave Macmillan, 2018).

[47] See ibid, Introduction, 'Understanding European Complexity', at 7.

[48] See ibid ch 3 ('What should be Democratized? The Peculiarity of Democracy in Europe'), at 73.

[49] 'The Argument from Transnational Effects I: Representing Outsiders through Freedom of Movement' (2010) 16 *ELJ* 315; 'The Argument from Transnational Effects II: Establishing Transnational Democracy' (2010) 16 *ELJ* 375.

[50] See J Habermas, 'Does the Contitutionalization of International Law still have a Chance' in idem, *The Divided West* (Cambridge: Polity Press, 2006) 113.

[51] C Joerges and J Neyer, 'From Intergovernmental Bargaining to Deliberative Political Processes: The Constitutionalisation of Comitology' (1997) 3 *ELJ* 273, reprinted in pt III, ch 12 of this volume.

ourselves as the authors of the legal provisions with which we are expected to comply. Under conditions of Europeanisation and globalisation and ever more growing interdependences, this is no longer conceivable. To cite Habermas himself:

> Nation-states ... encumber each other with the external effects of decisions that impinge on third parties who had no say in the decision-making process. Hence, states cannot escape the need for regulation and coordination in the expanding horizon of a world society that is increasingly self-programming, even at the cultural level ...[52]

It is difficult to reject these insights. The implications are, of course, controversial. Among the three just-named alternatives – state-building, down-scaling of integration, cooperation – I opt for the third. In the European case, we can build on European law's potential to compensate for the legitimacy deficits of national rule. European law can derive its own legitimacy from this function: its mandate is to implement the commitments of the Member States towards each other by two legal claims, namely, the requirement to take the interests and concerns of their neighbours into account when designing national policies, and by imposing a duty to cooperate. The very notion of cooperation indicates that this kind of rule cannot be some 'command and control' exercise, but must rely on the deliberative quality of cooperative interactions. Two important implications should be underlined. The first: there is no in-built guarantee that such cooperative efforts will, in the end, be successful; but such limitations need not be damaging *per se*; quite to the contrary, they may document mutual respect of essential, yet distinct, values and commitments of the other (the *ordre public* in the parlance of conflict of laws and private international law). The second implication is more drastic: socio-economic, institutional, political and cultural diversity is particularly strong and difficult to overcome. This, however, is by no means a plea for inactivity; it is, instead, a reminder that we have to distinguish 'justice within' consolidated polities, on the one hand, and 'justice between' them, on the other – and that we have to work in both spheres.[53] Last, but not least, it should, in view of the objections raised above against the discretionary mode of crisis governance, be underlined that the conflicts approach seeks to defend the idea of law-mediated legitimacy of public rule.

V. EPILOGUE

How much realism is in this 'united in diversity' vision? It is to be conceded that this perspective is a response to the social deficits of Europe's crisis politics

[52] Habermas, n 50, at 176.

[53] C Joerges, 'Social Justice in an Ever More Diverse Union' in F Vandenbroucke, C Barnard and G De Baere (eds), *A European Social Union after the Crisis*, (Cambridge: CUP, 2017), 92; available at: SSRN: http://ssrn.com/abstract=2697440.

and the normative fragility of its present constitutional constellation. The *praxis* which this vision envisages certainly depends, to invoke Böckenförde's famous dictum again,[54] on cultural and normative resources which cannot be produced wilfully or by some political or legislative fiat. European integration research used to be aware of such dependencies and has sought to identify them. As, for example, Joseph Weiler, in his insightful first reflection on supranationalism and intergovernmentalism, has underlined, the supremacy of European law was anything other than self-sustaining; instead, acceptance for its operation was held in precarious equilibrium, and dependent upon continuous political processes of intergovernmentalism and continuing commitment to the defence of the community spirit.[55] '*Fin-de Siècle* Europe', with its appeal to peace, prosperity and supranationalism, was a similar, only slightly more mundane, suggestion.[56] 'Political Messianism' is a more desperate, crisis-driven version.[57] Lawyers with their normative sensibilities are by no means the only ones who try to spell out what might hold societies in general and Europe in particular together. To take the two 'Polanyians' referred to before: *laissez faire*-liberalism, Polanyi has argued, is but a 'stark utopia'; it will provoke, and be accompanied by, protective counter-movements.[58] Dani Rodrik's trilemma theorem suggests that 'deep economic integration' among constitutional democracies will soon, rather than later, have to be either complemented by political union or downscaled. Can legal scholarship remain for long forgetful about the *proprium* of law? Can political science[59] refuse to consider whether the 'new normalcy' of the rule of economics, to take up Habermas' formula, 'deserves recognition'? Will Europe's constitutional courts continue to follow the lead of the CJEU when they are told that 'the financial stability of the euro area as a whole … and of the Union itself' is a commitment that trumps the essentials of their constitutional traditions? Will such messages incentivise the peoples of Europe to oppose populist demagogism?[60]

[54] 'Die Entstehung des Staates', n 3 above.

[55] 'The Community System: The Dual Character of Supranationalism' (1981) 1 *Yearbook of European Law* 257.

[56] JHH Weiler, 'Fin-de-Siècle Europe' in R Dehousse (ed), *Europe after Maastricht: An Ever Closer Union?* (Munich: CH Beck, 1994) 203.

[57] JHH Weiler, 'Europe in Crisis – On "Political Messianism", "Legitimacy" and the "Rule of Law"' (2012) *Singapore Journal of Legal Studies* 248; available at: SSRN:https://ssrn.com/abstract=2255263.

[58] Polanyi, n 4 above, at 3.

[59] Tellingly, political scientists who do not share the prevailing normative complacency in their own discipline search for support in legal academia – with limited success; see C Kreuder-Sonnen, 'Beyond Integration Theory. The (Anti-) Constitutional Dimension of European Crisis Governance' (2016) 54 *JCMS* 1350; idem, 'An Authoritarian Turn in Europe and European Studies?' (2018) 25 *JEPP* 452.

[60] This essay was finalised on 27 January 2020; this is a date at which the concern for financial stability signals a crisis rather than a noble commitment. Seemingly paradoxically, Europe's disintegration can even be observed in the populist movements; see I Krastev, *After Europe* (Philadelphia PA: University of Pennsylvania Press, 2017).

19

Conclusion – Part IV

I. OUTLOOK: THE REVISED POSTED WORKERS DIRECTIVE AND THE EUROPEAN PILLAR OF SOCIAL RIGHTS

IN THE INTRODUCTION to this part of the book, 'the Social' has been called the poor relation of the integration project. That, however, was to characterise the silence about labour and social policy in the Rome Treaty and the 'foundational period'. At present, 'the Social' might be better referred to as 'an unruly horse', although this unruliness is widely ignored or silenced. The proponents of a 'more social' Europe have never ceased to make their views and requests known. They placed great hopes in the Community Charter of the Fundamental Social Rights of Workers, adopted in 9 December 1989 by all Members States with the exception of the UK, now no longer part of the EU,[1] and further developed in the Charter of Fundamental Rights of the European Union,[2] which became legally binding with the ratification of the Treaty of Lisbon on 1 December 2009[3] and the commitment in the Treaty of Lisbon

> to work for the sustainable development of Europe based on balanced economic growth and price stability, a highly competitive social market economy, aiming at full employment and social progress, and a high level of protection and improvement of the quality of the environment. …[4]

More recently, the Commission solemnly proclaimed a European Pillar of Social Rights, with a view to 'building a fairer and more inclusive European Union'.[5] In its three chapters, the Pillar announces the promotion of 'equal opportunities and access to the labour market', 'fair working conditions', and 'social protection and inclusion'.[6] In view of the rigid austerity politics that Europe pursued

[1] Text available at www.eesc.europa.eu/resources/docs/community-charter--en.pdf.
[2] [2007] OJ C303/01, 1.
[3] Art 6 TEU.
[4] Art 3(3) TEU.
[5] See https://ec.europa.eu/info/strategy/priorities-2019-2024/economy-works-people/jobs-growth-and-investment/european-pillar-social-rights/european-pillar-social-rights-20-principles_en.
[6] See https://ec.europa.eu/info/sites/default/files/social-summit-european-pillar-social-rights-booklet_en.pdf.

during the financial crisis,[7] the Social Pillar was primarily viewed as a signal of good will and a symbolic use of politics.[8]

A more significant advance has been achieved in the revision of the Posted Workers Directive (PWD),[9] which seems to have initiated a retraction, on the part of the Court of Justice of the European Union (CJEU) of its *Laval* jurisprudence.[10] The key promise of this revision is to 'ensure the same pay for the same job at the same place'. This equal pay principle is to contain practices of 'social dumping' and direct wage competition between workers of different Member States. Unsurprisingly, Poland and Hungary have brought an annulment action against the revised Directive. Their concern is obvious. Both countries sought to defend their competitive advantages. The Directive, however, seeks a compromise. Posted workers, in important respects, profit from the better law of the guest state, while Poland and Hungary retain comparative advantages only to a very limited degree. The details can be left aside here. However, what does seem most remarkable here is that the CJEU, through its rejection of the Hungarian and Polish actions,[11] has implicitly strengthened the authority of the European legislature *vis-à-vis* the CJEU. Equally noteworthy, in the light of our argument on the legacy of conflicts law (private international law), are the considerations of Advocate General Manuel Campos Sánchez-Bordona: in his Opinion delivered on 28 May 2020,[12] he recalled the conflicts law aspects of the controversy, explaining:

Contrary to the Hungarian Government's submission, I believe that Article 3(1) of Directive 96/71 (concerning ordinary posted workers) and the new Article 3(1a) (concerning workers on long-term postings) are special rules on conflict of laws, which must be applied in conjunction with those of the Rome I Regulation.[13]

This implies the recognition of the mandatory character of the rules of worker protection. Both the original and the revised version of the PWD have overcome the traditional recognition of the autonomy of the parties to labour contracts to choose the applicable law.

[7] See pt V, ch 22 and pt I, ch 3.

[8] V Bogoeski, 'The EU Political Culture of Total Optimism is not Dead: Reflections on the European Pillar of Social Rights' in J Hien and C Joerges (eds), *Responses of European Economic Cultures to Europe's Crisis Politics* (San Domenico di Fiesole: EUI/RSCAS, 2018) 108, 174, available at http://cadmus.eui.eu/handle/1814/59884; see also S Garben, 'The European Pillar of Social Rights: Effectively Addressing Displacement?' (2018) 14 *ECLR* 210.

[9] Directive (EU) 2018/957 of the European Parliament and of the Council of 28 June 2018 amending Directive 96/71/EC concerning the posting of workers in the framework of the provision of services, [2018] OJ L173/16.

[10] See, on the following, V Bogoeski, 'The Revision of the Posted Workers Directive as a Polanyian Response to to Commodification of Labor in Europe' (2021) 2(1) *Global Perspectives* 18740.

[11] Case 620/18, *Hungary v European Parliament and Council of the EU*, ECLI:EU:C:2020:1001; and *Poland v EOP and Council of the EU*, ECLI:EU:C:2020:1000.

[12] ECLI:EU:C:2020:392.

[13] Ibid, para 194.

II. RELATED PUBLICATIONS

C Joerges and F Rödl, 'The "Social Market Economy" as Europe's Social Model?' in L Magnusson and B Stråth (eds), *A European Social Citizenship? Preconditions for Future Policies in Historical Light* (Brussels: Lang, 2005) 125.

C Joerges, 'The Rechtsstaat and Social Europe: How a Classical Tension Resurfaces in the European Integration Process' (2010) 9 *Comparative Sociology* 65.

Part V

The Contest on the Economic Constitution

20

Introduction: 'The Economic' in European Legal Scholarship

'IT'S THE ECONOMY, stupid!' – the slogan of Bill Clinton's presidential campaign in 1992 can be read as a wake-up-call or a correction of normative expectations. The year 1992 also saw the signing of the Maastricht Treaty, with the establishment of Economic and Monetary Union. The Treaty was widely welcomed. It seemed to promise progress towards an 'ever closer Union' among the peoples of Europe. With hindsight, however, it has more the feel of a wake-up call, albeit one without enduring confidence. Indeed, the year 1992 marks an unfortunate turning-point in the history of the integration project.

As underlined in chapter 21 and previously,[1] the Rome Treaty of 1957 had launched a European *Economic* Community which, through the Member States and the 'four (economic) freedoms' enshrined therein, would lead to a win-win situation. The programmed economic progress seemed compatible with the accomplishments of the welfare state in post-war Europe. The political dynamics within European societies and the erosion of governmental control were neither foreseen, nor foreseeable. 'The political of the economic' and its risks, the core concerns of Karl Polanyi's[2] economic sociology, were not in the mindset of European legal scholarship. Even the work of the European Convention during 2003 and 2004, concluded by the Draft Constitutional Treaty, did little to induce a new understanding. This is, of course, not to say that the steadily growing body of pertinent legislative acts, the jurisprudence of the Court of Justice (ECJ/CJEU), and administrative and other governmental activities would not have been comprehensively and carefully examined. What was lacking was a reflection on the constitutional importance of economic paradigms and rules. As late as 2020, a leading scholar of European constitutionalism wondered 'where's the "E" in Constitution?'.[3] Polanyi's economic sociology

[1] Eg, pt II, ch 8 and pt IV, ch 17.

[2] K Polanyi, The Great Transformation: The Political and Economic Origins of our Time [1944] (Boston, MA: Beacon Press,1957).

[3] N Walker, 'Where's the "E" in Constitution? A European Puzzle' in A Skordas, G Halmai and L Mardikian (eds), *Economic Constitutionalism in a Turbulent World* (Cheltenham: Edward Elgar, forthcoming), available at: https://ssrn.com/abstract=3642534.

could have provided some insights.[4] Markets are not autonomously functioning but 'socially embedded' entities. Economic law is concerned with the configuration of their institutional framing. The democratisation of these embedments within, between and beyond nation states is the core problem of the theories of economic law.[5]

The one and only school of thought to have continuously and intriguingly addressed this concern is Germany's ordoliberalism. This tradition, its merits as well as its weaknesses, is extensively discussed in this part of the book. Its greatest merit is the concern for the political and democratic legitimacy of economic law at all levels of governance. Its Achilles' heel, however, is the defence of competitive markets as 'really existing democracies' (Franz Böhm) and the 'discovery procedure of competition' as a means of acquiring and processing knowledge that would be superior to really existing democracies (Friedrich A von Hayek). This kind of legitimacy assumes that we have to reject the idea of economic democracy as a stark utopia. It has to concede, however, that elaborated concepts of an 'economic democracy' are unavailable. However, the pertinent debates in the Republic of Weimar,[6] as well as the legacy of Hermann Heller's social-democratic *Rechtsstaat*,[7] attract considerable attention in European law scholarship.[8]

[4] See the brief explanation by F Block, 'Towards a New Understanding of Economic Modernity' in C Joerges, B Stråth and P Wagner (eds), *The Economy as Polity: The Political Constitution of Contemporary Capitalism* (London: UCL Press, 2005) 3.

[5] For a recent contribution, see S Klein, 'European Law and the Dilemmas of Democratic Capitalism' (2000) 1 *Global Perspectives* 13378.

[6] See R Dukes, *The Labour Constitution: The Enduring Idea of Labour Law*(Oxford: OUP, 2014); PF Kjaer and N Olsen (eds), *Critical Theories of Crisis in Europe: From Weimar to the Euro* (London: Rowman & Littlefield, 2016); G Teubner, 'Transnational Economic Constitutionalism in the Varieties of Capitalism' (2020) 1 *Global Perspectives* 1342; G Gregoire, 'The Economic Constitution under Weimar. Doctrinal Controversies and Ideological Struggles', manuscirpt, University of Liege, 2021.

[7] See AJ Menéndez, 'Hermann Heller Now!' (2015) 21 *ELJ* 285 and the contributions of M Dawson, F de Witte, WE Scheuerman, A Somek, W Streeck and MA Wilkinson in the same issue.

[8] Traces of ordoliberalism are discernible in the commitment to a 'highly competitive social market economy' in Art 3.3 of the Lisbon Treaty; see, however, pt IV ch 24, section III.2.

21

The Market without the State? The 'Economic Constitution' of the European Community and the Rebirth of Regulatory Politics*

PRELIMINARY

THE EUROPEAN ECONOMIC Community is a phenomenon of law in three respects: It is a creation of law, it is a source of law and it is a legal order'.[1] German students of *Wirtschaftsrecht* (legal ordering of the economy), both theoreticians and practitioners, have always asserted that law ought to take primacy in the integration process. They have kept to this leadership claim even in times when integration was flagging and only jurists still took any serious interest in it. The very successes of the Community, by reviving the interest of the public and of social scientists in the integration process, are highlighting an unaccustomed volume of uncertainties in the law, and must, as this paper argues, arouse a willingness among jurists to take a varied and even experimental approach to institutional arrangements, decisional competences and the organisation of decision-making processes. This position will be developed here upon the basis of examples, specifically an analysis of the legal difficulties in coping with regulatory tasks in the Community. The term 'regulatory politics' is not a legal concept, nor does it fit in with the usual descriptions of economic policy actions in economic law based on distinctions between market and plan, competition and interventionism (see Section I). The alienation effect this may give rise to is intentional, for the Community is, in any case, no longer moving within conventional thought patterns in handling its 'regulatory'

* This essay was originally published in German: 'Markt ohne Staat? Die Wirtschaftsverfassung der Gemeinschaft und die regulative Politik' in R Wildenmann (ed), *Staatswerdung Europas? Optionen einer europäischen Union* (Baden-Baden: Nomos, 1991) 225; it was translated by Iain Fraser, EUI Florence, and published as *EUI Working Paper Law 1996/2*. It is available at https://cadmus.eui.eu//handle/1814/125 and also at http://eiop.or.at/eiop/pdf/1997-019.pdf.

[1] W Hallstein, *Die Europäische Gemeinschaft* (Düsseldorf: Econ, 1974) 33.

tasks. This will be shown in more detail herein with the example of two 'classical' policy areas, namely, competition policy on the one hand, and the new harmonisation policy in the removal of technical barriers to trade on the other (Section II below). In the current debate on the institutional and legal strategies to accomplish the Community's internal market project, differing concepts of integration policy are competing. They all operate with partly unclarified premises. They should therefore for the moment be treated as options with no claims to exclusivity (Section III below).

I. LEGAL STRUCTURES AND INTEGRATION POLICY

'Legally considered', the Community is nothing but an aggregation of nation states that have to a limited extent transferred powers to it. This (traditional perception of the) legal structure is a result of the history of the foundation of the Community. This original structure has put its stamp on the behaviour of actors in Community policy and has also determined the way in which the Community gradually gave itself a supranational legal constitution.

1. Starting Points and Approaches

There is no title for 'regulatory policy' in the text of the EEC Treaty adopted in 1957. The real issues it denotes were at the time debated partly not at all and partly in different forms. There was a vacuum in all the activities that appear as 'social regulation' in American heuristics of the regulatory debate. In 1957, the environment was not even a subject of interest in national policy; certainly, there was consumer protection policy,[2] but it was not taken into account as a European task; the sole exception, though admittedly of minor importance, was safety at work.[3] The Treaty provisions on control of the economy kept terminologically and factually to the state of the economic policy debate of the 1950s, with its twofold disjunction – between law and policy, economic sectors and exceptional areas: the Treaty proposed to implement the well-known 'four freedoms' (Articles 48 et seq, 52 et seq, 59 et seq, 67 et seq EEC). For economic policy, however, it was in principle the Member States that were competent. Their macroeconomic policies were defined in Articles 103 et seq EEC as 'a matter of common concern', and were kept together solely by agreements on coordination and cooperation. The Community was given genuine regulatory powers

[2] E Egner, 'Grundsätze der Verbraucherschutzpolitik' in B Biervert, WF Fischer-Winkelmann and R Rock (eds), *Verbraucherpolitik in der Marktwirtschaft* (Reinbek bei Hamburg: Rowohlt, 1956) 11.

[3] B Schulte, 'Risiken und Chancen für die Sozialpolitik im Europa der Zwölf' in U v Alemann, RG Heinze and B Hombach (eds), *Die Kraft der Region: Nordrhein-Weastfalen in Europa* (Bonn: JHW Dietz, 1990) 389 ff.

in competition policy. Yet the accepted areas known in domestic law remained untouched. Thus, transport policy was explicitly singled out as a Community task (Articles 74 et seq EEC) and a special regime was laid down for agriculture (Articles 38 et seq EEC).

The context of the freedoms aimed at bringing about the Common Market includes the legislative powers assigned to the Community pursuant to Article 100, 1st paragraph, EEC, wherever divergent legal and administrative provisions hinder market integration. But how are such powers to be handled in legislatively responsible fashion if competences for environmental, consumer and other regulatory policies are missing? How is Community competence for competition policy to be reconciled with Member State competence for economic policy? How are the macroeconomic effects of the four freedoms, namely a liberalisation of capital movements, to be coped with? What type of 'rationality' can be expected to emerge from such decision-making rules, and how can parliamentary democracies accept a '*législation des gouvernements*'? With all these questions the Community got along astonishingly well for astonishingly long. It used its legislative powers under Articles 100 and 235 EEC extensively, developed ambitious programmes for environmental and consumer policy, kept conflicts between the achievement of the freedoms and extension of its competition policy and Member State economic policy powers from coming to the surface, and successfully solved the problems of currency policy cooperation.[4]

The complex conditions for the legal stability, economic success and political acceptance of European integration must be left on one side here. It seems foreseeable at present that the new dynamics unleashed by the Commission's internal market programme will affect and intensify all the conflicts so far kept latent: the more decisively the Community checks national consumer and environmental provisions for their effect of restraining trade, the less can it do so purely in the name of a merely 'negative' policy directed towards achieving the internal market, and the more pressing will the question of the 'positive' legislative policy quality of this sort of influence become. The more decisively it proceeds against the dense network of national economic regulations, the more it will have to expect resistance based upon the Member States' residual economic policy powers. And this is true irrespective of whether national regulations are replaced by a competitive arrangement or by a European re-regulation. Finally, the example of the liberalisation of capital movements shows most clearly that the achievement of freedoms without a Europeanisation of regulatory instruments is not conceivable and creates pressure for the creation of macroeconomic policy powers.[5]

[4] F McDonald and G Zis, 'The European Monetary System: Towards 1992 and Beyond' (1989) 27 *JCMS* 183.

[5] T Padoa-Schioppa (ed), Effizienz, Stabilität und Verteilungsgerechtigkeit: Eine Entwicklungsstrategie für das Wirtschaftssystem der Europäischen Gemeinschaft (Wiesbaden: Gabler, 1988); N Horn, 'Bankrecht auf dem Weg nach Europa' (1989) Zeitschrift für Bankrecht und Bankwirtschaft 107; A Steinherr, 'Der europäische Bankensektor im integrierten Finanzmarkt' (1989) Zeitschrift für Bankrecht und Bankwirtschaft 121.

None of this is meant to assert some sort of inevitable logic of development. But when it comes to approaches which are normatively convincing and practically at least plausible,[6] then the question of the possibility of developing regulatory policies in the framework of the Community's legal structures becomes relevant.[7] However, everything depends on acknowledging that this query presents in fact a problem that needs to be addressed. The term 'regulatory policy' is not intended for the moment to denote anything more than the efforts to guarantee the social acceptability of the use of rights to act – the justification of these attempts at intervention and guidance. But also, and above all, the appropriateness and possibility of juridification of regulatory policy are not threatened thereby. Accordingly, the question of the Europeanisation of regulatory policy is not aimed at making Europe into a State, in the sense of replacing national regulations by European ones; instead, the point is rather to consider the Community's possibilities of successfully coping with the tasks that in part are accruing to it and in part have been taken over by it.

2. Legal Theories of Integration

The present debate in legal science about the future of the integration process displays all the features of a transitional state. In view of the downright inflationary growth of European law, the legal policy debate on all regulatory projects is intensifying, but so too is the endeavour to deal with the constitutional anomalies in the Community system. In such a stage of reorientation, it makes sense to start by recalling the traditional perspectives of legal theory of integration.[8] Re-constructively, it is easier to see what limits these theories came up against, to

[6] For corresponding questions in economic integration theory, see J Pelkmans, 'The Assignment of Public Functions in Economic Integration' (1982) 21 *JCMS* 97, and the report of the Netherlands Scientific Council for Government Policy, *The Unfinished European Integration* (The Hague, 1986) – evidently inspired by Pelkmans' thesis; for political sciences, see FW Scharpf, 'Regionalisierung des europäischen Raums. Die Zukunft der Bundesländer im Spannungsfeld zwischen EG, Bund, Kommunen' in Alemann, Heinze and Hombach (eds), *Die Kraft der Region*, n 3 above, 15.

[7] Nor is it solved in legal terms by the Treaty amendments put into force in 1987 by the Single European Act (SEA). The SEA formulated tasks for the Community in environmental, research, technology, regional and social policy that had already been taken up previously. The alterations in decisional rules through the majority principle of Art 100 a EEC and the extended rights of involvement by parliament pursuant to Art 149 (2) EEC did not in principle alter the legislative prerogatives of Council and Commission (for more details, see R Dehousse, '1992 and Beyond: The Institutional Dimension of the Single Market Programme' (1989) 1 *Legal Issues* of *European Integration* 109. The fact that the SEA's institutional pragmatism has merely favoured the new dynamics of integration but cannot lastingly consolidate it is confirmed also by the renewed debate on the 'limits to EC powers' (see E Steindorff, *Grenzen der EG-Kompetenzen* (Heidelberg: Verlag Recht und Wirtschaft, 1990).

[8] The choice presented here is necessarily selective. In particular, it neglects the controversies of the early period between constitutionalist-federalist and internationalist-international law approaches. For a more comprehensive survey, see P Behrens, 'Integrationstheorie. Internationale Wirtschaftliche Integration als Gegenstand politologischer, ökonomischer und juristischer Forschung' (1981) 45 *RabelsZ* 8 at 19 ff and 37 ff.

what extent they have already incorporated the move on from them in their own thinking, and the ways in which in current debates on how to handle the integration process from the legal viewpoint traditional thought patterns continue to operate.

*a) The Neoliberal Economic Order (*Ordnungspolitik*) as European Economic Constitutional Law*

It is among the achievements of German theory of the Community's economic constitution that it has never been content with merely positivist and pragmatic interpretations of the EEC Treaty but has always striven for a functional understanding of European law and a normatively consistent overall perspective on the integration process. The integration of the Member States and the consequential renunciation of sovereignty set the scene for the creation of a 'Law' which would dictate the substantive process and the substantive results of integration. This 'Law' is at its core '*economic*' constitutional law, since integration should be based on open markets and should aim for the creation of one common market; at the same time, this 'Law' is economic '*constitutional*' law, as it envisages that the opening up of markets should follow through the competitive process and that this common market should constitute a system of undistorted competition. The foundations of this interpretation were laid during the construction phase of the EEC and were further refined during the debates of the late 1970s.[9] That this theory did not accurately portray the construction phase of the EEC, nor the historical 'will' of the Member States that can be deduced from it, was well known by its promoters.[10] But nevertheless the fact that the agreement made among the founder states resulted in the development of a Treaty dominated by very strong anti-interventionist policies, and thus favoured the establishment of a liberal economic regime, has been interpreted as 'the cunning of reason' (*List der Vernunft*) – a term borrowed from Müller-Armack.[11] The interpretation of the EEC Treaty as an economic constitution committed to the advancement of market integration and the achievement of the principles of a market economy then gave a theoretical evaluation of this cunning of reason. This brought two results: on the one hand, the Community, through its interpretation as an order constituted by law and committed to economic freedoms, acquires a legitimacy

[9] See J Scherer, *Die Wirtschaftsverfassung der Europäischen Gemeinschaft* (Baden-Baden: Nomos, 1970); DW Rahmsdorf, 'Eine zweite Euro-Ordo-Debatte?' (1980) 3 *Integration* 156; and idem, *Ordnungspolitischer Dissens und europäische Integration* (Kehl-Straßburg: Engels, 1982).

[10] H vd Groeben, 'Zur Wirtschaftsordnung der Europäischen Gemeinschaft' [1981] in idem, *Die Europäische Gemeinschaft und die Herausforderungen unserer Zeit: Aufsätze und Reden 1967–1987* (Baden-Baden: Nomos, 1987) 201, at 217 ff.

[11] A Müller-Armack, 'Die Wirtschaftsordnung des Gemeinsamen Marktes' in idem, *Wirtschaftsordnung und Wirtschaftspolitik. Studien und Konzepte zur Sozialen Marktwirtschaft und zur Europäischen Integration* (Freiburg i.Br.: Rombach, 1964) 401, 405.

that protects it against all attacks motivated by democracy theory or constitutional policy.[12] On the other, the restriction of Community powers provokes an effect of blocking social policy moves considered illegitimate from the point of view of neoliberal order theory.[13]

This argument is not disconcerted by references to the contingencies of the unification process and the indeterminacies of the Treaty text,[14] since the very intention it pursues is to transcend the unclear or even contradictory compromise formulas of the text in a theoretically consistent conception. Accordingly, a critique that can satisfy the demands of European economic constitution theory needs to deal with its sociological, economic and integrational theoretical premises. The objections have been put forward often enough: there has been no success in establishing a dignity in the organisational principles of a market economy that sets them above the democratic process of constitutionally-structured societies;[15] but then the development of European economic policy too could not be legally immunised against the competition of other economic concepts;[16] this was said to be the case specifically because competition policy alone was not in a position to deal with the economic and social problems consequent upon market integration.[17]

b) The Communities as 'Special Purpose Associations (Zweckverbände) of Functional Integration'

Just as neoliberal theory explicitly referred to non-positive assumptions in its interpretation of the Community as a market economic legal constitution, so too does Ipsen in terming the Communities 'special purpose associations of functional integration'.[18] But by contrast with neoliberal theory, Ipsen does not envisage the law as the centre of a concept that envelops both an economic and a legal order. Ipsen's 'key concepts', while intended to take political and economic analysis into account, nonetheless presume an irreducible difference between the cognitive interests and statements of legal and non-legal disciplines.[19]

[12] E-J Mestmäcker, 'Macht, Recht, Wirtschaftsverfassung' (1973) 137 *Zeitschrift für das gesamte Handels- und Wirtschaftsrecht* 97; English translation: E-J Mestmäcker, 'Power, Law and Economic Constitution' (1973) 11 *The German Economic Review* 177.

[13] Idem, 'Politische und normativ-funktionale Legitimation der Europäischen Gemeinschaften' in idem, *Recht und ökonomisches Gesetz* (Baden-Baden: Nomos, 1972) 82.

[14] See P VerLoren van Themaat, 'Die Aufgabenverteilung zwischen dem Gesetzgeber und dem Europäischen Gerichtshof bei der Gestaltung der Wirtschaftsverfassung der Europäischen Gemeinschaften' in E-J Mestmäcker, H Möller and H-P Schwarz (eds), *Eine Ordnungspolitik für Europa: Festschrift für Hans von der Groeben* (Baden-Baden: Nomos, 1987) 425.

[15] K Homann, *Rationalität und Demokratie* (Tübingen: Mohr, 1988) 134 ff.

[16] Rahmsdorf, *Ordnungspolitischer Dissens und europäische Integration*, n 9 above, 103 ff.

[17] PR Krugman, 'Konzepte der wirtschaftlichen Integration in Europa' in Padoa-Schioppa *et al*, n 5 above, 113 ff.

[18] HP Ipsen, *Europäisches Gemeinschaftsrecht* (Tübingen: Mohr, 1972) 176 ff.

[19] Ibid, 976 ff and 983.

The originality and productiveness of Ipsen's concept lay in the fact that by comparison with constitutionalist-federalist perspectives of integration, on the one hand, and the reduction of the Community to an organisational form in international law, on the other, he defined their specific feature as the assignment of competences for specific areas which are correspondingly to develop the functionalist logic of the integration process and to be handled in a technocratic-bureaucratic fashion. In this view there can be no *a priori* rule-exception relationship between the specific task areas relying on the four freedoms and market principles on the one side, and the policy areas where the Community itself acts in 'regulatory' fashion on the other. Ipsen, therefore, uses the expression the 'economic constitution' of the Community merely for the relevant elements of primary law, a customs union committed to principles of competition, the four freedoms, the ban on discrimination in Article 7 EEC, as well as for planning that respects competitive and economic freedoms.[20] All this is certainly compatible with a neoliberal programme but does not require it as an unshakeable commitment. The social functions of law in the integration process and its detailed formulation instead remain contingent.[21]

Seeing the Community as a technocratic arrangement to solve specific economic and social policy tasks also points, however, to the dependence of this conception on the circumstances it was designed to address legally. Specifically, if the boundaries between comprehensive competence for the States and the partial Community competences become blurred, if the distinction can no longer be drawn, in deciding upon questions that arise, between 'organised creation of knowledge (*Wissensbildung*)' as a neutral consensus area and 'organised creation of aims (*Willensbildung*)' which is in need of legitimacy, then 'representation, legitimacy and consensus formation' must, Ipsen admits, be re-thought.[22] There was every occasion to do so, even in the 1970s.[23] But there is all the more reason to do so with the present dynamics of internal market policy: certainly, the Community is continuing to act on the basis of formally limited powers, only marginally expanded even by the SEA. But even in the classical areas related to market integration, its powers are so intermeshed horizontally with neighbouring and competing policy areas that the limits to competences can scarcely be used any more to derive substantive limitations on action, still less can rationality guarantees be employed for the content of policies. At the same time, the transfer of partial powers in no way means that they are now to be dealt with, or could be dealt with, autonomously and entirely at Community level. This is not some sort of 'de-concentration' process, in which the Community would

[20] Ibid, 176 ff.

[21] Ibid, 995 ff and 1054–55.

[22] Ibid, 1045.

[23] U Everling, 'Vom Zweckverband zur Europäischen Union – Überlegungen zur Struktur der Europäischen Gemeinschaft' in R Stödter and W Thieme (eds), *Hamburg – Deutschland – Europa: Festschrift für HP Ipsen* (Tübingen: Mohr, 1977), 597.

become dependent only on 'administrative aid' from the Member States,[24] but the inevitable establishment of mutual dependencies, if only because the steps towards integration usually cover only partial areas of a policy sphere and the Community, for all the steps towards completion and approximation, remains dependent on the Member States.

c) Legal Structures and Decision-making Processes

The question that can no longer be answered in Ipsen's approach – how the transference (out and) of powers can be kept reconcilable with Member States' political interests – lies at the centre of Weiler's approach to integration theories. Weiler developed his theory ten years after Ipsen, and thus against a different background of experience. The starting point for his analysis is an apparent paradox: while European law, in a continuing process of evolution, erected two constitutional structures, the Community went through one political crisis after another. This paradox between legal evolution and political erosion was resolved by Weiler in his discovery of mutual dependencies between the presumably divergent legal and political processes. He saw the decisive step to the establishment of these dependency relationships in the thesis set forth by the ECJ as early as the 1960s on the direct effect[25] and the supremacy[26] of European primary and secondary law.[27] These claims to validity were accepted by the courts of Member States, even if in part hesitantly and unwillingly. But the ECJ's leading decisions of the 1960s were followed by de Gaulle's empty chair policy, which in 1966 led to the Luxembourg compromise. The veto right of Member States claimed therein brought a radical reshaping of Community decision-making processes. At all levels – from the formulation of political objectives through the preparation, the adoption and then to the implementation of Community law – the Member States were able to secure extensive rights of participation.[28] It is precisely this development, which from the viewpoint of an interest in advancing integration looks merely like a phenomenon of decay, that Weiler interprets as a recipe for success. He views the influence of Member States on Community decision-making processes as legitimate, in accordance with the Community's overall structure as a combination of sovereign states; in practical political terms, it amounts to a counterweight to the building up of the supranational structure of constitutional law considered indispensable for the stability of the European system.

[24] Ipsen, n 18 above, 1052.

[25] ECR [1963] 1 – *Van Gend en Loos/Nederlandse Administratie der Belastingen.*

[26] ECR [1964] 585 – *Costa/Enel.*

[27] JHH Weiler, 'Supranational Law and Supranational System: Legal Structure and Political Process in the European Community', PhD Thesis, EUI, Florence, 1982, 69 ff.

[28] For details, see Weiler, ibid, 117 ff, 409 ff.

Just as in Ipsen's theorem of 'special purpose associations of functional integration', Weiler's theory of the supranational and intergovernmental dual structure of the Community is concerned with a normative programme founded upon analytical observations of the real world. Weiler's analytical statements have proven to be a great aid to interpretation.[29] The normative message is admittedly 'conservative': it states that the involvement of national political actors in the Community's political decision-making process is indispensable for the stabilisation and expansion of supranational legal structures; the Community's precarious 'dual structure' would be endangered either by ignoring political interests of Member States, or if the Member States ignored Community legal principles.

A defence of the status quo attained is not convincing once the equilibrium presupposed in this model of integration policy gets disturbed. Is the legislative policy activism of the new internal market policy indeed still controlled by the Member States? Has the Community, with its new harmonisation concepts, set in motion developments in which legislative policy responsibilities can no longer be called for? Is it still plausible to treat the integration process as merely or primarily affecting sovereign nation states and the institutionalised actors of the Community, and systematically neglect the formation of 'private systems of governments', of new political arenas, in the European context?

3. First Interim Observation

Academic legal theories do not represent the actual law. Nor are they, however, just arbitrary normative constructs. All academic legal theories of integration are similar in that, in their interpretation of the EEC Treaty, they refer to assumptions that are partly extralegal, partly empirical, and partly theoretical. They reflect what is possible and desirable under specific historical conditions. This explains the wide range in positions referred to, but also their convergence in relation to regulatory policy: neoliberal theory holds no legitimate place for economic (non-competition) or social regulation. In Ipsen's functionalist perspective, regulatory policy is assigned to a European expert technocracy. In Weiler's construction, it remains attached to the Member States and is at the mercy of their bargaining processes. If, then, the conclusion may be drawn from the dynamics of the integration process that there is a new need to structure it, this goes beyond the perspectives of integration theory to date.

[29] See, especially, S Krislov, C-D Ehlermann and JHH Weiler, 'The Political Organs and the Decision-Making Process in the United States and the European Community' in M Cappelletti, M Seccombe and JHH Weiler (eds), *Integration through Law*, vol 1: *Methods, Tools and Institutions* (Berlin–New York: Walter de Gruyter, 1986) 3; JHH Weiler, 'The European Community in Change: Exit, Voice and Loyalty' (1990) 3 *Irish Studies in International Affairs* 15.

II. PRACTICE AS A DISCOVERY PROCESS

The practice of law cannot await the further development of theory and the outcome of academic controversies as to the appropriateness of theoretical models of integration. It has to reach decisions even where there are no existing substantive criteria to justify the transformation of competing theoretical approaches into legally binding validity claims. This academic and theoretical legal agnosticism of practice does not simply condemn 'jurisgenerative politics' to arbitrariness, but forces it to do some production of its own. Certainly, non-theoretical validity can be ascribed to its processes of cognition and decision. But the reality images in legal theories can be measured against the problem content of legal conflict situations, legal conflicts re-constructed as forms of the debate on competing interpretative patterns, and decisions understood as institutionalised learning processes. Taking this approach, legal practice will be portrayed below in two classic policy fields of the Community. The first is concerned essentially with economic regulation, and the second essentially with social regulation.

1. Competition Policy: De-regulation Strategy or Economic Regulation?

Competition policy is rooted in Community primary law, and the Commission has its own administrative instruments and resources to implement it. This special position of competition policy in no way means that its present state was established as soon as the EEC Treaty came into force. It was only after a laborious process that the conditions for implementing competition policy could be created, and the principles of Articles 85 and 86 EEC could be successfully converted into legal rules and extended into what has since become a comprehensive system of European competition law. This growth process was bound up with reorientations of central categories and decisional criteria, through which competition policy responded to changing conflict patterns and took up new tasks. It is therefore not merely quantitative but also qualitative growth.

a) Jurisdiction and Supremacy

Pursuant to Articles 85 and 86 EEC, Community law is to check anti-competitive practices likely to 'affect trade between Member States'. This so-called interstate clause establishes the Community's jurisdiction and is intended to delimit it in relation to the area of validity of domestic antitrust law.

Supported by consensus on all sides, the Commission and the Court of Justice have in the course of time interpreted the criterion of jurisdiction, the restriction of trade, so extensively that it may even be termed functionless today.[30]

[30] E Steindorff, 'Spannungen zwischen deutschem und europäischem Wettbewerbsrecht' in *Schwerpunkte des Kartellrechts 1986/87* (Cologne-Berlin-Bonn-Munich: Carl Heymanns, 1988)

The logic of this interpretation is ultimately a consequence of integration itself. To the extent that the breaking down of barriers to trade is successful and Community internal trade becomes free, the question of restrictions on it loses its original meaning.[31] The potential general competence of European competition law has practical and administrative consequential problems simply arising out of the notoriously slight endowment of the competent Directorate General, DG IV. From the point of view of legal systematics, it means that Community competition law overlays the antitrust systems of Member States, making their harmonisation superfluous. Such a radical formulation of this consequence is usually avoided.[32] But on the logic of the case law on direct applicability and supremacy of Community law, it is undeniable,[33] even if the Court of Justice itself did not put it quite so drastically in its decision of principle over 20 years ago.[34]

b) Competition Policy as Economic Policy

The Community is competent for competition policy as a whole, but only to a limited extent for economic policy. This division of powers leads to a complex dispute at Community level and in relation to the Member States.[35] At Community level, the point is first of all the conceptual approach of competition policy itself. Nothing can be derived from the text of the EEC Treaty for the scholastic disputes among competition theoreticians about freedom of competition as an end in itself, the possibility and justification of instrumentalisation of competition law for economic and social policy, or the value of efficiency or distribution criteria. In particular, the underlying Article 85 EEC, in the prohibitory rules of paragraph 1 and the discretionary elements of paragraph 3, displays an indeterminacy typical of codifications. But the interpretation of the competition rules concerns not only competition policy as such; it is at the same time of importance for the Community's possibilities of economic policy action as a whole. For the more comprehensively the list of goals of competition

27, at 32–33; N Reich, 'Die Bedeutung der Binnenmarktkonzeption für die Anwendung der EWG-Wettbewerbsregeln' in JF Baur, KJ Hopt and KP Mailänder (eds), *Festschrift für Ernst Steindorff zum 70, Geburtstag am 13. März 1990* (Berlin–New York: Walter de Gruyter, 1990) 1065.

[31] J Faull, 'Effect on Trade between Member States and Community-Member State Jurisdiction' in B Hawk (ed), *Annual Proceedings of the Fordham Corporate Law Institute 1989* (New York: Transnational Juris, 1990) 485.

[32] M Zuleeg, 'Die Wirtschaftsverfassung der Europäischen Gemeinschaften' in Arbeitskreis Europäische Integration (ed), *Wirtschafts- und gesellschaftspolitische Ordnungsprobleme der Europäischen Gemeinschaften* (Baden-Baden: Nomos, 1990) 73.

[33] E Steindorff, 'Spannungen', n 30 above, 34–35; S Klaue, 'Einige Bemerkungen über die Zukunft der Zweischrankentheorie' in Baur et al (eds), *Festschrift für Ernst Steindorff*, n 30 above, 979.

[34] ECR [1969] 1 – Walt Wilhelm/Bundeskartellamt.

[35] There is an instructive survey in Mononopolies Commission (*Monopolkommission*), *Konzeptionen einer europäischen Fusionskontrolle, Sondergutachten 17* (Baden-Baden: Nomos, 1989) 387 ff.

policy is understood, the sooner the Community can make use of its competence for far-reaching regulatory purposes. The legal-technical machinery for this was created by the Court of Justice and the Commission through their handling of the prohibitory norms of Article 85 (1) EEC and the exemption possibilities of Article 85 (3) EEC. A formalistic, extensive application of Article 85 (1) EEC allows the prohibition of practices on which no definitive negative value judgement is to be pronounced. Instead, the definitive valuation comes about only in connection with the application of Article 85 (3) EEC – and this happens in the Commission's exclusive competency.[36] Its exclusive competence for exemption decisions and the broad catalogue of aims in Article 85 (3) EEC, including 'promoting technical or economic progress' and giving 'consumers a fair share of the resulting benefit', offer the Commission the possibility of combining exemptions from antitrust prohibitions with regulatory objectives, which must then in turn be respected by the Member States.

This technique has been tested in inconspicuous steps and in striking examples (see [Section II 1 c] below). A genuine dispute as to principle came out only in connection with European merger control. The prehistory of the present debates is instructive in this connection. In 1973 the Commission had already, following the ECJ decision in *Continental Can*,[37] presented a first draft regulation.[38] The draft fell into a sort of sleeping beauty slumber until a new ECJ judgment[39] disclosed possibilities for merger control by using the EEC Treaty competition rules in force. The Europeanisation of merger control then emerged as a development that could not be stopped. This situation was used by the Commission for a new initiative. The draft it submitted[40] was based upon the competence for competition regulations under Article 87 EEC, and additionally on the residual powers clause of Article 235 EEC, for the criteria named in Article 2 (4) of the draft for allowing mergers contained material for regulatory policy conflicts. The draft took off from the exemption regulations of Article 85 (3) EEC, extending them by further criteria (improvement of competitive structures and the taking of international competitiveness into account) and by a reference to the Community's general goals. By 1988 these already included the SEA title on social coherence (Article 130a EEC) and technology policy (Article 130f EEC). The regulatory policy criticism of the catalogue of objectives of merger control thus enriched was obvious. If the freedom of 'competition as a discovery process' counts as an end in itself, then there can be no industrial or social policy requirements of higher rank,[41] and the constructivist interventionism of

[36] Art 9 of Regulation 17/62.
[37] ECR [1973] 215 – *Euro Emballage Corp and Continental Can/Commission.*
[38] OJ C 92/1973, 1.
[39] ECR [1987] 4487 – *Philip Morris/Rothmans.*
[40] OJ C 130/1988, 4.
[41] Mononpolies Commission (*Monopolkommission*), *Konzeptionen einer europäischen Fusionskontrolle, Sondergutachten 17*, n 35 above, 67, 69–70, 77 ff.

technology policy in any case counts as a classical example of what Friedrich von Hayek would call a presumption of knowledge.[42] Translated into the language of economic constitutional law, this means that the competition competency norm of Article 87 EEC is sufficient to bring merger control into conformity with the competition rules of Articles 85, 86 EEC. If and because this competency norm is enough, reference to Article 235 EEC was misplaced.[43] Moreover, a regulation could not in any case amend Articles 85 and 86 EEC as primary Community law.[44]

The regulation finally adopted in December 1989[45] keeps the reference to Article 235 EEC, but is more reticent in its catalogue of objectives than the April 1988 draft. According to the 13th recital, the Commission is committed to the 'basic objectives of the Treaty pursuant to Art 2 thereof, including the objective of strengthening economic and social cohesion'; in the evaluative criteria of Article 2 (1) (b) of the regulation, 'promoting technical or economic progress' retained but an insignificant position. This is just the way legislation usually deals with conceptual difficulties, leaving the parties at dispute to their controversies.[46]

c) *Integration Policy as De-regulation Strategy?*

The dispute over the conceptual orientation of European competition policy and the legitimacy of regulatory objectives not only concerns the Community's own possibilities of action but at the same time contains considerable material for dispute in relation to the Member States. Two scenarios are relevant here: Community exemptions pursuant to Article 85 (3) EEC, broad interpretations of competition policy objectives, and industrial policy enrichments of merger control may clash with regulatory policy concepts in Member States – and in view of the supremacy principle, a Europe-legislated regulation should prevail over stricter domestic antitrust law. But the contrary is also true: in so far as Community law competition principles apply, their 'unitary application' and 'full effectiveness' is endangered not just by laxer antitrust practice, but

[42] See E-J Mestmäcker, 'Fusionskontrolle im Gemeinsamen Markt zwischen Wettbewerbspolitik und Industriepolitik' [1988] *Europarecht* 349, at 357 [his commitment to FA Hayek, The Pretence of Knowledge' (1989) 89 *The American Economic Review* 3 is clearly visible].

[43] Mestmäcker,'Fusionskontrolle', n 41 above, 365, ff;Steindorff, *EG-Kompetenzen*, n 7 above, 70–71, 114 ff; as against this, Monopolies Commission (*Monopolkommission*), *Fusionskontrolle*, n 35 above, 67 ff, 77 ff.

[44] E Steindorff, 'Kooperativer Unternehmenszusammenschluß und Kartellverbot' (1988) 152 *Zeitschrift für das gesamte Handels- und Wirtschaftsrecht* 57, at 64–65.

[45] OJ L 395/1989, 1.

[46] The Monopolies Commission (*Monopolkommission*), 'Achtes Hauptgutachten der Monopolkommission 1988/1989', Bt.-Drucksache 11/7582 v. 16.7.1990, at 15, took note of the regulation's compromise formulas, but expressed the expectation 'that the EC officials entrusted with applying the law have a clear competition approach to European merger control'. Whether this expectation will be fulfilled remains to be seen.

equally and even more so by regulations systematically located outside antitrust law – and Community law must then oblige Member States to take deregulation measures.

The first conflict pattern – the loosening up of national antitrust law by European competition law – has been well known since the Walt Wilhelm decision.[47/48] There was less clear awareness that the sequence of steps from a ban under Article 85 (1) to exemption under Article 85 (3) could amount to centralist re-regulation of national regulations;[49] and with remarkable nonchalance, regulatory elements of European exemption regulations, such as regulations to protect the weaker contractual party or consumers, are taken over into national contract law.[50] The archetypal situation, that is, the conflict between Community competition principles and national regulations, has recently moved into the centre of interest, thereby taking on the importance of a crucial question for European competition law.[51]

The starting point for this development is a judgment of 1977[52] in which the ECJ declared a Belgian regulation on the taxation of tobacco products, whereby taxes were to be calculated upon the basis of the retail prices indicated on the products, to be ineffective: the taxation system was guaranteeing the cigarette manufacturers' and importers' price policy more perfectly than could a market-dominating firm (or vertical mandatory price system). By introducing this system, Belgium was held to have infringed its loyalty obligations laid down in Article 5 (2) EEC. It was not until 1985 that the ECJ came back to this precedent. It questioned French book price maintenance, based on the '*loi Lang*',[53] though

[47] N 34 above.

[48] Again, it was only European measure control that compelled an intensification of debate. The resolution of the conflict in the regulation is diplomatic: only in cases of 'importance to the Community legislator' does the regulation claim absolute primacy (Art 21 (2)). If Member States wish to impose their national antitrust law in minor cases, they may do so. The 'German clause' of Art 9 also provides for reference of merger cases to national authorities where 'a market in this Member State includes all the characteristics of a separate market' (for more details, see E Niederleithinger, 'Das Verhältnis nationaler und europäischer Kontrolle von Zusammenschlüssen' (1990) *Wirtschaft und Wettbewerb* 721).

[49] Without causing much fuss in this connection at the time, the ECJ, in its Haecht II Judgment (ECR [1967] 543 – *Haecht/Wilkin-Janssen*), declared a regulation of beer sales based upon a Belgian royal decree to be in breach of competition. The exemption regulation adopted following this decision (OJ L 173/1983, 5) corresponds in its basic lines to the Belgian decree declared ineffective (and to selling practices tolerated in antitrust law elsewhere, particularly in the Federal Republic).

[50] See esp the Group Exemption Regulation 123/85 on motor vehicle sales and customer service agreements, OJ L 15/1985, 16, and the comments on it in H-J Bunte and H Sauter, *EG-Gruppenfreistellungsverordnungen* (Munich: CH Beck, 1988), Regulation no 123/85, no 76 et seq.

[51] Although the conflict situation is in no way new; see the example of franchising – liberal European competition law/national binding contract law – C Joerges, 'Franchise-Verträge und europäisches Wettbewerbsrecht' (1987) 151 *Zeitschrift für das gesamt Handels- und Wirtschaftsrecht* 195, at 218 ff.

[52] ECR [1977] 2115 – *GB-Inno-BM/ATAB*.

[53] ECR [1985] 1 – *Leclerc/Au blé vert*.

admittedly without concluding by declaring it ineffective. It thereby exclusively confirmed French price regulations for petrol that were administered directly by government officials.[54] There are only two sets of cases where the ECJ has shown itself to be more open: national permission for cartel agreements that made it easier for them to come about or that strengthened their effect[55] was held to breach the loyalty obligation, as was a delegation of price-setting powers to professional organisations or economic associations whose price policy was given the blessing of government offices.[56]

The German Monopolies Commission attaches far-reaching hopes to this case law: for the prohibition on delegation of government regulatory powers to corporatist self-regulatory associations could be interpretable as an approach to a 'general control of government action on the basis of its effects on the competition system'; a consequence of this approach would be an opening up of the possibility of 'assessing government measures in general on the criterion of compatibility with competition provisions'.[57] Wishful thinking? The Monopolies Commission[58] itself admits that the ECJ case law leaves many questions open. Not even its results are unambiguous. In the case of French book price maintenance, no infringement of the duties under Article 5 (2) EEC was found, and even a European confirmation of the special treatment of the book market was declared possible;[59] the importance of the '*Nouvelles Frontières*' decision becomes relative in the overall context of the rather cautious endeavours towards liberalising European air transport;[60] the *Cullet/Leclerc* and *Van Eycke/ ASPA* decisions can also be interpreted as explicit confirmation of the economic policy powers of Member States; the dislike for corporatist self-regulatory practices revealed in these cases, but also the *BNIC/Aubert* decision, contrasts strikingly with the approval of such arrangements both inside and outside (see Section II 2 below) European competition law. Even in the case of decisions that seem to point towards an instrumentalisation of European competition law for a de-regulation strategy, those very countervailing tendencies become effective that in the conflict between a 'weak' European and a 'stronger' national competition policy make the supremacy principle seem so problematical from a regulatory policy viewpoint.

[54] ECR [1985] 315 – *Cullet/Leclerc*.

[55] ECR [1986] 1457 – Ministère public/Asjes (Novelles Frontières); see ECR [1987] 3801 – VZW Vereniging van Vlaamse Reisbureaus/VZW Sociale Dienst van der Platselijke en Gewestelijke Overheidsdiensten.

[56] ECR [1987] 4789 – *BNIC/Aubert*; see ECR [1988] – *Van Eycke/ASPA*.

[57] Monopolies Commission (*Monopolkommission*), *Achtes Haiptgutachten* 1990, n 46 above, at 389.

[58] Ibid, 401.

[59] N 26 above; confirmed by ECJ in ECR [1988] 4468 – *L'Aigle Distribution*.

[60] See Monopolies Commission 1990, 'Achtes Hauptgutachten', n 46 above, 300 ff, 308 ff.

d) Second Interim Observation

The prospective theories of the integration process each have specific problems with the picture of competition law presented here. (1) There is clearly not a merely technical and bureaucratic administration of 'technical tasks' in Ipsen's sense. Particularly in the present debates on the re-employment of competition policy for industrial policy, on the applicability of innovative de-regulation strategies against regulatory protected zones and the replacement of national regulations by European ones, these are politically highly sensitive questions that are recognised and treated as such. (2) Can the Europeanisation of competition policy be understood as expansion of a supranational legal order carried out with the assent of the Member States? (3) Weiler has always tended to concede a special status to competition policy. But his analysis may prove to be more illuminating than he supposed. The influence of states seems considerably more massive than suggested by the genuine policy and administrative competencies of the Commission, and the mutual disputes over de-regulation in the Member States and re-regulation at European level confirm the Community's dependence on Member States' interests and competition policy conceptions.[61]

The practice of competition policy is hardest to fit into the interpretative framework of the neoliberal theory. The difficulties do not just stem from the effective power of legal practice over normative prescriptions. They rather concern the theoretical-normative premises of this conception. Obviously, the problems which European competition law and European competition policy are responding to by the integration of non-competition criteria are in principle, and rightly so, an objective of positively creative integration policy.[62] Policy 'may' understand the labour market and distribution policy effects of economic integration in the Member States and the divergent drifting of living standards

[61] More detailed case studies would probably confirm what V Schneider and R Wehrle, 'Vom Regime zum korporativen Akteur: Zur institutionellen Dynamik der Europäischen Gemeinschaft' in B Kohler-Koch (ed), *Regime in den intemationalen Beziehungen* (Opladen: Westdeutscher Verlag, 1988) 409, diagnosed on the example of their analysis of telecommunications policy: that the EC has grown into a corporate actor. This would mean that the balance assumed by Weiler between supranational constitutional structures and the Member States' possibilities of influence has shifted at the expense of the latter. Legal and institutional consequences of this finding are not discussed by Schneider and Wehrle.

[62] See PR Krugman, 'Konzepte der wirtschaftlichen Integration in Europa' in Padoa-Schioppa (ed), *Effizienz, Stabilität und Verteilungsgerechtigkeit*, n 5 above, 113. The formulations in the text have been kept deliberately cautious. They do not opt for the normative-legal adoption of recommendations from the camp of strategic commercial policy (on this tendency, see the survey and critique in K Stegemann, 'Wirtschaftspolitische Rivalitat zwischen Industriestaaten: Neue Erkenntnisse durch Modelle strategischer Handelspolitik?' in ME Streit (ed), *Wirtschaftspolitik zwischen ökonomischer und politischer Rationalität* (Wiesbaden: Springer, 1988) 3). It is, however, being suggested that strategic motives in negotiating processes at EC level are effective and that the Community can be given a disciplining function in controlling beggar-my-neighbour attitudes. What is particularly being asserted, though, is that controversies between economic schools are not to be decided without mediation in the name of the law.

in the Community as a mandate for action. Nor can the Community simply proceed in the name of an economic rationality allegedly built into the Treaty against national regulations that prove to be an obstacle to the achievement of a common competitive market – not just because jurists are accustomed and obliged to respect economically irrational regulations and/or ones that favour the interests of a particular clientele, but because diagnoses of market or government failure are as a rule theoretically controversial, and the question of whether or to what extent the market's control effects are socially acceptable must, in principle, be askable. The objection that the Community is not legitimated for a positive, shaping of economic and integration policy is certainly to be taken seriously.[63] But this also applies to the EEC Treaty's claim of a replacement inspired by neoliberal theory of the plurality of national governmental policies. Niederleithinger, in his critique of the extensive interpretation of the supremacy claims of European law over the competition policy of Member States, called for conflict solutions in which 'all legitimately competing objectives and viewpoints' are to be weighed up and 'competition restrictions as a part of Community policy' must be justified by the general Treaty objectives of Article 2 EEC.[64] This sort of comprehensive weighing up of clashing regulatory claims of the Community and the Member States might indeed act to settle disputes. But for the integration policy it would presuppose a readiness to 'mutual recognition' of differing regulatory policy concepts, and legally it would assume a conflict of laws reinterpretation of the supremacy principle.

2. New Harmonisation Policy: Market Integration or Social Regulation?

The Community's powers to harmonise the laws of Member States are enormously broad, and yet limited in a specific sense. According to the formulation in Article 100 EEC, the power for approximation of laws relates to 'such provisions as laid down by law, regulation or administrative action in Member States as directly affect the establishment or functioning of the Common Market'. This applies to the whole sphere of social regulatory law – consumer, labour and environmental law. The need for a 'positive' legislative policy by the Community in all these areas is confirmed by Article 36 EEC. According to it, the freedom of movement mentioned in Article 30 EEC has it limits in the case of provisions 'justified on grounds of public morality, public policy or public security; the

[63] E-J Mestmäcker, 'Auf dem Wege zu einer Ordnungspolitik für Europa' in Mestmäcker, Möller and Schwarz (eds), *Eine Ordnungspolitik für Europa: Festschrift für Hans von der Groeben*, n 14 above, 9, at 16 ff; see, also, Steindorff, *EG-Kompetenzen*, n 7 above, 18.

[64] K Schmidt, E Niederleithinger and P Schmidhuber, 'Die europäische Fusionskontrolle und ihr Verhältnis zum nationalen Recht – aus der Sicht des Bundeskartellamtes' in C-A Andreae (ed), *Wettbewerbspolitik an der Schwelle zum europäischen Binnenmarkt* (Cologne-Berlin-Bonn-Munich: Carl Heymansn, 1989) 79 and 87.

protection of health and life of humans, animals or plants'. But the powers and requirements of harmonisation are in no way covered by corresponding political and administrative competencies. The 1957 Treaty transferred very limited powers of action to the Community in the title on social policy. These have been expanded by the SEA (Article 118a EEC) and systematically augmented by the new environment policy powers. The changes in the approximation of laws provisions of Article 100a EEC, generally relating to the achievement of the internal market, do not however contain any explicit extensions of powers.[65] They merely combine the new majority decision procedure (Article 100a (1) EEC) with the obligation on the Commission 'in its proposals envisaged in paragraph 1 concerning health, safety, environment protection and consumer protection' to 'take as a base a high level of protection', while Member States retain powers of action even after a decision on harmonisation measures (Article 100a (4) and (5) EEC). This leaves the dilemma that marked even 'traditional' harmonisation policy unchanged: in order to implement its internal market policy, the Community must become involved in the same way about social regulations, but its powers to develop an independent regulatory policy remain limited and its possibilities of implementing such policies have not improved.

a) Old and New Harmonisation Policy

The intrinsically irresolvable tension between European legal approximation and national social regulation has not overly preoccupied practice and theory.[66] Since the 'General Programme to Eliminate Technical Barriers to Trade' of 1969,[67] approximation of laws has been entirely dominated by unification (approximation) of all provisions restricting intra-EC trade. Alongside this – and independently of it – the Community in the 1970s presented consumer and environmental policy programmes. The objectives of product regulation also certainly aimed at in these programmes remained unrealised. In particular, efforts at a separate European product safety policy have remained stuck at initial approaches (the setting up of accident information systems; mutual information by government authorities on product hazards).[68]

Admittedly, the 'traditional' harmonisation policy has also failed. Characteristically, the reasons held responsible for its failure have nothing to do with the regulatory one-sidedness of internal market policy. The decisive

[65] See Steindorff, *EG-Kompetenzen*, n 7 above, 94–95.

[66] But see K Hailbronner, 'Der "nationale Alleingang" im Gemeinschaftsrecht am Beispiel der Abgasstandards für Pkw' (1990) *Europäische Grundrechte-Zeitschrift* 101.

[67] OJ C 76/1969, 1.

[68] C Joerges, J Falke, H-W Micklitz and G Brüggemeier, *Die Sicherheit von Konsumgütern und die Entwicklung der Gemeinschaft* (Baden-Baden: Nomos, 1988) 282 ff. Translated version of the pertinent chapter: J Falke and C Joerges, 'The "Traditional" Law Approximation Policy Approaches to Removing Technical Barriers to Trade and Efforts at a "Horizontal" European Product Safety Policy' (2010) 6 *Hanse Law Review*, Special Issue, 31 ff.

weaknesses were instead seen exclusively in the notorious bottlenecks in the European legislative process: the hurdles of the unanimity rule of Article 100 EEC and the difficulty of using a harmonisation of 'legal and administrative provisions' to achieve the practically so-important transformation of private sets of norms in a way that would conform with integration.[69] This diagnosis then led to the treatment whereby harmonisation policy was renewed step by step:

- As early as 1983 the existing restriction of the approximation of laws to the legal and administrative provisions mentioned in Article 100 EEC was overcome, and its non-governmental appendage, namely technical standards, included. The so-called Information Directive of 28.3.1983[70] obliged Member States to provide early mutual information on legislative and standard-setting intentions. Since then, the Commission has been able to respond early to threatened market splitting by developing European solutions; in particular, it can guarantee the primacy of Community law anticipatorily by standstill orders.
- A second possible therapy was supplied by the *Cassis-de-Dijon* judgment of 1979,[71] with a statement that only those legal provisions that took into account actually 'mandatory requirements' justified restrictions on the free movement of goods guaranteed by Article 30 EEC, but that otherwise positive harmonisation measures could be done without. The 'new approach to technical harmonisation and standards'[72] drew a twofold conclusion from this: since only 'mandatory requirements' legitimated restrictions on freedom of trade by national law, harmonisation must in future concentrate on the unification of 'essential safety requirements'. Other 'positive' measures not belonging to this legislative policy core area could be left to the standardisation organisations, and the Community could content itself with procedural measures to guarantee the compatibility of the outcome of standardisation with the basic safety requirements.[73]
- The taking of decisions on the new type of directive was facilitated by Article 100a (1) EEC, introduced by the SEA. The sphere of application of this provision is, in so far as product regulations are concerned, very wide: in particular, it also covers environment policy provisions.[74] Admittedly, Article 100a (3) EEC obliges the Community to a 'high level of protection', and in accordance with Article 100a (4) and (5) EEC the Member States retain considerable possibilities of action.

[69] For details, see Joerges et al, *Die Sicherheit von Konsumgütern*, n 68 above, 272 ff, 346 ff.
[70] OJ L 109/1983 extended by the Directive of 22.3.1988, OJ L 81/1988, 75.
[71] ECR [1979] 649.
[72] Council Resolution of 7.5.1985, OJ C 136/1985, along with the 'conclusions on standardisation' of 16.7.1984 (Annex I) and the so-called Model Directive (Annex II).
[73] For more details, see Joerges et al, *Die Sicherheit von Konsumgütern*, n 68 above, 345 ff.
[74] As C-D Ehlermann already noted in his 'The Internal Market Following the Single European Act' (1987) 24 *CMLR* 361, at 383.

b) Successes and Difficulties

The stagnation of harmonisation policy was overcome by the 'new approach' and the European standardisation organisations have energetically taken up their new task. Admittedly, the expectation that the new harmonisation policy would be a de-regulation strategy was not fulfilled.[75] There has been deregulation purely in a sense of a 'de-nationalisation' and 'de-governmentalisation' of product safety law. The European standardisation organisations that are supposed to secure the harmonisation of standards in the place of the previously competent government representatives are plainly doing the job more quickly than was possible under an arrangement of national and Community law. But they are in turn likely to meet with difficulties in reaching agreement. At any rate, standardisation practice has rejected the idea of a 'mutual recognition' of national standards.

At the moment the Commission is endeavouring to perfect its standardisation policy at two levels. In a new Green Paper,[76] standardisation policy is explicitly committed to the objective of a technological conversion of Europe, and a shift of standardisation activity to European level is called for: European standardisation organisations are no longer to see themselves as assemblies of national delegations, but are themselves to organise the process of clarifying economic interests and technical possibilities.

In a complementary programme on standardisation, the building up of a European certification system is being pushed ahead. The practical importance of this programme can scarcely be over-estimated. Neither government offices nor 'the market' could just accept the conformity to standards of products. Conformity to standards must instead be positively established – that is, certified. But the special feature of the certification question lies in the fact that it cannot be handled along the lines of legislative or standardisation acts at European level. The certificates must necessarily be issued in de-centralised fashion – with the consequence that the equivalence of national practices must, in the interest of the recognition of such certificates by administrative offices in the Member States and by demanders of products, be guaranteed. Accordingly, the new directives contain detailed provisions on the issuing and recognition of certificates; but for that reason, too, the success of the new approach remains dependent on the success of the Commission's efforts to solve the certification

[75] I shall merely refer to the available theoretical explanations: an instructive sociological and political analysis can be found in E Bolenz, *Technische Normung zwischen 'Markt' und 'Staat'* (Bielefeld: Kleine, 1987); for an economic perspective, see G Pfeiffer, *Kompatibilität und Markt. Ansätze zu einer ökonomischen Theorie der Standardisierung* (Baden-Baden: Nomos, 1989); see, also, J Falke, 'Normungspolitik der Europäischen Gemeinschaften zum Schutz von Verbrauchern und Arbeitnehmern' (1989/90) 3 *Jahrbuch zur Staats- und Verwaltungswissenschaft* 176.

[76] EC Commission, Green Paper on the Development of European Standardization: Means for Faster Technological Integration in Europe (COM(90)456 final of 8.10.1990).

question: legally-binding requirements on the 'quality' of certification offices, the encouragement of their cooperation and the building up of a European agency to organise all this.[77] Here a strategy can be seen emerging in which the Community hopes, by using cooperative arrangements, to overcome not only its dependency on political assent by the Member States but also its administrative weakness.

c) Internal Market Policy and Social Regulation

The successes in the new harmonisation policy are impressive even now, and the conceptual imaginativeness with which the practical and legal difficulties are being approached is admirable. Precisely because of these successes, however, the problem of the relation between internal market-oriented approximation policy and social regulation, so long kept latent, now seems to be becoming acute. For environmentally motivated product regulation, this is emerging first in the fact that there is in principle no trust in the technique of reference to standards in this area.[78] But even with directly health-related product regulation, the differentiations known from national law continue to be retained. In law on medicines, the 'new approach' plays no part, and in foodstuffs law the regulatory structures have scarcely changed.[79]

It is noteworthy that not only is the extension in regulations on health protection advancing in these areas well known for their consumer policy sensitivity, but the Commission has now also systematically supplemented the whole new harmonisation programme with a draft directive on general product safety.[80] The complicated technical details can be left to one side here. The new directive is to apply to all products not already covered by special regulations, which are 'industrially manufactured, processed or agricultural, … new, used and reprocessed'. Member States are called on for legislative activities that go well beyond the existing state of product safety law. It provides for coordination of product

[77] For more details, see C Joerges and J Falke, 'Die Normung von Konsumgütern in der Europäischen Gemeinschaft und der Richtlinien-Entwurf über die allgemeine Produktsicherheit' in P-C Müller-Graff (ed), *Technische Regeln (Normen und Standards) – Bedeutung für die Vollendung des Binnenmarktes* (Baden-Baden: Nomos, 1991), Section II. 3; H-W Micklitz, 'Consumer Rights' in A Cassese, A Clapham and JHH Weiler (eds), *Human Rights and the European Community* (Baden-Baden: Nomos, 1991) 53.

[78] I Pernice, 'Auswirkungen des europäischen Binnenmarktes auf das Umweltrecht – Gemeinschafts (verfassungs-) rechtliche Grundlagen' (1990) 9 *Neue Zeitschrift für Verwaltungsrecht* 201, at 210 ff; by contrast, on national law, see H Voelzkow, J Hilbert and RG Heinze, 'Regierung durch Verbände – am Beispiel der umweltschutzbezogenen Techniksteuerung' (1987) 28 *Politische Vierteljahresschrift* 80; E Denninger, *Verfassungsrechtliche Anforderungen an die Normsetzung im Umwelt- und Technikrecht* (Baden-Baden: Nomos, 1990) 18 ff.

[79] What is, instead, to be noted is the attempt to coordinate national foodstuffs checks embarked on by Directive 89/397 (OJ L 186/1989, 23).

[80] A first draft (OJ C 193/1989, 1) has since been amended by the Commission,COM (90) 259 final, 11.6.1990; see Joerges and Falke, 'Die Normung', n 77 above, Section IV.

safety policy priorities and activities at Community level. In 'emergency cases' the Commission obtains powers of action of its own. One should hesitate with predictions on the fate of this draft. But there can be no doubt that the very logic of the matter requires the establishment of the second policy level to supplement systematically the existing one-dimensional harmonisation policy with its internal market policy orientation.

d) Third Intermediate Observation

The finding seems paradoxical: the new harmonisation policy, announced as a de-regulation strategy, at first produces cooperative arrangements between the Community and standardisation organisations, then forces cooperation among the national administrations, and finally leads to intensification of product safety law and to the establishment of a new policy area for the Community. These results seem less surprising, however, if the functions of standardisation are borne in mind. The cooperative relationships known particularly in German law between state and standardisation organisations in product regulation are to be explained upon the basis of the market-constituting function of standardisation, and at the same time are a response to the fact that the state, in an apparently irreversible development, is forced to take on increasingly wider protective tasks, yet cannot handle these tasks itself without coming to an agreement with economic interests.[81] These cooperative regulatory patterns have so far proved resistant to every critique on regulatory policy grounds.[82]

However, the Europeanisation of these national models remains in need of analysis and explanation. As long as the EC is an aggregate of states, interest representation can in principle not be given a new 'supranational' function.[83] If, as Weiler has shown, the Member States essentially determine the Community's decision-making processes, then this is not reconcilable with the (functional) delegation of legislative powers to supranational systems of 'private government'. These constitutional positions find support in political science analysis of the role of economic associations in Community policy.[84] Certainly, Ipsen already predicted that a shift of administrative competences to Community level would be bound to have effects on the organisation of interest representation.[85] In accordance with this prognosis, Kohler-Koch notes that reorganisations

[81] Bolenz, *Technische Normung zwischen 'Markt' und 'Staat'*, n 75 above 5 ff, 94 ff, 160 ff.

[82] See W Streeck and P Schmitter, 'Gemeinschaft, Markt und Staat – und die Verbände?' (1985) 25 *Journal für Sozialforschung* 133, on the one hand, and ME Streit, 'Ordnungspolitische Probleme einer Interessenvertretung durch Verbände' (1987) 36 *Zeitschrift fur Wirtschaftspolitik* 47, on the other.

[83] Ipsen, n 18 above, 1005.

[84] B Kohler-Koch, 'Vertikale Machtverteilung und organisierte Wirtschaftsinteressen in der Europäischen Gemeinschaft' in Alemann, Heinze and Hombach (eds), *Die Kraft der Region*, n 3 above, 221, at 225 ff

[85] Ipsen, n 18 above, 1005.

of associational cooperation aimed at 'increased efficiency ... with the greatest possible control by the Member Associations'.[86] The procedure of the new harmonisation policy in fact suggests a dual strategy. For the Member States remain present not only in the adoption of new directives, but also in all Commission decisions affecting standardisation policy in advisory or even regulatory committees (by representatives 'who may be supported by experts or advisors').[87] The European standardisation organisations are in turn combinations of national organisations.[88] Accordingly, at both national and European level there are indications of possibilities of the representation of interests that continue to be defined in primarily national terms. But for all this, decisions at Community level are taking on increasing importance, and this suggests legal and institutional consequences: to the extent that the functions of self-regulation are shifted to European standardisation organisations, functional equivalents for the mechanisms for regulating-self-regulation, found in national frameworks, must also be devised. Among these are measures to secure 'balanced' representation at European level,[89] and also governmental administrative control which must, in turn, be coordinated at Community level.

III. PROGRAMMES AND OPTIONS

The observations on the development of competition and standardisation policy confirm the thesis that the new dynamics of internal market policy point beyond the perspectives of academic legal theories of integration. This thesis admittedly remains destructive as long as it merely declares the analytical reference frameworks for those theories, and therefore also their normative claims, to be inadequate. Constructive counter-conceptions must satisfy further-reaching argumentational requirements. They must replace the integration policy models of legal science by more complex analytical assumptions, develop corresponding normative approaches and explain their relationship to the legal and institutional provisions of the EEC Treaty. Such justification claims do not merely overstrain the jurist as such. At a stage when the far-reaching changes in the framework conditions for the integration process must be dealt with, and new changes can be expected which could literally throw out of date from one day to the next the calculations and strategies of political actors, the effects of legal and institutional innovations can scarcely be predicted. In any case, the risk of speculative mis-assessments can be limited. If at the moment it cannot

[86] Kohler-Koch, n 84 above, at 226.

[87] Section 9 of the Model Directive; for more details, see Joerges et al, *Die Sicherheit von Kosumgütern*, n 68 above, at 345 ff.

[88] See Joerges et al, *Sicherheit von Kosumgütern*, n 87 above, at 360 ff.

[89] Ibid, 44 ff.

definitively be foreseen how and whether the economic policy threshold towards a European currency will be crossed, it is nonetheless certain that the new debates on the legitimacy of economic and social regulations and the delimitation of central and decentralised powers sparked off by the internal market policy programme will not come to a halt. If the efforts towards a specifically European federalism in a future European union still seem all too vague, it is nonetheless certain that particular framework conditions for a Europeanisation of regulatory policies will not change. And it is also certain that all considerations on the Europeanisation of regulatory policy will have to deal with the debates on the crisis of regulatory law.[90]

These preliminary observations should adequately establish the limited claim of, but also the justification for, the considerations below. These considerations do not pre-suppose any further-developed new guiding image of integration policy, and relate purely to the area of regulatory policy already covered by the integration process. They are not intended to set up any abstract models against the developments observable in this area, but instead aim to show what innovative strategies have already formed, or at least can be discerned in this development.

1. Achievement of the Internal Market and Regulatory Policy

The conceptions so emphatically and successfully advocated in the Commission White Paper on completion of the internal market from 1985 can be termed a specifically economic integration strategy: the internal market is to be aimed at because of its economic advantages, and is to be accomplished above all by guaranteeing rights of market access. This programme now, however, seems to be developing a peculiar dialectics that can be typified as a change in form of regulatory policy in Europe. Majone, in his studies on American and European regulatory policy, has worked out the traditional differences and drawn attention to more recent convergencies that can be observed.[91] The European forms of 'intervention' in the economy were and are much more comprehensive and ambitious than the controls of a 'regulatory state'. This is particularly true of the nationalisation of branches of industry, but tends to be so also for municipal and socialised enterprises, and corporatist interwinings between government offices

[90] See the documentation (and continuation) of this debate in G Teubner, 'Steuerung durch plurales Recht. Oder: Wie die Politik den normativen Mehrwert der Geldzirkulation abschöpft' in W Zapf (ed), *Die Modernisierung moderner Gesellschaften. Verhandlungen des 25. Deutschen Soziologentages 1990* (Frankfurt aM: Campus, 1991) 528.

[91] G Majone, 'Regulating Europe: Problems and Prospects' in T Ellwein, JJ Hesse, R Mayntz and FW Scharpf (eds), *Jahrbuch zur Staats- und Verwaltungswissenschaft 3* (1989) 159; idem, *Deregulation or Re-Regulation? Regulatory Reform in Europe and the United States* (London: Pinter/ New York: St. Martin's Press, 1990); idem, 'Cross-National Sources of Regulatory Policymaking in Europe and the United States' (1991) 1 *JEPP* 7.

and private organisations. By contrast, the American regulatory programmes are less comprehensive, though also more targeted: 'economic regulation' is no substitute for socialisation, but is intended merely to compensate for specific forms of market failure. 'Social regulation' is concerned with external effects, the protection of health and environmental interests, and the protection of workers and consumers.[92] The characteristic of this form of control is found by Majone in 'sustained and focused control exercised by a public agency over activities that are socially valued'.[93]

The regulatory semantics of the EEC Treaty – including the remnant of socialisation in Article 222 EEC – is clearly marked by the European traditions of influencing the economy. Not least because of the strength of these traditions and the differences between them, the object of a 'Common Market' for long seemed vague and utopian. The Community's integration prospect has, however, taken on clearer outlines through the internal market initiative and the SEA. It is in line with the logic of this programme for European policy to scarcely dream any longer of a 'harmonisation' of national traditions, but instead to be in principle questioning everywhere the continued existence of all regulatory forms where they seem incompatible with the creation of a unitary economic area.[94] But it correspondingly seems to fit the logic of consistent market integration for new forms to be sought to achieve regulatory goals, the justification for which is in principle not disputed. The 'regulatory state' is acquiring new topicality,[95] deriving precisely from the fact that its activities are not replacing market economy processes but are intended to 'accompany' them.

Certainly, the American conditions of regulatory policy differ considerably from the position in the EEC:

- By contrast with the USA, the implementation of a particular regulatory concept in Europe regularly comes up against differing traditions and patterns of interest.
- Economic differences in development and development interests have greater weight in Europe. They can be brought into decision-making processes at EC level as national economic interests. The resulting additional load on regulatory policy debates of appropriate regulatory forms and unification processes through standards and safety standards can be shifted only to a very limited extent onto abstract mechanisms for reaching agreement (transfer efforts).

[92] For more details, see, for example, MD Reagan, *Regulation. The Politics of Policy* (Boston MA–Toronto: Little, Brown & Co, 1987) 45 and 85 ff.

[93] Referring to P Selznick, 'Focusing Organisational Research on Regulation' in RG Noll (ed), *Regulatory Policy and the Social Sciences* (Berkeley CA: University of California Press, 1985) 363.

[94] See P-C Müller-Graff, *Binnenmarktziel und Rechtsordnung* (Bergisch-Gladbach/Cologne: Josef Eul, 1989) 38 ff; and on the case of competition policy, Section II 1 c above.

[95] See Majone, 'Cross-National Sources', n 91 above, at 22 ff.

- The question of whether market failure is responsible for wrong developments and to what extent it can be corrected by regulatory intervention is never free of dispute – neither between economic experts nor in the political process. This is even more true for all areas of social regulation. The establishment of safety standards or of threshold values for environmental pollution has a normative-practical dimension that scientific discourse cannot cognitively cope with, but on the other hand is brought to bear only in abbreviated form in economic and political interest bargaining.
- For regulatory policies in the sense of 'sustained and focused control', administrative competencies and resources, provided for only exceptionally by Community law, are necessary. The paradigm of EC regulatory policy is centralised legislation, with implementation through the legislation and administration of Member States. Simple following of American patterns is not possible within these structures.
- Last but not least, the American agencies are tangled up in all sorts of formal and informal networks from which they derive information and in which they agree on the securing and acceptance of their measure. Heclo has described this phenomenon as the breaking down of the 'iron triangle' of executive, parliamentary control and interest groups.[96] Majone interprets it as the move away from Weber's ideotype of the purpose of rationality of administrative action, explained on the basis of the scientific and normative policy complexity of regulatory policy, and justifies the move to a procedural rationality of administrative action. But at European level, this 'functional shift' in administration cannot be directly taken as a model.

2. Institutional Framework Conditions and Integration Policy Concepts

Despite these difficulties, the Europeanisation of regulatory policy is rapidly advancing in all areas of economic and social regulation. Its main institutional medium has developed more or less naturally: in an incomprehensibly vast multiplicity of advisory, administrative and regulatory committees, Commission and Member State officials come to agreement on the implementation of Community law. Relatively little is known about the mode of operation of this network of committees.[97] Structurally, this is administrative law-making, the

[96] H Heclo, 'Issue Networks and the Executive Establishment' in A King (ed), *The New American Political System* (Washington DC: American Enterprise Institute, 1978) 87, at 88 and 89.

[97] For a summary of the state of affairs, see W Meng, 'Die Neuregelung der EG-Verwaltungsausschüsse. Streit um die "Comitologie"' (1988) 49 *Zeitschrift für ausländisches öffentliches Recht und Völkerrecht* 208; for more up-to-date details in the area of product regulation, see H Bentlage, *An Advisory Board for Consumer Product Safety: The German Experience – European Perspectives* (Bremen: ZERP, 1990).

supranationality of which, entirely in line with Weiler's theses (see Section I 2 c above), remains tied to the involvement of Member States.

The effectiveness of comitology system certainly calls for more exact evaluation. From a constitutional viewpoint, however, this form of Europeanisation of regulatory tasks is questionable, if only because it takes place largely without public involvement and leaves the mediation of economic oppositions of interests and regulatory objectives at the mercy of non-transparent bargaining processes. In the Commission's more recent programmatic projects, the committee system has been squeezed aside by other concepts.

a) Regulatory Competition: Market Rationality as Arbitrator of Legislative Policy?

The Commission's White Paper on the completion of the internal market gained prominence for its reorientation of harmonisation policies.[98] In technical legal language this reorientation is termed 'mutual recognition', and in the jargon of regulatory discussion 'regulatory competition'. Following the *Cassis-de-Dijon* judgment,[99] the view came to prevail that in the EC the assumption should be the equivalence of the regulatory goals in health and consumer protection, so that the principle of 'host state control' could be replaced by that of 'home state control'.[100] 'Mutual recognition' as an alternative to positive harmonisation has subsequently been taken up, particularly in relation to free movement of services.

The idea is fascinating:[101] just as private economic action is subject to control by competition, so the constructivist 'presumptuousness of knowledge' that any legal intervention involves is made subject to indirect control. Member States may retain differing regulations; they must merely shape them and handle them in such a way that citizens of the EC market can 'choose' [under] which regulatory regime the products or services demanded or supplied [have been produced].

[98] Commission of the EC, Completing the Internal Market: White Paper from the Commission to the European Council of 14 June 1985, COM(85) 310 final.

[99] ECR [1979] 649.

[100] Commission, COM(85) 310 final, n 98 above, 58.

[101] It was developed in the recent American federalism debate as a critique of the centralism of the regulatory state (for a survey, see CW Sternberg, 'Regulatory Federalism: An Overview of American Experience', Typescript EUI Florence, 1990 (on file with author); see, also, the references in Joerges et al, *Die Sicherheit von Konsumgütern*, n 68 above, 243 ff). From the German debate, see, esp, *Wissenschaftlicher Beirat beim Bundesministerium für Wirtschaft*, '*Ordnungspolitische Orientierung für die politische Union*' (Bonn: Minstry of Economics, 1986); CJ Meyer-Schatz, 'Europäische Harmonisierung des Gesellschafts- und Kapitalmarktrechts 1989' (1989) 41 *Wirtschaft und Recht* 84; H Siebert, 'The Harmonization Issue in Europe: Prior Agreement or a Competitive Process' in idem (ed), *The Completion of the Internal Market* (Tübingen: Mohr, 1989) 53; JB Donges, 'Wieviel Deregulierung brauchen wir für den EG-Binnenmarkt?' (1990) 36 *Zeitschrift für angewandte Wirtschaftsforschung* 169.

However attractive this notion may seem, its practical difficulties, and those of principle, remain for the moment considerable. From the legal viewpoint, the obligation to recognise regulations of the state of origin is an equivalent to 'positive' harmonisation. From that viewpoint alone, the obligation can only subsist where it is rooted in primary Community law itself, or else positively prescribed in a directive. Two starting-points are available in primary Community law. The first is constituted by the checking of national measures for compatibility with the principle of free movement of goods since the *Cassis-de-Dijon* judgment. A complementary second approach lies in the theory of the economic constitution of the Community. If the Community is legally obliged to set up a system of undistorted competition, if, as the Monopolies Commission sees it (see Section II 1 above), in any case duties of regulatory self-restraint follow from the case law on Article 5 (2) EEC, then this may imply the less far-reaching obligation to open the national markets to suppliers from states with other regulatory systems. So far, however, in primary Community law duties of recognition are demonstrable only to a very limited extent. It is true particularly for the case law in Article 30 EEC, by which the substantive control of national regulations has remained extremely slight.[102] And the existing case law on Article 5 (2) EEC is still less able to support the far-reaching consequences the Monopolies Commission wishes to draw from it (See Section II 1 above).

These legal reservations are comprehensible: on the logic of regulatory competition, after all, the delimitation between competitive and non-competitive regulatory patterns should no longer be seen as a normative and legislative policy problem, but economic rationality should be allowed to make its way outside of political and legal procedures *vis-à-vis* the interests pursued by democratically legitimated legislators. Merely in consideration of these normative and legislative policy difficulties, there ought to be clarity at least as to the fields of application and mode of operation of regulatory competition. In the sphere of 'economic' regulations, the opening up of regulatory competition on economic regulations is in principle acceptable where no 'exogenous' regulatory objectives, like distributive justice or other social policy interests, are pursued.[103] But there must be further questions about how the actors concerned actually set in motion the game of regulatory competition and can exploit it – and a distinction must therefore be drawn between, say, the de-regulation of paternalistic regulations between 'professional' and 'private' demanders. In the recognition of foreign product regulations, the essential point is whether information on quality and safety differences adequately protects the product users concerned. In the sphere of so-called process regulation, in particular in the case of environmental and

[102] References in Falke and Joerges, 'The "Traditional" Law Approximation', n 68 above, Section II 2; from the recent case law, a noteworthy one is Case 382/88, judgment 7.3.1990 – *INNO-BM/ Confédération du Commerce Luxembourgois*, ECR [1990] I-00667 (on the checking of the German UWG against the Community's consumer policy programmes (!)).

[103] See Meier-Schatz, 'Europäische Harmonisierung', n 101 above.

work safety provisions, the principle of regulatory competition means that a regulatory interest recognised as legitimate 'politically' may indirectly, namely through the competitive advantages that may result from lower production costs with lower safety standards, fall into danger. But whether such consequences arise and to what extent they have to be tolerated is not something that can be predicted and assessed in general. But if they are not decidable *ex ante*, then regulatory competition itself proves in need of regulation. It would have to take the form of observing the successes and failures of regulations, and remain subject to checking. This sort of experimental, self-observing and improving legislative policy cannot, however, then simply be handed over to an anonymous mechanism.

b) European Corporatism: Europeanisation through the Self-Organisation of the Economy?

Regulatory policy relates its powers of resistance to de-regulatory strategies not only to the paternalistic inclinations of governmental actors, but also to the functional conditions of markets and the interests of the economy. This interplay of political regulatory claims and private regulatory interests can well be seen in the example of product regulation, so important for the achievement of the internal market (see Section II 2 b above): the 'new approach to technical harmonisation and standards' was set up as a de-regulation strategy in two respects. On the one hand, it was to unburden the Community legislator and exploit the standardisation capacities of private standardisation organisations. It was also, however, to encourage the mutual recognition of product regulations and national standards. This second element in the 'new approach' is hardly talked of any more. The so-called new harmonisation policy has since been proving to be a strategy to promote self-regulation mechanisms – in standardisation just as much as in the area of certification.

Just like the idea of regulatory competition, European corporatism has also since been moving in a legal no-man's land, and its practical chances of implementation are uncertain. Community law contains only one clear relevant rule on cooperation with private organisations in the European-law-making process: the ban on the delegation of law-making powers to actors not legitimated by the EEC Treaty.[104] Accordingly, the new standardisation policy must be located in a legal framework that forms a counterpart to the goal aimed at – to unburden the legislator – and at the same time covers up these contradictions by fictions: directives should be so precisely formulated that administrative authorities can be guided by them; the standards worked out by standardisation organisations

[104] Case 10-56, *Meroni & Co v High Authority of the European Coal and Steel Community*, Judgment of 16 June 1958, ECLI:EU:C:1958:8.

must be formally recognised by the Commission before they can develop the effects attributed to them.[105]

It is only in the Commission's most recent documents that a constructive alternative to this form of underpinning European corporatism is taking shape. The Green Paper on standards of 8 October 1990 states that standards are of too great importance 'to be left to the technical experts alone': 'Other interests, too, such as consumers, users and workers must equally be prepared to organise themselves more effectively to participate in European standardization.'[106] With such demands, the Commission wishes to take account of objections long discussed at national level to the self-regulatory handling of governmental tasks.[107] The normatively so plausible efforts at breaking down the European 'iron triangle' of Commission, Member States and standardisation organisations by pluralising standardisation procedures at Community level are, however, scarcely compatible with the institutional structures of the EC, and hard to put into practice.[108] Even the transformation of the European standardisation organisations into actors that replace the bargaining process between national delegations, and are themselves to organise the mediation between economic interests and technical possibilities, is an enormously ambitious project. If, over and above this, the feedback established at national level is to be taken as a model with further social actors at European level, then the Commission is postulating interest mediation processes for which the actors are not yet noticeably visible.

c) European Agencies: Regulatory Policy as 'Organised Formation of Knowledge'?

As a further possibility of guaranteeing the compatibility of internal policy objectives and regulatory claims, the setting up of European agencies is being discussed. Such proposals have already been put forward frequently, but have always failed – in both the economic and the social regulation spheres.[109]

The legal problems of establishing European agencies are considerable.[110] Community law does not have any powers to set up autonomous institutions not provided for in the Treaty; it is derived from the Community's organisational power. But the specific legal feature of the American agencies, namely the autonomous exercise of regulatory powers, is difficult to achieve within the legal

[105] For details on all this, see Joerges et al, *Die Sicherheit von Konsumgütern*, n 68 above, 380 ff.

[106] EC Commission, Green Paper, n 76 above, paras 29, 33; see 63 et seq.

[107] Most recently, see, in detail, E Denninger, *Verfassungsrechtliche Anforderungen* n 78 above 141 ff.

[108] See Joerges et al, *Die Sicherheit von Konsumgütern*, n 68 above, 401 ff.

[109] See the survey in M Hilf, *Die Organisationsstruktur der Europäischen Gemeinschaften* (Berlin-Heidelberg-New York: Springer, 1982) 147 ff.

[110] The most thorough discussion continues to be that in M Hilf, n 109, esp 293 ff; also detailed is J Schwarze in H vd Groeben, H v Boeckh, J Thiesing and CD Ehlermann (eds), *Kommentar zum EWG-Vertrag*, 3rd edn (Baden- Baden: Nomos, 1983) Art 235, paras 227 et seq.

structures of the EC, or only with restrictions: the EEC Treaty in principle only legitimates law-making by the Council – it makes no provision for the political responsibility of an agency equipped with discretionary powers. More or less far-reaching possibilities of transferring 'applicator, implementing and monitoring powers' can be derived from Article 235 EEC (and Article 100a EEC), but these powers must keep within the arrangement of competencies provided for in the EEC Treaty and may not cross the threshold into autonomous law-making. But the legal difficulties are not the only obstacle that all the efforts to set up independent agencies have so far encountered. The demands raised as early as the 1960s, and renewed in connection with the Europeanisation of merger control[111] for a European antitrust authority instead, failed partly because their regulatory policy goal, namely a consistent competition policy approach to merger control, could not be implemented (see Section II 1 b). The future European environmental agency[112] is to operate only as a body for scientific policy advice – here the Member States' interests in political action have won through. Also instructive is the fate of the Commission's endeavours to secure extension of its powers of action in 'implementation' of Community law, in connection with adoption of the SEA. In its decision of 13.7.1987,[113] the Council opposed these efforts and defended Member States' influence on the implementation of Community law.[114]

Yet the demand for central European agencies is highly plausible.[115] When regulations are seen as indispensable, then the establishment of a European central agency in principle corresponds to the interest of the industries concerned, insofar as these are in any case oriented towards the European market. This perception seems to be winning in the sphere of regulation of pharmaceuticals. This derives from a proposal made by the Commission in February 1990,[116] and apparently supported by the pharmaceutical industry,[117] to set up a European

[111] See Monopolies Commission, *Fusionskontrolle*, n 43above, and, on the earlier debate, Hilf, n 109 above, 147–48.

[112] OJ L 120/1990, 1.

[113] OJ L 197/1987, 33.

[114] See Joerges et al, *Die Sicherheit von Konsumgütern*, n 68 above, 337 ff, with references.

[115] For the case of safety of medicines, see D Hart, 'Drug Safety as a Means of Consumer Protection: The Approximation of Laws in the EC Medicinal Products Market and its Limitations' (1989) 12 *Journal of Consumer Policy* 343; E Kaufer, 'The Regulation of New Product Development in the Drug Industry' in Majone (ed), *Deregulation or Re-regulation?*, n 91 above, 153; D Hart and N Reich, *Integration und Recht des Arzneimittelmarktes in der EG* (Baden-Baden:Nomos, 1990) 36 ff and 119 ff.

[116] EC Commission, 'Proposal for a Council Regulation (EEC) laying down Community procedures for the authorization and supervision of medicinal products for human and vetinary use and establishing a European Agency for the Evaluation of Medicinal Products', Doc III/3603-1/90- EN 1990.

[117] See O May and G Wollnitz, 'Ein Miti ist noch keine Sünde. Zwischen Marktwirtschaft und Gesellschaftskonsens. Thesen zur Industriepolitik aus der Sicht der pharmazeutischen Industrie', *Frankfurter Allgemeine Zeitung* Nr 257/ 1990, 13; admittedly, these authors' advocacy of an agency that acts 'like a seal of approval' has two aspects: safety policy and industrial policy.

agency. In order to overcome the legal difficulties of the ban on delegating regulatory powers, the Commission proposal treats the evaluation of safety of medicines as an advisory activity, the findings being then passed on to the Commission for legal decisions.[118] In the most important working bodies of the new agency, however, there are not only academically trained experts but also representatives of Member States (Article 51 of the Draft). The Commission *must* deal with their objections and, where necessary, secure a Council decision (in the so-called regulatory committee procedure).[119]

The legal constructions found in the proposals to set up a European pharmaceutical agency are instructive. The interest in decisions that would apply Community-wide was to be made implementable by planning a discrepancy between form and function, between merely theoretically legal control possibilities and *de facto* processes of decision. Accordingly, the evaluation of safety of medicines is treated as a matter for expert advice that can and should be guided by supranational criteria. To that extent, the Commission proposal treats control of health risks as 'organised formation of knowledge'. Admittedly, it does not achieve this vision consistently. The consensus of the experts remains under political control: where differences of opinion cannot be eliminated, it falls back on the procedure known from the comitology system, of underpinning national rights of decision. This form of re-politicisation of scientific controversies is the price that regulatory policy has to pay for the institutional weakness of the EC.

3. Regulatory Networks: Mediation of Market Integration and Regulatory Policy?

The programmatic concepts of regulatory competition, European corporatism and the setting up of European agencies can readily be brought into connection with the paradigms of the academic legal theories of integration. Regulatory competition has to do with the correction of economic and social regulation by an arrangement for competition. The transfer of standardisation powers to private organisations and their experts, and still more the building up of European agencies as advisory bodies with *de facto* powers of decision, fits in with Ipsen's view of an institutionalisation of regulatory powers as 'organised formation of knowledge'. Finally, the possibilities of influence that Member States secure for themselves and through which they make the implementability of integration policy concepts relative confirm the realism of Weiler's theorem

[118] See, esp, Art 10 of the Draft, which says that the Commission will as a rule take up the new agencies' proposals without substantive verification of its own.

[119] Through the reference in Art 10 (4) to Directive 75/318 (OJ L 1477/1975, 1).

of the paradoxical concordance of supranational legal and intergovernmental decisional structures.

Yet the conclusion that the new dynamics of the integration process can be coped with in the framework of the traditional paradigms would be too hasty. In the further development of these concepts, problems that go beyond their limits are emerging, indeed in intensified form.

- The idea of regulatory competition overloads the integrating power of competitive processes. It would, if erected into generally binding programmes, call for the giving up of creative powers that all national political systems lay claim to and that were also embodied in the EEC Treaty – in however imperfect a form – alongside the internal market programme. But if regulatory competition is to be legitimated in normative constitutional terms only as a law-making policy that observes its own effects and intervenes correctively if necessary, then its legal policy function ought to consist in the institutionalisation of legislative policy as a learning process. In this area of economic regulation, such possibilities open up just because of the tension between Community competence for internal market and competition policy on the one hand, and the regulatory powers of Member States on the other. The competencies of Community law should then be grasped as commands to justify and to bring about compatibility, with national powers and regulatory differences to be removed neither by imperative de-regulation nor by re-regulation at Community level. In the area of social regulation, too, the idea of organised and regulated regulatory competition is applicable. Admittedly, it would in each case have to be verified whether, say, information policy measures were indeed functional as a substitute for uniform product regulations. And in the case of environmentally motivated process regulation and with protective standards in safety at work, the possibility must exist of responding to a 'race to the bottom' (see [Section III 2 a] above).
- European corporatism, discernible above all in standardisation policy, is – despite the Commission's declared willingness to work towards pluralisation of standardisation procedures – not an acceptable model for the Europeanisation of technology and product safety policy. Indeed, even standardisation policy in the narrower sense is systematically supplemented by two complementary intentions: on the one hand, to build up a certification system that has to be organised de-centrally and remains dependent on the assent of national bodies; on the other, by general product safety legislation, which in turn must be implemented by the Member States (see Section II 2 b and c above). The function of certification can be understood as substantive control in safety terms of European standards, while general product safety policy should organise the systematic determination of product risks, the updating of assessment criteria and intervention against hazardous products. Both tasks must necessarily be handled on a decentralised level. Community law can therefore reasonably only provide a framework that

ensures equal possibilities of action by Member States, but leaves to them both implementation of product safety law and the function of initiative in applying safety standards, and then organises the process of debate on divergent evaluation criteria. In this perspective, possibilities of harmonising internal market policy with social regulation and tying down the centralist corporatism of standardisation policy become visible: the working out of standards would be a European task, but the certification of safety conformity of products and general product safety policy would remain the primary responsibility of specialised agencies of Member States.

- The expansion of regulatory networks that differentiate between central and decentralised functions could also apply in areas where at present European agencies are being discussed. Thus, for medicaments regulation, it is foreseeable that the new European authority, if only because of its limited resources, will not be able to do without the expertise of national authorities in the case of licensing decisions, but particularly in the case of so-called follow-up market control. But this means that differences between medical schools and disputes as to the weighing-up of the risks and advantages of medicines cannot be silenced by setting up a European agency.[120] Just as in general product safety policy, the Europeanisation of medicament regulation can be conceived of in a regulatory network: the continued existence and initiative functions of national agencies would then be guarantees for the plurality of the scientific-normative discourse. The European decision-making level would then have to be shaped in such a way that disputes over assessment of risks did not simply lead to a political bargaining process.

All these considerations on the mediation between the economic logic of market integration and the normative logic of social regulation are certainly in need of greater precision. This is true particularly in relation to the topic of the 'regulatory network'. This concept is used in economics to describe the forms of cooperation 'between' enterprise and market, and in political science, following the corporatism debate, in analysing decentralised forms of organisation. Here it is used in order to respond to a specifically European problem: the need to find a way, difficult as it is, towards a Europeanisation of regulatory policies, *despite* the EC's institutional and political bottlenecks. The 'regulatory networks' that are to take up this task must link the Community with the Member States and overcome the legitimation deficits of their institutional structures. The hope that this can succeed is not an abstract speculation. It is thoroughly in line with the competency structure of the EEC Treaty to start from primary Community

[120] See E Kaufer, 'The Regulation of Drug Development: In Search of a Common European Approach', *EUI Working Paper No 89/411*, San Domenico di Fiesole, Florence, 1989, 163; D Hart and N Reich, *Integration und Recht des Arzneimittelmarktes in der EG* (Baden-Baden: Nomos, 1990) 45–46.

competence for the 'economy' and Member States' rights of action in order to 'regulate' it; the complexity and openness of the integration objectives in the EEC Treaty equally suit a search for alternatives to strategies of Euro-wide regulated de-regulation *and* for a centralisation of regulatory tasks. The 'regulated' regulatory competition and the building up of regulatory networks would certainly institutionalise tensions, because Member States' rights of action would mean a permanent threat to the unitary nature of market conditions. But the differentiation of decisional levels and functions and the differentiation of decisional tasks at the same time have unburdening effects: if national agencies are to seek forms of regulation that are as compatible as possible with integration, if they have to prove the justification for the interventions, if disputes about national protective measures can be kept free of strategic interest calculations, then the tension between market integration and regulatory policy may have thoroughly positive effects.

22

What is Left of the European Economic Constitution? A Melancholic Eulogy*

INTRODUCTION: THE MANY FACES OF AN HISTORICAL EVENT

'WHAT IS LEFT?' was the title of a series of articles in the *Frankfurter Allgemeine Zeitung*, which the social philosopher Stephen Lukes, then Professor at the European University Institute in Florence, had inspired after the fall of the Berlin Wall on 9 November 1989. The contributors to the series reflected on this event, and its historical dimensions and repercussions. Did the breakdown of the Soviet empire and the end of the Cold War also signal the end of the critique of capitalism and of the political left in the West? The title of the series was, indeed, a question. The authors were all from the West, all from the Left, and were concerned with the future of their political affiliations and the various facets of Social Democracy. *The Frankfurter Allgemeine Zeitung* appreciated these scrupulous questions and opened its *Feuilleton*, translating everything, without, however, finding a German equivalent for Stephen Lukes' melancholic *leitmotiv*.

The title of this essay insinuates that the queries raised in 1989 are still very much on the European agenda. This is certainly a discomforting message, one which is not in harmony with the recent seminal accomplishments of the integration progress, in particular, the deepened constitutionalisation of the European Union and the Union's enlargement towards Eastern Europe. But it is, at the same time, an unsurprising observation. Can the welfare state survive globalisation?[1] Can 'the' European social model survive Europeanisation?[2]

* Published in (2005) 30 *ELR* 461. The text is an elaboration of the introductory lecture of the Academy European Law – Session on European Union Law – at the European University Institute in Florence delivered on 5 July 2004. I am indebted to Marc Amstutz, Milena Büchs, Damian Chalmers, Yannis Karagiannis, Philip Manow, John McCormick, Rainer Nickel, Tommi Ralli, Florian Rödl and Stephen Weatherill for their encouraging comments and constructive suggestions.

[1] For a recent systematic overview, see S Leibfried and M Zürn, 'The Unravelling Golden Age State' in eidem (eds), *Transformations of the State?* (Cambridge: CUP, 2005).

[2] See, among many, C Offe, 'The European Model of "Social" Capitalism. Can it Survive European Integration?' (2003) 11 *Journal of Political Philosophy* 437.

The intensity of the debate on these issues is an indicator of their importance, and this importance is uncontested. Does this imply that the efforts to cure the 'democracy deficit' of the integration project will remain deficient if they fail to overcome Europe's 'social deficit'? It is one thing to agree with such a suggestion: it is quite another to identify an adequate theoretical framework in which the constitutional discourse can, and should, address it. The effort that this essay undertakes rests upon three interdependent (bundles of) premises.

The first: constitutionalism must reach down into the economic system and the social fabric of society. If it fails to do so, it loses its democratic credentials. This strong statement needs much explanation. Three references need to be given: one historical precedent is the debate within the *Staatsarechtslehre* of the Weimar Republic.[3] Not at the core, but significant, too, were the ideas of *Wirtschaftsdemokratie* (economic democracy) and *Sozialverfassung* (social constitution) as promoted by Franz Neumann, Hugo Sinzheimer, and Ernst Fraenkel.[4] All this was taken up after World War II under the new German constitution.[5] Just a *Sonderweg* of German constitutional theory? Certainly more than that. The tensions between law and social justice and its 'juridification' are of general importance.[6] And to take the argument a step further

[3] Particularly well documented in English by P Caldwell and W Scheuerman (eds), *From Liberal Democracy to Fascism: Legal and Political Thought in the Weimar Republic* (Boston MA: Humanities Press, 2000); A Jacobsen and B Schlink (eds), *Weimar: A Jurisprudence of Crisis* (Berkeley–Los Angeles CA–London, University of California Press Humanities Press, 2000); JP McCormick (ed), *Mass Democracy and Industrial Technology: Political and Social Theory from Nietzsche to Habermas* (Durham NC–London: Duke UP, 2002).

[4] See, on Franz Neumann, recently, M Iser and D Strecker (eds), *Kritische Theorie der Politik. Franz L Neumann – eine Bilanz* (Baden-Baden: Nomos, 2002). On Fraenkel, see WE Scheuerman, 'Social Democracy and the Rule of Law: The Legacy of Ernst Fraenkel', ibid, 74 ff.

[5] P Caldwell, 'Is a Social *Rechtsstaat* Possible? The Weimar Roots of a Bonn Controversy' in Caldwell and Scheuerman, n 3 above, 136.

[6] See the Special Issue of the *Canadian Journal of Law and Jurisprudence on Social Democracy* (Guest Editor: Colin Harvey); to cite just one contributor: R Burchill, 'The EU and European Democracy – Social Democracy or Democracy with a Social Dimension?' 185 ff, 186 argues: 'In addressing the "wider issues" of democracy, we are taken beyond the political sphere to engage with the social and economic organisation of society. Once we move in this direction, agreement about the nature, scope and content of democracy becomes very contentious. If the overall purpose of democracy is "to provide the conditions for the full and free development of the essential human capacities of all the members of the society" [referring to M Loughlin, 'Rights, Democracy, and Law' in T Campbell, K Ewing and A Tomkins (eds), *Sceptical Essays on Human Rights* (Oxford: OUP, 1992) 42 ff] … democracy needs to be something more than the existence of a few basic political procedures. By bringing the idea of "social" into the frame, we then begin to address the wider issues by incorporating the social and economic aspects of society into our understanding of democracy. However, as this involves making normative claims in relation to democracy, it is widely felt that this stretches the understanding of democracy too far.' And there is even more continuity with Weimar scholarship: 'Constitutionalisation' has become a quest which affects ever more spheres of 'secondary' law, including private law and under the label of 'societal constitutionalism'. See G Teubner, 'Societal Constitutionalism. Alternatives to State-centred Constitutional Theory?' in C Joerges, I-J Sand and G Teubner (eds), *Transnational Governance and Constitutionalism* (Oxford: Hart Publishing, 2004) 3. Continuity in the discussion of the tensions between the political objectives of social democracy and the rule of law in liberal democracies seems particularly relevant

into an uncharted sea: this debate is linked to the project of modernity itself: to the tension and conflict 'between the project of political modernity defined as collective self-determination, and economic modernity defined as the autonomous determination of the ways in which human needs are satisfied'.[7]

The second premise can be explained by a reference to 'Economy and Society', Max Weber's famous notion and project of a social theory which includes sociology of law. This type of sociologically informed jurisprudence is under-represented in the agenda of European constitutionalists. The law of the economy, of industrial relations, and the ever deeper involvement of the European Union with social policy[8] did not, of course, go unnoticed. But these matters were handed over to the experts in the fields that were under scrutiny.[9] The Theory of the European Economic Constitution to which the title of this essay alludes is a great exception. This theory is a truly constitutional response in its crafting of the interdependence of the *Rechtsstaat*, the ordering of the European economy, and the assignment of social policy to the nation states. In this way, the Theory of the European Economic Constitution has contributed to the *decoupling* (Scharpf)[10] of social policy from the European project.[11] This normative objection is, however, linked to a more 'sociological' critique. The theory's potential to guide the European project is exhausted, and the efforts to revive it have failed or are bound to be unsuccessful.

in the context of this paper. However, it is clear that it does not cover the relationship between constitutionalism and society comprehensively, and that it fails to specify the reasons for the deepening of the interest in a 'European social model'. What is true for both these traditions and the notion of an 'economic constitution' applies, of course, also to 'economic law'. This term cannot be adequately translated into English, as neither its ordoliberal nor its critical understanding – represented by titles such as *Wirtschaftsrecht als Kritik des Privatrechts* ('economic law as critique of private law'), by H-D Assmann, G Brüggemeier, D Hart and C Joerges (Königstein/Ts: Athenäum, 1980) – has an equivalent in the English-speaking world; see, very briefly, C Joerges, 'Economic Law, the Nation-State and the Maastricht Treaty' in R Dehousse (ed), *Europe after Maastricht: An Ever Closer Union?* (Munich: CH Beck, 1994) 29, 30–32.

[7] F Block, 'Towards a New Understanding of Economic Modernity' in C Joerges, B Stråth and P Wagner (eds), *The Economy as a Polity. The Political Construction of Modern Capitalism – An Interdisciplinary Perspective* (London: Glass House, 2004) ch 1.

[8] 'Creeping Europeanization' in the analysis of Offe, n 2 above.

[9] See the Review Essay of JP McCormick, 'Democratic Theory Confronts the European Union. Prospects for Constitutional and Social Democracy in a Supranational *Sektoralstaat*' (2006) 34 *Political Theory* 121.

[10] FW Scharpf, 'The European Social Model: Coping with the Challenges of Diversity' (2002) 40 *JCMS* 645, 646.

[11] A political science version of this thesis is Fritz Scharpf's well-known contention that democracies which prove to be unable to resolve problems of economic and social stability risk the loss of social legitimacy [eg, 'Democratic Policy in Europe' (1996) 2 *ELJ* 136], a thesis closely linked to Scharpf's famous analysis of Europe's 'political deficit': 'The Joint-Decision Trap: Lessons from German Federalism and European Integration' (1988) 86 *Public Administration* 239 ('Die Politikverflechtungs-Falle. Europäische Integration und deutscher Föderalismus im Vergleich' (1985) 26 *Politische Vierteljahresschrift* 323); for an update, see 'The European Social Model', n 10 above, and 'Problem-Solving Effectiveness and Democratic Accountability in the EU', *MPIfG Working Paper, No 03/1*, Cologne, 2003.

In an important sense, however, the exhaustion of the economic constitution is a mixed blessing. To anticipate the thesis which Section IV of this essay will defend: the erosion of the economic constitution did not pave the way to 'social Europe' or to the reconstruction of a European social democracy. Neither the commitments of the Constitutional Treaty to a 'social market economy' nor the new social rights or the turn to 'new modes of governance' are really trustworthy, and all are highly ambivalent. In particular, the 'Open Method of Coordination' threatens the very idea of constitutionalism, namely, the idea of law-mediated and rule-of-law bound governance. This argument is based upon a third premise which is 'conservative' in that it insists that European 'governance' practices must not take the rule of law lightly.

In the elaboration of this three-dimensional theoretical framework, this essay will take a re-constructive approach. The following section will first point to the origins of the theory of the economic constitution, and explain its specific notion of constitutionalism. It will then deal with the transformation of this theoretical heritage in post-World War II Germany into the 'social market economy' (*Soziale Marktwirtschaft*). The concluding part of this section will seek to explain why the theory of the economic constitution provided such an attractive design for the formative era of the European integration project. It will, however, be added that the importation of this theory into the European project came at a price. It prepared the ground for Europe's 'social deficit', which remains so difficult to overcome.

The leading proponents of this approach had fundamentally renewed their theoretical basis by the 1960s and 1970s, in such a way that they seemed well prepared for the new dynamics of European integration in the 1980s. However, the new dynamics and the striving for an 'ever closer Union' in the Maastricht Treaty led to a strengthening of European regulatory policies and a broadening of their scope, both of which were no longer compatible with the traditional and the renewed theoretical design. The support of the theory of the economic constitution which the German Constitutional Court's Maastricht judgment provided has proved to be a pyrrhic victory. The political constraints which this judgment confirmed damaged the economic viability of Europe and deepened the schism between national social models striving and institutionalised Europe.

The turn to new modes of governance presents itself as the most important remedy, which, thanks to the European Convention, even became a candidate for constitutionalisation. However, the account submitted in the final section will not be so positive.

There is not much left of the Economic Constitution, and there is not much of it which is Left either. But this resumé is not to announce an exercise in de-construction. Throughout the whole essay a background agenda will be pursued in each of its sections, which seek to reveal another dimension of the integration process. To indicate at least the perspective: markets, so the theory of the economic constitution argues, are not self-sustaining, they need institutional backing. Yes, but markets are social institutions which cannot be governed through some objective mechanism and do not simply respond to some functional needs – they are, in the last instance, 'polities'. The opening of our national economies (*Volkswirtschaften*) requires responses, on the one hand, to the erosion of the political powers of the nation state, and, on the other, to the risks of unaccountable transnational governance arrangements. It is the great merit of the theory of the European economic constitution to have addressed this challenge. Its responses, however, remained one-dimensionally restricted to an institutionalisation of economic rationality criteria at transnational levels of governance. The post-national constellations in which we find ourselves require more complex and socially more sensitive responses to the tensions between the opening of formerly national economies and the pre-requisites of social solidarity. Such answers are not readily available. They need to be discovered in reflective practices – and Europe's constitutionalisation needs, therefore, to be conceptualised as a process, in which Law has to supervise and to discipline the practices of governance.

WHAT IS AN ECONOMIC CONSTITUTION?

It is – or should have become – impossible to use the term constitutional law without reflecting the theoretical yardsticks which are invoked to assign specific functions and justify specific validity claims of 'constitutional' norms. It is hence insufficient to point to the supremacy doctrine, direct effect, or the resistance to change on the part of core elements of European law, to characterise them as constitutional.[12] This kind of definition is particularly popular among European lawyers, because it allows them to talk about a European constitution without discussing discrepancies with the juridification of political processes, institutional states, or the democracy deficits of European governance practices. The use of the word constitution in relation to European economic law is, then, nothing spectacular. But it is also empty, because such a notion does not inform us about the validity claims of the economic constitution, let alone its (normative) legitimacy.[13] This, and nothing less, is the promise and the aspiration of the theory of the economic constitution, and only because of these ambitions can it claim constitutional status.

[12] See C Möllers, 'Verfassungsgebende Gewalt – Verfassung – Konstitutionalisierung' in A von Bogdandy (ed), *Europäisches Verfassungsrecht. Theoretische und dogmatische Grundlagen* (Berlin-Heidelberg-New York: Springer, 2003) 1.

[13] 'Economic constitutional law consists of the constitutional rules that deal with economic matters.' This definition from J Baquero Cruz, *Between Competition and Free Movement: The Economic Constitutional Law of the European Community* (Oxford: Hart Publishing, 2002) 29, is not simply self-referential, because the author has first laid out a meta-positivist 'notion of constitution' which is 'inscribed within the Western legal tradition' (ibid, at 12). But it seems not sufficiently substantiated to provide a basis for determining the recognition which the internal market, European competition law and the four freedoms deserve.

In order to understand these ambitions, we have to take a detour and a glance, first, at the origins and, then, at the development of our notion.[14] The 'economic constitution' originated in the social turmoil and intellectual laboratory of Weimar – and this is so for very transparent reasons.[15] It was not so absurd, and was, at any rate, a widely held view that the economic crises and

[14] The literature in German is abundant, in English less so [recent analyses: DJ Gerber 'Constitutionalizing the Economy: German Neo-liberalism, Competition Law and the "New" Europe' (1994) 42 *AJCL* 25; W Sauter, *Competition Law and Industrial Policy in the EU* (Oxford: Clarendon, 1997) 26 ff, comprehensively, albeit with only scarce references to the legal 'branch' of ordoliberalism and *Ordnungstheorie*; C Mantzavinos, *Individuals, Institutions, and Markets* (Cambridge: CUP, 2001)]. For an early critical analysis, see C Friedrich, 'The Political Thought of Neo-Liberalism' (1955) 49 *APSR* 509. There is much less available in French. But there is the exceptional work of M Foucault, *Geschichte der Gouvernementalität II – Die Geburt der Biopolitik, Vorlesungen am Collège de France 1978–1979* (Frankfurt aM: Suhrkamp, 2004) in particular 201 ff; in English: *The Birth of Biopolitics. Lectures at the Collège de France 1978–1979* (Basingstoke: Palgrave Macmillan, 2008). For a recent comment, see L Azoulay, 'L'ordre concurrentiel et le droit communautaire' in M-A Frison-Roche (ed), *L'ordre concurrentiel, Mélanges en l'honneur d'Antoine Pirovano* (Paris: Dalloz, 2003) 277.

[15] In the account of Baquero Cruz, n 13 above, at 26, the meaning that this tradition gave to the concept is 'creating confusion and turning, as it were, against certain basic conceptions and functions of constitutionalism'. This harsh judgement is directed only at 'the original ordoliberal version defined in *The Ordo Mainfesto of 1936*' (signed by Franz Böhm, Walter Eucken, Hans Großmann-Doerth), in which he finds a 'strong Schmittian flavour'. It is difficult to understand, however, why we should assign the status of a foundational document to the 1936 *Manifesto* and neglect other, often more famous, writings (see nn 18 and 19 below). It seems equally problematical not to take into consideration how generations of scholars have developed the theory further and adapted it to the various phases of the European integration process. Baquero Cruz's note, made 'more in passing' on the Schmittian flavour, does, however, concern an interesting affinity (see n 25 below), although it is also problematical for two reasons. First, because it is, for obvious historical reasons, likely to evoke the wrong political and moral connotations. The ordoliberals were an opposition group in Nazi Germany. Their common – religious – concern over the *Reichskristallnacht* had brought the group together. Franz Böhm and Walter Eucken were members of the *Bekennende Kirche*. Some Members of the Freiburg School risked their lives in the resistance against Hitler. Großmann-Doerth, 42 years old in the *Manifesto* year of 1936, and drafted into the *Wehrmacht* in July 1939, died in 1944. Alexander Rüstow and Wilhelm Röpke had left Germany. On all this, see D Haselbach, *Autoritärer Liberalismus und Soziale Marktwirtschaft. Gesellschaft und Politik im Ordoliberalismus* (Baden-Baden: Nomos, 1991) and, more recently, P Manow, 'Ordoliberalismus als ökonomische Ordnungstheologie' (2001) *Leviathan* 179 ff, and his unpublished *Habilitationsschrift* on 'Social Protection and Capitalist Production. The Bismarckian Welfare State and the German Political Economy, 1880–1990', Cologne 2004, 76 ff, 93 ff) [now P Manow, *Social Protection, Capitalist Production. The Bismarckian Welfare State and the German Political Economy 1880–2015* (Oxford: OUP, 2020)]. And second, Baquero Cruz seems to misinterpret the 'Schmittian flavour'. The "strong state" that the ordoliberals asked for was certainly not a pluralist democracy (see KW Nörr, *Die Leiden des Privatrechts. Kartelle in Deutschland von der Holzstoffkartellentscheidung bis zum Gesetz gegen Wettbewerbsbeschränkungen* (Tübingen: Mohr Siebeck, 1994) 174). But this does not mean that they were striving for the same type of 'qualitatively strong' state which Carl Schmitt had called for in his famous 1932 speech ['Starker Staat und gesunde Wirtschaft. Ein Vortrag vor Wirtschaftsführern' ('A Strong State and a Healthy Economy. A Lecture for Business Leaders'), given on 23 November 1932, published, for example, in (1933) *Volk und Reich. Politische Monatshefte* 81]. Schmitt's strong state claimed the political primacy of politics over the economy, whereas the ordoliberals sought to impose a stable legal framework on the economy which the political system, for its part, was to respect (see R Wiethölter, 'Franz Böhm (1895–1977)' in B Diestelkamp and M Stolleis (eds), *Juristen an der Universität Frankfurt aM* (Baden-Baden: Nomos, 1989) 208. No economic

social tensions of post-World War I Germany were becoming out of control and that the Republic was threatened by strong and bitter opponents both from the radical right and from the radical left. Ordoliberalism sought a liberal answer to this crisis. This answer had to distance itself from the *laissez-faire* ideas which Alexander Rüstow discredited as 'paleo-liberalism'.[16] Two famous manifestos, often characterised as the foundational manifestos of ordoliberalism, were published at the peak of the crisis in 1932: Walter Eucken's '*staatliche Strukturwandlungen und die Krise des Kapitalismus*'[17] and Alexander Rüstow's '*Interessenpolitik oder Staatspolitik*'.[18] Other subsequently famous protagonists followed suit in the same year:[19] Franz Böhm's seminal monograph on *Wettbewerb und Monopolkampf* was published only one year later.[20] The answer was liberal in its rejection of the two state-focused contemporary competitors, the Historic School of Economics on the one side, and socialist ideas as propagated by the labour movement on the other.[21] It was post-*laissez-faire* in that it assigned the task of ensuring the *ordo* of the economic sphere to the state. Walter Röpke used the oxymoron 'liberal interventionism' to characterise this function.[22] The old paleo-liberal *Nachtwächterstaat* (*laissez-faire* state) was to be replaced by a 'strong state'.[23] And the intellectual *primus* of the constitutionalist Weimar Left immediately understood this: ordoliberalism is an *authoritarian* liberalism, Hermann Heller responded.[24] His response hit a nerve. Only recently, William E

theory remains the same over decades, however. On the development of the economic theory side of ordoliberalism, see, very lucidly, for example, C Mantzavinos, *Wettbewerbstheorie. Eine kritische Auseinandersetzung* (Berlin: Dunker & Humblot, 1993) and, more recently, his *Individuals, Institutions, and Markets*, n 14 above.

[16] 'Paläoliberalismus, Kollektivismus und Neoliberalismus in der Wirtschafts- und Sozialordnung' in K Förster (ed), *Christentum und Liberalismus – Studien und Berichte der Katholischen Akademie in Bayern*, vol 13, 149; see, also, his 'Interessenpolitik oder Staatspolitik?' in (1932) 6 *Der Deutsche Volkswirt* 169 ff; idem, 'Freie Wirtschaft – starker Staat' in F Bosse (ed), *Deutschland und die Weltkrise* (Schriften des Vereins für Socialpolitik 187) (Leipzig-Munich: Dunker & Humblot, 1932) 62.

[17] In (1932) 36 *Weltwirtschaftkliches Archiv* 297, reprinted in (1997) 48 *Ordo* 5.

[18] In 6 *Der Deutsche Volkswirt* (cited from the reprint in W Engels and H Froels (eds), *Querschnitte* (Düsseldorf: Wirtschaftswoche, 1986) 66).

[19] A Müller-Armack, Entwicklungsgesetze des Kapitalismus. Ökonomische, geschichtstheoretische und soziologische Studien zur modernen Wirtschaftsverfassung (Berlin: Junker und Dünnhaupt, 1932). On Müller-Armack's biography and work, see D Haselbach, Autoritärer Liberalismus und Soziale Marktwirtschaft. Gesellschaft und Politik im Ordoliberalismus (Baden-Baden: Nomos, 1991) 117 ff.

[20] Berlin 1933.

[21] W Abelshauser, Kulturkampf. Der deutsche Weg in die neue Wirtschaft und die amerikanische Herausforderung (Berlin: Kadmos, 2003) 158 ff.

[22] See W Röpke, *German Commercial Policy* (London: Longmans Green, 1934) 40 ff.; see, also, *Die Lehre von der Wirtschaft* (Vienna: Springer, 1937); on Röpke, see Glasman, n 30 below, 52 ff.

[23] A Rüstow in 1932 before the *Verein für Socialpolitik*: 'Einen starken Staat, einen Staat oberhalb der Wirtschaft, da, wo er hingehört' ('a strong state, a state situated at a level above the economy, as appropriate'), n 16 above; see Abelshauser, n 21 above, 159.

[24] H Heller, 'Autoritärer Liberalismus' (1933) 44 *Die Neue Rundschau* 289 ff [a strong *caveat* is to be added: Heller is exclusively dealing with Carl Schmitt's 'address to business leaders', cited in n 15 above].

Scheuerman has taken up Heller's line of argument and applied it to the institutional suggestions of the mastermind of the second generation of ordoliberals, the paleo-liberal economist and social philosopher Friedrich von Hayek.[25]

The Social Market Economy: An Economical Christian Project

But this is an anticipation of some of the aspects and developments to which we will have to return.[26] More important for the impact of ordoliberalism in post-war Germany is another dimension, which Philip Manow has carved out in a series of fascinating studies.[27] The social question which generated so much unrest in early capitalism was a challenge to the Christian churches, and the institutional varieties of European welfarism mirrored religious affinities. This is not major news concerning political Catholicism. But the story which Manow recounts about the importance of social Protestantism is new,[28] and this is of particular importance for the students of the 'economic constitution'. 'Ordo' is a Catholic notion. Yet the ordoliberals who embraced it – Walter Eucken, Alexander Rüstow, Wilhelm Röpke – were all strongly linked to Protestantism.[29] What both the Protestants and the Catholics sought was a third way between capitalism and socialism – and this alliance was the underpinning of Germany's post-war social market economy; this was their ecumenical project and became the common project of the Protestants and the Catholics in the Christian Democratic Union.

The Economic Constitution: 'Authoritarian Liberalism' Revisited?

The alliance of churches, political Protestantism and Catholicism in the early post-war years extended itself to the trade unions – Germany's social market

[25] WE Scheuerman, 'The Unholy Alliance of Carl Schmitt and Friedrich A Hayek' (1997) 4 *Constellations* 172; see n 57 below.

[26] Section III below.

[27] P Manow, 'Modell Deutschland as an interdenominational compromise', *Minda De Gunzburg Centre for European Studies, Working Paper 003/2001*; idem, 'Ordoliberalismus als ökonomische Ordnungstheologie', n 15 above; idem, '"The Good, the Bad, and the Ugly". Esping-Anderson's Sozialstaatstypologie und die konfessionellen wurzeln des westlichen Wohlfahrtsstaats' (2002) 54 *Kölner Zeitschrift für Soziologie und Sozialpsychologie* 203 (English version at www.mpi-fg-koeln.mpg.de/people/pm/download_de.html) and his revised *Habilitationsschrift, Social Protection,* Capitalist Production, n 15 above. *The Bismarckian Welfare State and the German Political Economy 1880–2015* (Oxford: OUP, 2020).

[28] 'New' is, of course, a relative concept. In the core ch 3.5 on 'Social Protestantism and the Redefinition of Social Reforms', Manow points not just to primary sources but also to an impressive range of historical studies.

[29] Manow, 'Ordoliberalismus', n 15 above; idem, 'Social Protection', n 15 above, at 76, fn 5. So was the great spokesman of the social market economy in the early Bonn Republic, Alfred Müller-Armack; on his religious background, see Haselbach, *Autoritärer Liberalismus*, n 15 above, 119.

economy was their common project and became a political, social and economic success.[30] But this alliance was not to last for long. Germany had overcome neither secularisation nor the political factioning which it had cultivated ever since the Kaiserreich. As Manow documents, the heritage of mistrust of Social Catholicism against economic liberalism resurfaced, and the old alliances between Catholicism, economic corporatism and Bismarckian welfarism were rebuilt.[31]

The Protestant Ordoliberals did not appreciate this restoration of patterns which looked all too similar to what they had tried to overcome back in the 1920s. And now, in the new Bonn Republic, they had another prestigious standing. The group had grown and its views dominated a good deal of academic life, public opinion, and the officious communications of the Christian Democratic government. Confidently and coherently, ordoliberalism revitalised its programme. A core element of its constitutional messages and perspectives was the theory of the 'economic constitution', the thesis that the constitution should respect the interdependence of a system of undistorted competition, individual freedoms and the rule of law – and protect this precious balance against discretionary political influence.[32]

The return of political Catholicism and ordoliberalism to their distinct routes/paths renewed an old schism – as well as other historical controversies. In his studies on the history of German private law in the Weimar and Bonn Republic, Knut Wolfgang Nörr[33] distinguishes two concepts in the (German) history of economic law: the 'organised economy' and the 'social market economy'. He downplays the tensions within the second camp, but rightly underlines that the co-existence of the 'organised economy' tradition, on the one hand, and ordoliberalism, on the other, amounted to the institutionalisation of a paradox: Germany cultivated both the ordoliberal credo and its concepts while the majority of its *Staatsrechslehrer* (professors of constitutional and administrative law) did not take the ordoliberal 'constitutionalisation' of the economy seriously.[34]

[30] For a concise analysis, see M Glasman, *Unnecessary Suffering: Managing Market Utopia* (London–New York: Verso, 1996) especially at 50 ff (on ordoliberalism) and 56 ff (on post-war Germany).

[31] Manow, 'Social Protection', n 15 above, 84 ff; Abelshauser, *Kulturkampf*, n 21 above, 93 ff.

[32] See, out of a rich literature, for example, G Brüggemeier, *Entwicklung des Rechts imorganisierten Kapitalismus*, vol 2 (Frankfurt aM: Syndikat, 1979) 322 ff (the reasons for the benign neglect of this book by Germany's *Rechtswissenschaft* are one of its well-kept secrets); F Kübler, 'Wirtschaftsrecht in der Bundesrepublik – Versuch einer wissenschaftshistorischen Bestandsaufnahme' in D Simon (ed), *Rechtswissenschaft in der Bonner Republik* (Frankfurt aM: Suhrkamp, 1994) 364.

[33] Die Republik der Wirtschaft. Teil I: Von der Besatzungszeit bis zur Großen Koalition (Tübingen: Mohr Siebeck, 1999) 5 ff; see, earlier his Zwischen den Mühlsteinen. Eine Privatrechtsgeschichte der Weimarer Republik (Tübingen: Mohr Siebeck, 1988), and Die Leiden des Privatrechts. Kartelle in Deutschland von der Holzstoffkartellentscheidung bis zum Gesetz gegen Wettbewerbsbeschränkungen (Tübingen: Mohr Siebeck, 1994).

[34] And *vice versa*: the ordoliberals dominated economic law and private law. They remained unimpressed by mainstream *Staatsrechtslehre*; even the explicit rejection of the theory of the economic constitution by the *Bundesverfassungsgericht* (BVerfGE 7, 377 – Investment aids) did not irritate them.

Nörr accordingly diagnoses 'a basic phenomenon in the history of the emergence of the Bonn Republic … [a] dual line, in economic policy and economic constitutional law'.[35]

Paradox or *List der Vernunft*? Yet the dual structure which Nörr finds so contradictory in theory proved to be very successful in practice. The social dimension of Germany's post-war market economy survived and flourished.[36] This is well-known and explains why 'a highly competitive social market economy' figures now in Article I-3 of the Constitutional Treaty, and also figures as one of the objectives of the European Union.[37] Its hopes for a pre-stabilised harmony between economic competitiveness and social solidarity are well-founded. In Manow's account of the German example, the success of the social market economy resulted from the inability of both *laissez-faire* and authoritarian liberalism to determine the policies of the Bonn Republic. Instead, Germany institutionalised 'a system of decentralized and functional interventionism'.[38] In Glasman's brilliant summary: 'No one "designed" post-war Germany, it was hewn out of far more durable and sophisticated moral and ethical materials than those provided by economic theory or any other social science methodology.'[39]

Ordoliberalism in the European Community: The Decoupling of Economic Integration from the Welfare State and its Social Policy

The real existing compromise, a *Wirtschaftsverfassung* with strong corporatist elements, the economic democracy aspirations in political Catholicism and the reconstruction of the Bismarckian welfare state under the Catholic Chancellor Adenauer were anathema to the leading Ordoliberals. They saw Germany again 'on the road to serfdom'. And, indeed, their institutional agenda, on which the quest for strong bodies dedicated to the defence of free competition and insulated from both the pluralism of interest groups and governmental political insinuations ranked so highly, was very often frustrated in Germany's *Verhandlungsdemokratie*.[40] Thus, it is small wonder that they embraced the

[35] Nörr, *Die Republik der Wirtschaft*, n 33 above, 84 (my translation).

[36] W Abelshauser, Die Langen Fünfziger Jahre. Wirtschaft und Gesellschaft in Deutschland 1949–1966 (Düsseldorf: Schwann, 1987).

[37] See C Joerges and F Rödl, 'The "Social Market Economy" as Europe's Social Model?', *EUI Working Paper Law No 2004-8* (www.iue.it.UB/law/04-8.pdf) on the Draft Treaty establishing a Constitution for Europe, CONV 850/03, Brussels, 18 July 2003; the amendment of Article I-3 by the EU Intergovernmental Conference on 22 June 2004 (Annex 3, doc. 82/04, is accessible at: www.statewatch.org/news/2004/jun/constitution-amendments-june22.pdf.

[38] Nörr, n 35 above, ch 3.6, at 96.

[39] N 30 above, 55.

[40] The *Kartellgesetz* was enacted only in 1957 under the chancellorship of Konrad Adenauer, with Ludwig Erhard, the strongest political ally of the ordoliberals, acting as its promotor; it was presented as 'the Basic Law of the Social Market Economy', but by no means did it realise the ordoliberal ideals comprehensively. See the re-construction of the whole process in G Brüggemeier, *Entwicklung des Rechts imorganisierten Kapitalismus*, vol 2 (Frankfurt aM: Syndikat, 1979) 383 ff.

integration project, supporting its establishment with all their considerable energy – and crafted their views into this emerging institution.

The formative phase of the European Economic Community has often been recounted in many languages and in various disciplines – especially by lawyers, political scientists, and historians.[41] The history of the European economic constitution is well documented.[42] I myself have published short versions of it on many occasions.[43] Let me repeat this much here: the affinities between

[41] Masterly by JHH Weiler for law [see his 'Transformation of Europe' (1991) 100 *Yale LJ* 2 ff; *The Constitution of Europe: 'Do the new Clothes have an Emperor?'* (Cambridge: CUP, 1999) 10 ff]; by A Moravscik for political science (*The Choice for Europe: Social Purpose/State Power from Messina to Maastricht* (Ithaca NY: Cornell UP, 1998) 86; for history by AS Milward (*The European Rescue of the Nation-State*, 2nd edn (London–New York: Routledge, 1999)). Interestingly enough, legal history has treated Europe with un-benign neglect, and equally revealing, none of the master tales cited takes note of ordoliberalism and its 'economic constitution'.

[42] ME Streit and W Mussler, 'The Economic Constitution of the European Community. From "Rome" to "Maastricht"' (1995) 1 *ELJ* 5; W Mussler, *Die Wirtschaftsverfassung der Europäischen Gemeinschaft im Wandel. Von Rom nach Maastricht* (Baden-Baden: Nomos, 1998); P Behrens, 'Die Wirtschaftsverfassung der Europäischen Gemeinschaft' in G Brüggemeier (ed), *Verfassungen für ein ziviles Europa* (Baden-Baden: Nomos, 1994) 73; for a recent summary, see A Hatje, 'Wirtschaftsverfassung' in von Bogdandy (ed), *Europäisches Verfassungsrecht*, n 12 above 683 ff. Valuable re-constructions in English include W Sauter, *Competition Law and Industrial Policy in the EU* (Oxford: Clarendon Press, 1997) 26 ff; DJ Gerber, 'Constitutionalizing the Economy: German Neo-liberalism, Competition Law and the "New" Europe' (1994) 42 *AJCL* 25. In a letter on the draft of the present article, Damian Chalmers (London) commented: 'How does all that relate to the real world? One point I have always thought is that France, Belgium, Italy were unconcerned by Ordoliberalism, because of Article 86 (ex Article 90 EC) which they saw as a derogation from its structures (particularly the seocnd paragraph) for all their public sector. Of course, that interpretation was shattered by Höfner, but a plausible interpretation of the first 15 years of integration was that it did follow the French model. None of the Treaty provisions were directly effective. Agriculture, external commercial policy, transport, coal and steel – huge parts of the trading regimes of the 6 – all proceeded on legislative harmonisation. It was only for a period from the mid 1970s to the mid 1990s, I would argue, that an ordoliberal model – with the development of Article 30 EC and Article 86 EC – began to get hegemony. Of course, during that period there was only limited harmonisation. Moreover, in the late 1970s, it was offset by substantial legislation in the labour and environmental law fields. My point is that there have been competing visions of the EC Treaty which have swapped predominance at different times.' A good question which can be complemented: if ordoliberalism is so important, why did hardly anyone outside Germany and hardly any political scientist become aware this? [Philip Manow, in the work cited in n 15 and n 27 above, is not covering Europe; but, see recently, Ph Manow, A Schäfer and H Zorn, 'European Social Policy and Europe's Center of Gravity, 1957–2003' *MPIfG Discussion Paper No 04/6*, Cologne, 2004; see, also, Ph Genschel, 'Markt und Staat in Europa' (1998) 39 *Politische Vierteljahresschrift* 55.] The easy answer would be: so few people read German. A more complex answer is: political scientists do not take normative theories seriously enough. Ordoliberalism itself, however, was always unimpressed by such benign neglect. After all, in Germany's advisory boards and institutions, lawyers and economists rank higher than political scientists. What is true for German economists working and advising in the ordoliberal tradition is, of course, not true for economists in general. Important books such as that of M Motta, *Competition Policy: Theory and Practice* (Cambridge: CUP, 2004) make no mention of the first or second or third generation of ordoliberals, nor of the legal or of the economic proponents.

[43] Ever since 'Markt ohne Staat?' ['The Market without the State? The "Economic Constitution" of the European Community and the Rebirth of Regulatory Politics'], reprinted as ch 21 of this volume.

ordoliberalism and the integration project of 1958 were manifold – for a series of reasons. As a concept, ordoliberalism appeared particularly appropriate for the legitimisation and orientation of the integration project. The freedoms guaranteed in the EEC Treaty, the opening up of national economies, and anti-discrimination rules and the commitment to a system of undistorted competition, were interpreted as a 'decision' which supported an economic constitution that matched the ordoliberal conceptions of the framework conditions for a market economic system (at least to the degree that the many departures from the system might be classified as exceptions, and a blind eye could be (had to be!) turned to the original sin of the Common Agricultural Policy. The fact that Europe had started its integrationist path as a mere economic community lent plausibility to ordoliberal arguments – and even required them: in the ordoliberal account, the Community acquired a legitimacy of its own by interpreting its pertinent provisions as prescribing a law-based order committed to guaranteeing economic freedoms and protecting competition by supranational institutions. This legitimacy was independent of the state's democratic constitutional institutions. By the same token, it imposed limits upon the Community: discretionary economic policies seemed illegitimate and unlawful.[44]

Thus, the prospects for institutionalising an ordoliberal style economic constitution looked bright. But what about Germany's social market economy? In one of his recent pertinent analyses, FW Scharpf hypothesises about 'the road not taken' back in 1950s. 'Where would we now be,' he asks, 'if, in the 1956 negotiations leading to the Treaties of Rome and the creation of the EEC, the French (Socialist) Prime Minister Guy Mollet had had his way? Mollet, supported by French industry, had tried to make the harmonisation of social regulations and fiscal burdens a pre-condition for the integration of industrial markets. Could attempts to harmonise social policies have succeeded or would they have blocked European integration altogether?'[45] An interesting question, but, as Scharpf himself adds, an unanswerable one.

We can only know what was actually accomplished, namely, the 'decoupling' of the social dimension from the institutionalisation of the Europeanised 'system of undistorted competition'. This was quite to the liking of the ordoliberals. In their view, the European level of governance could not, and, indeed, should not, be burdened with political tasks that required the legitimation provided by the institutions of constitutional democracies. Regardless of one's affinity

[44] Significant, here, is A Müller-Armack, 'Die Wirtschaftsordnung des Gemeinsamen Marktes' in *Wirtschaftsordnung und Wirtschaftspolitik* (Freiburg i.Br.: Rombach, 1966) 401 ff. For a topical restatement, see J Drexl, 'Wettbewerbsverfassung' in von Bogdandy, n 12 above, 747.

[45] FW Scharpf, 'The European Social Model: Coping with the Challenges of Diversity' (2002) 40 *JCMS* 645, at 645 ff; see, also, Manow, Schäfer and Zorn, 'European Social Policy and Europe's Centre of Gravity, 1957–2003' n 42 above, 16 ff, and their reference to Milward, *The European Rescue*, n 41 above, 213 ff.

for the argument, it is coherent and compatible with the institutional order of the European Economic Community as it was originally conceived.[46] The ordoliberal European polity has a twofold structure: at supranational level, it is committed to economic rationality and a system of undistorted competition. At national level, re-distributive (social) policies may be pursued and developed further.

To summarise: Europe was constituted as a dual polity. Its 'economic constitution' was un-political in the sense that it was not subject to political interventions. This was its constitutional-supranational *raison d'être*. Social policy was treated as a categorically distinct subject. It was a domain of political legislation and, thus, had to remain national. The social embeddedness of the market could, and should, be accomplished by the Member States in differentiated ways – and, for a decade or so, the balance seemed stable.[47]

THE AMBIVALENCES OF THE POST-1985 DEVELOPMENTS

The Delors Commission's 'White Paper on Completion of the Internal Market' of 1985[48] is widely, and with good reason, perceived as a turning point and breakthrough. After years of stagnation, the integration project developed a new dynamic – thanks to the well-chosen focus of all political energies. The evaluations of the Commission's initiative and of the processes it triggered are, of course, controversial. The protagonists of a European 'economic constitution' responded very positively at first (1). However, the Maastricht Treaty of 1992, which was to transform the Community into an 'ever closer Union', met with strong critique precisely because of the broadening of the European ambitions (2). Monetary Union, as agreed upon in Maastricht and then interpreted affirmatively by the German Constitutional Court, opened up yet another page (3).

[46] E-J Mestmäcker is the uncontested and outstanding intellectual head of the ordoliberal tradition. He has recently published his most important essays on the constitutionalisation of the economy in the EU, entitled *Wirtschaft und Verfassung in der Europäischen Union. Beiträge zu Recht, Theorie und Politik der europäischen Integration* (Baden-Baden: Nomos, 2003). The time span ranges from 1965 to 2001. All the stages of the integration process are considered and all major issues discussed. Less impressive in terms of theoretical grounding, however, is the new edition of his *Europäisches Wettbewerbsrecht* (Munich: CH Beck, 1974); E-J Mestmacker and H Schweitzer, *Europäisches Wettbewerbsrecht*, 2nd edn (Munich: CH Beck, 2004).

[47] It may be worth noting that the whole construct has structural affinities, or is at least compatible with, JHH Weiler's analysis of the co-existence of, and interdependence between, legal supranationalism and political intergovernmentalism in the EEC (see n 41 above) and path-breaking 'The Community System: The Dual Character of Supranationalism' (1981) 1 *Yearbook of European Law* 257.

[48] Commission of the EC, 'Commission White Paper to the European Council on Completion of the Internal Market', COM(85) 310 final of 14 June 1985.

'Invasions of the Market'?

The Commission's Internal Market initiative could be interpreted as an effort to strengthen and prioritise the institutionalisation of economic rationality in the integration project.[49] This interpretation was, of course, shared and promoted by observers committed to the ordoliberal tradition. The reasons were explained in pertinent publications of ordoliberal strongholds, such as the Advisory Board of the German Ministry of the Economics[50] and the Monopolies Commission.[51]

The White Paper had presented its rejection of traditional harmonisation policies as a consequence of the – at the time already legendary – *Cassis de Dijon* judgment[52] and the new emphasis on the principle of mutual recognition. In conjunction with the strengthening of the four freedoms, this legal background could be interpreted as providing a framework which would further processes of regulatory competition and hence expose national legislation to economic rationality tests. The ECJ's readiness to supervise national legislation under Article 30 (now 28) was complemented by new developments in competition law and policy. The attention shifted from market failures to regulatory failures, from the control of the anti-competitive practices of private actors to anti-competitive regulation and state aid. And from such premises, the plea for de-regulation and privatisation followed with a compelling logic.

How did this re-orientation fit into the ordoliberal economic constitution? It did not fit into it at all. But traditional ordoliberalism had already been thoroughly revised by its leading exponents in the late 1960s. Their theoretical allegiance shifted from Walter Eucken to Friedrich A von Hayek. The latter's '*Wettbewerb als Entdeckungsverfahren*'[53] became the new manifesto and credo of a new generation of scholars working in the ordoliberal tradition.[54] The legal and policy implications of the revised theoretical framework were spelled out in great detail, first at national but soon also at European level. However, these implications cannot be dealt with here. The second generation is, at any rate, in

[49] Joerges, 'Economic Law, the Nation-State and the Maastricht Treaty', n 6 above, 37 ff.

[50] Wissenschaftlicher Beirat beim Bundesministerium für Wirtschaft, *Stellungnahme zum Weißbuch der EG-Kommission über den Binnenmarkt* (Schriften-Reihe 51) (Bonn, 1986).

[51] Monopolkommission, 'Achtes Hauptgutachten der Monopolkommission 1988/1989', BT-Drucksache 11/7582 of 16 July 1990, 401.

[52] Case 120/78, ECR [1979] 649 – *Cassis de Dijon*.

[53] (Competition as discovery procedure) Kiel 1968, reprinted in FA von Hayek, *Freiburger Studien. Gesammelte Aufsätze* (Tübingen: Mohr Siebeck, 1969) 249.

[54] The leading economist of the Freiburg School in that period was Erich Hoppmann. The most important and fascinating among the many lawyers is Ernst-Joachim Mestmäcker, a disciple of Franz Böhm (see nn 17 and 48 above); also noteworthy in the present context is his [Mestmäcker's] submission to the European Convention – see the 'Report to the European Convention on Economic Liberties', submitted by E-J Mestmäcker on 29 October 2002, which is available on the Convention Website ([the submission was a defence of Ordnungspolitik] but did apparently not come to the attention of the Working Group VI on Economic Governance/*Ordnungspolitik*; see Section V.1 below).

one important sense, faithful to the ordoliberal tradition. The framework within which the integration project is supposed to develop further is un-political in that it is not subjected to political debate or deliberation. This framework again seeks to institutionalise economic liberties and economic rationality. It does so more flexibly, but also more comprehensively than was originally envisaged by the ordoliberal school. It therefore deserves to be called an 'economic constitution'.[55]

The hopes that leading exponents of the school articulated corresponded to the expectations that many critics had retained of the new orientation of the integration project. This schism between proponents and opponents forms part of a wider debate concerning the benefits and the costs of market governance.[56] This debate is, of course, relevant for an assessment of the 1992 project. But it is not 'directly applicable', simply because the implementation of this project disappointed the hopes of its proponents as much as it did not confirm the anxieties of its critics. What had started out as a collective effort to strengthen Europe's competitiveness and accomplish this objective through new (de-regulatory) strategies soon led to the entanglement of the EU in ever more policy fields and the development of ever more sophisticated regulatory machinery.[57] It was, in particular, the concern of the European legislation and the Commission with 'social regulation' (health and safety of consumers and workers, and environmental protection) which proved to be irrefutable. The weight and dynamics of these policy fields had been thoroughly underestimated by the proponents of the 'economic constitution'.[58]

[55] The turn from Walter Eucken to Friedrich A von Hayek, and, in particular, the shift of emphasis from private to public distortions of competition, affects the role of the state and state institutions. WE Scheuerman argues in a recent essay [n 25 above] that the differences are not as significant as most observers assume. Indeed, von Hayek shared the ordoliberal, and, for that matter, the Schmittian mistrust in the institutions of pluralist polities and their performance. But this convergence in the analysis does not extend to the consequence. Both may share the view that welfare interventionism leads into a 'quantitatively' strong state (see Schmitt, n 15 above). But Hayek certainly did not opt for the 'qualitatively' strong state Carl Schmitt welcomed after 1933. This is not what Scheuerman insinuates. He is instead concerned with the chain of events that a radical dismantling of the welfare state, and the social and political risks of von Hayek's 'curious institutional proposal' in *Law, Legislation and Liberty* (Scheuerman is referring to vol 3, Chicago IL: 1979, 113), entails.

[56] For a recent summary of the 'case against the market', see S Lukes, 'Invasions of the Market' in RW Dworkin et al (eds), *From Liberal Values to Democratic Transition: Essays in Honor of János Kis* (Budapest–New York: CEU Press, 2004) ch 4.

[57] For a comprehensive account, see V Eichener, *Entscheidungsprozesse in der regulativen Politik der Europäischen Union* (Opladen: leske+Budrich, 1997).

[58] 'Underestimated' is an empirical concept and hence not a sufficient basis for an evaluation of the neo-ordoliberal agenda. It would also be too simplistic to suggest that economic theories might, in principle, be incapable of addressing and dealing adequately with the problems of the 'risk society' (see K-H Ladeur, *Negative Freiheitsrechte und gesellschaftliche Selbstorganisation* (Tübingen: Mohr Siebeck, 2000) especially at 171 ff; A Arcuri, 'The Case for a Procedural Version of the Precautionary Principle Erring on the Side of Environmental Preservation', *NYU Law School Global Law Working Paper 9/04*. What remains true, however, is that the protagonists of the 'economic constitution' have remained silent and thereby contributed to the devaluation of their approach.

Erosions of the Market?

The praise of the Internal Market Programme was not to last long: the preparation and adoption of the Maastricht Treaty in 1992, widely perceived as a deepening and consolidation of the integration project, met with fierce criticism.[59] The reasons are manifold and – within the (neo)-ordoliberal theoretical framework – are comprehensible and conclusive. How can one continue to assign a constitutive function to the 'system of undistorted competition', when the promotion of that system is only one among many other competing objectives and its relative weight has to be determined in political processes?[60] How can one reconcile the commitment to competition as the discovery procedure in economic affairs with the acknowledgement of industrial policy as a constitutionally legitimated concern? The Maastricht Treaty was the end of the 'economic constitution'. From then onwards, the ordoliberal school re-defined itself as an oppositional movement.[61] This is not to say that its adherents would have given up their cause. Quite to the contrary. They continued to develop the approach further and to explore all the possibilities of strengthening its (now relative) weight and impact.[62] The turn was one from self-confident identification with the integration project to a critique of its course.

Rules *versus* Politics? Monetary Union, the Maastricht Judgment and the Stability Pact

A grand opportunity to promote the ordoliberal cause seemed to arise in the context of the objections against the Maastricht Treaty, which were brought to the Constitutional Court in Germany (*Bundesverfassungsgericht*).[63] Their legal framing was interesting, if not elegant, and fits well into the first set of premises named in the Introduction:[64] the competences of the European Community,

[59] See Mussler, n 42 above, 166 ff; Streit and Mussler, 'The Economic Constitution …', n 42 above; P Behrens, 'Die Wirtschaftsverfassung der Europäischen Gemeinschaft' in Brüggemeier, n 41 above, 73 ff; W Mussler, *Die Wirtschaftsverfassung der Europäischen Gemeinschaft im Wandel. Von Rom nach Maastricht* (Baden-Baden: Nomos, 1998) 166 ff; most elegantly, E-J Mestmäcker, 'On the Legitimacy of European Law' (1993), reprinted in idem, n 46 above, 133.

[60] See Articles 2 [and 3(1) (g) TEC as amended by the Treaty of Maastricht].

[61] See, particularly clearly, Streit and Mussler, n 42 above; Behrens (as cited in n 59 above).

[62] P Behrens, 'Das wirtschaftsverfassungsrechtliche Profil des Konventsentwurfs eines Vertrags über eine Verfassung für Europa' in *Festschrift Ulrich Immenga* (Munich: CH Beck, 2005) is somewhat more cautious with the tone of his assessment of the Convention's Draft Constitution than he was with the Maaastricht Treaty (n 61 above). But the gist of the argument is the same. The multiplicity of constitutional commitments read in conjunction with the consistency postulate of Article III-1 renders the weight of the system of undistorted competition indeterminate.

[63] Judgment on the Maastricht Treaty of 12 October 1993, *Entscheidungen des Bundesverfassungsgerichts* 89, 155 = [1994] 1 *CMLR* 57.

[64] Text accompanying nn 2 et seq.

now the European Union, are enumerated and thus limited. They were, nevertheless, considerable and entailed, so the plaintiff argued, a disempowerment of the nation state. Was such a disempowered state still a democratic constitutional state under its own constitution? In its response to this query, the *Bundesverfassungsgericht* promised to defend Germany's constitutional democracy against the erosion of ever more statehood. But the judgment ended up legalising European integration, confirming the constitutional legitimacy of ordoliberal institutional ideas and curtailing the control that Member States had over their economies.

How was this achieved and why did hardly anybody notice it? The essential paradox in the Court's reasoning is readily apparent. True, the *Bundesverfassungsgericht* called it a constitutional 'must' that the German Parliament retain 'essential' competencies. But then the Court took an argumentative turn which was, in its substance, strictly ordoliberal: economic integration was qualified as a non-political phenomenon occurring autonomously outside the Member States. All Monetary Union needed was a functional legitimacy based upon the institutionally guaranteed commitment to price stability and provisions against excessive fiscal deficits. With such an institutional design, the Court concluded, economic integration would not be exposed to further questioning of its democratic legitimacy. To put it slightly differently: Europe could remain a 'market without a state' while its sub-units, once called the 'Masters of the Treaties' (*Herren der Verträge*), would be downgraded to 'states without markets'.[65]

This reading is obviously inspired by the interpretative framework used in this essay. Outside Germany (and also inside Germany in the public law factions of European scholarship), the paradoxical side of the Court's argument went unnoticed. Instead, the *Bundesverfassungsgericht*'s defence of nation state democracies was blamed as echoing Schmittian ideas.[66] Even if this were so, the point underlined here seems more critical. The Court's reasoning implied that Germany was, as a matter of its constitutional law, barred from joining the monetary union, unless all of Europe subscribed to Germany's monetary philosophy.

[65] C Joerges, 'States without a Market? Comments on the German Constitutional Court's Maastricht-Judgment and a Plea for Interdisciplinary Discourses', *NISER Working-Paper*, Utrecht, 1996, also at: http://eiop.or.at/eiop/texte/1997-020.htm. Clearly, one has to ask how seriously the Court wanted to be taken when imposing these restraints. 'Not too literally' is the answer one can infer from the *Bundesverfassungsgericht*'s response to the subsequent complaint against the entry into the third phase of Monetary Union: the competent political institutions can rely on a prerogative in the assessment of the economic and monetary situation. See *Entscheidungen des Bundesverfassungsgerichts* 97, 350.

[66] See JHH Weiler, 'Does Europe Need a Constitution? Reflections on Demos, Telos and the German Maastricht Decision' (1995) 1 *ELJ* 219 (also in O Due, M Lutter and J Schwarze, *Festschrift für Ulrich Everling*, vol 2 (Baden-Baden: Nomos, 1995) 1651).

There is little reason to be proud of the imposition of ordoliberal concepts on the rest of Europe. There is much more reason to believe that this was only, and at best, a pyrrhic victory. In terms of economic policy and political democracy, the most problematical aspect of the 1992 amendments concerns fiscal policy. They seek to ensure a budgetary reasonableness and discipline not through a political process but through 'juridification', namely, the rules laid down in Article 104 and in the Protocol 'On the Excessive Deficit Procedure and the Monitoring of these provisions by the European Commission'. The replacement of fiscal policy with pre-fabricated, albeit, in many respects, indeterminate rules, mirrors the precarious political legitimacy of the whole construct. Fiscal policy is economic policy. And if it is nevertheless political, some actors, identifiable to the citizen, should be accountable for it. Framework rules and their 'implementation' through the European Commission constitute the typical pattern. Wherever Europe needs to organise a policy field in which the legal powers and/or administrative resources at the European level of governance are insufficient, it will (have to) resort to such techniques.

This indicates that the Member States are neither able nor willing to comply with an institutional compromise, which was born out of the need to find a non-political supranational answer to a policy area which was once a core area of national sovereignty and parliamentary control. Not only Germany, once the self-confident promoter of rule-bound stability, but also France, The Netherlands, and six out of the new Member States are exceeding the 3 per cent deficit limit. Could it be that the assumptions on which these rules of the Stability Pact build are shaky? Barry Eichengreen, an American observer of Europe's monetary policy during the negotiations of the Maastricht Treaty,[67] holds such an opinion. One of the mild formulae he uses is that the 3 per cent 'numerical threshold is not well grounded in theory'.[68] In a more recent analysis, he has renewed his critique of 'the folly of treating all deficits alike and of taking an arbitrary figure like 3 per cent of GDP as the threshold above which this suddenly becomes a problem'.[69] However, he is just one economist among many. What is uncontroversial, however, is the 'fact' that there is controversy about the reasonableness of the rules that the Member States have signed.

Lawyers are not supposed to examine the reasons, but are supposed to obey authorities, Immanuel Kant once remarked somewhat sarcastically.[70] In a

[67] See his 'Should the Maastricht Treaty be Saved?' (*Princeton Studies in International Finance no 74*), Princeton NJ, 1992.

[68] In his *Working Paper PEIF-6* on 'Institutions for Fiscal Stability', which he prepared for the Munich Economic Summit of 2–3 May 2003. At times, his language is stronger: the '3 percent ceiling is at best silly and at worst perverse' – which he wrote in a contribution to *DIE ZEIT* of 20 November 2003.

[69] 'Europe, the Euro and the ECB: Monetary Success, Fiscal Failure' (2005) 27 *Journal of Public Policy* 427.

[70] I Kant, 'The Contest of Faculties' in idem, *Political Writings* (Hans Reiss, ed, 2nd edn, Cambridge/New York, CUP, 1991).

field so strongly infiltrated by non-legal expert knowledge and so difficult to programme in advance by sound and stable criteria, there are other reasons for being cautious about taking decisions *qua* law.[71] Would institutional actors be well advised not to search for legal answers?

That is a question which the ECJ had to deal with in a recent judgment.[72] On 27 January 2004, the European Commission had brought an action against the Council of the EU before the ECJ.[73] The Commission asked the Court to declare *inter alia* that the (economic and financial affairs) Council's refusal, in its 'conclusions' of 25 November 2003, 'to adopt the formal instruments contained in the Commission's recommendations pursuant to Article 104(8) and (9) EC … was unlawful and should be annulled'. The Commission had initiated an excessive deficit procedure in relation to Germany in November 2002, and the Council had confirmed, by a decision of 21 January 2003, that an excessive deficit existed. An excessive deficit procedure had also been initiated in relation to France in April 2003, and the existence of an excessive deficit been confirmed by the Council on 3 June 2003. The Commission then recommended the Council on 8 October 'to establish that the French Republic had undertaken no effective action', and on 21 October 'to decide, under Article 104(9) EC, to give notice to the French Republic to take measures to reduce its deficit';[74] Germany was treated likewise.[75] The Council took a vote on the requests without achieving the majority required in Article 104(13). It also took votes on the Commission's recommendations under Article 104(9) EC. In its conclusions, the Council explained that it had 'decided not to act, at this point in time, upon the basis of the Commission Recommendation for a Council decision under Article 104(9)' and 'agreed' to hold the Excessive Deficit Procedure 'in abeyance for the time being'.[76]

What could one expect the ECJ to do? To go by the book? To be cautious with powerful Member States?[77] The ECJ did not indicate what it thought about the controversy on the soundness of the Stability Pact. Instead, it underlined the high importance that all institutional actors had attached to it.[78] It observed that

[71] MJ Herdegen, 'Price Stability and Budgetary Restraints in the Economic and Monetary Union: The Law as Guardian of Economic Wisdom' (1968) 35 *CMLR* 9.

[72] On the following, see R Streinz, C Ohler and C Herrmann, 'Todgesagte leben länger – oder doch nicht? Der Stabilitäts- und Wachstumspakt nach dem Beschluß des Rates vom 25.11.2003 über das Ruhen des Defizitverfahrens gegen Frankreich und Deutschland' (2004) 57 *Neue Juristische Wochenschrift* 1553, and the re-construction of the events in paras 7 et seq of the ECJ judgment (Full Court) of 13 July 2004 in Case C-27/04 – *Commission v Council*, ECLI:EU:C:2004:436.

[73] Case C-27/04; see OJ C 354 of 7 February 2004.

[74] Case C-27/04, paras 9–10.

[75] Case C-27/04, paras 11–12.

[76] Case C-27/04, para 20.

[77] See the *Bundesverfassungsgericht*'s cautious, if not evasive, response to the 'four professors' asking it to examine the legality of the Community's allegedly much too lax application of the Maastricht convergence criteria (see *Entscheidungen des Bundesverfassungsgerichts* 97, 350 and n 65 above).

[78] Case C-27/04, paras 67 et seq.

it was simply not legally foreseen in the pertinent provisions to hold procedures 'in abeyance', and concluded that

> the Council's conclusions adopted in respect of the French Republic and the Federal Republic of Germany respectively must ... be annulled in so far as they contain a decision to hold the excessive deficit procedure in abeyance and a decision modifying the recommendations previously adopted by the Council under Article 104(7) EC.[79]

It also underlined, however, that the Council has 'a discretion' and that 'it may, in particular on the basis of a different assessment of the relevant economic data, of the measures to be taken and of the timetable to be met by the Member State concerned, modify the measure recommended by the Commission'.[80] Hence, the Commission's 'action is inadmissible in so far as it seeks annulment of the Council's failure to adopt the formal instruments contained in the Commission's recommendations pursuant to Article 104(8) and (9) EC'.[81]

Could the Court have done more? Should it have indicated that the restraints that the Stability Pact imposes on democratically legitimised governments should be re-considered in the light of Europe's current efforts to address its democracy deficit? It is worth noting that the ECJ exercised more prudence than most of the commentators on the Draft Constitutional Treaty, who simply defended the views which the Maastricht rules had incorporated, and warned against any softening of that discipline. Thus, Paul Kirchhof, co-author of the Maastricht judgment,[82] wonders whether the expectation, expressed in Article I-29(2), that the Central Bank should support general economic policies in the Union, might weaken its dedication to the price stability objective.[83] Peter Behrens, in his careful textual analysis, appreciates that the pertinent provisions have not significantly changed.[84] The widely articulated[85] concern about the wording of Article 1-3(3) in the Draft Treaty found its resonance: after the amendment by the Intergovernmental Conference of June 2004, 'price stability' is now named among the objectives to which that provision assigns constitutional dignity. Can we sleep well again? 'The stability pact is dead and gone,'[86] argued Barry Eichengreen at the beginning of the controversy. Compliance with it would further damage the German economy, in particular. This would not be in the European interest. Who knows that? Maybe, we lawyers should not take responsibility for decision-making in which we risk discrediting the law.[87]

[79] Case C-27/04, para 97.

[80] Case 27/04, para 80.

[81] Case 27/04, para 36

[82] N 63 above.

[83] P Kirchhof, 'Europa auf dem Weg zu einer Verfassung?' (2003) *Zeitschrift für Staats- und Europawissenschaften* 358, at 379.

[84] N 62 above, in Section V.4.

[85] Most prominently by the ECB: Opinion of the European Central Bank of 19 September 2003 on the draft Treaty establishing a Constitution for Europe (CON/2003/20), para 8.

[86] Hence, the title of his contribution in *DIE ZEIT*, n 69 above.

[87] See Herdegen, n 73 above.

The constitutional risk inherent in a misconceived 'juridification' of monetary and fiscal policy responsibilities is to create a vacuum in which political actors cannot be held accountable and the very idea of law-mediated legitimacy gets destroyed.[88] The sad concluding message is that the Maastricht Treaty and the Maastricht judgment were a pyrrhic victory for a twofold reason: (1) Maastricht confirmed the decoupling of the social from the economic constitution, thereby deepening Europe's social deficit. (2) Rather than establishing the supremacy of law over monetary and fiscal policy, Maastricht has 'de-juridified' the economic constitution – and now it seems that the effort to cure the social deficit has run into the same trap.

ARE WE ABOUT TO BRING THE LAW TO TRIAL? SOME QUERIES WITH THE OPEN METHOD OF COORDINATION

What, then, is left of the European Economic Constitution and what is Left of it? If we think about the '*l*' in small letters, we might conclude: not very much! An abstract normative idea is losing ground in conceptual debates and in European political arenas. But when we take a capital letter '*L*', a widespread reaction is that there are prospects for a new mode of governance which seems tailored to overcome Europe's social deficit, namely, the Open Method of Coordination (OMC).

The Career of the Concept

Like everything else in this world, the OMC has its precursors.[89] But it is *cum grano salis* safe to take the Lisbon Council of 2000 as the birthday of the OMC.[90] This Council was primarily dedicated to knowledge society issues and

[88] See F Snyder, 'EMU Revisited: Are we Making a Constitution? What Constitution are we Making?', *EUI Working Paper Law 98/6* (abbreviated version in P Craig and G de Búrca (eds), *The Evolution of EU Law* (Oxford: OUP, 1999) 417 ff); M Everson, 'The Constitutional Law of the Euro? Disciplining European Governance' in P Beaumont and N Walker (eds), *Legal Framework of the Single European Currency* (Oxford: Hart Publishing, 1999) 119 ff. B Eichengreen, in a note to the author of 23 March 2005, considered the outcome entirely predictable and, for better or worse, unavoidable. His analysis (see n 69 above) is at least compatible with the argument that the 'juridification' aspired to by the Stabilty and Growth Pact was a failure. He argues: 'I see the EU as still too politically decentralized for there to be a willingness to infringe on sensitive fiscal prerogatives. If and when the constitution is ratified and leads subsequently to significant steps in the direction of political integration, I think the issue can be revisited.'

[89] One could name here the coordination of economic policies under Article 99. The Stability Pact is of another quality, however, because it restricts the ways leading to sustainable budgetary policies quite strictly. Much more important, however, is the more general 'turn to governance' in the EU (see, extensively, C Joerges, 'The Law in the Process of Constitutionalising Europe', *EUI Working Paper Law 4/2002*, and C Joerges and M Everson, 'Law, Economics and Politics in the Constitutionalization of Europe' in EO Eriksen, JE Fossum and AJ Menéndez (eds), *Developing a Constitution for Europe* (London–New York: Routledge, 2004) 162, at 173 ff.

[90] http://europa.eu.int/council/off/conclu/mar2000/index.htm.

to setting very ambitious goals for Europe in pertinent industries. However, it also renewed the agenda of 'Social Europe' and tried to turn what, until then, had been perceived as a deficit, namely, the lack of genuine European competences and the unavailability of the traditional 'Community method', into a virtue. The OMC, so Jonathan Zeitlin argues, promises to be

> an attractive model of how a non-coercive form of policy coordination emphasizing mutual learning and exchange of good practices could be applied to a politically sensitive field such as social protection which is characterized by wide institutional variations across EU Member States, where harmonization is considered by many to be neither practicable nor desirable.[91]

A European Employment Strategy was the first objective. Employment is a pressing problem in so many European states. At the European level of governance, it cannot be directly addressed with the means that the Union has at its disposal. But it can be discussed, non-binding objectives substantiated, and guidelines offered. These recommendations can then be adapted in the Member States to their specific contexts. This type of implementation cannot be subjected to the controls through which the Community seeks to ensure compliance with its legislative frameworks and policies. But the activities at Member State level can be 'benchmarked' and evaluated. The accompanying hope is that this will open chances for mutual learning and better performance.[92]

The OMC approach has since been applied to other areas, such as social inclusion and pensions. It has even become something like a *Leitbild* on the political Left.[93] It has also attracted much attention in the Convention Process. The final report of Working Group VI on 'Economic Governance' stated: 'The Working Group considers that the Open Method of Coordination has proved to be a useful instrument in policy areas where no stronger coordination instrument exists.'[94] Such positive evaluations were shared by other Working Groups.

[91] J Zeitlin, 'Comments on Jacobsson and Vifell, Employment Policy Co-ordination: Between Deliberation and Discipline?', manuscript, Madison WI, 2004.

[92] As was underlined at the Lisbon summit, the OMC procedure is 'a fully decentralised approach' which can be applied 'in line with the principle of subsidiarity; the Union, the Member States, the regional and local levels, as well as the social partners and civil society can and should be actively involved, using variable forms of partnership'. Presidency Conclusions, Lisbon European Council, 23–24 March 2000 (http://europa.eu.int/council/off/conclu/mar2000/index.htm).

[93] Most prominently: M João Rodrigues, Professor at the University of Lisbon and Special Adviser to the Prime Minister, Coordinator of the Lisbon Council (see her edited *The New Knowledge Economy in Europe*, (Cheltenham: Edward Elgar, 2002)), and F Vandenbroucke, 'Promoting Active Welfare States in the EU', Lecture at the University of Wisconsin of 0.10.03, available at: http://eucenter, wisc.edu/Conferenves/OMCnetOcto3; see, also, his 'Foreword' in G Esping-Andersen et al (eds), *Why we Need a New Welfare State* (Oxford: OUP, 2003) viii–xxiv.

[94] CONV 516/1/03 Working Group XI on Social Europe: 18, 19; see 'Tomorrow Europe', July 2003, no 17, at 3: 'Those opposed to including such a reference had advanced three sets of arguments: the fear of incorporating an intergovernmental method liable to compromise the definition of hard-won competences; a lack of transparency and democratic control; but also a lack of legitimacy owing to the involvement of a large number of experts in the process.' More recent evaluations

The quest for 'constitutionalisation' through the Constitutional Treaty was but a logical step.[95]

There has never been unanimity, however, in the evaluation of the OMC within the Convention or elsewhere. Milena Büchs,[96] in a comprehensive and particularly thoughtful analysis of pertinent debates, distinguishes between three types of issues: (1) One concerns the efficacy of the OMC. What made Working Group VI believe that the OMC had proved to be a useful instrument? (2) Such primarily empirical enquiries are complemented by analyses of the relations between the political structures of the EU, the dilemmas of European social policy and the search for explanations of why the OMC may overcome, or fail to overcome, these impasses. (3) The third debate concerns the legitimacy of the OMC in both senses of this term: Will the OMC find acceptance, eg, because of the beneficial outcome it generates for the majority of Europeans? Do the OMC practices deserve recognition because they strengthen democracy and enhance the normative quality of EU governance?

Output Legitimacy?

Uncertainty about the effects of the OMC is unsurprising,[97] and statements which present it as something like a *Wunderwaffe* that will win the battle against Europe's social model are not to be taken literally. David M Trubek, however, one

have become more sceptical. Thus, S Colligon, R Dehousse, J Gabolde, M Jouen, P Pochet, R Saleis, R-U Sprenger and H Zsolt de Sousa, 'The Lisbon Strategy and the Open Method of Co-ordination. 12 Recommendations for an Effective Multi-level Strategy', *Notre Europe Policy Paper no 12*, Paris 2004, conclude that the OMC 'has developed in a somewhat haphazard fashion … the EU is present in an unprecedented range of areas, but is not endowed with the instruments that would enable it to malke a difference' (19). Similarly, W Schelkle, 'Understanding New Forms of European Integration: A Study in Competing Political Economy Explanations' in E Jones and A Verdun (eds), *Political Economy Approaches to the Study of European Integration* (London: Routledge, 2005).

[95] See G de Búrca and J Zeitlin, 'Constitutionalizing the Open Method of Coordination. A Note for the Convention', *CEPS Policy Brief No 31*, March 2003; CF Sabel and J Zeitlin, 'Networked Governance and Pragmatic Constitutionalism: The New Transformation of Europe', manuscript, New York–Madison, WI, 2003. See http://eucenter.wisc.edu/OMC/index.htm.

[96] New Governance in European Social Policy: The Open Method of Coordination (Basingstoke: Palgrave Macmillan, 2007).

[97] Output legitimacy is a widely suggested rationale for the OMC. This is problematic not only in view of the uncertainties of its effects, but also in view of the principled objections against this distinction (see B Peters, 'Public Discourse, Identity, and the Problem of Democratic Legitimacy' in EO Eriksen (ed), *Making the Euro-Polity: Reflexive Integration in Europe* (London: Routledge, 2004). The use in the text refers to distinctions between objections against the efficacy of the method and its recognition as a legitimate alternative to law-bound governance. For a strong critique of output-oriented defences of the OMC, see A Schäfer, *Die neue Unverbindlichkeit: Wirtschaftspolitische Koordinierung in Europa* (Frankfurt aM: Campus, 2004). He insists that we should first seek to explain why and in which institutional and political context OMC was adopted, and argues that the softness of the Method reflects the divergence of national views and strategies as well as the unwillingness to commit national systems to policy changes. In his analysis, OMC complements the

of the Method's most eloquent exponents, stresses that we should understand the emergence of the OMC as a potentially workable response to the dilemmas of national welfare state politics, and design our research agendas accordingly. We should analyse its potential to 're-calibrate' social policies in a more flexible, participatory, experimental mode and to accomplish this objective as a multi-level governance system.[98] The OMC, we read in a recent paper, will

> create transnational expertise networks that: transmit new ways of thinking about social policy across borders; broaden participation in such transnational policy networks to ensure legitimacy and effectiveness; merge technical insight with practical knowledge and new normative visions; combine a problem-solving technical approach with participatory deliberation; facilitate lower level experiments; produce learning through decentralized experimentation, wide-spread bench-marking, exchange of best practices, and peer review; bring various policy worlds together; foster public-private cooperation; and avoid a race to the bottom via multi-lateral surveillance and shaming …

though it was added therein that such claims must be 'subjected to rigorous testing'.[99]

Normative Queries

It is difficult not to agree with such an understanding of the OMC. And yet, we must consider the risks that we run once this machinery is set in motion. This is, in particular, Claus Offe's disquieting objection:[100] The OMC has effects, but not the promised ones. It will instead destroy the non-Anglo-Saxon modes of welfarism in Europe. How should the Law know? But it is by no means exceptional for lawyers and law to be confronted with contests over issues they do not understand and with uncertainties over the implications of their decisions. They

turn from Keynesianism to Monetarism as institutionalised in the harder Monetary Union and the Stability Pact; it thus confirms the old schism between the welfare state(s) and economic integration.

[98] DM Trubek and J Mosher, 'New Governance, EU Employment Policy, and the European Social Model' in C Joerges, Y Mény and JHH Weiler (eds), *Mountain or Molehill?, Symposium on the Commission White Paper on Governance*, New York University School of Law 2001, accessible at: www.iue.it/RSC/e-texts/WPgovernance.pdf [also in J Zeitlin and D Trubek (eds), *Governing Work and Welfare in a New Economy: American and European Experiences* (Oxford: OUP, 2003) 51]; DM Trubek and L Trubek, 'Hard and Soft Law in the Construction of Social Europe: the Role of the Open Method of Coordination' (2005) 11 *ELJ* 343.

[99] Not so rigorous but with some reserves: B Bercusson, 'Social Rights in the European Constitution', manuscript, London 2004: 'It remains to be seen whether the OMC, hitherto criticised as to its effectiveness when implemented by Member States' administrations in the field of employment policy, is appropriate for the Work Programme of the Social Partners on Employment. If joint opinions and other non-regulatory instruments continue to be ineffective, their failure may imply other, more rigorous steps towards effectiveness, including regulatory agreements and/or legislation' (at 21).

[100] N 7 above; similarly, D Chalmers and M Lodge, 'The Open Method of Coordination and the European Welfare State', *ESCR Discussion Paper 11*, London (LSE) 2003.

should, therefore, understand their task of designing responses to such difficulties. The OMC is an institution designed to find, not to implement, solutions. Is it a good design?

(i) Democratic Experimentalism?

The theoretical background on which the advocates of the OMC rely has been developed outside European frameworks.[101] then tried out in American administrative law,[102] before [it was] presented in Europe[103] and the merger with OMC occurred.[104]

It is important to remember that the whole approach of democratic experimentalism received its inspiration from a societal sphere, which European constitutionalism tends to treat with (un-) benign neglect, namely, the organisational practices of private business. In a daring and fascinating move,[105] Charles Sabel and his followers have applied the lessons to be learnt from the Japanese variety of capitalism about their practices of benchmarking, the need to adapt to incessant change,[106] the commitment to permanent experimentation, an interest and a readiness in mutual learning from independent monitoring, the establishment of systems of measurement and evaluation, etc, to *administrative bodies*, and argued that their regulatory practices should follow these examples from economy and society. Democratic experimentalists promise that 'a successful institutionalization of the principles of benchmarking, simultaneous engineering, and independent monitoring allows us to tackle volatility and diversity best' – not just within firms.[107]

[101] See the re-construction by WE Scheuerman, 'Democratic Experimentalism or Capitalist Synchronization? Critical Reflections on Directly-Deliberative Polyarchy' (2004) 17 *Canadian Journal of Law and Jurisprudence* 101, at 108 ff; see, earlier, CF Sabel, 'Bootstrapping Reform: Rebuilding Firms, the Welfare State, and Unions' (1995) 23 *Politics & Society* 5 ff; J Cohen and CF Sabel, 'Sovereignty and Solidarity: EU and US' in J Zeitlin and DM Trubek (eds), *Governing Work and Welfare in a New Economy: European and American Experiments* (Oxford: OUP, 2003) 345.

[102] MC Dorf and CF Sabel, 'A Constitution of Democratic Experimentalism' (1998) 98 *Columbia Law Review* 267.

[103] J Cohen and CF Sabel, 'Directly-Deliberative Polyarchy' (1997) 3 *ELJ* 313.

[104] See J Scott and DM Trubek, 'Mind the Gap: Law and New Approaches to Governance in the European Union' (2002) 8 *ELJ* 1. O Gerstenberg and CF Sabel, 'Directly-Deliberative Polyarchy, An Institutional Ideal for Europe?' in C Joerges and R Dehousse (eds), *Good Governance in Europe's Integrated Market* (Oxford: OUP, 2002) 289; J Zeitlin and DM Trubek (eds), *Governing Work and Welfare in a New Economy*, n 101 above.

[105] See, in particular, CF Sabel, 'Learning by Monitoring: The Institutions of Economic Development' in N Smelser and R Swedberg (eds), *The Handbook of Economic Sociology* (Princeton NJ: Princeton UP, 1994) 137.

[106] 'High-speed capitalism' is the category Scheuerman uses referring to David Harvey, *Justice, Nature and the Geography of Difference* (Oxford: Wiley-Blackwell, 1996) when explaining his own analytical basis and normative perspectives; see, also, WE Scheuerman, 'Reflexive Law and the Challenges of Globalization' (2001) 9 *Journal of Political Philosophy* 81.

[107] Scheuerman, n 106 above, at 111. See O Gerstenberg, 'Law's Polyarchy: A Comment on Cohen and Sabel' (1997) 3 *ELJ* 343; see, also, R Schmalz-Bruns, 'Deliberativer Supranationalismus. Demokratisches Regieren jenseits des Nationalstaats' (1999) 6 *Zeitschrift für Internationale Beziehungen* 185, at 236–38.

At first sight, this message might look like a strange loop which begins in the public sphere, then goes into the private realm, and then brings messages from there to its point of departure. Have we not all been taught to use all sorts of legal instruments – company law, antitrust, and economic regulation – to tame private enterprise? Why is there such a widely felt need to extend the reach of fundamental rights into the private sphere if private governance develops superior qualities anyway? Are all the quests for a constitutionalisation of the sub-constitutional spheres of the legal system and the search for a 'societal constitutionalism' superfluous?[108] In an ironic sense, democratic experimentalism can be called a methodological heir to first-generation ordoliberalism. It invokes qualities inherent in the economic sphere as a yardstick that public governance should respect and internalise; and the affinities with the Hayekian discovery procedure may seem even stronger because von Hayek has substituted the strong state of the ordoliberals for the smoother governance of general legal rules.[109] These affinities are, however, very limited. Whereas ordoliberalism sought to protect the *ordo* of the economy through a strong state which would rigorously enforce laws against restrictive business practices and abuse of private power, democratic experimentalism is relying on political processes, softer modes of coordination, and the subtle power of transparency and exposure to public critique. And, in contrast to the Hayekian discovery process, the proposals to 'institutionalise' democratic experimentalism invoke the imagination not just of entrepreneurs and market participants but also of deliberating political citizens, and trust in their readiness to engage in problem-solving and in their interest to learn from one another.

'Sweet melodies', to be sure. The question is, however, whether we should listen to them and trust 'a law so "soft" as to be no law at all'?[110] This soft supranational power may not be so innocent, opines Alexander Somek. The 'new modes of governance', he observes,

> are marked by two characteristics: first, they are informal in that they are based on information-gathering, the drawing up of 'action-plans', the allocation of public praise for 'best practice' and the shaming of under-achievers; second, even though they have been designed for special policy areas, they are nonetheless 'holistic', which means, in the words of the European Commission, that they commit 'Governments as a whole, as well as a wide range of stakeholders'.

[108] On this notion, see n 6 above.

[109] See, for a systematic analysis, H-G Graf, *'Muster-Voraussagen' und 'Erklärungen des Prinzips' bei F.A. von Hayek* (Tübingen: Mohr Siebeck, 1978); M Amstutz, *Evolutorisches Wirtschaftsrecht* (Baden-Baden: Nomos, 2001) 30 ff and 219 ff; C Mantzavinos, 'Das institutionenökonomisch-evolutionäre Wettbewerbsleitbild' (2005) 225 *Jahrbücher für Nationalökonomie und Statistik/Journal of Economic and Statistics* 205.

[110] Everson, 'The Constitutional Law of the Euro?, n 88 above, 120.

A diffuse soft power, critics observed, is exercising its hold without being constrained by the norms which govern competence allocation.[111] Similar concerns have been articulated by Marc Amstutz on a systems theory basis. His concern is the law's *proprium*, namely, its function and task to respond to conflicts which cannot be resolved in the societal sub-systems in which they originate.[112] In a discourse theory version, what may function at the level of local 'government councils' will be much more difficult to achieve when experimentalists meet with national, European and international standardisation bodies,[113] or face administrators who are keen to promote the institutional prestige and power of their organisations, or welfare bureaucracies which seek to defend their own practices and/or the political interests of their superiors. Can we really believe that arrangements will be found, implemented and sustained, in which stakeholders engage with sufficient intensity and continuity in the definition and discussion of their concerns so that legitimacy can be said to rest on the deliberative processes of all the affected parties? Democratic experimentalism asks us to take the traditional virtues of the rule of law lightly. It asks us to loosen the ties between law and enforcement, and, instead, to trust that our societies will manage with far fewer governmental powers. But it does not tell us how we might find the post-national criteria that will enable and legitimate a 'benchmarking' of national experiences, histories, and aspirations. It fails to explain how an exposure to the experiences of others might lead to coordinated policies and how they might be implemented against unconvinced opponents. More importantly, it fails to address the risks that its own implementation in the EU entails. There is nothing wrong with bureaucracies and experts exchanging experiences and learning about new possibilities. There is a great deal wrong with building up opaque networks which get entrusted with the task of seeking to carry through what they have learned or agreed upon in democratic societies. Such a model of governance may be soft because it no longer relies on mandatory provisions. It is, for the same reason, strong because it risks empowering the executive and removing the virtues of democratic accountability, of rule-bound public governance and its judicial control.[114] Should we, by taking the rule of law so lightly, promote executive governance instead of deliberate polyarchy?

[111] A Somek, 'Constitutional Theory as a Problem of Constitutional Law. On the Constitutional Court's Total Revision of Austrian Constitutional Law' (1998) 32 *Israel Law Review* 567.

[112] M Amstutz, 'Zwischenwelten. Zur Emergenz einer interlegalen Rechtsmethodik im europäischen Privatrecht' in C Joerges and G Teubner (eds), *Rechtsverfassungsrecht, Recht-Fertigung zwischen Privatrechtsdogmatik und Gesellschaftstheorie* (Baden-Baden: Nomos, 2003) 213.

[113] An interesting exception is the interpretation of the 'New Approach' offered by J Scott, 'International Trade and Environmental Governance: Relating Rules (and Standards) in the EU and the WTO' (2004) 15 *EJIL* 307.

[114] Similar objections have been raised by democratic experimentalists, and in a similar vein by E-J Mestmäcker, 'Wandlungen in der Verfasstheit der europäischen Gemeinschaft' in idem, *Wirtschaft und Verfassung*, n 46 above, 49, at 69 ff against comitology and the idea of 'deliberative supranationalism' as defended by this writer. Why the OMC should be a democratically superior mode of

Scheuerman has complemented these sceptical queries by a sociological observation. He summarises one key assumption of democratic experimentalism as the assertion 'that we increasingly encounter evidence of diversity in terms of local conditions and regulatory needs'. He confronts this claim with the tendencies of 'high-speed' capitalism

> to compress and even 'annihilate' geographical space or distance. High-speed social activity dramatically heightens the possibilities for interaction across both geographical and the existing political divides, opening the door to historically unprecedented opportunities for simultaneity and instantaneousness in human experience.[115]

Democratic experimentalists, he continues, fail 'to provide an adequate place in their theory, in both normative and institutional terms, for those facets of contemporary social experience poorly captured by its repeated references to local diversity in social conditions'.[116]

(ii) Bringing the Eighties Back In?

The turn to soft governance in the EU and the turn away from the very idea of law-mediated governance are risky. And it seems that this risk is not really necessary. It may be an all too hasty disregard of the alternatives that were elaborated decades ago. The intense debates of the 1970s about the failures of welfare-state juridification strategies were guided by normative concerns about the intrusion of bureaucratic machineries into the economy and the life-world. It was the broadly experienced disappointment with 'purposive' legal programmes *and* a new sensitivity towards 'intrusions into the life-world' through a juridification of social policy goals that triggered the search for models of legal rationality that would fill the gaps left open by formalist legal techniques, and, at the same time, cure the failures of the law's grip on social reality on the basis of some 'grand theory' (such as economic theories of law, systems theory or discourse theories).[117] 'Proceduralisation' and 'reflexive law' were, at the same time,

governance than comitology is difficult to understand. Comitology operates in much narrower and better-defined realms. Its social and legal embeddedness is more intense. Its successful 'constitutionalisation' is imperfect but seems at least conceivable; see C Joerges, '"Comitology and the European Model?" Towards a *Recht-Fertigungs-Recht* in the Europeanisation Process' in EO Eriksen, C Joerges and J Neyer (eds), *European Governance, Deliberation and the Quest for Democratisation*, EUI-RSCA/Arena (Arena Report 2/2003. Oslo), 501.

[115] 'Democratic Experimentalism', n 106 above, 119 ff.

[116] Ibid, 120.

[117] See G Teubner, 'Substantive and Reflexive Elements in Modern Law' (1983) 17 *Law and Society Review* 239; R Wiethölter, 'Materialisation and Proceduralisation of Law' in G Teubner (ed), *Dilemmas of Law in the Welfare State* (Berlin–New York: DeGruyter, 1986) 221; R Wiethölter 'Proceduralisation of the Category of Law' in C Joerges and DM Trubek (eds), *Critical Legal Thought: An American-German Debate* (Baden-Baden: Nomos, 1989) 501; J Habermas, *Between Facts and Norms* (Cambridge MA: The MIT Pres, 1998) 427 ff; idem, 'Paradigms of Law' in M

concerned with very practical matters, namely, the problems of implementation and compliance. Discrepancies between legal programmes – especially between 'purposive' legislation designed to achieve specific objectives and the actual impact of such laws on society – were a core concern of legal sociology, of effectiveness and implementation research.[118] The normative and the pragmatic critique of purposive programmes and of command-and-control regulation have motivated a search for alternatives such as self-regulation and soft law. Such strategies responded to the same concerns that the proponents of the OMC now invoke. But they sought to keep the rule of law alive.

A RESUMÉ

So much for the critique. And what has the critic to offer instead? The law is a normative exercise; the whole discipline is engaged in the production of valid answers which distinguish between the legal and the illegal, and equate this distinction with justice as opposed to injustice. Ambivalent messages are not particularly welcome and are difficult to endure.

And yet the uncertainties of the state of the (European) Union may require exactly that – at least if lawyers seek to take up the three issues denoted in the introduction:[119] Does the constitutionalisation of Europe reach out into the 'Economy and Society'? Are there alternatives to the OMC alternative to the exhausted economic constitution? Can we ensure that European governance remains rule-bound and its legitimacy continues to be meditated by law?

The Constitutional Treaty

The obvious first object is to look for answers to these questions in the new Constitutional Treaty as amended on 22 June 2004,[120] in particular in the provisions that promise to reach out into 'Economy and Society': the 'social market economy' has become a constitutional objective,[121] and access to services of

Rosenfeld and A Arato (eds), *On Law and Democracy: Critical Exchanges* (Berkeley–Los Angeles CA: University of California Press, 1998) 13. Earlier German contributions include R Wiethölter, 'Entwicklung des Rechtsbegriffs' in V Gessner and G Winter (eds), *Rechtsformen der Verflechtung von Staat und Wirtschaft* (Opladen: Verlag für Sozialwissenschaften, 1982) 82 ff; C Joerges and G Brüggemeier (eds), *Workshop zu Konzepten des postinterventionistischen Rechts*, *Zentrum für Europäische Rechtspolitik, Materialien 4*, Bremen 1984, 25.

118 Famously summarised and analysed by G Teubner, 'Juridification – Concepts, Aspects, Limits, Solutions' in idem (ed), *Juridification of Social Spheres* (Berlin–New York: DeGruyter, 1987) 3.

119 Text accompanying nn 4 et seq.

120 N 37 above.

121 According to Article 1-3 (3) CT the 'Union shall work for … a highly competitive social market economy'.

general economic interest is recognised and respected[122] by Article II-36, which incorporates the new 'social rights'.[123] Last but not least, elements of the OMC can be seen in various places.[124] We find a first reference in Article I-1(4), which states: 'the Union may adopt initiatives to ensure the coordination of the Member States' social policies'; Part III (Policies and Functions) refers to the OMC four times, once in the section on Social Policy (Article III-107), and once in Chapter V Section 1, on Public Health (Article III-179).[125]

Most of these topics have already been mentioned, and those not mentioned are too big to be dealt with *en passant*. Suffice it to restate here that the invocation of the 'social market economy' in the Constitutional Treaty is conceptually flawed, and is, politically, an all too risky promise, because it may raise expectations which it will subsequently fail to deliver. Instead of saying 'flawed', one might also say 'empty': the historical compromise that the concept once embodied is no longer alive. Not even the ordoliberal component of this legacy was present in the deliberations of the Convention. However, one linguistic detail does deserve a particular mention here: '*Ordnungspolitik*' was the German name of Working Group VI. The English name was 'economic governance'. Was this an innovative translation? Not really. It was the Convention Secretariat who was responsible for the introduction of the term, in which someone remembered the fierce controversies between market-compatible '*Ordnungspolitik*' and market-correcting interventionist 'industrial policy' in the Maastricht Intergovernmental Conference. A case of 'linguistic-discursive path-dependency', according to Andreas Maurer,[126] which became definite when Joschka Fischer and Dominique de Villepin submitted a common position on *Ordnungspolitik* just before Christmas 2002,[127] when Working Group VI had already closed its files.[128]

Will the 'social rights' serve as an *Ersatz*? The easy answer is that this is difficult to predict, and that we should wait and see what the ECJ tells us. This answer sounds easy but is not trivial. It is not trivial because it implies that we, the

[122] Article II-36; this is an important signal, because it confirms the right of Member States to pursue distributional objectives. The compatibility of such policies with the opening of national or regional markets to 'foreign' competitors is a complex issue of constitutional importance. It is one of the many fields where 'constitutionalisation' has to occur incrementally.

[123] The Rights' Charter as solemnly declared in Nice was incorporated into the Constitutional Treaty which now contains social rights, especially in Title IV on solidarity.

[124] Article I-14 (4): 'the Union may adopt initiatives to ensure co-ordination of Member States' social policies'; Part III, section on Social Policy (Article III-107 CDT), on Public Health (Article III-179 CDT). The assignment of a *competence* 'to promote and coordinate the economic and employment policies of the Member States' has been repealed. Article I-11(3) as amended on 22 June 2004 (n 37 above) reads: 'The Member States shall coordinate their economic and employment policies …'.

[125] See the following section.

[126] In a letter to the author; Andreas Maurer is Head of the Research Group on European Integration of the German Institute for International and Security Affairs in Berlin.

[127] CONV 470/02.

[128] A detail, but a noteworthy one, after decades of disagreement between the German proponents of *Ordnungspolitik*, on the one hand, and the French defenders of *planification*, on the other.

citizens, should entrust the Court with the shaping of a 'social Europe'. Should the Court take over where the citizens' representatives in the Convention and elsewhere failed to produce clear constitutional guidance? These are puzzling and, to a certain extent, worrying consequences, which are hardly reconcilable with the inherited notions of democracy and of the normative weight of constitutional norms. In addition, we have to assume that the Constitutional Treaty could serve as a sufficiently stable basis for daring activism. This is a somewhat heroic assumption with regard to the social rights in the light of Article II-52 (5), which provides:

> The provisions of this Charter which contain principles may be implemented by legislative and executive acts taken by Institutions and bodies of the Union, and by acts of Member States when they are implementing Union law, in the exercise of their respective powers. They shall be judicially cognisable only in the interpretation of such acts and in the ruling on their legality.[129]

Constitutionalisation as Process

'L'éssentiel est invisible pour les yeux' is the comfort that Antoine de Saint Exupéry's *Petit Prince* gives us. What is likewise invisible, because it seems so unexciting and trivial, is the performance of the European machinery, the innumerable, small and not so small indicators of good European governance. Europeanisation is an instigator of countless innovative projects. Directly behind or lying in the shadow of grand designs, such as that of the theory of the economic constitution or directly-deliberative polyarchy, there is another Europe at work. It is not so easy to discover, not so coherent, and often ambivalent. But we can approach it in three steps:

(1) One is analytical and interdisciplinary. We have some well-discussed and elaborated hypotheses about the structures of the European multi-level system of governance and the conceptualisation of this system in legal categories.
(2) The second step concerns our experiences with and insights into the Europeanisation processes. Nobody can claim to know and understand the complex processes of Europeanisation in their entirety. But if one studies some of them in some depth, one will discover patterns of change in both successful learning processes and in failures.[130] The 'law of the European

[129] See G de Búrca, 'Fundamental rights and Citizenship' in B de Witte (ed), 'Ten Reflections on the Constitutional Treaty for Europe', *San Domenico die Fiesole: RSCASAEL Working Paper, 2003*, 11, 22 ff.

[130] I refrain from an effort to elaborate the following remarks in the abstract. They need to be substantiated and concretised in the context of much more detailed analyses of specific fields. For a recent attempt, see C Joerges, 'The Challenges of Europeanization in the Realm of Private Law: A Plea for a New Legal Discipline' (2004) 24 *Duke Journal for Comparative and International Law* 149; available also at www.iue.it/PUB/law04-12.pdf.9.

economy' which becomes visible in such endeavours is very different – and much more interesting – than the law in the books. Europeanisation functions as an instigator of change and learning. It is an exercise in transformation, and modernisation.

(3) There is a theoretical background to this kind of cautious optimism. One, under-estimated, virtue of law is its concreteness, the need to take decisions and give reasons for them to actors, litigants, experts and to the wider public; the chance and, indeed, duty to reconsider what once seemed settled. Law is a Product guided by reasoning, it is *Recht-Fertigung* which reflects the justice and fairness of its production processes.[131] In such perspectives, 'constitutionalisation' can be conceived not as merely being the writing of a text and its formal acceptance by those who govern us and/or us, the people.

Can we expect 'constitutionalisation as process' not only to ensure the compatibility of open markets with regulatory concerns and preserve the social dimension of private law, but also to overcome Europe's social deficit? This seems highly unlikely but is not inconceivable. 'All political projects are inherently unrealistic, in that they strive for a not yet realized objective.' This was Wolfgang Streeck's response[132] to the lecture which Jürgen Habermas delivered in Hamburg on 26 June 2001.[133] The philosopher argued that a European constitution could help to defend the 'European social model'. Streeck substantiated his response: too much voluntarism will downgrade a project to mere wishful thinking. This is why it should be accompanied by empirical research. And, at some point, we should be prepared to take the discrepancies which we find between our aspirations and our observations seriously. But when and how? 'Constitutionalisation as process' is no answer to these questions. Nevertheless, it is a response to the state of the integration project which seeks to take the core idea of constitutionalism seriously.

[131] See R Wiethölter, 'Just-ifications of a Law of Society' in O Perez and G Teubner (eds), *Paradoxes and Inconsistencies in the Law* (Oxford: Hart Publishing, 2005) 65.

[132] 'Das "soziale Europa" und seine Verfassung: Fragen zu einem politischen Projekt', manuscript, Cologne 2001. The paper has not been published. But W Streeck has explained his position more comprehensively elsewhere. See, eg, 'From Market-Making to State-Building? Reflections on the Political Economy of European Social Policy' in S Leibfried and P Pierson (eds), *European Social Policy: Between Fragmentation and Integration* (Washington DC: Brookings Publications, 1995) 389; idem, 'The Internationalization of Industrial Relations in Europe: Prospects and Problems' (1998) 26 *Politics and Society* 429.

[133] 'Warum braucht Europa eine Verfassung? Nur als politisches Gemeinwesen kann der Kontinent seine in Gefahr geratene Kultur und Lebensform verteidigen', first published in *DIE ZEIT* of 29 June 2001, reprinted in J Habermas, *Zeit der Übergänge* (Frankfurt aM: Suhrkamp, 2001) 104 ff; English translation 'Why Europe Needs a Constitution' in EO Eriksen, JE Fossum and AJ Menéndez (eds), *Developing a Constitution for Europe* n 89 above, 19.

23

*Europe's Economic Constitution in Crisis and the Emergence of a New Constitutional Constellation**

I. INTRODUCTION

THE EUROPEAN UNION rides through troubled waters. Its original reliance on law as the object and agent of the integration project and on the 'economic constitution', which the Economic and Monetary Union (EMU) – as accomplished by the Treaty of Maastricht – expected to complete, have proven unsustainable. Following the financial and sovereign debt crises, individuals perceive the EMU, with its commitments to price stability and monetary politics, as a failed construction precisely because of its reliance on inflexible rules. The European crisis management seeks to compensate for these failures by means of regulatory machinery which disregards the European order of competences, takes power from national institutions, and burdens – in particular – Southern Europe with austerity measures; it establishes pan-European commitments to budgetary discipline and macroeconomic balancing. This abolishes the ideal of a legal ordering of the European economy, while the economic and social prospects of these efforts appear gloomy and the Union's political legitimacy becomes precarious. A fictitious debate between Carl Schmitt and Jürgen Habermas addresses the present critical constellation, in which a number of Schmittian notions seem alarmingly realistic. This essay pleads for a more modest Europe committing itself to 'united in diversity', the motto of the ill-fated Constitutional Treaty of 2003.

*This paper dates back to a presentation given at the Center for Transnational Studies (ZenTra) at the Faculty of Law of the University of Bremen in the summer term of 2012. An elaborated version ('Europas Wirtschaftsverfassung in der Krise') was published in (2012) 51:3 *Der Staat* 357. It was translated by Sandra H Lustig, Hamburg, and Matthew G Harris, Buchen/Odw. The paper was then presented in ever-revised versions at the *Trentième anniversaire de l'Association internationale de droit économique* on 8–9 November in Wroclaw, on 15 January 2013 at the Centre for European Law and Governance at the University of Amsterdam, and on 21 March 2013 at the conference on European Citizenship in Uppsala. The version presented there was published in (2014) 15 *German Law Journal* 985.

II. PRELIMINARY NOTE ON THE COURSE OF THE DEBATE

Europe faces troubling times. Constructive suggestions – such as the federal finality that Joschka Fischer sought to promote in his legendary lecture at the Humboldt University in Berlin[1] more than ten years ago – no longer sound credible. They now stand in contrast with the endless and frenzied crisis management that has placed its stamp of rigid austerity policy on the 'periphery' of what was to evolve into an 'ever closer Union'. The rule of law and the project of 'integration through law' are at stake, concepts which characterised and connected European law scholarship transnationally[2] in the formative phase of the integration project and for a good while thereafter. Europe is far from hosting 'the most competitive, knowledge-based economy in the world' as the Lisbon Council proclaimed in the year 2000;[3] its economy stands at the core of the present crisis. European constitutionalism, which dominated academic discussions for a decade and thoroughly neglected the inherently political dimensions of the 'economic', has been silenced.

Paradoxically, the same holds true for Germany's ordoliberalism and its project of an 'economic constitution'. According to this school of thought, the legitimacy of the European project rested upon the legal ordering of the economy,[4] the economic freedoms of the EEC Treaty – a system of undistorted competition – and an economic policy 'complying with justiciable criteria'.[5] These stood as the potential cornerstones of this order, to orient the integration process in a way by which the European polity would be legitimised by – and reduced to – an economic *ordo* whose validity did not depend upon democratic

[1] 'Vom Staatenverbund zur Föderation – Gedanken über die Finalität der europäischen Integration' ['From Confederacy to Federation: Thoughts on the Finality of European Integration'], Rede am 12 Mai 2000 in der Humboldt-Universität in Berlin, reprinted in C Joerges, Y Mény and JHH Weiler (eds), *What Kind of Constitution for What Kind of Polity? Responses to Joschka Fischer* (Florence: Robert Schuman Centre, EUI Florence and Cambridge MA: Jean Monnet Chair at Harvard Law School, 2000), available at: www.jeanmonnetprogram.org/papers/00/symp.html and http://cadmus.eui.eu/handle/1814/17255.

[2] A chapter from JHH Weiler's PhD thesis, published as 'The Community system: the dual character of supranationalism' in (1981) 1 *YBEuLaw* 1, 257 was ground-breaking – and then the major work he orchestrated: M Cappelletti, M Seccombe and JHH Weiler (eds), *Integration through Law* (Berlin–New York: de Gruyter, 5 vols, 1986–88).

[3] See Presidency Conclusions of the Lisbon Council of 23–24 March 2000, available at: www.europarl.europa.eu/summits/lis1_en.htm.

[4] See, for a critical account, C Joerges, 'What is Left of the European Economic Constitution? A Melancholic Eulogy' (2005) 30 *EL Rev* 461; idem, 'Europe after Ordoliberalism: A Philippic' in T Biebricher and F Vogelmann (eds), *The Birth of Austerity: German Ordoliberalism and Contemporary Neoliberalism* (London–New York: Rowman and Littlefield, 2017) 197.

[5] E-J Mestmäcker, 'Macht-Recht-Wirtschaftsverfassung' (1973) 137 *Zeitschrift für das gesamte Handelsrecht und Wirtschaftsrecht* 97, at 106. The essay is the elaboration of the lecture which he gave at the Verein für Socialpolitik conference in Bonn in 1972 and was immediately translated: 'Power, Law and Economic Constitution' (1973) 11 *German Economic Review* 177.

credentials, let alone upon the transformation of Europe into a fully-fledged federal state.[6]

This idea guided and accompanied ordoliberalism's path to Europe. Nobody championed or developed it more consistently than Ernst-Joachim Mestmäcker. One of his seminal essays explained that the pressure to harmonise, stemming from integration, would become stronger.[7] A Common Monetary Policy would mean 'ultimately giving up' the opportunity to maintain far-reaching differences between the economic orders.[8]

The Community for which the original ordoliberal concepts were conceived – and to which Mestmäcker referred – looks nothing less than idyllic from today's perspective. It was both smaller and more homogeneous than the current Union. For this reason alone, the incorporation of the project of integration through law, particularly its commitments to a legal ordering of economic policy (*Ordnungspolitik*), no longer seem viable. By now, individuals see the symptoms of a deep crisis, and the necessity for developing new perspectives for the European project appears irrefutable. One cannot reverse the course of history, but one can analyse and try to understand how and why the configuration of the relationship between law and politics in the integration project has contributed to the 'integration failure' which we are now witnessing in the current crisis. This essay proceeds in five steps.

The first step, taken somewhat in haste, concerns the Weberian notion of the nation-state and its pursuit of power through economic strength. The second involves the taming of the self-same nation-state by law and the de-coupling of the European economic constitution from the labour and social constitutions of the nation-states, which presents itself to the one – the ordoliberal – side as nothing but a logical implication of the establishment of a European economic order, while other political quarters perceive this disconnection as a threat to the legacy of the welfare state. This is followed by an analysis of the various dimensions of the integration project's problems, referring to Karl Polanyi's economic sociology. The next section elaborates on these remarks, dealing with

[6] See M Wegmann, *Früher Neoliberalismus und Europäische Integration* (Baden-Baden: Nomos, 2002); this is a reconstruction of Europe's ideational (economic) history. It corresponds instructively to W Fikentscher's magnum opus on *Wirtschaftsrecht* (economic law). Decades before the studies on global and European governance, and analyses of the relation between the levels and the impact of transnational governance on national statehood became *en vogue* in political science and 'constitutionalism beyond the state' became everybody's concern, Fikentscher conceptualised his *Wirtschaftsrecht* (Munich: CH Beck, 1983) in truly transnational and constitutional perspectives and composed the two monumental volumes accordingly: the first volume is dedicated to *Weltwirtschaftsrecht* (global economic law) and *Europäisches Wirtschaftsrecht* (European economic law); national economic law (*Deutsches Wirtschaftsrecht*) is presented upon that basis. This conceptualisation documents the truly universalist commitments of the ordoliberal tradition which Wegmann emphasises in her re-construction of the ordoliberal tradition.

[7] E-J Mestmäcker, Key Note at the Verein für Socialpolitik Conference on 'Macht-Recht-Wirtschaftsverfassung' [Power-Law-Economic Constitution] (1972); Mestmäcker, n 5 above, at 109.

[8] Mestmäcker, n 5 above, at 109.

the establishment and the crisis of Europe's EMU and including an overview of Europe's new 'crisis law' and its assessment by the German Constitutional Court (FCC) and the Court of Justice of the European Union (CJEU). The dramatic nature of our current situation will then be illustrated by means of a fictitious debate between Carl Schmitt and Jürgen Habermas. In the analysis of this debate, Carl Schmitt's theorems will prove to be frighteningly realistic: 'But where danger threatens, that which saves from it also grows.'[9] What kind of regime did Europe impose on itself, and what does this mean for European citizenship? These challenges will be addressed in the Epilogue, which will also tentatively consider an alternative vision to both the frightening as well as the possibly merely voluntarist scenarios on the future of the European integration project.

III. MAX WEBER'S *NATIONALSTAAT*

The steps towards European integration after World War II document how we overcame our bellicose past. At the same time, the designers of the project wanted to rein in the economic militancy of the nation-state. Max Weber formulated his perception of that nation-state in his 1895 inaugural Freiburg address as follows:

> Our successors will not hold us responsible before history for the kind of economic organization we hand over to them, but rather for the amount of elbow-room we conquer for them in the world and leave behind us. Processes of economic development are in the final analysis also power struggles, and the ultimate and decisive interests at whose service economic policy must place itself are the interests of national power, where these interests are in question. The science of political economy is a political science. It is a servant of politics, not the day-to-day politics of the individuals and classes who happen to be ruling at a particular time, but the lasting power-political interests of the nation. And for us the national state is not, as some people believe, an indeterminate entity raised higher and higher into the clouds in proportion as one clothes its nature in mystical darkness, but the temporal power-organization of the nation, and in this national state the ultimate standard of value for economic policy is 'reason of state'. There is a strange misinterpretation of this view current to the effect that we advocate 'state assistance' instead of 'self-help', state regulation of economic life instead of the free play of economic forces. We do not. Rather we wish under this slogan of 'reason of state' to raise the demand that for questions of German economic policy – including the question of whether, and how far, the state should intervene in economic life, and when it should rather untie the economic forces of the nation and tear down the barriers in the way of their free

[9] Friedrich Hölderlin, *Patmos. Dem Landgrafen von Homburg überreichte Handschrift*, 1802 (quoted from Friedrich Höderlin, *Werke* (Salzburg-Stuttgart: Bergland, 1954) 379; English translation by Michael Hamburger in Friedrich Hölderlin, *Selected Poems and Fragments* (London: Penguin Books, 1994) 243).

development – the ultimate and decisive voice should be that of the economic and political interests of our nation's power, and the vehicle of that power, the German national state.[10]

'It was not the agreement of many audience members with the following remarks, but their dissent that prompted me to publish them', Weber wrote in the preliminary notes to the publication of his lecture.[11] This text has weathered these concerns well. He developed a profoundly thought-through argument – in terms of economic theory, sociology, and history – and, despite all its jingoistic pronouncements, it also stands as a critique of the lack of political capacity of the German political class.[12] The martial tone of Weber's lecture clearly spells out a target of the European project, as people understood it later, particularly in Freiburg when that city had become the intellectual *Heimat* of the Ordoliberal School.

IV. THE CIVILISING ACCOMPLISHMENT AND ASYMMETRY OF THE EEC TREATY

In his seminal lecture of 1972, Mestmäcker explained succinctly how ordoliberalism had liberated itself from the legacy of Weber's *Nationalstaat*. He stated:

> What is historic about the EEC Treaty is that it integrates the internationality of economic relationships into the internationality of law and political institutions. In this sense, the EEC Treaty includes an economic constitution ... Expressed in terms of state and society, the EEC takes as its starting-point the law of bourgeois society and its institutions as the first manifestation of the universal in the international realm.[13]

This all came at a price. The liberation from the Weberian *Nationalstaat* came about through the imposition of legal commitments and constraints on the political autonomy of sovereign states. Due to these constraints, it became possible 'to conceptualise an economic policy that can be bound to legal and constitutional norms'.[14] Not only are the contents of economic policy affected

[10] M Weber, 'The National State and Economic Policy'; the translation by Ben Fowkes of the Freiburg Inaugural Address, given in 1895, was published in (1980) 9 *Economy and Society* 428 (with the passage cited at 438).

[11] M Weber, *Der Nationalstaat und die Volkswirtschaftspolitik. Akademische Antrittsrede* (Freiburg–Leipzig: Mohr Siebeck, 1895) 1–2.

[12] See R Aldenhoff, 'Nationalökonomie, Nationalstaat und Werturteile. Wissenschaftskritik in Max Webers Freiburger Antrittsrede im Kontext der Wissenschaftsdebatten in den 1890er Jahren' in G Sprenger (ed), *Deutsche Rechts- und Sozialphilosophie um 1900* (Stuttgart: Franz Steiner Verlag, 1991) 79.

[13] Mestmäcker, n 5 above, at 108–09.

[14] Ibid, at 102.

by these demands, but so are the competencies of legislation and its scope,[15] and the details of free collective-bargaining and co-determination.

This touches upon a sensitive issue. Even if we assume that the Treaties of Rome have established a European economic constitution, they nonetheless remain silent concerning labour and social law. This is why a functional equivalent of the 'social *Rechtsstaat*', in the sense of Article 20(1) German Basic Law or of the 'social market economy', as Alfred Müller-Armack programmatically developed it,[16] could not establish itself at the European level. Fritz W Scharpf considers the implications of this finding – the separation of the economic and social constitutions – to be a design-flaw that places Europe's social integration at long-term risk.[17] These statements are sociologically based, and meant in a socio-political way. A different question concerns explaining how this decision came about; another concerns whether such explanations are normatively instructive and what legally-binding effect may be granted to this initial situation. People widely view the reduction of the European social and labour constitution to the EEC Treaty's principle of non-discrimination as a successful negotiation on the part of Germany, supposed to have been worth attaining at the expense of agricultural policy. Now, the parties agreed upon the *quid pro quo* under the influence of the welfare promises of the Ohlin Report,[18] impressing the political left at the time and taking place in the era of 'embedded liberalism',[19] in which the opening up of national economies seemed compatible with the establishment of welfare-state systems.[20]

What does all this mean in legal terms? Is this an irreversible 'decision' about the alternatives of a planned economy versus a market economy? Or is this a constitutional compromise, similarly to how Hermann Heller found the Weimar Constitution to be a compromise; permanently binding guidelines for

[15] Ibid, at 103.

[16] See A Müller-Armack (ed), *Wirtschaftsordnung und Wirtschaftspolitik. Studien und Konzepte zur sozialen Marktwirtschaft und zur europäischen Integration* (Freiburg i.Br.: Rombach, 1966); idem, *Genealogie der sozialen Marktwirtschaft. Frühschriften und weiterführende Konzepte* (Bern: Haupt, 1974).

[17] FW Scharpf, 'The Asymmetry of European Integration, or Why the EU cannot be a "Social Market Economy"' (2010) 8 *Socio-Economic Review* 211, with references to his earlier works. In the legal literature pointedly, see, eg, F Rödl, 'Zur Idee demokratischer und sozialer Union im Verfassungsrecht der EU' ['The Idea of a Democratic and Social Union in the Constitutional Law of the EU'] in J Bast and F Rödl (eds), *Wohlfahrtsstaatlichkeit und soziale Demokratie in der EU; Europarecht Beiheft 1, 2013* (Baden-Baden: Nomos, 2013) 179.

[18] International Labour Organization, 'Social Aspects of European Economic Co-operation: Report by a Group of Experts' (1956) 74 *International Labour Review* 99.

[19] JG Ruggie, 'International Regimes, Transactions and Change: Embedded Liberalism in the Postwar Economic Order' (1982) 36 *International Organization* 375.

[20] For a critical discussion of Ruggie's later views, see C O'Brien, 'The UN Special Representative on Business and Human Rights: Re-embedding or Dis-embedding Transnational Markets?' in C Joerges and J Falke (eds), *Karl Polanyi, Globalisation and the Potential of Law in Transnational Markets* (Oxford: Hart Publishing, 2011) 323.

developing the relationship between the economic and labour constitutions in Europe?[21] Both positions suffer from the same difficulty. They treat the results of political negotiations as though they were the results of an assembly convened to draw up a constitution. So, is this merely a piece of history, whose further course is to be accepted as a kind of normative fact that we no longer can influence retroactively? This sequence of question marks indicates that there is no conclusive answer available. The constitutional configuration of the integration project is in permanent flux. Consolidated constitutional democracies too have to adapt to changing contextual conditions. But they tend to be more disciplined in the processes of adaptation.[22] In the EU Treaty, changes have become so burdensome that they are no longer conceivable. This is why the European *praxis* resorts to ever more evasive techniques and informal transformations of its order.

To put this slightly differently: European integration is a project without a defined *finalité*; it is adjusting to the dynamics of a development whose decoding is impossible without extra-legal means. We encounter such undertakings everywhere. Undoubtedly, the resort to Karl Polanyi – which now follows – is so far unusual. We submit that this is a promising encounter.

V. SYMPTOMS OF EUROPE'S CRISIS IN THE LIGHT OF KARL POLANYI'S ECONOMIC SOCIOLOGY

Karl Polanyi is one of the three Viennese *émigrés* who grappled with fascism towards the end of World War II. The other two are Friedrich August von Hayek[23] and Karl Popper.[24] Polanyi took up the issue in his brief monograph, first published in 1944.[25] His analysis is specific, 'embedded' in a re-construction of the core instability of industrial capitalism. This analysis lays heavy emphasis on the role played within capitalist society by three 'fictitious commodities': money, labour, and land. These three fictitious commodities denote 'goods' (*Waren*) which nonetheless pre-date and transcend 'the market', and whose subsequent 'commodification' not only provokes crises both within and around

[21] Thus Florian Rödl, 'Labour Constitution' in A v Bogdandy and J Bast (eds), *Principles of European Constitutional Law* (Oxford: Hart Publishing, 2nd ed. 2010) 605; S Giubboni, *Social Rights and Market Freedoms in the European Constitution: A Labour Law Perspective* (Cambridge: CUP, 2006) 7 ff.

[22] In principle, Hans Peter Ipsen's term 'continuous re-configuration' (*Wandelverfassung*), means nothing else; see his 'Europäische Verfassung – Nationale Verfassung' (1987) *Europarecht* 195, at 201.

[23] FA von Hayek, *The Road to Serfdom* (Chicago IL: University of Chicago Press, 1944).

[24] K Popper, *The Open Society and its Enemies* (London: Routledge, 1945).

[25] K Polanyi [1944], *The Great Transformation: The Political and Economic Origins of our Time* (Boston MA: Beacon Press, 2001). On Polanyi's topicality, see, eg, J Beckert, 'The Social Order of Markets', *MPIfG Discussion Paper 07/6*, Cologne, 2007; W Streeck, *Reforming Capitalism. Institutional Changes in the German Political Economy* (Oxford: OUP, 2009); F Block, 'Karl Polanyi and the writing of The Great Transformation' (2003) 32 *Theory and Society* 275.

capitalism, but also proves to be an impetus for counter-movements to the market.[26] In view of the chronic instability within the EMU, the steady erosion of national labour and social constitutions, and continuing conflicts in the area of energy policy, Polanyi's theses and conclusions have gained a remarkable degree of general topicality. The following analysis limits itself within this paradigm to the European 'integration through law project', and to the question of what European law has experienced, is experiencing, and what it has precipitated. This is not a matter, for example, of a generalised condemnation of market processes, at least not for strong voices in the Polanyian tradition.[27] Polanyi's thesis that treating fictitious goods as marketable products cannot come about smoothly is anything but comforting: the marketisation of labour, land, and money, he warned, will trigger crises and counter-movements. In view of the present state of the European Union, the erosion of the labour and social constitution, and the looming conflicts about the future of atomic energy, Polanyi's diagnoses are astonishingly topical.[28]

In the present constellation of conflict inter-dependencies, we must remain sensitive towards pertinent problems in their specific contexts. Drawing a line from Polanyi's fictitious commodities to atomic energy is a stretch and may go too far, but it is not absurd to regard atomic energy as a non-marketable good.[29] In any case, the insight that the economic success of this type of energy is due not to natural evolutionary processes, but to the establishment of markets by political fiat instead, is irrefutable. European law plays an unfortunate role here. The Euratom Treaty of 1957[30] was in a position to declare atomic energy the technology of the future *par excellence*, but did not Europeanise it, leaving the decision about its use to the nation-states.[31] The Treaty of Lisbon did not change

[26] Polanyi, *The Great Transformation*, n 25 above, at 69 ff.

[27] See A Ebner; '*Governance and Public Policy*', habilitation thesis, Erfurt 2007 (ch 2); idem, 'Transnational Markets and the Polanyi Problem' in Joerges and Falke (eds), *Karl Polanyi*, n 20 above, 19, at 29 ff.

[28] See C Joerges, 'Law and Politics in Europe's Crisis: On the History of the Impact of an Unfortunate Configuration' (2014) 21 *Constellations* 249. The growing interest in Polanyi and the renaissance of economic sociology is due to current events, but is nonetheless more robust. See references in n 25 above.

[29] Polanyi states: 'To allow the market mechanism to be the sole director of the fate of human beings and their natural environment, indeed, even of the amount and use of purchasing power, would result in the demolition of society … [N]o society could stand the effects of such a system of crude fictions even for the shortest stretch of time unless its human and natural substance as well as its business organization was protected against the ravages of this satanic mill'. See Polanyi, *The Great Transformation*, n 25 above, at 73.

[30] Euratom Treaty, Consolidated Version of the Treaty Establishing the European Atomic Energy Community, Consolidated version, OJ C 84 of 30 March 2010, 1.1 [hereinafter Euratom Treaty].

[31] The silence of the Euratom Treaty is deafening: The EAEC Treaty did not grant the Community the competence to 'authorise the construction or operation of nuclear installations'. See *Commission v Council*, CJEU Case C-29/99, 2002 ECR I-11281/11311, para 89. See, for a critique, C Joerges, 'The Timeliness of Direct Democracy in the EU – and the Contest over Atomic Energy in Conflicts-law Perspectives' in J Busch et al (eds), *International Constitutional Law in Legal Education. Proceedings of the Erasmus Intensive Programme NICLAS 2010–2012* (Vienna: Facultas, 2014) 89.

this in any way,[32] with the consequence that a phasing-out of atomic energy in Europe could only take place if all the Member States were to implement it, a scenario that definitely is nowhere in sight.

The consequences of de-coupling the labour and economic constitutions from one another either remained unobserved for a long time, or parties presented them as being rectifiable. The notion that a 'European social model' would take the place of the diverse variants of the Western European welfare states stood as no more than a pale utopian dream. This became apparent after the enlargement towards the East. At that juncture, the socio-economic disparities became so pronounced that a continuation of integration was feasible only in the form of negative integration by reducing the social protection provided by welfare states. This strategy was initiated by the European Commission in collaboration with actors representing relevant interests in both the old and new Member States. The *Viking*, *Laval*, and *Rüffert*[33] decisions are the most striking legal, partial victories, which can be viewed together as a confirmation of the decision to treat an economic constitution as a 'pure' market constitution and as the abandonment of the common European constitutional compromise. One must also keep in mind, though, what this means with regard to the acceptance of the project of integration. If Polanyi's diagnoses are correct, then we must anticipate counter-movements seeking to restore perspectives calling for social protection, and such signals are becoming ever more visible after Europe's transformation into an 'austerity union'.

VI. THE CRISIS OF ECONOMIC AND MONETARY UNION AND THE EUROPEAN RULE OF LAW

These very brief remarks must suffice so that space remains for the financial crisis that overshadows everything now.[34]

A. Juridification of Monetary Union

The financial crisis concerned the EMU as it took shape in the 1992 Treaty of Maastricht. The EMU was doubtless a political project, albeit one strictly

[32] Consolidated Version of the Treaty on the Functioning of the European Union, Art. 194, 26 October 2010, 2010 OJ (C 326) 47 [hereinafter TFEU].

[33] *International Transport Workers' Federation v Viking Line ABP*, CJEU Case C-438/05, 2007 ECR I-10779; *Laval un Partneri Ltd v Svenska Byggnadsarbetareförbundet*, CJEU Case C-341/05, 2007 ECR I-11767; *Rüffert v Land Niedersachsen*, CJEU Case C-346/06, 2008 ECR I-01989.

[34] An extensive discussion is to be found in C Joerges, 'United in Diversity as Europe's Vocation and Conflicts Law as Europe's Constitutional Form' in R Nickel and A Greppi (eds), *The Changing Role of Law in the Age of Supra- and Transnational Governance* (Baden-Baden: Nomos, 2012) 125; available also at: http://papers.ssrn.com/sol3/papers.cfm?abstract_id=1723249.

insulated against the influence of daily politics and entrusted instead to the medium of law. It was not '*alternativlos*' (without alternative), as is claimed today. In the 1970s, the Werner-Davignon Plans had attempted to synthesise the economic and social constitutions[35] During these years, a general departure from Keynesianism came about; Keynesianism had been legally anchored in Germany in the 1967 Stability Act (*Stabilitätsgesetz*),[36] realising the 'magical quadrant' – price stability, high employment, balance of payments, and appropriately increasing economic growth – a balancing act that seemed very precarious to many renowned German constitutionalists at the time because it had to be entrusted to the evaluation and discretionary decision-making of the political authorities. While German traditionalists worried about rule-guided *Ordnungspolitik*, in Great Britain, the post-war welfare-state *acquis* was revoked. Such a background constellation provided a strong political basis for a new European consensus that was expressed in the project of the single market and the turn to monetarist concepts. Paradigm shifts of this kind do not simply follow theoretical reason, nor should their effective rejection be regarded as evidence of the success of the prevailing paradigm without further ado.[37]

In the case of Europe's economic-policy orientation, individuals can discern two stages of re-orientation. First, Commission President Jacques Delors obtained broad support for his project of a single market, perceived as an institutionalisation of economic rationality: a commitment to principles designed to guide all political action.[38] The Monetary Union and the Stability Pact[39] were understood as complementary projects, as institutionalising an independent central bank outside all political spaces and beyond the institutional structure of the Union, designed to consummate the new architecture and fossilise a supranational economic constitution.

This understanding is deeply flawed. What the Treaty of Maastricht has established through the separation of Europeanised monetary policy from national

[35] H Schulz-Forberg and B Stråth, *The Political History of European Integration. The Hypocrisy of Democracy-through-Market* (London–New York: Routledge, 2010) 43 ff.

[36] C Joerges, 'The Idea of a Three-dimensional Conflicts Law as Constitutional Form' in C Joerges and E-U Petersman (eds), *Constitutionalism, Multilevel Trade Governance and International Economic Law* (Oxford: Hart Publishing, 2011) 413, at 420 ff (reprinted in pt VI, ch 27 of this volume).

[37] For the 1970s, see M Glasman, *Unnecessary Suffering. Managing Market Utopia* (London–New York: Polity Press, 1996) 96 ff; for the present, C Crouch, *The Strange Non-Death of Neoliberalism* (London: Polity Press, 2011) passim, and PA Hall, 'Commentary, Brother, Can You Paradigm?' (2013) 26 *Governance* 189.

[38] See MR Lepsius, 'Institutionalisierung und Deinstitutionalisierung von Rationalitätskriterien' in G Göhler (ed) *Institutionenwandel, Leviathan Sonderheft 16/1996* (Opladen: Westdeutscher Verlag, 1997) 57; regarding application to Europe, see idem, 'The European Union as a Sovereignty Association of a Special Nature' in C Joerges, Y Mény and JHH Weiler (eds), *What Kind of Constitution for What Kind of Polity?*, n 1 above, 213.

[39] Resolution of the European Council on the Stability and Growth Pact, OJ C 236 of 02.08.1997; Art 126 TFEU (ex-Art 104 EC Treaty) in conjunction with Protocol No 12.

fiscal and economic policy can best be characterised as a 'diagonal conflict'. This notion requires an explanatory remark:[40] monetary policy has become an exclusive competence of the Union (Article 3(1) c TFEU). With this provision, the Union claims supremacy in the policy area conferred to it, a conferral which did not include economic and fiscal policies. However, the exercise of these policies by the Member States can have effects which destruct the operation of monetary policy as administered by the European Central Bank (ECB). As experienced so drastically after 1992, the potential and actual tensions between monetary policy and the national policies cannot be controlled. This tension is not a vertical conflict for which arguably the supremacy principle could provide a response. It is a 'diagonal conflict' in the just-defined sense, because both the Union and the Member States are certainly interested in the functioning of their economies, but the powers required to accomplish this objective are attributed to two distinct levels of governance with often irreconcilable policy preferences. The type of conflict resolution foreseen in Article 119 TFEU is 'the adoption of an economic policy which is based on the close coordination of Member States' economic policies' as substantiated in Article 121 TFEU, and has proved to unworkable; this deficiency cannot be cured under the provisions of the Treaty of Maastricht and the soft law of the Stability Pact.

The decision by the FCC on the Treaty of Maastricht literally had a decisive part in making this misfortune come about, when it declared replacing politics by legal rules to be a *sine qua non* for Germany's participation, both in terms of content and institutionally.[41] The remarkably complex reasoning of the Court's Second Senate first dealt with the plaintiff's argumentation that the European Union had, under the new provisions, such far-reaching competence that the nation-states were no longer in a position to discharge important tasks. This called the continuing existence of 'democratic statehood' into question. This argumentation also referred to monetary policy. But the Court then responded by occupying the spaces for democratically shaping policy with law. In so doing, it embraced the – in this instance, compatible – ordoliberal and monetarist theorems, and gave them a legal form: economic integration, the Court said, was an apolitical process that both could and was permitted to take shape autonomously and beyond the Member States. Monetary Union was constituted appropriately *via* a constitutional duty to guarantee price stability and regulations to counter

[40] See C Joerges, 'Rethinking European Law's Supremacy: A Plea for a Supranational Conflict of Laws' in B Kohler-Koch and B Rittberger (eds), *Debating the Democratic Legitimacy of the European Union* (Lanham MD: Rowman & Littlefield, 2007) 311 at 318 ff; see, also, G Teubner, *Constuitutional Fragments* (Oxford: OUP, 2012) at 158 ff.

[41] Bundesverfassungsgericht [BVerfG – Federal Constitutional Court], Case No 2 BvR 2134/92 & 2 BvR 2159/92, 89 BVerfGE 155 (Oct 12, 1993). See, for a critique, C Joerges, 'States Without a Market: Comments on the German Constitutional Court's Maastricht-Judgment and a Plea for Interdisciplinary Discourses', *NISER Working Paper*, 1996, available at: http://eiop.or.at/eiop/pdf/1997-020.pdf; M Everson, 'Beyond the Bundesverfassungsgericht: On the Necessary Cunning of Constitutional Law' (1998) 4 *ELJ* 389.

excessive budget deficits. In this way, the objections to the democratic legitimacy of economic integration seemed to resolve themselves. In the public-law divisions of European legal studies in both Germany and in the larger quarters of European constitutionalism, scholars either did not even realise this, or they did not deem it worthy of mention.[42]

B. Processes of Erosion

In Mestmäcker's account, what is at stake is a power struggle between the political and the economic. In that contest, in his view, it is law that deserves the highest authority.[43] Yet this authority proved unable to prevail. The situation is more dramatic today. But the rules agreed upon were flawed in substance, and if they had been enforced, this would have caused harm. In line with this widely shared view, the very short life of the new legal edifice did not give rise to much concern.[44] When Germany, France, and The Netherlands, as well as others, failed to respect the rules of the Stability Pact, the Commission's much-vaunted efforts to take action against them dwindled into nothing. Barry Eichengreen, a renowned US observer of European monetary policy since the negotiations on the Treaty of Maastricht,[45] commented frankly on the breach of the law: 'How can one expect compliance with a threshold which has no sound conceptual basis?'[46] Occasionally, he used even stronger language,[47] and was by no means alone in voicing such principled criticism.[48] The Monetary Union was poorly designed, and the enforcement of its rules would not prevent the damage but increased it.

Things were to become much worse during the current crisis. The Union experiences a state of emergency where the law is losing its integrity. The all-too-meagre points of reference provided in Article 122(2) TFEU, amended under

[42] Instead, the Court was confronted with its talk of an 'association of states', its announcement that it would refuse to follow *ultra vires* legal acts, but, above all, the statement that its democratic rule pre-supposes that a 'relatively homogeneous people' has the opportunity 'to give legal expression to what unifies them – intellectually, socially, and politically'. JHH Weiler, 'Does Europe Need a Constitution? Reflections on Demos, Telos and the German Maastricht Decision' (1995) 1 *ELJ* 219; see, below, text accompanying nn 44–50.

[43] See E-J Mestmäcker, 'Europäische Prüfsteine der Herrschaft und des Rechts' (2007) 58 *ORDO: Jahrbuch für die Ordnung von Wirtschaft und Gesellschaft* 3 (re-stating his position).

[44] See C Joerges, 'What is Left of the European Economic Constitution: A Melancholic Eulogy' (2005) 30 *EL Rev* 461, 465 (reprinted in ch 22 of this volume).

[45] B Eichengreen, *Should the Maastricht Treaty be Saved?* (Princeton, NJ: International Economics Section, Department of Economics Princeton University, 1992) 74.

[46] B Eichengreen, 'Institutions for Fiscal Stability', *Working Paper PEIF No* 6, 2003, available at: https://econpapers.repec.org/paper/cdlbineur/qt34p6v7pt.htm.

[47] 'The 3% cap is at best ridiculous and at worst perverse', *DIE ZEIT* (20 November 2003), www.zeit.de/2003/49/Oekonom_I.

[48] See, with many references, G Majone, 'Rethinking European Integration after the Debt Crisis', *UCL Working Paper No 3*, 2012, available at: www.ucl.ac.uk/european-institute/analysis-publications/publications/WP3.pdf.

the simplified revision procedures of Article 48(6), which 'shall not increase the competences conferred on the Union in the Treaties',[49] must justify incalculable solidarity payments.[50] The ECB is disregarding its statutes as they used to be read;[51] parliaments are convened to make fast-tracked decisions that cannot be meaningfully discussed; Greece and other members of the Union are being told that their sovereignty is now 'limited'. Changes of government take place under exceptional circumstances. Polanyi and his analyses of monetary policy are only rarely mentioned during all this. Yet bear in mind his qualification of money as a fictitious commodity,[52] and of the risks of destroying the social conditions under which market societies can function.[53] Ordoliberal and monetarist standards were Europeanised in the legal constitution of the Monetary Union, although it was not possible to Europeanise their societal conditions for functioning that had developed over time. Majone explains his opinion that the Central Bank is a 'constitutional monstrosity' by reasoning that the Bank is supposed to pursue its stated goal of price stability in a political vacuum, and it is unable to take the Union's socio-economic disparities into account while doing so.[54] As Scharpf adds, the institutionalised inabilities to do anything other than react to instability and imbalance with intensified austerity programmes not only threatens the well-being of European citizens, but also endangers the social acceptance of the Union.[55]

C. Reactions

The pace at which crisis summits are being held – and the drafting of more and more new legislation and regulatory complements – is breathtaking.[56] It is both

[49] Council Decision 2011/199, 2011 OJ (L 91) 1 (amending Art 136 TFEU with regard to a stability mechanism for Member States whose currency is the euro).

[50] See Section VI.C.2.2.1 below, text accompanying nn 88 et seq (evaluating the Constitutional Court's decision on Greece). The reasons provided in plaintiff Peter Gauweiler's constitutional complaint by Dietrich Murswiek are available at: www.jura.uni-freiburg.de/institute/ioeffr3/forschung/gutachten.

[51] M Seidel, 'Der Euro – Schutzschild oder Falle?', *ZEI Working Paper No B01*, 2010.

[52] 'Money … is merely a token of purchasing power which, as a rule, is not produced at all, but comes into being through the mechanism of banking or state finance', Polanyi, *The Great Transformation*, n 25 above, at 72; see S Frerichs, 'From Credit to Crisis: Max Weber, Karl Polanyi, and the Other Side of the Coin' (2013) 40 *Journal of Law and Society* 7.

[53] W Streeck, 'The Crises of Democratic Capitalism' (2011) 71 *New Left Review* 5; see, also, the revised version as *MPIfG Discussion Paper 11/15*, Cologne 2011, www.mpifg.de/pu/mpifg_dp/dp11-15.pdf, and A Supiot, 'A Legal Perspective on the Economic Crisis of 2008' (2010) 149 *International Labour Review* 151.

[54] See G Majone, Europe as the Would-be World Power: The EU at Fifty (Cambridge: CUP, 2009).

[55] FW Scharpf, 'Monetary Union, Fiscal Crisis, and the Preemption of Democracy', *MPIfG Discussion Paper 11/11*, Cologne 2011, 5.

[56] See Economic and Financial Affairs, Council of the European Union, available at: www.consilium.europa.eu/press/press-releases/economic-and-financial-affairs?lang=en&BID=93 (updating information continuously).

important and meritorious to record all this precisely,[57] so that we can become aware of the tensions between our inherited concepts and methodological tools, and the present European *praxis*. Here, though, we must limit ourselves to a few highlights.

In March and May 2010, the Commission developed the 'Europe 2020 Strategy'[58] and the 'European Semester',[59] respectively. These were followed by the European Financial Stability Facility (EFSF) Framework Agreement[60] in June 2010, and by the European Council's 'Euro Plus Pact'[61] in March 2011. Simultaneously, upon the basis of the simplified revision procedures laid down in Article 48(6) TEU, the European Council also decided on 25 March 2011 to add a new paragraph 3 to Article 136 TFEU, which permitted the establishment of a stability mechanism and the granting of financial assistance, effective 1 January 2013.[62] This was followed in November 2011 by a bundle of legislative measures aimed at re-enforcing budgetary discipline on the part of the Member States. The package is supposed to go down in history under the catchy title of the 'Six Pack', and entered into force on 13 December 2011.[63] The high point of all this is the Treaty on Stability, Coordination and Governance (TSCG), drafted in December 2011, approved at an informal meeting of the European Council on 30 January 2012,[64] and signed on 2 March 2012 by twenty-five out of the then twenty-seven Member States. A debt brake according to the German model has been introduced, and will be subject to judicial review by the CJEU in the form of institutional borrowing, with one Member State bringing action against another. Support from the European Stability Mechanism (ESM) – a permanent crisis fund – will be available only to countries in the euro area that have signed the pact. The TSCG has been ratified by the required number of Member States and entered into force on 1 January 2013. Two further Regulations submitted back in November 2011 – the 'Two-Pack' – were adopted with parliamentary blessing in March 2013. They provide 'for monitoring and assessing draft budgetary plans

[57] Suffice it here to refer to just a few examples from the torrent of literature. C Calliess, 'Perspektiven des Euro zwischen Solidarität und Recht – Eine rechtliche Analyse der Griechenlandhilfe und des Rettungsschirms' (2011) 14 *Zeitschrift für Europarechtliche Studien* 213; M Ruffert, 'The European Debt Crisis and European Union Law' (2011) 49 *CMLRev* 1777; see, also, N Scicluna, *European Union Constitutionalism in Crisis* (London–New York: Routledge, 2015) 120 ff.

[58] Communication from the Commission, COM (2010) 2020 final (3 March 2010).

[59] Communication from the Commission, COM (2010) 250 final (12 May 2010).

[60] The Framework Agreement was concluded by the ECOFIN Council and confirmed by the European Council, Brussels on 17 June 2010. Council Conclusion No 2 of 17 June 2010, EUCO 13/10.

[61] Council Conclusion No 3 of 25 March 2011, Annex I, EUCO 10/11.

[62] Council Decision 2011/199, 2011 OJ (L 91) 1 (amending Art 136 TFEU with regard to a stability mechanism for Member States whose currency is the euro).

[63] Council Regulations 1173–1177/2011, 2011 OJ (L 91) 1; Council Directive 2011/85, 2011 OJ (L 91) 1.

[64] See the Communication of the euro area Member States as well as the Treaty on Stability, Coordination and Governance in the Economic and Monetary Union in the version of 20 January 2012, available at: http://european-council.europa.eu/media/639235/st00tscg26_en12.pdf.

and ensuring the correction of excessive deficit of the Member States in the euro area' and 'the strengthening of economic and budgetary surveillance of Member States experiencing or threatened with serious difficulties with respect to their financial stability in the euro area'.[65]

There is much to scrutinise here: the legal problems, their treatment in legal scholarship, the analysis and interpretation of what has been established. The law-politics relationship is particularly challenging. Lawyers – practitioners and academics alike – have all traditionally sought to remain on good terms with political power.[66] When it comes to Articles 122–126 TFEU, our discipline can apparently not resist helping political and institutional actors by taking the letter of the law so lightly as to run afoul of it. But just as legally wayward spirits will sometimes fail to finesse a fine legal point and must withdraw without achieving anything, jurisprudence is facing problems that seem to lie beyond the reach of its methodological means and conceptual potential. We are not going to re-construct these discussions in any detail here, but merely underline three particularly disturbing constitutional issues which will be discussed in the following Sections 1–3. These are:

1. The establishment of new regimes of economic governance outside the institutional frameworks of the Treaties and of national constitutions, for which two German lawyers[67] have coined the notion of *völkerrechtliches Ersatzunionsrecht*; the main difficulty here is that *Ersatzunionsrecht* legalises departures from the European Treaties without their amendment.
2. The problem of whether the means by which these regimes have been established may be used to intervene into national constitutions and imposed upon democratically legitimated governments which require financial support; with this practice, Europe's crisis management is following international examples.[68] The German Constitutional Court was confronted with

[65] See Press Release, European Parliament, Green light for economic governance 'two pack' (12 March 2013), www.europarl.europa.eu/pdfs/news/expert/infopress/20130312IPR06439/20130312IPR06439 _en.pdf.

[66] See M Stolleis, 'Reluctance to Glance in the Mirror: The Changing Face of German Jurisprudence after 1933 and post-1945 in C Joerges and NS Ghaleigh (eds), *Darker Legacies of Law in Europe: The Shadow of National Socialism and Fascism over Europe and its Legal Traditions* (Oxford: Hart Publishing, 2003) 1; Stolleis' observations concern primarily, but by no means exclusively, Germany's Nazi period.

[67] RA Lorz and H Sauer, 'Ersatzunionsrecht und Grundgesetz – Verfassungsrechtliche Zustimmungsgrundlagen für den Fiskalpakt, den ESM-Vertrag und die Änderung des AEUV (2012) 65 *Die öffentliche Verwaltung* 573, cited in the judgment of the German Constitutional Court of 12 September 2012, n 89 below, at para 257 of the German version and para 226 of the English version.

[68] Pertinent practices have been exercised by central banks and the IMF long before the financial crisis. They have been characterised as a feature of the global capital market: 'The new conditionality of the global economic system – the requirements that need to be met for a country to become integrated into the global capital market – facilitates the task of instituting a certain kind of monetary policy.' S Sassen, 'De-Nationalized State Agendas and Privatized Norm-Making' in K-H Ladeur (ed), *Public Governance in the Age of Globalization* (London: Routledge, 2004) 51, 56.

the query of whether such practices can be employed among the Member States of the Union and/or are even required by Germany's constitution; the main difficulty here is that unelected authorities exercise controls to which the democratic bodies of the state under supervision agree under enormous external pressures.

3. A third issue is often obscured as a simple matter of methodological interpretation. The difficulty here is that the conceptual basis for EMU is disregarded and replaced by a new type of economic governance. If the EMU suffers from a design defect and the implementation of the law as it stands seems to cause harm, can its rationale be replaced by some alternative, and who is empowered to decide upon such emergencies? The CJEU did not shy away from handing down clear answers to the queries in the *Pringle* case on 27 November 2012.[69]

1. *Community Method v Union Method and* Ersatzunionsrecht

The special feature of the European system – as Joseph HH Weiler explained in his seminal 1981 essay – is the simultaneity and balance of supranational law and inter-governmental policy.[70] Weiler thus characterised a precarious relationship, but certainly did not seek to grant the Member State governments *carte blanche* to suspend their commitments to Community (now Union) law whenever they believed that doing so would be irrefutable and expedient. And precisely this is the historical achievement of the Treaties of Rome: that they endeavoured to rein in the power-political actions of the Weberian nation-state by legal means. The differences between different modes of interaction in the Union have been quite thoroughly explored.[71] The move from arguing and deliberative problem-solving to bargaining and the strategic pursuit of 'national' interests, and the replacement of the old Community method in which the law provided institutional and procedural protection to the weaker actors make a real difference. Thanks to its domination by the Council, the new 'Union method' faithfully mirrors the power asymmetries in the Union. Should the law care? Mark Dawson and Floris de Witte are among the few[72] who have raised this issue.[73]

[69] *Pringle v Ireland*, CJEU Case C-370/12 (27 November 2012), available at: http://curia.europa.eu.

[70] Weiler, 'The Community System', n 2 above.

[71] C Reh, 'European Integration as Compromise: Recognition, Concessions and the Limits of Cooperation' (2012) 47 *Government & Opposition* 414.

[72] There are more, but they are rare. For another noteworthy exception with a great sensitivity for the hybrid nature of the Union praxis, see E Chiti and PG Teixeira, 'The Constitutional Implications of the European Responses to the Financial and Public Debt Crisis' (2013) 50 *CMLR* 683, 685, 690. Chiti and Teixeira, throughout their analyses, assess what they lucidly describe through functional and normative yardsticks and thereby soften their critique; their conclusion is nonetheless uncompromising on this point: the new hybrid method 'tends to set aside the role of EU institutions in exercising their respective competences within a democratic framework based on EU law in favour of power-based intergovernmental relations'. Ibid, at 708. But this is precisely the reason why not only democracy but also the rule of law in its core transnational function – as we have underlined it in Section II – is at stake.

It is simply amazing that it has become the rule among lawyers not to take these issues seriously. To be sure, the Member States of the Union have conferred their sovereignty only in 'limited fields' and retain political autonomy where this does not occur. But they nonetheless remain bound by their common commitments, in particular to democracy and the rule of law (Article 2 TEU). This is why the sovereignty that they have retained does not empower them to enter into *qualsiasi* agreement. The Fiscal Compact requires from its signatories[74] changes of fundamental constitutional importance, and the modes of their implementation are anything but consensual.[75] The methodological reasons invoked in various modes replicate what could be observed earlier in European law, namely, a resort to legal formalism which shields law from justifying to what extent it is used:[76] 'Intergovernmental cooperation permits Member States to exercise reactive crisis management, but Union law does not provide an instrument for doing so.'[77] 'Major sections of the Euro rescue package,' Thym added in his review of

[73] M Dawson and F de Witte, 'Constitutional Balance in the EU After the Euro-Crisis' (2013) 76 *MLR* 817, at 838. They conclude that 'the rise of executive control via the European Council, the increasing ease of making Treaty and legislative reforms without consulting smaller member states, and the creation of eternal fiscal rules uncontrollable by national parliaments, unable to be fully discussed and legitimated, is now in danger of desensitising the Union'. Ibid, at 842. Indeed, and it is true 'that the Union's existing response … does not bode well for the future'. Ibid, at 844. What remains to be explained is Europe's apparent political inability to organise a legally robust response to these insights. See discussion below.

[74] Least from Germany, which has in 2009 constitutionalised the *Schuldenbremse* (debt brake) in Art109 Basic Law. Constitutional provisions, however, are easier to amend than the TFEU and multilateral treaties.

[75] Suffice it here to point to the analysis submitted by political scientist M Höpner and lawyer F Rödl, 'Illegitim und rechtswidrig: Das neue makroökonomische Regime im Euroraum' *ZBW – Leibniz-Informationszentrum Wirtschaft* 219; similarly, J Bast and F Rödl, 'Jenseits der Koordinierung? Zu den Grenzen der EU-Verträge für eine Europäische Wirtschaftsregierung' (2012) 39 *Europäische Grundrechte-Zeitschrift* 269. The authors demonstrate in detail that the Council's power of surveillance in accordance with Art 136(1)(b) lacks sanctions. Art 136(1)(b) does *not* provide for the sanctions which the new regime establishes. Although the coordinating competencies in accordance with Art 121(3) and (4) TFEU provide for reporting requirements on the part of the Member States as well as recommendations by the Commission, Art 121(6) TFEU does not permit mandatory sanctions. Indeed, the multilateral surveillance in accordance with Art 121(3) and (4) TFEU contains provisions for reports, recommendations, and warnings, but no security deposits (whether or not they bear interest) or fines. Art 121(6) is aimed at removing the right to regulate the details of the procedures in accordance with Art 121(3) and (4) TFEU. The assumption that the Council could reject recommendations from the Commission concerning surveillance only with a qualified majority – but also that such a shift in the institutional structure would be up for negotiation by the Member States – is untenable. This arrangement has created a hybrid of justice and injustice by establishing a regulatory machinery which is not provided for in the Union's legal framework and is to be superimposed on the Member States' institutions and political procedures. See also A Fischer-Lescano, 'The European TSCG and EU Law' Bremen 2012, available at: www.eunews.it/wp-content/uploads/2012/09/2012_09_06_Fischer-Lescano; and L Oberndorfer, 'Der Fiskalpakt – Umgehung der 'europäischen Verfassung und Durchbrechung demokratischer Verfahren?' (2012) *Juridikum* 168.

[76] See C Joerges, 'A New Alliance of De-Legalisation and Legal Formalism? Reflections on the Response to the Social Deficit of the European Integration Project' in H Brunkhorst (ed), *Demokratie in der Weltgesellschaft. Soziale Welt Sonderband 18* (Baden-Baden: Nomos, 2009) 437.

[77] D Thym, 'Euro-Rettungsschirm: zwischenstaatliche Rechtskonstruktion und verfassungsgerichtliche Kontrolle' (2011) 25 *Europäische Zeitschrift für Wirtschaftsrecht* 167; and idem,

the Greece decision of 7 September 2011, were 'designed as intergovernmental macro-financial assistance' and 'should therefore [*sic*] not be measured against European-law standards'.[78] This move has its methodological precursors in the widely-acclaimed resort to the Open Method of Coordination (OMC) in the field of social policy. Its liberation from the straitjacket of the 'Union method' and the replacement of hard law by soft law were explicitly targeted at the attainment of social objectives which were unattainable under the old regime.[79] The present case, although, is much more dramatic. While the OMC did not accomplish the noble objectives that its proponents had envisaged, the resort to the 'Union method' amounts to a deep transformation of the European constitutional constellation. The stakes are higher not only for this reason, but also because the organisers of the new modes of economic governance fail to provide any theoretical framework within which the means that would be employed to bring the deeply affected Member States 'back on track' become visible and comprehensible.[80] It is far from clear how the new regime might accomplish

'Annotation to Bundesverfassungsgericht, judgment of 7.9.2011' (2011) 66 *Juristenzeitung* 148; as a student of the *Darker Legacies of Law in Europe*, I cannot refrain from a plea for linguistic sensitivity. It is one thing for JHH Weiler to introduce 'total law' as a trademark, or for Loïc Azoulai to write about 'total harmonisation'; Germans cannot disregard the connotations of such terms. The same holds true for the establishment of secondary legal regimes. Germans are as free as anybody else to approve such developments, but they should make it clear that they are aware of the shadow of Ernst Fränkel's *Doppelstaat* and Franz Neumann's *Behemoth*.

[78] (2011) 66 *Juristenzeitung* 1011, 1014 (my translation). This is, by now, the dominant position in European constitutional scholarship. This is a recent *acquis*, however. As late as 2011 – and hence in the middle of the crisis – de Witte considered that the German constitutional court might declare the EFSF to be incompatible with German constitutional law and an ultra vires act in contravention of the 'no-bailout' provision of Art 125 TFEU, see B de Witte, 'The European Treaty Amendment for the Creation of a Financial Stability Mechanism' (2011) *European Policy Analysis* 1, 6. This was, indeed, a widely-shared concern. B de Witte has clarified his position on various occasions, particularly succinctly in L Azoulai et a., 'Another Legal Monster? An EUI Debate on the Fiscal Compact Treaty', *EUI Working Papers Law No 09* (2012). His argument is far more sophisticated than the one cited in the text. But is not possible to come to terms with the TSCG simply because that Treaty states in Art 2 No 2: 'This Treaty shall apply in full to the Contracting Parties whose currency is the euro. It shall also apply to the other Contracting Parties to the extent and under the conditions set out in Article 14.' In the draft circulated until 2 March 2012, one could read: 'This Treaty shall apply insofar as it is compatible with the Treaties on which the European Union is founded and with European Union law. It shall not encroach upon the competence of the Union to act in the area of the economic union.' What happened to the compatibility with the Union's primary law, one wonders. We must reckon with conflicts between the law of the Union as enshrined in the Treaties on the one hand, and the Fiscal Compact and the regulatory machinery established in response to the crisis on the other. The Fiscal Compact in its latest version simply assumes that, in such conflicts, it will prevail.

[79] See DM and LG Trubek, 'Hard and Soft Law in the Construction of Social Europe: The Role of the Open Method of Co-ordination' (2005) 11 *ELJ* 343, and the critique in C Joerges, 'Integration Through De-Legalisation?' (2008) 33 *EL Rev* 219 (reprinted in pt III, ch 13 of this volume).

[80] By contrast, the proponents of the OMC relied on the weak premises of deliberative polyarchy and/or democratic experimentalism: 'In deliberative polyarchy, problem-solving depends not on harmony and spontaneous co-ordination, but on the permanent disequilibrium of incentives and interests imperfectly aligned, and on the disciplined, collaborative exploration of the resulting differences'. J Cohen and CF Sabel, 'Sovereignty and Solidarity: EU and US' in K-H Ladeur (ed), *Public Governance in the Age of Globalization*, n 68 above, 168. This is a formula which

what its organisers envisage and promise. Furthermore, the asymmetry between fully-harmonised monetary policy and nation-state competence in economic and fiscal policy diagnosed above remains unaffected. Above all, the stark socio-economic disparities – which have deepened since the Eastern enlargement – remain in place, as do the conflicts resulting from these disparities. As just underlined above, Europe's crisis management operates without conceptual guidance. And this is anything but fortuitous, as this crisis management is intergovernmental and must hence follow the logic of finding compromises between actors with different interests, institutional preferences, and political perspectives.[81]

2. *Constitutional Guardianship I: Mutual Non-recognition of the Budgetary Power of National Parliaments?*

The German Federal Constitutional Court is by no means the only forum[82] in which Europe's constitution has been tested.[83] Yet nowhere else does this occur with such regularity, and although the Court has, indeed, gained the reputation of a dog 'that barks but does not bite',[84] the anxieties of the many publics in both the EU and elsewhere, awaiting its decisions on the management of the financial crisis, are easy to explain: this Court supervises the economically most powerful Member State whose government underlines again and again how seriously it takes every judicial pronouncement. The FCC is, of course, well aware of all this. The mere fact that it is exposed to political scrutiny from many

is very close to many methodological pronouncements within the conflicts-law approach and its plea for a proceduralisation. See nn 31, 33 above. The proponents of the latter approach diagnose, sadly, that conflicts-law constitutionalism has become a critic which can no longer be presented as a re-constructive approach. See C Joerges and M Weimer, 'A Crisis of Executive Managerialism in the EU: No Alternative?' in G de Búrca, C Kilpatrick and J Scott (eds), *Critical Legal Perspectives on Global Governance: Liber Amicorum for David M Trubek* (Oxford: Hart Publishing, 2014) 295. The most prominent proponents of OMC and democratic experimentalism see, apparently, no reason for such modesty and re-design. See CF Sabel and J Zeitlin, 'Experimentalism in the EU: Common Ground and Persistent Differences' (2012) 6 *Regulation and Governance* 410.

[81] For a deepened analysis, see Majone, 'Rethinking European Integration', n 48 above; Scharpf, 'Monetary Union', n 55 above; idem, 'Legitimacy Intermediation in the Multilevel European Polity and its Collapse in the Euro Crisis', *MPIFG Discussion Paper 12/6*, Cologne 2012. What both authors implicitly confirm is the validity of Polanyi's insights in the social embeddedness of the economy. See nn 25–28 above.

[82] The following passages on the crisis jurisprudence of the GCC and the CJEU draw on M Everson and C Joerges, 'Who is the Guardian for Constitutionalism in Europe After the Financial Crisis?' in S Kröger (ed), *Political Representation in the European Union. Democratic in a Time of Crisis* (Abingdon–New York: Routledge, 2014), also available at: http://ssrn.com/abstract=2287111.

[83] See F Fabbrini, 'The Euro-Crisis and the Courts: Judicial Review and the Political Process in Comparative Perspective' (2014) 32 *Berkeley J Int'l L* 64.

[84] JHH Weiler, 'The "Lisbon Urteil" and the Fast Food Culture' (2009) 20 *EU J Int'l L* 505, 505 (commenting on Bundesverfassungsgericht [BVerfG – Federal Constitutional Court], Case No 2 BvE 2/08, 2 BvE 5/08, 2 BvR 1010/08, 2 BvR 1022/08, 2 BvR 1259/08, 2 BvR 182/09 (30 June 2009), available at: www.bverfg.de/entscheidungen/ es20090630_2bve000208en.html [hereinafter Judgment of 30 June 2009].

quarters and that its pronouncements are assessed politically means that it is *de facto* performing a political role. But the source of the Court's authority is its legal mandate and the quality of its exercise. It is not just the outcome of a litigation that matters. In this respect Joseph Weiler hit the nail on the head with his respectful ridicule. Indeed, how realistic was it to expect that the Court would help Mr Brunner and his *DM-Partei* overturn the Treaty of Maastricht in 1993?[85] Would Karlsruhe have been in a position to put a sad end to the Treaty of Lisbon, which had been negotiated with so much effort by so many actors over so many years?[86] And yet these judgments did matter. In particular, the significance of the Treaty of Maastricht decision, which had for the first time raised the previously rather staid discussion about Europe to the level of a true constitutional debate, and which had – albeit only indirectly – imposed Germany's economic philosophy upon the rest of Europe,[87] can hardly be overstated.

Hardly anybody had serious doubts as to the outcome of the proceedings on the rescue package for Greece,[88] and on the ESM Treaty and the Fiscal Compact.[89] What observers were nevertheless anxious to learn was how the FCC would perform the balancing between law and politics, and thereby define its own constitutional guardianship.

2.1. The Rescue Package for Greece

The plaintiffs in this litigation were the usual suspects: a group of professorial economists and Dr Gauweiler, a member of the *Bundestag*, as representing the Bavarian branch of the Christian Democratic party (CSU). They challenged both German and European legal instruments, as well as further measures related to attempts to solve the current financial and sovereign debt crisis in the area of the European Monetary Union.[90]

My reading of the judgment on the Greek rescue package focuses on three concerns. The first is the tension between the financial crisis management and the German constitution. In this regard, the message of the Court is strong

[85] See BVerfGE 155 (1993) [*Brunner v European Union Treaty* [1994] 1 CMLR 57].

[86] See the Lisbon Judgment of 30 June 2009, available at www.bundesverfassungsgericht.de/entscheidungen/es2009063

[87] See Section VI.D.I below.

[88] Bundesverfassungsgericht [BVerfG – Federal Constitutional Court], Case No 2 BvR 987/10, 2 BvR 1485/10, 2 BvR 1099/10 (7 September 2011), available at: www.bverfg.de/entscheidungen/rs20110907_2bvr098710en.html [hereinafter Judgment of 7 September 2011].

[89] Bundesverfassungsgericht [BVerfG – Federal Constitutional Court], Case No 2 BvR 1390/12 (12 September 2012), available at: www.bundesverfassungsgericht.de/entscheidungen/rs20120912_2bvr139012en.html [English translation], www.bundesverfassungsgericht.de/entscheidungen/rs20120912_2bvr139012.html [German] [hereinafter Judgment of 12 September 2012].

[90] Namely, the Währungsunion-Finanzstabilisierungsgesetz (Monetary Union Financial Stabilisation Act), which grants the authorisation to provide aid to Greece, and the Gesetz zur Übernahme von Gewährleistungen im Rahmen eines europäischen Stabilisierungsmechanismus (Act Concerning the Giving of Guarantees in the Framework of a European Stabilisation Mechanism).

in principle, but not so constraining in practice: Budgetary powers are a core responsibility of the parliament and a central element of democratic self-rule.[91] This is why the *Bundestag* must remain 'the place in which autonomous decisions on revenue and expenditure are made, even with regard to international and European commitments'.[92] But this is where the law's prerogatives end; parliament enjoys wide latitude in the exercise of its responsibilities, a political prerogative which the Court will respect.[93] A second concern is the compliance with the order of competences. The Court recalls its famous dictum from the Maastricht Judgment: legal instruments that disregard the order of competences (*ausbrechende Rechtsakte*) do not apply in Germany.[94] But this *monitum* is actually soft, because it needs to be read in the light of the *Mangold/Honeywell* decision.[95] The Court refrained, though, from considering the request for a preliminary ruling under Article 267 TFEU with a view to having the CJEU examine the compatibility of the rescue measure/s with Article 125 TFEU. Instead, it contented itself with assuring that Monetary Union was designed to be a 'stability community' and hence is one.[96] And we, the citizens? We cannot, in a constitutional democracy, be obliged to comply with European commands that exceed the competences conferred to the Union. Hence, we need to accept that our government takes its commitments to our financial interests seriously.[97] 'A crafty and blandishing wink of the eye', comments M Ruffert.[98] In fact, the Court is examining only whether Germany has met its 'integration responsibility' (*Integrationsverantwortung*), and then leaves the question unanswered of 'under what conditions constitutional complaints against non-treaty changes of primary Union law can be based upon Article 38 Paragraph 1 Sentence 1 German Basic Law'.[99] The intergovernmental decisions were not 'sovereign acts of German public authorities', 'notwithstanding other possibilities for legal review', which is why they could not be challenged.[100]

[91] Judgment of 7 September 2011 at paras 121–23.

[92] Ibid, at para 124.

[93] Ibid, at paras 130–32.

[94] Ibid, at para 116 (referencing the decisions on Maastricht [BVerfGE 89, 155, 175] and Honeywell [BVerfGE 126, 286, 302 ff]); in the Maastricht decision, see, also, paras 129 and 137 on commitment to the stability concept.

[95] Bundesverfassungsgericht [BVerfG – Federal Constitutional Court], Case No 2 BvR 2661/06 (6 July 2010), www.bundesverfassungsgericht.de/entscheidungen/rs20100706_2bvr266106en.html.

[96] Judgment of 7 September 2011, at para 129. The Court adds: 'In this connection, particular mention should be made of the prohibition of direct purchase of debt instruments of public institutions by the European Central Bank, the prohibition of accepting liability (bailout clause) and the stability criteria for sound budget management (Articles 123 to 126, Article 136 TFEU).' Ibid. This remark attracted considerable attention but has not been taken too seriously by the ECB.

[97] Ibid, at para 98.

[98] M Ruffert, 'Die europäische Schuldenkrise vor dem Bundesverfassungsgericht – Anmerkung zum Urteil vom 7. September 2011' [2011] Europarecht 842, at 844.

[99] Judgment of 7 September 2011, at para 109.

[100] Ibid, at para 116.

Is it adequate to consider the decision's 'lasting merit' to be the fact that it 'honestly recognized the limits of its own substantive expertise'?[101] Wise judicial self-restraint is hardly a proper reading of this rescue package judgment – certainly not if it is read in conjunction with the follow-up judgment of 12 September 2012.

2.2. The ESM Treaty and the Fiscal Compact

This litigation was more spectacular by far. Not only the usual plaintiffs, but also the parliamentary group of *Die Linke* and 37,000 citizens – among them very prominent figures – had filed constitutional complaints with which they primarily requested a temporary injunction, which would inhibit the entering into force of the statutes passed by the *Bundestag* and the *Bundesrat* on 29 June 2012 as measures to deal with the sovereign debt until the decision of the FCC in the principal proceedings.

The outcome was as usual. The government, Brussels, and the market were relieved. The resonance in academic quarters was unusually positive. On closer inspection, though, the judgment turns out to be highly problematical. Its ambivalence stems, unfortunately, from the Court's renewed defence of the budgetary power of the German *Bundestag* as a democratic essential. As in the previous judgment, one wonders about the *de facto* importance of this principle. Again, the Court underlined that the *Bundestag* enjoyed wide latitude which the judiciary had to respect.[102] Through this move, the rights of the *Bundestag* were re-defined in a proceduralising mode: the Parliament must be adequately informed, enabled to deliberate, and prevented from delegating its evaluation. It is far from clear, though, to what degree these *caveats* will enable the German Parliament to exercise effective supervision of its government and its transnational activities.[103] Even more important and questionable is the Court's complacency with the rest of the Union. In the pertinent passages, the Court once again strengthened the link between the *Bundestag*'s budgetary responsibility and a distinctly German philosophy of stability (eg, price stability and the independence of the ECB above all).[104] As a consequence, the nature of the

[101] See Thym, 'Annotation', n 72 above, at 1015.
[102] Judgment of 12 September 2012, at para 180.
[103] See C Geyer, 'Anatomie einer Hintergehung' [Anatomy of a Deceit] *Frankfurter Algemeine Zeitung* 21 June 2012, at 29.
[104] The Judgment of 12 September 2012 in the English translation reads, at para 220: 'In view of the transfer of monetary sovereignty to the European System of Central Banks, the German *Bundestag*'s overall budgetary responsibility is safeguarded particularly by the fact that the European Central Bank subjects itself to the strict criteria of the Treaty on the Functioning of the European Union and of the Statute of the European System of Central Banks with regard to the independence of the Central Bank and to the priority of monetary stability (see BVerfGE 89, 155 <204–205, 207 ff>; 129, 124 <181–182>). In this context, an essential element of safeguarding the constitutional requirements resulting from Article 20(1) and (2) in conjunction with Article 79(3) of the Basic Law in European Union Law is the prohibition of monetary financing by the European Central Bank

EMU as a stability community (*Stabilitätsgemeinschaft*) is even seen as being protected by the 'eternity clause' of Article 79(3) of the German Basic Law as an unamendable core of Germany's constitutional identity. Thus, the stability principles become the core of a refurbished European economic constitution.[105] All this – the Court hopes – will protect the democratic rights of German citizens. Non-German citizens of the Union, however, should not be amused at all. Why is budgetary autonomy not understood as a 'common' European constitutional legacy, respect for which is demanded by Article 4(2) TEU?

The one-sidedness of this argument is all the more disappointing as the Court, in an earlier paragraph of its judgment, had opened another and more constructive perspective: the Court explained that 'Article 79(3) seeks to protect those structures and procedures which keep the democratic process open'.[106] The Court did not indicate that it would be prepared to address the tensions between democratic commitments and the integration process, which would include the concerns of all the Member States. Instead, the Court's reasoning leads to a strengthening of the links between economic stability and social austerity. This form of judicial self-restraint seems even more questionable in the light of – or rather, in the shadow of – the Maastricht Judgment discussed above.[107] Once again, the FCC imposes German views on the rest of Europe, albeit in a significantly modified move. While the Maastricht judgment assumed that Europe's economic constitution could be an essentially legal project, the new judgment is moving from law to governmental and executive managerialism, with requirements defined mainly by Germany and its Northern allies. To put it slightly differently, we find it deplorable that the FCC acted as (only) the guardian of the German constitution. The qualification of financial assistance as a matter not of European monetary but of national economic policy,[108] as well as the somewhat euphemistic statements on the respect of the stability commitments,[109] are anything but robust indicators of truly European commitments. They are embedded in the conditionality of existing crisis management. The FCC talks about democratic essentials – Jürgen Habermas has observed – but has Germany in mind.[110] The one-sidedness of its decision seems, indeed, obvious – and difficult to overcome. The German Court is not entitled to act as the Guardian of Europe. What we would expect, although, is a readiness to define Germany as

(see BVerfGE 89, 155 <204–205>; 129, 124 <181–182>).' Paragraph 170 reads: '... Since the Federal Finance Minister is delegated to the Board of Governors and a Permanent Secretary to the Board of Directors, it is guaranteed, together with the Act for Financial Participation in the European Stability Mechanism, that the overall budgetary responsibility of the German *Bundestag* is safeguarded.'

[105] See ibid, paras 219–20, 232–33, 239–79, 300–19.

[106] Ibid, at para 206 in the English extract, para 222 in the German original.

[107] See text accompanying n 82 above.

[108] Judgment of 12 September 2012 at para 169 [English version].

[109] Ibid, at para 201.

[110] J Habermas, 'Three Reasons for "More Europe"' in idem, *The Lure of Technocracy* (Cambridge: Polity, 2015) 80.

a Member of a Union in which the concerns of all the Member States and their democratic rights deserve recognition. Only then would the Court document an understanding, or *Integrationsverantwortung*, which might reflect common European commitments.[111]

3. *Constitutional Guardianship II: The Methodological Failures of the CJEU in the* Pringle *Case*

Thomas Pringle, Member of the Irish Parliament, raised a series of objections against the involvement of his government in the ESM Treaty. Of particular interest in the present context is his assertion that the ESM constitutes an autonomous and permanent international institution, designed to evade restrictive provisions in the TFEU in relation to economic and monetary policy, and amounts to a usurpation of competences which were not conferred on the Union. This argument concerns the transformation of the European economic constitution through *Ersatzunionsrecht*, which we have discussed in Section III above. It is intrinsically linked to Pringle's concern with the rule of law. He argued the new regime has suspended the principle of legal protection. His complaint was rejected in the first instance, but, on appeal, the Irish Supreme Court, in a judgment of 17 July 2012,[112] decided to stay proceeding and submit a reference for a preliminary ruling to the CJEU. The CJEU (Full Court) handed down its judgment on 27 November 2012.[113]

The argument upon which the following analysis focuses is based upon the Court's reading of the bailout prohibition of Article 125 TFEU, and the emergency exception in Article 122(2) TFEU, through which the unrestrained new mode of economic governance is justified; these are key provisions of the economic constitution established under the Treaty of Maastricht and their re-vision through the judiciary is, hence, about the structuring of a new constitutional constellation. The reasons for this transformation have been addressed throughout the previous sections. It has, by now, become a *communis opinio* that European monetary policy – with its pre-defined objectives and institutional frameworks – cannot operate in tandem with the multitude of national actors that are pursuing economic and fiscal policies under a very loosely-constructed machinery of European supervision. The message of the *Pringle* judgment is in line with that which we have observed thus far; the failures of the past justify the efforts of Europe's crisis management which can, therefore, be legalised. The Court's attitude is certainly understandable; its reasoning, however, suffers from serious flaws.

[111] For a similar critique, see H Deters, 'National Constitutional Jurisprudence in a Post-National Europe: The ESM Ruling of the German Federal Constitutional Court' (2014) 20 *ELJ* 204.
[112] *Pringle*, n 69 above.
[113] Ibid.

The main flaw is the Court's failure to address the implications of its own explanation of the conceptual background to the 'no-bailout' clause:

> The prohibition laid down in Article 125 TFEU ensures that the Member States remain subject to the logic of the market when they enter into debt, since that ought to prompt them to maintain budgetary discipline. Compliance with such discipline contributes, at Union level, to the attainment of a higher objective, namely, maintaining the financial stability of the monetary union.[114]

This is, indeed, a fair re-statement of an ordoliberal legacy that we can still identify within the Maastricht EMU. Except, the Court is then silent with regard to the philosophy underlying our current cure to the failures of the past. This is by no means to suggest that the Court should have advocated an ordoliberal renaissance. Nonetheless, what truly disappoints in its presentation of the new modes of economic governance is the lack of any kind of conceptual deliberation about their background and their adequacy. As we have argued in Section III, the new modes of European economic governance amount to nothing less than a deep transformation of the state of the European Union. To put it slightly differently: is the CJEU legitimated to depart from the law as it stands and to replace it with a new regime?

The Court finds an easy answer:

> Since Article 122(1) TFEU does not constitute an appropriate legal basis for any financial assistance from the Union to Member States who are experiencing, or are threatened by, severe financing problems, the establishment of a stability mechanism such as the ESM does not encroach on the powers which that provision confers on the Council.[115]

This is, in itself, a daring assumption. But precisely if one subscribes to the 'bicycle theory' of Europe, and concedes that the constant re-writing of its law is an irrefutable necessity,[116] then one must, all the more, insist both upon an explanation of the new objectives and deliberation on the adequacy of the means which they are employing.

Prior to the *Pringle* judgment, Kaarlo Tuori had developed a transformative theory, which sought to anchor the disregard of the economic philosophy underlying the EMU in a 'second order *telos*':[117]

> [A] teleological interpretation should heed not only the particular telos of the no-bailout clause but also the more general objective of the regulative whole

[114] Ibid, at para. 135.
[115] Ibid, at 116.
[116] See Section V above, with the reference to HP Ipsen in n 22.
[117] See, on the defence of the CJEU, P Craig, 'Pringle: Legal Reasoning, Text, Purpose and Teleology' (2013) 20 *Maastricht J of Comp & Eur L* 3, at 10. Craig characterises the Court's reasoning on Art 15 as 'tenuous' and then uses the two authors cited in the text to strengthen the judicial argumentation, whereas I feel that they reveal its weaknesses further. Ibid, at 8.

> Article 125(1) is part of. And this 'second-order' telos of the no-bailout clause undoubtedly includes the financial stability of the euro area as a whole. This argument supports the legal impeccability of Member-State assistance, in spite of the no-bailout clause and the inapplicability of the emergency provision in Article 122(2) TFEU. But it also justifies and even presupposes, at least to a certain extent, the 'strict conditionality' of assistance.[118]

Tuori's argument can be read as a search for rationality, an effort to shield the law, its production, and its application against its replacement by pure politics. His argument was not available to the Court, and the *Pringle* judgment was obviously not available when Tuori developed it. It is all the more illuminating that the core of his *telos* theory is present in the judgment; in the paragraph already cited, the Court invokes 'the logic of the market' as the rationale of the new regime, and underlines that it is precisely this logic which requires strict conditionality.[119]

In an essay seeking to understand and explain what makes resorting to *topoi* and theorems from economics so attractive for legal scholarship, jurisprudence, and the judiciary in transnational constellations in which the modes of legitimation as we know them from constitutional democracies are not available, Michelle Everson has deciphered the 'processes by which law has transformed itself into an economic technology'.[120] The *Pringle* judgment provides a stunning illustration of her analysis. There is no sinister conspiracy at work in the argumentation of the Court and its supporters, but a serious and desperate effort to defend the law's *proprium*. The tragedy of all these moves remains that 'the logic of the market' fails to deliver the kind of objective orientation which the lawyers hope for. The clearest and, at the same time, most disquieting confirmation of that dilemma can be read in Advocate General Kokott's view:

> Given the mutual interdependence of the Member States' individual economic activities which is encouraged and intended under European Union law, substantial damage *could be* caused by the bankruptcy of one Member State to other Member States also. That damage *might possibly be* so extensive that an additional consequence would be to endanger the survival of monetary union, as submitted by a number of parties to the proceedings.
>
> There is no question here of finding that such a danger to the stability of the monetary union exists or *of examining how such a danger should best be combated*. It must only be emphasized that a broad interpretation of Article 125 TFEU would, also in such circumstances, deprive the Member States of the power to avert the bankruptcy of another Member State and of the ability thereby to attempt to avert damage to

[118] KH Tuori, 'The European Financial Crisis – Constitutional Aspects and Implications', *EUI Working Paper Law 2012/28*, 34.

[119] '[T]he activation of financial assistance by means of a stability mechanism such as the ESM is not compatible with Article 125 TFEU unless it is indispensable for the safeguarding of the financial stability of the euro area as a whole and subject to strict conditions,' *Pringle*, n 69 above, para 135.

[120] M Everson, 'The Fault of (European) Law in (Political and Social) Economic Crisis' (2013) 24 *L & Critique* 107.

> themselves. In my opinion, such an extensive restriction on the sovereignty of the Member States to adopt measures for their own protection cannot be founded on a broad teleological interpretation of a legal provision the wording of which does not unambiguously state that restriction.[121]

The rescue measures are political decisions; they need no legal justification: *auctoritas, non veritas, facit legem*. The replacement of law by discretionary political fiat is pure Schmittianism. It is, therefore, unsurprising that the deeply undemocratic nature of conditionality goes unnoticed or fails to be commented upon.

3.1. An Interim Conclusion

What would have happened to the European Union had its Court of Justice found that Thomas Pringle's concerns about Europe's crisis management were well-founded; that the support mechanisms which the EFSF and the ESM have established interfere with the exclusive European competence for monetary policy; that the amendment of Article 136 TFEU was not possible under the simplified revision procedure enshrined in Article 48(6) TEU; that new policies being adopted and pursued by the Member States jeopardised the primacy of price stability; that the no-bailout provision of Article 125 TFEU prohibited the granting of financial assistance to Member States whose currency is the euro; that the functions assumed by the Commission, the ECB, and the IWF were irreconcilable with the principles on the conferral of powers laid down in Article 13 TFEU; or that the mandate allocated to the CJEU in the ESM Treaty exceeded judicial powers? It is simply impossible to predict the dire consequences.

It is equally difficult to determine what the judgment has accomplished, in terms both of its contribution to the taming of the crisis *and* its effect on Europe's constitutional constellation and the role of law. The situation of the FCC is not much different. The Court could not clarify the factual uncertainties of the financial crisis, and no normative guidance was available to help the Court assess the risks of partisanship for or against the European *praxis*. The German Court decided to (re-)delegate responsibility for present and future consequences to the political process. The European Court elected to prioritise textual formalism over conceptual reasoning – as though Ernst Steindorff never wrote about the politics of law[122] – and without justifying its departure from the type of teleological interpretation on which it tends to rely so heavily.[123] These are but methodological shortcomings. The substantive theoretical default of

[121] View of AG Kokott delivered on 26 October 2012, ECLI:EU:C:2012:675, at paras 139–40; see the *Pringle* judgment, n 69 above.

[122] E Steindorff, 'Politik des Gesetzes als Auslegungsmaßstab im Wirtschaftsrecht' in *Festschrift für Karl Larenz* (Munich: CH Beck, 1973) 217; idem, 'Wirtschaftsordnung und Steuerung durch Privatrecht?' in *Festschrift für Ludwig Raiser* (Tübingen: Mohr Siebeck, 1974) 62.

[123] See, generally, G Beck, *The Legal Reasoning of the Court of Justice of the EU* (Oxford: Hart Publishing, 2013).

both courts is their disregard for Europe's commitments to democracy and the rule of law. This unfortunate complacency is inherent in the politics of conditionality to which both courts subscribe.[124] To rephrase this critique: Do these courts and the academics supporting them 'place a thin veneer of legality on the political which allows the executive to do what it wants'?[125] Do they consciously, or at least implicitly, re-construct the contemporary conditions in which political guidance and rule are provided by the executive, rather than representative institutions, and in which law can no longer be understood as a body of rules but must, instead, content itself with providing standards which are sufficiently vague to empower policy-makers to act according to their understanding of what needs to be done?[126]

At this point, the critique must reflect upon its own premises, particularly its assumption that the integrity of law could have been defended. It is precisely this speculation which may be overly simplistic and naïve. But how can this be determined? Perhaps it would be best to step back and observe these issues from a more removed perspective.

D. A Fictitious Debate between Carl Schmitt and Jürgen Habermas

Europe's financial crisis is not an expression of a faulty way of dealing with prevailing law, but an expression of the imperfection of Europe's legal design – including its configuration of the law-politics relationship. A rare, albeit superficial, consensus has emerged regarding this critical evaluation. Beyond this consensus, the crisis has generated challenges for all disciplines engaged in European studies. This is why it would be presumptuous to venture legal and constitutional policy hypotheses here based upon some definite assessment as to the causes of the crisis, as well as forecasts regarding its further course, intending to provide a blueprint for Europe's future constitutional architecture. The following deliberations will examine these ongoing contestations from a distance, in the form of a fictitious debate between Carl Schmitt and Jürgen Habermas. Considering these names, it may be appropriate to begin by stating

[124] See M Ioannidis, 'EU Financial Assistance Conditionality after "Two Pack"' (2014) 74 *Heidelberg Journal of International Law* (ZaöRV) 61; M Everson, 'An Exercise in Legal Honesty: Re-writing the Court of Justice and the Bundesverfassungsgericht' (2015) 21 *ELJ* 474: '[C]onditionality irrevocably undermines the status of the Member States as "Masters of the Treaties" … Just as the Federal Government within Germany respects the democratic integrity of the *Länder* which make up the federal state, the Federal Republic of Germany cannot, in its relations within the European Union, contract with "slaves". It cannot enter into partnership with anything other than fully sovereign states.'

[125] D Dyzenhaus, *The Constitution of Law: Legality in a Time of Emergency* (Cambridge: CUP, 2006) 103.

[126] E Posner and A Vermeule have underlined that they seek to reconstruct Schmitt's work in 'generizable social-scientific terms'; see their 'Demystifying Schmitt' *Univ of Chicago, Public Law Working Paper No 333* (2010) available at: http://ssrn.com/abstract=1723191.

positions.[127] My personal theoretical home is the discourse theory of law, in both German and European law.[128] It is for an adherent of the Habermasian theory of law and democracy all the more disturbing that Carl Schmitt seems to have gained alarming topicality, not only with his concept of the state of exception and his theorem of a commissarial dictatorship, but also with his theory of the *Großraum* and the diagnosis concerning the 'hour of the executive'.

1. *Carl Schmitt's Shadow Over Europe*

In view of the European dimension of the financial crisis, it seems best to begin with the theory of the *Großraum*, a notion which was explicitly, albeit not exclusively, designed to capture the European constellation. Carl Schmitt selected a memorable occasion to present it: from 29 March 1939 to 1 April 1939, still half a year before the war against Poland, but after the *Anschluss* of Austria and the invasion of Bohemia and Moravia (the *Sudetenland*), at the *Reichsgruppe Hochschullehrer des Nationalsozialistischen Rechtswahrer-Bundes* (Reich section of professors in the National Socialist Association of Lawyers) convened in Kiel. Also during this time period, the Institute for Politics und International Law was celebrating its 25th anniversary. Thus, Carl Schmitt gave his lecture entitled '*Völkerrechtliche Großraumordnung mit Interventionsverbot für raumfremde Mächte. Ein Beitrag zum Reichsbegriff im Völkerrecht*' ('The *Großraum* Order of International Law with a Ban on Intervention for Spatially Foreign Powers: A Contribution to the Concept of *Reich* in International Law') amidst this momentous setting.[129]

The core argument of Schmitt's keynote was that the *jus publicum europaeum*, which had made the sovereign state its central concept, was no longer in line with the *de facto* spatial order of Europe.[130] Following the model of the Monroe Doctrine, a specific 'space' (the *Raum*) had to become the conceptual

[127] An explanatory follow-up to the remarks on *Ersatzunionsrecht* in Section VI.C.1 above may be in place here. For obvious reasons, Germans are particularly concerned about the lasting impact of Schmitt and another 'hour of the executive'. This is by no means to say that the search for administrative legitimacy of European rule as pursued by PL Lindseth (see the references to his work in n 143 below and his recent 'Equilibrium, Demoi-cracy, and Delegation in the Crisis of European Integration' (2014) 15 *German Law Journal* 529 or by Deirdre Curtin (see her Chorley Lecture on 'The Challenge of Executive Democracy in Europe' (2014) 77 *MLR* 1) would operate in the shadow of that legacy.

[128] See C Joerges, 'The Science of Private Law and the Nation-State' in F Snyder (ed), *The Europeanization of Law. The Legal Effects of European Integration* (Oxford: Hart Publishing, 2000) 47; idem, 'Reflections on Habermas' Postnational Constellation' in C Ungureanu, K Guenther and C Joerges (eds), *Jürgen Habermas*, vol 2 (Burlington VT: Ashgate, 2011) XI.

[129] The lecture was published as early as April 1939 in the Institute's series; its 4th edition of 1941 refers to translations into five languages. The quotations in the following are either our own translations of the extremely carefully annotated reprint in G Maschke, *Carl Schmitt, Staat, Großraum, Nomos. Arbeiten aus den Jahren 1916–1969* (Berlin: Duncker & Humblot, 1995), 269, or, as the title reproduced in this text, from *Carl Schmitt: Writings on War*, edited and translated by Timothy Nunan (Cambridge: Polity Press, 2011) 75.

[130] For more detail on the following, see C Joerges, 'Europe a *Großraum*? Shifting Legal Conceptualisations of the Integration Project' in Joerges and Ghaleigh, n 65 above, 167 (reprinted in pt VII, ch 32 of this volume).

basis for international law, with the *Reich* constituting the order of that space. To quote directly: 'The new ordering concept for a new international law is our concept of the *Reich*, with its *Volk*-based, *völkisch Großraum* order.' But what does this mean for the internal order of the *Großraum*? Schmitt refers to the elasticity of the concept of international law, which could also cover the inter-*völkische* relations within a *Großraum* as well. What the *Großraum* requires and constitutes is an 'order that excludes the possibility of intervention on the part of spatially foreign powers and whose guarantor and guardian is a nation that shows itself to be up to this task'.[131]

This claim to leadership was, in Schmitt's words, 'situational',[132] and the overall notion of the *Großraum*, as he underlined in discussions with his Nazi contemporaries, rivals, and critics, was a 'concrete, historical and politically contemporary concept' (*konkreter geschichtlich-politischer Gegenwartsbegriff*).[133] But in so doing, he emphasised elements which he claimed to be valid long-term. The obviousness of the *Großraum* concept, he argued, resulted from transformations dominated by technical, industrial, and economic developments. Thus, Schmitt outlined, albeit somewhat apocryphally, an erosion of the territorial state as the harbinger of the necessity to adapt international law to the factual re-structuring of international relations and the replacement of classical international law by norm systems which, today, would affirmatively be called 'governance structures', or, distanced and critically, 'managerialism'.[134] He underlined two phenomena in particular, namely, the economic interdependencies beyond state frontiers (*Großraumwirtschaft*), and the specific dynamics of technology-driven developments ('technicity' [*Technizität*]).[135] Schmitt had already published on both topics prior to 1933.[136]

[131] See Nunan (ed and trans), n 129 above, at 110. Contemporary reactions attested to how the theory of the *Großraum* with its 'German Monroe doctrine' suited Nazi policy; for this reason, the theory is considered Schmitt's way of indicating his return as a leading legal thinker; see L Gruchmann, *Nationalsozialistische Großraumordnung. Die Konstruktion einer 'deutschen Monroe-Doktrin'* (Stuttgart: DVA, 1992) 11 ff; WE Scheuerman, *Carl Schmitt. The End of Law* (Lanham MD–Boulder CO–New York–Oxford: Rowman & Littlefield, 1965) 161 ff and 169 ff.

[132] On the theoretical understanding, but also the determination with which Schmitt championed this claim of leadership, lucidly H Hofmann, *Legitimität gegen Legalität. Der Weg der politischen Philosophie Carl Schmitts* (Berlin: Duncker & Humblot, 2nd edn 1992) 215 ff; later O Eberl, 'Großraum und Imperium. Die Entwicklung der "Völkerrechtlichen Großraumordnung" aus dem Geiste des totalen Krieges' in R Voigt (ed), *Großraum-Denken. Carl Schmitts Kategorie der Großraumordnung* (Stuttgart: Steiner, 2008). More complacently, in contrast, H Dreier's appreciation in 'Wirtschaftsraum – Großraum – Lebensraum. Facetten eines belasteten Begriffs' in H Dreier, H Forkel and K Laubenthal (eds), *Festschrift 600 Jahre Würzburger Juristenfakultät* (Berlin: Duncker & Humblot, 2002) 47.

[133] Carl Schmitt, *Writings on War*, n 129 above, at 107.

[134] M Koskenniemi, 'Constitutionalism as Mindset: Reflections on Kantian Themes about International Law and Globalization' (2007) 8 *Theoretical Inquiries in Law* 9, at 16; idem, 'Miserable Comforters: International Relations as New Natural Law' (2009) 15 *European Journal of International Relations* 395, at 411.

[135] *Carl Schmitt, Writings on War*, above n 129; on the notion of technicity, see JP McCormick, *Carl Schmitt's Critique of Liberalism: Against Politics as Technology* (Cambridge: CUP, 1997) 42-46, 92-105.

[136] Infamous and important, Carl Schmitt, *Starker Staat und gesunde Wirtschaft. Ein Vortrag vor Wirtschaftsführern* (delivered on 23 November 1932) (1933) 2 *Volk und Reich*, 81; translation:

Schmitt was silent on the internal 'order' of the *Großraum* during the years of war. In the 1941 edition of the *Großraum*, he remained sibylline[137] and only published his famous '*Nomos der Erde im Völkerrecht des Jus Publicum Europaeum*' in 1950, which he had written prior to 1945.[138] But the topic continued to haunt him.[139] When considering Schmitt's theories within the context of the financial crisis, not only must his diagnoses of the loss of nation-state sovereignty and the de-legalisation of their relationships be taken seriously. His observations on the increase of executive power – broadly supported by comparative legal research – must also be taken into account.[140] But here, above all, we are concerned with his theorems of the state of emergency[141] and the (commissarial) dictatorship.[142] Ernst-Wolfgang Böckenförde was the first to take up the term 'state of emergency',[143] and others followed. 'The European Stability Mechanism,' writes Ulrich Hufeld, has 'the format of a constitution-breaching

'Strong State and Sound Economy: An Address to Business Leaders' in R Christi, *Carl Schmitt and Authoritarian Liberalism*, (Cardiff: University of Wales Press, 1998) Annex 212.

137 The preliminary remarks to the 4th edition (Berlin 1941) include the famous motto: 'We are like mariners on a continuing journey, and no book can be more than a log book.'

138 C Schmitt, *Der Nomos der Erde im Völkerrecht des Jus Publicum Europaeum* [1950], reprinted by Duncker & Humblot, Berlin, 1988 [*The Nomos of the Earth in the International Law of the* Jus Publicum Europaeum, trans GL Ulmen (New York: Telos Press Publishing, 2008)].

139 C Schmitt, 'Die legale Weltrevolution. Politischer Mehrwert als Prämie auf juristische Legalität und Superlegalität' (1978) 17 *Der Staat* 321. In this tribute to the French economic theorist François Perroux, who examined apparently related economic dimensions of space, we read at 328: 'Heute geht es um das der wissenschaftlich-technisch-industriellen Entwicklung adäquate politische System der Gesellschaft' ['Today, we have to consider the potential of the society's political system to keep pace with scientific-technical-industrial developments.'] 'Today the adage is *cujus industria, ejus regio or cujus regio, ejus industria*.' One page thereafter he continues: 'Die industrielle Gesellschaft ist an eine Rationationalisierung gebunden, zu der auch die Verwandlung des Rechts in Legalität gehört' ['Industrialised society is bound to rationalisation, including the transformation of law into legality'].

140 C Schmitt, 'Vergleichender Überblick über die neueste Entwicklung des Problems gesetzgeberischer Ermächtigungen (legislative Delegationen)' (1938) 6 *Zeitschrift für ausländisches öffentliches Recht und Völkerrecht* 252; on this, of course under the impression of the American understanding of the executive, see PL Lindseth, *Power and Legitimacy. Reconciling Europe and the Nation-State* (Oxford: OUP, 2010) 62 ff. Lindseth has underlined the importance and topicality of this aspect of Schmitt's work already in his essay on 'The Paradox of Parliamentary Supremacy: Delegation, Democracy and Dictatorship in Germany and France, 1920s–1950s' (2004) 113 *Yale LJ* 1343, 1354, 1382.

141 JP McCormick, *Carl Schmitt's Critique*, n 135 above, 122 ff; E Kennedy, 'Emergency Government within the Bounds of the Constitution: An Introduction to Carl Schmitt, "The Dictatorship of the Reich President according to Art 48 WRV"' (2011) 18 *Constellations* 284.

142 C Schmitt, *Die Diktatur. Von den Anfängen des modernen Souveränitätsgedankens bis zum proletarischen Klassenkampf* [1921] (Berlin: Dunker & Humblot, 5th reprint, 1989). As examples from the copious literature cf the explanations in Hofmann, n 132 above), at 62 ff (state of emergency) and 70 ff (dictatorship).

143 E-W Böckenförde, 'Kennt die europäische Not kein Gebot? Die Webfehler der EU und die Notwendigkeit einer neuen politischen Entscheidung' *Neue Züricher Zeitung*, 21 June 2010; see, also, E-W Böckenförde, 'Wissenschaft, Politik, Verfassungsgericht' (2012) 67 *Juristenzeitung* 197.

measure along the lines of Carl Schmitt's conceptualization of contrasts',[144] and adds a quotation from Schmitt's 1928 *Constitutional Theory*:

> Such breakout entities are, by nature, measures, not norms … Their necessity arises from the particular circumstances of an individual case, an unexpected abnormal situation. If, in the interest of the whole, such renegade entities are formed, the superiority of the existential over mere normativity is apparent. Whoever authorised such acts and is capable of acting, is sovereign.[145]

In a tone of urgency, Frank Schorkopf calls the calamity that we are dealing with a 'crisis without an alternative';[146] a constellation in which the actors, including the governments and the executive branches, 'merely have power within the existing conditions, but not over them'.[147] Anna-Bettina Kaiser arrives at her position following a precise reconstruction of the debates around Article 48(2) of the Weimar Constitution.[148] The handling of this provision and the extensive interpretation of Article 122(2) TFEU today are in her view equally dubious and can be placed at the same level.[149] Furthermore, the rules laid down in the Six-Pack, the Two-Pack, and the TSCG must not be sugar-coated.[150] Yet is the academic community fulfilling its responsibility by merely accepting that the provisions of the EMU are dysfunctional, and abstracting from the dilemma of the political in the EU?

We cannot escape from Carl Schmitt's shadow that easily. The concept of 'commissarial dictatorship' is most plausible to except to. After all, in the current management of the crisis, the actors are not alone. They must come to an arrangement not only at a supranational level, but also between the levels of the multilevel governance system, as well as internationally – the dictator has been replaced by technicity. But how comforting is this? The fact remains that the new form of European government collides with democratically legitimised institutions and processes. Thus, it is anything but comforting that the new European practice coincides with ideas of prominent American constitutionalists who draw upon Carl Schmitt in order to turn away from James Madison

[144] U Hufeld, 'Zwischen Notrettung und Rütlischwur: der Umbau der Wirtschafts- und Währungsunion in der Krise' (2011) 34 *Integration* 117, at 122.

[145] C Schmitt, *Verfassungslehre* [1928] (Berlin: Duncker & Humblot, 10th edn 2010) 107 (this author's translation, 2010).

[146] F Schorkopf, 'Gestaltung mit Recht – Prägekraft und Selbststand des Rechts in einer Rechtsgemeinschaft', (2011) 136 *Archiv des öffentlichen Rechts* 323, at 341 ff; idem, 'Finanzkrisen als Herausforderung der internationalen, europäischen und nationalen Rechtssetzung' (2012) 71 *Veröffentlichungen der Vereinigung der Deutschen Staatsrechtslehrer* 183.

[147] Schorkopf, 'Finanzkrisen', n 146, at 225.

[148] A-B Kaiser, 'Die Verantwortung der Staatsrechtslehre in Krisenzeiten – Art. 48 WRV im Spiegel der Staatsrechtslehrertagung und des Deutschen Juristentages 1924' in UJ Schröder and A von Ungern-Sternberg (eds), *Zur Aktualität der Weimarer Staatsrechtslehre* (Tübingen: Mohr Siebeck, 2011) 119.

[149] Ibid, at 140.

[150] See Section VI.C above.

and argue the case for a plebiscitary democracy in place of a representative one; theorists who advocate delegating political power to the executive in case of need.[151] And are we, perhaps, exchanging Scylla for Charybdis? Anyone who observes the busy activities of the Commission's Services – their tireless production of additional lists of criteria for ever more policy fields, in ever more regions – will remember Carl Schmitt's words about the 'total' but by no means 'strong' state, which he linked with a polemic against all technocratic efforts that believe they can decide 'all issues according to technical and economic expert knowledge following supposedly purely substantive, purely technical and purely economic considerations'.[152] Ironically, Schmitt's late essay,[153] quoted above, provides a situational, theoretical interpretation of this. Reading Hans Peter Ipsen's 1,000-page tome on European law, Schmitt confessed, he was 'stricken with deep sorrow', for the following reason: the approach of European law, which 'legalises' a technocratic-functional administration of European associations, has no concept of a 'legitimate political' project.[154] Therefore, one cannot speak of the rule of law (*Rechtsstaatlichkeit*), much less of democracy. Now, one must take into account what *Rechtsstaatlichkeit*[155] and democracy meant to

[151] EA Posner and A Vermeule, *The Executive Unbound. After the Madisonian Republic* (Oxford: OUP, 2011) at 8: 'When emergencies occur, legislatures acting under real constraints of time, expertise, and institutional energy typically face the choice between doing nothing at all or delegating new powers to the executive to manage the crisis'; the book is riddled with such pronouncements; on this see N Urbinati, *Democracy Disfigured, Opinion, Truth, and the People* (Cambridge MA: Harvard University Press, 2014) ch 4; for a critical discussion of the empirical dimensions and claims of *The Executive Unbound*, see AZ Huq, 'Binding the Executive (by Law or by Politics)' (2012) 79 *U Chi L Rev* 777. In an earlier essay, Posner and Vermeule underlined that they seek to re-construct Schmitt's work in 'generizable social-scientific terms'; see Posner and Vermeule, n 126 above. I am by no means the only one to underline, and to relativise, the topicality of Schmittian notions in the present state of the European project: 'Without a modicum of legitimacy derived from any European treaties, the austerity dictates of the Troika (comprised of the EU, the ECB, and the IMF) have insinuated themselves as the sovereign acts in the distinctly Schmittian sense of the term, ie, as extra-legal decisions on the exception', M Marder, 'Carl Schmitt and the De-Constitutionalisation of Europe', contribution to Conference on 'Europe after the Euro-crisis: Legitimacy, Democracy and Justice', organised by the Institute for Democratic Governance, Bilbao, 2–3 September 2013 (ms on file with the author).

[152] C Schmitt, 'Die Wendung zum totalen Staat' ['The Turn to the Total State'] (1931) *Europäische Revue*, quoted according to the reprint in Carl Schmitt, *Positionen und Begriffe im Kampf mit Weimar-Genf-Versailles, 1923–1939* (Berlin: Duncker & Humblot, 3rd reprint 1988) 146. On this, see, also, Carl Schmitt, *Der Hüter der Verfassung* [1932] (Berlin: Duncker & Humblot, 2nd edn 1969) 78 ff; on all this, see WE Scheuerman, n 131 above, 85 ff.

[153] C Schmitt, 'Die legale Weltrevolution. Politischer Mehrwert als Prämie auf juristische Legalität und Superlegalität' (1978) 17 *Der Staat* 335.

[154] On the recourse to the duality of legality and legitimacy in the present context, see R Mehring, 'Der "Nomos" nach 1945 bei Carl Schmitt und Jürgen Habermas' *Forum historiae iuris*, available at: www.forhistiur.de/zitat/0603mehring.htm, paras. 20-26.

[155] On the theory of the *Rechtsstaat*, see I Maus, *Rechtstheorie und Politische Theorie im Industriekapitalismus* (Munich: Fink, 1986). Schmitt's differentiation of the categories of 'formal' and 'political' concepts of law and legislation (Schmitt, *Verfassungslehre*, n 145 above, at 143 ff), between the generality of laws and the concrete political act of will, leads him to executive and governmental law-making in the contribution mentioned in n 140 above; see Hofmann, n 132 above, 83 ff.

Schmitt. In *Constitutional Theory*, he writes that democracy 'is a state form that is consistent with the principle of identity (eg, of the concretely existing people identified with itself as a political unit)' – and consequently, it cannot apply to an ethnically diverse Europe.[156] After all this, Jürgen Habermas' reply is all the more important.[157]

2. *The Crisis as Opportunity According to Jürgen Habermas*

In view of the crisis, Jürgen Habermas has brought his prestige and powerful eloquence to bear. His countless public interventions have been published across Europe in many languages. 'Democracy is at stake', he has warned time and time again,[158] and Europe risks establishing a post-democratic regime of 'executive federalism'.[159] These drastic messages, though, are always accompanied by signals of hope and political appeals. He intends listeners to view the crisis as an opportunity to strengthen the European project. The 'strength' which he advocates is not merely Europe's managerial potential; to Habermas, 'more Europe' also means a deepening of Europe's democratic credentials.

In contrast to so many commentators on the debate regarding the financial crisis and the future of Europe, in his passionate pronouncements Habermas pursues a demanding and coherent agenda based upon his long-term explorations of the many facets of the European project. His work on this theoretical basis started with the essay 'Citizenship and National Identity',[160] just prior to

[156] Schmitt, *Verfassungslehre*, n 145 above, 223 (1928) (reprinted in 2010); see UK Preuß, 'Die Weimarer Republik – ein Laboratorium für neues verfassungsrechtliches Denken' in A Göbel (ed), *Metamorphosen des Politischen: Grundfragen politischer Einheitsbildung seit den 20er Jahren* (Berlin: Akademie Verlag, 1995) 177 ff, 180 ff.

[157] This exploration is no contribution to the *les-extrêmes-se-touchent* debate around the relationship of Habermas to Schmitt [for an attempt to update it, see E Vollrath, 'Proteus und Medusa. Die politische Apperzeption der deutschen Staatsrechtslehre im Werk von Jürgen Habermas' (1996) 37 *Politische Vierteljahresschrift* 197; see also Mehring, n 154 above]. I let this matter rest in order to be able to discuss how Habermas counters Schmitt's diagnoses and which reasons he uses to support his argument.

[158] Succinctly, eg, in the features section of the *Frankfurter Allgemeine Zeitung* of 4 November 2011 entitled 'Rettet die Würde der Demokratie' ('Rescue the dignity of democracy'). A number of these statements are reprinted in J Habermas, *Zur Verfassung Europas: Ein Essay* (Berlin: Suhrkamp, 2011) 97; a more recent example is his essay in *Le Monde* of 27 October 2011 [English version available at: www.presseurop.eu/en/content/article/1106741-juergen-habermas-democracy-stake]. Habermas's entire work is comprehensively documented and updated weekly in the 'Habermas Forum': at www.habermasforum.dk. A great number of his pertinent essays have recently been reprinted in the journal *Blätter für deutsche und internationale Politik* 3/2014, 85-416 under the title *Der Aufklärer Jürgen Habermas* at the occasion of his 85th birthday on 18 June 2014. They can be downloaded freely at http://habermas-rawls.blogspot.dk/2014/06/e-book-der-aufklarer-jurgen-habermas.html.

[159] See J Habermas, 'A Pact for or against Europe?' in U Guérot and J Hénard (eds), *What does Germany Think about Europe*? (Berlin: European Council on Foreign Relations, 2011) 83, available at: http://habermas-rawls.blogspot.it/2011/07/habermas-pact-for-or-against-europe-in.html.

[160] J Habermas, 'Citizenship and National Identity', first published separately as *Staatsbürgerschaft und nationale Identität* (Zurich: Erker, 1991), reprinted as Annex II to *Between Facts and Norms* (Cambridge MA: The MIT Press, 1999) 491.

the publication of his *magnum opus* on legal theory.[161] Since then, Habermas has ceaselessly occupied himself with the European project, both as a citizen and a theoretician. As a theoretician, he conceives of the process of Europeanisation as a challenge to his theory of the democratically-constituted nation-state; from the perspective of the citizen, he views the process as a response to the catastrophes of the twentieth century, for which Germany bears so much responsibility. This intent is manifested in the project, as well as the objective to defend democratic welfare-state accomplishments in the processes of globalisation and European integration. As a theoretician on the constitutionalisation of Europe, Habermas seeks to accomplish a type of analysis that not only grasps the facticity of the processes of Europeanisation, but also achieves a normative concept that both provides criteria and identifies the institutional conditions for the question of whether the configurations emerging in the process of Europeanisation 'deserve recognition'.[162]

Following his more recent interventions as a citizen, Habermas has approached this aspiration again.[163] He identifies the institutional causes for the crisis and states his polemics against the crisis management in Europe in terminology that critically transforms Schmitt's affirmative observations on the steadily growing power of the executive into critical objections to the present course of the process of Europeanisation.[164] 'Post-democratic executive federalism' is the term he uses to denote – and to criticise – Europe's *praxis*.[165] The European Union must not continue on the path it has taken due to the pressure of the crisis, but cease to coordinate the relevant policies in the gubernative/governative-bureaucratic style which has been customary until now and take the path of adequate democratic legalisation.

The theoretical core of Habermas' essay is found in the reasons he gives for this postulate, in which Habermas specifically continues deliberations by Armin von Bogdandy, Claudio Franzius, and Ulrich K Preuß.[166] He places a dual role for Europe's citizens alongside the recognition that these rights are equally rooted

[161] Faktizität und Geltung. Beiträge zur Diskurstheorie des Rechts und des demokratischen Rechtsstaats (Frankfurt aM: Suhrkamp, 1992).

[162] For a re-construction of Habermas' works, which, however, seeks to (re-) interpret the author for his own ends, see Joerges, *Reflections on Habermas' Postnational Constellation*, n 128 above.

[163] J Habermas, 'The Crisis of the European Union in the Light of a Constitutionalization of International Law' (2012) 23 *EJIL* 335. In the preface to his most recent book, on *The Lure of Technocracy*, n 110 above, Habermas expresses some discontent with the fact that his public interventions did not make it into the general academic discourses.

[164] *Pringle*, CJEU Case C-370/12 at para 296; see Section VI.C.3 above.

[165] See, eg, J Habermas, 'Bringing the Integration of Citizens into Line with the Integration of States' (2012) 18 *ELJ* 485.

[166] 'Basic Priciples' in A v Bogdandy and J Bast (eds), *Principles of European Constitutional Law*, 2nd edn (Oxford: Hart Publishing, 2010) 13, 44; C Franzius, *Europäisches Verfassungsdenken* (Tübingen: Mohr Siebeck, 2010) 49 ff; C Franzius and UK Preuß, *Die Zukunft der Europäischen Demokratie* (Berlin: Heinrich Böll Foundation, Berlin 2012) 33 ff, available at: www.boell.de/downloads/Zukunft_Europaeische_Demokratie.pdf.

in the democratic constitutional state: they remain citizens of their states, but become citizens of the Union as well. With this construct, Europe's ability to be a democracy becomes more theoretically plausible. In addition, however, the construct promises to provide criteria for democratic constitutionalisation of European governance and to come to terms with its functional requirements. But it is precisely at this point that it remains under-specified. It is difficult to imagine which institutional architecture might satisfy Habermas' normative ideas.[167] As long as extreme uncertainties as to the causes of the crisis and the possibility of its democratic cure persist, it is even more difficult to understand which kind of practical guidance they might provide. We are witnessing instead a re-emergence of age-old animosities in Europe's publics, the rise of populist movements and an erosion of the legitimacy of the governments in precisely those countries most deeply affected by the crisis. It remains unclear how a political European leadership with secure democratic legitimation could be established. 'Until these questions and problems are addressed,' American political scientist John McCormick noted in much more tranquil times, 'Schmitt's work and career haunts the study of European integration like a spectre.'[168]

VII. EPILOGUE: FROM 'ONE SIZE FITS ALL' TO 'UNITED IN DIVERSITY!'

The debate on the transformation of Europe's constitutional constellation, its new *Verfassungswirklichkeit*,[169] has only just begun and is bound to continue. Pertinent characterisations oscillate between Executive Federalism (Jürgen Habermas),[170] a Distributive Regulatory State or New Sovereignty with Largely Unfettered Power of Rule (Damian Chalmers),[171] a *Konsolidierungsstaat* (Consolidating State, Wolfgang Streeck),[172] Authoritarian Managerialism (Christian Joerges and Maria Weimer),[173] an Unconstrained Expertocracy

[167] N Scicluna, *EU Constitutionalism*, n 57 above, at 1 who submits: 'So far it has proved difficult, if not impossible, to have a full and inclusive debate on the lofty ideal of "political union" while the Eurozone crisis is still in its emergency phase. As long as this state of emergency persists, European politicians and officials will continue to be heavily focused on the pragmatic, day-to-day steps that (in their opinions) are necessary to save it.' See, also, N Scicluna, 'EU Constitutionalism in Flux? Is the Eurozone Crisis Precipitating Centralisation or Diffusion? (2012) 18 *ELJ* 489.

[168] JP McCormick, 'Carl Schmitt's Europe: Cultural, Imperial and Spatial, Proposals for European Integration, 1923–1955', in Joerges and Ghaleigh (eds), n 65 above, 133 at 141.

[169] The contrast between *Verfassungsrecht* (constitutional law) and *Verfassungsswirklichkeit* (constitutional reality) is another problematical German legacy – again with root in Schmitt, *Verfassungslehre*, n 145 above, 107.

[170] Habermas, 'A Pact for or against Europe?', n 159 above.

[171] D Chalmers, 'The European Redistributive State and the Need for a European Law of Struggle' (2012) 18 *ELJ* 667; and idem, 'European Restatements of Sovereignty', *LSE Working Paper No 10*, 2013.

[172] W Streeck, Buying Time: The Delayed Crisis of Democratic Capitalism (Cambridge: Verso, 2014) 97–164.

[173] Joerges and Weimer, 'A Crisis of Executive Managerialism in the EU: No Alternative?', n 80 above.

(Fritz W Scharpf),[174] an Unbound Executive (Deirdre Curtin),[175] and *Krisenkapitalismus* (Crisis Constitutionalism, H-J Bieling).[176] None of these characterisations are in line with the ever-so positive and optimistic presentation of the integration project which we have been reading for decades.[177] Among the features underlined include the lack of a theoretical/conceptual paradigm; a radical disregard of Friedrich A von Hayek's warnings against the 'pretence of knowledge',[178] a disregard of the rule of law, and a thorough de-legalisation of governance.[179]

What does all this mean for European citizenship? What was once a cherished accomplishment is now characterised by inequalities between the North and the South, the social exclusions of a large part of the European population, and political disempowerment. The present calamities are not without precursors,[180] but the ambivalences of the vision of transnational, albeit nationally dis-embedded, citizenship have, by now, become increasingly apparent and disquieting. I am not trying to go, in this already overly lengthy paper, into any detailed analysis and refer instead to the contributions by Giubboni.[181] Just as it is misconceived to subject a socio-economically and politically diverse Union to the discipline of one currency, the construction of a uniform 'European social model' is a similarly misconceived project.[182]

All foregoing, disheartening diagnoses notwithstanding, this epilogue should not conclude without an outline of what has been announced in the introductory remark: 'But where danger threatens, that which saves from it also grows.'[183] The present state of the Union is unsustainable. The efforts to force Member States and their citizens into the straitjacket of new economic governance are bound to

[174] FW Scharpf, 'Political Legitimacy in a Non-optimal Currency Area' in D Chalmers, M Jachtenfuchs and C Joerges (eds), *The End of the Eurocrats' Dream: Adjusting to European Diversity* (Cambridge: CUP, 2016) 29.

[175] D Curtin, 'The Challenge of Executive Democracy in Europe' (2014) 77 *MLR* 1.

[176] H-J Bieling, 'Das Projekt der Euro-Rettung und die Widersprüche des europäischen Krisenkonstitutionalismus' (2013) 20 *Zeitschrift für Internationale Beziehungen* 89.

[177] For a critique of the European 'political culture of total optimism' and its weak underpinnings, see G Majone, *Rethinking the Union of Europe Post Crisis: Has Integration Gone too Far?* (Cambridge: CUP, 2014) 74–80.

[178] FA v Hayek, Nobel Memorial Lecture (11 December 1974), available at: http://pavroz.ru/files/hayekpretence.pdf.

[179] This is why law should not be called the culprit here; but see KA Armstrong, 'New Governance and the European Union: An Empirical and Conceptual Critique' in *Liber amicorum DM Trubek*, n 80 above, 249.

[180] See M Everson, 'A very Cosmopolitan Citizenship; but who Pays the Price?' in M Dougan, NN Shuibhne and E Spaventa (eds), *Empowerment and Disempowerment of the European Citizen* (Oxford: Hart Publishing, 2013) 145.

[181] S Giubboni, 'European Citizenship, Labour Law and Social Rights in Times of Crisis?' (2014) 15 *German Law Journal* 935.

[182] It is worth noting that very similar disappointments are also becoming a concern in the accession states; see, for an instructive analysis, B Bugaric, 'Europe Against the Left? On Legal Limits to Progressive Politics', *LEQS Paper No 61* (2013).

[183] Höderlin, n 9 above.

fail. The Euro-crisis, somewhat paradoxically and inadvertently, underlines the urgent need for pluralistic variety – the toleration of disagreement and contestation – rather than an ever-more centralised executive Europe. The failures of Europe generate growing unrest and protest among dis-empowered citizens who are exposed to austerity measures, experienced as hopeless and, to a considerable degree, useless suffering. They increasingly provoke the political public, national parliaments, and even the European Parliament. It will become progressively more apparent that it is impossible for the great majority of signatories of the Fiscal Compact to comply with the requirements imposed upon them. It will also become ever more apparent that it is simply impracticable for the great majority of signatories to comply with the requirements imposed upon them, and the '*die neue Umständlichkeit*' (cumbersomeness) of all these procedures will affect their impact.[184]

Hence, there is room for manoeuvre. And yet, to date, any substantial transformation of the established regime remains out of sight. Is it nevertheless conceivable that, in the not-too-distant future, the new policy coordination within the annually repeating European Semester, the reporting and multilateral surveillance obligations, the macro-economic imbalance procedures, and the responses to country-specific recommendations will lead to new assessments of the weight of socio-economic diversity. Growing awareness of the social embeddedness of markets, acknowledgement of the different regulatory, social, and economic cultures in the Member States, may well generate a search for innovative responses to Europe's complex conflict constellations – and sooner or later, even to the developments of standards and criteria which discipline authoritarian managerialism.

It would be absurdly pretentious to promise a 'solution' to these difficulties. But we must not shy away from the construction of projects which seek to respond to the problems which we have identified. The project which I have pursued for more than a decade is 'conflicts-law constitutionalism'.[185] Its analytical and normative core can be briefly summarised as follows: as long as the shape of a pan-European democracy lacks contours, and the conditions for its realisation remain entirely unclear, we must explore alternatives which take into account the difficulties the European project must not, and cannot, avoid.

How should we respond to the reality that the socio-economic disparities in the expanded Union are not melting away? Which conclusions should be drawn from the insight that the neo-liberal interventions to which the 'varieties of capitalism' in the Union have been exposed have repeatedly disintegrative effects? If it is impossible to construct a uniform welfare-state model, is it then advisable to dismantle Europe's welfare-state traditions altogether? If it is not our

[184] For a thorough re-construction, see B Braams, *Koodinierung als Kompetenzkonflikt* (Tübingen: Mohr Siebeck, 2013) 15.

[185] See nn 31 and 33 above.

goal to suppress the painful memories of Europeans, to not iron out the differences between their bitter historical experiences, to not waste the wealth of their cultures, must not tolerance therefore determine the status of European citizens, tolerance which is established in law and based upon the principle of mutual acceptance? These questions are not merely rhetorical. They have a normative point of reference in the optimistic 'motto' of the ill-fated Treaty establishing a Constitution for Europe as 'United in Diversity',[186] which need not remain an empty phrase. My proposal for putting this motto into practice is as follows: Europe must find its constitutional form in a new type of 'conflicts law', which is characterised by two guiding principles. Firstly, the supranational European conflict of laws is to require Member States of the Union to take their neighbours' concerns seriously – in this respect, it aims at compensating the structural democratic deficits of nation-statehood. Secondly, this European conflicts law should structure cooperative solutions to problems in specific areas – thereby reacting to the inter-dependencies of modern societies. Suffice it here to underline three points.

We should shift our attention from the democratic deficit of the EU to the structural democracy deficit of its Member States. Nation-states continuously, and unavoidably, violate the principle that those affected by their laws can 'in the last instance' understand themselves as their authors. The Member States of the Union can be requested to take the impact of their own policies on other jurisdictions into account and *vice versa* – they can expect that their concerns be included in the decision-making processes of the others. In the Union, these commandments correspond to the common commitments to democracy which European law is legitimated to implement. European law has the vocation, and some potential, to compensate these deficits. It can derive its legitimacy from its capacity to correct the democracy deficits of Member States.[187]

The second vocation and task stems from the erosion of the potential of the nation-state to resolve problems autonomously. In the Union, this dependence upon the other transforms itself into duties of cooperation which European law is legitimated to organise. The 'constitutionalisation of co-operation'[188] must then seek to derive its validity from the normative credentials of the very interactions that it organises.

[186] Draft European Constitutional Treaty, Arts 1–8 (16 December 2004).

[187] It seems worth noting that Habermas expresses the same ideas in his recent work on the constitutionalisation of international law: 'Nation-states … encumber each other with the external effects of decisions that impinge on third parties who had no say in the decision-making process. Hence, states cannot escape the need for regulation and coordination in the expanding horizon of a world society that is increasingly self-programming, even at the cultural level'. J Habermas, 'Does the Contitutionalization of International Law still have a Chance?' in idem, *The Divided West* (Cambridge: Polity, 2007) 113, at 176.

[188] C Joerges, PF Kjaer and T Ralli, 'A New Type of Conflicts Law as Constitutional Form in the Postnational Constellation' in eidem (eds), *Conflicts Law as Constitutional Form in the Postnational Constellation*, (2011) 2:2 *Transnational Legal Theory*, 'Special Issue on Conflicts Law as Constitutional Form in the Postnational Constellation' 153.

Conflicts-law constitutionalism was meant to be elaborated further and to proceed as a 're-constructive project'. For example, a re-conceptualisation of European law which would, to a considerable degree, be compatible with European law as it stood, and be able to orient its further development. The re-constructive status was based upon its sociological premises which reflect the European constellation more adequately than the orthodoxy of European law. It seems, indeed, overdue to re-consider the integration project in the light of Europe's ever-growing diversity, to take the conflicts which this diversity generates into account, and to re-orient Europe's agenda from harmonisation and unity to the management of complex conflict constellations.

The last point is the most difficult to defend. Following the financial crisis, such hopes and ambitions are obviously unrealistic, with substantial backing in already existing European law. This bold assertion has suffered numerous setbacks. For example, through the de-legalisation and de-formalisation of European governance.[189] At present, under the pressures of European crisis management, it continues to dwindle, and conflicts-laws constitutionalism is, for the time being, a merely critical project.[190] What can nevertheless be explored are the conflict constellations which the new modes of economic governance and the imposition of austerity politics on a large part of the Union generate – together with the space for counter-movements which the unfortunate state of the Union may generate. That, though, requires another project.

[189] See nn 73 and 76 above.

[190] See Joerges and Weimer, 'A Crisis of Executive Managerialism in the EU: No Alternative?' n 80 above.

24

Conclusion – Part V

I. OUTLOOK: A STATE OF EXCEPTION AS EUROPE'S 'NEW NORMALCY'?

TO PARAPHRASE THE introduction to this part of the book: 'It's been the Economy, stupid!' A huge, still steadily increasing number of monographs, edited volumes and journal articles confirm the topicality of Neil Walker's query about the 'E' in the debates on a European economic constitution.[1] The recent awareness of the importance of the economy, which the cited slogan highlighted, was, of course, triggered by the impact of the financial and state debt crises. The challenge on which the contributions to this part focused is the 'meta-economic', the political dimension of the economy, which requires that the seemingly technical problems of economic governance be addressed in a broader normative framework. A democratisation of the social embeddedness of the economy, we submitted in the introduction, constitutes and has to be understood as the core problem of the 'law of economic integration'.

The debate is intense,[2] but the prospects for widely-shared promising answers are anything but bright. Recent contributions that are not prepared to accept the present situation as Europe's new normalcy[3] oscillate between corrections of the practices of European crisis politics,[4] quests for an 'emergency constitution'[5] and 'targeted measures of disintegration that reduce the EU's supranational

[1] N Walker, 'Where's the "E" in Constitution? A European Puzzle' in A Skordas, G Halmai and L Mardikian (eds), *Economic Constitutionalism in a Turbulent World* (Cheltenham: Edward Elgar, forthcoming), available at https://ssrn.com/abstract=3642534.

[2] Suffice it to mention here K Tuori and K Tuori, *The Eurozone Crisis: A Constitutional Analysis* (Cambridge: CUP, 2014); C Kaupa, *The Pluralist Character of the European Economic Constitution* (Oxford: Hart Publishing, 2016); D Adamski, *Redefining European Economic Integration* (Cambridge: CUP, 2018); Y Drossos, *The Flight of Icarus: European Legal Responses Resulting from the Financial Crisis* (Oxford: Hart Publishing, 2020); PG Teixeira, *The Legal History of the European Banking Union: How European Law Led to the Supranational Integration of the Single Financial Market* (Oxford: Hart Publishing, 2020).

[3] See B de Witte, 'Euro Crisis Responses and the EU Legal Order' (2015) 11 *European Constitutional Law Review* 434.

[4] Eg, M Dawson and F de Witte, 'Constitutional Balance in the EU after the Euro-Crisis' (2013) 76 *MLR* 817.

[5] See C Kreuder-Sonnen, 'Does Europe Need an Emergency Constitution?' (2021) 57 *European Journal of Political Research* 989.

character'.[6] We submitted, in Part I, chapter 3, that legal science should learn to take not only the law but also the limits of judicial decision-making seriously.[7] The idea of 'conflicts-law as Europe's constitutional form' is a proposition that seeks to protect the normative integrity of law while avoiding its overburdening. This proposition is explored in the following part of the book.

II. RELATED PUBLICATIONS

'"Brother, can you paradigm"?, Review Essay of Kaarlo Tuori and Klaus Tuori. *The Eurozone Crisis. A Constitutional Analysis* (Cambridge: CUP, 2014)' (2014) 12 *International Journal of Constitutional Law* 769.

C Joerges and M Weimer, 'A Crisis of Executive Managerialism in the EU: No Alternative?' in G de Búrca, C Kilpatrick and J Scott (eds), *Critical Legal Perspectives on Global Governance – Liber Amicorum for David M Trubek* (Oxford: Hart Publishing, 2014) 295.

[6] 'Can Disintegration be Democratic? The European Union Between Legitimate Change and Regression' (2020) 68 *Political Studies* 582; idem, 'The Democratic Ambivalence of EU Disintegration: A Mapping of Costs and Benefits' (2021) *Swiss Political Science Review*, available at: https://doi.org/10.1111/spsr.12455.

[7] Chapter I.2, Section, text accompanying n 20 ff, and G Lübbe-Wolff, 'Transnational Judicial Interactions and the Diplomatization of Judicial Decision-Making' in C Landfried (ed), *Legitimacy, Effectiveness, and Judicial Methods of Decision-Making* (Cambridge: CUP, 2019) 233.

Part VI

Conflicts Law as Europe's Constitutional Form

25

Introduction: Semantics and Concepts

EUROPEAN LAW NEEDS to be understood as 'conflicts law'. This message is clearly not easily comprehensible. Call it a 'law of norm-collisions', I was advised after the introduction of the term and its use in a number of publications. It was too late to change terminology. The latter term may indeed be less irritating. However, the integration project is constantly concerned with legal diversity, and Europeanisation is the process that responds to diversity, be it through harmonisation, the adoption of common rules or more complex arrangements. 'Norm collision' may sound more comforting than 'conflicts law', but it does not eliminate the problems that the term 'conflicts' denotes more drastically. Each and every step towards harmonisation or uniformity, and the search for some compromise solution has to consider the pros and cons of the jurisdictions concerned. Only in very specific circumstances will the elimination of diversity generate the kind of win-win situation the advocates of market-building tend to promise. Law should be impartial, but it also has to respond to social problems and controversies. Legal change will hence see winners and losers. What is true within national societies is, with important modifications, true between the Member States. The difference is that controversies within societies are replaced by differences between polities. The representatives of these polities will have to aggregate the costs and benefits of Europeanisation in their assessment of European initiatives and judicial dispute settlement. The difference between domestic and European law-making, significant as it is, in no way affects the adequacy of a characterisation of European law as conflicts law. Indeed, it seems more than adequate to refer to conflicts-law methodology in the handling of conflicting objectives within consolidated national systems.[1]

There is, however, another barrier to this understanding: 'conflicts law', or, in the Continental parlance, 'private international law', is concerned only with a specific segment of national legal systems. The 'juridification' of our societies has generated a host of sub-disciplines, each one of which has to take the

[1] Pioneering in this respect were R Wiethölter, 'Begriffs- oder Interessenjurisprudenz:– falsche Fronten im IPR und Wirtschaftsverfassungsrecht. Bemerkungen zur selbstgerechten Kollisionsnorm' in A Lüderitz and J Schröder (eds), *Festschrift für Gerhard Kegel* (Frankfurt aM: Metzner, 1977) 213; and G Teubner and A Fischer-Lescano, 'Regime-Collisions: The Vain Search for Legal Unity in the Fragmentation of Global Law' (2004) 25 *Michigan Journal of International Law* 999.

specifics of its legal field into account. The rules of private international law cannot without further ado be applied – to name just two examples – to international labour relations, let alone to fields of administrative law and governance. European law could – in its foundational phase – neglect this kind of fragmentation simply because of its respect for national autonomy, or, to put it European legal terms, because of the lack of Community competences. The deepening of European integration has affected ever more segments of national legal orders. European law has had to respond. It has done so through the development of new techniques of Europeanisation, such as the formation of transnational governance systems and the establishment of European agencies.[2]

Does the resort to the notion of 'conflicts law' become obsolete or less plausible in the light of these transformations? The core problem of the pre-European disciplines did not disappear. The problem in a nutshell is this: Which legal system is to be applied where the facts of a case (*Sachverhalt*) are related two different legal systems, each of which is democratically legitimated according to its own constitutional rules and claims application upon that basis and in line with its own rules of private international law? This problem will persist as long as Europe remains 'less than a federation', and would, as the example of the United States shows, not necessarily go away even if it became one.

The understanding of European law as conflicts law builds upon these observations. The core idea was first submitted in an analysis of the European committee system ('comitology') in the foodstuffs sector,[3] and the suggestion that Europeanisation should not be criticised as an erosion of national democratic accomplishments but instead be developed into a transnational correction of democratic deficits of national governance. These deficits result from the failure of national law to take the concerns of European citizens into account – non-national citizens who are affected by national laws and policies but who nonetheless have no say in national political will formation.[4]

The first contribution to this part of the book (chapter 26) elaborates on these arguments and generalises them, with the suggestion that conflicts law is the proper 'form' of European constitutionalisation. The second contribution (chapter 27) responds to the Europeanisation of regulatory activities through the internal differentiation and distinction of three dimensions of conflicts law. Finally, chapter 28 explores the potential of the conflicts-law approach to cope with the legitimacy problems of the legal ordering of international trade relations.

[2] See the contributions in pt III of this volume.

[3] See C Joerges and J Neyer, 'From Intergovernmental Bargaining to Deliberative Political Processes: The Constitutionalisation of Comitology' (1997) 3 *ELJ* 273, reprinted in pt III, ch 12 of this volume.

[4] The argument is contested but has prominent partisans, most notably J Habermas, 'Does the Constitutionalization of International Law Still Have a Chance?' in J Habermas, *The Divided West* (Cambridge: Polity Press, 2007) 113, at 176.

26

*United in Diversity as Europe's Vocation and Conflicts Law as Europe's Constitutional Form**

PRELIMINARY REMARKS

'UNITED IN DIVERSITY' was the fortunate motto of the otherwise unfortunate Draft Constitutional Treaty.[1] This motto deserves to be kept alive, despite, or even because of, this failure and the retreat of European politics from overt constitutional ambitions. It is even safe to say that, precisely through these failures, the need to come to grips with the challenges that it articulates have become more obvious. The core problem from which this chapter departs can be simply stated: the Member States of the European Union (EU) are no longer autonomous. They are, in many ways, inter-dependent and hence depend upon cooperation. However, Europe has not transformed into a federation, and it *cannot* become a federation as long as its constituent actors do not agree to the federal vision. Should we, nevertheless, keep the federal perspective alive? The reaction to this question cannot be uniform. In view of the histories of European democracies, their uneven potential and/or willingness to pursue objectives of distributional justice, to respond to economic and financial instabilities, and to cope with environmental challenges, differentiating answers suggest themselves. 'Social Europe' is probably the most delicate among these challenges, as long as it remains, at best, unclear whether and, if so, how, a European federation might respect and re-construct the embeddedness of

* Published in R Nickel and A Greppi (eds), *The Changing Role of Law in the Age of Supra- and Transnational Governance* (Baden-Baden: Nomos, 2014) 125. Core arguments in this chapter were first presented in the Workshop 'The Changing Role of Law in the Age of Supra- and Transnational Governance' on 18–19 November 2009, at the Universidad Carlos III de Madrid; they were developed further in the Opening Lecture of the 'New International Constitutional Law and Administrative Studies' Summer School on 5 July 2010, at the Central European University in Budapest. I would like to express my gratitude to my commentators in Madrid (Patricia Mindus, Turin, Agustín José Menéndez, Leon and Andrea Greppi, Madrid, Carlos III) and the discussants at the Summer School in Budapest. They all have inspired very significantly the elaboration of the present text.

[1] Article I-8 Draft European Constitutional Treaty (OJ C 310/1, 16/12/2004).

Europe's welfare state traditions. This example is by no means exceptional. The sustainability of the whole European project seems to depend upon the construction and institutionalisation of a 'third way' between or beyond the defence of the nation state, on the one hand, and federalist ambitions, on the other. This essay will explore the potential of the conflicts law approach to provide perspectives within which this challenge can be met.

This is not only an immodest, if not overly ambitious, suggestion; it is also one which must not be misunderstood as a sceptical retreat from the European project. As a precautionary move, the chapter will, in its first section, recall Max Weber's classical [inaugural lecture]. It will use this reference to re-construct the lasting merits and accomplishments of the integration project. It will also, in Section II, address the legitimacy *problématique* of this project's institutional design and discuss three significant theoretical efforts of the foundational period to cope with this challenge. The following Section III will analyse the responses of these three theories to the post-foundational dynamics of the integration project. Arguing that all three of these traditions realise an exhaustion of their potential to cope with Europe's present challenges, Section IV will present the conflicts-law approach as an alternative response to Europe's legitimacy *problématique*. Two follow-up sections, one on the recent labour law jurisprudence of the European Court of Justice (ECJ/CJEU) (Section V), the other on its response to the conflict between the Czech Republic and Austria on atomic energy (Section VI), will illustrate the operation of the conflicts-law approach. The concluding Section VII will summarise its problems and perspectives.

I. MAX WEBER'S NATION STATE

Back in 1895, Max Weber gave his inaugural address in the University of Freiburg, then situated in Bismarck's *Kaiserreich* of 1871. The address was published in an enlarged version under the title 'The National State and Economic Policy'.[2] It became a real classic and has now regained a fascinating topicality for two reasons. The first concerns the object of the field study, which Weber used to explain some of his more abstract theoretical positions and provocative political views. The field study dealt with the reasons for, and implications of, the migration of workers. It is of stunning topicality – and the analysis which Weber delivered excels through a precision and subtlety which is difficult to find in the current debates, at least in legal quarters. However, Weber also used this case to explain and defend a vision of the political and economic commitments of the nation state which is, at best, a contrast to the European vocation – but is,

[2] *Der Nationalstaat und die Volkswirtschaftspolitik* (Freiburg i.Br: CA Wagner, 1895) [citations here are from Ben Fowkes' translation in (1980) 9 *Economy and Society* 420].

nevertheless, at least negatively instructive because it helps us to realise to what degree this vision is still alive in contemporary debates and legal arguments.[3]

Weber drew upon the empirical work which he had undertaken in 1892, while still a *Pivatdozent* in Berlin, in the context of a major Enquete of the *Verein für Sozialpolitik* (Association for Social Reform) on the situation of the agrarian work force in the German *Reich*. He had focused there on 'the posting of workers' from Poland to the Prussian Province of West-Prussia. His multi-faceted analysis addressed the transformation of pre-modern patriarchical structures into a capitalist agrarian economy, identified the pressures which these processes exerted on the landowners, and described the incentive structure which fostered the import of 'cheap labour' from the neighbouring regions of Poland and from the deeper East Galicia.[4] The capability of the Poles to endure the poor working conditions and the social situation in the new agrarian economy, so Weber observed, was fostering the gradual increase of the Polish and the decrease of the German share. The great theorist of occidental rationalism felt deeply irritated. Weber expressed his concern about the decline of 'German-ness' (*Deutschtum*) in West Prussia. And, equally irritating in EU-perspectives, he called for corrective state measures: a closure of the borders to migrating workers, and the purchase of land by the state.

Even more irritating, however, is what he submits as his 'subjective' position – the value judgements nurturing his political advice:

> And the nation State is for us not an indefinite something that one feels one can place all the higher the more its essence is shrouded in mystical gloom, but the worldly power organisation of the nation, and in this nation State is raison d'état for us, the ultimate value criterion on economic considerations too. It does not mean to us, as a strange misunderstanding believes: 'state assistance' instead of 'self-help', national regulation of economic life instead of the free play of economic forces, but we want through this slogan to raise the demand that for questions of German national economic policy – including the question whether and how far the State should interfere in economic life or whether and when it ought instead to set the nation's economic forces free to develop themselves and tear down restraints on them – in the individual case the last and decisive vote ought to go to the economic and political power interests of our nation, and its bearer, the German State.[5]

Strong words, indeed. Even Weber's audience in Freiburg was apparently upset, and Weber distanced himself later from this strong language.[6] What

[3] See the stunning example of the Austrian *Oberster Gerichtshof* discussed in Section VI.2.1 below.

[4] See the fascinating reconstruction of Weber's analysis of the underlying transformation processes by O Agevall, 'Science, Values, and the Empirical Argument in Max Weber's Inaugural Address' (2004) 4 *Max Weber Studies* 157.

[5] The translation is not taken from the source in n 2 above, but was done by Iain F Fraser, Florence.

[6] See Max Weber's letter to his brother Alfred, cited in R Aldenhoff-Hübinger, 'Max Weber's Inaugural Address of 1895 in the Context of the Contemporary Debates in Political Economy' (2004) 4 *Max Weber Studies* 143, at 146 note 8. [Weber's contribution to the *Kirchentag* of 1894 cited by R Aldenfoff is reprinted in WJ Mommsen (ed), *Max Weber. Gesamtausgabe*, vol 1.4 (Tübingen: Mohr Siebeck, 1993) 313; the citation is from p 340; the translation is by R Aldenhoff.]

motivated his polemic? Rita Aldenhoff, in her very instructive comments on the address, starts her analysis with a quotation from Weber's contribution to the *Verhandlungen des 5. Evangelisch-sozialen Kongresses* held in Frankfurt in 1894. There, Weber had stated his normative premises quite succinctly:

> We do want … to shape the conditions of life in a way that makes people feel good, but such that, under the pressure of the unavoidable struggle for life, the best in them, the physical and psychological qualities that we want to save for our nation, will be preserved. Well … these are value-judgements and they are changeable. Anyway, there is an irrational element.

Is this a pure nationalist talking? 'German-ness', as defined, can neither be understood as some form of brutal nationalism; nor does it have anything in common with the *homo economicus*, as we know from mainstream economic theorising. Weber's *homini* are human beings; he exposes them to demands of a different quality. What is, at any rate, noteworthy is the care which Weber takes to differentiate between theoretical, economics, and the political orientations which should in his view inform the *Volkswirtschaftspolitik* (economic policy-making). When he diagnoses the readiness of migrant workers from Poland to accept the hardships of their new existence in the 'host state', he is, in fact, describing what we would call a 'race to the bottom' and questioning precisely the 'willingness to starve the most' as the underlying mechanism.[7] There is a very critical dimension in Weber's position, in that he rejects any claim to 'objective validity' of arguments presented in the name of economics; such arguments tend to camouflage normative judgements and political choices – a cardinal sin in the eyes of Weber's epistemology. This is not to defend the substance of Weber's pronouncements. We have reasons to remain irritated when reading about the 'role played by physical and psychological racial differences between nationalities [*sic*!] in their struggle for existence'.[8] But Rita Aldenhoff's reference to Weber's trans-economic *Menschenbild* is a stringent defence of Weber the methodologist against Weber's political polemics. The methodologist remains of great topicality in his critique of spurious claims, not only of the historical school, but also of neo-classical economics[9] – and their negligent contemporary use in misguiding rationalisations of the integration project as a whole and so many of its segments.

[7] See Agevall, n 4 above, at 174.

[8] This opening statement of the inaugural address is a core reference in the debates on Weber's nationalism, see, for example, K Palonen, 'Was Max Weber a "Nationalist"? A Study in the Rhetoric of Conceptual Change' (2001) 1 *Max Weber Studies* 196. Weber's nationalism and his political interventions have later nurtured the suspicion of a *liaison dangereuse* with Carl Schmitt (see K Ebelbrekt, 'What Carl Schmitt picked up in Weber's Seminar: A Historical Controversy Revisited' (2009) 14 *The European Legacy* 667; the young Jürgen Habermas, who had helped to provoke this debate, has clarified his assessment, suggesting that it seems more appropriate to call Carl Schmitt Max Weber's 'natural son' (see the reference in K Engelbrekt at 668).

[9] See Agevall, n 4 above, at 172–74.

II. THE EUROPEAN RESPONSE TO THE FAILURES OF WEBER'S NATION STATES AND THE *PROBLÉMATIQUE* OF ITS INSTITUTIONAL DESIGN

The project of European integration can be understood and re-constructed as a response to the failures of the Weberian nation state, and, more generally and in broader perspectives, to Europe's bitter experiences in the twentieth century. After 50 years of integration, however, we are confronted with massive challenges: ever since the turn to majority voting in the Single European Act of 1987, the compatibility of European rule with its democratic commitments is discussed with ever increasing intensity. In the aftermath of the French and the Dutch referenda of 2005, concerns over its neo-liberal tilt and the social deficit, ie, the compatibility of its institutional design and the welfare traditions of European democracies moved to centre stage. The Irish '*No*' of 2008 to the Treaty of Lisbon was perceived as an erosion of the permissive consensus that had backed the progress of integration. During the present financial crisis the instability of Europe's economic constitution became apparent. All of these unresolved issues and queries seem to suggest that we can no longer be so sure about the sustainability of the European project but have to re-consider our premises.

It would, of course, be absurd to assume that conceptual re-orientations, in an academic legal exercise such as the one we are undertaking, could produce ready-made answers to the type of problems just named, or lead to immediate practical changes. The ambitions which we pursue when suggesting a new way of thinking are much more modest. But, in their conceptualisation of the integration project, they propagate a change of paradigmatic proportions. To summarise and accentuate how they contrast with prevailing views, European law tends to be portrayed as an ever growing and ever more comprehensive body of rules and principles of steadily richer normative qualities. This edifice is expected to come together through successive steps of legal integration. Such visions of the integration project and process rest, in part explicitly, in part implicitly, on daring assumptions about the social functions of law and its powers – and its leitmotif. Giandomenico Majone has recently characterised this conundrum as Europe's 'operational code': the 'priority of integration over all other competing values'.[10] One need by no means subscribe to his diagnosis in all of its aspects when realising that, law can, indeed, use this operational code on its 'integration through law' path only if, and as long as, it insulates itself from many specifics of national orders, from inherited varieties of conflict patterns and institutional mechanisms within economy and society – and even from the aspirations of its Member States and their governments.

[10] Thus, G Majone, *Europe as the Would-be World Power: The EU at Fifty* (Cambridge: CUP, 2010) 1.

The messages which we are going to submit under the title of the 'conflicts law alternative' differ from the prevailing visions most markedly in two respects. As the recourse to the notion of conflicts law indicates, the approach assigns primacy to the resolution of conflicts arising out of Europe's diversity rather than the establishment of a unitary legal regime. Equally important, the approach takes account of the ongoing contestation about the kind of polity which the integration process is to generate. This contestation is not different in principle from the ongoing domestic contests about the proper political order – with the important difference, however, that the law of constitutional democracies provides a framework which channels political contestation, while, in contrast, the law of the integration process cannot build upon this type of legitimating framework. The modesty of the pragmatic ambitions which have underlined must not be understood as some complacent gesture. Quite to the contrary, we believe that the type of thinking and counter-visions which we seek to promote rests on quite solid grounds in the deeper structures of the European fabric. Its most widely-known reference point is the 'unity in diversity' motto of the Draft Constitutional Treaty.[11] Further precursors and allies can be named, such as Joseph Weiler's juxtaposition of 'Europe as unity' v 'Europe as community',[12] and Kalypso Nicolaïdes' vision of a European '*demoi*-cracy'.[13] All that is original about the conflicts-law approach is the plea for a resort to legal categories derived from conflict-of-laws traditions and conflict-of-laws methodologies in the legal re-construction of the 'unity in diversity' challenge.

What kind of validity can our plea for re-orientation claim? The binary right/wrong, legal/illegal, lawful/unlawful codes in which the legal system operates, and to which lawyers appeal in their doctrinal argumentation, cannot be relied upon in our considerations without further ado. All of the important theories of legal integration have operated on horizons which that code cannot reach directly. They reflected the historical context of the integrations project, they sought to cope with the specifics and deficiencies of its institutional design – and, indeed, they continue with similarly comprehensive reflections when addressing Europe's present challenges. The conflicts-law approach situates itself on an equivalent conceptual level. Just like its interlocutors in the legal integration theory, it seeks to re-construct both the accomplishments of the integration project and its present *impasses* and crises, and to evaluate the pros and cons of the competing visions against such a background. It is of crucial importance to underline two limitations of this kind of exercise. It would, for one, be a misunderstanding to expect from the re-constructions of historical contexts and assumptions that they would reveal 'the true story' – a Leopold Rankan tale of

[11] See n 1 above.

[12] See Sections II.3 and III.2.3 below.

[13] K Nicolaïdis, 'The New Constitution as European "*Demoi*-cracy"?' (2004) 7 *Critical Review of International Social and Political Philosophy* 76.

'*wie es wirklich gewesen ist*'. What we seek to understand is the meta-positive assumptions on which legal conceptualisation of the integration project have relied, and from which they sought to derive normative guidance on their contributions to its operation. We will, then, necessarily, and deliberately so, have to proceed selectively, albeit not arbitrarily. Our re-construction will depart from, and be restricted to, three schools of thought of long-term significance. Each of the three approaches has some *fundamentum in re*: each of them can claim to conceptualise important elements of Europe's integration law, and each of them can provide normative reasons for its specific conceptualisation: the model of European rule (*Sozialmodell*) which it defends and promotes. It is a further characteristic of our re-construction that we take account of both the internal developments of each of these models and the continuous contestation among them, along with the ups and downs in terms of their practical impact. We will also argue, however, that all three have, notwithstanding their remarkable viability, deficits in common, which exhaust their potential to cope with the present challenges that Europe faces.

One aspect which the three models have in common can be stated negatively. They were perfectly aware of the discrepancy between the European and the national level of governance, and did not conceive of the European Economic Community as a constitutional democracy in being. What they have in common is a search for legitimate governance beyond nation-state confines and frames. Their messages on the modes of transnational governance, however, differ significantly: (1) 'Europe should be institutionalised as a technocratic regime and be restricted to that function'. (2) 'Europe's vocation is the establishment of an "economic constitution" which is to protect individual freedoms and to discipline the exercise of political power'; and (3) 'Europe has accomplished and should preserve an equilibrium between a supranational legal order and ongoing political bargaining'. We will in this section focus on the foundational period, underline a common deficit; the further development of the three approaches and their potential to cope with the 'transformations of Europe' will be addressed in a separate section (III).

II.1. Europe as Technocratic Administration: Hans Peter Ipsen and Ernst Forsthoff

Hans Peter Ipsen was the influential founding father of European Law in Germany. He was a very remarkable protagonist of Germany's legal scholarship. The Nazi period had left him, to paraphrase Hans Ulrich Jessurun d'Oliveira,[14]

[14] HU Jessurun d'Oliveira, 'An Anecdote, a Footnote' in H-P Mansel et al (eds), *Festschrift fürErik Jayme* (Munich: Sellier. European Law Publishers, 2004) 387. Oliveira, writing in 1968, referred to Hans Dölle, from 1954 onwards one of the Directors of the Max-Planck Institute für auländisches und internationals Privatrecht in Hamburg; on Ipsen, see C Joerges, 'Europe a Großraum? Shifting

'not totally flawless' (*nicht ganz fleckenlos*). His post-war work on the Basic Law of the young German democracy, however, documents very clearly democratic commitments in general, and commitment to the *Sozialstaatlichkeit* of the new order in particular.[15] He had started to work on European law at the age of 50 – and helped to establish *Europarecht* as a new legal discipline.[16] Precisely his democratic commitments may explain both Ipsen's sensitivity for the precarious legitimacy of the European system, on the one hand, and the affinities between his own response and the work of one of Germany's most famous contemporary constitutionalists, namely, Ernst Forsthoff, on the other. These affinities are, at first sight, somewhat surprising in view of the differences in their constitutional theorising;[17] they are, nevertheless, plausible in view of Ipsen's search for a type of rule whose validity was not dependent on democratic legitimacy. The communities were to confine themselves to administering questions of 'knowledge', but leave truly 'political' questions to democratic and legitimated bodies.[18] The characterisation of the European Communities as '*Zweckverbände funktionaler Integration*' (organisations with functionally-defined objectives) was path-breaking. With this theory, Ipsen rejected both further-reaching federal integration notions *and* earlier interpretations of the Community as a mere international organisation. He saw Community law as a *tertium* between (federal) state law and international law, constituted by its 'objective tasks' and adequately legitimised by their solution.[19] This theory had an implicit answer to the queries about 'the social' on offer. Ernst Forsthoff had, in his contribution to the so-called *Sozialstaatskontroverse*, argued that the realisation of social objectives had to operate outside the rule of law; the

Legal Conceptualisations of the Integration Project' in C Joerges and NS Ghaleigh (eds), *Darker Legacies of Law in Europe: The Shadow of National Socialism and Fascism over Europe and its Legal Traditions* (Oxford: Hart Publishing, 2003) 167, at 182, fn 92) reprinted in pt VII, ch 32 of this volume.

[15] Suffice it here to point to HP Ipsen, 'Über das Grundgesetz' (1949), reprinted along with all of his later essays in idem, *Über das Grundgesetz* (Tübingen: Mohr Siebeck, 1988) 1.

[16] See idem, 'Der deutsche Jurist und das Europäische Gemeinschaftsrecht' in *Verhandlungen des 43. Deutschen Juristentages* (Munich: CH Beck, 1964), vol 2 L 14 ff; idem, *Europäisches Gemeinschaftsrecht* (Tübingen: Mohr Siebeck, 1972) 176 ff; very remarkable, in the present context, is his rejection of the idea of an economic constitution at both European and national level: ibid, at 563–66.

[17] See idem, *Über das Grundgesetz*, n 15 above, reprinted also in E Forsthoff (ed), *Rechtsstaatlichkeit und Sozialstaatlichkeit* (Darmstadt: Wissenschaftliche Buchgesellschaft, 1968) 16; and E Forsthoff, 'Begriff und Wesen des sozialen Rechtsstaats' (1954) 12 *Veröffentlichungen der Vereininigung deutschen Staatsrechtslehrer* 8.

[18] *Europäisches Gemeinschaftsrecht*, n 16 above, at 1045.

[19] See HP Ipsen, *Verfassungsperspektiven der Europäischen Gemeinschaften* (Berlin: Walter de Gruyter, 1970) 8 ff, and the interpretation by M Kaufmann, *Europäische Integration und Demokratieprinzip* (Baden-Baden: Nomos, 1997) 300 ff and 312 ff; see, also, M Bach, *Die Bürokratisierung Europas. Verwaltungseliten, Experten und politische Legitimation in Europa* (Frankfurt aM: Campus, 1999) 38 ff.

provision of welfare was hence, by virtue of the very nature of social policies, characterised as an administrative task, which was incompatible with the commitment to the *Rechtsstaat* ('rule of law') in the Basic Law.[20] This was not a principled objection against welfare policies. What is, nevertheless, difficult to conceive is how the European *Zweckverband* with its transnational machinery might actively pursue the type of activities which welfare states administer domestically. In more principled terms, it seemed, at any rate, inconceivable that the type of a 'hard' legal *Sozialstaats*-commitment, which Forsthoff's opponents understood as a constitutive dimension of the Federal Republic's democracy,[21] would be institutionalised at European level.

II.2. Europe's Economic *Ordo*: Walter Eucken and Franz Böhm

The notion of the 'social market economy' was formally introduced into Europe's constitutional parlance by a joint motion of Joschka Fischer and Domenique Villepin in the course of the debates on the Constitutional Treaty.[22] Their initiative was meant to calm down the anxieties over what was perceived as a neo-liberal tilt in the constitutional project. The clause on the social market economy has fulfilled this function quite well in the general public, and in the constitutional discourses of both lawyers[23] and political scientists.[24] The vague notion of the 'social' and simultaneously 'competitive' market economy of the Convention and the Treaty of Lisbon is situated at a great distance from the

[20] Forsthoff, 'Begriff und Wesen des sozialen Rechtstaates', n 17 above.

[21] The so-called *Sozialstaats*-debate is an evergreen in German constitutionalism; for recent contributions, see O Eberl, 'Soziale Demokratie in Europa und zwischen Konstitutionalismus und Etatismus' in A Fischer-Lescano, F Rödl and CU Schmid (eds), *Europäische Gesellschaftsverfassung. Zur Konstitutionalisierung sozialer Demokratie in Europa* (Baden-Baden: Nomos, 2009) 245; A Fischer-Lescano, 'Europäische Rechtspolitik und soziale Demokratie' in Friedrich-Ebert-Stiftung, (2010) *Internationale Politikanalyse*, available at: https://library.fes.de/pdf-files/id/ipa/07082.pdf; C Joerges, '*Rechtsstaat* and Social Europe: How a Classical Tension Resurfaces in the European Integration Process' (2010) 9 *Comparative Sociology* 65.

[22] See the references in C Joerges, 'What is Left of the European Economic Constitution? A Melancholic Eulogy' (2005) 30 *EL Rev* 461, at 486; reprinted in pt V, ch 22 of this volume.

[23] See, for example, FC Mayer, 'Die Rückkehr der Europäischen Verfassung? Ein Leitfaden zum Vertrag von Lissabon' (2008) *Zeitschrift für öffentliches Recht und Völkerrecht* 1141, at 1165 ff; idem, 'Der EuGH und das soziale Europa' in *Internationale Politikanalyse* (Berlin: Friedrich-Ebert-Stiftung, 2009) 7, and the contributions to: U Neergaard, R Nielsen and L Roseberry (eds), *Integrating Welfare Functions into EU Law – From Rome to Lisbon* (Copenhagen: DJØF Publishing, 2009), and, most prominently, the German Constitutional Court's judgment of 30 June 2008 on the Treaty of Lisbon. Bundesverfassungsgericht, file no 2 BvE 2 / 08, 2 BvE 5 / 08, 2 BvR 1010 / 08, 2 BvR 1022 / 08, 2 BvR 1259 / 08 und 2 BvR 182 / 09, paras 195 et seq; the provisional English translation is available at: www.bundesverfassungsgericht.de/entscheidungen/es20090630_2bve000208.en.html.

[24] See, for example, U Liebert, 'Reconciling Social with Market Europe? The EU under the Lisbon Treaty' in D Schiek, U Liebert and H Schneider (eds), *European Economic and Social Constitutionalism after the Treaty of Lisbon* (Cambridge: CUP, 2011) 47.

original and fairly precise contours of Germany '*sozialer Marktwirtschaft*'.[25] As the most important protagonist of the concept, Alfred Müller-Armack, explained repeatedly, the social market economy was to provide a 'third way' beyond economic liberalism, on the one hand, and beyond socialism, on the other. There was conditioning of this model by requirements of 'competitiveness'; quite to the contrary, the governance of market mechanisms was subjected to commands of social justice.[26]

Müller-Armack and his political allies were keen to underline the compatibility of their vision with the ordoliberal school of economics, and the essential role assigned to economic freedoms and the protection of an undistorted system of competition by law and strong politically-independent enforcement authorities. The development of ordoliberalism as an economic theory and vision of a political order had started in the early 1920s as a counter-move against the strong cartelisation of the German economy and its corporatist links with a weak political system. The school survived National Socialism; it was perceived as one among the German traditions not contaminated by National Socialism and therefore entitled to broad public recognition and influence. The details need not concern us here. What is important to note, however, is our concern for the social dimension of the European project, the initial compatibility of ordoliberalism and the model of the social market, and the dissolution of this alliance, which was replaced by a new alliance between the second generation of ordoliberalism and Anglo-Saxon neoliberalism.

The leading protagonists of the Freiburg School, the intellectual *Heimat* of Germany's post-war ordoliberalism in both economic and legal scholarship, namely, Walter Eucken and Franz Böhm, derived from the dual commitments to the idea of an 'undistorted system of competition', on the one hand, and to the promise of social justice and security, on the other, a challenging task: the dual commitment required institutionalising specific, albeit inter-dependent, orders, namely, a legally-structured order of industrial relations and of social security ('*Arbeits- und Sozialverfassung*') along with the legally guaranteed economic *ordo*, the 'economic constitution' (*Wirtschaftsverfassung*). In this sense, the economic order the protagonists of the 'social market economy' envisaged was meant to be 'socially embedded'.

The 'really existing social market economy', however, was never as coherently realised as their conceptual *Vordenker* would have liked to see it. Even

[25] See, on the following, P Manow, 'Modell Deutschland as an Interdenominational Compromise', *Minda De Gunzburg Centre for European Studies, Working Paper 003/2001*; A Ebner, 'The Intellectual Foundations of the Social Market Economy. Theory, Policy, and Implications for European Integration' (2006) 33 *Journal of Economic Studies* 206.

[26] See, the references in C Joerges and F Rödl, '"Social Market Economy" as Europe's Social Model?' in L Magnusson and B Stråth (eds), *A European Social Citizenship? Preconditions for Future Policies in Historical Light: Preconditions for Future Policies from a Historical Perspective* (Brussels: Peter Lang, 2005) 125.

its economic core institution – its *Wirtschaftsverfassung* – was, by no means, a theoretically uncontested and legally consolidated project. The strongest practical challenge to the Freiburg style of *Ordnungspolitik* was the *renaissance* of Germany's corporatist traditions already in the early years of the Bonn Republic. The Federal Republic was characterised by permanent tensions between *Theorie und Praxis*: striking discrepancies between the officious rhetoric of *Ordnungspolitik*, on the one hand, and the ongoing bargaining between the political system and the political and economic actors, on the other – a German *Lebenslüge*, to be sure, albeit an economically successful and socially beneficial arrangement.[27] The perception of this discrepancy will have influenced the (ordo-) liberal 'turn to Europe', which implied a retraction from their earlier more global political preference.[28] The European level of governance promised to ensure stronger barriers against the *renaissance* of Germany's corporatist traditions and its political opportunism in economic affairs than the institutional pillars of Germany's *Ordnungspolitik*.

II.3. Europe as Community: Joseph HH Weiler

In his very first publication on European issues,[29] Joseph Weiler presented a vision, which he substantiated and defended in his PhD thesis,[30] then retold, refined and complemented in his seminal narrative on the 'Transformation of Europe':[31] Europe has, in its foundational period, so Weiler argued, managed to establish an equilibrium between legal supranationalism and political intergovernmentalism. His portrayal of European integration was inspired by his teachers in international law, on the one hand, and by the work of Erik Stein, on the other, but it was path-breaking and unique in its doctrinal lucidity and its sensitivity for the European synthesis of 'the political' and the law.

Weiler's *œuvre* is a powerful critique of the type of national state which Weber's inaugural address describes.[32] Nowhere, however, did he talk about

[27] Well documented by W Abelshauser, Die Langen Fünfziger Jahre. Wirtschaft und Gesellschaft in Deutschland 1949–1966 (Düsseldorf: Schwann, 1987).

[28] The scepticism and resistance of leading ordo-liberals has been re-constructed and explained in detail by M Wegmann, Fruher Neoliberalismus und europaische Integration: Interdependenz der nationalen, supranationalen und internationalen Ordnung von Wirtschaft und Gesellschaft (1932–1965) (Baden-Baden: Nomos, 2002) especially at 351 ff, for the importance of the political and social constitution for the project of economic integration (359–66).

[29] JHH Weiler, 'The Community System: The Dual Character of Supranationalism' (1981) 1 *Yearbook of European Law* 257.

[30] Idem, Il sistema comunitario europeo: struttura giuridica e processo politico (Bologna: Il Mulino, 1985).

[31] Idem, 'The Transformation of Europe' (1990-91) 100 *Yale Law Journal* 2403.

[32] See the thorough analysis by D Gaus, 'Legitimate Political Rule without a State? An Analysis of Joseph HH Weiler's Justification of the Legitimacy of the European Union qua Non-statehood', *RECON Online Working paper 2008/12*, available at: www.reconproject.eu/projectweb/portalproject/RECONWorkingPapers.html.

something akin to 'social Europe'. Even in the concluding passages on democracy in Europe and the legitimacy of the integration project of the 'Transformations of Europe', there is no mention of the possibility that democracy might presuppose social justice and that Europe's socially-defined legitimacy might erode through a destruction of welfare state traditions. And yet, even though Weiler's value-laden work is characterised by a considerable distance from technocratic precepts and economic rationalisation of the European Community, his visions seem surprisingly compatible with the benign neglect of the 'social deficit' of the European order in European legal studies during the foundational period. To be sure, Weiler's re-construction of the Europe as a Janus-headed polity was not meant as a conceptualisation which would exclude Europe's engagement in social issues as a matter of (legal) principle. It is, nevertheless, true that, thanks to the *Realpolitik*-kernel of his analysis, 'social Europe' was an unlikely option, and one of very limited significance, anyway. It was highly unlikely simply because its advent was dependent on unanimous inter-governmental voting; it was, by the same token, of little concern, as the later tensions between the integrationist objective and the legacy of European welfarism were still dormant.

II.4. Three Concluding Observations

As an interim summary, we can put on record an ambivalent legacy of the foundational period. On its bright side, we note the turning away from the Weberian nation state; less fortunate, however, was the benign neglect of the welfarist commitments of West European democracies. Both aspects deserve some further comments.

II.4.1. The Taming of Weber's National State

The designers of the EEC Treaty were both realistic and wise enough to understand that the darker legacy of the European political and economic nationalism would not fade away with the end of the war. Their objectives, however, were institutionalised prudently. The three foundational theories which we have sketched out have understood these messages and integrated them into their conceptualisation of the European project: no discrimination on grounds of nationality, no resorting to the political power of the state as an instrument of parochial economic advantages, common economic freedoms in the pursuit of economic prosperity – this was the lesson Europe seemed to have learned.

II.4.2. The Neglect of the Welfare State Legacy of European Democracies

We have defined the second communality of the early legal-integration theories negatively. It is more troubling, because the institutionalisation of welfare commitments could be, and was in fact, widely understood as a 'second pillar' of Europe's democratic conversion, a societal shield providing protection against a rebirth of the social anxieties which nationalist movements had instrumentalised. Why is it, we are both inclined and entitled to ask, that precisely the welfare state traditions of European democracies are not visible in the legal theories of European integration? Why does it need historians like Alan Milward[33] and Tony Judt[34] to remind Europe's legal academia that welfare traditions are what Europeans *do* have in common and what distinguishes their collective memories from that of American citizens? Why does it need political-scientists like Fritz Scharpf[35] and Giandomenico Majone[36] to remind European constitutionalists, albeit in very different perspectives, of the structural asymmetries in their constitutional visions? How is it that a scholar of the format and sensitivity of Joseph Weiler, in his seminal narrative on the 'Transformation of Europe',[37] fails to address the issue of 'social Europe' and, even in his comment on the Treaty of Maastricht, continues to present 'prosperity' as Europe's second value without ever referring to social justice. What he offers, instead, is quite in line with his appeal to 'Community', a somewhat metaphorical uploading of the notion of 'prosperity' with a 'solidarity' dimension: a soft power, which he expects to control 'the demonic at the statal economic level'.[38] Is it by chance that, in European constitutionalism, it took primarily labour lawyers to remind us of the importance of 'the social' for democratic constitutionalism?[39]

The omission of a 'social dimension' in the conceptualisation of the European project seems not so much a surprising omission, as a downright failure. During the foundational period, welfare state policies and practices were, of course, controversial in many respects, but they were understood as *national* affairs. Only with hindsight have the implications and effects of this constellation

[33] A Milward, *The European Rescue of the European Nation-State*, 2nd edn (London: Routledge, 2000) 21 ff.

[34] T Judt, *Postwar: A History of Europe since 1945* (New York: The Penguin Press, 2005) 791 ff; idem, *Ill Fares the Land* (New York: The Penguin Press, 2010) 127 and passim.

[35] See, for example, FW Scharpf, 'The European Social Model: Coping with the Challenges of Diversity' (2002) 40 *JCMS* 645, at 645–46, and, recently, 'The Asymmetry of European Integration – Or Why the EU cannot be a Social Market Economy', *MPIfG Working Paper 09/12*, available at: www.mpifg.de.

[36] *Europe as the Would-be World Power*, n 10 above, 128 ff. Majone is well aware, however, of the foundational moment; see his classic *Regulating Europe* (London-New York: Routledge, 1996) 1: 'At the end of the period of reconstruction of the national economies shattered by the war income redistribution and discretionary macroeconomic management emerged as the top policy priorities of most Western European governments …'

[37] N 31 above; see, in particular, 2476 ff.

[38] See JHH Weiler, 'Fin-de-Siècle Europe' in R Dehousse (ed), *Europe After Maastricht: An Ever Closer Union?* (Munich: CH Beck, 1994) 203, at 208 ff.

[39] See B Bercusson, 'Social Policy at the Crossroads: European Labour Law after Maastricht' in Dehousse (ed), n 38 above, 149; S Giubboni, *Social Rights and Market Freedoms in the European Constitution: A Labour Law Perspective* (Cambridge: CUP, 2006); B Bercusson, S Deakin, P Koistinen, Y Kravaritou, U Mückenberger and A Supiot, 'A Manifesto for Social Europe' (1997) 3 *ELJ* 189.

become so clearly visible. Stefano Giubboni, who has re-constructed both the mindset of the 'founding fathers' and the political bargaining over the Treaty of Rome carefully, concludes that we have to understand this outcome not as a mere failure but as a 'historical compromise'.[40] The parties to this compromise are said to have trusted in the wisdom of eminent economists who expected very positive effects from an opening of national *Volkswirtschaften*;[41] they may also have trusted in the sustainability of a constellation which eminent political scientists were to characterise as an politically and socially 'embedded liberalism'.[42] Such positive expectations seem compatible with stringent transnational regulation where such interventionism were held to be indispensable, ie, in agricultural policy. Legal scholarship, however, treated this socially extremely important and economically extremely costly domain as an 'exception' in the European edifice, which did not deserve, and did not, in fact, attract, closer academic scrutiny for a very long time to come.[43]

II.4.3. Historical Indeterminacy and the Indispensability of Theory in Legal Argumentation

The differences in the re-construction of the foundational constellation between the institutional generalists in European legal scholarship, on the one hand, and a later generation of labour law constitutionalists, on the other, are quite illuminating: Brian Bercusson, writing under the impression of the Treaty of Maastricht, put all his hopes on the 'outstanding importance' of what was accomplished therein.[44] Stefano Giubboni,[45] writing a decade later, complemented the projection of positive signals into the European development in his comments on the later Treaty amendments and the (Draft) Constitutional Treaty;[46] in addition, he started to seek legally relevant backing for his views in the 'compromise' which he read into the Treaty of Rome:

> [T]he apparent flimsiness of the social provisions of the Treaty of Rome (and of the slightly less meagre ones of the Treaty of Paris) was in reality consistent with the

[40] Giubboni, n 39 above, 7.

[41] See, most notably, the 'Ohlin Report': International Labour Organization, 'Social Aspects of European Economic Co-operation. Report by a Group of Experts' (1956) 74 *International Labour Review* 99.

[42] JG Ruggie, 'International Regimes, Transactions and Change: Embedded Liberalism in the Postwar Economic Order' (1982) 36 *International Organization* 375; see J Steffek, *Embedded Liberalism and its Critics: Justifying Global Governance in the American Century* (New York: Palgrave Macmillan, 2006).

[43] Until F Snyder, *Law of the Common Agricultural Policy* (London: Sweet & Maxwell, 1985); for a comprehensive recent analysis, see K Zurek, *European Food Regulation after Enlargement: Facing the Challenges of Diversity* (Leiden: Nijhoff, 2011) 149 ff.

[44] Bercusson, 'Social Policy at the Croosroads', n 39 above, 183.

[45] *Diritti Sociali e Mercato. La Dimensione Sociale dell'Integrazione Europea* (Bologna: Il Molino, 2003); (English version in n 39 above).

[46] Giubboni, *Social Rights*, n 39 above, at 94.

> intention, imbued with the embedded liberalism compromise, not only to preserve but hopefully to expand and strengthen the member States' powers of economic intervention and social governance: ie, their ability to keep the promise of protection underlying the new social contract signed by their own citizens at the end of the war.[47]

Lasciate ogni speranza is, instead, the main message of Florian Rödl,[48] writing after *Viking* and *Laval*, as far as the actual development of the Union is concerned. He renews, however, the defence of 'Social Europe' by the re-construction of the foundational constellation as a legally significant 'compromise'. It seems, indeed, plausible to argue that the premises of the negotiators and their understanding of the EEC Treaty should be taken into account in the interpretation of Treaty provisions such as Article 153 (5) TFEU (ex-Article 137 (5)), which stipulates that 'the provisions of this Article shall not apply to pay, the right of association, the right to strike and the right to impose lock-out'.[49] The legal surplus of such suggestions seems minimal, however, and is a shaky ground for far-reaching conclusions as to the Union's social commitments. The Treaty of Rome has mentioned, in its Title III of Part Three, significant social fields, and Member States were, as Article 118 EEC Treaty confirms, expected to cooperate closely. It is also true that distributional and income policies were foreseen in an important part of the European Economy, namely, agriculture. Agustín José Menéndez[50] reads these provisions as strong elements of a federal structure foreshadowing the strengthening of the federalisation of Europe, whereas, in Giandomenico Majone's view,[51] they confirm that the social-policy domain, was 'considered to be outside the competence of the supranational institutions'.[52] Both of these readings are based upon the same historical evidence. Both of them can claim to be valid – but they need to base their claims upon re-constructions which are informed by non-historical theoretical premises.

What we can more safely suggest is simply that the negotiators operated on the assumption of some kind of 'embedded liberalism' and its sustainability, so that the protagonists of welfare policies could live with the compromise. If such expectations proved to be wrong, legal reasoning must not assume that conclusive normative arguments can be derived from 'historical facts'; it must, instead, engage in conceptual deliberations and controversies. It must become

[47] Ibid, at 16.

[48] F Rödl, 'Labour Constitution' in A v Bogdandy and J Bast (eds), *Principles of European Constitutional Law* (Oxford: Hart, 2010) 605; for a very similar argument, see L Niglia, 'Form and Substance in European Constitutional Law: The "Social" Character of Indirect Effect' (2010) 16 *ELJ* 439.

[49] On the doctrinal controversies on this provision, see Section V.3.2. below.

[50] 'United they Diverge? From Conflicts to Constitutional Theory? Critical Remarks on Joerges' Theory of Conflicts of Law' in R Nickel and A Greppi (eds), *The Changing Role of Law*, n * above, 241.

[51] Majone, *Europe as he Would-be World Power*, n 10 above, 131 ff.

[52] Ibid, 132.

aware of the non-historical normative and analytical issues underlying historical re-constructions like those we have just mentioned. These issues are complex and sensitive: Does democratic governance, as a matter of principle, require that the objectives of social justice can be pursued by the political system? If so, is it at all conceivable that welfare policies can be successful institutionalised at European level, or is it, in view of the diversity of socio-economic conditions, political traditions and preference, more promising to preserve their variety?

III. HINDSIGHT AND FORESIGHT

We have started this chapter by listing some enormous challenges which Europe is facing today. The 'social deficit', which we have traced back to the institutional design of the Treaty of Rome, is just one of them, albeit one of particular importance in view of the collateral damage in terms of the social acceptance of the Union and the growing risks of populism and xenophobia. The social deficit furthermore illustrates particularly drastically the *impasses* of European politics, which result from the reliance of the integration project on the so-called Community Method. We will – in the first step of this section – illustrate these difficulties briefly, before we again take up the discussion of the three legal conceptualisations of the integration project. The development of these conceptualisations mirror, so we will argue, the practical *impasses* of European politics. It is important not to misunderstand the exercise we are undertaking as some fundamental critique, not even as a further characterisation of Europe as a 'faltering project'.[53] Instead, its objective is to pave the way for a paradigm shift which would defend the Union's accomplishments and, at the same time, open new perspectives.

III.1. Fragile Pillars of 'Social Europe'

The story of Social Europe has much in common with Michael Ende's most famous fairy tale.[54] Every move in the process of economic integration was accompanied by counter-moves towards a social re-imbedding of the European polity. These counter-moves did not just occur through the conferral of new competences to the Community in treaty amendments and subsequent legislative arenas. The ECJ, in particular through its anti-discrimination jurisprudence, operated as a progressive instigator, and the reference procedure was often

[53] See J Habermas, 'European Politics at an Impasse. A Plea for a Policy of Graduated Integration' in idem, *Europe: The Faltering Project* (Cambridge: Polity Press, 2009) 78.
[54] M Ende, *The Neverending Story* (New York: Penguin Books, 1983).

enough prudently and successfully used by labour law networks.[55] However, most of the changes were piecemeal, with no comprehensive long-term background agenda.

Social aspirations were more explicitly articulated in the aftermath of the Treaty of Amsterdam. The contours of what was to constitute Europe's 'social dimension', however, remained vague. Key concepts from national welfare states appeared in official documents without an equivalent institutional background. This held true for Germany's '*soziale Marktwirtschaft*',[56] for France's '*services publiques*',[57] and TH Marshall's notion of 'social rights'.[58] The only transnational European innovation was the 'Open Method of Coordination' which the Lisbon Council of 2000 brought to bear in new areas of social policy.[59] Even Fritz W Scharpf initially suggested that this alternative to the traditional community method 'could hold considerable promise'.[60] Sophisticated theorists were persuaded by the prospect of a seemingly democratic 'learning through monitoring'.[61] This initial enthusiasm was to fade away with the rather modest accomplishments of the Treaty of Lisbon, on the one hand, ambivalent or inconclusive practical experiences,[62] and, last but not least, the recent dis-embedding moves in the labour law jurisprudence of the ECJ, on the other.[63]

III.2. The Foresight of Theory: Three Retractions

The rejection of all the constitutional ambitions in the Treaty of Lisbon and the present impasses of the integration *praxis* are also observable in the legal

[55] See S Sciarra (ed), Labour Law in the Courts: National Judges and the European Court of Justice (Oxford: Hart Publishing, 2001).

[56] See references in nn 25, 26 and 35 above.

[57] See the comparative account in M Krajewski, *Grundstrukturen des Rechts öffentlicher Dienstleistungen* (Heidelberg: Springer, 2010) 55 ff; for European level, see U Neergard, 'Services of General (Economic) Interest: What Goals and Values Count?' in Neergard et al, n 23 above, at 191.

[58] TH Marshall, 'Citizenship and Social Class' in idem, *Class, Citizenship and Social Development* (Westport CT: Greenwood Press, 1973) 65.

[59] See, for an analysis of the legal meaning of coordination powers, B Braams, 'Die Kompetenzordnung im Vertrag von Lissabon' in I Pernice (ed), *Der Vertrag von Lissabon: Reform der EU ohne Verfassung?* (Baden-Baden: Nomos, 2008) 115.

[60] See FW Scharpf, 'European Governance: Common Concerns vs The Challenge of Diversity' in C Joerges, Y Mény and JHH Weiler (eds), *Mountain or Molehill? A Critical Appraisal of the Commission White Paper on Governance*, EUI Florence/NYU Law School 2002, 1, at 9, available at: www.eui.eu/RSCAS/Research/OnlineSymposia/Governance.shtml.

[61] CF Sabel and J Zeitlin, 'Learning from Difference: The New Architecture of Experimentalist Governance in the European Union' (2008) 14 *ELJ* 271.

[62] For a recent comprehensive evaluation on legal theory perspectives, see M Dawson, *New Governance and the Proceduralisation of European Law: The Case of the Open Method of Coordination* (Cambridge: CUP, 2011); for an analysis in social theory perspectives, see PF Kjaer, *Between Governing and Governance: On the Emergence, Function and Form of Europe's Postnational Constellation* (Oxford: Hart Publishing, 2010).

[63] See Section V.2 below.

integration theory. Tellingly enough, this holds true for all of the three conceptualisations that we have sketched out above. This observation seems all the more significant as these three models – technocratic rule, economic rationality, and the community vision – were not chosen at random. They represent quite comprehensively the evolutionary options among which the integration project can choose and kept oscillating. All of them have been continuously present since the foundational period. They have been developing, even mutating, within their particular perspectives, be it in their responses to changing contexts, be it through mutual observation and political learning. We can neither try to document the continuities and innovations within each tradition, nor discuss the affinities between them in any detail. It is sufficient, for our argument, to characterise crucial transformations within each of them – and to underline telling parallels in their diagnosis of the current *impasses*.

III.2.1. Technocracy without Efficiency: Majone's Critical Turn

The importance of the technocratic tradition in the *praxis* of the integration project can hardly be over-estimated. Its weight was bound to increase with the involvement of the European Community in ever more regulatory policies, which were to be organised at transnational levels without the backing of a consolidated democratic order. How else than through an 'objective' and expertise-based conceptualisation of its enormous tasks could the European Community hope to ensure the acceptance of its involvement in ever more problem-solving activities? The by far most interesting and influential work which renewed and refined the technocratic legacy is that of Giandomenico Majone.[64] It is unique not only in its clarity and its coherence, but also in its reflections of the option for an alternative to the democratic constitutionalism of the Member States of the European Union. Majone's famous conceptualisation of Europe as a 'regulatory State'[65] which operates essentially through non-majoritarian institutions was conceived as ensuring the credibility of commitments to in principle uncontested policy objectives. Welfare policies pose additional problems. The Union's failure to institutionalise a comprehensive social policy results partly from the 'reluctance of the member states to surrender control of a politically salient and popular area of public policy'; equally important is the factual difficulty and political impossibility of replacing the variety of European welfare

[64] Who confronted Europe's integration studies right upon his return to Europe with essays like 'Regulating Europe: Problems and Prospects' (1989) 3 *Jahrbuch zur Staats- und Verwaltungswissenschaft* 159; 'Cross-national Resources of Regulatory Policymaking in Europe and the United States' (1991) 11 *JPP* 79, and has kept working on the perspectives outlined therein ever since (see, most recently, his *Europe as the Would-be World Power*, n 10 above.

[65] G Majone, 'The European Community as a Regulatory State', 1994-V/1 *Collected Courses of the Academy of European Law* (The Hague–Boston MA–London: Martinus Nijhoff, 1996) 321.

state models and traditions with some integrated European scheme.[66] Not only does Majone respect the primacy of constitutional democracies; he is equally, and with increasing urgency, underlining the fallacy of an ever more perfect and comprehensive subjection of the integration project to its 'operational code', the principle 'that integration has priority over all competing values',[67] and also the camouflage strategies which he calls 'integration by stealth'.[68] This is an alarming retraction from his earlier trust in the problem-solving potential of the European project. His warnings by no means reflect a change of theoretical premises. Majone continues to underline that Europe is not legitimated to pursue the type of distributional politics which welfare states have institutionalised.[69] He does not retract his plea for regulatory efficiency. His critical turn is, instead, motivated by the *inefficiencies* which he observes in the Union's operations. His quest for more modesty in Europe's ambitions ('*Geht's nicht eine Nummer kleiner?*')[70] summarises these observations. His adaption of the 'unity/ united in diversity' formula[71] is an implication of these insights, to which we will return in the following Section IV.

III.2.2. What is Left of the Economic Constitution: Ordoliberal Concerns

An institutionalisation of economic rationality is most widely perceived today, either affirmatively or critically, as Europe's main agenda.[72] This perception has gained prominence since the legendary White Paper on the Completion of the Internal Market.[73] At that stage of the integration process, the ordoliberal tradition had experienced a deep transformation. That mutation had started at national level with the move of Friedrich von Hayek from Chicago to Freiburg, and his promotion of a version of neo-liberalism situated between the Freiburg School's orthodoxy, on the one hand, and the Chicago School's normative complacency, on the other. Von Hayek's notion of 'competition as a discovery process' captures the essence of his messages best. They have led the second generation of ordoliberal

[66] Majone, *Europe as the Would-be World Power*, n 10 above, at 144.

[67] Ibid, 1.

[68] See his Dilemmas of European Inregration: The Ambiguities and Pitfalls of Integration by Stealth (Oxford: Oxford University Press, 2005).

[69] Majone, *Europe as the Would-be World Power*, n 10 above, 128 ff.

[70] Ibid, 170 ff.

[71] Ibid, 205 ff.

[72] See, on the one hand, the contributions on European economic law in v Bogdandy and Bast, n 48 above by A Haltje, 'The Economic Constitution within the Internal Market', 589, and J Drexl, 'Competition Law as Part of the European Constitution', 659, which are strongly indebted to the ordoliberal tradition; and M Höpner and A Schäfer, 'A New Phase of European Integration: Organized Capitalisms in Post-Ricardian Europe' (2010) 33 *West European Politics* 344, on the other. Such theoretical controversies vary, of course, as strongly as Europe's varieties of capitalism.

[73] European Commission, 'White Paper to the European Council on Completion of the Internal Market', COM (85) 310 final, 14 June 1985.

scholars to re-define the objectives and the methods of national and European competition law. Attention shifted from the control of economic power to the protection of entrepreneurial freedom and the critique of anti-competitive regulation. What happened in the 1970s had been not anticipated, but it was analysed with an amazing precision a good number of years ago by Michel Foucault in the course of the lectures that he delivered at the *Collège de France*.[74] There, Foucault characterised the ordoliberal vision of the strong state which is committed to the protection of the competitive ordering of the market as new type of *gouvernmentalité*, namely, the acceptance of market governance by the political system and the whole of society.[75] There are remarkable affinities between the second generation ordoliberalism and the Chicago School when it comes to practical issues of competition law and policy, but they have never led to a real merger of the two schools. The heirs of Eucken and von Hayek did not subscribe to the Chicago understanding of economic output efficiency and 'consumer welfare' but continued to define and defend the 'system of undistorted competition' as the core of Europe's 'economic constitution'.[76] They witnessed, however, a steady decline of the impact of their visions, which became clearly visible in the substantial broadening of European economic policies in the Treaty of Maastricht,[77] the so-called 'modernisation' of European competition law[78] and the move towards a 'more economic approach'.[79] The weakening of their ideational power was symbolically confirmed when French Prime Minister Nicolas Sarkozy saw to it that the Union's commitment to 'a system ensuring that competition is not distorted' was not included in Article 3 TFEU (ex Article 2 TEU) but moved back into Protocol 27 of the Treaty of Lisbon.[80]

[74] M Foucault, *Naissance de la biopolitique. Cours au Collège de France* (Paris: Seuil/Gallimard, 2004), in particular, the lecture of 7 February 1979, 105, and that of 14 February 1979, 135.

[75] '[A]u lieu d'accepter une liberté du marché, définie par l'État et maintenue en quelque sorte sur surveillance étatique … eh bien, disent les ordolibéraux, il faut entièrement retourner la formule et se donner la liberté du marché comme principe organisateur et régulateur de l'État … Autrement dit, un État sous surveillance du marché plutôt qu'un marché sous surveillance de l'État', *Biopolitique* (note 7), Lecture 5, at 120.

[76] See E-J Mestmäcker, *Wirtschaft und Verfassung in der Europäischen Union. Beiträge zu Recht, Theorie und Politik der europäischen Integration* (Baden-Baden: Nomos, 2003), with a collection of essays written from 1965 to 2001 and his recent critique of R Posner in *A Legal Theory without Law: Posner v Hayek on Economic Analysis of Law* (Tübingen: Mohr Siebeck, 2007), also available at: http://papers.ssrn.com/sol3/papers.cfm?abstract_id=1168422.

[77] See ME Streit and W. Mussler, 'The Economic Constitution of the European Community. From "Rome" to "Maastricht"' (1995) 1 *ELJ* 5.

[78] H Schweitzer, 'Competition Law and Public Policy: Reconsidering an Uneasy Relationship: The Example of Art 81' (1 December 2007), available at SSRN: http://ssrn.com/abstract=1092883.

[79] See D Schmidtchen, M Albert and S Voigt (eds), *The More Economic Approach to European Competition Law* (Tübingern: Mohr Siebeck, 2007).

[80] Legally speaking, the removal looks insignificant, as, for example, Peter Behrens has underlined in 'Der Wettbewerb *im* Vertrag von Lissabon' (2008) 21 *Europaische Zeitschrift für Wirtschaftsrecht* 193; the [black letter] law's truth, however, is not the whole truth.

III.2.3. Unity Without Community: JHH Weiler's Constitutional Complacency

Joseph Weiler's early work can in hindsight be identified as truly path-breaking in that it synthesised, in a novel way, Europe's constitutive historical move towards a common peaceful future, the construction of a supranational legal alternative to the role of international law in the system, while remaining aware of the political embeddedness and dependency of these accomplishments. The great normative perspectives and the sensitive realism in his design of an equilibrium between 'legal supranationalism' and 'political intergovernmentalism', however, became gradually ever more apparent as Weiler sought to develop his construct and vision further in the light of European experiences, accomplishments and failures. In his seminal article on the 'Transformation of Europe', he delivered an insightful diagnosis of the problematical implications of majority voting in terms of Europe's legitimacy.[81] He was among the first to realise the normative and political ambivalences of the completion of the Internal Market by the Delors Commission:

> [T]o regard the Community as a technological instrument is, in the first place, to under-estimate the profound political choice and cultural impact which the single market involves – a politics of efficiency, a culture of market.[82]

We can summarise the foregoing observations in a second interim conclusion: the *impasses* of the integration *praxis* are mirrored and foreshadowed by the exhaustion of the main theoretical perspectives which have accompanied and oriented legal reflections, theoretical conceptualisations and the prescriptive modelling of Europe's *finalité*. Where practice and theory concur so significantly in their retroactive moves, it seems about time to consider an alternative paradigm.

IV. EUROPE'S LEGITIMACY PROBLEM REVISITED: THE CONFLICTS LAW ALTERNATIVE

Europe's 'operational code' is to prioritise integration 'over all other conceivable values including democracy'.[83] 'United in Diversity', the motto of the Constitutional Treaty, has become Majone's new *leitmotiv*.[84] The legal form of this motto is the re-conceptualisation of European law as a new type of supranational conflicts law. That approach, however, seeks to open much broader perspectives than Majone envisages in his plea for a political modesty. Rather

[81] Weiler, 'The Transformation of Europe', n 31 above, at 2461 ff.
[82] Idem, 'Fin-de-Siècle Europe', n 38 above, 215.
[83] Majone, *Europe as the Would-be World Power*, n 10 above, 1.
[84] Ibid, 205 ff.

than repeating this argument once more,[85] commentary is here restricted to a depiction of its five core messages.[86]

IV.1. Conflicts Law as Democratic Commandment

The entire construction is built upon a sociological observation with normative implications. Under the impact of Europeanisation and globalisation, contemporary societies experience an ever stronger schism between decision-makers and those who are impacted upon by decision-making. This schism is explained by Niklas Luhmann within his sociological risk theory; according to Luhmann, the problem arises because decision-making on risks is always characterised by the fact that the potential damage is not simply borne by individual decision-makers, nor is it only suffered by the persons profiting from the decision.[87] Luhmann's sociological observation is normatively disquieting in democratic orders. Suffice it here to point to Jürgen Habermas' first essay on European integration,[88] which he published prior to the completion of his discourse theory of law and democracy,[89] and later elaborated in greater detail:[90] increasingly, constitutional states are unable to guarantee the inclusion of all of those persons who are impacted upon by their policies and politics within their internal decision-making processes. The democratic notion of self-legislation, however, which postulates that the addressees of a law should be able to understand themselves as its authors, demands 'the inclusion of the other'.

IV.2. The Supranationality of European Conflicts Law

This plea for a new understanding of EU law, must not, the connotations of its terminological origin notwithstanding, serve as a retraction from supranationalism

[85] For early versions, see C Joerges, 'The Europeanisation of Private Law as a Rationalisation Process and as a Contest of Legal Disciplines – An Analysis of the Directive on Unfair Terms in Consumer Contracts' (1995) 3 *ERPL* 175; idem, 'The Impact of European Integration on Private Law: Reductionist Perceptions, True Conflicts and a New Constitutionalist Perspective' (1997) 3 *ELJ* 378; idem, '"Deliberative Supranationalism": Two Defences' (2002) 8 *ELJ* 13.

[86] In the following I draw on C Joerges, 'Integration through Conflicts Law: On the Defence of the European Project by Means of Alternative Conceptualisation of Legal Constitutionalisation' in R Nickel (ed), *Conflict of Laws and Laws of Conflict in Europe and Beyond – Patterns of Supranational and Transnational Juridification* (Antwerp: Intersentia, 2010) 377.

[87] N Luhmann, *Soziologie des Risikos* (Berlin: Walter de Gruyter, 1991); colourfully and laconically summarised in, for example, idem, *Das Recht der Gesellschaft* (Frankfurt aM: Suhrkamp, 1995) 141–43.

[88] J Habermas, *Staatsbürgerschaft und nationale Identität* [Citizenship and National Identity] (Zurich: Erkner, 1991), reprinted in idem, *Faktizität und Geltung* (Frankfurt aM: Suhrkamp, 1992) 632.

[89] Idem, Between Facts and Norms. Contributions to a Discourse Theory of Law and Democracy (Cambridge MA: The MIT Press, 1998) 491.

[90] Idem, 'The European Nation State: On the Past and the Future of Sovereignty and Citizenship' in idem, *The Inclusion of the Other* (Cambridge: Polity Press, 1998) 105.

as such. Quite to the contrary, it furnishes a justification for the validity of the supranational jurisdiction – albeit one which is, just like the three models of legal integration theory discussed above,[91] at the same time depicting the limits of supranational rule. To rephrase its sociological and normative basis slightly: as a consequence of their manifold degree of inter-dependence, the Member States of the European Community/Union are no longer in a position to guarantee the democratic legitimacy of their policies. A European law that concerns itself with the amelioration of such external effects, ie, which seeks to compensate for the failings of the national democracies, may induce its legitimacy from this compensatory function. With this, European law can, at last, free itself from the critique that has accompanied it since its birth; a critique that states that it is *not* legitimate. It can thus operate to strengthen democracy within a contractual understanding of statehood, without needing to establish itself as a democratic state.[92]

IV.3. Convergence, Re-construction, Critique

Clearly, such a democratic exoneration of European law is only plausible to the exact degree that it may be re-constructed within this perspective, or that it may

[91] Sections II.1.3 and III.2.

[92] The argument has been taken up or reinvented repeatedly: see, for example, R Howse and K Nicolaïdis, 'Democracy without Sovereignty: The Global Vocation of Political Ethics' in T Broude and Y Shany (eds), *The Shifting Allocation of Authority in International Law: Considering Sovereignty, Supremacy and Subsidiarity* (Oxford: Hart Publishing, 2008) 163; K-H Ladeur, 'The State in International Law' in C Joerges and J Falke (eds), *The Social Embeddedness of Transnational Markets* (Oxford: Hart Publishing, 2011). It has also provoked critique, in particular by A Somek, 'The Argument from Transnational Effects I: Representing Outsiders Through Freedom of Movement' (2010) 16 *ELJ* 315; idem, 'The Argument from Transnational Effects II: Establishing Transnational Democracy' (2010) 16 *ELJ* 375. It will become apparent from our exemplary discussion in Sections V and VI that, in our understanding, Part I of Somek's argument fails to acknowledge the conflicts-law framework of the argument, which is 'emebedded' in the Habermasian notion of the 'co-originality' of private and public autonomy; the whole point of the conflicts approach is about the defence of co-originality against the supremacy of 'economic freedoms' (see Section V.1 below and the references in n 102); Part II of the argument seeks to take the interdependence *problématique* too lightly. As F Rödl has recently put it: 'The border-crossing interdependence of national societies generates types of problems that can no longer be solved by the States on their own or through their consensual cooperation, but require a unitary political space that corresponds to the continental or even global scope of the problems' ('Democratic Juridification without Statization: Law of Conflict of Laws instead of a World State', ms Frankfurt aM, 2010; on file with the author); see, also, his 'Regime-Collisions, Proceduralised Conflict of Laws and the Unity of the Law: On the Form of Constitutionalism Beyond the State' in Nickel, *Conflict of Laws*, n 86 above, 263. To argue that the conflicts approach conceptualises the interdependence problem adequately is not to suggest, however, that it would generate good answers to all true conflicts – see Section IV.2.3 below. Also, to refer to Habermas is not to suggest that the discourse theory of law has a privileged access to a query which is raised by others, lawyers and political theorists alike, in similar ways; see N Nic Shuibhne, 'The Resilience of Market Citizenship' (2010) 47 *CML Rev* 1597, and R Bellamy, 'The Liberty of the Post-moderns? Market and Civic Freedom within the EU', *LEQS Paper No 01/2009*, available at: www2.lse.ac.uk/europeanInstitute/LEQS/LEQSPapers.aspx. For a summary of the constitutional debate since Maastricht and a critical analysis of the 'social surplus' of the ECJ's social rights-jurisprudence, see M Everson, 'European Citizenship and the Dillusion of the Common Man', in Nickel, *Conflict of Laws*, n 86 above, 135.

be furnished with a conflicts-law orientation. This, however, is already, often enough, the case: European law has given legal force to principles and rules which serve the purpose of supranational 'recognition' – the non-discrimination principle, the supranational definition and the demarcation of legitimate regulatory concerns, the demands for justification for actions that are imposed upon national legal systems, and the proportionality principle – which supplies a legal yardstick against which respect for supranationally-guaranteed freedoms may be measured – and the demand that all public exercise of power pays due regard to fundamental rights. All these principles and rules may be understood as a concretisation of a supranational conflicts law, which guarantees that the actions of the Member States are reconcilable with their position within the Community. This is not to say, however, that the solutions to the conflicts at which European law has actually arrived are always convincing. Our re-construction of European law in the normative perspectives just outlined will reveal tensions between 'facticity' and 'validity', as well as failures and missed opportunities – the conflicts approach shares this type of experience with the three approaches from which it seeks to replace.

IV.4. Internal Differentiation of Conflicts Law within Europe's Multi-level System: The Idea of a Three-dimensional Conflicts Law

The metaphor of the multi-level system asserts that European 'rule' cannot be organised hierarchically. This argument is reflected not only within the apportionment of competences within the EU, but also by the fact that vast discrepancies exist in the operational resources available at each ruling level. Accordingly, we are able to distinguish between three forms of legal collision – vertical, 'diagonal' and horizontal. Diagonal collisions are an important and unique feature of multi-level systems. They are a constant feature of life within the EU, since the competences required for problem-solving are, at times, to be found at the level of the EU itself and, at other times, at the level of the Member States. This division of competences gives rise to two forms of potential conflict – on the one hand, between divergent EU and national political orientations, and, on the other, between divergent interest constellations in the Member States – so that very particular mediation arrangements must be identified. This need for mediation is true for all multi-level systems, but is particularly pressing in the case of the EU, where the existence of diagonal conflict has had, as its corollary, the evolution of a particularly intense degree of administrative cooperation, the institutionalisation of advice-giving instances, and the systematic construction of non-governmental cooperative relationships. This infrastructure may be understood as furnishing the integral components of a conflicts law, a law that may no longer restrict itself to the individual adjudication of situational cases of conflict, and which must, instead, constantly busy itself with the finding of general solutions to universal problems. At the same time, such conflicts law must be methodologically and organisationally open to evolution, which has seen the development of post-interventionist regulatory practices and legal forms within national law. Accordingly, we may identify three types of European conflicts law, which operate in three dimensions:[93] conflicts law of the 'first order' is flanked, on the one hand, by a conflicts law which, most specifically in the realm of European comitology, has concerned itself with the elaboration of material (substantive) regulatory options, and, on the other hand, by a conflicts law which governs the supervision of para-legal law and self-regulatory organisation.

IV.5. Conflicts Law as Proceduralising Constitutionalism

It follows from the preceding sections that it would be factually and normatively mistaken to regard European law as a system of law dedicated to the incremental construction of a comprehensive legal edifice. Europe must, at last, take the motto of the Draft Constitutional Treaty[94] to heart, and learn to accept the fact that its diversity will accompany it far into the future, so that conflict born of diversity will continue to characterise the process of European integration. It must further concede that this 'process' should be overseen by a conflicts law, which, by virtue of its identification of the principles and rules that govern conflict, will generate the law of the European multi-level system. Europeanisation is not simply a process of change; it is also a learning process. Law cannot pre-determine the substance of such processes, but may yet secure its own normative character, by virtue of its self-dedication to the processes of law-making/legal-justification (*Recht-Fertigung*), which mirror and defend the justice and fairness within law.[95] This understanding is by no means simply some Teutonic idiosyncrasy.[96] It is akin to, for example, Antje Wiener's notion of 'the invisible constitution'[97] or Deirdre Curtin's concept of the 'living constitution'.[98]

[93] See, for more detail, C Joerges and F Rödl, 'Reconceptualising the constitution of Europe's post-national constellation – by dint of conflict of laws' in I Lianos and O Odudu (eds), *Regulating Trade in Services in the EU and the WTO. Trust, Distrust and Economic Integradtion* (Cambridge: CUP, 2012) 762; C Joerges, 'The Idea of a Three-dimensional Conflicts Law as Constitutional Form', reprinted in ch 27 of the present volume. For similar terminological usage, though built upon a different conceptual base, see PF Kjaer, 'Three-dimensional Conflict of Laws in Europe', ZERP-DP 2/2009, available at: www.zerp.uni-bremen.de/; see, also, Kjaer, n 62 above, 141 ff.

[94] Article I-8 Draft European Constitutional Treaty, n 1 above. The formula was dispensed with by the Lisbon Treaty on the Functioning of the EU.

[95] See R Wiehölter, 'Just-ifications of a Law of Society' in O Perez and G Teubner (eds), *Paradoxes and Inconsistencies in the Law* (Oxford: Hart Publishing, 2005) 65, available at: www.jura.uni-frankfurt.de/ifawz1/teubner/RWTexte/justum.pdf.

[96] See M Everson and J Eisner, *The Making of the EU Constitution: Judges and Lawyers Beyond Constitutive Power* (Abingdon: Routledge-Cavendish, 2007), in particular 41 ff.

[97] A Wiener, The Invisible Constitution of Politics: Contested Norms and International Encounters (Cambridge: CUP, 2008).

[98] D Curtin, *Executive Power of the European Union. Law, Practices and the Living Constitution* (Oxford: OUP, 2009).

Could it be that these daring ideas are realistic in the sense that they represent the only conceivable type of responses to the challenges to which the European project is exposed? In his comments on the conflicts-law approach, Andrea Greppi has identified these difficulties with radical clarity.[99] The proceduralisation of law risks forgoing all substance, in particular a commitment to social justice. Its openness and plea for deliberative problem-solving risks being seized by the logic of technocratic managerialism. To summarise these concerns and hopes in a citation:

> Whether intentionally or unintentionally, legal theory and philosophy suggest that they contain a remedial potential which in fact they lack, and necessarily must lack, to the extent that they fail to incorporate the inchoate values of individuals and institutions in society, the phenomenon Ernst Cassirer called the 'constitution that is written in the citizens' minds'.[100]

V. THE DEEPENING OF EUROPE'S LEGITIMACY PROBLEM BY THE ECJ'S LABOUR LAW JURISPRUDENCE

As indicated, the conflicts-law approach is not meant as an artificial juxtaposition to positive European law, but it does claim to take up the legacy of legal realism and, hence, to articulate that law's 'real life'. This, however, is by no means a purely affirmative exercise. Both of the case studies in the following sections will use the approach to raise objections or to articulate reserves against important decisions of the ECJ.

V.1. The Example of *Cassis de Dijon*

The conflicts-law approach advocates mitigation between controversies over diverging policies and complex interest configuration. With this aspiration, the approach departs markedly from the traditional treatment of public law provisions in private international law, international public and administrative law. Europe has, as Jona Israël put it, the chance and vocation to transform the *comitas* (voluntary and diplomatic coordination) among its states and societies into a legally-binding commitment to cooperative problem-solving.[101] This has been accomplished in countless cases – more or less convincingly. The ECJ's

[99] 'Procedure and Substance in Postnational Constitutionalism. "Montesquieu or Sieyes?"' in Nickel and Greppi (eds), *The Changing Role of Law*, n * above, 211.

[100] V Grosswald Curran, 'Law's Past and Europe's Future' (2005) 6 *German Law Journal* 483, at 486, available at: www.germanlawjournal.com. The reference is to E Cassirer's posthumously published *The Myth of the State* (New Haven CT: Yale University Press, 1946) 91.

[101] J Israël, *European Cross-Border Insolvency Regulation* (Antwerp-Oxford: Intersentia, 2005) 123, 150–52 and 323–34.

legendary *Cassis de Dijon* judgment of 1979[102] may serve to illustrate this point. The ECJ's response to the controversy between Germany and France over Germany's prescriptions on a minimum percentage of alcohol in liquor was as plausible as it was trifling: the confusion of German consumers could be avoided, and a reasonable degree of protection against erroneous decisions by German consumers could be achieved, by simply disclosing the lower alcohol content of the competing French liqueur.

Damian Chalmers and Agustín José Menéndez have raised objections of different weight. As Chalmers rightly underlines, the 'centre of gravity' of the case was in Germany and concerned conflicts of interest between a German distributor (REWE) and German liquor producers.[103] This is so, but it does not affect the involvement of the ECJ in a conflict constellation which is *within* the European multi-level system. Chalmers' critique touches upon the upgrading of economic freedoms to constitutional rights which entitle those affected to a supervision of national legislation by the ECJ. This move of the ECJ was anything but trivial, because the Court has assumed *en passant* the constitutional functions. This kind of power is inherent in any supranational supervision of national public law. Its constitutional sensitivity control becomes apparent when we re-construct the issue in the framework of the discourse theory of law. Economic freedoms belong to the sphere of private autonomy and deserve recognition as constitutional rights. However, within consolidated constitutional democracies, the recognition of the constitutional status of the private sphere is complemented by the constitutional recognition and protection of political rights. Both spheres must be understood in the conceptualisation of Jürgen Habermas as 'co-original'.[104] The issue, then, is of whether the ECJ has gone a step too far when complementing the recognition of the constitutional status of economic freedoms by its authoritative definition of the kind of concerns which are deemed to be compatible with the establishment of a common European market. It is this latter query to which Menéndez refers in his critique of the constitutional ambitions of the conflicts-law approach.[105]

[102] Case 120/78, ECR [1979] 649.

[103] 'Deliberative Supranationalism and the Reterritorialization of Authority' in B Kohler-Koch and B Rittberger (eds), *Debating the Democratic Legitimacy* (Lanham MD: Rowman & Littlefield, 2007) 329, at 334.

[104] J Habermas has developed this notion in the context of his theory of democratic constitutionalism; see his *Between Facts and Norms*, n 89 above, 118 ff. Very convincingly, in my view, R Nickel and F Rödl have suggested its application 'beyond the state': see R Nickel, 'Private and Public Autonomy Revisited: Jürgen Habermas' Concept of Co-Originality in Times of Globalisation and the Militant Security State' in M Loughlin and N Walker (eds), *The Paradox of Constitutionalism* (Oxford: OUP, 2007) 147; F Rödl, 'Private Law Beyond the Democratic Order? On the Legitimatory Problem of Private Law "Beyond the State"' (2008) 56 *AJCL* 743.

[105] See AJ Menéndez, 'When the Market is Political: The Socio-economic Constitution of the European Union between Market-making and Polity-making' in R Letelier and AJ Menéndez (eds), *The Sinews of Peace: Reconstituting the Democratic Legitimacy of the Socio-Economic Constitution of the European Union*, Oslo: *ARENA Report No 7*, Oslo 2009, 39.

This point is well taken,[106] but it in no way affects the reading of *Cassis* as a conflicts law case. The ECJ handed down a ruling on a complex conflict constellation. This ruling does provide a legal framework for this conflict. This 'is' conflicts law, albeit not necessarily good law.[107]

V.2. A Market Community? The ECJ's Recent Labour Law Jurisprudence

The much-debated recent labour law jurisprudence of the ECJ provides a line of cases in point. It is difficult for anybody aware of Continental private and public international law or Anglo-Saxon conflict of laws *not* to realise the discrepancies between the latter disciplines and the decisions which the ECJ handed down under European law. This is not, in itself, deplorable. What deserves closer scrutiny, however, is the contents of the principles and rules which the ECJ has invoked and developed in its responses to the conflict constellations which were referred to it.

V.2.1. Viking, Laval, Rüffert

These three cases are, by now, so well-known that it should suffice here to summarise their contents very briefly.

The first case was decided on 11 December 2007.[108] Finnish seafarers, employed on the ferry *Rosella*, become aware of the intention of their employer to flag out to Estonia. Since they ware afraid of losing their jobs or being forced to accept lower wages, they tried to challenge their employer by threatening to strike. This was legal under Finnish law. But, so their Finnish employer argued, such action was incompatible with its right of free establishment as enshrined in Article 43 EC.

The response of the ECJ is conciliatory in its tone, but is, in fact, quite rigid. The ECJ underlined that the 'right to take collective action, including the right

[106] See, a good while ago, E Steindorff, 'Probleme des Art 30 EWG' (1984) 148 *Zeitschrift für das gesamte Handelsrecht und Wirtschaftsrecht* 338.

[107] There is no space in this lengthy essay to review related approaches which share this insight. GM Conway's PhD thesis on 'Values and Conflicts of Norms in EU Law and the Legal Reasoning of the European Court of Justice' (Brunel, 2010; available at: file:///C:/Users/C1681~1.JOE/AppData/Local/Temp/FulltextThesis.pdf), however, deserves exceptional treatment [see, also, his 'Conflicts of Competence Norms in EU Law and the Legal Reasoning of the ECJ' (2010) 11 *German Law Journal* 966, available at: www.germanlawjournal.com/index.php?pageID=11&artID=1280]. With his notion of 'conflict of norms', Conway has chosen a term which, very fortunately, avoids connotations and confusion which the 'conflicts law' approach tends to provoke. Conway also does not engage extensively in constitutional deliberations. It is all the more remarkable and enlightening that his analyses documents the omnipresence of conflicts and the need for legal responses in all spheres of the law of the EU.

[108] Case C-438/05, *International Transport Workers' Federation, Finnish Seamen's Union v Viking Line ABP, OÜ Viking Line Eesti*, judgment of 11 December 2007, [2007] ECR I-10779.

to strike … [is] a fundamental right which forms an integral part of the general principles of Community law'.[109] Earlier, however, the Court had fundamentally re-configured the traditional balance between economic freedoms at European level and social rights at national level, explaining that the Member States,

> Para 40. … [although] still free, in principle, to lay down the conditions governing the existence and exercise of the rights in question … must nevertheless comply with Community law …
>
> Para 41. Consequently, the fact that Article 137 EC does not apply to the right to strike or to the right to impose lock-outs is not such as to exclude collective action such as that at issue in the main proceedings from the application of Article 43 EC.

The second case was decided only one week later.[110] Laval, a company incorporated under Latvian law, had won the tender for a school building on the outskirts of Stockholm. In obtaining the tender, it had profited from the differences in the wage levels of Latvia and Sweden. In May 2004, when work was to start, and after Laval had posted several dozens of its workers, the Swedish trade unions resorted to hostile actions against Laval with such determination and intensity that Laval gave up.

The unions had acted legally according to Swedish law, but the Court referred to Directive 96/71/EC concerning the posting of workers in the framework of the provision of services.[111] This Directive requires, with respect to a number of essential working conditions, that foreign workers are not to be disadvantaged. According to Article 3, workers are to be guaranteed the minimum rates of pay. According to the general principle of the same Article, the rates of pay must be laid down either 'by law, regulation or administrative provision' or 'by collective agreements which have been declared universally applicable within the meaning of paragraph 8'. Sweden, however, had refrained from changing its pertinent laws but relied on the exceptions listed in Article 3 paragraph 8 (providing therein the absence of a system for declaring collective agreements or arbitration awards universally applicable). It left the determination of wage levels to collective agreements concluded among the undertakings themselves. The Court argued that, in this respect, Sweden was in breach of (secondary) Community law.[112]

In the third judgment, which was handed down in April 2008, the ECJ further entrenched its position.[113] *Rüffert* concerned the legality of a tender proffered by one of the German *Länder*, Lower Saxony, which contained a clause indicating

[109] Case C-438/05 (*Viking*), para 44.

[110] Case C-341/05, *Laval un Partneri Ltd v Svenska Byggnadsarbetareförbundet, Svenska Byggnadsarbetareförbundet, avd. 1, Svenska Elektrikerförbundet*, judgment of 18 December 2007, [2007] ECR I-11767.

[111] Directive 96/71/EC OJ 1996, L18/1.

[112] See paras 70–71 of the judgment.

[113] Case C-346/06, *Rüffert v Land Niedersachsen*, Judgment of 3 April 2008, [2008] ECR I-01989.

that the public authorities were bound to respect existing collective-bargaining agreements, so that tendering firms would also be required to abide by the relevant collective-bargaining agreements. The ECJ held that Lower Saxony's legislation was irreconcilable with Article 49 EC since it prevented foreign service-providers from benefiting from lower wage costs within their country of origin.

The vital point within the judgment is its evaluation of the protective purpose of the clause committing the public authorities to respect collective agreements: in this connection, the Court held that 'contrary to the contentions of Land Niedersachsen and a number of the Governments, such a measure cannot be considered to be justified by the objective of ensuring the protection of workers'.

This finding is all the more remarkable in view of a prior pertinent decision of Germany's Constitutional Court, which had explained only in 2006:[114]

> The combating of unemployment, together with measures that secure the financial stability of the social security system, are particularly important goals, for the realisation of which the legislator must be given a relatively large degree of decisional discretion, and especially so under current, politically very difficult, labour market conditions.[115]

V.2.2. *Dissenting Opinions in Luxembourg and their Disregard*

In all of the three cases, the Court's Advocate Generals – Poiares Maduro in *Viking*, Mengozzi in *Laval*, Bot in *Rüffert* – had submitted Opinions which differed, more or less significantly, from the Court's later judgments. In two more recent cases, the signals of dissent were becoming stronger and more articulate.

The first case concerns the applicability of Directive 2004/18 to a German pension scheme for public employees, and has considerable affinities with *Rüffert*.[116] The German scheme foresaw the involvement of trade unions in the transformation of parts of their remuneration into pensions ('*Entgeltumwandlung*'). The European Commission found the involvement of the trade unions in the selection of insurers to be compatible with the Directive.

The Opinion which Advocate General Verica Trstenjak delivered on 14 April 2010 does not directly question the Court's labour law jurisprudence.[117] She explicitly refrains from supporting Germany's quest for an '*Albany* exclusion',[118] and confirms the applicability of the economic freedoms. She then adds, however, that the social right to collective bargaining and the freedoms

[114] Bundesverfassungsgericht, – 1 BvL 4/00 – (First senate, 16 July 2006), available at the Court's website at: www.bverfg.de/entscheidungen/ls20060711_1bvl000400.html.

[115] Para 103 (translation by the author; references to earlier judgments omitted).

[116] Case C-271/08, *European Commission v Federal Republic of Germany*, ECLI:EU:C:2010:426.

[117] See, in particular, paras 196 et seq, on the *Rüffert* case.

[118] See her discussion of Case C-67/96, *Albany International BV v Stichting Bedrijfspensioenfonds Textielindustrie* [1999] ECR I-5751 in paras 54 et seq.

are of equal weight, and invokes the principle of proportionality as a guide for its resolution.[119] The conflict is to be resolved at the level of primary law, and that resolution has then to guide the interpretation of secondary legislation. This leads her to question the validity of the Commission's reading of the said Directive and to suggest that the complaint be dismissed.[120]

The second case concerns the compatibility of Belgian requirements relating to the posting of workers in Belgium with the Posted Workers Directive.[121] It is, in this respect, closer to *Laval*. Advocate General Cruz Villalón, in his Opinion of 5 May 2010, characterises this Directive as a response to the conflicts between social values and economic freedoms which the internal market is bound to generate,[122] and then complements the argument of his Slovenian colleague by a reference to Articles 9 and 3 TFEU, suggesting that, under the Treaty of Lisbon, social protection is no longer to be understood as an exception from the economic freedoms but as commitment of general validity. Like his colleague, he then invokes the proportionality principle to resolve these tensions.[123]

The two Opinions move the conflict between economic freedoms and social rights to the European level and thereby strengthen Europe's judicial supranationalism. The premises and implications of this projection are difficult to understand. Both cases concern policy fields in which national law has not been replaced but is only partially affected by European prerogatives. The prospects for a clarification of such queries, however, do not seem bright. In its judgment of 15 July 2010 the ECJ (Grand Chamber) rather flatly rephrases what has been stated in *Viking* and *Laval*:

> [W]hile it is true that the right to bargain collectively enjoys in Germany the constitutional protection conferred, generally, by Article 9(3) of the German Basic Law upon the right to form associations to safeguard and promote working and economic conditions, the fact remains that, as provided in Article 28 of the Charter, that right must be exercised in accordance with European Union law.
>
> Exercise of the fundamental right to bargain collectively must therefore be reconciled with the requirements stemming from the freedoms protected by the FEU Treaty, which in the present instance Directives 92/50 and 2004/18 are intended to implement, and be in accordance with the principle of proportionality.[124]

[119] See paras 186 et seq.

[120] See para 237.

[121] Case C-515/08, *Vítor Manuel dos Santos Palhota and Others*. The judgment of the ECJ case dates from 7 October 2010.

[122] Para 38.

[123] Paras 52 et seq.

[124] Case C-271/08, paras 43–44. In Case C-515/08, n 121 above, the ECJ handed down its judgment on 7 October 2010. The Court confirmed that 'overriding reasons relating to the public interest capable of justifying a restriction on the freedom to provide services include the protection of workers' and 'recognised that the Member States have the power to verify compliance with the national and European Union provisions' (paras 47–48) without mentioning the TFEU and the Charter. In their proportionality analysis of the Belgian legislation, the AG and the ECJ concurred.

V.3. The Conflicts Law Alternative

What is wrong about all this? There is no space here to comment on the Europe-wide discussion of this jurisprudence. The following remarks will be restricted to some aspects which illuminate the specifics of the conflicts-law approach.

V.3.1. *Sweden's Social Democratic Sonderweg*

Patricia Mindus[125] has, after her review of social and legal integration theories, turned to a dimension of the *Laval* case which she is extremely well-equipped to take up withsuch sophistication: the *Laval* litigation does indeed illustrate aspects of 'the Swedish *Sonderweg*', such as the legal status and social function of *kollektivavtalssystemet*, which the Swedish legislature did not want to (dare to?) touch when implementing the Posted Workers Directive. She argues very convincingly that the 'Swedish model' is, by now, politically contested, and not only under pressure exerted by some 'kleptomaniac competence extension' of the ECJ. In a conflicts-law language, Sweden has to become aware of the tensions between its *Sonderweg* and its European commitments. The Union and its highest Court must defend these commitments which are, at the same time, Community entitlements – and also be aware of the instrumentalisation of European law and court proceedings in internal Swedish power battles[126] – the *Laval* case was, after all, initiated and financed in Sweden.[127] This is an instructive explanation of the background and the implication of *Laval*. It is also, at the same time, an instructive illustration of the conflict patterns which the Europeanisation process generates. This observation confirms the assertion that European law 'is' conflicts law. But is *Laval* 'good conflicts law'? The constellation is structurally the same as in *Cassis de Dijon*,[128] but so much more dramatic. The message of the conflicts-law approach is seemingly abstract: the law should civilise the contest over divergent policies and interests without assuming the mandate to streamline Europe's diversity.

V.3.2. *Conflicts Law's Prudence*

'Judicial restraint' v 'judicial activism' is a misleading dichotomy here, and does not at all exhaust the potential of the traditions on which the conflicts-law approach builds.

[125] P Mindus, 'Theorizing Conflicts and Politicisation in the EU'in Nickel and Greppi (eds), *The Changing Role of Law*, n * above, 195.

[126] Ibid, text accompanying fnn 35 et seq.

[127] Battle is on-going in Swedish politics, legislation and jurisprudence. In a judgment of 2 December 2009 the Swedish *Arbetsdomstolen* imposed 'exemplary damages' on the trade unions that had taken action against *Laval*. See the annotation by N Reich, 'Laval "Vierter Akt"' (2010) 21 *Europäische Zeitschrift für Wirtschaftsrecht* 21.

[128] See Section V.1 above.

Antoine Lyon-Caen, the doyen of French labour law, has, without resorting to the conflict of law or private international law terminology, recalled one core message:

> Dans les sociétés d'Europe de l'Ouest, le droit du travail s'est constitué par émancipation du droit du marché, dénommé moyennant les variations terminologiques qu'il importe de ne pas oublier: liberté du commerce ici, freedom of trade ailleurs ... Ce n'est pas que des règles sur le travail n'existaient pas avant cette émancipation, mais elles relevaient d'avantage d'une police du travail, partie plus ou moins autonome d'une police du ou des marchés.[129]

There is a categorical difference between economic law and labour law, Lyon-Caen argues. The most basic notion which conflicts law has at its disposal is 'characterisation'[130] and, Ernst Rabel's universalist visions notwithstanding, characterisation has, according to the prevailing view, to take the views of the forum seriously. The categorical difference is not written in stone and not pre-given as some transpositive *ordo*, but deeply rooted, albeit in a variety of forms, in the history of industrial and democratised societies.

The European law parallel is the principle of enumerated competences. Awareness of this parallel is no longer widespread among European law scholars. This is unfortunate, because the sensitivity of the elder discipline for the specifics of legal fields provides some guidance in the interpretation of such opaque provisions as Article 137 (5) EC (now 153 (5) TFEU).[131]

The prudence suggested by conflicts law coincides with what we have noted in our references to the discourse theory of law and democracy.[132] What the ECJ did in the perspective of this theory was to disregard the autonomy and cooriginality of private and political autonomy, and to assign supremacy to economic freedoms over political citizenship. The conflicts law approach does, of course, pretend to have delivered an elaborated re-construction of this inter-dependence at European level. What its understanding of the constitutionalisation strongly suggests, however, is to respect the variety in Europe's social

[129] 'In West European Societies Labour Law was constituted as an alternative to the law of the market. It developed terminological distinctions which one must not disregard: *liberté de commerce* here, freedom of trade there. To be sure, legislation relating to work had been in place pror to that emancipatory move, but pertinent rules were meant to control work in a way which was more or less akin to laws policing the market or markets in general' (translation by the author) – thus A Lyon-Caen, 'Droit communautaire du marché v.s. Europe sociale', Contribution to the Symposium on *The Impact of the Case Law of the ECJ upon the Labour Law of the Member States*, Berlin, 26 June 2008, organised by the Federal Ministry of Labour and Social Affairs, available at: www.bmas.de/portal/27028/2008__07__16__symposium__eugh__lyon-caen.html.

[130] E Rabel, 'Das Problem der Qualifikation' (1931) 5 Rabels Zeitschrift für ausländisches und internationales Privatrecht 241.

[131] See v Bogdandy and Bast, 'The Federal Order of Competences' in eidem, *Principles*, n 48 above, 275, at 294, fn 144; but see also, for example, Conway, 'Values and Conflicts of Norms in EU', n 107 above, ch 5.6, 285 ff.

[132] See nn 92 and 102 above.

models and to promote their coordination in the light of practical experiences. It seems perfectly justified to further the efforts of the new Member States to exploit their competitive advantages. It is by no means plausible, however, that 'direct wage competition'[133] would signal and achieve solidarity with these countries, and further both the prosperity within, and distributional justice among, Europe's diverse regions. It may be that, through the opening of the Western markets for cheap labour, we foreclose the chances for accession states to build up their own social model. Should we really assume that the Swedish employer organisations seek to give a hand to the development of Estonia by the kind of strategies they pursued with Laval and the financing of the lengthy litigation in that case? European law should know more about the social price to be paid for the bringing of cheap labour to Old Europe before engaging in the flattening of Europe's diversity.[134]

'Restraint' v 'activism' is not the proper frame for these issues. The type of prudence which the conflicts law approach requires is as at least as demanding as, but not identical with, what we expect from the constitutional courts of consolidated nation states or federations in their supervision of legislation. To this issue, we will have to return.

VI. CONFLICTS LAW OR COMMUNITY METHOD? RESPONSES TO UPPER AUSTRIA'S CONCERNS WITH ATOMIC ENERGY

The protection of 'health and life of humans, animals and plants' was mentioned as a legitimate regulatory concern in Article 36 EEC Treaty and complemented by the recognition of environmental protection as a matter of 'general interest' in the aftermath of *Cassis de Dijon*. Environmental issues are, indeed, the best conceivable case for the theoretical and normative core of the conflicts-law approach. Nowhere is it more evident that national decision-making has external effects, and that those affected in another territory

[133] See F Rödl, 'Transnationale Lohnkonkurrenz: ein neuer Eckpfeiler der "sozialen" Union?' in A Fischer-Lescano et al (eds), *Europäische Gesellschaftsverfassung. Zur Konstitutionalisierung sozialer Demokratie in Europa* (Baden-Baden: Nomos, 2009) 145.

[134] Tellingly enough, in the US, nobody seems to doubt that, in cases in which an enterprise from a poorer and lower-wage State brings its workers to a higher-wage, more generous State, the latter's higher labour standards apply to those workers. Communication from Professor Cynthia Estlund, NYU Law School. The mindset of European constitutionalists seems quite firmly closed against alarming evidence and argument which would question their practical wisdom. This holds true for the empirical findings and sociological analyses in Neil Fligstein's prize-winning *Euro-Clash: The EU, European Identity and the Future of Europe* (Oxford: OUP, 2008), and, equally, for their legal implications. Rödl, n 133 above, and M Everson are among the few who have complained 'about the dire consequences of forcing a working-class into wage competition with itself' and 'the exclusion in the name of "social justice" and the aid of "proportionality"' of a 'European working-class from any possible site of political contestation, within which its antagonistic interests might be presented and asserted': Everson, n 92 above, at 159.

are regularly excluded from intra-state/domestic decision-making processes. Nowhere does it seem more plausible to establish a transnational regime with the potential to correct such failures Last but not least, environmental issues are, often enough, of such political sensitivity that it makes sense to insist on the kind of horizontally-inclusive constitutionalism which the conflicts law advocates.

European law and pertinent theoretical conceptualisations were, for a long time, far from respecting such insights. The unanimity rule governed in environmental policies. Political scientists provided us with the distinction of product and process regulation, which seemed to rationalise the autonomy of national preference-building. However, since Maastricht, environmental protection has become a commitment of constitutional dignity – and has retained this status ever since.[135]

It should hence be easy to provide plausible evidence militating in favour of our claim that the conflicts-law approach is not something external to the integration project but a dimension of it which can be re-constructed in Europe's political and legal development. However, the discussion here will be restricted to one recent example of particular sensitivity, namely, the litigation over the Temelín nuclear power plant, between its operator ČEZ, a power-supply undertaking in the Czech Republic, and the Austrian Land of Oberösterreich, owner of a piece of land located at a distance of just 60 km from Temelín. The Temelín saga had two main stages.

VI.1. Case C-343/04: *Land Oberösterreich v ČEZ*

The Temelín nuclear plant was authorised by Czecheslovakian authorities back in 1985, and was brought into operation upon a trial basis and has, since 2003, been working at full capacity.

The Austrians complained about ionising radiation emanating from the plant. They framed their complaint in private law categories and the controversy was hence, at this first stage, fought out as a genuine horizontal conflict under the pertinent rules of private international law and the jurisdictional provisions of the Brussels Convention of 1968.

The *Land Oberösterreich* brought its action before the *Landgericht* Linz, seeking an order that ČEZ put an end to the actual or potential nuisance relating to the ionising radiation emissions potentially emanating from the Temelín power plant, in so far as they exceeded those to be expected from a nuclear power station operated in accordance with current generally-recognised technological standards. Upper Austria based this request upon the *actio negatoria* of § 364 (2)

[135] See Article 11 TFEU.

of the Austrian Civil Code.[136] Advocate General Poiares Maduro, in his Opinion of 11 January 2006, and the ECJ, in its judgment of 18 May 2006,[137] therefore turned to the pertinent provisions of the Convention. They hence asked: Are rights *in rem* at issue here so that the Austrian courts can invoke Article 16 of the Convention and claim exclusive jurisdiction? Is this matter instead to be qualified as a tort in the sense of Article 5 III, governed by the *lex loci delicti* ('the place where the harmful event occurred')?

The answer given by the ECJ to the question so framed sounds plausible:

> [I]t cannot be considered that an action such as that pending before the national court should in general be decided according to the rules of one State rather than the other and in conclusion: this is no case of exclusive Austrian *in rem* jurisdiction.[138]

Plausible as it sounds, one remains puzzled: if Austrian standards must not govern, does it follow that the defendant can operate the plant according to the standards of the Czech Republic without regard for the Austrian concerns? That would constitute a democracy failure of the type described above.[139] Advocate General Poiares Maduro, in one of his scholarly opinions, was digging much deeper: the courts of both interested states should be able to claim exclusive jurisdiction for the analysis of the statutory restrictions on ownership over immovable property located in their respective territories.[140] This, however, implies that the risk of conflicting judgments.[141] 'In such cases the judgment to be delivered must pay special attention to the transnational character of the situation.'[142] This may sound a bit sibylline, but it indicates, in fact, the need for a conflicts-law response:

> If the national legal system allows the protection of property either through a property rule or a liability rule, the transnational dimension of the case and the possible difficulty of making a full cost-benefit analysis may be relevant to such a choice. Secondly, the same concern for the consideration of the transnational character of the situation may be relevant in seeking a balance of all relevant elements with respect to the assessment of the amount of damage or the assessment of the risk that such damage may occur.[143]

The ECJ found a quite comfortable way out, explaining merely that Austria cannot claim exclusive jurisdiction. This was only a preliminary end of the saga's first chapter.

[136] § 364 (2) of the Austrian Civil Code states: 'The owner of land may prohibit his neighbour from producing effects, emanating from the latter's land, by effluent, smoke, gases, heat, odours, noise, vibration and the like, in so far as they exceed normal local levels and significantly interfere with the usual use of the land. Direct transmission, without a specific legal right, is unlawful in all circumstances.'

[137] [2006] ECR I-04557.

[138] Case C-343/04, para 36.

[139] Section IV.1.

[140] Para 90.

[141] Para 91.

[142] Para 93.

[143] AG Maduro in Case C-343/04, [2006] ECR I-4584, at 4559 (para 95).

VI.2. Case C-115/08: *Land Oberösterreich v ČEZ as*

The Czech Republic and Austria have apparently taken Maduro's advice seriously. Both states

> ... declared that they would fulfil the series of bilateral obligations, including safety measures, monitoring free movement rights and the development of energy partnerships, set out in a document known as 'The Conclusions of the Melk Process and Follow-Up', which was concluded in November 2001.[144]

VI.2.1. The Shadow of Weber over Austria's Oberster Gerichtshof

But this agreement did not stop Upper Austria from pursuing its complaint further. In April 2006, they obtained a judgment from the *Oberster Gerichtshof*, which was based upon the exception from § 364 (2) adopted in § 364a. This provision reads:

> However, if the interference is caused, in excess of that level, by a mining installation or an officially authorised installation on the neighbouring land, the landowner is entitled only to bring court proceedings for compensation for the damage caused, even where the damage is caused by circumstances which were not taken into account in the official authorisation process.

The Austrian Court's judgment is as traditional as it is interesting in the reasons stated for the refusal to recognise the authorisation of the Czech plant. Such authorisations, the Court explained, have to weigh conflicting considerations and interests. This weighing, however, occurred in a foreign jurisdiction, and there was hence 'no reason why Austrian law should restrict the property rights of Austrian landowners purely in the interests of protecting a foreign economy and public interests in another country'.[145] This can be read as a tribute to the political nature of decisions on high-risk activities and the need for a democratic basis of such decisions. A principled refusal of Austrian courts to recognise the legitimacy of foreign authorisation is a blatant breach of European commitments. Unsurprisingly, both the ECJ and its Advocate General concurred in the conclusion. They differed, however, significantly and illuminatingly, in the reasoning upon which they based this conclusion. They shared the same quandary in their responses to the true conflict underlying the controversy between the two neighbours: Austria, after a referendum held in 1978, committed in its constitution to the rejection of atomic energy and confirmed its position by an unanimous parliamentary vote in 1997. Austria's neighbours are not entitled to reverse this position. On the other hand, Austria must not impose its views in its neighbours.

[144] AG Maduro, ibid, 4559 (para 3).

[145] Thus the report on the judgment of the Austrian *Obrerster Gerichtshof* at para 51 of the judgment in Case C-115/08, [2009] ECR I-10265.

VI.2.2. Administrative Suprantionalism in the ECJ's Grand Chambre

When confronted with the differences between Austria and the Czech Republic, the ECJ started to search for a resolution at a higher legal level. That search, however, did not lead to conclusive results. True, the EAEC Treaty of 1957, in its Title II, contains 'provisions designed to encourage progress in the field of nuclear energy'. Neither this Treaty nor any other provision of European law grants the competence 'to authorise the construction or operation of nuclear installations'.[146] All that Articles 30–31 EAEC provide for are procedures for the coordination of national standards for the protection of dangers from ionising radiation.[147] The gap between these Articles remains puzzling. The way the ECJ takes out of this dilemma is troubling: The principle of prohibition of discrimination on grounds of nationality precludes, so the ECJ explains, legislation of a Member State under which an undertaking in possession of the necessary official authorisations for operating a nuclear power plant situated in the territory of another Member State may be the subject of an action for an injunction. Then follows a concession:

> [T]he national court must, as far as is at all possible, interpret [the domestic legislation] in a way which accords with the requirements of Community law. Where application in accordance with those requirements is not possible, the national court must fully apply Community law and protect the rights conferred thereby on individuals ...
>
> In the last instance, however, the national court is bound to protect the rights which Community law confers on individuals.[148]

VI.2.3. AG Poiares Maduro's Flirt with Conflicts Law

The Opinion which Advocate General Maduro delivered to the Court on 22 April 2009 is indefinitely more elegant. Maduro does not seek an escape route to public law of spurious supranational validity. The way he frames the *problématique* is a variant of the 'argument from external effects':

> This case may be characterised as one which turns on the question of reciprocal externalities. On the one side, Austria and, in particular, the Land Oberösterreich believe they are victims of an externality imposed on them by ČEZ and the Czech authorities in installing a nuclear power plant next to the Austrian border without taking into account the risks imposed on those living on the other side of the border. On the other side, ČEZ and the Czech Republic argue that it is the interpretation of Austrian law made by the Austrian Supreme Court that imposes on them an externality by

[146] Ibid para 103.
[147] Ibid paras 111 et seq.
[148] Ibid paras 138, 140.

> requiring them to close the Czech nuclear power plant simply to protect the interests of Austrian citizens and without taking into account the situation in the Czech Republic.[149]

Not only the diagnosis, but also the suggested therapy is very much in line with the conflicts-law approach. Maduro defines the law's proper objective as

> making national authorities, insofar as is possible, attentive to the impact of their decisions on the interests of other Member States and their citizens since this goal can be said to be at the core of the project of European integration and to be embedded in its rules.[150]

He arrives at his solution in two bold steps. The first is an upgrading of the economic freedoms which he had already prepared in his PhD thesis, and later on famously developed further.[151] Maduro transforms the 'argument from external effects' into a legal duty to respect the extra-territorial interests of economic actors:

> [T]he rules of free movement aim at eliminating any restriction imposed by a Member State on economic activity in or with another Member State. A cross-border element is required but that cross-border element does not need to involve an actual hindrance of free movement from or to the State imposing the measure. It is sufficient that the extraterritorial application of that State measure may affect economic activity in another Member State or between other Member States.[152]

This move implies that it is up to Austria to justify the impact of its restrictive views on the Czech Republic. In this respect, he seems to proceed more subtly than the ECJ. The duty to take the impact of Austrian decisions on its neighbours into account is indeed an implication of the 'argument from external effects'. It is also worth noting that the Advocate General does not camouflage the lacunae of European law in the present constellation.[153] That argument, however, works both ways. The Czech Republic must take the concerns of its neighbours seriously. This is precisely the type of 'true' conflict which should, according to the conflicts of law's theory of the American conflicts scholar Brainerd Currie, be resolved by a higher legislative authority (by Congress in the American federal system).[154] Advocate General Maduro does not refer to such theorising, but he is perfectly aware of the *problématique* to which Brainerd Currie responded in

[149] AG Maduro in Case C 115/08, para 1.

[150] Ibid.

[151] Very markedly, for example, in *Viking*, n 108 above, and in his Opinion in Case C-210/06, *Cartesio Oktató és Szolgáltató bt*, delivered on 22 May 2008.

[152] Thus, AG Maduro in para 16 of his Opinion in Case 115/08, delivered on 22 April 2009.

[153] Ibid, paras 1 and 13.

[154] B Currie, 'The Constitution and the Choice of Law: Governmental Interests and the Judicial Function' in idem, *Selected Essays on the Conflict of Laws* (Durham NC: Duke University Press, 1958) 188, at 272.

such an uncomfortable way. He implicitly subscribes to the 'true conflict' analysis with his notion of 'reciprocal externalities'[155] – and then seeks to avoid Currie's *non possumus* in a search for a reconciliation of both concerns:

> In balancing the achievement of public policy goals, such as protection of human health and property rights, with the restriction of rights protected by Article 43 EC and other free movement provisions which a refusal to recognise a Czech authorisation will entail, the Austrian court must take account of the fact that Community law specifically authorises the development of nuclear installations and the development of nuclear industries in general. It must also give weight to the fact that the authorisation granted to the Temelín facility by the Czech authorities was granted in accordance with the standards established by the relevant Community law.[156]

The first step in the argument sounds nothing but logical, the second, however, is not easily to reconcile with the Advocate General's observation that 'the EAEC rules are only aimed at regulating the conditions under which a nuclear facility should be authorised to operate'.[157] It is by no means clear why such regulations should trump Austria's constitutionalised 'no' to atomic energy. The democracy gap which we have observed in the ECJ's labour law jurisprudence re-surfaces again and the answers remain unsatisfactory. The non-discrimination principle alone must not outrule Austria's principled objections against nuclear energy. The economic freedoms which the Treaty grants to Czech citizens must not trump the political rights of Austrian citizens. This constellation is even more intricate than the conflicts between national labour law and European freedoms. There, we have argued that European law would be well advised to respect national welfare traditions. This type of solution is unavailable in the present conflict. European law can neither legitimise nor prohibit nuclear energy. One may argue that *de facto* irrevocable decisions like that on atomic energy should never be taken. But such a normative argument must not be transformed into a legally-binding decision by judicial *fiat*. At the end of the day, Advocate General Maduro, but equally the ECJ, gave the only possible answer to an irresolvable *problématique*.

VII. THE 'GEOLOGY' OF CONTEMPORARY LAW AND THE PROJECT OF A THREE-DIMENSIONAL CONFLICTS LAW

'United in Diversity', *unitas in pluralitate*, the motto of the Constitutional Treaty, transposes the European ambitions and perspectives of the conflicts-law approach. Neither the significance of this motto, nor its translation into the language and proceduralising methodology of the conflicts-law approach is

[155] AG Maduro, Case 115/08, n 152 above, para 1.
[156] AG Maduro, ibid, para 16.
[157] AG Maduro, ibid, para 13.

confined to Europe's postnational constellation. The need to cope with conflicting policies and to ensure the legitimacy of their 'weight' and coordination is present at all levels of governance, in the international system as well as within constitutional democracies. At all levels, this *problématique* has provoked a turn to 'proceduralisation', and fostered the insight that legal decision-making cannot be deductive but must be constructive, and must derive its legitimacy from the quality of the procedures guiding its decision-making processes. The identification of this *problématique* at all levels of governance and in the 'diagonal conflicts constellations' between them, which multi-level constellations generate, is just one message of the conflicts-law approach, which these concluding remarks wish to underline. Equally important is a second message which requires a three-dimensional differentiation of the conflicts-law approach. The title of this section alludes to this second message. 'Geology' is a term borrowed from Joseph Weiler, who introduced it to explain transformations of international law of paradigmatic importance.[158] 'International law as Regulation' is a notion which he contrasts with 'international law as Transaction' and 'international law as Community'. To Weiler, it represents 'a new mode of international law, specific in its normativity and legitimacy'. This latter insight corresponds to the grand debates on the new functions and normative qualities of the law of post-*laissez-faire* welfare states, which dominated the agenda of the pre- and post-1968 generations.

VII.1. Post-interventionist Law and the Turn to Regulation and Governance

These two generations witnessed, or participated in, two big waves of theorising. The first wave was preoccupied with the social deficits and methodological flaws of 'legal formalism'; the replacement of formalism by substantive rationality criteria was the slogan of the day.[159] 'Law as regulation' was not the then prevailing terminology; substantive rationality was to be carried into law through 'interventionism'. As all this did not really work out, a second wave of theorising was initiated: substantive rationality was replaced by post-interventionist programming, in particular through reflexive law and the quest for a proceduralisation of the category of law.[160]

These moves sought to come to grips with the law's assumption of, and involvement in, ever new tasks and problem-solving activities. The search for

[158] JHH Weiler, 'The Geology of International Law – Governance, Democracy and Legitimacy' (2004) 64 *Heidelberg Journal of International Law (ZaöRV)* 547, at 552.

[159] See C Joerges, '*Politische Rechtstheorie* and Critical Legal Studies: Points of Contacts and Divergencies' in C Joerges and DM Trubek (eds), *Critical Legal Thought: An American-German Debate* (Baden-Baden: Nomos, 1989) 597, at 611 ff.

[160] Ibid, 626 ff; and previously G Brüggemeier and C Joerges, 'Workshop zu Konzepten des postinterventionistischen Rechts' (1984) 4 *Zentrum für Europäische Rechtspolitik Bremen, Materialien*.

post-interventionist programming ('governance structures' is the now widely-used term) and legal methodologies sought – or should have sought – to reconcile the erosion of formerly 'conditional' legal programmes with the legacy of the rule of law and the idea of law-mediated legitimacy of democratic rule. Nobody has characterised this new challenge as pointedly as Rudolf Wiethölter in one of his early essays: '"Purposive programming" is the living law and legal conditio sine qua non (Lebenselexier) of modern democracies', he submitted back in 1973,[161] and complemented this message in 1977 through the discovery of the affinities or structural analogies with conflict of laws.[162] In the meantime, he had already proclaimed the need for a 'proceduralisation of the category of law'.[163]

Practice, sociological research and theoretical reflections did not come to a standstill. We have, for many years now, accustomed ourselves to ever more sophisticated regulatory programming, and we have, more recently, witnessed a turn to 'governance', a notion encompassing a grand variety of widely used cooperative arrangements between governmental and non-governmental actors. There is no space and no need to elaborate on all this here. The only observation to be underlined concerns the structural parallels in the national and the postnational constellations. The geology which Joseph Weiler has depicted in international law can be observed at all levels, even within constitutional law. Parallel structures generate similar challenges. Regulatory politics need to be institutionalised and governance arrangements established within the EU and beyond its 'borders'. The practical challenges and normative problem that these developments pose, however, vary considerably.

VII.2. The Need for a Three-dimensional Conflicts Law

Throughout the preceding sections, we have dealt with primary and secondary European law, on the one hand, and the legal systems of the Member States, on the other. The sociological background analytics, the normative premises of the doctrinal fabric of the conflicts approach can, quite plausibly, claim to capture the distinctiveness of the EU multi-level system and its vertical, horizontal and

[161] See his '*Rechtswissenschaft in Kritik und als Kritik*' [*Critique of Legal Science and Legal Science as Critique*] (Mainz: Universitätschriften, 1973), available at: www.jura.uni-frankfurt.de/l_Personal/em_profs/wiethoelter/RWTexte/KritikalsRecht_Sonderdruck.pdf.

[162] R Wiethölter, 'Begriffs- oder Interessenjurisprudenz – Falsche Fronten im IPR und Wirtschaftsverfassungsrecht: Bemerkungen zur selbstgerechten Kollisionsnorm' in A Lüderitz et al (eds), *Festschrift für Gerhard Kegel* (Frankfurt aM: Metzner, 1977) 213; G Teubner, 'Dealing with Paradoxes of Law: Derrida, Luhmann, Wiethölter' in O Perez and G Teubner (eds), *Paradoxes and Inconsistencies in the Law* (Oxford: Hart Publishing, 2005) 41 [partisan positions are cited there in fn 5]; to be added to this list is now G Conway, 'Values and Conflicts of Norms in EU Law', n 107 above, ch 1 and passim.

[163] 'Materialization and Proceduralization in Modern Law' in G Teubner (ed), *Dilemmas of Law in the Welfare State* (Berlin–New York: Walter de Gruyter, 1986) 221.

diagonal conflicts adequately. With regard to the last, it should have become particularly apparent why the conflicts-law approach cannot be reduced to the choice of a particular legal order. However, European conflicts law is also distinct in the conceptualisation of 'vertical' and 'horizontal' conflicts. Its rules and principles are supranationally valid, and, in this respect, stronger than the legal regimes established by international law; equally unique is the degree to which European law has transformed the *comitas* among Member States into binding legal commitments.[164] This conflicts-law system, however, is by no means comprehensive. The structural reasons have just been addressed: the transformations which have occurred at national level in the turn to regulation and governance are also under way in the EU and in the international system.

Regulatory politics in the EU have led to the establishment of complex transnational non-legislative quasi-administrative regimes, which we have characterised as a *second dimension of conflicts law*. It responds to the irrefutable need to accompany the Europeanisation of the economy by transnational regulatory politics which must operate outside the administrative-law frameworks that nation states have at their disposal. These have triggered the cooperation of national bureaucracies with networks of epistemic communities with the European Commission in the much-criticised – but also much-praised – comitology system, and the establishment of ever more European agencies, most of whom are without genuine decision-making powers. The conflicts-law approach seeks, here too, to defend the idea of the rule of law and law-mediated legitimacy. Its constitutional hopes and perspectives focus on the quality of transnational decision-making and its anchoring in, and supervision by, democratically legitimated actors – hence, again, on a proceduralisation of law.[165]

The *third dimension of conflicts law* reacts to the 'privatisation' of regulative tasks and the development of new 'governance arrangements', which can also be observed at national level, but which are, unsurprisingly, particularly important at transnational levels.[166] Any sharp differentiation between primarily administratively-anchored regulative forms, with which the conflicts law of the second dimension is concerned, and the primarily private regimes is not possible, because of the participation of expert communities and societal actors in both of them. What the law needs to be concerned about is the regulative function which both types exercise, and what it has to consider is its potential to ensure their legitimacy. The conflicts-law approach in its third dimension therefore does not qualify these regimes complacently and without further ado

[164] For a comparison with WTO law, see Howse and Nicolaïdis, 'Democracy without Sovereignty', n 92 above, and Joerges, 'Three-dimensional Conflicts Law', n 93 above.

[165] See C Joerges and M Everson, 'Re-conceptualising Europeanisation as a Public Law of Collisions: Comitology, Agencies and an Interactive Public Adjudication' in CH Hofmann and AH Türk (eds), *EU Administrative Governance* (Cheltenham: Edward Elgar, 2006) 512.

[166] See O Dilling, M Herberg and G Winter, Responsible Business: Self-Governance and Law in Transnational Economic Transaction (Oxford: Hart Publishing, 2008).

as transnational 'law'. Instead, it seeks to develop and promote the impact of normative yardsticks for their recognition by democratic legal orders; it furthermore builds upon the law's shadow, particularly the interests of non-statal orders in external recognition and their ensuing readiness to subject themselves to a stringent procedural discipline.[167]

VII.3. The Mandate of the ECJ in Conflicts-Law Perspectives

Critical assessments of the ECJ, like those that have been submitted above, are apparently difficult to digest even in the relatively progressive law quarters of European law scholarship, and with the critics stigmatised as 'enemies'.[168] The circle of potential addressees is widening. It not only includes political organisations such as trade unions, but may also encompass those who argue that the ECJ operated outside good legal manners in the *Mangold* case,[169] and it without further ado includes the German Constitutional Court after its pronouncements on the Treaty of Lisbon.[170] The discovery of such enemies may [instead] signal more of a crisis of the court, and the Dominicans among its academic allies, than some malicious anti-European scepticism among the ECJ's critics. It should be recalled that the first seminal article on the constitutionalising activity of the ECJ has explained the Court's success by the fact that the ECJ operated 'tucked away in the fairytale Kingdom of Luxembourg'.[171] Eric Stein's most famous disciple warned as early as 1994 that the 'extended honeymoon' between the Court and its interlocutors may have come to an end.[172] We know, indeed, too much about the context and the conditions which have fostered the broad acceptance of the Court's jurisprudence to simply assume that the Court's performance and the Court's recognition by its interlocutors will remain stable.[173]

Should the impact of the ECJ have resulted from the belief in its non-partisanship and the non-political nature of its adjudication, and the beneficial effects of these beliefs, the conflicts-law approach has to plead guilty to the accusation of not respecting this fiction. This unmasking of what cannot be

[167] Thus is the conclusion of the extensive inquiries of H Schepel, The Constitution of Private Governance: Product Standards in the Regulation of Integrating Markets (Oxford: Hart Publishing, 2005) 223.

[168] See FC Mayer, 'Der EuGH als Feind? Die Debatte um das soziale Europa in der europäischen Rechtsprechung' (2009) 14 *Integration* 247.

[169] See D Grimm, 'Die große Karlsruher Verschiebung' in *Frankfurter Allgemeine Zeitung*, 9 September 2010, Nr 209, p 8.

[170] N 23 above.

[171] E Stein, 'Lawyers, Judges and the Making of a Transnational Constitution' (1981) 75 *AJIL* 1.

[172] JHH Weiler, 'The Least Dangerous Branch: A Retrospective and Prospective of the ECJ in the Arena of Political Integration' in idem, *The Constitution of Europe. 'Do the New Clothes Have an Emperor?'* (Cambridge: CUP, 1999) 188, at 206.

[173] A Vauchez, 'The Transnational Politics of Judicialization. *Van Gend en Loos* and the Making of EU Polity' (2010) 16 *ELJ* 1.

concealed anyway, builds upon both so many conclusive analyses of the ECJ in particular and the politicisation of the integration project as a whole.[174] The state of the Union is too critical and the integration project too precious to benefit from this type of critical exchange. Europe and its Court would deserve a more serious effort. Lawyers and political scientists have produced very strong analyses of the Court's performance and impact.[175] It is nevertheless stunning to observe how cautious the *maître penseurs* of constitutional and legal theory operate when it comes to define the theoretical basis and legitimate functions of the ECJ.[176] What these analyses do not include is a political theory of the kind and of the quality of the theorising on constitutional courts and their legitimacy. The conflicts-law approach cannot claim to fill this gap conclusively. The distinction, however, between the supervision of political powers within constitutional democracies, on the one hand, and the compensation of democracy failures of nation states by European law, on the other, should at least provide some new orientation for further research.

[174] See the path-breaking study by A-M Burley (Slaughter) and W Mattli, 'Europe before the Court: A Political Theory of Legal Integration' (1993) 47 *International Organization* 41; and, for the politicisation thesis, M Zürn, "On the Politicisation of the EU" (2006) 47 *Politische Vierteljahreschrift* 242.

[175] See, recently, K Alter, *The European Court's Political Power: Selected Essays* (Oxford: OUP, 2009) 34 ff.

[176] Suffice it to point here to M Rosenfeld, 'Comparing constitutional review by the European Court of Justice and the US Supreme Court' (2008) 4 *International Journal of Constitutional Law* 618; at 633, we read: 'In spite of the remarkable success ... that the ECJ has had with national judges, it does have a vertical division-of-powers legitimacy problem. ... Unlike the US Constitution, ... the EU treaties do not address the supremacy issue. It is the ECJ itself that has ruled that Community law is supreme in its landmark Costa decision'. Does Rosenfeld provide us with an answer, or instead a re-statement of the problem?

27

*The Idea of a Three-Dimensional Conflicts Law as Constitutional Form**

IN THE EPILOGUE to the first edition of this volume,[1] the conflicts-law approach was already presented as an alternative conceptualisation of the law in post-national constellations. The argument was presented somewhat cautiously and inductively. It referred to developments in both European and World Trade Organization (WTO) law, and suggested their re-interpretation. It also underlined the compatibility of the suggested re-orientation with conceptualisations of the 'post-national constellation' in European studies and various strands of International Relations theory. It then alluded, albeit very tentatively, to analyses of the dynamics of modern markets in contemporary strands of economic sociology.[2] The renewed presentation in this chapter will build on recent endeavours both to refine and to broaden the scope of the whole argument.[3] However, the approach remains for the time being merely a project, albeit one with a quite substantiated agenda. Our emphasis here will be on the *clarification* of this agenda, its premises and its aspirations, rather than on a discussion of neighbouring or competing approaches.

* Published in C Joerges and E-U Petersmann (eds), *Constitutionalism, Multilevel Trade Governance and International Economic Law*, 2nd edn (Oxford: Hart Publishing, 2011) ch 15, 413.

[1] C Joerges and E-U Petersmann (eds), *Constitutionalism, Multilevel Trade Governance and Social Regulation* (Oxford: Hart Publishing, 2006) ch 18, 491–527.

[2] See, the introductory section of my Epilogue, n 1 above, with its four programmatic background theses at 492–99.

[3] These include C Joerges, 'Integration through Conflicts Law: On the Defence of the European Project by Means of Alternative Conceptualisation of Legal Constitutionalisation' in R Nickel (ed), *Conflict of Laws and Laws of Conflict in Europe and Beyond: Patterns of Supranational and Transnational Juridification*, (Antwerp–Oxford: Intersentia, 2010) 377; C Joerges and F Rödl, 'Zum Funktionswandel des Kollisionsrechts II: Die kollisionsrechtliche Form einer legitimen Verfassung der post-nationalen Konstellation' in G-P Calliess, A Lescano-Fischer, D Wielsch and P Zumbansen (eds), *Soziologische Jurisprudenz: Festschrift für Gunther Teubner* (Berlin: Walter de Gruyter, 2009) 765; C Joerges, 'Judicialization and Transnational Governance: The Example of WTO Law and the GMO Dispute' in B Iancu (ed), *The Law/Politics Distinction in Contemporary Public Law Adjudication* (Utrecht: Eleven International Publishing, 2009) 67; C Joerges, 'Rethinking European Law's Supremacy: A Plea for a Supranational Conflict of Laws' in B Kohler-Koch and B Rittberger (eds), *Debating the Democratic Legitimacy of the European Union* (Lanham MD: Rowman & Littlefield, 2007) 311.

The argument will proceed in six steps: we will start with terminological remarks which seek to substantiate and to understand the term 'conflicts law', and endeavour to defend its use in post-national constellations (Section I). In the subsequent section, the discussion of all post-, inter- and transnational connotations of the notion will, however, be suspended. Instead, the focus will be on the substantive and methodological developments in the legal systems of constitutional democracies. This move is of central importance for the whole argument for two reasons. The first concerns our terminology and the use of the conflicts-law notion *within* the legal systems of nation states. The second concerns the above-mentioned transformation processes, which have, in the light of the increase of regulatory tasks and then through the adoption of new forms of governance, affected profoundly both the social functions of law and its methodological orientations (Section II). Only after these terminological clarifications in the first section and the re-construction of legal transformation in the second section will the chapter turn to the European [Section III] and the trans-European [Section IV] levels of governance.

The conflicts-law approach will be used at both levels – with an important refinement. It will be submitted that the 'geological' transformations that have been re-constructed within the legal systems of constitutional democracies necessitate the development of a differentiated, three-dimensional conflicts-law approach with *the first* reflecting the interdependence of the formerly more autonomous jurisdictions, *the second* dimension responding to the rise of the regulatory state, and *the third* dimension considering the turn to governance – in particular, the inclusion of non-governmental actors in regulatory activities and the emergence of para-legal regimes. It seems obvious, however, that the elaboration of these perspectives should distinguish between Europe and the international system. In the European Union, which will be discussed in Section III, the conflicts-law approach can build – in all of its three dimensions – upon legal commitments, regulatory and administrative competences, which are not available and cannot be pasted onto the transnational level. The need to respond to regulatory concerns and to generate transnational governance structures is, nevertheless, irrefutable at all levels of governance. Hence, there is a basis for a three-dimensional conflicts law, albeit one which takes the discrepancies between the European and the international constellation into account. 'Irrefutable need' is a notion with normative, as well as functional, connotations. The functional dimension will be examined in the analytical frameworks of economic sociology, within which we seek a non-legal basis for our understanding of markets as 'social institutions'. The Polanyian notion of the 'always socially embedded' economy is a particularly challenging conceptualisation of both the non-legal foundations *and* the dependencies of markets, not only those of the formerly national economies, but also contemporary 'markets beyond the state'. This contextual background does not provide the 'solution' to the functional and normative issues of transnational governance. It is, nevertheless, both instructive and of significance for the broader debate on constitutionalism beyond the state – which is, according to eminent scholars, 'the central challenge faced by international philosophers in the 21st century'.[4] Our own perspectives are ambitious: we understand the conflicts-law approach as the proper constitutional form of law-mediated transnational democratic governance; as a *democratic* perspective which is not dependent on the establishment of a European state or a world republic.[5] Instead, Karl Polanyi's economic sociology will be invoked as a sociological basis of this vision. It seems to us that Polanyi's analyses of the recurrent tensions between dis-embedding strategies and re-embedding counter-moves capture the unruliness of the post-national constellation adequately – thereby providing new perspectives for an understanding of the potential of law to contribute to the social embedding of transnational markets (Section V).

I. INTRODUCTORY OBSERVATIONS ON THE METHODOLOGICAL NATIONALISM OF TRADITIONAL CONFLICT OF LAWS AND THE INSTITUTIONAL DIMENSIONS OF THE CHOICE-OF-LAW *PROBLÉMATIQUE*

The presentation of the substantive and methodological arguments which we are going to submit in this chapter has first to address the irritations which our terminology is bound to, and, indeed, meant to, generate. These irritations will be twofold. With the notion of conflicts law, we recall connotations of a tradition from which we will distance ourselves because of its striking 'methodological nationalism'. Notwithstanding this, we will then argue that European law should be re-conceptualised with the help of a modernised understanding of this tradition. Move and counter-move are even *meant* to provide new perspectives on institutional core problems and the constitutionalisation of transnational governance.

I.1. The Legacy of Classical Private International Law and its Methodological Nationalism

The history of 'modern' private international law is said to commence in Germany in 1849 by a Copernican turn against pre-modern legal traditions with

[4] P Allot, 'The Emerging Universal Legal System' (2001) 3 *International Law Forum du droit international* 12, at 16; A Moravcsik, 'Is there a "Democratic Deficit" in World Politics? A Framework for Analysis' (2004) 39 *Government and Opposition* 336, uses even stronger language. Constitutionalism 'is emerging as one of the central questions – perhaps the central question – in contemporary world politics', at 336.

[5] See the references in n 3 above, and F Rödl, 'Demokratische Verrechtlichung ohne Verstaatlichung: Kollisionsrecht statt Globalstaat' in O Eberl (ed), *Transnationalisierung der Volkssouveränität. Festschrift für Ingeborg Maus* (Stuttgart: Franz Steiner Verlag, 2011) 271.

the publication of Volume VIII of von Savigny's famous treatise,[6] and, in the United States, with Joseph Story's legendary *Commentaries*.[7] The – in many respects – congenial conceptualisations of private international relations by these two founding fathers should, notwithstanding their seemingly technical and doctrinal emphasis, be understood in the broader context of the political history of the sovereign nation state. The 'juridical' conceptualisation of international relations by the various legal disciplines was based upon the same paradigm as traditional theories of international relations. To give a very brief account,[8] traditional (public) international law (*ius gentium*) was confined to the ordering of inter*state* relations. National public law – in particular, administrative law – was conceptualised as an emanation of the power of the sovereign; hence, a truly 'international' public law was inconceivable, and *inter*national public and administrative law was, instead, confined to the delineation of the sphere of application of national provisions. It had to operate 'one-sidedly', because, in the heyday of legal positivism, any subjection to the commands of the law of another sovereign seemed inconceivable.[9]

In contrast, private international law in the von Savigny tradition was more universalistic in its orientations. Its universalism was, however, based upon an understanding of private law as the organiser of strictly private relations in a – by definition – apolitical (civil) society. The private law orders of civilised (Christian) nations could be treated as equivalent, and the application of foreign law was not perceived as involving, let alone threatening, the sovereignty of the *forum* state. This type of universalism is fully compatible with the refusal to support foreign regulatory objectives. Such 'political' dimensions are beyond private law. Friedrich Carl von Savigny, Germany's *maître penseur* of all times, knew, of course, about public law and the public order. But to incorporate what we now call regulatory or political objectives into the legal order was about realising non-legal (*außerrechtliche*) values, and thus was stepping outside the law. If private international law were to engage in such activities, it would, in his understanding, cease to be law at all.[10]

Why should one be aware of this legacy? The traditional dichotomies of private law and public (including administrative) law are generally firmly held

[6] FC von Savigny, *System des heutigen römischen Rechts* (Berlin: Veit, 1849).

[7] J Story, *Commentaries on the Conflict of Laws*, 3rd edn (Boston MA: Little & Brown, 1846).

[8] This history is no longer well known but very well explored. See, recently, A Mills, 'The Private History of International Law' (2006) 55 *International & Comparative Law Quarterly* 1.

[9] See K Vogel, *Der räumliche Anwendungsbereich der Verwaltungsrechtsnorm* (Frankfurt aM: Metzner, 1965) 176; for alternative traditions, see C Tietje, *Internationalisiertes Verwaltungshandeln* (Berlin: Duncker & Humblot, 2001).

[10] J Israël, *European Cross-Border Insolvency Regulation* (Antwerp–Oxford: Intersentia, 2004) at 102; R Michaels, 'Globalizing Savigny? The State in Savigny's Private International Law and the Challenge of Europeanization and Globalization' in M Stolleis and W Streeck (eds), *Aktuelle Fragen politischer und rechtlicher Steuerung im Kontext der Globalisierung* (Baden-Baden: Nomos, 2007) 119, at 129–30.

to be outdated. And, in fact, the disciplines of international private, economic and administrative law all became aware of the post-*laissez-faire* transformations of the 'private law society', the intrusion of regulatory objectives into our legal systems. They took them, albeit often hesitantly, into account in the choice-of-law process. But even where this happened, any move beyond a 'unilateral' or 'one-sided' determination of the international sphere of the application of domestic law (the *lex fori*) towards some transnational cooperative legal responses for all the jurisdictions concerned remained enormously challenging, if at all conceivable. This hesitancy is often expressed as a refusal to comply with the commands of a foreign sovereign. However, it need not be based upon nationalist parochialism. Good 'constitutional' reasons can be invoked – in particular, queries regarding the validity claims of foreign law which is not generated in, and legitimated by, domestic democratic processes, and which therefore simply seem irreconcilable with the principles and rules to which the forum state owes its constitutional allegiance.

It should be readily apparent how deeply the prerogatives of European law have both affected and transformed the normative ordering enshrined in these disciplinary traditions – including their 'methodological nationalism', ie their entanglement in the concepts and methodologies of presumably sovereign nation states and their difficulties to envisage and to conceptualise in their categories a legitimate transnational order. European law imposes on the Member States of the Union the duty to 'recognise' mutually not only foreign private law, but also – to a large extent – the mandatory provisions of foreign 'sovereigns' *regardless* of their 'private' or 'public' legal nature. It has overcome both the 'one-sidedness' (*Einseitigkeit*) of international administrative law *and* the disregard for 'foreign' concerns and interests by national polities. The argument that we submit will neither deny nor obfuscate the presence of conflicts of laws and of interests in Europe. However, we do claim that Europe has institutionalised what, in an important respect, is a revolutionary 'new type of conflicts law'. Before submitting our plea for a re-conceptualisation of European law from such perspectives,[11] and before examining to what degree equivalent accomplishments are conceivable at international level through WTO law,[12] we need to take further preparatory steps.

I.2. Institutional Dimensions of the Choice-of-Law Problem

In order to illustrate the emergence and the institutional delicacy of the choice-of-law problem, we will take another historical detour and recall the ardent critique of traditional conflict of laws by Brainerd Currie, the highly contested leader of the American 'conflict of laws revolution' of the 1960s.[13] This is not to

[11] Section III.

[12] Section IV.

[13] Currie's work is collected in B Currie, *Selected Essays on the Conflict of Laws* (Durham NC: Duke University Press, 1963).

insinuate that his positions could, or even should, be revitalised after more than half a century. His rigid arguments remain nevertheless instructive, and deserve to be taken seriously,[14] in particular, for two inter-related reasons.

The first has already been addressed.[15] Laws, statutes and even common law rules, Currie argued, should be read as pursuing some form of policy. At first sight, this message may sound like a trivial confirmation of the widely accepted insights of American Legal Realism. On closer inspection, however, his views turn out to be more subversive because they build upon daring conceptualisations of the links between law and the political system.[16] These aspects and assaults on the traditional notions of private law in general, and the citadel of private international law in particular, which they imply, come to the fore where Currie substantiates the implications of this seemingly trivial realist insight into intra-state settings: the application and implementation of policy-guided laws, he submitted, will often be backed by the 'governmental interests' of that state, which courts must not disregard. In a nutshell:

> If the court finds that the forum state has an interest in the application of its policy, it should apply the law of the forum, even though the foreign state also has an interest in the application of its contrary policy ...[17]

This is, he explained, because

> choice between the competing interests of co-ordinated states is a political function of a high order, which ought not, in a democracy, to be committed to the judiciary: ... the court is not equipped to perform such a function; and the Constitution specifically confers that function upon Congress.[18]

[14] See, for example, L Kramer, 'Vestiges of Beale: Extraterritorial Application of American Law' (1991) *Supreme Court Review* 179; it is not by chance that sometimes the titles of his essay allude to seminal articles by Currie; see, in particular, L Kramer, 'More Notes on Methods and Objectives in Conflict of Laws' (1991) 24 *Cornell International Law Journal* 245; idem, 'Rethinking Choice of Law' (1990) 90 *Columbia Law Review* 277. See, more recently, PS Berman, 'Towards a Cosmopolitan Vision of Conflict of Laws: Redefining Governmental interests in a Global Era' (2005) 153 *Pennsylvania Law Review* 1819, at 1845 ff; and, for a thoughtful evaluation which covers and contrasts American and European approaches, see H Muir Watt, 'Choice of Law in Integrated and Interconnected Markets: A Matter of Political Economy' (Sept 2003) 7.3 *Electronic Journal of Comparative Law*, available at: www.ejcl.org/ejcl/73/art73-4.html.

[15] Section I.1.

[16] See C Joerges, *Zum Funktionswandel des Kollisionsrechts. Die 'Governmental Interest Analysis' und die Krise des Internationalen Privatrechts* (Berlin-Tübingen: Walter de Gruyter/Mohr Siebeck, 1971) 38. These intricate relations between law, politics and the judicial function are often interpreted too simplistically, even by A Fischer-Lescano and G Teubner, 'Regime-Collisions: The Vain Search for Legal Unity in the Fragmentation of Global Law' (2004) 25 *Michigan Law Review* 999, in their critique of the governmental interest analysis at 1023.

[17] B Currie, 'Notes on Methods and Objectives in the Conflict of Law' in idem, *Selected Essays on the Conflict of Laws*, n 13 above, 177, at 183–84. See, for another brief summary, his 'Comment on *Babcock* v *Jackson*' (1963) 63 *Columbia Law Review* 1233, at 1242 ff. [See also idem, 'The Disinterested Third State' (1963) 28 *Law & Contemporary Problems* 754, where Currie quotes Justice Roger R Traynor, who, regarding the weight to be accorded a presumption, mused 'Can you weigh a bushel of horsefeathers against next Thursday?']

[18] Idem, 'The Constitution and the Choice of Law: Governmental Interests and the Judicial Function' in idem, *Selected Essays on the Conflict of Laws*, n 13 above, 188, at 272.

It has often been underlined, in particular by adherents of the governmental interest approach,[19] that Currie later softened his position somewhat when he recommended a 'moderate and restrained interpretation'.[20] This concession, Currie's opponents, as well a good number of his followers, have argued, needs to be interpreted as a retreat from his original position. 'Weighing' and 'balancing' is to be acknowledged as an inherent dimension of the judicial function, and hardly anybody hesitates to 'weigh a bushel of horsefeathers against next Thursday'. This type of softening of Currie's radicalism fails to consider that his argument was not epistemological but institutional. His resistance to any judicial derogation from the *lex fori*, where the governmental interests of the forum state are affected, should not be understood as a merely parochial defence of the 'self-interested state'. If there is a kernel of truth in the realist lessons about the political quality of modern law, it is only conclusive to insist on the involvement of politically accountable bodies in the 'weighing' and 'balancing' processes which characterise modern law production and upon which its legitimacy seems to depend. The topicality of Currie's argument should then become apparent. Within the legal systems of constitutional democracies, we have found ways and means to ensure the presence of the political system in, or its correcting re-entry into, the administration of law. We are also becoming aware of the difficulty of establishing equivalent processes at European and at international level. What we are witnessing here is a de-coupling of the legal system from the political system, which then nurtures anxieties about judicialisation and bureaucratisation phenomena. To this issue, we will return.[21] Before considering this query further, however, we have to take a closer look at the 'geology' of national law. This detour is an indispensable step in our turn to conflicts law, which seeks to explain why this law has to become 'three-dimensional'.

II. THE GEOLOGY OF THE LAW OF CONSTITUTIONAL DEMOCRACIES: FROM 'LAW AS REGULATION' TO 'LAW AS GOVERNANCE' AND THE DEFENCE OF THE RULE OF LAW THROUGH PROCEDURALISATION

'Geology' is a term borrowed from Joseph Weiler, who introduced it to explain transformations of international law of paradigmatic importance.[22] 'International law as Regulation' is a notion which he contrasts with 'international law as Transaction' and 'international law as Community'. It represents 'a new mode of international law, specific in its normativity and legitimacy'. This latter insight corresponds to the grand debates on the new functions and

[19] See, for example, Kramer, 'Vestiges of Beale', n 14 above.

[20] B Currie, 'The Disinterested Third State' (1963) 28 *Law & Contemporary Problems* 754.

[21] Section IV.1(c) below.

[22] JHH Weiler, 'The Geology of International Law – Governance, Democracy and Legitimacy' (2004) 64 *Heidelberg Journal of International Law* (*ZaöRV*) 547, at 552.

normative qualities of the law of post-*laissez-faire* welfare states, which dominated the agenda of the pre- and post-1968 generations.

II.1. The Post-interventionist Law of Constitutional Democracies

We can discern two waves in these debates. The first wave was embedded in a critique of the social deficits and methodological flaws of 'legal formalism'. Carried away by a broad social reform agenda, learned jurists engaged in a critique of 'formal rationality' in private and administrative law, which they sought to replace with substantive rationality criteria.[23] 'Law as regulation' was not the then prevailing terminology, but it was a core concern of the reformist movement, articulated and analysed in a specific parlance, namely, as a shift from 'conditional' to 'purposive' legal programming. Such grand theoretical concepts were invoked to articulate the paradigmatic importance of the reformist project. Contemporary accounts were, of course, controversial. The ambitious perspectives were perceived as the 'Achilles' heel' of the whole movement, in particular by Niklas Luhmann, who had invented the dichotomy in his sociology of law.[24] Such moves, Niklas Luhmann observed from his proverbial ironic distance, were bound to fail because they were at odds with the functioning of the legal system in functionally differentiated societies.[25] Alternative theoretical assessments are conceivable, Rudolf Wiethölter objected, and their realisation can build upon the 'fact' that 'purposive programming' is the living law and legal *conditio sine qua non* of modern democracies;[26] although, he added, we have to become aware of the ambivalences, and learn how to discipline the 'political administration' that it has established, and we also have to understand it as a potential and ongoing counter-movement against the shadows of German law's undemocratic past.

These controversies could not be, and were not, resolved. Instead, the attention shifted in the 1980s to the failures and to the fallacies of social reform projects. Economists provided theories of regulatory failures, sociologists and political scientists uncovered failures in the implementation of political programmes, and legal theorists, who became aware of all this, started a new

[23] See C Joerges, 'Politische Rechtstheorie and Critical Legal Studies: Points of Contacts and Divergencies' in C Joerges and DM Trubek (eds), *Critical Legal Thought: An American-German Debate* (Baden-Baden: Nomos, 1989) 597; re-published as 'SocioTheoretically Based Legal Science and Critical Legal Studies: Points of Contact and Divergencies' (2011) 12 *German Law Journal* 554, available at: www.germanlawjournal.com/index.php?pageID=11&artID=1333.

[24] N Luhmann, *Rechtssoziologie*, vol II (Reinbek bei Hamburg: Rowohlt, 1972), at 227 ff; see, later, idem, *Das Recht der Gesellschaft* (Frankfurt aM: Suhrkamp, 1993) at 195–204.

[25] Concise and beautifully ironic is his look at the doctrinal art of jurists in N Luhmann, *Rechtssystem und Rechtsdogmatik* (Stuttgart: Kohlhammer, 1974).

[26] See R Wiethölter, *Rechtswissenschaft in Kritik und als Kritik* (Mainz: Universitätschriften, 1973); and idem, 'Wirtschaftsrecht' in A Görlitz (ed), *Handlexikon zur Rechtswissenschaft* (Munich: Ehrenwirth, 1972) 531, at 531.

search for the concepts of a 'post-interventionist' law.[27] The search was again inspired by grandiose social theories (*Gesellschaftstheorien*). Jürgen Habermas had revealed how the law of the welfare state contributed to a 'colonisation of the lifeworld'.[28] It became ever more apparent that economic and social processes were embedded in a much more complex way in modern societies than the dichotomies that pitted market and state, economy and intervention, law and economics in (quasi-) oppositional relations. Systems theory embarked upon the long-term project of re-constructing the functions of law in its own terms.[29] For the time being, however, it seemed both possible *and* constructive to suspend the efforts to anchor legal conceptualisations faithfully in 'grand theories, and to focus, instead, on a re-design of 'legal rationality', which would be sufficiently sensitive towards the new insights into the failures of legal interventionism, while, nevertheless, avoiding a regression into the formalist traditions. 'Proceduralisation of the category of law'[30] and 'reflexive law'[31] became the two main reference points in the efforts to re-conceptualise the law's 'geology'.

The long-term impact and the practical importance of these endeavours do not so much stem from their theoretical ambitions, or their conceptual elegance, let alone from some German idiosyncrasies, but primarily from the broad range of contextual studies which they have inspired. They triggered the search for soft-law and regulatory alternatives to command and control regulation; they realised that the law of constitutional democracies is, on the one hand, expected to operate effectively and to organise economic and social regulation accordingly, but that, on the other hand, it still needs to maintain its responsiveness to wider social legitimacy concerns; they engaged in the re-fashioning of the constitutional and administrative legal spheres and the development of constructive and legitimate synergies between markets and hierarchies.

This section is not meant to contribute new insights into legal theory and legal sociology. Its objective is to pave the way for a systematic move in the elaboration of the conflicts-law approach. This objective both necessitates and justifies a drastic simplification of the conceptualisation of the law's

[27] See G Brüggemeier and C Joerges, '*Workshop zu Konzepten des postinterventionistischen Rechts*' (Bremen: Zentrum für Europäische Rechtspolitik, Materialien 4, 1984).

[28] J Habermas, *Theorie des kommunikativen Handelns*, vol II: *Zur Kritik der funktionalistischen Vernunft* (Frankfurt aM: Suhrkamp, 1981) at 522 ff; idem, 'Law as Medium and Law as Institution' in G Teubner (ed), *Dilemmas of Law in the Welfare State* (Berlin: Walter de Gruyter, 1985) 203.

[29] See Teubner (ed), *Dilemmas of Law*, n 28 above, and his 'Juridification – Concepts, Aspects, Limits, Solutions' in idem (ed), *Juridification of Social Spheres* (Berlin–New York: Walter de Gruyter, 1987) 3.

[30] R Wiethölter, 'Proceduralisation of the Category of Law' in Joerges and Trubek (eds), *Critical Legal Thought: An American-German Debate*, n 23 above, 501; J Habermas, *Between Facts and Norms. Contributions to a Discourse Theory of Law and Democracy* (Cambridge MA: The MIT Press, 1999 [1992]), at 414.

[31] G Teubner, 'Substantive and Reflexive Elements in Modern Law' (1983) 17 *Law and Society Review* 239.

contemporary 'geology', namely, the distinction between 'law as regulation' and 'law as governance'. The distinction is not categorical but gradual. It is meant to underline the dimensions of post-interventionist law, which are omnipresent and even inter-dependent, even though they have different weight in 'regulatory programmes' and 'governance arrangements'.

One characteristic feature of modern post-interventionist law is its dependence upon non-legal expertise. Wolfgang Schluchter has conceptualised this move by distinguishing between '*Amtsautoritat*' and '*Sachautoritat*' respectively;[32] institutionally-derived authority as opposed to authority based upon some specific expertise which is supposed to strengthen the merits of decisions taken by administrators, regulators, and, of course, legislatures. Typically, this kind of 'cognitive opening' of law will be accompanied by a 'practical opening', namely, the resort to the management capacities and the knowledge resources of non-governmental actors and organisations. Both openings present a challenge to the rule of law. Expertise does not simply generate 'objective' answers to normative questions pre-fabricated by law. The inclusion of societal actors in the preparation and implementation of policy programmes cannot be reduced to a servicing function, but will open participatory mechanisms and channels of influence.

In what respects and to what degrees these developments seem either challenging or deplorable, and what kind of responses they require, depends upon the theoretical perspectives from which they are observed. Jürgen Habermas, in his *magnum opus* on legal theory, seems very deeply concerned, if not embarrassed:

> When faced with political decisions relevant to the whole of society, the State must be able to perceive, and if necessary assert, public interests as it has in the past. Even when it appears in the role of an intelligent advisor or supervisor who makes procedural law available, this kind of law-making must remain linked back to legislative programs ina transparent, comprehensible and controllable way.[33]

Habermas' *monitum*, which reflects core messages of his discourse theory of law, cannot be 'applied' literally to the law of regulatory politics and governance arrangements. Habermas' concession that legislation has to resort to procedural techniques of supervision implies that the idea of law-mediated governance needs to be re-defined and adjusted so that it can continue to provide orientation in the assessment of both regulatory practices *and* the development of new modes of governance. The 'proceduralisation' of the category of law implies a shift to the 'constitutionalisation' of regulatory bodies and of de-centralised arenas of law production.[34] The extension of constitutionalism into both dimensions has

[32] W Schluchter, *Aspekte bürokratischer Herrschaft. Studien zur Interpretation der fortschreitenden Industriegesellschaft* (Frankfurt aM: Suhrkamp, 1972, reprint 1985) 145.

[33] Habermas, *Between Facts and Norms*, n 30 above, at 441.

[34] See, in different terminology, FI Michelman, *Brennan and Democracy* (Princeton NJ: Princeton University Press, 1999) 34 (Law of law-production), and R Wiethölter, 'Just-ifications of a Law of Society' in O Perez and G Teubner (eds), *Paradoxes and Inconsistencies in the Law* (Oxford: Hart

only recently become a widespread concern, although it responds to much older and broader developments which can be observed, albeit in specific varieties, in all constitutional democracies. To document these parallels, it may suffice here to refer to Jody Freeman's analysis of 'The Private Role of Public Governance',[35] on the one side of the Atlantic, and to Harm Schepel's discovery and defence of a 'Constitution of Private Governance' in the realms of standardisation, on the other.[36] Freeman suggests defining 'governance as a set of negotiated relationships between public and private actors'. One of the examples that she discusses is *regulatory* standard-setting,[37] which is usually presented as an *aliud* to the generation of standards by private organisations. Freeman, however, notes:

> In truth, agencies routinely promulgate rules developed, not internally, but by private parties. Private standard-setting groups are so well integrated into the standard-setting process that their role appears to give neither administrators nor legal scholars pause. However, by adopting privately generated standards after a cursory notice and comment process, agencies may effectively (if not formally) share their standard-setting authority. In this sense, even traditional regulation illustrates public/private interdependence.[38]

Harm Schepel has reviewed equivalent phenomena at national, European and international levels. His notion of a 'constitution' of such regimes is based upon the two dimensions of legitimate governance to which the conflicts law seeks to respond:

> The sociological question of the law's recognition of private governance is, then, indissolubly connected with a normative question of democratic theory: can law recognise legal validity and democratic legitimacy outside the constitution, without constitutional political institutions and beyond the nation state?[39]

II.2. Intra-state Conflicts Law

We will return to the sociological dimension of the legitimacy of transnational governance in the section on economic sociology.[40] For now, it suffices to underline again that we can observe – even within constitutional states, many decades

Publishing, 2005) 65, available at: www.jura.uni-frankfurt.de/ifawz1/teubner/RW.html; see, for a transcultural interpretation, M Everson and J Eisner, *The Making of the EU Constitution: Judges and Lawyers Beyond Constitutive Power* (Abingdon: Routledge-Cavendish, 2007), in particular at 41 ff.

[35] J Freeman, 'The Private Role in Public Governance' (2000) 75 *New York University Law Review* 543.

[36] H Schepel, *The Constitution of Private Governance: Product Standards in the Regulation of Integrating Markets* (Oxford: Hart Publishing, 2005).

[37] Freeman, 'The Private Role in Public Governance', n 35 above, at 638 ff.

[38] Ibid, at 639 (footnote omitted).

[39] Schepel, *The Constitution of Private Governance*, n 36 above, at 2.

[40] Section V below.

before both globalisation and privatisation attracted so much attention – the emergence of a 'geology' of legal layers, each 'specific in its normativity and legitimacy'.[41] This is the basis of our plea for a three-dimensional conflicts law in post-national constellations.

Before exploring these issues, we have to emphasise an analogy and a difference between the laws of the nation-state democracies and those of transnational constellations. The analogy concerns the similarity of transnational and intra-national conflicts, while the difference concerns the means available for their resolution. The first point on the observation of national legal systems in conflicts-law perspectives is of crucial importance for our whole argument. The analogy suggests itself because what we are witnessing in the domestic legal systems of constitutional democracies are precisely the same difficulties which have caused the 'crisis of private international law' and led Brainerd Currie to open bankruptcy procedures over the inherited doctrines of his beloved discipline. Not only internationally, but also domestically, we are confronted with conflicting policies. These conflicts quite regularly concern constitutionally endorsed objectives, which may have been concretised in much detail in environmental, labour market or consumer protection laws but tend to jeopardise each other.

Rudolf Wiethölter, in a kind of summa of his own private international law scholarship which he dedicated to his academic mentor,[42] was the first[43] to uncover these structural similarities, or, rather, challenging implications, of the intrusion of policy commitments into legal programmes. The most prominent answer to the response – on the part of constitutionalists – to these methodological and substantive difficulties is the search for '*praktische Konkordanz*';[44] legal theorists have established an '*Optimierungsgebot*';[45] while the Community legislature provided '*Querschnittsklauseln*' (such as Article 11 TFEU, ex Article 6 TEC on Environmental Protection Requirements). It is not incidental that all these terms are German and pose apparently considerable obstacles to translators.[46] To my mind, the main reason is the need to perform a genuinely

[41] Weiler, 'The Geology of International Law', n 22 above.

[42] R Wiethölter, 'Begriffs- oder Interessenjurisprudenz: Falsche Fronten im IPR und Wirtschaftsverfassungsrecht – Bemerkungen zur selbstgerechten Kollisionsnorm' in A Lüderitz and J Schröder (eds), *Internationales Privatrecht und Rechtsvergleichung im des 20. Jahrhundrets: Bewahrung oder Wende? Festschrift für Gerhard Kegel* (Frankfurt aM: Metzner, 1977) 213, at 232.

[43] Partisan positions are cited in G Teubner, 'Dealing with Paradoxes of Law: Derrida, Luhmann, Wiethölter' in Perez and Teubner (eds), *Paradoxes and Inconsistencies in the Law*, n 34 above, 41, at 42, fn 5.

[44] K Hesse, *Grundzüge des Verfassungsrecht der Bundesrepublik*, 20th edn (Heidelberg: CF Müller, 1999) at para 72.

[45] R Alexy, *Theorie der Grundrechte* (Frankfurt aM: Suhrkamp, 1985) at 75–76.

[46] *Praktische Konkordanz* is 'practical concordance'; *Optimierungsgebot* seems to be an 'optimising maxim'; *Querschnittsklausel* is a 'clause improving a general obligation'.

political task *outside* regular legislative and judicial processes.[47] This may be a daring assertion, but it helps us to understand the dilemmas at transnational levels. Even within the EU, the interaction between the political system and the judicial system has become ever more deficient.[48] At international level, and in particular at WTO level, we are confronted with the *problématique* of fragmentation, which does, indeed, pose – as Jürgen Bast has argued – a fundamental problem to democratic legitimacy.[49]

Conflicts-law issues, we can conclude, are present at *all* levels of governance. They pose problems everywhere. Their intricacies, however, become more disquieting from level to level. The legally significant differences and their sociological background are such that we will deal with Europeanisation and WTO law in two separate sections.

III. EUROPEAN LAW AS CONFLICTS LAW

'The democratic deficit of international law and global governance ... is crucial because it de-legitimises international law and offers a reason for states not to apply and observe international law.'[50] This is a lucid re-statement of a widely, albeit not universally, shared thesis. The normative core message of the conflicts-law approach departs from an antithesis. The difference can best be illustrated by the European example, which is so intensively pre-occupied with the European 'democracy deficit'. The debate on the democratic constitutionalisation of the European polity, we submit, should be turned upside down, ie, re-conceptualised fundamentally. It should depart from the insight that democracy – as nation states organise it – is *necessarily* deficient, whereas European law has the potential to cure such deficits. Thus, Europe is not the problem but the potential cure, a pre-condition for legitimate governance, a point which Jürgen Neyer and I submitted for the first time back in 1997.[51]

[47] 'Discovery procedure of practice' was a notion used against von Hayek's 'competition as discovery procedure'; see, for example, C Joerges, 'Quality Regulation in Consumer Goods Markets: Theoretical Concepts and Practical Examples' in T Daintith and G Teubner (eds), *Contract and Organization* (Berlin: Walter de Gruyter, 1986) 142; for more sophisticated views, see K-H Ladeur, *Kritik der Abwägung in der Grundrechtsdogmatik. Plädoyer für eine Erneuerung der liberalen Grundrechtstheorie* (Tübingen: Mohr Siebeck, 1974); A Fischer-Lescano, 'Kritik der praktischen Konkordanz' (2000) 41 *Kritische Justiz* 166.

[48] See the references in n 93 below.

[49] J Bast, 'Das Demokratiedefizit fragmentierter Internationalisierung' in H Brunkhurst (ed), *Demokratie in der Weltgesellschaft*, *Soziale Welt*, Sonderband 18 (Baden-Baden: Nomos, 2009) 185.

[50] A Peters, 'Dual Democracy' in J Klabbers, A Peters and G Ulfstein, *The Constitutionalization of International Law* (Oxford: OUP, 2009) ch 6 at 263.

[51] C Joerges and J Neyer, 'From Intergovernmental Bargaining to Deliberative Political Processes: The Constitutionalisation of Comitology' (1997) 3 *ELJ* 273, at 293; and C Joerges, 'The Impact of European Integration on Private Law: Reductionist Perceptions, True Conflicts and a New Constitutional Perspective' (1997) 3 *ELJ* 378, at 390.

Even then the argument was not fundamentally new. Jürgen Habermas identified it as the core normative problem of supranational decision-making in his very first essay on European integration.[52] In the same year, Niklas Luhmann addressed the discrepancy between '*Entscheidungszuständigkeit*' (political decision-making powers) and '*Entscheidungsbetroffenheit*' (affectedness by political decisions), without framing it as a democracy problem, in his sociological analysis of risks.[53] The argument clearly has some appeal. But it needs an analytical framework which will allow one to situate it in the wider field of European studies, and it needs to be specified so that its normative orientations can be operationalised in legal arguments.

III.1. Multilevel Governance as Analytical Paradigm in European Studies and the Misery of Methodological Nationalism

The study of European integration in legal quarters is one in which resorting to political science has, by now, become routine. The present interdisciplinary opening of the academic legal world is – to a considerable degree – the result of the rise of the European 'regulatory state' and its subsequent 'turn to governance'.[54] But the foundations for trans-disciplinary endeavours were laid much earlier.

[52] J Habermas, *Staatsbürgerschaft und nationale Identität* [*Citizenship and National Identity*] (Zurich: Erker, 1991), reprinted as Annex II to *Between Facts and Norms*, n 30 above, 491, at 503: the citizens today experience 'an ever greater gap being passively affected and actively participating'.

[53] N Luhmann, *Soziologie des Risikos* (Berlin: Walter de Gruyter, 1991) [*Risk: A Sociological Theory* (New Brunswick NJ: Transaction, 2005)]. The substance of these arguments can, eg, be found in R Howse and K Nicolaïdis, 'Democracy without Sovereignty: The Global Vocation of Political Ethics' in T Broude and Y Shany (eds), *The Shifting Allocation of Authority in International Law: Considering Sovereignty, Supremacy and Subsidiarity* (Oxford: Hart Publishing, 2008) 163, at 167: '[Our] horizontal reading of subsidiarity and supremacy follows directly from the limits of the notion of sovereignty in a world where laws and actions within a polity increasingly have external effects. Supremacy and subsidiarity therefore can be defined in a dialectic way as complementary principles to deal with the fundamental conundrum of transnational democracy. Supremacy serves as a meta-norm of conflict of laws between Member States such as to enhance the representation of foreigners inside the jurisdiction of every Member State, and to ask when and to what extent these interests should trump the domestic social contract.' Similarly, T Cottier, 'The Legitimacy of WTO Law' in L Yueh (ed), *The Law and Economics of Globalization* (Cheltenham: Edward Elgar, 2009) 11, at 15: 'The principles of the WTO, much as those of EU law … compensate for deficiencies in domestic democratic processes as these do not inherently take into account the interests of those not represented by the electorate. WTO law, in other words, addresses a structural failure inherent in the principles of representation. It ensures that democratic processes take into account interests that are not formally represented.' Similarly, much earlier, A von Bogdandy, 'Law and Politics in the WTO – Strategies to Cope with a Deficient relationship' (2001) 5 *Max Planck Yearbook of United Nations Law* 609, at 666: '[M]ore and more purely domestic decisions are having a transnational impact: when a sovereign decision affects the economic interests of people in other states, their interests must be taken into account …'

[54] As proclaimed by the European Commission in 'European Governance. A White Paper', COM(2001) 428 final of 25 July 2001, [2001] OJ C287/5, available at: europa.eu.int/comm/governance/index_en.htm.

Some decades ago, William Wallace had already famously realised and explained why Europe was 'less than a federation' but 'more than a regime'.[55] Lisbeth Hooghe and Gary Marks pioneered the efforts to define positively the European Community's status between the two poles by the notion of 'multilevel governance *sui generis*'.[56] The contours of that notion, however, remain puzzling for both political scientists[57] and academic jurists, both of whom seek to loosen the ties of their inherited categories with the nation state and to transform the notion of 'governance' into a legal category.[58] Michael Zürn has characterised this situation dramatically as a 'misery of methodological nationalism'.[59] His diagnosis is so valuable because it rests upon robust descriptions of the irreversible transformations of the contexts of policy-making in the European, and extra-European post-national, constellation. The nation state is quite clearly no longer in a position to define its political priorities autonomously (as a 'sovereign'), but is, instead, forced to coordinate them transnationally. The citizens of constitutional democracies can no longer be sure of whether and, if so, how they can be – in the last instance – the authors of the laws which they are expected to adhere to, while the nation states to which they belong have become accountable to transnational bodies by which their politics are subject to evaluation.

The conflicts-law approach, so we assert, offers new perspectives for the understanding of the Union's *sui generis* characteristics. This is because the multilevel 'system' is portrayed as a web of potentially conflictual and unstable relationships, rather than some new coherent entity.

The conflicts-law approach

> distinguishes between vertical, horizontal, and diagonal legal conflicts in the EU, ie, conflicts about which legal norms apply to a given case.[60] These three types of legal conflict can be applied to MLG [multilevel governance] generally. Vertical conflicts are conflicts between legal regimes at different territorial levels; they occur both between national law and EU legislation, and between EU law and WTO rules. In horizontal conflicts, the injunctions of different national laws to a given case diverge. Horizontal legal conflicts occur typically in the context of transactions involving the movement

[55] W Wallace, 'Less than a Federation, More than a Regime: The Community as a Political System' in H Wallace and W Wallace (eds), *Policy-Making in the European Community*, 2nd edn (Oxford: OUP, 1983) 403.

[56] G Marks, L Hooghe and K Blank, 'European Integration since the 1980s: State-Centric versus Multi-level Governance' (1996) 34 *JCMS* 343.

[57] See, instructively, B Kohler-Koch and B Rittberger, 'Review Article: The "Governance Turn" in EU Studies' (2006) 44 *JCML Annual Review* 27.

[58] This is by now a transnational debate; see, among the contributions in English by authors from Germany, H Hofmann and A Türk (eds), *EU Administrative Governance* (Cheltenham: Edward Elgar, 2006).

[59] Michael Zürn, 'The State in the Post-National Constellation – Societal Denationalization and Multilevel Governance', *ARENA Working Paper, 35/1999*, Oslo; see, very similarly, Habermas, *Citizenship and National Identity*, n 52 above.

[60] See Joerges, 'The Impact of European Integration', n 51 above, at 378; CU Schmid, 'Vertical and Diagonal Conflicts in the Europeanisation Process' (2000) 8 *ERevPL* 155.

of persons, goods, or finances across national borders. Diagonal legal conflicts finally occur if regimes at two different levels that apply to different aspects of a given case make contradictory demands.[61]

The pure diversity of these conflict constellations militates against any hierarchical re-construction of the European polity – and the variety within the European constellation suggests a differentiating, three-dimensional approach in their legal conceptualisation. In a nutshell: the compensation of democratic deficits of nation states is the primary task of European conflicts law – the essence of its 'first dimension'. However, the European Union has not only to unburden itself from its nationalist and parochial legacy, but it also has to provide constructive responses to its increasingly inter-dependent regulatory tasks and problems, ie, it has to establish cooperative frameworks which ensure that its performance as a transnational regulatory machinery 'deserves recognition' – this is the challenge of the second dimension of its conflicts law. Last, but not least, it has to realise that its steadily widening tasks and commitments overburden its administrative capacity, so that the resort to non-legal expertise and the inclusion of non-governmental bodies in the management of public affairs are becoming irrefutable. We are, in fact, witnessing a multitude of new governance arrangements which compensate for the lack of a political hierarchy in the Union and rely on the self-regulatory schemes and/or the cooperation of non-governmental actors – this is why a third dimension of conflicts law needs to develop mechanisms which ensure the proper performance of these modes of transnational governance.

III.2. The Three-dimensional Fabric of European Conflicts Law

The elaboration of our suggestions in the following sections cannot be comprehensive. We will, instead, illustrate the three dimensions of the conflicts-law approach with the help of enquiries into European primary law, regulatory mechanisms and governance arrangements of exemplary importance. Our objective is again twofold: we will seek to document to what degree the conflicts-law approach reflects in its three dimensions, on the one hand, the 'facticity' of the European Union polity, and how it can, on the other hand, be used to ensure its legitimacy. In all of these enquiries it should then once more become apparent why the juridification of the Europeanisation processes needs to build upon a proceduralisation of the category of law.[62]

[61] R Mayntz, 'The Architecture of Multi-level Governance of Economic Sectors', *MPIfG Discussion Paper 07/13*, Cologne, at 23–24.

[62] The notion of a three-dimensional conflict of laws as Europe's constitutional design is also used by PF Kjaer, 'Three-dimensional Conflict of Laws in Europe' (Bremen: *ZERP DP 2/2009*); idem, *Between Governing and Governance: On the Emergence, Function and Form of Europe's Post-National Constellation* (Oxford: Hart Publishing, 2010) 141. Kjaer's theoretical framework is

(a) *Conflicts Law I: Horizontal Constitutionalisation of the European 'Bund'*

'Conflict of laws' and its Continental equivalent have come of age. The discipline seems to have lost much of its former prestige, and is *terra incognita* for the majority of the academic European law community. The conflict of laws issues which were present in so many leading cases in our teaching materials were hardly ever noticed. The most spectacular example is the legendary *Cassis de Dijon* case of 1979.[63] There, the European Court of Justice (ECJ) held that a German ban on the marketing of a French liqueur – the alcohol content of which was lower than its German counterpart – was incompatible with the principle of the free movement of goods (then Article 30 EC Treaty, now Article 41 TFEU). The ECJ's response to the conflicts between French and German policies was as convincing as it was trifling: the confusion of German consumers could be avoided, and a reasonable degree of protection against erroneous decisions by German consumers could be achieved, by disclosing the low alcohol content of the French liqueur. With this observation, the Court defined *en passant* its constitutional competence to review the legitimacy of national legislation which presented a non-tariff barrier to free intra-Community trade in a new way. This move was of principled theoretical importance and had far-reaching practical impact.

The ECJ's holding is, of course, mainly perceived as confirming the constitutional status of the economic freedoms, and imposing restrictions on the regulatory autonomy of Member States. Precisely this reading leads to the type of queries which were immediately articulated – for example by Ernst Steindorff[64] – and have never satisfactorily been answered: Are the European freedoms meant to impose a neo-liberal economic constitution which would replace, erode or transform the welfare traditions of European constitutional democracies?[65] To date, the critique directed against the ECJ is bitter: What

sociological not only in his approach to the integration process, but also in his analysis of the functions of law and the specifics of constitutions. He does not seek to translate his analyses of the integration process into legal categories with specific normative connotations and into a legal methodology which reflects these normative concerns and seeks to guide the law's operations accordingly. These differences come to the fore in all of the three dimensions of conflicts law. The notion of 'diagonal conflicts', which reflects the asymmetric distribution of powers in the European multilevel system, goes unnoticed in his distinction between horizontal and vertical collisions (but see Mayntz, n 61 above). The sociological imprint is more clearly visible in the 'third dimension', namely, Kjaer's notion of conflicts between functionally differentiated systems which have no legal equivalent. See, also, the discussion of G Teubner's 'societal constitutionalism', 'Societal Constitutionalism: Alternatives to State-Centred Constitutional Theory?' in C Joerges, I-J Sand and G Teubner (eds), *Transnational Governance and Constitutionalism* (Oxford: Hart Publishing, 2004) 3; see, also, D Grimm, 'Gesellschaftlicher Konstitutionalismus – Eine Kompensation für den Bedeutungsschwund der Staatsverfassung?' in M Herdegen, HH Klein, H-J Papier and R Scholz (eds), *Staatsrecht und Politik, Festschrift für Roman Herzog zum 75. Geburtstag* (Munich: CH Beck, 2009) 67.

[63] Case 120/78, *Cassis de Dijon* [1979] ECR 649.

[64] E Steindorff, 'Probleme des Art 30 EWG' (1984) 148 *Zeitschrift für das gesamte Handelsrecht und Wirtschaftsrecht* 338.

[65] See, recently, M Höpner and A Schäfer, 'Grenzen der Integration – wie die Intensivierung der Wirtschaftsintegration zur Gefahr für die politische Integration wird' (2010) 33 *Integration* 3; and their edited volume, *Die Politische Ökonomie der Integration* (Frankfurt aM–New York: Campus, 2008).

kind of constitutional mandate can the ECJ invoke and implement in its control of Member State policies?[66] Fritz Scharpf, a prominent opponent, had, some 15 years earlier, submitted a more accommodating alternative interpretation of the Court's jurisprudence, by suggesting that the ECJ was mainly quite prudently mitigating the difference between the respect of national political autonomy and the protection of the integration project.[67] In the same spirit, the conflicts-law approach suggests that the excitement over the ECJ's jurisprudence is unnecessary because its celebrated argument can be translated into the language of a European conflicts law. This translation reveals nothing less than a European conflicts revolution which was more radical than its American predecessor of the 1960s: the ECJ required Germany to 'recognise' (ie, to apply!) foreign public law. It considered whether Germany could plead an *ordre public* exception, but concluded that the German 'requirements relating to the minimum alcohol content of alcoholic beverages do not serve a purpose which is in the general interest'.[68] What the ECJ imposed was a 'meta-norm', which started from the premise that both France and Germany were committed to the objective of free intra-Community trade and were hence bound to accept limitations to their political freedom, as long as they did not substantially interfere with essential regulatory concerns.[69] Last, but not least, the conflicts-law approach allows one to come to terms with the adjudicative functions of the ECJ. It is much easier to understand why the ECJ must arbitrate in cases of conflicts in the European *Bund* than it is to accept that the ECJ, whose holdings enjoy a *de facto* definite validity, can transform itself into Europe's highest authority, at times even its *pouvoir constituant*.

[66] See R Herzog and L Gerken, "Stoppt den EuropäischenGerichtshof" *Frankfurter Allgemeine Zeitung*, 8 September 2008, p 8; FW Scharpf, 'The Only Solution is to Refuse to Comply with ECJ Rulings' (2008) 4 *Social Europe Journal* 16.

[67] FW Scharpf, 'Community and Autonomy: Multi-level Policy Making in the European Union' (1994) 1 *JEPP* 219.

[68] But, so D Chalmers has objected, the *Cassis* case 'was, after all, not between the French producers of Cassis de Dijon and the German authorities. The parties to the dispute were exclusively German. It was between Rewe, a German distributor, and the German regulatory authorities. It was not only the parties to the dispute that were domestic, the centre of gravity of the dispute was also domestic. Cassis de Dijon is not a widely sold drink. Instead, it was used as the touch paper to resolve a wider redistributive question between German distributors and German producers.' (D Chalmers, 'Deliberative Supranationalism and the Reterritorialization of Authority' in Kohler-Koch and Rittberger (eds), *Debating the Democratic Legitimacy*, n 3 above, 329, at 334.) It is certainly true and also unsurprising that interested actors are trying to instrumentalise European law continuously and often successfully: if the law were to rubberstamp such practices, the conflicts-law approach would indeed collapse. But more benevolent readings of European law are usually possible and plausible. The parties to the *Cassis* proceedings may have been after a 'Faustian Pact' with DG III; see, on this notion, BG Peters and J Pierre, 'Multi-level Governance and Democracy: A Faustian Bargain?' in I Bache and M Flinders (eds), *Multi-level Governance* (Oxford: OUP, 2004) 75; however, the ECJ's holding remains convincing and unaffected by such practices – and the conflicts-law reading of *Cassis* remains a sound choice.

[69] B Currie, 'The Disinterested Third State' (1963) 28 *Law & Contemporary Problems* 754.

Cassis was an easy case because Germany's consumer protection philosophy was not credible. But the messages of this judgment were anything but trivial. With the imposition of a legal duty to recognise the validity of foreign law regardless of its private law or public law 'nature', the ECJ had established a horizontal constitutional bond between the Member States. Equally important, the ECJ neither *imposed* a bond which would forge the Member States into a uniform legal structure, nor did it assume any comprehensive European power or grant itself the powers of a regular constitutional court. Scharpf's formula captures this self-restraint well. The Court required the Member States both to recognise and to respect a mitigating function which only a Community court could credibly exercise: neither can the Community blatantly disregard the regulatory priorities of national polities and insist upon an abolition of non-tariff obstacles to free trade, nor can its Member States unilaterally and autonomously invoke exceptions to the disciplining requirements of free trade. The establishment of an independent judiciary body entrusted with the task of identifying the rules and principles under which the free trade objective and the respect for legitimate regulatory concerns become compatible does, to use Habermas' formula, 'deserve recognition'.[70]

All of these reasons militate in favour of a re-conceptualisation of mutual recognition jurisprudence from the perspectives of the conflicts-law approach. Jona Israël has characterised these developments as a transformation of voluntary and diplomatic coordination into a legal duty of cooperative problem-solving.[71] In quite the same vein, Christoph Schönberger has revitalised the notion of the German '*Bund*',[72] thereby building on Carl Schmitt's *Verfassungslehre*.[73] This notion assumes – just like the conflicts approach – a *horizontal* constitutionalisation of the Union. This use of the notion of *Bund* is by no means to be equated with the kind of '*konkrete, seinsmäßige*' (concrete and substantial) homogeneity[74] which Carl Schmitt read into the *Bund*. One can also safely

[70] J Habermas, 'Remarks on Legitimation through Human Rights' in idem, *The Postnational Constellation: Political Essays* (Cambridge MA: The MIT Press, 2001) 113, at 113.

[71] J Israël, *European Cross-Border Insolvency Regulation* (Antwerp-Oxford: Intersentia, 2005) at 123, at 150–52 and 323–34. See, also, the concise restatement of the doctrinal historical background and discussion of its *problématique* in the coordination of regulatory policies by R Wai, 'Conflicts and Comity in Transnational Governance: Private International Law as Mechanism and Metaphor for Transnational Social Regulation through Plural Legal Regimes' in Joerges and Petersmann (eds) *Constitutionalism, Multilevel Trade Governance and Social Regulation*, n 1 above, 251.

[72] C Schönberger, 'Die Europäische Union als Bund. Zugleich ein Beitrag zur Verabschiedung des Staatenbund-Bundesstaat-Schemas' (2004) 129 *Archiv des öffentlichen Rechts* 81, at 88 ff. On predecessors and followers, see C Franzius, *Europäisches Verfassungsrechtsdenken* (Tübungen: Mohr Siebeck, 2010), at 62–68.

[73] First published in 1929, cited here after the 10th edn (Berlin: Duncker & Humblot, 2010): 'The *Bund* is a stable association [of states], grounded on a freely entered into agreement, serving the common purpose of political self-preservation of all the *Bund* members, an association by virtue of which the general political status of each individual member will be changed in view of the common purpose' (*Verfassungslehre* ibid at 366).

[74] 'Any *Bund* rests on an essential assumption, namely, the *Homogeneity of all Bund-members*, ie, it presupposes a substantive uniformity which underlies the concrete, mutual understanding of

assume that Schmitt was far from considering the need to compensate the democracy failures of nation states. The use of the notion and understanding of a horizontal constitutionalisation through conflicts law as a legal basis is, instead, indebted to the vision of 'united in diversity' as once envisaged by the motto of the Union in the Draft Constitutional Treaty.[75]

(b) Conflicts Law II: Constitutionalising Europe's 'Political Administration'

'Horizontal constitutionalism' cannot, however, be reduced to the compensation of democracy failures in parochial national decision-making. The European *Bund* has also created the 'positive' duty of its Member States to engage cooperatively, and participate actively, in the administration of regulatory programmes. This positive commitment is a result of the opening of national markets, the establishment of the internal market – and the insight that markets will always transform into embedded social institutions: markets both generate and require regulatory frameworks in which they can operate. This is a lesson to be learned from the institutional development of all constitutional democracies. With the 'completion' of the European internal market as designed by the White Paper of 1985,[76] this lesson was taught again. The institutional forms which have been used and generated in this process vary with regard to the intensity of bureaucratic cooperation, the role of expertise, the involvement of non-governmental actors, and the interaction between the European Commission and the Council. Within this rich variety comitology remains the most fascinating phenomenon. The practical importance of this machinery is as obvious as its political sensitivity and salience. This is why the normative core of democratic constitutionalism, namely, the commitment to the idea of law-mediated legitimacy, requires the establishment of a legal framework that generates legitimate rule. To summarise its role,[77] there are, first, stringent functional needs for this system. It has been

the Member States and thus guarantees that the extreme case of a conflict within the *Bund* does not occur', *Verfassungslehre* ibid, at 375 f; for a detailed analysis, see M Avbelj, 'Theory of European Bund' (PhD Thesis, EUI, Florence, 2009), ch 3, at 109 ff.

[75] Art IV-1 of the DCT, [2004] OJ C 310/1 of 16 December 2004. That vision of *unitas in pluralitate* is quite Habermasian and can content itself with his 'constitutional patriotism' as recently re-formulated in J Habermas, *Zwischen Naturalismus und Religion* [*Between Naturalism and Religion*] *Philosophische Aufsätze* (Frankfurt aM: Suhrkamp, 2005) at 111: 'Contrary to a widely spread misunderstanding, constitutional patriotism means that citizens embrace the principles of the Constitution not only in their abstract content but also concretely, out of their own national historical context. If the moral content of fundamental rights is to take practical root, the cognitive process does not suffice. Moral intuitions and the universal agreement which arises as indignation towards massive human rights violations, as such, would suffice only for the very superficial integration needs of the politically created world society citizenry. Between state citizens arises in truth a solidarity – as always partially abstract and legally-mediated – only when the principles of justice find an entry point into the network of cultural value-orientation.'

[76] European Commission, 'White Paper to the European Council on Completion of the Internal Market', COM(85) 310 final, 14 June 1985.

[77] Joerges and Neyer, 'Comitology', see n 51 above.

quite stringently documented that this system performs – in spite, or, indeed, because, of its de-centralised modes of operation – reasonably well. However, such performance rests on contingent grounds. This is why comitology needs to be 'constitutionalised', ie, stabilised and supervised by an adequate legal framework.

Comitology committees, which are composed of administrative practitioners and experts from the Member States, are supposed to support the Commission in the 'implementation' of European legislative programmes; they are also involved in the continuous process of amending the existing legislation, filling legislative gaps and preparing new initiatives. These committees embody the functional and structural tensions which characterise internal market regulation. They hover between 'technical' and 'political' considerations, between the functional needs and the ethical/social criteria which inform European regulation. Their often very fluid composition not only reflects upon the regulatory endeavour to balance the rationalisation of technical criteria against broader political concerns, but also forcefully highlights the schisms that exist among the political interests of those engaged in the process of internal market regulation. Even where they are explicitly established to support and oversee the implementing powers delegated to the Commission, committees are deeply involved in political processes and often resemble 'mini-councils', in that they are the forum in which the balancing of European market-building against the concerns of the individual Member States has to be achieved.[78] The notion of 'political administration' reflects these activities best[79] – it is not by chance that this oxymoron was coined in the 1970s to characterise the new law of 'purposive programming'.[80]

'Political administration' is a term through which the comitology system can be distinguished from, and defended against, such notions as 'administration without government' or 'technocratic deliberation'. The rise and success of the committee system is attributable to its potential to organise the administration of the internal market cooperatively, rather than by a fusion of national bureaucracies or the institutionalisation of a hierarchically-structured command-and-control machinery. These are still primarily descriptive characterisations. The normative challenge, however, concerns the normative quality of its operation. It is precisely this challenge which the 'second dimension' of conflicts law seeks to address through a 'constitutionalisation' of transnational cooperation. Categorical differences between the constitutionalisation of administrative law in democratic states and a federation, on the one hand, and the search for mitigating meta-norms as advocated within the first dimension

[78] See, in much more detail, C Joerges and E Vos (eds), *EU Committees: Social Regulation, Law and Politics* (Oxford: Hart Publishing, 1999).

[79] C Joerges, '"Good Governance" through Comitology?' in Joerges and Vos (eds), n 78 above, at 311.

[80] See Section II above.

of conflicts law, on the other, do, indeed, continue to exist in the absence of the transformation of transnational cooperation into a single democratically-governed polity, but, nevertheless, one needs to ensure that regulatory policies can be pursued transnationally. The second dimension of conflicts law does not control the external effects of national political decision-making, but is to be understood as a response to their inability to accomplish regulatory objectives autonomously and in isolation.

A broad range of issues needs to be considered when such perspectives are pursued and substantiated.[81] It should be underlined that there are no built-in guarantees that comitology will develop further along such lines.[82] De-parliamentarisation, bureaucratisation and judicialisation are all side-effects

[81] They include the selection of the expert circles, the establishment of ties with parliamentary bodies with civil society, and the reversibility of decisions taken in the light of new knowledge or changes in social preferences; see C Joerges and M Everson, 'Re-conceptualising Europeanisation as a Public Law of Collisions: Comitology, Agencies and an Interactive Public Adjudication' in Hofmann and Türk (eds), *EU Administrative Governance*, n 58 above, 512; with quite similar intuitions, L Viellechner, 'Können Netzwerke die Demokratie ersetzen?' in S Boysen et al (eds), *Netzwerke: 47th Assistententagung Öffentliches Recht* (Baden-Baden: Nomos, 2008) 36, at 48 ff. The most recent analysis in political science which reviews what is by now an impressive number of pertinent studies is GJ Brandsmas, 'Backstage Europe. Comitology, Accountability and Democracy in the EU' (PhD Thesis, Amsterdam, 2010).

[82] See C Joerges, 'Integration through De-legalisation?' (2008) 33 *EL Rev* 219, at 297 ff (reprinted in pt III, ch 13 of this volume); more optimistic, however, E Vos, '50 Years of European Integration, 45 Years of Comitology' in A Ott and E Vos (eds), *Fifty Years of European Integration: Foundations and Perspectives* (The Hague: TMC Asser Press, 2009) 31, at 49 ff. Unfortunately, the most recent steps towards reform of comitology upon the basis of Arts 291 and 290 TFEU as suggested by the Commission do not nurture such hopes. Both the Communication of 9 December 2009 [COM(2009) 673 final] on delegated acts and the proposal on the exercise of implementing powers of 9 March 2010 [COM(2010) 83 final] seek to strengthen the Commission's role significantly. The first-named Communication underlines the Commission's belief its belief that '[d]elegations of power should in principle … be of indefinite duration' (para 3.2), that it 'enjoys a large amount of autonomy' in implementing its powers (para 4.1). Furthermore, the Commission expects that the legislator, in exercising a right to revocation provided for in a pertinent legislative act, be under a 'duty to explain the reasons behind it' (para 5.2). On 16 December 2010 an agreement has been reached between the EP and Council on the new regulation of the Commission's implementing powers; see the Commission Communication IP/10/1735 and the Plenary Report on the legislative resolution of the European Parliament of 16 December 2010. This strengthening of the powers of the European Commission seemed inconceivable at the beginning of the inquiries into the possibilities of a constitutionalisation of comitology; see, for example, C Joerges, 'Scientific Expertise in Social Regulation and the European Court of Justice: Legal Frameworks for Denationalized Governance Structures' in C Joerges, K-H Ladeur and E Vos, *Integrating Scientific Expertise into Regulatory Decision-Making: National Traditions and European Innovations* (Baden-Baden: Nomos, 1997) 295, at 324. The legal system must continue its search for guarantees of regulatory reasonableness, procedural safeguards and the protection of rights. This search should be complemented by the institutionalisation of political accountability. Such institutional innovations would have to correspond to the emerging structures of governance beyond intergovernmentalism and below orthodox supranationalism. One conceivable step might be the entrustment of parliamentary committees, composed of both European Parliament members and national delegates, with the task of regularly reviewing the experiences of Community and national officials, of organising hearings to which experts and non-governmental organisations would be invited, and of initiating legislative action at the European and national level.

both of Europeanisation and, even more so, of globalisation.[83] The factual strength of these tendencies does not, however, invalidate the critique of techno-cratic reason. Instead, it necessitates its re-design and *Aufhebung* in new visions of democratic administration and governance. Such perspectives do exist,[84] and Europe seems better equipped than any international arena to establish regimes under which transnational governance can derive its legitimacy from an institutional design in which European citizens can understand transnational governance activities as a product of the ensemble of both EU *and* national policy-making. It is precisely because of both these tendencies and the need for modern modes of governance to liaise with non-governmental bodies that the conflicts-law approach needs to develop its third dimension, namely, the means and yardsticks for the supervision of non-governmental regimes.

(c) Conflicts Law III: The Irresistible Rise of Para-legal Regimes and the Need for their Legal Supervision

The most ingenious among the strategies of European market-building was 'the new approach to harmonisation and standards'.[85] The new approach was a sophisticated reaction to a profound dilemma. Free trade in the Common Market depended upon the 'positive' harmonisation of countless regulatory provisions. The legislative harmonisation was a Sisyphean task, which remained a nightmare even after the old unanimity rule of Article 100 EC Treaty was replaced by qualified majority voting in Article 100a EC Treaty as introduced by the Single European Act of 1987. Judicial governance – as promoted by the *Cassis de Dijon* decision of 1979 – could only proceed selectively and required a bundle of accompanying measures in order to exert practical effects.[86] Seemingly

[83] See D Chalmers, 'Administrative Globalisation and Curbing the Excesses of the State' in Joerges and Petersmann (eds), n 1 above, 351.

[84] See, recently, EC Fisher, *Risk Regulation and Administrative Constitutionalism* (Oxford: Hart Publishing, 2007) and Joerges and Petersmann (eds), n 1 above, 327; see, also, D Curtin, *Executive Power of the European Union: Law, Practices and the Living Constitution* (Oxford: OUP, 2009) passim, conclusions at 277–304.

[85] The story of the new approach has often been told; see, for example, J Falke and C Joerges, '"Traditional" Harmonisation Policy, European Consumer Protection Programmes and the New Approach', *EUI Working Paper Law 91/14*, available at: www.iue.it/LAW/WP-Texts/Joerges91; recently and brilliantly, H Schepel, *The Constitution of Private Governance: Product Standards in the Regulation of Integrating Markets* (Oxford: Hart Publishing, 2004) 225; see, previously, J Falke and C Joerges, 'The New Approach to Technical Harmonization and Standards, its Preparation through ECJ Case Law on Articles 30, 36 EEC and the Low-Voltage Directive, and the Clarification of its Operating Environment by the Single European Act', *EUI Working Paper Law No 91/13*, San Domenico di Fiesole, 1991, re-issued in G Brüggemeier, J Falke, C Joerges and H-W Micklitz (eds), 'European Product Safety, Internal Market Policy and the New Approach to Technical Harmonisation and Standards' (2010) 6 *Hanse Law Review* 289, available at: www.hanselawreview.org/pdf10/HanseLRVol6No02.pdf.

[86] See SK Schmidt, 'Mutual Recognition as a New Mode of Governance' (2007) 14 *JEPP* 667; K Nicolaïdis, 'Trusting the Poles? Constructing Europe through Mutual Recognition' (2007) 14 *JEPP* 682.

paradoxically, self-regulation, a technique very widely used in Germany, in particular, was by no means easier to live with. Voluntary product standards were 'private' obstacles to trade, which the Community legislature could not overcome by legislative *fiat*.

The new approach managed to overcome that *impasse* through a series of interrelated measures: European legislation was confined to laying down 'essential safety requirements', while the task of detailing the general requirements was delegated to the experts of both European and national standardisation organisations. The involvement of non-governmental actors involved a *de facto* 'delegation' of law-making powers, which could not be openly admitted. Harm Schepel[87] cites, with a somewhat ironic undertone, a leading representative of the standardisation community, who stated that the new approach

> makes it possible to distinguish better between those aspects of Community harmonisation activities which fall within the province of the law, and those which fall within the province of technology, and to differentiate between matters which fall within the competence of public authorities and those which are the responsibility of manufacturers and importers.[88]

This language both covers and hides the political dimensions of standardisation. This is small wonder, because the advocates of the new approach had to present their project in legally-acceptable clothes. They were perfectly aware of the limited guidance that 'essential safety requirements' can offer in the standardisation process. But they had good reason to trust in the responsibility of the standardisation community, and the engineers of the approach were happy to see their creation functioning so smoothly.[89] Do we have to conclude that 'private transnationalism' had replaced public legislation and administration? That would be too simplistic. The new 'private transnationalism' did not operate in a vacuum. Interaction between the standardisation community, the Commission and national officials remained intense. Product liability law, tort law and competition law retained powerful multi-faceted potential for control and supervision, while national and European public authorities retained the means to intervene if their trust were disappointed.[90] It is in the shadow of the law that 'private transnationalism' flourishes; it is by no means an autonomous legal order.

[87] Schepel, *The Constitution of Private Governance*, n 36 above, at 65.

[88] F Nicolas, *Common Standards for Enterprises* (Luxembourg: Office of Official Publications, 1995) at 94.

[89] See Schepel, *The Constitution of Private Governance*, n 36 above, at 37 ff, 101 ff and 225 ff; J Falke, 'International Standards for the Elimination of Barriers to Trade – An Analysis of the Agreements and of the Discussion of Standardisation Policy', Report Commissioned by the Commission for Occupational Health and Safety and Standardisation [KAN] (Bremen: Zenrum für Europäische Rechtspolitik, 2001).

[90] See C Joerges, H Schepel and E Vos, '"Delegation" and the European Polity: The Law's Problems with the Role of Standardisation Organisations in European Legislation', *EUI Working Paper Law 9/1999*, available at: www.iue.it/LAW/WP-Texts/law99_9.pdf; Schepel, *The Constitution of Private Governance*, n 36 above, at 234–56, 309–38 and 347–400.

Why should this order, to take up the Habermasian formula, 'deserve recognition'?[91] As Harm Schepel has shown in his ground-breaking analysis, the new arrangements proved to function as a highly civilised polity. Widely-accepted and stable procedures have emerged, which synthesise legal principles, professional standards and participation opportunities, and lead repeatedly to consensual problem-solving. Significantly, European standardisation has refrained from centralisation, and, with its non-unitary network structure, it guarantees that national delegations can make their viewpoints heard. Not only the national and European bureaucracies – in particular, the European Commission – but also courts are always latently, and, at times, actually, present. Information systems which alert pertinent bodies to product risks, product safety and product liability law can be invoked, and European competition law has the potential to supervise the internal constitution of standardisation bodies. The law's strong shadow is complemented by internal operational modes. The reason for the success of Europe's standardisation project, Schepel concluded, was that its procedures followed a political, and not merely economic or scientific, rationale. Fair procedures, transparency, openness and balanced interest representation are the principles according to which consultations within the respective institutions are assessed.[92]

Can all this be plausibly characterised as a dimension of conflicts law? The example of European standardisation is not radically different from the comitology pattern. Undoubtedly, the role of non-governmental actors is significantly stronger here. But the step to be taken is not too difficult. Conflict of laws has, throughout its long history, dealt with the acceptability of the laws of 'foreign' jurisdictions. Once we recognise that our statal law cannot operate autonomously but is dependent upon the norm generation in non-statal spheres, we need to re-define its scope. This re-definition must not copy the privatisation patterns by which private international law theory and practice have de-coupled transnational private governance arrangements from any significant public scrutiny. The recognition of para-legal arrangements must be conditioned by their normative quality. The criteria to be applied will primarily concern norm-generation processes, and their implementation will have to engage in various legal areas such as anti-trust and tort law. This, then, is the model for the constitutionalisation of private governance.[93]

[91] J Habermas, 'Remarks on Legitimation through Human Rights' in idem, *The Postnational Constellation: Political Essays* (Cambridge MA: The MIT Press, 2001) 113.

[92] Schepel, *The Constitution of Private Governance*, n 36 above, at 223. Transnational governance arrangements need to adapt continuously to changing contexts, respond to new experiences, refine and renew their machinery. It is fascinating to observe that European standardisation is coping successfully with these challenges. See, for a detailed analysis, J Falke, 'Produkt- und Lebensmittelsicherheit in der Europäischen Union und in der WTO' in J Falke and C Joerges (eds), *Handelsliberalisierung und Sozialregulierung in transnationalen Konstellationen* (Baden-Baden: Nomos, 2011) 31, at 62 ff.

[93] The parallel to the recognition of foreign law and foreign judgments seems obvious, but it is rarely drawn. But see E Schanze, 'International Standards – Functions and Links to Law' in P Nobel (ed), *International Standards and the Law* (Bern: Stämpfli, 2005) 84, esp at 90–91.

We conclude that the conflicts-law approach to European law is not a purely contra-factual normative fantasy. We have, however, to warn against any Panglossian wishful thinking. In all of its three dimensions, the conflicts-law approach to European law is under stress. It is threatened by new tendencies in European primary and secondary law, which promote a very orthodox and centralist reading of supremacy.[94] Similarly, the prospects for a constitutionalisation of the second dimension of conflicts law are by no means promising.[95] However, in the field of standardisation, promising prospects for innovative further refinements of 'good' transnational governance have been identified.[96] One intervening variable of crucial importance for its future development is, of course, the globalisation process, to which we now turn.[97]

IV. CONSTITUTIONALISING TRANSNATIONAL GOVERNANCE THROUGH CONFLICTS LAW

The revolutionary (so-to-speak) transformative move in European law, in our conceptualisation, both implies and pre-supposes a radical break with methodological nationalism. Seemingly paradoxically, but in fact, for very stringent reasons, private international law – its *quasi* cosmopolitan name notwithstanding – is inextricably linked to the nation state, and even the proponents of an un-political 'spatial' justice as a methodological *credo* of the discipline do not overcome this legacy.[98] There are, of course, theoretical alternatives, but in practical terms, the most important chance for a re-orientation towards cosmopolitanism is provided by WTO law – ironically, a fragment of international law and hence, according to the still prevailing view, a dangerous threat to the law's unity.

[94] See, for private law, H-W Micklitz and N Reich, 'Crónica de una muerte anunciada' (2009) 46 *MLR* 471; for labour law, see C Joerges and F Rödl, 'Informal Politics, Formalised Law and the "Social Deficit" of European Integration: Reflections after the Judgments of the ECJ in *Viking* and *Laval*' (2009) 15 *ELJ* 1, reprinted in pt IV, ch 16 of this volume.

[95] Joerges, 'De-legalisation', n 82 above; and Vos, '50 Years', n 82 above.

[96] Falke, 'Produkt- und Lebensmittelsicherheit', n 92 above.

[97] The following sections draw on the previous edition and two more recent essays: C Joerges, 'Judicialization and Transnational Governance: The Example of WTO Law and the GMO Dispute' in B Iancu (ed), *The Law/Politics Distinction in Contemporary Public Law Adjudication* (Utrecht: Eleven International Publishing 2009) 67; C Joerges, 'A New Type of Conflicts Law as the Legal Paradigm of the Postnational Constellation' in C Joerges and J Falke (eds), *Karl Polanyi: Globalisation and the Potential of Law in Transnational Markets* (Oxford–Portland OR: Hart Publishing, 2011) 153.

[98] See the analysis in F Rödl, 'Weltbürgerliches Kollisionsrecht. Über die Form des Kollisionsrechts und seine Gestalt im Recht der Europäischen Union', PhD Thesis, EUI, Florence, 2008, Teil 1 B.II.

The potential importance of European experiences for the understanding of WTO law and transnational governance is not widely acknowledged. The obvious institutional discrepancies between both systems are one reason for the hesitancy to enter into systematic comparisons; the fact that they are studied by different scholarly communities is probably of similar weight. But there is a growing body of bridging enquiries[99] which discuss the affinities and functional similarities: both institutions have to balance free-trade objectives and regulatory concerns, or, as the Appellate Body in the *Hormones* case put it, 'the shared, but sometimes competing, interests of promoting international trade and of protecting … life and health'.[100] The non-tariff barriers to trade, to which the proponents of international free trade increasingly had to pay attention in the last decades, are requirements which the EU tends to recognise as legitimate restrictions on the freedom of intra-Community trade. Both the Sanitary and Phytosanitary Measures (SPS) Agreement and the Technical Barriers to Trade (TBT) Agreement are institutionalised responses to health and safety concerns, and the legitimacy of the trade restrictions which result from environmental policies is explicitly recognised in the Preamble to the WTO Agreement.

Our discussion of these parallels in this section will deal with conflict resolutions under these agreements. We will, on the one hand, contrast juridified and judicialised modes with inter-governmental, diplomatic and political conflict resolution. In the present context, our analysis will focus on 'product' – as opposed to 'process' – regulation, and the governance patterns in this area. Both of these distinctions refer to separate debates, but are, nevertheless, inter-dependent. Clearly, product regulation is more closely linked to the realisation of free trade than process regulation, because product-related mandatory requirements can hinder the importation of goods directly, while process regulation need not affect the quality of the output of production. Stricter and more costly standards can be a competitive disadvantage, and conflicts arising from such differences are often primarily economic. However, the distinction is of limited use: environmental and safety-at-work requirements may relate to the product itself; low environmental standards may have external effects on other countries; safety-at-work standards may have a human rights basis; and, last but not least, international agreements often do not apply the

[99] See G de Búrca and J Scott (eds), *The EU and the WTO: Legal and Constitutional Issues* (Oxford: Hart Publishing, 2001); J Scott, 'Mandatory or Imperative Requirements in the EU and the WTO' in C Barnard and J Scott (eds), *The Law of the Single European Market: Unpacking the Premises* (Oxford: Hart Publishing, 2002) 269; and J Scott, 'International Trade and Environmental Governance: Relating Rules (and Standards) in the EU and the WTO' (2004) 15 *European Journal of International Law* 307.

[100] *EC-Measures Concerning Meat and Meat Products*, Report of the Appellate Body, 16 January 1998, WT/DS26/AB/R & WT/DS48/AB/R, para 177.

product/process distinction. Here, it is sufficient to mention the 'measures necessary for the protection of human, animal or plant life or health' in the Preamble and in Article 2.1 of the SPS Agreement. Nevertheless, it seems plausible to assume that the juridification of transnational product regulation will be more intense than transnational standardisation in the field of safety at work and environmental protection. The latter can, presumably, be better explained by political processes, while the former will more often be dictated by functional necessities.

IV.1. Re-Interpreting WTO Law as Conflicts Law

As argued in the previous section,[101] the celebrated jurisprudence of the ECJ on Article 41 (ex Article 28 TEU), which seeks to 'harmonise' the principle of freedom of intra-Community trade with respect for the legitimate regulatory concerns of EC Member States, can be understood as a modernisation, if not a revolution, of traditional conflict of laws principles. Our re-interpretation has pointed to the 'non-discrimination' between mandatory provisions of public and private law, and based the ECJ's interventions in the law of the Member States upon meta-norms which the jurisdictions involved can accept as a supranationally valid yardstick for evaluating and correcting their legislation. It is submitted that the same interpretative scheme can be applied to the reports of the WTO Appellate Body, which assess the compatibility of health-and-safety-related non-tariff barriers to trade with the SPS Agreement.[102] With regard to the SPS Agreement, this interpretation does not seem far-fetched. That Agreement does not invoke some supranational quasi-legislative authority. It can be understood as a framework within which WTO Members may seek a resolution for conflicts arising from the extra-territorial impact of their regulatory policies. An elaboration of these parallels is more than some doctrinal *l'art pour l'art*. As in European law, the conflicts approach should be understood as a potentially more convincing way of justifying the validity claims of transnational law, which would take some tensions out of the debate on the 'constitutional' status of WTO law. It would also allow a re-definition of the functions of the Appellate Body; its operation as 'a court in all but its name'[103] is easier to accept – and, in fact, better to understand – if one acknowledges its conflict-resolving tasks. It is precisely for these reasons that we propagate the understanding of conflicts law as 'constitutional form'.

[101] Section III.2.(a).

[102] See, on these parallels, Wai, 'Conflicts and Comity', n 71 above.

[103] JHH Weiler, 'The Rule of Lawyers and the Ethos of Diplomats: Reflections on the Internal and External Legitimacy of WTO Dispute Settlement' (2001) 35 *Journal of World Trade* 191.

(a) Hormones: Political Sensitivity in Legal Conflict Resolution

The transatlantic conflict over hormones in beef[104] – widely discussed in this volume[105] – provides an instructive example. The US and most of the Member States of the EU are in disagreement regarding the administration of growth-promoting hormones to beef-producing cattle. Can both parties agree to expose their practices to a science-based analysis of the health risks which the consumption of hormone-enhanced beef may entail? The requirement in the SPS Agreement that the measures of the WTO Members must not be 'maintained without sufficient scientific evidence' (Article 2.2) and that it must be 'based on' a risk assessment (Article 5) seems to suggest exactly that. But, as the actors involved know all too well, science, for a variety of reasons, cannot provide comprehensive answers to all the dimensions of the transnational conflicts constellation. Science does not typically answer unambiguously and exactly the questions that policy-makers and lawyers are concerned with. Scientific debates are categorically distinct from ethical and normative deliberations. And, last but not least, consumer anxieties about (scientifically speaking) marginal risks may be so considerable that policy-makers may not be able to neglect them.[106]

All these difficulties militate against accepting the standards of 'sound science' as a transnational 'regulatory' authority. However, they do not stand in the way of extending the conflicts-law approach to WTO law. Nor do they jeopardise the insight that – when dealing with regulatory differences – the pursuit of a meta-norm might be more convincing than the search for some substantive ruling of transnational validity. Even when the meta-norms, which one can identify, remain vague and indeterminate, they may, nevertheless, further the search for a fair compromise. The hesitancy, even the refusal, to hand down an authoritative holding on the substance of the hormones litigation, must hence not be equated with a refusal to answer questions which the litigants are expecting. The answers which WTO law can legitimately give must, instead, reflect the limits of its own law-making powers. This is, indeed, what the Appellate Body

[104] *EC-Measures Concerning Meat and Meat Products (Hormones)*, Report of the Appellate Body, 16 January 1998, WT/DS26/AB/R and WT/DS48/AB/R.

[105] See C Gerstetter, 'The Appellate Body's "Response" to the Tensions and Interdependencies between Transnational Trade Governance and Social Regulation' in Joerges and Petersmann (eds), n 1 above, 111; A Herwig, 'The Precautionary Principle in Support of Practical Reason: An Argument against Formalistic Interpretations of the Precautionary Principle' in Joerges and Petersmann (eds), n 1 above, 301.

[106] Lawyers and political scientists look at decision-making through very different lenses – but their insights into science remain unaffected: see T Hüller and ML Maier, 'Fixing the Codex? Global Food-safety Governance Under Review' in Joerges and Petersmann (eds), n 1 above, 267; Herwig, 'The Precautionary Principle', n 105 above, at 304 ff; E Fisher, 'Beyond the Science/Democracy Dichotomy: The World Trade Organisation Sanitary and Phytosanitary Agreement and Administrative Constitutionalism' in Joerges and Petersmann (eds), n 1 above, 327; on European practices, see J Corkin, 'Science, Legitimacy and the Law: Regulating Risk Regulation Judiciously in the European Community' (2008) 33 *EL Rev* 359.

did. It accepted, in principle, the need to integrate regulatory policies into the system of free trade. However, it nonetheless shied away from telling the litigants whether the Americans or the Europeans had found the proper universally valid answer. The Appellate Body even understood and respected the limits of science-based positive criteria – and found a prudent way out of an apparent dilemma. By pointing to the need for a risk analysis, without determining the definite meaning of that specific yardstick, it was, nevertheless, able to structure the ongoing controversy, and generated a generally civilised conduct of the ongoing conflict.[107] However, this jurisprudential caution is in striking contrast with the Panel Report in the GMO case.

(b) The Example of the GMO Dispute: Methodological and Substantive Failures

Genetically Modified Organisms (GMOs) are the most technologically advanced and the most controversial of all foodstuffs, if not of all consumer products. As is well known, the US and the EU, again the main actors in the dispute, differ in their regulatory approaches to GMOs in two significant respects: while the US focuses on the health risks posed by food, the EU follows a more comprehensive approach, placing an additional and greater emphasis upon environmental risks. *Unless* evidence exists which confirms a risk, the US authorities *will* approve products. In contrast, the 1992 Treaty on European Union constitutionalised the 'precautionary principle', so that all legislative, administrative and judicial decision-making within Europe must respect the notion that *any* indistinct hazard must be guarded against (Article 191(2) TFEU, ex Article 174(2) EC).[108]

Again, we have to ask whether this type of conflict can be resolved properly by 'science'? It has, of course, to be underlined that EU's precautionary principle does not provide much guidance. Small wonder that the Appellate Body, in the *Hormones* case, had found that '[the precautionary] principle has not been written into the SPS Agreement as a ground for justifying SPS measures that are otherwise inconsistent with the obligations of Members set out in particular

[107] The Report of the Appellate Body of 16 October 2008 on the *Continued Suspension of Obligations in the EC–Hormones Dispute* (*Complainant: EC*), WT/DS320/AB/R is equally cautious. It confirmed that the inclusion of the risks of an abuse in the administration of hormones in EU law is compatible with Art 5.1 of the SPS Agreement (at paras 548–55, 617–19) and refused to determine definitely what level of uncertainty is uncertain enough where WTO Members base precautionary measures on Art 7.1 of the SPS Agreement (at paras 617–19, 685–86, 701–03).

[108] See, in detail, G Shaffer and MA Pollack, 'Reconciling (or Failing to Reconcile) Regulatory Differences: The Ongoing Transatlantic Dispute over the Regulation of Biotechnology' in DM Andrews, MA Pollack, G Shaffer and H Wallace (eds), *The New Transatlantic Agenda and the Future of Transatlantic Economic Governance* (Florence: European University Institute, 2005) 167; A Herwig, *WTO Law, GMO Food Safety and Consumer Choice: The Limits of Legal Control* (Leiden: Nijhoff Publishers, 2010); M Weimer, 'Applying Precaution in Community Authorisation of Genetically Modified Products: Challenges and Suggestions for Reform' (2010) 16 *ELJ* 624.

provisions of that Agreement'.[109] But, by this rejection of the European enigma, it did not empower another emperor without clothes. The GMO panel takes a very different step. Recalling 'that, according to the Appellate Body, the precautionary principle has not been written into the *SPS Agreement* as a legitimate ground for justifying SPS measures', the panel proceeds to explain that 'even if a Member follows a precautionary approach', its SPS measures need to be 'based on a ("sufficiently warranted" or "reasonably supported") risk assessment'.[110] This is a strange constitutionalising move. It seems readily apparent that the WTO panel is not prepared to recognise the constitutional commitment of any of its Members to the precautionary approach: WTO standards trump European constitutional commitments – this is the implication and the message.

It is instructive to contrast the European and the WTO constellations at this point. Although the ECJ has imposed significant burdens on Member States when invoking their autonomy in risk assessments, the Court has refrained from drawing any rigid lines. Why such self-restraint? Could it be that the ECJ did not want to settle the dispute on GMOs, but respected a framework within which competing positions are continuously discussed and negotiated? The most problematical aspect of the Panel Report is that it seeks to de-legitimate even this type of indeterminate response to scientific controversies and political contestation.

Exercising prudence of a different kind, the panel decided that the SPS Agreement was applicable to the authorisation of GMOs, and could then point to Article 8 SPS Agreement, whose provisions require that applications must be processed without 'undue delay'. This, again, is a strategic manoeuvre of fundamental importance. The private right of applicants seeking authorisation for their products trumps political sensitivities. In substantive terms, the Panel Report has disregarded the sensitivity of the GMO issue, which democratically legitimated legislatures cannot neglect; in methodological terms, it has disregarded the discrepancy between traditional conditional programming and the purposive programming of regulatory politics. In both respects, the Report failed to take the logic of 'political administration' into account, ie, the 'normative fact' that time is needed for a democratically meaningful debate on political and ethical sensitive issues. On what grounds should WTO law be legitimated to disregard the enormous difficulties of the Union to settle its conflicts? The GMO panel found that completion of the approval process had been 'unduly delayed' in 24 cases. Accordingly, it requested that the EU bring its measures 'into conformity with its obligations under the SPS Agreement', in effect asking the EU to complete approval procedures for all outstanding applications.

The panel's critique of EU Member State autonomy in relation to safeguard measures was equally indirect but effective. France, Germany, Austria, Italy, Luxembourg and Greece were told that their bans on the marketing and

[109] See n 104 above, at para 124.
[110] Para 7.0365 fn 1905 of the Appellate Body report, n 107 above.

importation of EU-approved biotech products were incompatible with WTO law. Again, the panel arrived at this result in an indirect way. It did not question the validity of the European regulatory framework and/or its institutional balancing. It nonetheless opined that since the EU's scientific committee had judged the relevant biotech products to be safe, the named states had failed to undertake risk assessments that would 'reasonably support [their] prohibitions' under the SPS Agreement. SPS standards overrule Europe's precarious institutional settlement. Could it be that no authority (certainly not a WTO panel) is entitled to interfere with such politically – and legally – sensitive issues in the name of sound science?

(c) Regulatory Prudence through WTO Conflicts Law as Response to Fragmentation

Our affirmative reading of the *Hormones* case endorses the hesitancy of the Appellate Body to hand down any definite substantive decision, whereas our critique of the GMO Report complains about an illegitimate assumption of decision-making powers by that body. The basis of both the affirmation *and* the critique is the same: the WTO simply lacks the legitimate power to take a definite stance on true conflicts which concern matters of high political sensitivity and far-reaching economic implications. Positively put, our objection is a *defence* of both the rule of law and of the expectation that judicial and administrative bodies need – in the last instance – to be legitimated by us, the peoples.

This defence should be understood in the light of the differences and the discrepancies of the various levels of the interaction of law and politics within constitutional democracies and in post-national constellations. Responses to conflicts between competing policy objectives have to be found as a matter of routine in democratic orders. Contrary to the nation-state system with its comprehensive competences and mechanisms to deal with legally unresolved conflicts in political and legislative arenas, the possibility of organising equivalent processes beyond the nation states is limited. Within the European Union, transnational regulatory and administrative techniques to organise cooperative responses are available via the 'second dimension' of conflicts law. At the WTO level, however, equivalent coordinating mechanisms are simply unavailable – and this entails the risk that fragmentation will be strategically exploited to erode the accomplishments of post-*laissez-faire* regulatory endeavours.[111]

[111] This concern is shared by many contributors to the present volume; see, in particular, J Pauwellyn, 'Non-Traditional Patterns of Global Regulation: Is the WTO "Missing the Boat"?' in Joerges and Petersmann (eds), n 1 above, 199; for an impressive recent analysis of the risks of fragmentation, see E Benvenisti and GW Downs, 'The Empire's New Clothes: Political Economy and the Fragmentation of International Law' (2007) 60 *Stanford Law Review* 595.

All this provokes the follow-up question of whether the law may be required *not* to take definite substantive decisions. An exercise of this kind of restraint should not be misinterpreted as a return to the 'state of nature' and refusal to enter into a Kantian *Rechtszustand* ('lawful condition').[112] What we need to acknowledge are both factual *and* normative limitations to the 'legalisation' and 'judicialisation' of transnational conflicts resolution, which reflect the varying intensities of positive commitments. Seen from such perspectives, the Panel Report in the GMO litigation should not be rationalised through the duty of judicial and *quasi*-judicial bodies to hand down decisions. Quite to the contrary, a Report reflecting the WTO's precarious legitimacy in the assessment of regulatory policies is precisely what the mandate of the WTO requires – and what the litigants are entitled to receive.

> Global governance must live with a constant potential for mutual challenge of decisions with limited authority that may be contested through diverse channels until some (perhaps provisional) closure might be achieved.[113]

IV.2. Second Order Conflicts Law and its Affinities with Global Administrative Law (GAL)

The emergence of a regulatory layer of international law, 'specific in its normativity and legitimacy',[114] has functional equivalents in the European polity, but has not been institutionalised in the same modes at the international level. Against the background of the WTO jurisprudence just reviewed, its specificity can be substantiated further. Our reading of this jurisprudence in conflicts-law perspectives is based upon the apparent search for meta-norms which the jurisdictions involved can accept as a supra-nationally valid yardstick for evaluating, modifying or even correcting their legislation and policies. Since WTO law cannot establish legal equivalents to the European regulatory machinery through which general principles or legislative frameworks are concretised, it is bound to develop some functional *Ersatz*. 'Delegation of regulatory authority'[115] did occur, albeit in a limited and indirect way; legal commitments are 'softer' and coordinative activities typically informal.[116] The two Agreements complementing the WTO

[112] I Kant, 'Perpetual Peace. A Philosophical Sketch' in idem, *Political Writings*, H Reiss (ed) (Cambridge: CUP, 1991 [1796]) 93.

[113] N Krisch, 'The Pluralism of Global Administrative Law' (2006) 17 *EJIL* 247, at 266. See, more recently, idem, 'Global Administrative Law and the Constitutional Ambition', *LSE Law, Society and Economy Working Papers*, available at: www.lse.ac.uk/collections/law/wps/wps.htm.

[114] See Weiler, 'The Geology of International Law', n 22 above, at 552.

[115] See T Büthe, 'The Globalization of Health and Safety Standards: Delegation of Regulatory Authority in the SPS Agreement of the 1994 Agreement Establishing the World Trade Organization' (2008) 71 *Law and Contemporary Problems* 219, at 226.

[116] See the analysis of U Ehling, 'Environmental Policies and the WTO Committee on Trade and Environment: A Record of Failure?' in Joerges and Petersmann (eds), *Constitutionalism, Multilevel Trade Governance and Social Regulation*, 1st edn, n 1 above, 437.

framework are the outstanding devices. They operate in different ways. Where SPS measures adopted by WTO Members are in conformity with the international standards, guidelines and recommendations of organisations specified in that agreement or identified by the SPS Committee, compliance with WTO law is presumed.[117] In contrast, the TBT Agreement, which refrains from identifying such organisations, contains prescriptions as to their operation. Legal 'softness' is not to be equated with practical weakness, however. These mechanisms have proved to be remarkably powerful.

Their proper juridification is the challenge which the 'second dimension' of conflicts law has to address. It follows from the very notion of law from which this chapter departs[118] that we cannot simply equate the facticity of transnational governance and the functioning *telle quelle* of its mechanisms with 'law'. As in the case of European governance, the law's truth and justice need to be discerned in the concrete operations in place. The concrete is, at the same time, the nitty-gritty, at international, even more so than at European level. We can safely assume only that at *both* the European *and* the WTO level of governance, the factually existing regulatory 'layer' reflects practically irresistible needs – *and* that this facticity is exposed to the quest for 'fair and just' problem-solving. Complex as the mechanisms certainly are, legal practice and legal scholarship should not, and cannot, avoid addressing the normative query: the potential of transnational governance to ensure that its practices 'deserve recognition'. Pertinent contributions rarely use such Habermasian terms – but are, nevertheless, often enough compatible with his regulative ideas.

The most important suggestions have been developed in the context of the Global Administrative Law project (GAL) at NYU Law School.[119] Its protagonists have underlined that they deliberately refrain from designing a global constitutional vision;[120] Richard Stewart has explicitly objected to any transplanting of

[117] For details, see J Scott, The WTO Agreement on Sanitary and Phytosanitary Measures: A Commentary (Oxford: OUP, 2007) 246.

[118] See Section II.

[119] See B Kingsbury, N Krisch and RB Stewart, 'The Emergence of Global Administrative Law' (2005) 68 *Law and Contemporary Problems* 15. The project is enormous in its scope. It has, of course, predecessors and allies. It has, for example, been suggested that 'WTO law could be construed as concretizing what might be implicit in an adequate constitutional understanding of a State in an interdependent world', by A von Bogdandy, 'Legitimacy of International Economic Governance: Interpretative Approaches to WTO law and the Prospects of its Proceduralization' in S Griller (ed), *International Economic Governance and Non-Economic Concerns: New Challenges for the International Legal Order* (Vienna–New York: Springer, 2003) 103, at 134. See, earlier, R Howse and K Nicolaïdis, 'Legitimacy and Global Governance: Why Consitutionalizing the WTO is a Step too Far' in RB Porter et al (eds), *Efficiency, Equity, Legitimacy: The Multilateral Trading System at the Millenium* (Washington DC: Brookings Institution Press, 2001) 227. The core GAL group seems to me much closer to the distinction between various dimensions of conflicts law as suggested here. Because of the precarious legitimacy of substantive WTO decision-making, the 'first dimension' of conflicts law is indispensable – and equally irrefutable is, in view of the 'privatisation' of regulatory tasks, the need for the development of conflicts law's third dimension.

[120] B Kingsbury, 'The Concept of "Law" in Global Administrative Law' (2009) 20 *EJIL* 23.

EU models, such as that of a constitutionalised comitology, to global level.[121] And yet, considerations in the GAL project on a deepened 'juridification' of transnational governance arrangements and practices seem to reflect nothing else and nothing less than the possibility of a 'law of law-production'.[122] In a recent essay, Richard Stewart and his collaborators have even developed a three-dimensional pattern of their project, which seems to have very much in common with the three-dimensional conflicts law.[123] The affinity with the first dimension of conflicts law is first apparent from their definition of the objective of GAL disciplines to 'cure political externalities by protecting foreign citizens and firms against local discrimination and exploitation',[124] and then, even more so, from their conceptualisation of the 'inter-public' tensions between WTO law and the regulatory standards developed by other global bodies. Situations in which such public entities 'bump up against each other' will multiply; Benedict Kingsbury therefore predicts that GAL will have to generate 'conflict of laws arrangements' as GAL's 'horizontal dimension'.[125]

The affinity with conflicts law's second dimension is apparent from the suggestion to subject transnational WTO governance practices more strongly to procedural legal principles which all affected parties can accept, their American legacy notwithstanding.[126] This suggestion is accompanied by Benedict Kingsbury's defence of the law's normative *proprium*, which underlines that the qualification of norms as law 'is not a value-neutral statement'.[127] It seems reasonably safe to generalise upon the basis of GAL's most important considerations and yardsticks: transnational governance must be organised as a cooperative venture of the jurisdictions concerned; cooperation must respect democratically legitimated concerns. It must specify this respect through requirements pertaining to the organisation and working procedures of the bodies involved in the preparation of standards and recommendations. It must be prepared to respect normative and ethical objections, and to take the socio-economic asymmetric implications of transnational ruling into account. This implies decisional restraints and strategies in the form outlined at the end of the previous section.[128]

[121] 'Mars or Venus? Accountability and the Discontents of Globalization: US and EU Models for Regulatory Governance', mimeo 06 (on file with author).

[122] See, for this term, n 34 above.

[123] RB Stewart and MR Sanchez-Badin, 'The World Trade Organization and Global Administrative Law' in Joerges and Petersmann, n* above, ch 16, in particular Section II.3.

[124] Ibid, Section V.

[125] Kingsbury, 'The Concept of "Law" in Global Administrative Law', n 120 above, at 56; the reconstruction of this passage as a resort to conflict of laws doctrines which would govern these relationships by conflicts of law doctrines by M-S Kuo, 'Inter-public Legality or Post-Public Legitimacy? A Reply to Benedict Kingsbury' (2009) 20 *EJIL* 997, is, in my view, a misunderstanding of both Kingsbury's argument and of the proponents of conflicts law.

[126] See Stewart and Sanchez-Badin, 'The World Trade Organization and Global Administrative Law', n 123 above.

[127] Kingsbury, 'The Concept of "Law" in Global Administrative Law', n 120 above, at 26.

[128] Section IV.1.

IV.3. Para-legal Regimes: 'Facts Without Norms'?

Para-legal regimes are of paramount importance in the globalising economy – and the most complicated challenge to the conflicts-law project.[129] Since the approach submitted here places so much emphasis on the potential of democratically-legitimated law to supervise and to control both the involvement of non-governmental actors *and* the practices of governance, even with the EU, how can the transnational arena – where the law's shadow is obviously, on the whole, less clearly visible than at national and European level – be something other than the 'Achilles' heel' of the whole approach? It all depends, however, on what we know about the phenomena under scrutiny. Through the observation of para-legal regimes from the perspectives of conflicts-law methodologies, we do, at least, gain access to yardsticks for their recognition. The emergence of these regimes can be related to the basic premises of the approach, and their evaluation can be oriented accordingly. The impossibility of those affected by nation-state decision-making to participate in decision-making processes and the inter-dependencies of once territorially separated societies both necessitate and justify transnational decision-making. The type of regulatory problems that are of paramount importance in transnational markets requires the inclusion of non-governmental organisations (NGOs) and of expert knowledge. From such perspectives, it is simple, one-sided and reductionist to qualify these para-legal regimes as an alternative to state law and as a threat to the survival of that law. If one then considers the prerequisites for the recognition of these arrangements, one can again resort to conflicts-law thinking. The generation of norms and standards needs to respect the concerns of all the jurisdictions affected, and it will, at the same time, have to take the political dimensions of markets into account.

Any systematic exploration of these mechanisms is beyond the scope of this chapter.[130] The perspectives in which they should be undertaken should, however, be identical with those that we have articulated.[131] Conflicts law can build upon

[129] The phrase 'Facts Without Norms' in the title of this section is Christoph Humrich's; see his 'Facts without Norms? Does the Constitutionalisation of International Law still have a Discourse-Theoretical Chance?' in C Ungureanu, K Günther and C Joerges (eds), *Jürgen Habermas*, vol II: *Law and Democracy in the Postnational Constellation* (Farnham: Ashgate Publishing, 2011) 323.

[130] They are being intensively discussed in the context of the Bremen project, see, in particular, A Herwig, 'Transnational Governance Regimes for Food derived from Bio-Technology and their Legitimacy' in Joerges, Sand and Teubner (eds), *Transnational Governance and Constitutionalism*, n 62 above, 199; Hüller and Maier, 'Fixing the Codex?', n 106 above; Falke, 'Produkt- und Lebensmittelsicherheit', n 92 above; see, recently, MD Masson-Matthee, *The Codex Alimentarius Commission and its Standards* (The Hague: TMC Asser Press, 2007); D Bevilacqua and J Duncan, 'Towards a New Cosmopolitanism: Global Reflexive Interactive Democracy as a New Mechanism for Civil Society Participation in Agri-food Governance' (2009) 10 *Global Jurist* (Advances), Art 2, available at: www.bepress.com/gj/vol10/iss1/art2.

[131] Section III above. In his earlier writings, Gunther Teubner framed these issues in a similar way: 'If we abandon the old practice to obscure the *de facto* law-making in all kinds of "private governments" and bring to light that what they are doing is producing positive law which we *nolens-volens* have to obey, then we ask more urgently than before the question: What is this "private legal

the politicisation of the economy, and on the not-so-trivial power of states and the shadow of their laws. Conflicts within the economy cannot be settled by experts, and will certainly not be settled spontaneously. The elaboration of regimes which strike a fair balance between the economic interests concerned and mediate between the diverging political orientations will be dependent on the power of states to impose discipline on transnational norm generation and to defend exit options. This power is by no means negligible.

Its normative strength and also its political and legal prospects rest upon the recognition of, and respect for, diversity. This starting point is normatively stringent simply because political preference and priorities cannot be uniform around the globe. However, the main factual obstacles here are not discretionary preferences, but the hard realities of socio-economic diversity. Concerns stemming from socio-economic asymmetries are omnipresent in transnational governance. They are the real 'Achilles' heel' of the uniformity of ambitions in transnational law. Even within the European Union, the exclusion of pertinent considerations in the evaluation of the tensions between free access to all parts of the European market and regional interests has become normatively indispensable.[132] This implies that it may be often impossible to find solutions to disputes which deserve recognition by all affected jurisdictions. Why should this be a weakness rather than the strength of the conflicts-law approach?

regime's" democratic legitimation? At the same time, we see how naïve it would be to demand a formal delegatory link of private governments to the more narrow parliamentary process. Rather, we are provoked to look for new forms of democratic legitimation of private government that would bring economic, technical and professional action under public scrutiny and control. That seems to me is the liberating move that the paradox of global law without the state has actually provoked: an expansion of constitutionalism into private law production which would take into account that "private" governments are "public" governments' – thus his 'Breaking Frames: The Global Interplay of Legal and Social Systems' (1997) 45 *American Journal of Comparative Law* 149, at 159. However, one wonders what could constitute and characterise these 'new forms of democratic legitimation'? In his more recent work, Teubner seems to radicalise the equation of *de facto* law-making with positive law, which is already present in the cited passage. 'Spontaneous self-validation' of transnational private regimes (*Zivilverfassungen*) seems an all too mysterious process. In a recent essay, however, Teubner uses formulae which take up his earlier intentions and seem close to our suggestions: '[I]n order for private ordering to qualify as genuine law, it is not sufficient that the pertinent behavioural rules are alloyed to the notion of legal or illegal. Instead, the rules must themselves be subjugated to a process, in which they are judged according to the legal code. This reflexive process requires certain institutional precautions, in particular, the development of actors or instances, who or which are responsible for the establishment, modification, interpretation and implementation of the primary norm formation. Fundamental to this is the growth of the central level of internal control and implementation organs, which mediates between the two other normative levels, thusly grounding the legal character of the corporate code.' And, later, he even adds: 'One important condition for the success of corporate codes is their interaction with national legal systems. The effectuation of this interaction should be one of the most important tasks.' See, for a more elaborate discussion, Joerges and Rödl, 'Zum Funktionswandel des Kollisionsrechts II: Die kollisionsrechtliche Form einer legitimen Verfassung der post-nationalen Konstellation', n 3 above, 765; F Rödl, 'Regime-collisions, Proceduralised Conflict of Laws and the Unity of the Law: on the Form of Constitutionalism beyond the State' in R Nickel (ed), *Conflict of Laws and Laws of Conflict*, n 3 above, 263.

[132] See K Zurek, *Europen Food Regulation after Enlargement: Facing the Challenges of Diversity* (Leiden: Martinus Nijhoff, 2011).

V. THE LEGACY OF KARL POLANYI

Throughout this chapter, we have operated upon the basis of implicit assumptions about the institutional and social embeddedness of markets – within the former '*Volkswirtschaften*' (national economies) and our – by now – Europeanising and globalising economies. These assumptions, so the 'unsubstantiated fourth theses' of the previous edition has indicated,[133] can be backed by a broad range of traditions of political economy,[134] economic sociology,[135] political sociology,[136] various strands of systems theory,[137] and theories of the knowledge society.[138] Related endeavours can be observed in the search for a normative social theory basis in international relations[139] and in the exuberant inter-disciplinary debates on transnational governance[140] – and, last but not least, in human rights-based economic constitutionalism, as defended by Ernst-Ulrich Petersmann.[141]

The *locus classicus* – and, by now, also topical – reference point of pertinent discussions is, as Robert Wai has noted,[142] Karl Polanyi's *Great Transformation*.[143] Polanyi's analyses of the rise of capitalism are instructive for lawyers because

[133] *Constitutionalism, Multilevel Trade Governance and Social Regulation*, n 1 above, at 496–99.

[134] F Block, 'Towards a New Understanding of Economic Modernity' in C Joerges, B Stråth and P Wagner (eds), *The Economy as Polity: The Political Constitution of Contemporary Capitalism* (London: UCL Press, 2005) 3.

[135] See, out of a booming disciplinary renaissance, J Beckert, *Beyond the Market: The Social Foundations of Economic Efficiency* (Princeton NJ: Princeton University Press, 2002).

[136] N Fligstein, 'Markets as Politics: A Politico-Cultural Approach to Market Institutions' (1996) 61 *American Sociological Review* 656.

[137] H Willke, 'Dekonstruktion der Utopie' in idem, *Atopia. Studien zur atopischen Gesellschaft* (Frankfurt aM: Suhrkamp, 2001) 7 (his argument concerns the utopia of the pure market).

[138] N Stehr, *Wissenspolitik. Die Überwachung des Wissens* (Frankfurt aM: Suhrkamp, 2003) 222.

[139] See, most explicitly, P Nanz, 'Democratic Legitimacy of Transnational Trade Governance: A View from Political Theory' in Joerges and Petersmann, n 1 above, 59 (ch 2); and R Nickel, 'Legal Patterns of Global Governance: Participatory Transnational Governance', ibid, 157.

[140] See, for example, M Zürn, 'Democratic Governance Beyond the Nation-State: The EU and Other International Institutions' (2000) 6 *EJIR* 183; for recent contributions in German literature, see B Herborth and P Niesen (eds), *Anarchie der kommunikativen Freiheit: Jürgen Habermas und die Theorie der internationalen Politik* (Frankfurt aM: Suhrkamp, 2007); R Kreide and A Niederberger (eds), *Transnationale Verrechtlichung, Nationale Demokratien im Kontext globaler Politik* (Frankfurt aM–New York: Campus, 2008); N Deitelhoff and J Steffek (eds), *Was bleibt vom Staat? Demokratie, Recht und Verfassung im globalen Zeitalter* (Frankfurt aM–New York: Campus, 2009). Pertinent contributions in English can no longer be documented in a footnote. The debate on the constitutional quality of the WTO is an easier case, mirroring, however, the controversies in international and European law. See, for a recent critical survey, JL Dunoff, 'Constitutional Conceits: the WTO's "Constitution" and the Discipline of International Law' (2006) 17 *EJIL* 647.

[141] 'Multilevel Trade Governance in the WTO requires Multilevel Constitutionalism' in Joerges and Petersmann, n 1 above, 5; see the analysis by A Herwig and T Hüller, 'Towards Normative Legitimacy of the World Trade Order' in C Joerges and PF Kjaer, *Transnational Standards of Social Protection. Contrasting European and Transnational Governance*, Oslo: RECON-REPORT No 4 (2008) 223, at 237 ff.

[142] See n 71 above, such casual remarks are indicative of a real revival; see, Teubner, 'Societal Constitutionalism', n 62 above, at 12.

[143] K Polanyi, *The Great Transformation: The Political and Economic Origins of Our Time* (Boston MA: Beacon Press, 1957 [1944]).

they identify patterns which we continue to observe within nation states, in the European and also in transnational contexts: markets are contested social institutions. This is plainly visible from the political controversies and legal litigation over their proper ordering. Polanyi's messages reach beyond these phenomena. The proponents of the self-regulating market, he warns us, expose the economy and society to economic and social risks, which, in turn, will provoke, and, indeed, may be dependent upon, counter-movements which strive for stability and protection. There is neither an invisible hand at work, which would ensure prosperity and social integration as a lasting effect of the expansion of market rationality, nor will the double movement somehow find some stable social equilibrium automatically. Stability will, in the last resort, be dependent upon political action. Our fascination with Polanyi's analysis stems precisely from his refusal to provide us with recipes upon which states and societies could complacently rely or derive instructions in the disciplines of social and economic engineering. 'Polanyi's message is decidedly *not* that a market economy works better, or works only, if it is underpinned by a network of non-economic, community-type social relations'.[144] What kind of conflicts, then, does the economy harbour, and what means are at the disposal of state and/or society to discipline these processes and their agents? The answers to this query are, of course, not uniform.

Fred Block can be quoted as an authority among those who derive from Polanyi's work the need for reformist welfare state politics:

> Once it is recognised and acknowledged that markets are and must be socially constructed, then the critical question is no longer the quantitative issue of how much state or how much market, but rather the qualitative issue of how and for what ends should markets and states be combined and what are the structures and practices in civil society that will sustain a productive synergy of states and markets.[145]

This argument, Alexander Ebner objects,[146] downplays the Polanyian critique of the commodification of labour, land and money. Protagonists of the 'always socially embedded market' and the political messages associated with it tend to disregard the distinction between policies which stabilise the market mechanism and the counter-movements which strive for its replacement.

Indeed, the Polanyian concept of embeddedness is not associated with the rules of the market as such. Rather, it is the content of these rules with regard

[144] W Streeck, *Reforming Capitalism: Institutional Changes in the German Political Economy* (Oxford: OUP, 2009) at 247.

[145] Thus, in a contribution to the Workshop on 'The Economy as a Polity' at the European University Institute, 12–13 May 2003; this passage was not included in the later publication: Block, 'Towards a New Understanding of Economic Modernity', n 134 above, at 3–16. It remains, nevertheless, alive in topical contributions; see, for example, JA Caporaso and S Tarrow, 'Polanyi in Brussels: European Institutions and the Embedding of Markets in Society' (2009) 63 *International Organization* 593.

[146] A Ebner, 'Transnational Markets and the Polanyi Problem' in Joerges and Falke (eds), *Karl Polanyi, Globalisation and the Potential of Law in Transnational Markets*, n 97 above, 19.

to the commodity fiction regarding labour, land and money that matters. A Polanyian viewpoint thus implies an integrated perspective on embeddedness and commodification: the former addresses types of social integration and the latter is concerned with the socio-ecological substance of commodity production.[147]

When contrasted with the contestation which one observes in concrete 'cases', this dichotomy seems too schematically and opaquely constructed. The phenomena which, for example, Nico Stehr characterises as 'moralisation' and 'politicisation' of today's markets,[148] are, however, more ambiguous and more multi-faceted. Consumers, once portrayed as rent-seeking monads in the models of economic theory, are increasingly more adequately portrayed as politically-active market citizens by consumer policy analysts and historians.[149] The much-cited 'greening' of consumers affects one of Polanyi's 'false commodities'; legislation protecting consumers in cases of over-indebtedness is directly involved with the kind of social protection which labour law sought to ensure – and hence affects a second 'false commodity'. Such evidence may appear anecdotal but is, nonetheless, certainly compatible with the suggestions of Polanyians, who underline that 'congealed into every market exchange is a history of struggle and contestation'.[150] Polanyi's conceptualisation of the 'economy as instituted process'[151] captures precisely these dynamics, 'a universal *tendency* for societies to self-protect against "unregulated" market exchange' (emphasis added),[152] which Streeck's explains by a

> *fundamental* tension between stable social integration and the operation of self-regulating markets, [with] the latter inevitably eating away at the former unless society mustered the capacity and the will to put markets in their place and keep them there.[153]

Economic Sociology cannot generate conclusive answers to the problems which the law and legal scholarship have with the juridification of transnational governance. However, the Polanyian legacy does provides a key to the

[147] Ibid, Section 3, 26–33.

[148] *Moral Markets: How Knowledge and Affluence Change Consumers and Products* (Boulder CO: Paradigm Publishers, 2008); see, also, N Stehr, C Henning and B Weiler (eds), *The Moralization of the Markets* (New Brunswick NJ: Transaction Publishers, 2006).

[149] See M Everson, 'Legal Construction of the Consumer' in F Trentmann (ed), *The Making of the Consumer* (Oxford–New York: Berg, 2006) 99; M Everson and C Joerges, 'Consumer Citizenship in Postnational Constellations?' in K Soper and F Trentmann (eds), *Citizenship and Consumption* (New York: Palgrave Macmillan, 2008) 154.

[150] G Kippner, 'Opening Remarks on Embeddedness' in idem et al, 'Polanyi Symposium: A Conversation on Embeddedness' (2004) 2 *Socio-Economic Review* 109, at 112.

[151] K Polanyi, 'The Economy as Instituted Process' in M Granovetter and R Swedberg (eds), *The Sociology of Economic Life*, 2nd edn (Boulder CO–San Francisco CA–Oxford: Westview Press, 2001 [1957]) 31–50.

[152] S Randles, 'Issues for a Neo-Polanyian Research Agenda in Economic Sociology' (2003) 13 *International Review of Sociology* 409, at 424.

[153] Streeck, *Reforming Capitalism*, n 144 above, at 247–48.

conceptualisation of the economy as polity – and to the double movement of '*Rechtswissenschaft in Kritik und als Kritik*' (Critique of legal science and legal science as critique).[154] Thus, Rudolf Wiethölter's formula both captures and mirrors real-world tensions and their controversial conceptualisations. It re-phrases the kind of tensions which Karl Polanyi re-constructed in his analyses of dis-embedding strategies and re-embedding counter-movements.

[154] See Wiethölter, n 26 above.

28

*A Conflicts-Law Response to the Precarious Legitimacy of Transnational Trade Governance**

STRUCTURING OUR ARGUMENT

THE RECENT NEGOTIATIONS over comprehensive mega-regional free trade agreements exemplify the challenges and consequences of an increasing political transnationalisation. Focusing on the permanent reduction of non-tariff barriers through the convergence of legal orders, these agreements increasingly constrain the policy autonomy of national governments and put a strain on domestic democratic and societal institutions. By moving and blurring the line where domestic prerogatives end and external obligations begin, and by creating permanent transnational governance arrangements, these treaties have proven much more legitimacy-sensitive than past agreements. This article/essay outlines the implications for national decision-making and democratic politics. Our objective is the establishment of a framework within which these challenges stemming from 'deep' economic integration and transnational governance can be substantiated and meaningfully addressed.

The theoretical frame and background of our argument, which we sketch out in Section I, builds on Karl Polanyi's work on the social embeddedness of markets, John Gerard Ruggie's reception of Polanyian premises in his theory of embedded liberalism and his analyses of the transformations of the trade system, and proceeds to Dani Rodrik's 'trilemma thesis', which provides, in our view, a congenial complement to their pathbreaking insights. We are far from suggesting that theories developed at such temporal distance and in such a variety of disciplines can be merged seamlessly and then 'applied' to contemporary phenomena. Instead, we argue that the traditions to which we refer have remained topical in their conceptualisations of markets, politics, and law, and that these insights can help us in a reconstruction of the post-war development of the international trade system. We furthermore submit that they remain

* Co-Author Fabian Bohnenberger. Published in M Hirsch and A Lang (eds), *Research Handbook on the Sociology of International Law* (Cheltenham: Edward Elgar, 2020) 37.

important with respect to core issues in the debates about the prevailing modes of transnational trade governance and the tensions between economic globalisation and democratic legitimacy.

We illustrate these ideas in Section II, where we discuss how the frontier of bilateral and regional trade negotiations has transcended national borders and moved deep into the arena of domestic politics and societal choices. To be sure, the most controversial so-called 'mega-regional trade agreement', the Transatlantic Trade and Investment Partnership (TTIP) between the European Union and the United States, has been removed quite abruptly from the political agenda. It seems nevertheless unlikely that the upheaval in American politics will constrain the so far irresistible proliferation of bilateral trade agreements and 'mega-regional agreements'. The EU–Canada Comprehensive Economic and Trade Agreement (CETA), which was approved by the European Parliament on 15 February 2017, underlines this trend towards increasingly broader and deeper trade agreements, and we will discuss CETA's implications in some depth. It is not only the asymmetric distributional consequences but also the price that is paid in terms of democratic control and national autonomy in order to reap the benefits of this type of transnational governance that has created legitimacy problems and – in combination with treaty negotiations behind closed doors – generated political unrest. Our discussion will briefly explore core features of this new trade agenda, which will simultaneously provide an acid test for our theoretical framework. Finally, Section III introduces a model of transnational legitimacy – an approach we dub 'conflicts-law constitutionalism' – which we understand as an *aliud* to the democratic legitimacy of constitutional states, on the one hand, and purely functionalist or economic models of transnational ordering, on the other.

I. THE FRAMEWORK: POLANYI, RUGGIE AND RODRIK

I.1. Polanyi and Ruggie on the Social Embeddedness of the Market and International Trade

Karl Polanyi's magisterial work *The Great Transformation*, with its exploration of 'the political and economic origins of our time',[1] has made a lasting impression, in particular with two of its messages: first, the capitalist market economy is not an evolutionary accomplishment but a political product – '*laissez-faire* was planned'.[2] The second – namely the theorem of the 'always socially embedded economy' – is implicit in Polanyi's analyses. It follows stringently from the

[1] K Polanyi, *The Great Transformation: The Political and Economic Origins of Our Time* [1944] (First Beacon, MA: Beacon Press, 1957) (hereinafter, KP, *GT* 1957).

[2] '… planning was not', ibid, 147.

first, but is much broader: markets require institutional backing and continuous political management. 'The political' is inherent in 'the economic' – markets are polities.[3] Unsurprisingly, Polanyi was not concerned with the markets for sophisticated consumer goods and services, as we know them today. His analysis focuses on 'land, labour and money', three goods which were not produced to be sold on markets but were, nevertheless, 'marketed', and subjected to market governance, as though they were regular commodities. With regard to these three fictitious commodities, '*embeddedness*' denotes a precarious constellation. The politically imposed commodification of the three fictitious commodities cannot be expected to be accomplished easily; instead, such 'political' moves will spark crises and provoke 'counter-movements' – an insight of uncomforting topicality.[4] Transnational governance was, in his world, primarily realised through the gold standard – 'the faith of the age', as Polanyi put it to underline the strong belief that this mechanism would ensure a control of exchange rates and balanced international accounts.[5]

Our markets today are politicised; they reflect a broad variety of societal concerns.[6] Pertinent measures will, at the same time, reflect a variety of political preferences and socio-economic conditions. John G Ruggie was among the first to highlight these interdependencies succinctly; in the seminal elaboration of his findings, he underlined the indebtedness of this approach to Karl Polanyi. Ruggie's paper became famous for its analyses of the trade system and its awareness of the interdependencies between Western societies in the post-World War II system. Ruggie characterised this period of the GATT Agreement, the Bretton Woods System, and the foundational period of the (then) European Economic Community (EEC), as the age of a politically and socially 'embedded liberalism'.[7] The validity of his analysis and the adequacy of the notion that he coined was very widely recognised.[8] Its importance for our argument should be obvious: both post-war trade regimes, the GATT and the EEC, established frameworks which left 'the participating states with very considerable freedoms to pursue

[3] For a stringent explanation, see F Block, 'Towards a New Understanding of Economic Modernity' in C Joerges et al (eds), *The Economy as Polity: The Political Construction of Modern Capitalism* (London: UCL Press, 2005) 3.

[4] See C Joerges, 'Law and Politics in Europe's Crisis: On the History of the Impact of an Unfortunate Configuration' (2014) 21 *Constellations* 249.

[5] KP, *GT*, 1957, 25; see, for an instructive analysis, S Frerichs, 'The Law of Market Society: A Sociology of International Economic Law and Beyond' (2016) 23 *Finnish Yearbook of International Law* 173.

[6] See, for example, N Stehr et al (eds), *The Moralization of the Markets* (London: Routledge, 2009); on the latter aspect, see, also, Section I.3 below.

[7] JG Ruggie, 'International Regimes, Transactions and Change: Embedded Liberalism in the Postwar Economic Order' (1982) 36 *International Organization* 375.

[8] This is not to suggest that 'embedded liberalism' was a globally accepted concept; see J Steffek, *Embedded Liberalism and its Critics: Justifying Global Governance in the American Century* (Basingstoke: Palgrave Macmillan, 2006) especially at 43 ff.

their regulatory objectives and distributional policies'. This last conclusion is submitted by Dani Rodrik. His reiteration of Ruggie's observation reads:

> The considerable manoeuvring room afforded by these trading rules allowed advanced nations to build customized versions of capitalism around distinct approaches to corporate governance, labor markets, tax regimes, business-government relations, and welfare state arrangements. What emerged in a phrase coined by the political scientists Peter Hall and David Soskice, were 'varieties of capitalism'.[9] The United States, Britain, France, Germany, or Sweden were each market-based economies, but the institutions that underpinned their markets differed substantially and bore unmistakably national characteristics.[10]

I.2. Rodrik and the Tensions between Economic Globalisation and Democratic Politics

Rodrik's work is deeply influenced by Polanyian ideas, an intellectual indebtedness that he recently described in more detail and which led him to observe that '[i]n my own writings on economic development and globalization, I felt often that I was simply restating the main themes of the Great Transformation for our current era'.[11]

The historical and contextual dimensions of Rodrik's analysis of trade relations and his understanding of markets as social institutions document these affinities clearly.[12] Both scholars underline the social and institutional environment of markets, ie, the establishment of legal frameworks and governance arrangements within which markets can function, as well as the formal and social norms which support their functioning.

Rodrik's seminal work on globalisation has so far rarely been taken into account by students of international trade law.[13] In our view, his writings provide an exceptionally lucid access not only to the general debate on the pros and cons of free international trade, but also to the systemic choices prevailing in the international trade system. This holds particularly true for Rodrik's 'trilemma

[9] PA Hall and D Soskice (eds), *Varieties of Capitalism: The Institutional Foundations of Comparative Advantage* (Oxford: OUP, 2005).

[10] D Rodrik, *The Globalization Paradox: Democracy and the Future of the World Economy* (New York: Norton, 2011) (hereinafter Rodrik, GP, 2011).

[11] See his foreword to KP Levitt's 'From the Great Transformation to the Great Financialization', available at: http://rodrik.typepad.com/dani_rodriks_weblog/2017/03/a-foreword-to-kari-polanyi-levitt.html.

[12] See the sections from Polanyi's *Great Transformation* reprinted in NH Barma and SK Vogel (eds), *The Political Economy Reader: Markets as Institutions* (Abingdon: Routledge, 2008) 121.

[13] A notable exception is Robert Howse, who is engaged in an ongoing exchange with Rodrik; see his 'Further Considerations on Dani Rodrik, The Globalization Paradox' (2013) 11 *I•CON* 813–815, and, most recently, 'The World Trade Organization 20 Years on: Global Governance by Judiciary' (2016) 27 *EJIL* 9.

thesis', which he submitted in 2011.[14] With this thesis, he asserts the impossibility of the simultaneous pursuit of economic globalisation, democratic politics, and national determination (autonomy), describing a situation in which only two of the goals can be achieved. The tensions increase with the move towards what Rodrik characterises as 'deep' economic globalisation, namely, the trend of international trade law – and, of course, European market integration law – to reach *beyond* the prohibition of discriminatory practices into the domestic regulations of WTO members and the Member States of the EU.

Often enough, Rodrik does not shy away from pointed normative statements.[15] Although his views on deep economic integration remain somewhat ambivalent, he voices a preference for a system which prioritises national autonomy and democratic legitimacy over free trade and access to foreign markets. 'Hyperglobalization' would, in his view, 'require shrinking domestic politics and insulating technocrats from the demands of popular groups',[16] as well as invoke 'clashes with democracy for the simple reason that it seeks not to improve the functioning of democracy but to accommodate commercial and financial interests seeking market access at low costs', thereby overriding other social and political objectives.[17] There is a well-explored and well-explained empirical background to this stance, namely, Rodrik's scepticism towards the general validity of the promises that tend to be attributed to trade liberalisation,[18] and 'the false economic promise of global governance'.[19] But his normative scepticism is context-dependent, and he is aware of the strength of political and economic motivation to 'conclude one trade agreement after another'.[20] We will come back to his position in Section III.

I.3. Hall and Soskice on the *Varieties of Capitalism*

Every assessment of the political price to be paid in order to achieve deep integration has to take into account a further complication to which Rodrik alludes only loosely in his reference to the 'Varieties of Capitalism' studies: an opening of national economies and the exposure to the requirements of free market access not only affects insulated regulations but, in the long run, also the entire institutional and normative framework of the economy. This is a long-term and not-so-easily visible challenge that has rarely been addressed in the legal debates

[14] Rodrik, *GP*, 2011; Rodrik summarised his argument lucidly in *Social Europe* of 14 January 2014, available at www.socialeurope.eu/2014/01/globalization-paradox.

[15] See his much visited weblog: http://rodrik.typepad.com.

[16] Rodrik, *GP*, 2011, 189.

[17] Rodrik, *GP*, 2011, 205.

[18] See, for example, Rodrik, *GP*, 2011, 76 ff.

[19] See his blog entry of 11 August 2016, available at: http://drodrik.scholar.harvard.edu/links/false-economic-promise-global-governance.

[20] Rodrik, *GP*, 2011, 190.

among the experts of international trade law – and it is all the more remarkable that Polanyi was already aware of these difficulties. Its presence is nevertheless irrefutable.

Because real-world markets synthesise local cultural orientations and the outcomes of political contestation, their institutionalisation will differ considerably from one polity to another. The work on the varieties of capitalism, as initiated in 2011 by Peter A Hall and David Soskice, has validated this insight again and again.[21] The five main institutional variations which these studies identified all concern 'the way in which firms resolve the coordination problems they face'.[22] These characteristics are hardly ever directly and never comprehensively affected by the provisions that open national markets. This is because they build, to a significant degree, upon 'social norms', which tend to be surprisingly resistant.[23] And yet, the exposure to competitive pressures from foreign jurisdictions may, in the long run, exert eroding effects. Is this a normative challenge which the law has to take seriously? It is a challenge which is rarely noticed at all. Wolfgang Streeck, Fritz W Scharpf and Jürgen Habermas are notable exceptions, with the first-mentioned two responding in the affirmative and the latter rejecting the validity of the argument.[24] Polanyi's perception of these challenges is simply amazing. The pertinent passage of the *Great Transformation* deserves to be cited in full:

> [W]ith the disappearance of the automatic mechanism of the gold standard, governments will find it possible to … tolerate willingly that other nations shape their domestic institutions according to their inclinations, thus transcending the pernicious nineteenth century dogma of the necessary uniformity of domestic regimes

[21] PA Hall and D Soskice, 'An Introduction to Varieties of Capitalism' in eidem (eds), *Varieties of Capitalism: Institutional Foundations of Comparative Advantage* (Oxford: OUP, 2001) 1.

[22] Hall and Soskice, ibid, 6–8. The variables are industrial relations; vocational training and education; corporate governance; inter-firm relations; and relations between firm and their employees.

[23] See W Abelshauser, 'Europa in Vielfalt einigen. Eine Denkschrift', available at wwwhomes.uni-bielefeld.de/wabelsha/Denkschrift.pdf; G Teubner, 'Idiosyncratic Production Regimes: Co-evolution of Economic and Legal Institutions in the Varieties of Capitalism' in J Ziman (ed), *The Evolution of Cultural Entities: Proceedings of the British Academy* (Oxford: OUP, 2001) 161; idem, 'Transnational Economic Constitutionalism in the Varieties of Capitalism' (2015) No 2 *The Italian Law Journal*, available at www.theitalianlawjournal.it/teubner.

[24] See W Streeck, *Re-Forming Capitalism: Institutional Change in the German Political Economy* (Oxford: OUP, 2009) 246 ff; FW Scharpf, 'After the Crash: A Perspective on Multilevel European Democracy' (2015) 21 *ELJ* 384: 'In European constitutional democracies, these diverse socioeconomic configurations – which for purposes of the present discussion may be collapsed into the rough distinction between "social-market" and "liberal-market" political economies – have become constitutive parts of the legitimate social order. Since the end of the post-war period, these normatively salient configurations have changed in response to internal moral and social changes and to the external challenges of global capitalism and of European integration.' The recognition of the normative validity of this type of 'social acquis' is rejected by J Habermas, 'Demokratie oder Kapitalismus? Vom Elend der nationalstaatlichen Fragmentierung in einer kapitalistisch integrierten Weltgesellschaft' (2013) *Blätter für deutsche und internationale Politik* 59, at 61 ff.

> within the orbit of world economy. Out of the ruins of the Old World, cornerstones of the New can be seen to emerge: economic collaboration of governments and the liberty to organize national life at will.[25]

What Polanyi submits is a vision of a transnational ordering which synthesises the functional necessities of international markets with the normative concerns prevailing in the participating polities. Fred Block highlights the period of embedded liberalism as the best example, which, for him, is the so-to-speak 'crowning moment of Polanyi's alternative history',[26] because the unprecedented global economic expansion at that time would testify to the ability of market societies to combine economic dynamism with expanding social rights and protection for the citizenry. But this may be a somewhat wishful reading; in Ruggie's more critical words:

> Polanyi's prediction of the end of capitalist internationalism does not stand up well against the subsequent internationalization of production and finance … yet [Polanyi] had been correct in the essential fact that a new threshold had been crossed in the balance between 'market' and 'authority', with governments assuming much more direct responsibility for domestic social security and economic stability.[27]

At any rate, Polanyi's vision seems perfectly compatible with the perspective which Rodrik elaborates and defends in his work on globalisation and the above-cited trilemma thesis: the autonomy of polities is curtailed if they are compelled, in the name of free trade, to accept standards or other prescriptions which do not mirror their own preferences; economic integration and national self-determination do not go hand in hand. Would a resolution of this conflict presuppose the establishment of a transnational democracy? Would this require the establishment of decision-making procedures which would reflect and implement some common will of all the members of the WTO? This suggestion leads us into a dead-end alley. Do we have to conclude that a commitment to democracy implies that we have to go without the economic advantages of free trade?

I.4. Living with a Trilemma: A Glance at the Responses in the International Trade System

In the final sections of his seminal article, Ruggie discusses the advent of new challenges to the balancing of national autonomy and international economic integration in the golden age of 'embedded liberalism' in depth. Under the GATT 1948 regime, he observed, objections to free trade were essentially

[25] KP, *GT*, 1957, 253.

[26] Fred Block, 'Introduction' to Karl Polanyi, *The Great Transformation* (Boston MA: Beacon Press, 2001) xxxv ff.

[27] Ruggie, 'International Regimes', n 7 above, 338.

economic, and tariffs were a nation state's primary means of protecting its interests. However, tariffs had been substantially reduced by the early 1970s – and, in this respect, the GATT was remarkably successful. What the trade community witnessed was a steady increase of so-called 'non-tariff barriers' to trade, which reflected a wide range of domestic concerns for the health and safety of consumers, and the protection of workers and the environment. Ruggie's remarks on these new obstacles to free trade are anything but hostile. He acknowledged that these developments both represent and further a new type of social embeddedness of markets, but also realised that trade liberalisation had to renew its conceptual frame: domestic regulatory objectives that are generally embedded in a nation state's legal system, sometimes at constitutional level, were now confronted with external objections as to both their protectionist implications and their regulatory reasonableness. Writing in 1982, Ruggie could not predict how the international trade system would adapt to this new constellation a decade later under the pressures of re-ascendant market liberalism by transforming the GATT 1948 into the WTO 1994. The institutional change created more effective means for dispute resolution and established a number of special agreements, such as the Agreement on the Application of Sanitary and Phytosanitary Measures (SPS) and the Agreement on Technical Barriers to Trade (TBT), with rules for balancing the economic concerns of free trade with the social concerns of regulatory policy.

The ambivalences of these developments are readily apparent. The creation of non-tariff barriers reflected the move towards more 'social regulation', such as consumer protection, safety at work, and environmental concerns, and had its democratic credentials. The new challenge was to defend these accomplishments at the transnational level. The particular promise of the new framework, including the TBT and SPS Agreements, was to further institutionalise a specific way of policy-making based upon scientific evidence and expertise, cleansed of the pushing and shoving of everyday politics. We will discuss the scholarly debates on these tensions between trade liberalisation and democratic legitimacy and the search for genuinely transnational legitimation in our concluding section (IV) after a brief analysis of the not so scholarly controversies over 'mega-regional trade agreements' in the next section.[28]

[28] The potential advantages of the EU in the search for valid responses to the tensions between economic integration and democracy seem overwhelming. The EU has considerable legislative competences – 'albeit in limited fields' – which are exercised within European-wide political processes and legitimated on that basis. It has no genuine administrative powers but it can build on the services of the European Commission and the support by well-organised advisory networks and the cooperation with a host of national institutions. The prevailing mode of operation of this complex regulatory machinery is technocratic: executive and managerial. For systematic analyses of the affinities and discrepancies between Europe's 'completion' of its internal market and the international trade system, see J Falke and C Joerges (eds), *Handelsliberalisierung und Sozialregulierung in transnationalen Konstellationen* (Baden-Baden: Nomos, 2013), with extensive reference to studies undertaken a project on 'Trade liberalisation and social regulation in transnational structures' in the

II. THE EXEMPLARY IMPORTANCE OF MEGA-REGIONAL TRADE AGREEMENTS

The shift towards mega-regional trade agreements has profoundly affected the discussions on international trade. In the light of the political and normative conceptions of the relationship between state and markets outlined in Section I, we now focus on the apparent tensions between the new modes of transnational treaty governance and autonomous national democratic decision-making. The following analysis discusses the core institutional innovations envisioned in the finalised Comprehensive Economic and Trade Agreement (CETA) and the earlier TTIP negotiations – the failure of the latter notwithstanding – and points to normative sensitivities in preparation of our theoretical analysis and legal characterisation in Section III.

II.1. The Move towards Mega-regional Trade Agreements

Deadlock in the multilateral negotiations in the Doha Development Agenda framework and the complexities of twenty-first-century trade[29] have precipitated the rise in selective associations between WTO member states. Initiatives such as the TTIP and the CETA constitute but the latest and most prominent attempts to broaden market liberalisation and create new rules outside the WTO. The negotiations have focused on the removal and alignment of non-tariff barriers, which includes placing more substantial constraints on national governments' discretionary policy space while creating some form of institutionalised governance arrangements between the signatories. As 'living' agreements, these treaties are much more forward-looking than previous initiatives, and envision ongoing cooperation on regulatory and other matters.

In contrast to existing trade deals, the proposed mega-regional agreements have produced an unprecedented societal backlash aimed at stopping the negotiations. The objections against the legitimacy of the new agreements are based upon their reach beyond the reduction or elimination of the traditional hurdles to international commerce into spheres which Rodrik characterises as deep economic integration: the harmonisation or mutual recognition of standards and risk assessment procedures, and the creation of respective procedures and governance venues. In this regard, the current debate about free trade is essentially about preserving national autonomy in decision-making and

context of 'The Collaborative Research Centre Transformations of the State' at the University of Bremen from 2003 onwards. Comprehensive information is available at www.sfb597.uni-bremen.de/pages/forProjektBeschreibung.php?SPRACHE=en&ID=1.

[29] R Baldwin, '21st Century Regionalism: Filling the Gap between 21st Century Trade and 20th Century Trade Rules' (Working Paper ERSD-2011-08), available at www.wto.org/english/res_e/reser_e/ersd201108_e.pdf.

standard-setting, as well as the particular normative assumptions that guide these powers. In other words, while domestic distributional questions play a role, it is not only demands for social protection that have driven people to the streets or to sign petitions: the critics are afraid that deep trade agreements could lead to a redefinition of the legitimate social purposes in pursuit of which state power is expected to be employed in domestic contexts.

These concerns directly relate to more fundamental questions about the domination of the political sphere by narrow economic interests, technocratic decision-making processes, and the delegation of authority to transnational levels of governance. The negotiations on the TTIP and the CETA acted as catalysts for a broader debate which engages with these issues and reflects broader societal concerns with the role of the state in creating and overseeing globalising markets, managing externalities and holding the precarious balance between different actors. As the need for new rules has grown in international trade and there are also good reasons to increase the cooperation on regulatory and other issues between trade partners, the key question is how this can be achieved without circumscribing the decision-making autonomy of the EU and its Member States, and thereby bypassing or weakening democratically legitimated legislative and regulatory procedures. While confining the following remarks to the new mode of governance which the final CETA and provisional TTIP agreements represent in an exemplary fashion, we will take a look at two of the most interesting – and controversial – developments in terms of balancing the imperatives for transnational governance with national democratic politics. The first section discusses the potential implications of institutionalised regulatory cooperation in these agreements; the second part offers further insights into the tensions between investor–state dispute settlement and democratic government.

II.1.1. The Right to Regulate and its Basis in Normative Dimensions of Regulatory Governance

In the context of the CETA and the TTIP, the negotiators expected the largest economic gains from intensified cooperation on regulatory issues.[30] While average tariffs are already low in the transatlantic context, differences in product standards, testing requirements, certification procedures, and domestic health and safety regulations remain costly for producers and exporters on both sides. Decades of transatlantic cooperation and the recent negotiations of both agreements have, however, shown that greater convergence in behind-the-border barriers is hard to achieve in practice: while the creation of uniform norms could greatly simplify trade, harmonisation remains extremely difficult and the

[30] J Francois, 'Reducing Transatlantic Barriers to Trade and Investment. An Economic Assessment (Final Project Report)', 2013, available at http://trade.ec.europa.eu/doclib/docs/2013/march/tradoc_150737.pdf.

scope of common objectives fairly limited.[31] Instead, attempts at using mutual recognition of the existing approaches of both sides dominated proposals for regulatory cooperation in the TTIP. The CETA only contains provisions aimed at forward-looking cooperation and has no direct impact on existing regulation. The creation of common standards remains most likely in fields of future regulatory activity.

More interesting are the cross-cutting 'horizontal' commitments on how the participating states should conduct domestic regulatory activities. The relevant draft chapter for the TTIP has been singled out by analysts as an 'innovative approach to international trade treaty-making containing a framework for future bilateral regulatory cooperation',[32] and CETA features similar, albeit generally weaker, language. The chapters[33] include commitments to transparency, mutual consultation, evaluations and periodic review – in short, 'good regulatory practices' – and the obligation to inform the other party early on about any planned regulatory acts with a significant impact on trade or investment. Additional clauses spell out requirements on assessing the impact on trade and investment for planned regulation and, in the more ambitious TTIP draft, the opportunity for any interested party to petition any regulatory authority for the issuance, amendment, or repeal of any regulation, as well as the requirement to maintain procedures to promote periodic reviews of regulations affecting transatlantic trade and investment.

Regulatory cooperation remains voluntary and the agreements – as well as the CETA Joint Interpretative Instrument (JII), which was adopted to accommodate numerous concerns from EU Member States – highlight the 'right to regulate' of the signatories. At the same time, however, the fundamental aim of regulatory cooperation is to 'prevent and eliminate unnecessary barriers to trade and investment'.[34] While the agreements do not foresee any changes to legislative or standard-setting processes, the provisions on regulatory cooperation suggest

[31] In TTIP, negotiations on mutual recognition or harmonisation of sectorial provisions were very difficult and progress did not meet the EU's expectations. Sectoral annexes were discussed for the following sectors: cars, pharmaceuticals, chemicals, cosmetics, ICT, pesticide, engineering, medical devices and textiles. See http://trade.ec.europa.eu/doclib/press/index.cfm?id=1553.

[32] A Alemanno, 'The Regulatory Cooperation Chapter of the TTIP. Challenges and Opportunities' (2015) 18 *JIEL* 625, available at https://ssrn.com/abstract=2651091.

[33] For the CETA, see Chapter 21, available at: http://trade.ec.europa.eu/doclib/docs/2014/september/tradoc_152806.pdf. The discussion is so far less intensive than the debate on the TTIP; for a particularly comprehensive analysis, see P-T Stoll, TP Holterhus and H Gött, 'Die geplante Regulierungszusammenarbeit zwischen der Europäischen Union und Kanada sowie den USA nach den Entwürfen von CETA und TTIP', Göttingen 2015, available at www.abl-ev.de/fileadmin/Dokumente/AbL_ev/Welthandel/2015_Rechtsgutachten_TTIP_CETA_Regulierungszusammenarbeit.pdf. For the TTIP, see Greenpeace leaks draft chapter name: 'Initial Provisions for Chapter [EU: Regulatory Cooperation] [US: Regulatory Coherence, Transparency, and Other Good Regulatory Practices]' as of April 2016, available at: https://ttip-leaks.org/ttip/regulatory-cooperation, hereinafter 'Leaked Draft of TTIP Chapter on Regulatory Co-operation'.

[34] CETA Article 21.2 (4a).

a shift in the discourse and normative assumptions that underpin and steer the work of regulators. Will this enhanced exchange lead to mutual learning and better regulation for the benefit of all? Or will it curtail regulatory autonomy, abetting arrangements on the lowest common denominator and a situation in which trade liberalisation comes at the expense of legitimate regulatory activity?

The implications for the way in which we regulate in Europe depend heavily on the mechanisms and new institutional venues that are created to facilitate the operations of a 'living agreement'.[35] The signatories of the CETA have high expectations to 'minimise unnecessary divergences in regulations',[36] and Chapter 21 contains explicit objectives to reduce differences in regulation through ongoing bilateral discussions and the establishment of a Regulatory Cooperation Forum (RCF) and a Joint Committee. Pursuant to CETA Article 21.6, the RCF will provide an institutionalised platform for technical dialogue between the parties on regulatory policy and joint initiatives, without the power to adopt legally binding decisions.[37] The TTIP agenda also envisioned a Regulatory Cooperation Body composed of experts who would continuously work towards regulatory convergence. Access and membership would have a significant impact on what kind of concerns these institutions would prioritise in dealing with existing and future regulation, and what regulatory culture would dominate joint undertakings. Both venues intend to comprise the relevant officials and regulators of both sides and 'may by mutual consent invite other interested parties to participate in the meetings'.[38]

An intensifying exchange on regulatory policy and joint reviews of regulatory initiatives in these new treaty bodies indicate a potential shift in the normative assumptions that have guided regulatory activity. The emphasis of these agreements on cost–benefit analysis in regulatory policy-making and scientific methodologies – that gain importance for drawing the line between what is perceived as 'disguised protectionism' and what is perceived as rewarding domestic regulation – aims at changing the way in which knowledge is used while regulating. Mutual learning between regulators should therefore, from a more nuanced perspective, not simply be understood as acquiring more or better knowledge, but also as aligning normative assumptions that guide regulatory action.[39] Given our initial concern for national democracy, these exchanges are

[35] The German Constitutional Court, in its judgment of 13 October 2016 on CETA, underlined that the validity of this innovation will be examined thoroughly in the further proceedings (2 BvR 1368/16, paras 30–31, 71).

[36] CETA Article 21.4.

[37] According to Article 26.2, the RCF would only have such powers if these were explicitly stated in the agreement. Article 21.6 does not grant such powers to the RCF.

[38] CETA Article 21.6 (3); a similar statement can be found in leaked draft of TTIP chapter on regulatory cooperation.

[39] M Bartl, 'TTIP's Regulatory Cooperation and the Politics of "Learning"', *Social Europe*, 26 November 2015, available at www.socialeurope.eu/2015/11/ttips-regulatory-cooperation-and-the-politics-of-learning.

uncontroversial as long as they only affect domestic regulation that is intentionally protectionist and in violation of trade obligations. The problem, however, arises when non-discriminatory regulations are challenged: food safety measures that are not based upon scientific evidence, environmental regulations or even wage and labour laws are but a few examples.

However, while some of the treaty obligations intrude into domestic regulatory affairs, we have to keep in mind that the particularly sensitive parts of regulatory processes are unlikely to be subject to strong disciplines. Governments have recognised the sensitivity of the issue and any commitments will be modest in terms of real enforceability. What we can nevertheless observe is a shift of policy-making activities to new governance arrangements which cannot but operate as a type of anonymous expert administration working on functionally limited tasks. While it can be argued that this is primarily 'technical' work that is already the domain of experts and requires little democratic oversight, recent protests should act as a constant reminder that these standards represent societal choices that can be highly political.

From our perspective on the new modes of transnational treaty governance, the outcome for national democracy remains highly ambivalent and fully reflects the uncertainties of the negotiation processes and treaty provisions. However, the procedural and substantive requirements of the agreements clearly indicate a growing emphasis on the executive and technocratic elements in government that are likely to undercut public deliberation, remove regulatory governance further from democratic oversight, and may reduce the reactiveness of national governments to public opinion. We can be sure of the need to supplement or to revise our regulatory approaches and standards in the future; the 'life' of the CETA and the proposed TTIP will be filled by technocratic expertise.[40] This trend is problematic because it creates the need for new procedural rules, accountability relationships, avenues for judicial control, and exit options. While the sheer complexities of European governance have already fostered a turn towards politically unaccountable, technocratic problem-solving,[41] this same tendency dominates the disciplines of the new agreements on regulatory cooperation. Our worry is that, so far, the treaties seem to produce further advances on

[40] For a detailed instructive analysis, see J Falke, 'Hohe Standards beibehalten und nicht-tarifäre Handelshemmnisse abbauen. (Wie) geht beides?', Loccum: EAL-Tagung 5/15 (on file with the authors).

[41] 'Comitology', once praised as heralding a turn to 'deliberative supranationalism', has slowly but steadily disappointed pertinent hopes. This cannot be attributed to some sinister political conspiracy. It is due to the sheer amount of decisional issues that have to be resolved, which increased dramatically with the Eastern enlargement of the Union and became ever more complicated due to the ever deepening socio-economic and political diversity which fostered this technocratic turn; see n 40 above and the comments on the recent reform initiative of the European Commission by Maria Weimer: *No More Blame Game: Back to the Future of Comitology, VerfBlog*, 2017/2/18, available at http://verfassungsblog.de/no-more-blame-game-back-to-the-future-of-comitology, and DOI: http://dx.doi.org/10.17176/20170218-165503.

what is called 'good regulatory practices' without adding much with regard to the broader implications that this process has for state and democratic control of regulatory policy.

II.1.2. Investor–State Dispute Settlement and Democratic Government

Investor–state dispute settlement (ISDS) was the most controversial aspect of the TTIP and remains highly contested in the CETA. The extrajudicial mechanism was once intended to protect foreign investments in countries with less sophisticated legal systems.[42] This justification, so the critics argue, cannot be invoked in the transatlantic context.[43] ISDS touches upon general questions on the relationship between the state and the market and individual investors' rights *vis-à-vis* democratic politics and the right to regulate. While the strong European opposition to ISDS seems at least somewhat hypocritical after the existing investment agreements of the Member States promoted the system globally, the CETA and the TTIP represent the first instances in which the system could credibly threaten the decision-making of European governments.

Responding to public opposition, the European Commission has implemented significant changes to the dispute settlement mechanism in the CETA[44] and proposed further reforms in the TTIP.[45] In addition, the Commission

[42] For a critical account, see D Schneiderman, *Constitutionalizing Economic Globalization: Investment Rules and Democracy's Promise* (Cambridge: CUP, 2008); idem, *Resisting Economic Globalization: Critical Theory and International Investment Law* (Basingstoke: Palgrave Macmillan, 2013); idem, 'The Global Regime of Investor Rights: Return to the Standards of Civilised Justice?' (2014) 5 *Transnational Legal Theory* 60. According to United Nations Conference on Trade and Development (UNCTAD), over 3,000 bilateral investment treaties are already in place, many of which include elements of ISDS (UNCTAD Investment Policy Hub: http://investmentpolicyhub.unctad.org/IIA).

[43] See, for example, P Eberhardt, 'Investment Protection at a Crossroads: The TTIP and the Future of International Investment Law' in *Dialogue on Globalization*, Friedrich-Ebert-Stiftung, Berlin, 2014, available at: http://library.fes.de/pdf-files/iez/global/10875.pdf, and the many contributions to the symposium 'A Critical View on Investment Protection in TTIP', organised by Isabel Feichtner and Markus Krajewski, available at http://verfassungsblog.de/en/category/focus/a-critical-view-on-investment-protection-in-ttip.

[44] The CETA establishes a 'Tribunal' composed of a 15-person roster whose 'members ... shall possess the qualifications required in their respective countries for appointment to judicial office, or be jurists of recognised competence' (CETA Article 8.27). Although the exact procedure is to be specified by a joint EU–Canadian committee at a later time, the text also envisions an Appellate Tribunal to hear appeals to first-instance decisions (Article 8.28). Besides altering how the judges are appointed, the CETA also strengthens the ethical safeguards applicable to decision-makers (Article 8.30), provides that regulatory activity 'which [merely] negatively affects an investment or interferes with an investor's expectations' is not constitutive of a breach (Article 8.9), and looks towards establishing a multilateral investment court (Article 8.29).

[45] European Commission, 'Commission proposes new Investment Court System for TTIP and other EU trade and investment negotiations', September 2015, http://europa.eu/rapid/press-release_IP-15-5651_en.htm. The Commission proposal envisages an Investment Court System consisting of a first instance Tribunal and an Appeal Tribunal, which would include a more transparent and permanent selection of judges. In addition, the Commission has emphasised the need for stricter rules that ensure policy space for states to regulate in the public interest. However, for US business

clearly stated its vision to develop further the current system into a Multilateral Investment Court.[46] Overall, the EU reform proposals take great pains in trying to address public concerns while preserving the general nature of the existing system. Ensuring policy space and reaffirming control by the contracting parties over the interpretation of the agreement are core objectives, but it remains questionable whether these reforms sufficiently address the systemic risks that ISDS poses for democratic governance.[47] The reforms provide answers to serious and well-known drawbacks, ranging from the definition of concepts such as indirect expropriation to the deterrence of frivolous claims and a more transparent selection of judges.[48] However, many problems of the current regime, such as the lack of clarity of the rights of states *vis-à-vis* foreign investors and the inexistence of enforceable investor obligations under international law, can only be tackled through a wider reform of substantive standards.[49] Likewise, achieving coherence will not be possible if many thousands of agreements continue to exist; a Multilateral Investment Court system, as ultimately envisaged by the Commission, would require more fundamental reform than presently suggested.

From our perspective on the impact of mega-regional agreements on democratic decision-making, ISDS arbitration tribunals seem to be a prime example of a disembedding effort that explicitly removes certain elements of economic governance from the reach of open political deliberation and judicial scrutiny. It not only separates but also intentionally places (foreign) economic interests above – potentially conflicting – domestic political and social concerns. This is a calculated political move by the host government to attract investment, which follows the overall neoliberal logic of self-regulating markets and highlights the role of investor sentiment in the context of interconnected, globalising economies. In comparison, the creation of a new Multilateral Investment Court outside the existing European court system would also deprive the courts of the Member States of some of their powers in relation to the interpretation and application of European Union law, and the European Court of Justice (ECJ) of

associations such as the American Chamber of Commerce to the EU, 'the European Commission's proposal appears to weaken rather than strengthen investment protection.' See American Chamber of Commerce in Europe, 'AmCham EU response to EU proposal for investment protection and Court System for TTIP', 2016, available at www.amchameu.eu/system/files/position_papers/amcham_eu_response_to_eu_proposal_for_investment_protection_and_court_system_for_ttip_-_26.02.2016.pdf.

[46] See the CETA IIJ and with regard to the TTIP: European Commission, 'Commission proposes new Investment Court System for TTIP and other EU trade and investment negotiations', September 2015, available at http://europa.eu/rapid/press-release_IP-15-5651_en.htm.

[47] SW Schill, 'Reforming Investor-State Dispute Settlement (ISDS): Conceptual Framework and Options for the Way Forward', available at http://e15initiative.org/wp-content/uploads/2015/07/E15-Investment-Schill-FINAL.pdf.

[48] M Krajewski, 'Modalities for Investment Protection and Investor-State Dispute Settlement (ISDS) in TTIP from a Trade Union Perspective', Friedrich-Ebert-Stiftung, EU Office Brussels (2014), available at http://library.fes.de/pdf-files/bueros/bruessel/11044.pdf.

[49] Schill, n 47 above.

some of its powers to reply, by preliminary ruling, to questions referred by those courts.[50] While the CETA JII tries to alleviate concerns, it does not alter the CETA arbitration mechanism or substantially change the rights and obligations of the parties. In its rulings on various demands for preliminary injunctions against CETA,[51] the German Constitutional Court has not yet assessed ISDS on its merits, but has instead stated that, because most of the agreement's provisions on investment protection (Chapter 8) fall within the jurisdiction of the Member States, they cannot be subject to any decision on the preliminary application of the agreement. The Court has not been asked to assess similar provisions in other agreements.

The CETA and the TTIP called attention to a mechanism that has existed for many years, but it is only now that the application of ISDS against EU Member States has become likely that real concerns about the system's legitimacy are being raised. ISDS establishes a privileged and powerful mechanism for foreign investors to bring claims against governments, that fundamentally affects how domestic law is developed, interpreted, and applied. For many, this influence now 'requires that the ISDS system be reformed to make it more democratic and to subject the existing system to an appropriate degree of state and democratic control'.[52] However, while suggesting some relevant steps to re-assert democratic control over ISDS, the current proposals also expose a further shift towards transnational venues: initiatives such as the one aimed at establishing a Multilateral Investment Court system show the inherent appeal of transnational solutions for resolving the conflicts between interconnected, globalised markets and geographically limited government.

II.2. Responses to the Tensions between Autonomy and Interdependence

Deep international trade agreements provide clear evidence of the ever-increasing tensions between independence and interdependence in ever more salient policy domains. Their proposed governance arrangements raise concerns about the future of state and democratic control of decision-making and standard-setting processes. Dani Rodrik, to whose analyses of globalisation we have referred in the theoretical framing of our argument, considers two avenues to resolve the tensions between economic integration and national self-determination: globalising democratic governance along with markets, or re-thinking trade and

[50] Deutscher Richterbund, 'Stellungnahme zur Errichtung eines Investitionsgerichts für TTIP – Vorschlag der Europäischen Kommission vom 16.09.2015 und 12.11.2015', February 2016, available at www.drb.de/fileadmin/docs/Stellungnahmen/2016/DRB_160201_Stn_Nr_04_Europaeisches_Investitionsgericht.pdf.

[51] German Constitutional Court Decision on CETA (13 October 2016; 2 BvR 1368/16 paras 8, 54, 58, 70) and Decision on CETA (07 December 2016; 2 BvR 1444/16 paras 6, 23–25).

[52] Schill, n 47 above.

investment agreements to expand the space for democratic decision-making at national level.[53] At the same time, he remains deeply sceptical of any proposal to create accountable global governance. His main concern is that we are dealing with problems rooted deep in divisions among different societies in terms of preferences, circumstances, and capabilities; in his view, this is exactly the 'embeddedness' that creates the difficulties with hyperglobalisation in the first place. 'Global governance can make only a very limited contribution,' he writes, 'and only if it focuses on enhancing domestic decision-making rather than constraining it.' Otherwise, global governance would embody a yearning for technocratic solutions that override and undermine public deliberation.[54] Instead, he recommends a thin layer of simple and transparent international rules to regulate the interactions between nations,[55] and calls for 'updating … the Bretton Woods compromise for the 21st century' – a vision that safeguards the considerable benefits of a moderate globalisation while explicitly recognising the virtues of national diversity and the centrality of national governance. This would mean carving out greater policy space for individual countries to re-structure their economies, and address domestic concerns regarding inequality and distributive justice.[56] At WTO level, he suggests a revision of the WTO's Agreement on Safeguards into an 'Agreement on Developmental and Social Safeguards'.[57] Rodrik is frank about the implications: 'this requires placing some sand in the wheels of globalization'.[58]

Most importantly, Rodrik's reasoning illustrates the impossibility of overcoming the trilemma between economic globalisation, democratic politics, and national determination (autonomy). In trying to reconcile global markets and transnational governance arrangements with political authority at national level, he opts for both safeguarding and extending the space for national deliberation and decision-making. In his view, this increases the legitimacy and resilience of the world trading system, and renders it more responsive to domestic societal needs. The conflicts-law approach, which we submit in Section III is, in many ways, indebted to Rodrik's argument, but seeks to take it a step further: our approach does not seek to overcome socio-economic and political diversity by some substantive transnational regime, but responds to diversity

[53] Rodrik, *GP*, 2011, 206.

[54] Rodrik, 'The False Economic Promise of Global Governance', Project Syndicate, available at www.project-syndicate.org/commentary/global-governance-false-economic-promise-by-dani-rodrik-2016-08. See, also, Rodrik, *GP*, 2011 (212, 228), where he remains critical of global electoral accountability and therefore the legitimacy of new forms of governance that could be instituted at this level.

[55] Rodrik, for example, writes: '[t]he scope of workable global regulation limits the scope of desirable globalization', see Rodrik, *GP*, 2011, 323.

[56] Rodrik, *GP*, 2011, 206, 236–237.

[57] Rodrik, *GP*, 2011, 254.

[58] Rodrik, 'A Progressive Logic of Trade', *Social Europe*, 15 April 2016, available at: www.socialeurope.eu/progressive-logic-trade.

with procedural safeguards which guarantee the necessary space to search for cooperative problem-solving and fair compromises. We will hence not pretend to have found the solution to Rodrik's trilemma, merely a way to live with it.

III. THE CONFLICTS-LAW ALTERNATIVE

In the preceding sections, we first re-constructed the conflict constellation of the international trade system, and then analysed the governance arrangements which mega-regional trade agreements are about to establish. What we now present is a legal approach which is not only adequately informed sociologically, but also provides a framework within which trade disputes and transnational governance arrangements can be normatively assessed.

'We are all Polanyians now' – what Germany's leading economic sociologist claims[59] is the wide recognition of Polanyi's understanding of the sociological context and political contents of the establishment and functioning of markets. His argument applies, albeit in differentiated modes, to the markets of nation states with well-defined territorial borders, to international markets as they emerged through international trade and were reshaped during the age of 'embedded liberalism', to conglomerates such as Europe's internal market of politically autonomous polities, and finally to transnational markets which operate under the no longer 'one-dimensional economic' regime of the WTO. The passage from the concluding sections of *The Great Transformation* which we have cited above at some length[60] reflects a vision of transnational ordering which synthesises the functional necessities of international markets with the normative concerns prevailing in the participating polities. This, we submit, is precisely what international trade law should seek to accomplish. Mutual toleration of diversity and readiness to cooperate do not deny but rather presuppose that the diversity among these orders reflects a diversity of political orientations and will generate a diversity of economic interests which will conflict and may be difficult to reconcile. We have specified the development of these conflict constellations in two steps, first by exploring the ever-increasing role of non-barriers to trade. Where such 'barriers' result from democratically legitimated choices, their elimination must be politically legitimated as well. Recourse to the assumed mutual advantages of free trade is an answer which fails to take the need for the political legitimacy of free trade seriously enough. The same holds true for a harmonisation of diverging standads: 'one-size' solutions cannot do justice to the social and political contexts which have generated the policies in the jurisdictions concerned. It is precisely this constellation that Dani Rodrik's trilemma thesis mirrors. 'Deep' economic integration comes at a democratic price.

[59] J Beckert, 'The Great Transformation of Embeddedness: Karl Polanyi and the New Economic Sociology', *MPIfG Discussion Paper 07/1*, Cologne 2007, available at www.mpifg.de.

[60] See Sections I.1, I.3 and n 1 above.

With our reference to the varieties of capitalism studies, we have argued that a further critical implication of free trade regimes needs to be considered. This implication is not as readily apparent as the trade-induced modifications or reversal of social regulation. They are nevertheless of the utmost, albeit more indirect and subtle, importance. The operation and performance of our market economies are determined by, and dependent upon, institutional infrastructures. These features are anything but uniform. Their defining characteristics cannot be recomposed at random; such re-arrangements would risk damaging the efficacy of established configurations. Policy-makers, trade negotiators, and jurists should recognise this destructive potential of free trade arrangements: 'these diverse socioeconomic configurations … have become constitutive parts of the legitimate social order'.[61] We need to understand the normative fabric of our economic orders as a 'social *acquis*' which is, of course, subject to changes, but deserves to be protected against politically illegitimate intrusions.[62]

'Conflicts-law constitutionalism', so we submit in the following, is well-suited to deal with all of these concerns and arguments. We have to refrain from space-consuming comparisons and delineations of our conceptualisation of legitimated transnationalism from related approaches such as economic constitutionalism, global administrative law, or societal constitutionalism,[63] and proceed instead to an unmitigated defence of conflicts law as the 'constitutional form' of legitimate transnational governance – and apologise for the extensive references to our own previous work.

III.1. Europeanisation

The approach was first submitted as an alternative to the European 'Treaty Constitutionalism' as established by the foundational jurisprudence of the ECJ[64] and the rhapsody of efforts to assign to European law a constitutional legitimacy worthy of primacy over the constitutional orders of the EU Member States. The conflicts-law approach suggests that this kind of argumentation should be turned upside down. The analytical premise is the interdependence between the Member States, which the integration project has established and

[61] Scharpf, 'After the Crash', n 24 above, 384.

[62] C Joerges, 'Private Law in Europe's Political Economy after the Financial Crisis' in M Ruffert (ed), *European Economy and People's Mobility. Project Conference of the Jean Monnet Centre of Excellence Jena* (Tübingen: Mohr Siebeck, 2016) 101 (reprinted in pt II, ch 8 of this volume).

[63] For recent concise summaries, see G Teubner, *Constitutional Fragments: Societal Constitutionalism in Globalization* (Oxford: OUP 2014) (hereinafter Teubner, *Fragments*, 2014) 114 ff, 158 ff); and PF Kjaer, *Constitutionalism in the Global Realm: A Sociological Approach* (Abingdon: Routledge, 2014) 2 ff, 65 ff, 78 ff.

[64] For a recent summary and critique, see D Grimm, 'Europe's Legitimacy Problem and the Courts' in D Chalmers et al (eds), *The End of the Eurocrats' Dream: Adjusting to European Diversity* (Cambridge: CUP, 2016) 241.

continuously deepened. The normative core argument is the commitment of these states to recognise each other as democratically legitimated equals.

III.1.1. Analytical Framing and Normative Assumptions

The analytical premise and the normative argument go hand in hand. Because of the interdependences between the Member States, none of them can restrict the impact of its policies and legislative measures to their own territories; by the same token, each and every one of them will experience exposure to the policies and measures pursued by its neighbours. For anyone with sympathies for the Habermasian argument that the citizens of democracies must be able to interpret themselves as the political co-authors of the law with which they are expected to comply, it follows that EU Member States are democratically deficient.[65] The constitutional dilemma of the European project is then not the democracy deficit of the Union, but the inability of its Member States to ensure democratic accountability.

It is precisely this point that Dani Rodrik's trilemma thesis concerns. In his conceptualisation, European democracy can only be definitely resolved by the establishment of a fully-fledged European federal state; this, however, is (nearly) as unlikely to happen as the transformation of the UN into a state-like global order.[66] But here the conflicts approach envisages a totally different solution:

> We must conceptualise supranational constitutionalism as an alternative to the model of the constitutional nation-state which respects that state's constitutional legitimacy but at the same time clarifies and sanctions the commitments arising from its interdependence with equally democratically legitimised states and with the supranational prerogatives that an institutionalisation of this interdependence requires.[67]

To rephrase this 20-years-old assertion slightly: European law has the potential to compensate the legitimacy deficits of national rule, and it can derive its own legitimacy from this function: European law exists to implement the commitments of the Member States towards each other by two legal claims, namely, the requirement to take the interests and concerns of their neighbours into account when designing national policies, and by imposing a duty to cooperate.

[65] See this endorsement: 'Nation-states … encumber each other with the external effects of decisions that impinge on third parties who had no say in the decision-making process. Hence, states cannot escape the need for regulation and coordination in the expanding horizon of a world society that is increasingly self-programming, even at the cultural level …', J Habermas, 'Does the Constitutionalization of International Law still have a Chance?' in idem, *The Divided West* (Cambridge: Polity Press, 2007) 113, 176.

[66] See D Rodrik, 'The Future of European Democracy' in L v Middelaar and PV Parijs (eds), *After the Storm: How to Save Democracy in Europe* (Tielt: Lannoo Publishers, 2015) 53.

[67] C Joerges and J Neyer, 'From Intergovernmental Bargaining to Deliberative Political Processes: The Constitutionalisation of Comitology' (1997) 3 *ELJ* 273, 292 f.

III.1.2. Conceptual Refinements and Doctrinal Elaboration: The Three Dimensions of the Conflicts-law Approach

Just like the formerly national economies, Europeanising and globalising markets are to be understood as 'polities': they are exposed to the functionally equivalent transformations of their institutional frames, regulatory challenges, and normative claims. The best known and most intensively adjudicated and discussed field is 'social regulation'. The integration project experienced an extensive Europeanisation of pertinent activities from the mid-1980s; international trade law had to cope with a steady increase of 'non-tariff barriers to trade'. But the international trade system was in no position to copy the regulatory machinery of the EU. It had to resort to the establishment of transnational governance arrangements – an alternative of which the EU started to make intensive use from 2001.[68] The affinities of these developments with phenomena first observed within national legal systems are readily apparent. Legal systems had to be adjusted both institutionally and in their methodologies to purposive regulatory programmes ('*Zweckprogramme*' in Luhmannian parlance)[69] and because of the increase in complex administrative tasks whose fulfilment critically depends on pertinent expert knowledge, it became equally indispensable for law to adjust to forms of self-regulation, namely, the inclusion of non-governmental actors in regulatory policy, and the increased need to make use not only of expert knowledge, but also of the managerial potential of non-governmental organisations.

The conflicts-law approach responds to a twofold challenge: it seeks to capture the specifics of post-national conflict configurations, while adapting the methodology of traditional conflicts law to the 'turn' to regulation and governance.

Three Types of Conflicts in the European Multi-level System

The discipline of conflicts of law (or, in Continental Europe, private international law) is a jurisdiction selection exercise. Its objective is to determine the applicable law in cases where two or more jurisdictions are involved. In the European multi-level system, this objective has by no means become obsolete. Quite to the contrary, due to the intensity of commercial and other activities, multi-state constellations in which the laws of different Member States claim application abound. Often enough, 'horizontal' conflicts cannot be meaningfully resolved by the selection of one particular jurisdiction but require innovative compromises over substantive issues.[70] 'Vertical' conflict constellations, in

[68] European Commission 2001, 'European Governance. A White Paper', COM(2001) 428 final of 25 July 2001, OJ 2001, C 287/5, available at http://europa.eu.int/comm/governance/index_en.htm.

[69] See, eg, N Luhmann, *Recht und Automation in der öffentlichen Verwaltung* (Berlin: Duncker & Humblot, 1966) 36 ff; idem, *Das Recht der Gesellschaft* (Frankfurt aM: Suhrkamp, 1993) 195 ff.

[70] For an exemplary elaboration, see A Riles, 'Managing Regulatory Arbitrage: A Conflict of Laws Approach' (2015) 47 *Cornell Int'l LJ* 63.

which European law claims supremacy over national law, are demanding in another way – namely, in that they involve a discussion of the merits and scope of supremacy. But the most challenging constellations are 'diagonal' conflicts, where European law covers an issue only selectively and the Member States have retained potentially competing competences. Tensions between European competition law, which legalises vertical restraints, and national contract law, according to which such restraints are unfair, are a well-known example,[71] but the most dramatic illustration is the conflict between European Monetary policy and the prerogatives of the Member States in fiscal and economic policy.[72] Here it is particularly obvious that a response cannot be conceptualised in terms of simply selecting the applicable law.[73]

Three Types of Responses

Horizontal conflict constellations remain the main province of conflict-of-law rules. Wherever legal systems pursue regulatory objectives, the adequacy of such rules is questionable. Where European law expects Member States to recognise their standards mutually, such recognition may presuppose substantive or procedural innovations.[74] The need for the redemption of national through transnational solutions is obvious where transnational regulatory politics have to cope with divergences of policy orientation, socio-economic differences, and the distributional implications of social regulation. Substantive decisions are typically the only conceivable response. However, they need to be understood and designed functionally as conflicts law, which responds to the interdependence of problem scenarios, the erosion of national regulatory potential, and the concomitant necessity of, and duty of, cooperation. A well-known and extensively studied example is that of European comitology.[75] The irrefutable need for transnational regulatory policies has, furthermore, encouraged the cooperation of bureaucracies, the establishment of agencies, and the transfer of decision-making tasks (or their preparation) to epistemic communities on a much wider scale. Here, too, the concern with the preservation of constitutional democratic

[71] See C Joerges, 'The Impact of European Integration on Private Law: Reductionist Perceptions, True Conflicts and a New Constitutionalist Perspective' (1997) 3 *ELJ* 378.

[72] See C Joerges, '*Pereat iustitia, fiat mundus*: What is Left of the European Economic Constitution After the OMT-litigation' (2016) 23 *Maast J Eur & Comp L* 99, also available at http://ssrn.com/abstract=2691929.

[73] See, very similarly, PS Berman, 'Choice of Law and Jurisdiction of the Internet: Towards a Cosmopolitan Vision of Conflict of Laws Redefining Governmental Interests in a Global Era' (2005) 153 *U Pa L Rev* 1819.

[74] See the discussion of the *Cassis de Dijon* jurisprudence in C Joerges, 'Rethinking European Law's Supremacy: A Plea for a Supranational Conflict of Laws' in B Kohler Koch and B Rittberger (eds), *Debating the Democratic Legitimacy of the European Union* (Lanham MD: Rowman & Littlefield, 2007) 311.

[75] See C Joerges and E Vos, *EU Committees: Social Regulation, Law and Politics* (Oxford: Hart Publishing, 1999).

interpretive motifs remains central. Conflicts-law constitutionalism remains committed to the idea of law-mediated legitimacy and must not be equated with technocratic notions of governance. 'Conflicts law' of the second dimension is hence concerned with the organisation and supervision of cooperative problem-solving. Given that it cannot prescribe that such solutions will always be achieved, it must therefore consider the recognition and delimitation of exit options for the participating jurisdictions.[76]

The third dimension of conflicts law reacts to the privatisation of regulative tasks and the development of new 'governance arrangements', which include non-governmental actors, and makes use of their knowledge and managerial expertise. A sharp differentiation (primarily) of all the administratively anchored regulative forms seems neither possible nor desirable. However, the conflicts-law approach should not relinquish its normative claims. It does by no means subscribe to self-justifying ruling powers, which no longer distinguish between the facticity of transnational governance and the development of criteria under which such practices 'deserve recognition'. Such criteria can be identified in international civil procedural law and its requirements for recognition of judgments and arbitration awards. It must, however, above all, develop techniques and criteria for dealing with non-state institutions and para-legal regimes. European law offers templates for potential supervision structures and indirect forms of control.[77]

III.2. Conflicts Law in the Light of Globalisation

As underlined at the beginning of the preceding section, our approach understands conflicts law as a variant of constitutionalism. Even though its specific analytical features and normative ambition have been developed in the debates over legitimacy of the European Union, its basic messages and arguments can be transferred to the international system. This is, in particular, the case with respect to the conceptualisation of conflict reconciliation and transnational legitimacy lacking a superordinate political authority. Conflicts law *is* the proper form of transnational constitutionalism.[78] It is also true with respect to both the

[76] See, in more detail, C Joerges and M Everson, 'Re-conceptualising Europeanisation as a Public Law of Collisions: Comitology, Agencies and an Interactive Public Adjudication' in HCH Hofmann and AH Türk (eds), *EU Administrative Governance* (Cheltenham: Edward Elgar, 2006) 512; for an exemplary elaboration, see M Weimer, 'Risk Regulation and Deliberation in EU Administrative Governance – GMO Regulation and its Reform' (2015) 21 *ELJ* 622.

[77] C Joerges, H Schepel and E Vos, '"Delegation" and the European Polity: The Law's Problems with the Role of Standardisation Organisations in European Legislation', *EUI Working Paper in Law 9-1999*, available at www.iue.it/LAW/WP-Texts/law99-9.pdf.

[78] It may all sound more idiosyncratic than it really is. See, for example, J Bomhoff, 'The Constitution of the Conflict of Laws' in H Muir Watt and DP Fernández Arroyo (eds), *Private International Law and Global Governance* (Oxford: OUP, 2015), also available as *LSE Law, Society and Economy Working Papers 4/2014* at http://ssrn.com/abstract=2376171; F Rödl, 'Weltbürgerliches

distinction of conflict and the three modes of conflict resolution. The juridification of the European Union is, of course, deeper and its political processes and administrative capacities have, of course, no equivalents in the international system. The conflicts approach can nevertheless claim international validity. It must suffice here to document this with the help of some remarks on WTO law.[79]

The whole body of WTO law which determines the legality of behind-the-border controls of WTO members can be re-conceptualised as (horizontal) conflicts law. The analogy with EU law rests upon the commitments enshrined in the WTO treaties. To be sure, their ties are much looser than those within the EU, and the authority of the ECJ to subject the Member States to mutual recognition and respect is much stronger than that of the Appellate Body. But it is precisely the intrusion into the regulatory prerogatives of WTO members which militates in favour of a balancing of economic interests and political concerns – and it is a practice which can be observed in landmark cases such as the hormones dispute,[80] although there are less fortunate examples.[81] The WTO has no political authority to adjudicate on the substance of these conflicts. Unsurprisingly, both the Appellate Reports and the Panel Reports document adjudicatory restraint.[82] The same holds true where the traditionally dimensional reading of WTO law as a facilitator of free trade is confronted with normative claims enshrined in other international regimes.[83] The affinities are also clearly visible in the resort to the proportionality principle.[84]

Kollisionsrecht. Über die Form des Kollisionsrechts und seine Gestalt im Recht der Europäischen Union', PhD thesis, EUI, Florence, 2008. For a very similar argument, see, also, R Howse and K Nicolaïdis, 'Democracy without Sovereignty: The Global Vocation of Political Ethics' in T Broude and Y Shany (eds), *The Shifting Allocation of Authority in International Law. Considering Sovereignty, Supremacy and Subsidiarity. Essays in Honour of Professor Ruth Lapidoth* (Oxford: Hart Publishing, 2008) 162.

[79] In the context of the Collaborative Research Centre 'Transformations of the State' at the University of Bremen, over a period of 12 years, Josef Falke and I have conducted a project on 'Trade Liberalisation and Social Regulation' on which the present text draws in many ways. Out of the publication in that project, see only J Falke and C Joerges (eds), *Handelsliberalisierung und Sozialregulierung in transnationalen Konstellationen* (Baden-Baden: Nomos, 2013); C Joerges, PF Kjaer and T Ralli, 'Conflicts Law as Constitutional Form in the Postnational Constellation' (2011) 2 *Transnational Legal Theory* (special issue); C Joerges, 'The Idea of a Three-dimensional Conflicts Law as Constitutional Form', reprinted in pt VI, ch 27 of this volume.

[80] Appellate Body Report, European Communities – Measures Concerning Meat and Meat Products (Hormones) ('EC – Hormones'), WT/DS26/AB/R and WT/DS48/AB/R, adopted 13 February 1998.

[81] The GMO Panel Report: European Communities – Measures Affecting the Approval and Marketing of Biotech Products ('Ec-Biotech), WT/DS291/R, WT/DS292/R, WT/DS293/R (29 September 2006).

[82] This is not to say that these reports would always offer fortunate solutions. See the positive evaluation of the hormones case and the critique of the panel report in the GMO litigation.

[83] Examples include the Tuna/Dolphin and Seal Products cases. See Appellate Body Report, United States – Measures Concerning the Importation, Marketing and Sale of Tuna and Tuna Products, WT/DS381/AB/R (16 May 2012) and *European Communities – Measures Prohibiting the Importation and Marketing of Seal Products*, W/DS400/R and WT/DS401/R, circulated 25 November 2013.

[84] See A Herwig and C Joerges, 'The Precautionary Principle in Conflicts-law Perspectives' in G van Calster and D Prévost (eds), *Research Handbook on Environment, Health and the WTO* (Cheltenham: Edward Elgar, 2013) 3.

Modern markets are inconceivable, so we have argued, without regulation. Global Administrative Law reflects this irrefutable need comprehensively.[85] We characterise the establishment of transnational regulatory activities as the 'second dimension' of conflicts law. Since WTO law cannot establish legal equivalents to the European regulatory machinery, it is bound to develop some functional *ersatz*. 'Delegation of regulatory authority' does occur, albeit in more limited and indirect modes. The SPS and the TBT Agreements are the outstanding devices. Legal 'softness' is not to be equated with practical weakness, however. These mechanisms have proved to be remarkably powerful.[86] Yet we must not derive from the pure facticity of transnational governance its normative validity. Transnational governance must be organised as a cooperative venture of the concerned jurisdictions; cooperation must respect democratically legitimated concerns. It must specify this respect through requirements pertaining to the organisation and working procedures of the bodies involved in the preparation of standards and recommendations. It must also be prepared to respect normative and ethical objections, and to take the asymmetry of socio-economic backgrounds into account.[87]

The 'third dimension' of conflicts law reacts to the privatisation of regulative tasks and the development of new governance arrangements, which can also be observed at national level but which are, unsurprisingly, particularly important at transnational levels.[88] Their legitimacy *problématique* is, in principle, the same as that of their European equivalents and has its analogies in the recognition of foreign judgments and international arbitration.[89] These are yardsticks which rely on the requirements of democratically legitimated orders. The conflicts approach can furthermore build upon the law's 'shadow', ie, the interests of non-state orders in external recognition and their ensuing readiness

[85] For an authoritative self-description, see B Kingsbury et al, 'Symposium: The Emergence of Global Administrative Law' (2005) 68 *Law Contemp Probl* 15.

[86] An under-explored equivalent to our understanding of proactive and creative problem-solving through conflicts law is the waiver power under Article IX (3)Abs 3 WTO, provided this competence is not understood and restricted to the granting of an exception in view of some hardship but as a means to soften constructively 'interest and value conflicts within societies and among states' (see, for this reading, I Feichtner 'The Waiver Power of the WTO: Opening the WTO for Political Debate on the Reconciliation of Competing Interests' (2009) 20 *EJIL* 615, 644. She argues that the *praxis* of waivers is essentially in line with such an understanding. The first to have made the students of European integration aware of this power is FW Scharpf, who suggests, as an equivalent, that the governments of Member States be entitled to request the Council to opt for the disregard of ECJ judgments which are, in their assessment, damaging; see his 'Legitimität im europäischen Mehrebenensystem' (2009) 37 *Leviathan* 244, 274 with fn 24.

[87] In a very similar vein, see B Kingsbury, 'The Concept of "Law" in Global Administrative Law' (2009) 20 *EJIL* 23.

[88] See O Dilling et al, *Responsible Business. Self-Governance and Law in Transnational Economic Transactions* (Oxford: Hart Publishing, 2008).

[89] This parallel is rarely realised; but see E Schanze, 'International Standards – Functions and Links to Law' in P Nobel (ed), *International Standards and the Law* (Bern: Stämpfli, 2005) 84, at 90–91.

to subject themselves to a stringent procedural discipline. Templates are, again, available. To date, the best example is still standardisation.[90]

IV. REGULATORY COOPERATION IN THE CETA IN CONFLICTS-LAW PERSPECTIVES

In our concluding section, we apply our conflicts-law approach to the provisions on regulatory cooperation in Chapter 21 of the CETA, which remains one of the most contested issues in the new agreements.[91] Two observations convince us that this can serve as an acid test for our framework. First, the need for this new type of cooperation seems functionally irrefutable. Standards and their epistemic basis are not written in stone. Technological innovation, new insights into the risk of products and production processes, and changing political preferences, all need to be continuously taken into account and require an adaptation of regulatory practices. This is why a comprehensive trade agreement such as the CETA has been envisioned as a 'living agreement'.[92] On the other hand, it is precisely this innovative move that generates considerable tensions between trade liberalisation and democratic legitimacy. Regulatory cooperation has the potential to replace the legitimated bodies and procedures of the jurisdiction concerned by transnational arrangements which entrust a new transnational body, whose efficacy is furthered by a thinning of its accountability, with the preparation of legislative acts and/or decision-making powers. Such activities are, often enough, anything but 'merely technical'. Proactive discussions on the need and means of regulatory action will have to deal with regulatory philosophies and principles of constitutional weight. The policies agreed upon and the rejection or approval of standards are bound to generate distributional effects, which are attributed to the jurisdictions concerned but will affect both the economic sectors and the citizens within these jurisdictions in different ways and with different intensities. There is an inherent risk in the establishment of transnational bodies that they will resort to expert knowledge as the prime justification of their policies and downplay the political dimensions of their activities. It is hence anything but surprising that commentators have objected – sometimes vigorously – to regulatory cooperation and that, in particular, the German Constitutional Court has announced its determination to exercise strict scrutiny.[93]

Regulatory cooperation pertains to the 'second dimension' of the conflicts-law framework. 'Regulation' has become a layer of international law,

[90] As explained in Harm Schepel's magisterial study on *The Constitution of Private Governance – Product Standards in the Regulation of Integrating Markets* (Oxford: Hart Publishing, 2005), passim.

[91] The full text is referred to in n 33 above.

[92] See Section II.1 above.

[93] See Bartl, n 39 above.

Joseph Weiler has argued, which is 'specific in its normativity and legitimacy'.[94] It is an activity upon which all modern markets depend. As long as both the Member States of the EU and Canada exchange products and services, both have to deal with the regulatory concerns and practices of the other. But regulatory cooperation is a *proactive* mechanism which goes beyond the resolution of conflicts regarding divergences in individual standards. To be sure, this cooperation can have considerable benefits: it is a chance for constructive dialogue and mutual learning. However, to what degree and how this potential will be realised remains to be seen. But what is unavoidable is the disembedding and alienation of this regulatory cooperation from domestic political processes.

This *problématique* is, in essential respects, akin to that of the European committee system ('comitology'), which has been quite thoroughly studied and intensively discussed. Early evaluations have praised this system: comitology has managed to transform strategic intergovernmental bargaining over safety standards in the foodstuffs sector into deliberative political processes[95] by creating procedures which tend to promote reason-giving and learning. These positive evaluations were attributed to the specific conditions of a much smaller and more homogeneous Community at that time – a situation in which distributive issues could often be neglected – which allowed agreement, in principle, on regulatory objectives. But comitology is a moving target. After the Treaty of Lisbon and due to the conditions of its operation in a union of 28 Member States, its characterisation as 'deliberative supranationalism' has lost its former plausibility.[96]

Nonetheless, the fate of comitology seems instructive. The move from deliberative problem-solving to technocratic governance is the risk that we envisage as the future *praxis* of the regulatory cooperation prescribed in the CETA. This risk may not be unavoidable, however. The life of this living agreement will be determined by two irreconcilable tendencies. On the one hand, the CETA underlines in Article 21.2 that regulatory cooperation will be undertaken only 'on a voluntary basis' and is not meant to limit 'the ability of each Party to carry out its regulatory, legislative and policy activities'. At present, there is no explicit transfer of regulatory powers. However, this confirmation of political autonomy is clearly at odds with the objective of avoiding barriers to trade.[97] The body which is supposed to reconcile these contradictions is the RCF established under Article 21.6, which will be entrusted with the organisation of a broad range

[94] JHH Weiler, 'The Geology of International Law – Governance, Democracy and Legitimacy' (2004) 64 *Heidelberg J Int'l L* (*ZaöRV*) 547, 552.

[95] Joerges and Neyer, n 67 above.

[96] See n 41 above.

[97] See, for the case of the TTIP, M Bartl and E Fahey, 'A Postnational Marketplace: Negotiating the Transatlantic Trade and Investment Partnership (TTIP)' in E Fahey and D Curtin (eds), *A Transatlantic Community of Law: Legal Perspectives on the Relationship between the EU and US Legal Orders* (Cambridge: CUP, 2014) 210.

of cooperative activities. These include the consultation with 'stakeholders and interested parties' as further specified in Article 21.8. What is envisaged here is the establishment of complex machinery which will need to develop rules and routines under which the living agreement can operate. Its effectiveness will be conditioned by the streamlining of these interactions. This is not, in itself, worrisome. Re-active conflict resolution under the present WTO regime is cumbersome and, due to its time- and resources-consuming complexity, a barrier to constructive cooperation. But we are concerned with the organisation of the Forum and its activities. We wonder whether the consultation and influence channels will be sufficiently responsive to the notorious diversity of inner-EU preferences and interests. Commentators on the CETA fear that the new body 'would create a set of institutions and processes for foreign governments (and their corporate lobbyists) to have a say in the creation of new domestic regulations'.[98] Our concern reaches beyond such imbalances. The CETA is a 'mixed agreement' with a host of tensions between Union and residual Member State competence. It is simply unclear whether and, if so, how the democratic accountability of the envisaged regulatory cooperation can be guaranteed, and how the involvement of the European and national parliaments can be ensured in the envisaged Regulatory Cooperation. In view of the sensitivities of so many regulatory issues to be dealt with and the diversity of the preferences and interests within the Union, it highly likely that any measures proposed by the Commission will remain controversial among the Member States. In such cases, oversight, flexibility, and exit options must be available.[99]

When we started to work on this chapter, we assumed that the trend towards mega-regional agreements would be irresistible. After the popular protest movement was replaced by presidential obstruction, we felt less sure. At the time of completion of our work, we are witnessing a return to large trade deals and a reconfiguration of trade alliances. What remained a constant in all these ups and downs, however, is the precarious legitimacy of transnational trade governance. We conclude that transdisciplinary frameworks within which this *problématique* can be addressed are badly needed.

[98] S Sinclair et al (eds), 'Making Sense of the CETA: An Analysis of the Final Text of the Canada-European Union Comprehensive Economic and Trade Agreement' (Berlin/Ottawa: Canadian Centre for Policy Alternatives, 2nd edn, 2016), available at www.policyalternatives.ca/sites/default/files/uploads/publications/National%20Office/2016/09/Making_Sense_of_CETA_2016.pdf; similar Stoll et al, n 33 above, 27 ff.

[99] See the arguments submitted in Section II.2 above.

29

Conclusion – Part VI

I. PERSPECTIVES: DEMOCRACY-ENHANCING CONFLICTS LAW

As UNDERLINED IN the introduction to this part of the book (chapter 25), the idea of 'conflicts law as constitutional form', submitted in the contributions to this part, pursues methodological, theoretical and conceptual objectives that not only concern European law and the international legal disciplines, but also deserve recognition even within national legal systems. They furthermore seek to make these legal arguments connectable with Polanyian economic sociology and its awareness of 'the political' in 'the economic'. It is precisely through these reorientations that they aim at a social democratisation of economy and society.

The scholarly majority does certainly not share our understanding of conflicts law. That understanding has, however, significant affinities with approaches in the theory of international relations,[1] political science[2] and, last but not least, within pertinent legal scholarship.[3] It is, even after so many years, still a 'work in progress'. Two issues seem to deserve continued attention. One, namely the 'justiciabilty' of transnational conflicts, has been addressed in chapter 3 ('Where

[1] eg, RO Keohane, S Macedo and A Moravcsik, 'Democracy-Enhancing Multilateralism' (2009) 63 *International Organization* 1.

[2] eg, JP Vogler, 'The Political Economy of the European Union: An Exploration of EU Institutions and Governance from the Perspective of Polycentrism' in P Boettke, B Herzberg and B Kogelmann (eds), *The Political Economy and Social Philosophy of Vincent and Elinor Ostrom* (London–New York: Rowman & Littlefield International, 2020) 145.

[3] In particular, the 'PILLAGG' (private international law and global governance) project initiated by H Muir Watt (see her 'Private International Law beyond the Schism' (2011) 2 *Transnational Legal Theory* 347); the works of JA Bomhoff (see, eg, his essay on 'The Constitution of the Conflict of Laws' *LSE Legal Studies Working Paper No 4/2014*, available at https://ssrn.com/abstract=237617; J Corkin (see, eg, his 'Experimental Constitutionalism in the EU: Co-ordinating Legal Difference through Mutual Recognition, Mutual Law and Mutual Learning' in C Joerges and C Glinski (eds), *The European Crisis and the Transformation of Transnational Governance: Conflicts-Law Constitutionalism and Authoritarian Managerialism* (Oxford: Hart Publishing, 2014) 359); M-S Kuo, 'On the Constitutional Question in Global Governance: Global Administrative Law and the Conflicts-Law Approach in Comparison' (2013) 2 *Global Conflicts* 437; and the essays collected in C Joerges, PF Kjaer and T Ralli (eds), 'Conflicts Law as Constitutional Form in the Postnational Constellation' (2011) 2 *Transnational Legal Theory* (Special Issue). Numerous contributions 'do' conflicts law implicitly; see, eg, CF Sabel and O Gerstenberg, 'Constitutionalising an Overlapping Consensus: The ECJ and the Emergence of a Coordinate Constitutional Order' (2010) 16 *ELJ* 511.

the Law Runs Out'), chapter 13 ('Integration through De-legalisation?') and chapter 23 ('Europe's Economic Constitution in Crisis and the Emergence of a New Constitutional Constellation'). The second issue concerns the potential of transnational interventions to compensate for the democratic failings of nation states, the core idea submitted in 'From Intergovernmental Bargaining to Deliberative Political Processes: The Constitutionalisation of Comitology' (chapter 12). In a recent article,[4] political economist Dani Rodrik, building on the Keohane et al article cited above,[5] suggested distinguishing between 'globalisation enhancing global governance' and 'democracy enhancing global governance'.[6] The analogy with European integration is obvious. Rodrik substantiates his suggestion with a formula that corresponds to our plea for a correction of democracy deficits of the Member States through European law. He argues that that 'the policy failures that exist arise not from weaknesses of global governance, but from distortions of domestic governance'.[7] He continues, 'As a general rule, these domestic failures cannot be fixed through international agreements or multilateral cooperation.'[8] This twofold reserve is an innovative move. Governance failures must be corrected where they occur. In view of their manifold causes and forms, they cannot be eliminated by transnational *fiat*. What the supranational level should do, instead, is to further self-corrections at national level, 'with global oversight restricted to procedural safeguards – such as transparency, accountability, use of scientific/economic evidence – intended to reinforce democratic deliberation'.[9] The suggestion is less intrusive than our request that European oversight should see to it that the Member States consider the external effects of their laws and the concerns of others. Is it all too soft and too optimistic about the democratic quality of national democratic will-formation? These processes are indeed anything but perfectly deliberative. Reliance on transnational market governance is not superior. Markets can neither generate nor process the kind of knowledge that the reasonable solution of complex interdependencies requires. Centralised expertise, on the other hand, as the prevailing mode of transnational governance lacks sensitivity for local specifics and cannot accomplish democratic legitimacy.

[4] D Rodrik, 'The Right Scope of Global Governance and Democracy Enhancement' (2021) 2 *Revue européenne du droit*, available at https://geopolitique.eu/en/articles/the-right-scope-of-global-governance-and-democracy-enhancement.

[5] See n 1 above.

[6] See Rodrik, n 4 above; and D Rodrik, 'The Future of European Democracy' in L van Middelaar and Ph Van Parijs (eds), *After the Storm. How to save democracy in Europe* (Tielt: Lannoo Publishers, 2015) 53.

[7] Rodrik, n 4 above, 3.

[8] Ibid.

[9] Ibid 10. Building on these suggestions, see C Joerges, 'Responding to Socioeconomic Diversity in the European Union (and to Steven Klein's Essay) with Democracy-Enhancing Conflicts Law' (2021) 2 *Global Perspectives* 18788.

II. RELATED PUBLICATIONS

M Everson and C Joerges, 'Re-conceptualising Europeanisation as a public law of collisions: comitology, agencies and an interactive public adjudication' in HCH Hofmann and AH Türk (eds), *EU Administrative Governance* (Cheltenham: Edward Elgar, 2006) 512.

C Joerges and F Rödl, 'Reconceptualising the constitution of Europe's post-national constellation – by dint of conflict of laws' in I Lianos and O Odudu (eds), *Regulating Trade in Services in the EU and the WTO. Trust, Distrust and Economic Integration* (Cambridge: CUP, 2012) 762.

Part VII

Vergangenheitschuld (Guilt about the Past) and the Duty to Remember

30

'Darker Legacies of Law in Europe' – Problems with a Research Project

VERGANGENHEITSSCHULD IS THE title of a book by Bernhard Schlink,[1] which assembles 'essays on a German theme', a theme present in all of his literary[2] work and also in his academic publications.[3] My Italian colleague Massimo La Torre and I could not know about these essays when we announced, in November 1998, at the Law Department of the European University Institute, Florence, a seminar on 'The National Socialist and Fascist Heritage of Legal Thought in Europe' and submitted an application for the funding of a project under the same title to the annual meeting of the Institute's Research Council. We had produced a scandal, noted with negative effects even far away in the Berlaymont. We modified the title of our application and thereafter received 1,500,000 Lira (ie €800) for the further preparation of our project.

We did not understand what we had done to cause such anger. Our German–Italian initiative was meant to address the *Vergangenheitschuld* of our countries. However, we learned that there was more to it. Beyond Germany's and Italy's *Vergangenheitsschuld*, our project was bound to address a series of thorny issues: the complicity with National Socialism and Fascism outside the borders of our countries; the presence of this dark past in anti-democratic and anti-liberal traditions in our countries and elsewhere, in particular in some of the accession states of Eastern Europe; the persistence of anti-Semitism in the old Member States. 'You are damaging the dignity of the integration project', we were told. This seems to be the crux of the matter. Michael Stolleis, the most renowned among Germany's legal historians studying the Nazi past,[4] observed 'you have transformed the German guilt into a pan-European problem'.

[1] *Vergangenheitsschuld. Beiträge zu einem deutschen Thema* (Zürich: Diogenes, 2007); English translation: *Guilt about the Past* (Toronto: House of Anansi Press, 2000).

[2] Including, most famously, *The Reader* (New York: Vintage International, 1995).

[3] A Jacobson and B Schlink, *Weimar: A Jurisprudence of Crisis* (Berkeley, CA–London: University of California Press, 2000); many more listed at http://schlink.rewi.hu-berlin.de/schlink.

[4] See his *Geschichte des öffentlichen Rechts in Deutschland*, vol 3: *Staats- und Verwaltungsrechtswissenschaft in Republik und Diktatur 1914–1945* (Munich: CH Beck, 1999).

Our seminars and related activities met first with rather modest, but later at times with lively interest. We some managed to raise sufficient funds for an international conference.[5] The proceedings were published in 2003.[6] The book met with very considerable interest,[7] and our series of seminars and workshops continued.[8] The first contribution to this part of the volume (chapter 31) is a paper presented at the 'The Simon Bond International Wannsee Seminar' in July 2002.[9] The invitation to this talk was a response to the above-mentioned project and the EUI conference on 'The National Socialist and Fascist Heritage of Legal Thought in Europe'.[10] The paper given in Berlin in 2002 drew on my contribution to the EUI conference of 2000, reprinted here in chapter 32. There are hence overlaps between the two texts. Both of them are reproduced in their original versions so that they remain understandable on their own. The third essay (chapter 33) is a translation of my contribution to a conference on '"Schmerzliche Erfahrungen" der Vergangenheit und der Prozess der Konstitutionalisierung Europas', in October 2006 in Berlin.

[5] 'Perceptions of Europe and Perspectives on a European Order in Legal Scholarship During the Era of Fascism and National Socialism', EUI Florence, 29–30 September 2000.

[6] C Joerges and NS Ghaleigh (eds), *Darker Legacies of Law in Europe. The Shadow of National Socialism and Fascism over Europe and its Legal Traditions*, with a Prologue by M Stolleis and an Epilogue by JHH Weiler (Oxford: Hart Publishing, 2003).

[7] (2006) 7 *German Law Journal* 71 published a collection of 23 reviews with an introduction by D Augenstein, available at https://germanlawjournal.com/volume-07-no-02/.

[8] See, eg, C Joerges (guest ed), 'The Darker Side of a Pluralist Heritage: Anti-liberal Traditions in European Social Theory and Legal Thought', Special Issue of (2003) 14:3 *Law and Critique*; C Joerges and P Blokker (eds), 'Confronting Memories: European "Bitter Experiences" and the Constitutionalisation Process', Special Issue of (2005) 6 *German Law Journal*, available at https://germanlawjournal.com/volume-06-no-02/.

[9] Conference on 'Tyranny, Justice and the LAW: The Nazis and Beyond', co-sponsored by Touro Law School, Central Islip, NY and Free University Berlin.

[10] N 5 above.

31

*Continuities and Discontinuities in German Legal Thought**

INTRODUCTORY REMARK

THIS CONTRIBUTION IS a quite personal response to the topic that this panel addresses: I am not going to analyse the impact of the past on the *praxis* of law in post-war Germany in general, but will only talk about German legal science and Germany's legal academia. Likewise, mine is a personal perspective: How did Germany's past affect my identity as a student in the 1960s, as a university assistant in the early 1970s, and as a law professor thereafter? How did, and how does, Germany's past affect my education, my research, my teaching, my writing?

This focus may seem to lie somewhat outside the context which the organisers of this panel had in mind when defining its topic. And yet, not being a historian or otherwise specifically qualified to deal with contemporary history, my biographical framework may very well be appropriate, and, in some respects, unavoidable. To cite a well-known passage from Jürgen Habermas' contribution to the *Historikerstreit*:

> Our own life is linked to the life context in which Auschwitz was possible not by contingent circumstances but intrinsically. Our form of life is connected with that of our parents and grandparents through a web of familial, local, political, and intellectual traditions that is difficult to disentangle – that is, through a historical milieu that made us what and who we are today. None of us can escape this milieu, because our identities, both as individuals and as Germans, are indissolubly interwoven with it. This holds true from mimicry and physical gestures to language and into the capillary ramifications of one's intellectual stance … we have to stand by our traditions, then, if we do not want to disavow ourselves …[1]

My contribution reflects a degree of shock as regards the long-term effects of the Third Reich. The shock stems from the insight of my generation – I was born

* Contribution to the conference on 'Tyranny, Justice and the Law: the Nazis and Beyond' organised by the Touro Law Center, New York, Free University, Berlin, The Touro Institute on Human Rights and the Holocaust, 7–10 July 2002, Berlin.

[1] J Habermas, 'On the Public Use of History' in idem, *The New Conservatism* (Cambridge MA: The MIT Press, 1990) 233.

in 1943 – that Germany's past was present in so many aspects of our lives and that we had to try and confront these links if we were to understand our possible futures; both our personal futures and that our country.

These are the steps in which I am going to address the continuities and discontinuities in Germany's legal thought:

1. An academic one, namely, a characterisation of the theoretical challenges Nazi law poses;
2. A more personal narrative, namely, a retrospective on how my generation became aware of these issues;
3. Some reflections on the intellectual history of legal science in post-war Germany, its 'reluctance to glance in the mirror',[2] as well as its failure to integrate the 'third legal culture' that German emigrants had developed in their encounters with their host countries, especially in United States;
4. The risks inherent in such confrontations with the past and the difficulty that we face when trying to arrive at an unambiguous conclusion.

I. CONTINUITY AND DISCONTINUITY: LEGAL ACADEMIA IN THE THIRD REICH

German research on *The Law under the Swastika*, to cite the English title of Michael Stolleis' collection of essays, and of academic life in the *Third Reich*[3] is by now impressive. The insights we get are devastating. But the picture is by no means uniform. Germany's academics adapted to the new 'order' created by the Nazi state. In significant numbers, they sought to define a new '*völkisch*' legal culture,[4] to find concepts which would capture the new power constellation: '[J]urisprudence reflected the spirit of the times and implementing such reflection in a wealth of proposals, small and large. In this, it remained a creative force, with prolific publication occurring until well into the war years.'[5] And, at the same time, elements of Germany's older legal culture survived, were cultivated – and not only in niches such as legal history.

[2] 'Reluctance to Glance in the Mirror – The Changing Face of German Jurisprudence after 1933 and post-1945' is the title of an essay by Michael Stolleis, to whom I am deeply indebted. The essay is published in C Joerges and NS Ghaleigh (eds), *Darker Legacies of Law in Europe: The Shadow of National Socialism and Fascism over Europe and its Legal Traditions* (Oxford: Hart Publishing, 2002) 1.

[3] M Stolleis, *Law under the Swastika* (Chicago IL: Chicago University Press, 1998).

[4] The term is from MR Lepsius, 'Juristen in der sozialwissenschaftlichen Emigration' in M Lutter, EC Stiefel and MH Hoeflich (eds), *Der Einfluß deutschsprachiger Emigranten auf die Rechtsentwicklung in den USA und in Deutschland* (Tübingen: Mohr/Siebeck, 1993); see, also, M Rainer Lepsius, *Kultur und Wissenschaft in Deutschland unter der Herrschaft des Nationalsozialismus* in idem, *Demokratie in Deutschland* (Göttingen: Vandenhoeck & Ruprecht, 1995) 119.

[5] Stolleis, 'Reluctance to Glance in the Mirror', n 2 above.

I refrain from referring to pertinent historical studies. Instead, I cite a few passages from JHH Weiler's novel *Removed (chiaroscuro)*.[6] This is the story of a young German law professor, a professorial celebrity's (Steinmann) former assistant, who re-constructs the reasons for his master's early retirement. The few passages reprinted here seem to me to tell more than many references to academic writings would:

> The University register provided some missing details … [They] did not satisfy my curiosity. So I got the idea of reading all of Steinmann's publications from that period. But soon may project grew. I decided to read the entire corpus of our legal literature during the twelve years. This was not as huge a task as it may seem to you. The academic legal world was far smaller those days and much less was published.[7]

The findings:

> A part of the literature was patently beyond the pale. I read it with the detachment of a criminal pathologist: Article after article seeking to provide the jurisprudential foundation for the New Order. But this stuff, written by evil people, from which I felt alien and estranged, was not the worst. It was far more depressing to read the numerous articles which addressed with zeal the laws brought in by that New Regime, applying to them the technical apparatus of the professional lawyer, clarifying their meaning, working out their implications, filling in the legislative gaps.[8]
>
> But my worst days, in the beginning at least, were those in which all I read was totally removed from the grimness of the epoch, problems in contract and delict, negotiable instruments and criminal liability. Some of the articles written in 1942 could have been written in 1932 or 1952.
>
> This confrontation with the normal, the banal, the ordinary and the trite was the wellspring of my understanding of that period and from it emerged the clearest images of the world in which Steinmann and his colleagues lived. It was a world of talent and mediocrity, of ambition and commitment, of scholars developing their careers; so it had always been and so it will remain …[9]

This is the narrative. Why is it academically challenging to observe that the destruction of Germany's legal culture by the protagonists of the 'New Order' and elements of the first legal culture existed side by side? Both the search for and obedience to the 'New Order', as well as the survival of a seemingly regularly functioning legal system, were apparently inextricably linked. 'Was Nazi law Law'? Should we distinguish between a realm of pure and shameless power on the one hand and the realm of the 'banal' and the 'ordinary' on the other?

[6] Typescript, Cambridge MA, 1991. German translation by Michael Cochu: *Der Fall Steinmann* (Bremen: Bettina Wassmann, 1998; 2nd edn Munich: Piper, 2000).

[7] Weiler, *Removed*, n 6 above, 84–85.

[8] [Ibid, 76; the text continues with examples such as 'Was the property of the child of an Aryan woman from a first marriage who later married a Jew and was adopted by him, subject to the new laws concerning Jewish property?' and more of this kind.]

[9] Ibid, 86–87.

These are controversial issues that are not simply of historical significance. I cite just one – highly pertinent – recent analysis:

> Politically, the years 1930–3 and 1945–9 unquestionably constituted breaks. But were they also intellectual breaks? Was there autonomous law or legal thinking [in both 'cultures'] during National Socialism, with the consequence that the literature and ideas of those times stand suspect in principle of being influenced or stamped by National Socialism? Or is there a continuity in legal thinking from the Weimar Republic to National Socialism, with the consequence that particular lines of tradition from the 1920s that do not as such have anything to do with National Socialism appear in a questionable light? Why were many lawyers around 1933 prepared voluntarily to abandon the values of democracy, fundamental rights and the rule of law in favour of a comparatively open, unspecified ideology? Why did many not adequately recognize the National Socialist ideology's specific effect of destroying law, thereby becoming involved in the self-destruction of legal science too?[10]

Disquieting issues. The 'New Order' the Nazi ideology envisaged cannot be called law, Oliver Lepsius argues. The jurisprudential protagonists of that 'order' testified to the contrary. Did they know better? Can we hold them responsible? This conference will take up these issues. My contribution will address them in the 'concluding' section.

II. THE PAST RE-SURFACES

Such questions seem to suggest themselves to educated minds. But this was not always the case. It was only in 2001, to take just one example, that the German Association of Teachers of Public Law (*Vereinigung der Deutschen Staatsrechtslehrer*) dedicated a meeting to the question of how the Nazi seizure of power was perceived in contemporary 'constitutional' jurisprudence.[11]

Why so late? Does it make sense to articulate one's indignation? Michael Stolleis writes:

> In retrospect, we can recognize in the founding of the Federal Republic a distinct pattern of defensive 'common values' in which the 'others' were excluded by these values. For German lawyers after 1945, who formed an even more specific professional community of shared values, this meant having to band together in order to gain a foothold and dispel the criticism levelled, for example, at their involvement in National Socialism. Through tacit coalition and active association, virtually all the

[10] O Lepsius, 'The Problem of Perceptions of National Socialist Law or: Was there a Constitutional Theory of National Socialism?' in Joerges and Ghaleigh (eds), *Darker Legacies of Law in Europe*, n 2 above, 19. But see, also, D Fraser, '"The outsider does not see al the game …": Perceptions of German Law in Anglo-American Legal Scholarship, 1933–1940', ibid, 87.

[11] See the essays by H Dreier and W Pauly on 'Die deutsche Staatsrechtslehre in der Zeit des Nationalsozialismus' (2001) 60 *Veröffentlichungen der Vereinigung der Deutschen Staatsrechtslehrer* 9–72 and 73–101.

> lawyers who had practiced in the Third Reich were reinstated in public office and private law firms. There were hardly any abrupt breaks or dismissals. Like the rest of the nation, they were reluctant to look back into the abyss.[12] Only those considered to have gone beyond the pale were excluded, but even that was not public knowledge.[13] In an essay published anonymously in November 1949, Carl Schmitt invoked a theme that typifies the spirit of the time: 'amnesty, the power of forgetting'.
>
> What this new departure meant was that Germany's recent history under National Socialism could be disregarded or, at most, remembered only as a time marred by a regrettable perversion of justice. The legal authors of those years kept silent about their earlier publications. Their pupils adjusted the bibliographies. Librarians were instructed to sift out the writings from the relevant period and stash these away in the vaults. In a way, the Allies did the same in the immediate post-war period, and had lists drawn up by 'untainted' specialists.[14]

This broad consensus, to which Stolleis points, was rarely disturbed by dissonant voices until the 1960s. This was a decade of intellectual and political unrest. As announced, I now turn to my own history.

When I started my studies of law at the University of Frankfurt in the summer term of 1962, everything still looked well ordered. Beginning to study meant that in the foreseeable future you would either occupy an 'A 13' *Beamten*-position, become a lawyer in order to make more money, or, in the case of failure, work for an insurance company. Studying itself, however, was mostly a boring exercise.

Not always, however, and not for long. In 1963, a certain Rudolf Wiethölter had accepted his *Ruf* to Frankfurt (he found himself as number 3 b on the list that the faculty had suggested to the ministry). The man was a shock. He started to mention the past of people like Karl Larenz, the most famous of all teachers of private law in the Republic; he advised us to read Josef Esser, rather than Larenz; he admired Franz Wieacker deeply, but also made us wonder about the non-treatment of the Nazi period in Wieacker's seminal *Privatrechtsgeschichte der Neuzeit*.[15]

A second event: thanks to Heinrich Kronstein, one of the very few emigrants from Germany who held a professorial position at a German university,[16] I received a scholarship to study law at the Georgetown University Law Center during the 1966/67 academic year. I attended a course on civil procedure.

[12] N Frei, *Vergangenheitspolitik: Die Anfänge der Bundesrepublik und die NS-Vergangenheit* (Munich: CH Beck, 1996).

[13] M Stolleis, 'Die Vereinigung der Deutschen Staatsrechtslehrer: Bemerkungen zu ihrer Geschichte' in (1997) *Kritische Vierteljahresschrift für Gesetzgebung und Rechtswissenschaft* 339, concerning the inner debates around the acceptance of former members of the NSDAP.

[14] Stolleis, 'Reluctance to Glance in the Mirror', n 2 above.

[15] ... *unter besonderer Berücksichtigung der deutschen Entwicklung* (2nd edn, Göttingen: Vandenhoeck & Ruprecht, 1967) [*A History of Private Law in Europe: with particular reference to Germany* (Oxford: Clarendon Press, 1995)].

[16] On the biographical background, see E Rehbinder, 'Heinrich Kronstein' in B Diestelkamp and M Stolleis (eds), *Juristen an der Universität Frankfurt aM* (Baden-Baden: Nomos, 1989) 253.

One day, the civil procedure teacher, who spoke with a strong German accent, Professor Jakobi, stepped down to me and told me that he and my father had been assistants of the legendary Martin Wolff at the famous Berlin law faculty.

These were two of the more personal turning-points. The third was generational, namely, the publication of Bernd Rüthers's *Habilitation* entitled *Die unbegrenzte Auslegung* in 1998.[17] Is it by chance that this book appeared at the height of the student revolution?

It is once more stunning to observe how well Joseph Weiler's novel characterises the German mood of the time:

> In the mid-60s he [Steinmann] gave, twice only, a seminar on the History of Public Law from Weimar to the Present. The title of the seminar alone was enough to raise some eyebrows. Even today serious historical research is considered as ending with Weimar. Raised eyebrows turned into consternation when it was reported that he was dealing with the work of living authors. It was still the mid-Sixties and the fun had not yet begun. Only eleven students enrolled in the seminar in the first year, seventeen in the second … Apparently, Steinmann made them examine publication lists as they appeared in *Festschriften* and other reference works approved by the authors. They then checked these against biographies culled from libraries and legal indexes, retrieving the Articles the authors had chosen to forget in their official lists … [Comment of] a lawyer now practicing in Stuttgart: 'Steinmann's seminar? Communist propaganda!' In the third year, 1968, over two hundred students enrolled in the Seminar. Steinmann promptly and permanently cancelled it …[18]

As to the responses to the 1968 unrest, the novel notes:

> Most members of the faculty during the 1968 events were, of course, outraged by the disturbances. Those who were afraid to denounce Communism explicitly, spoke against 'all forms of totalitarianism'. Everybody, hard liners and soft liners, affirmed the need to 'stand up for principles'.[19]

Such a long time has elapsed since these events. Are we now better able to understand, to explain the long silence? To cite Michael Stolleis once more:

> The reluctance to glance in the mirror after 1945 … is hardly surprising, given what we know about the psychology of memory. Every author writes 'in his time', and every writer feels that his own work is more coherent and free from influence than it really is. No-one wants to have his life's work declared worthless. These are understandable attitudes …[20]

[17] B Rüthers, *Die unbegrenzte Auslegung – Zum Wandel der Privatrechtsordnung im Nationalsozialismus* (Tübingen: Mohr Siebeck, 1968).

[18] Weiler, *Removed*, n 6 above, 18.

[19] Ibid, 23.

[20] Stolleis, 'Reluctance to Glance in the Mirror', n 2 above, 12. It follows a citation from Friedrich Nietzsche, *Jenseits von Gut und Böse, Viertes Hauptstück*: '"This I have done," says my memory. "This I cannot have done," says my pride and remains intractable. In the end, memory gives in.'

III. THE RETURN TO THE 'FIRST LEGAL CULTURE' AFTER THE WAR

In a symposium in 1991 honouring the German emigrants to the US,[21] no less than four contributors dealt with the work of Friedrich Keßler (hereinafter Kessler). Kessler, not a Jew himself, but husband to a Jewish wife, hence a '*jüdisch Versippter*', did not divorce; he left Germany in 1934. His American career was nothing less than phenomenal.[22] He was affiliated with the Realist movement, became Professor at Yale, was the author of the Kessler and Gilmore casebook on *Contracts*.[23] Kessler, the emigrant, was often invited back to Germany. From 1952 onwards, he published quite regularly and visibly. Legions of students who took their LLMs at Berkeley and many professors who spent some time in the US met with him, discussed with him. What was the impact of all this back home? It was my task at the symposium to document this influence. In the end, I called my essay 'History as Non-History'.[24] The term 'non-history' was intended to describe the impact of Kessler's work on legal scholarship in Germany. This non-history, I argued, was a disquieting story. Disquieting and telling in at least two exemplary respects.

The first: Kessler's non-history stands for the whole history of the discipline from which he had emigrated in 1933 and which he had re-defined during his American career. Kessler's contribution to a 'third legal culture' found no entry into his *Heimatland* during the immediate post-war period. Germany's post-war jurisprudence was neither ready nor able to listen to the lost son. The collapse of the *Third Reich* in 1945 had meant the end of the State of the *Volksnation* and of that State's *Rechtserneuerung*. Legal texts record the need to loosen the entanglements of private legal science with National Socialism, to distinguish between the undamaged relics and untenable remnants of tradition and the desire to arrive at a positive attitude towards the constitution of the democratic state and social rule of law. Anyone taking up a text from the post-war period ought to remember the external conditions and internal constitution of legal science in those early years.

The science of private law managed, following the uncertainties of the immediate post-war years, to adjust to the new political and social reality of the Federal Republic. Germany's *Privatrechtswissenschft* regained its self-confidence, and legal theory again became a sort of holiday activity deemed not really useful to the core task of the discipline, namely, the doctrinal work on private law.

[21] Lutter et al (eds), *Der Einfluß deutschsprachiger Emigranten*, n 4 above.

[22] See 'Tributes: Friedrich Kessler' (AT Kronman, JK McNulty, C Joerges and GL Priest) (1995) 104 *Yale Law Journal* 2129.

[23] F Kessler and G Gilmore, *Contracts: Cases and Materials*, 2nd edn (Boston MA and Toronto: Little, Brown and Company, 1970) (the 1st edn – with Malcom Sharp – dated from 1953).

[24] C Joerges, 'History as Non-History: Divergencies and Time Lags between Friedrich Kessler and German Jurisprudence' (1994) 42 *AJCL* 163.

This newly found self-confidence could do without inquiry into the reasons for the departure of Kessler not just from Nazi Germany, but also from the first German culture in which he had grown up during the Weimar Republic, and without too serious an investigation into the emergence of what sociologist Rainer M Lepsius[25] has called a third legal culture, namely, the sometimes, and, in the case of Kessler, the outstandingly, productive result of encounters between the intellectual heritage of the German emigrants and that of their new *Heimat*.

But Kessler's non-impact is telling in yet another respect. The Kessler and Gilmore casebook,[26] and even more so his earlier writings of the 1940s, stands for a strand of Legal Realism and what the later allies of that movement call a 'progressive critique' of formalism in American law. The rejection of this kind of legal thinking in Germany goes hand in hand with a much broader *Verarmung* of German jurisprudence. When the Nazis removed Jewish academics from the German universities, this also meant an anti-liberal and anti-socialist *Gleischaltung* in legal thought and the extinction of younger disciplines such as the sociology of law. The 'fight against the Jewish spirit'[27] was, after all, not just a process of racial selection, but also one which impacted upon methodical, legal, and social-critical approaches to legal science overall.

All this had a lasting heritage. It was only in the mid-1960s that new debates on the theoretical bases of private law began to emerge. The pre-democratic past, dealt with only provisionally in the immediate post-war years, also returned to the stage. In private law, this happened when Bernd Rüthers initiated a discussion on the 'changes in the private legal system under National Socialism'[28] – and not with the distance of a historian, but as a 'problem of the present'.

IV. WHY SO LATE AND AT WHAT PRICE?

Academic life in Germany has normalised and is flourishing – no other European academic community is comparably so prolific. But why did all this happen so late, and what price did we pay for this belated return to normality?

I return to a narrative, a concluding story on Hans Peter Ipsen, born in 1907 in Hamburg, the *Doyen* of European law in Germany, successful supervisor of 140 PhD students and no less then seven *habilitation* theses. Tributes of the law faculty of Hamburg honouring Hans Peter Ipsen were published in

[25] N 4 above.

[26] Kessler and Gilmore, *Contracts. Cases and Materials*, 2nd edn, n 23 above.

[27] C Schmitt, 'Die deutsche Rechtswissenschaft im Kampf gegen den jüdischen Geist' (1936) *Deutsche Juristen-Zeitung* 1195.

[28] *Die unbegrenzte Auslegung*, n 16 above.

2001, three years after his death.[29] One contributor, Professor Gert Nicolaysen from Hamburg, addressed Ipsen's biography.[30] Ipsen was 25 years old when the Nazis seized power in 1933. His main academic teacher, Kurt Perels, a Jewish Professor of Public Law, committed suicide in the same year. Ipsen passed his 2nd state exam in 1934, and became a *Verwaltungsbeamter* in Hamburg. In 1936, he handed in his *Habilitation* thesis on '*justizlose Hoheitsakte*' (judiciary free sovereign acts);[31] he was appointed *Dozent* a year later,[32] joined the Nazi party on 1 May 1937,[33] and was appointed as a Professor on 9 February 1940. As Nicolaysen – and Ipsen himself in the letter just cited – underline,[34] the local *Rechtswahrerbund* (the National Socialist Association of Lawyers) had resisted his earlier appointment. Still in 1940, the German Military Administration of Brussels appointed Ipsen, Commissioner of the (Flemish) Colonial University of Antwerp and subsequently, in May 1941, *commissaire* of the (Wallonian) Free University in Brussels. He was in charge when the university decided to close its doors rather than accept the appointment of three collaborators as professors. In 1945, Ipsen was dismissed from his professorial position by the military government of Hamburg. In December 1946, he returned to his university position.

There is no mention of such matters in the 35 contributions to the *Festschrift für Hans Peter Ipsen zum 70. Geburtstag*,[35] or in the later memorial by Helmut Quaritsch.[36] An assessment of Ipsen's activities as a commissioner of the Free University of Brussels is, in fact, not so easy. Nicolaysen[37] writes: 'When I applied for a position to work with Ipsen, he himself handed over to me things that had been written on him, in Belgium and elsewhere ... Had I found anything compromising, I would not have accepted the position'.[38] The Belgian documents and publications I have seen, however, are not at all favourable.[39] 'Commissioner

[29] Fachbereich Rechtswissenschaft der Universität Hamburg (ed), *Hans Peter Ipsen. 1907–1998* (Münster-Hamburg-London: Lit, 2002).

[30] G Nicolaysen, 'Lebensbild Hans Peter Ipsen', ibid, 33 at 39.

[31] HP Ipsen, *Politik und Justiz. Das Problem der justizlosen Hoheitsakte* (Hamburg: Hanseatische Verlagsanstalt, 1937).

[32] According to most of the biographies I have seen; H Quaritsch, however, in his memorial 'Hans Peter Ipsen zum Gedenken' (1998) 123 *Archiv des öffentlichen Rechts* 1, at 19, gives a later date: 1939.

[33] On 1 May 1937, according to a letter by Ipsen in which he responds to a resolution taken by the Faculty of Law of the Free University of Brussels on 27 February 1960.

[34] N 29 above, at 39.

[35] R Stödter and W Thieme (eds), *Hamburg, Deutschland, Europa: Beiträge zum deutschen und europäischen Verfassungs-, Verwaltungs- und Wirtschaftsrecht; Festschrift für Hans Peter Ipsen zum 70. Geburtstag* (Tübingen: Mohr, 1977).

[36] N 31 above.

[37] 'Zu Leben und Werk' in Fachbereich Rechtswissenschaft der Universität Hamburg (ed), *Hans Peter Ipsen. 1907–1998*, n 28 above, 5, at 7 (my translation); more details in n 92 of ch 32 of this volume.

[38] In his 'Lebensbild Hans Peter Ipsen', n 29 above, at 33, at 39 ff, Nicolaysen presents a more detailed account and defence of the activities in Belgium.

[39] Most of them were made available to me by David Fraser from Sydney, who is carrying out a major project on the collaboration in Belgium under the German occupation; as a first result, see D Fraser, 'The Fragility of Law: Anti-Jewish Decrees, Constitutional Patriotism, and Collaboration Belgium 1940–1944' (2003) 14 *Law and Critique* 253.

Ipsen of Hamburg University' is called 'a henchman of the Nazi party'.[40] In 1960, when Ipsen was invited to lecture in Luxembourg, a letter of Professor Hames of 2 March 1960 opined that 'cette nouvelle … souleva une revolte'. The Luxembourg Faculty of Comparative Law had been approached by Professor van Ryn from Brussels: 'Je suis certain d'interpreter les sentiments de tous mes collègues en affirmant que la conduite de M Ipsen pendant toute cette période, et quelles que fussent les circonstances exceptionelles de l'époque, n'a pas été dignes d'un professeur de l'Université'.

Ipsen himself, in his response to the letters that he received from Luxembourg and Brussels,[41] called the accusation that he was an ardent partisan of the Nazis 'absurd', and pointed, *inter alia*, to the postponement of his appointment as a professor in Hamburg.[42]

This is a case of exemplary importance for two reasons. Our factual knowledge is imperfect. It could be improved, to be sure. But it is doubtful whether further inquiries into Ipsen's political attitudes and his behaviour in Brussels will enable us to come to a safe moral assessment. It is not just that the occupied will underline, and maybe glorify, their *resistance*, whereas the occupiers will underline their involvement in military occupation, and maybe downplay their own initiatives. Who am I to judge? A vexing question.[43] To cite once again from Stolleis:

> There was probably also a sense of shame, for the most part suppressed but nevertheless subconsciously present, at having succumbed so readily to the spirit of the times. This sense of shame easily co-exists with an aversion towards those who were born late enough to feel righteous and who so often took the moral high ground in expressing their surprise at the behaviour of their elders. It was a gesture of accusation that not only sealed the lips of the older generation, but proved academically unproductive, for the oft-repeated talk of the older generation's alleged failure was a moralist stance that obscured more than it enlightened. It defined the problem primarily as a moral one, linking it to a single 'misled' generation, and thereby not only avoiding an actual historical explanation, but also distorting the view of their own conformity and capacity to adapt. That is something the older generation was only too happy to point out to the revolutionary generation of 1968 at every opportunity.[44]

What remains possible, however, is to follow the career of the 'hero' of JHH Weiler's novel and to study what Ipsen has written. This is, in the present case, a

[40] In a publication for the Belgian Government Information Center in New York of 1947 ['The Universities under the Occupation' in J-A Goris (ed), *Belgium under Occupation*, Moretus Press]; similarly in her assessment, M-R Thielemans, 'Un commissaire allemand pour l'Université' in A Espy-Meyer, A Dierkens and F Scheelings (eds), *25.11.1941. l'Université Libre de Bruxelles ferme ses portes* (Brussels: Archives de l'ULB, 1991) 25; see, also, H Liebrecht, *L'Université de Bruxelles et la guerre* (Brussels: La renaissance du livre (no year)) esp at 35 ff, 93 ff.

[41] N 31 above.

[42] See text accompanying n 32 above.

[43] See JP Reemtsma, *'Wie hatte ich mich verhalten?' und andere nicht nur deutsche Fragen* (Munich: CH Beck, 2001).

[44] Stolleis, 'Reluctance to Glance in the Mirror', n 2 above.

revealing experience. Ipsen's *Habilitation* on the '*justizlosen Hoheitsakte*' is not just a work in comparative law. It is an analysis of the ideological and political background of the separation of powers ideas. Germany's New Order, or so he explains quite emphatically,[45] has left this tradition far behind.[46] Three types of acts stand out that are to be removed from judicial *Schutzpowers* of review:[47] the '*Schutzhaftanordnung*' (internment in a concentration camp); the '*Säuberung des Beamtentums*' (cleansing of the *Reich*'s civil service); the 'Reinigung der von der Deutschen Arbeitsfront beseitigten Gewerkschaften von politisch Unzuverlässigen' (cleansing of the trade unions). Ipsen certainly pays tribute to the political context that generated such requirements. To be sure, 'contextual' considerations can again come in: Ipsen could not, surely, be expected to give up his career. Perhaps what he wrote can be read more benevolently and did not really reflect his inner beliefs anyway. Be that as it may, this *Politik und Justiz* is a bad piece. I am not aware of any theoretical and methodological standard which would provide us with a defence of the type of thinking presented in this *Habalitationsschrift.*

My generation, who grew up in democracies, should not be self-righteous. How, then, should we face the past? In grief, ashamed, or both? Let us look at Steinmann's reaction to the quest of his colleagues to 'stand up for principles':

> Here legend has it that Steinmann's only intervention in one such meeting was to say, turning to one of the senior members whose eagerness to stand up for principles pushed him to stand up during his speech, 'Karl, sit down; don't you think it's too late for our generation to stand up?'[48]

[45] Ipsen, *Politik und Justiz*, n 31 above, 200 ff.

[46] See M Stolleis, *Geschichte des öffentlichen Rechts in Deutschland. Dritter Band 1914-1945* (Munich: CH Beck, 1999) 336.

[47] Ipsen, *Politik und Justiz*, n 31 above, 218 ff.

[48] Weiler, *Removed*, n 6 above, 19.

32

Europe a Großraum? *Shifting Legal Conceptualizations of the Integration Project**†

I. QUERIES

A NASTY TOPIC! NUMEROUS queries obtrude. Why deal with Europe from such perspectives? There are many answers to this sort of question, some of which are easy. The integration project is a response to the bitter experiences of the past for all Europeans, and for the Germans in particular. It is a way of *Vergangenheitsbewältigung*, as Germans call their efforts to face the past. This is true of a manifold range of topics, which encompass the shape of the European institutions and include many individual policy sectors, both old and new, such as the return of neo-nationalist and xenophobic movements, and even the sad destiny of the German language. Everywhere and at every moment, Germany, its culture as a whole, its academic disciplines, political moves and ambitions, come up against German history. Such encounters are, indeed, often nasty, polemic or, at the very least, unpleasant.[1] And this will remain so, especially in the more immediate future as the EU's eastern enlargement recalls disturbing old notions of '*Mitteleuropa*', and arouses concerns about Germany's role in the enlarged and enlarging *Großraum* economy.[2]

* Published in C Joerges and NS Ghaleigh (eds), *Darker Legacies of Law in Europe: The Shadow of National Socialism and Fascism over Europe and its Legal Traditions* (Oxford: Hart Publishing, 2003) 167; translated from German by IL Fraser, EUI Florence. I am grateful for many suggestions, warnings and corrections. Since the list is so long, I shall make explicit mention only of Bardo Fassbender (St Gallen), Ingo Hueck (Berlin), Oliver Lepsius (Münster), Philip Manow (Bremen) and John P McCormick (Chicago), who helpfully criticised a draft of this paper.

† 'Großraum', literally, 'greater space', was a term in use in a variety of contexts long before its adoption by Carl Schmitt. The connotations of the concept that Schmitt intended are better captured by a term like 'sphere of influence'. We use italics and leave the term *Großraum* untranslated.

[1] Sometimes it is all of these things at once, eg, J Laughland, *The Tainted Source: The Undemocratic Origins of the European Idea* (London: Warner, 1997) 11 and 142.

[2] On the notion of *Mitteleuropa* and its complex history, see PMR Stirk, 'Ideas of Economic Integration in Interwar Mitteleuropa' in idem, *Mitteleuropa. History and Prospects* (Edinburgh: Edinburgh University Press, 1994) 86; J Brechtefeld, *Mitteleuropa and German Politics: 1848 to the Present* (Houndmills–London: Macmillan, 1996). B Kletzin, *Europa aus Rasse und Raum. Die nationalsozialistische Idee der Neuen Ordnung*, 2nd edn (Münster: Lit, 2002) 13; P Chiantera-Stutte,

The past will not lie down, nor, indeed, should it be allowed to. It is, of course, true that the competence to discuss the consequences of history falls more to historians, political scientists and politicians than to lawyers. And yet *Vergangenheitsbewältigung* cannot be left to particular disciplines. National Socialist and Fascist ideologies and practices had an impact on the whole of social and human science; their impact on law was particularly strong, and is embarrassing because of the involvement of both the law and lawyers in the exercise of state authority. The 'duty to remember',[3] which follows from such involvement, implies the task of following and deciphering the traces that the past has, or may have, left in the individual disciplines. Europe is, one should add, a special case in important respects. Ideas resonating from National Socialism cannot be directly relevant in a discipline which constituted itself only after the founding of the European Communities in the late 1950s. But what about more indirect and more subtle undercurrents? All of the legal disciplines that later contributed to the legal conceptualisation of the European Community had been infected by '*völkisch*' legal thinking in Germany. There was a National Socialist practice of international law and a National Socialist-inspired theory of it, the striving for a '*völkisch*' 'legal renewal' [*Rechtserneuerung*] permeated the *Staatsrecht*, constitutional law, administrative law, and the whole body of private and economic law. Both vague and elaborate visions of the historical role and/or position and mission of Europe in general, and Germany in particular,[4] complement the picture. And, to be sure, scholars who documented their allegiance more or less industriously made themselves heard.[5]

Europe, nevertheless, remains a special case – in a very special sense even for the *völkisch* movement. The notion of Europe had been widely discussed in the 1920s in many variants. There was a European radical right with projects of their own. After the National Socialist seizure of power, 'Europe' was to remain a political issue. All thoughts about a future common Europe were, however, gradually abolished and then more or less radically rejected.[6] They were first overlaid by the grand National Socialist project to conquer the Continent militarily, and,

'The Ambiguous Heritage of Mitteleuropa: The Resurfacing of Mitteleuropa as a Counterimage of the EU in Austrian Populism' (2003) 14 *Law and Critique* 325.

[3] P De Greiff, 'Redeeming the Claims of Justice in Transitions to Democracy', unpublished manuscript, Princeton NJ, 2001.

[4] For the quasi official (Nazi party) position, see FA Six, *Das Reich und Europa – eine poltischhistorische Skizze* (Schriftenreihe der NSDAP. Gruppe 4 Vol 5, 1943); FA Six, *Europa – Tradition und Zukunft* (Hamburg: Hanseatische Verlagsanstalt, 1944).

[5] Not just in law; suffice it here to mention the so-called *Kriegseinsatz* of German human and social sciences, organised by international lawyer Paul Ritterbusch, see F-R Hausmann, *Deutsche Geisteswissenschaft' im Zweiten Weltkrieg. Die 'Aktion Ritterbusch' (1940–1945)* (Dresden–Munich: Dresden University Press, 1998); see Section II.1 below.

[6] See the documents cited in the essay of M Salewski, 'Ideas of the National Socialist Government and Party' in W Lipgens (ed), *Documents on the History of European Integration*, vol 1 (*Continental Plans for European Union 1939–1945*) (Berlin–New York: de Gruyter, 1985) 37; see, also, the references in n 12 below.

as defeat in the war became clear, became obsolete and downright undesirable politically.[7] All this may explain why the European integration project attracted scarcely any attention in the *Vergangenheitsbewältigung* of legal historians and in other disciplines. Nevertheless, the more indirect impact, as already hinted at, of the anti-liberal and anti-democratic legal concepts so highly rated in National Socialism represent a disquieting heritage. These elements did not simply emerge from nothing only after 1933, nor did they simply disappear without trace after 1945. We should be prepared to reckon not just with ruptures in legal thinking, but, equally, with continuity. This observation cannot, of course, claim any originality. But its implications are complex. For the years after 1933, MR Lepsius[8] distinguishes between three German academic cultures: 'the one that dominated under National Socialism; the one that was oppressed and silenced in Germany; and the one in emigration'.

In the last political attitudes and theoretical orientations remained alive in the German tradition that had represented 'modernity' and were, until 1933, able to come out openly against the anti-individualism and anti-democratic strands. The protagonists of these traditions, who had often welcomed the new regime with great hopes and with much naïvety, were now, after the National Socialist seizure of power, looking forward to the acceptance and flourishing of their ideas under the *aegis* of the new regime.[9]

It is these contrasts, parallels, continuities and re-configurations in legal thinking and their impact upon the conceptualisation of Europe in legal science that have to be discussed below. This is a highly complex venture. In searching for traces in the German legal tradition, distinctions between 'modernity' and 'anti-modernism', as used by MR Lepsius, are helpful, yet do not provide a sufficiently reliable yardstick. This dichotomy has proven to be illuminating in political philosophy, sociology and constitutional law.[10] It is normatively

[7] E Siebert, 'Entstehung und Struktur der Auslandswissenschaftlichen Fakultät an der Universität Berlin (1940–1945)' (1996) 15 *Wissenschaftliche Zeitschrift der Humboldt-Universität zu Berlin. Gesellschafts- und Sprachwissenschaftliche Reihe* 19, at 33.

[8] MR Lepsius, 'Juristen in der sozialwissenschaftlichen Emigration' in M Lutter, CE Stiefel and MH Hoeflich (eds), *Der Einfluß deutschsprachiger Emigranten auf die Rechtsentwicklung in den USA und in Deutschland* (Tübingen: Mohr, 1993) 19, at 30; see, also, MR Lepsius, 'Kultur und Wissenschaft in Deutschland unter der Herrschaft des Nationalsozialismus' in idem, *Demokratie in Deutschland* (Göttingen: Vandenhoeck & Ruprecht, 1995) 119.

[9] For the interesting case of the history of constitutional thought, see A Lübbe, 'Die deutsche Verfassungsgeschichtsscheibung unter dem Einfluß des Nationalsozialismus' in M Stolleis and D Simon (eds), *Rechtsgeschichte im Nationalsozialismus. Beiträge zur Geschichte einer Disziplin* (Tübingen: Mohr, 1989) 63. It took more than half a century for the Association of German Teachers of Public Law ('*Staatsrecht*') to dedicate a meeting to contemporaneous responses to, and reflections on, the *Machtergreifung*; see the two reports by H Dreier and W Pauly, 'Die deutsche Staatsrechtslehre in der Zeit des Nationalsozialismus' (2001) 60 *Veröffentlichungen der Vereinigung der Deutschen Staatsrechtslehrer* 9–72 and 70–101 – and the comment by B Schlink, 'Unfähigkeit der Staatsrechtswissenschaft zu trauern?' in idem, *Vergangenheitsschuld und gegenwärtiges Recht* (Frankfurt aM: Suhrkamp, 2002) 124.

[10] See, famously, K Sontheimer, *Antidemohratisches Denken in der Weimarer Republik* (Munich: Nymphenburger Verlagsanstalt, 1962).

committed to the abiding idea of the democratic constitutional state. That yardstick, the end of the 'German exceptionalism' (Germany's so-called political and intellectual *Sonderwege*) is valuable and yet insufficient when it comes to the construction of Europe if, and indeed because, the European integration project is bound to establish unprecedented polity.

Concomitant uncertainties determine today's debates. However, even these uncertainties have their traditions. Europe's *faiblesse*, the complaint about its political and social diversity, the hopes invested in its unification, have long been talked about: 'it's reputation as poor, its social order decried … let Europe unify, become a legal unity' – runs a 1929 kind of Euro-barometer.[11] This paper will, however, refrain from any attempt to sift through the errors and confusion of the movements of thought about Europe which circulated in the 1920s, and were first selectively taken up and then abandoned under National Socialism.[12] It will rather seek to reconstructs the origins and the content of ideas on the ordering of Europe; it will be concerned with what MR Lepsius has called the 'institutionalising of rationality criteria'.[13] That looks like an impossible, at best paradoxical, effort for two interrelated reasons. First, it seems problematical to apply a label like 'rationality' to the thinking influenced by, or trying to grasp intellectually, National Socialist ideologies.[14] Second, it is particularly unlikely that there will be any space left for thoughts about the proper ordering under a regime seeking to conquer the whole of Europe. And indeed, the only intellectual contribution worth mentioning stems from the *Third Reich's* 'crown jurist'[15] Carl Schmitt. And even that contribution is only indirectly pertinent. The *Großraum* debate Carl Schmitt sparked off in 1939 was, first of all, about the destruction of classical international law. And even if one acknowledges a constructive dimension in Carl Schmitt's 'European Monroe Doctrine', it is nevertheless striking that he himself remained largely silent as to the *internal order* of the *Großraum*. However, the Schmitt of the *Großraum* theory is not the whole Schmitt. In his diagnoses and theses on the erosion of the international law system of states by spheres of influence – the *Großräume* – Schmitt referred briefly, albeit rather apocryphally, to general developments that were affecting

[11] H Jahrreiß, *Europa als Rechtseinheit* (Leipzig: Robert Noske, 1929) Preface.

[12] Nn 4–6 above; P Kluke, 'Nationalsozialistische Europaideologie' (1955) 3 *Vierteljahreshefte für Zeitgeschichte* 240; J Elvert, '"Germanen" und "Imperialisten" – Zwei Europakonzepte aus nationalsozialistischer Zeit' (1992) 5 *Historische Mitteilungen der Ranke-Gesellschaft* 161; Hausmann, *Aktion Ritterbusch*, n 5 above, 84.

[13] MR Lepsius, 'Max Weber und das Programm einer Institutionenpolitik' (1995) 5 *Berliner Journal für Soziologie* 327.

[14] See, on this *problématique*, O Lepsius, 'The Problem of Perceptions of National Socialist Law or: Was there a Constitutional Theory of National Socialism?' in C Joerges and NS Ghaleigh (eds), *Darker Legacies of Law in Europe*, n * above, 19.

[15] On that title, A-M Gräfin von Lösch, *Der nackte Geist. Die Juristische Fakultät der Berliner Universität im Umbruch von 1933* (Tübingen: Mohr, 1999) 430; B Rüthers, 'Reinhard Höhn, Carl Schmitt und andere – Geschichten und Legenden aus der NS-Zeit' (2000) 53 *Neue Juristische Wochenschrift* 2866, at 2868.

traditional understandings of state constitutions and governance. These diagnoses were written before the *Machtergreifung*; they dealt with what Schmitt perceived as the crises of the Weimar Republic. It is hence through the linkages between Schmitt's *Großraum* concept and his writings that this paper seeks to shed light on the continuities and discontinuities of legal thinking. All this may make this paper look overly concerned with Schmittian ideas. Yet it is not just the general paucity of pertinent contributions from the National Socialist period that necessitates a discussion of the *Großraum* theory. Schmitt is the weightiest exponent of anti-liberal thought in the German tradition – and this is in itself reason enough for taking both his ideas and their impact seriously.[16]

II. RUPTURE: CARL SCHMITT'S *GROßRAUM* THEORY

In the years following the seizure of power, the *Third Reich*, despite its withdrawal from the League of Nations and other international organisations, did not simply disregard international law in its external presentations. Furthermore, international law was more intensively observed and commented upon in the outside world than other disciplines.[17] For these reasons, the discipline continued to enjoy some protection against the *völkisch* renewal of legal thought.[18] Schmitt paid attention to international law very soon after the *Machtergreifung*,[19] although his really intensive concern with it commenced, however, only after he had fallen out

[16] This concern is different from JP McCormick's essay on 'Carl Schmitt's Europe:Cultural, Imperial and Spatial Proposals for European Integration, 1923–1955' in C Joerges and NS Ghaleigh (eds), *Darker Legacies of Law in Europe*, n * above, 133; McCormick deals with Schmitt's visions of Europe, which he presented from 1923 to 1955 in ever new variants.

[17] See VL Gott, 'The National Socialist Theory of International Law' (1938) 32 *American Journal of International Law* 704; JW Garner, 'The Nazi Proscription of International Law' (1939) 33 *American Journal of International Law* 112; JH Herz, 'The National Socialist Doctrine of International Law and the Problems of International Organization' (1939) 54 *Political Science Quarterly* 536; and analyses by D Fraser, '"the outsider does not see all the game ...": Perceptions of German Law in Anglo-American Legal Scholarship, 1933–1940' in C Joerges and NS Ghaleigh (eds), *Darker Legacies of Law in Europe*, n * above, 17; Fraser reveals the indignant responses to Garner by C Schmitt; see *Völkerrechtliche Großraumordnung mit Interventionsverbot für raumfremde Mächte. Ein Beitrag zum Reichsbegriff im Völkerrecht*, 4th edn, 1941, reprinted in G Maschke (ed), *Carl Schmitt, Staat, Großraum, Nomos. Arbeiten aus den Jahren 1916–1969* (Berlin: Duncker & Humblot, 1995) 269, 302. Maschke's reprint is very carefully annotated (321ff) and contains an annex on the impact of Schmitt's essay (341 ff).

[18] See R Wolfrum, 'Nationalsozialismus und Völkerrecht' in FJ Säcker (ed), *Recht und Rechtswissenschaft im Nationalsozialismus* (Baden-Baden: Nomos, 1992) 89, 95; M Stolleis, *Geschichte des öffentlichen Rechts in Deutschland*, vol 3: *Staats- und Verwaltungsrechtswissenschaft in Republik und Diktatur 1914–1945* (Munich: CH Beck, 1999) 382 and 384; I Hueck, 'Die deutsche Völkerrechtswissenschaft im Nationalsozialismus' in D Kaufmann (ed), *Geschichte der Kaiser-Wilhelm-Gesellschaft im Nationalsozialismus. Bestandsaufnahme und Perspektiven der Forschung* (Göttingen: Wallstein, 2000) 490; B Fassbender, 'Stories of War and Peace. The Writing of the History of International Law in the "Third Reich" and After' (2002) 13 *EJIL* 479, 492.

[19] C Schmitt, Nationalsozialismus und Völkerrecht (1934), cited after the reprint in G Maschke (ed), C Schmitt, *Frieden oder Pazifismus? Arbeiten zum Völkerrecht und zur internationalen Politik 1924–1978* (Berlin: Duncker & Humblot, 2nd edn 2005) 391.

of official, albeit not of Hermann Göring's, favour. Tragedy, irony, justice? Schmitt had broken with the former German legal culture, without establishing himself safely enough in the new hierarchies. Despite its '*situativem*' opportunism, the impact of the *Großraum* theory was to be limited both in the political arena and in contemporary academic international law.[20]

II.1. The Theory

From 29 March to 1 April 1939, ie, after the *Anschluß* of Austria until the invasion of Bohemia and Moravia, but before the war against Poland, the '*Reichsgruppe Hochschullehrer des Nationalsozialistischen Rechtswahrer-Bundes*' [Reich section of professors in the National Socialist Association of Lawyers] met in Kiel. At the same time, the Institute for Politics and International Law was celebrating its twenty-fifth anniversary. Paul Ritterbusch was both the chairman of the professorial league and the rector of Kiel University.[21] This was the setting in which Carl Schmitt presented his new theory of international 'law':[22] the '*Großraum* order in international law, with a ban on intervention for powers from outside the sphere. A contribution on the concept of the *Reich* in international law.'[23] The paper appeared in the Institute's publications series as early as April 1939, and in 1941 had its fourth edition.[24]

The core ideas of the lecture were that the *jus publicum europaeum*, which had made the sovereign state its central concept, was no longer in line with the *de facto* spatial order of Europe. Referring to the example of the American Monroe Doctrine, Schmitt explained that a specific 'sphere/space' had to become the conceptual basis for international law, with the *Reich* constituting the order of that space. Self-confidently, Schmitt declared:

> When, in autumn 1937, I presented my report on the turn to a discriminating concept of war, the overall political situation was still markedly different from today's …

[20] For comprehensive analyses, see L Gruchmann, *Nationalsozialistische Großraumordnung. Die Konstruktion einer deutschen Monroe-Doktrin* (Stuttgart: Deutsche Verlags-Anstalt, 1962); M Schmoeckel, *Die Großraumtheorie. Ein Beitrag zur Geschichte der Völkerrechtswissenschaft im Dritten Reich, insbesondere der Kriegszeit* (Berlin: Duncker & Humblot, 1994).

[21] Ritterbusch was soon entrusted with organising the '*Kriegseinsatz*' of the human and social sciences, an effort to document the usefulness of academic work for the *Reich* in its war; see Hausmann, *Aktion Ritterbusch*, n 5 above, at 11.

[22] The quotation marks are not intended merely to indicate taking a distance, but to point to a problem that affects Carl Schmitt's jurisprudence as a whole, mainly his rejection of a concept of law involving general validity claims: in international law, he indicated this with his '*quis judicabit*' question, and otherwise most sharply with his distinction between friend and foe.

[23] For the orginal German title of the *Völkerrechtliche Großraumordnung*, see n 17 above.

[24] Maschke's reprint is the fourth edition; on the context of Schmitt's lecture, see Hausmann, *Aktion Rittersbusch*, n 5 above, at 44 f and 253 ff; idem, 'Carl Schmitt und die deutschen Romanisten' (1999) 23 *Romanistische Zeitschrift für Literaturgeschichte* 409 and 414; G Balakrishnan, *The Enemy: An Intellectual Portrait of Carl Schmitt* (London–New York: Verso, 2000) 226.

> Having delivered my report, I was asked to substantiate what new order was to substitute the state order ... Today, I can give the answer. The new ordering concept for a new international law is our concept of the *Reich*, with its *Volk* based, *völkisch Großraum* order.[25]

The German *Reich* had been introduced by Schmitt a page earlier as

> a *Großraum order* dominated by particular ideological ideas and principles that exclude intervention by powers foreign to the area, whose guarantor and guardian is a people that has proved itself capable of this task.[26]

The only people that came into question as a 'guarantor and guardian' were the Germans. This meant acknowledging *de jure* a *Großraum* in which states could no longer claim equal respect, a situation which Germany had just set in motion *de facto*. And Schmitt went on praising the *Führer*, who had 'given the idea of our *Reich* political reality, historical truth and a great international future'.[27] The political success of such an exemplary demonstration of *konkretes Ordnungsdenken à la* Schmitt seemed pre-destined. Yet, although the echoes to Schmitt's messages were considerable,[28] they did not find political acclaim.

II.2. Controversies

Opponents, like those who had, in 1936, already halted Schmitt's career as 'crown jurist', made themselves heard again.[29] Objection was taken to his statement that 'the new international law approach, its reference to the concept of the *Volk* notwithstanding, retained elements of order stemming from the state concept'. In his brief review, Werner Best explained that the *Völker* [peoples, national communities] with their 'supra-personal, supra-temporal overall essentialities' were to replace the 'concept of the abstract state' or 'economic interest formations', and the *Großraum* to be understood as an 'order of *volk* orders [national communities]'.[30]

This criticism was taken seriously – so seriously that Schmoekel is able to use this dichotomy of '*völkisch*' as against 'statist' to re-construct the whole

[25] Schmitt, *Großraum*, n 17 above, at 306.

[26] Ibid, at 305.

[27] Ibid, at 306.

[28] See the annotations by Maschke, n 17 above, 321, and the references in Schmoeckel, n 20 above, at 152; Brechtefeld, n 2 above, at 55.

[29] See Rüthers, 'Reinhard Höhn', n 15 above; idem, *Carl Schmitt im Dritten Reich. Wissenschaft als Zeitgeist-Verstärkung*, 2nd edn (Munich: CH Beck, 1990) 81; v Lösch, *Der nackte Geist*, n 15 above, at 429 and 448.

[30] W Best, 'Völkische Großraumordnung' (1940) 10 *Deutsches Recht* 1006; in more detail, idem, 'Grundfragen einer deutschen Großraumverwaltung' in *Festschrift für Heinrich Himmler zum 40. Geburtstag* (Darmstadt: Wittlich, 1941) 33.

contemporary debate.[31] The contrast between the two reference points is theoretically important and politically nothing less than dramatic. Schmitt's reminder that the existing concept of the state contains a minimum of reliable organisation and internal discipline, and that this organisational minimum constitutes the real basis of everything that has been seen as the concrete order of the 'international community', appeals to values which Schmitt himself had substantially discredited but which he, having fallen in disgrace, seems to have re-discovered.[32]

The support Schmitt found, particularly from Ernst Rudolf Huber, goes in a similar direction. Schmitt's statements on how both of his quests, for the preservation of the basic elements of international law on the one hand, and for the legal recognition of the new power structure of Germany's power politics in the *Großraum* on the other, could co-exist had remained ambiguous. Schmitt[33] had previously ventured ideas on a consolidation of both elements somewhat provisionally in a review essay on the second edition of Heinrich Triepel's *Hegemonie. Ein Buch von führenden Staaten* [*Hegemony: A Manual on States that Lead*].[34] He refrained from further elaborating his idea in his *Großraum* essay, but contented himself with underlining the elasticity of the notion of international law, which, as he explained, could also cover 'inter-*völkische* relations within a *Großraum*'. His famous disciple, Huber, however, took the key National Socialist concept of *Führung* much more seriously as a legal concept.[35] *Führung*, he argued, was to be understood as a concept of general significance in the new order, which offered an alternative to such categories as power and rule:

> Führung implies rule, but it is more: it goes further by setting people moving from within ... the awakening of the inward urge to action on one's own responsibility within a pre-designed action plan is the distinguishing feature of true leadership.

This applied between peoples [*Völkern*, ethnic communities] no less than between individuals [as *Volksgenossen*]:

> Political leadership is, then, the responsible determination of a closed unity of life, growing directly out of the basic forces of the community and based on a symbiosis of authority and power.[36]

[31] Schmoeckel, n 20 above, 174; see the documentation in Maschke, n 17 above, 343 ff, and on contemporary 'state law' [*Staatsrecht*], Stolleis, *Geschichte des öffentlichen Rechts in Deutschland*, vol 3, n 18 above, 361; Pauly, n 9 above, at 76.

[32] See D Dyzenhaus, 'Leviathan in the 1930s: The Reception of Hobbes in the Third Reich' in JP McCormick (ed), *Mass Democracy and Industrial Technology. Political and Social Theory from Nietzsche to Habermas* (Durham NC–London: Duke UP, 2002) 163, 171.

[33] C Schmitt, 'Führung und Hegemonie' (1939), reprinted in Maschke, n 17 above, 225.

[34] (Stuttgart-Berlin: Kohlhammer, 1938); see, also, Schmoeckel, n 20 above, at 117.

[35] ER Huber, 'Herrschaft und Führung' (1941) 11 *Deutsches Recht* 2017. See, on the broader discussion, O Lepsius, Die gegensatzaufhebende Begriffsbildung. Methodenentwicklungen in der Weimarer Republik und ihr Verhältnis zur Ideologisierung der Rechtswissenschaft unter dem Nationalsozialismus (Munich: CH Beck, 1994) 93 ff; and, for a sociological analysis, drawing upon Weber's concept of charismatic domination and leadership, see RM Lepsius, 'Das Modell der charismatischen Herrschaft und seine Anwendbarkeit auf den "Führerstaat" Adolf Hitlers', in idem, Demokratie in Deutschland, n 8 above, 95.

[36] The tone of his conclusion [in an essay on this topic published in the same year (ER Huber, 'Bau und Gefüge des Reiches' (1941) 6 *Deutsche Rechtswissenschaft* 22, at 31)] does not survive

This sounds, as is characteristic for this author, quite conciliatory.[37] The difference between a *völkisch* order entirely devoid of law and the proponents of a state-structured international legal system is indeed important, even terribly so. The writings of the radical *völkisch* school – Werner Best, Reinhard Höhn, and Wilhelm Stuckart, a group which contributed prominently to the Himmler *Festschrift* of 1941 – are not merely a disaster in academic terms. Werner Best[38] did not shrink from explaining the necessity, as a law of life, for the *Führungsvolk* to destroy totally (or expel totally from its sphere) undesired peoples. 'Annihilation and expulsion' do not, 'according to historical experience, contradict the laws of life if they are done totally.'[39] Best's contemporaries and comrades did not, apparently, ever publish such sentences, neither before nor after 1941 or 1942.[40] So the dichotomy was merely ideological when Schmitt set to minimise his differences with Best:

> [It] … can be left open whether the relationships emerging between a Reich and a *Großraum* can still be called 'international law', whether other words and designations are more proper, and whether the inter-people [*zwischenvölkische*] relationships developing within a *Großraum* had not, as Werner Best suggested, more properly to be termed as the '*völkisch* (instead of international law) order of the *Großraum*'.[41]

Huber once again managed to find a pleasant formula for the new order:

> For political theory as for legal theory, the decisive problem is how the idea of the Reich, in its adaptation to the *Großraum* principle, differs from the imperialism of the others against whom we have honourably and uprightly fought … The vital difference can only lie in the fact the old imperialism was a formation of pure power and naked interest, concealed behind the high sounding talk of the equal rights of all nations; for the concept of the Reich, what must, instead, be decisive is that it is a structure of graduated order in which the leading power takes over open responsibility for the preservation of the overall order and the existence of all the members. For power becomes Law only by being understood as a responsibly boned function *vis à vis* a living whole entrusted to it … The most important aspect of the Reich's task will thus be to make German leading power [*Führungsgewalt*] responsible for solving prime European questions beyond the state boundaries of the Reich.[42]

translation into a living language: 'Politische Führung ist sonach: *die aus den Grundkräften der Gemeinschaft unmittelbar erwachsende, auf der Verbindung von Autorität und Macht beruhende verantwortliche Bestimmung einer geschloßenen Lebenseinheit*' (italics in the original).

[37] And must be read in the context of Huber's efforts to identify a 'constitution' of the National Socialist state; see, comprehensively, R Walkenhaus, *Konservatives Staatsdenken. Eine wissenssoziologische Studie zu Ernst Rudolf Huber* (Berlin: Akademie Verlag, 1995) esp at 234.

[38] On his biography, see U Herbert, *Best. Biographische Studien über Radikalismus, Weltanschauung und Vernunft*, 1903–1989, 3rd edn (Bonn: JHW Dietz, 1996).

[39] Best, 'Grundfragen', n 30 above, at 42; in the same sense, idem, 'Großraumordnung und Großraumverwaltung' (1942) 32 *Zeitschrift für Politik* 406; see Herbert, n 38 above, at 283.

[40] See Dreier, n 9 above, at 39 (Best is not cited there, but Dreier's observation is neither surprising nor illuminating anyway).

[41] Schmitt, N 33 above.

[42] Huber, 'Bau und Gefüge des Reiches', n 36 above, at 31.

In the dark shadow of such artistic linguistic exercises, the internal shape of the *Großraum* remains clearly discernible. If, in contrast with the uncompromisingly *völkisch* school, the 'order' of the *Großraum* is not presented as a naked power structure,[43] the implications of a graded legal capacity of the 'states' in the *Großraum* and also for its inhabitants are drastic enough:[44] in line with the 'existential determination of the people by its natural biological vitality and its spiritual and historical character', which distinguishes the '*volk* comrade' [*Volksgenosse*] and his 'German or species-related [*artverwandtes*] blood'. In consequence, the old category of citizenship, which had once included alien racial groups, is to be replaced by that of the '*Reich* citizen' [*Reichsbürger*]; below this species, we find mere '*Reich* members', who enjoy a status of 'protection and obligations' and therefore owe obedience but not 'loyalty' and military service. Among the *Reich* members – we are to distinguish further between '*Volk* members' and the 'racially alien' – there is 'citizenship' for '*Volk* groups' (who owe the German *Volk* and *Reich* obedience); and there is *Reich* citizenship for groups with a 'culture of their own'. Then there are *Volk* members living outside the *Reich* frontiers to whom the *Reich* owes duties of protection.[45] 'No theoretician presupposed that the governments or inhabitants of the *Großraum* "states" would have to consent to the new order', observes Schmoeckel.[46] This aspect of the *Großraum* should be taken into account by those who present Carl Schmitt's position as actually being in contrast to the purely *völkisch* concepts.[47]

Franz Neumann, in his *Behemoth*,[48] presented the *Großraum* theory as a toolkit for the regime. However, very soon after its presentation at the '*Aktion Ritterbusch*' in Spring 1939, this new instrument was already outdated. Schmitt, the '*situative*' thinker, responded in the 1941 edition, when Germany occupied ever-greater spaces, by adding an epigraph to his paper: 'We are like mariners on a continuing journey, and no book can be more than a log book.' He was well aware of the implications of the changed situation within the *Großraum*.

[43] Schmitt, n 3 above: 'The *Großraum* order is, then, neither a "state" nor "international law" phenomenon in the sense hitherto usual. Accordingly, the "legal" [characterisation of] the rules for the lasting relationships between the peoples of the *Großraum* … is without real importance …'

[44] Huber's summary is reprinted in AJ Jacobson and B Schlink (eds), *Weimar: A Jurisprudence of Crisis* (Berkeley–Los Angeles CA: University of California Press, 2000) 330.

[45] N 42 above, at 26. It should be added that Huber did not adopt the anti-Semitic phraseology. And, in his relentless search for a conciliatory formula, he suggested a '*Kriegsverfassung*' (war constitution), which would 'govern' the creation of the *Großraum* (see R Walkenhaus, *Konservatrives Staatsdenken*, n 37 above, at 242).

[46] *Großraum*, n 17 above, at 274.

[47] See JH Kaiser, 'Europäisches Großraumdenken. Die Steigerung geschichtlicher Größen als Rechtsproblem' in H Barion, E-W Böckenförde, E Forsthoff and W Weber (eds), *Epirrhosis. Festgabe für Carl Schmitt*, vol 2 (Berlin: Duncker & Humblot, 1968) 319.

[48] F Neumann, *Behemoth. Struktur und Praxis des Nationalsozialismus 1933–1944*, ed by G Schäfer (Frankfurt aM: Fischer, 1984) 198.

III. CONTINUITIES: ELEMENTS OF INTERNAL ORDERING

In his reply to Best and his *völkisch* admonitions, Carl Schmitt had presented his *Großraum* as a 'concrete, historical and politically contemporary concept' [*konkreten geschichtlich-politischen Gegenwartsbegriff*] rooted 'essentially not in the state but in the technical, industrial and economic sphere'.[49] The revised editions of the Kiel lecture contain corresponding passages.[50] Schmitt was now referring, albeit apocryphally, to debates and theorems which lent support to his theses on the erosion of the territorial state, a harbinger of the necessity to adapt international law to the factual re-structuring of international relations and the replacement of classical international law by norm systems which one would call governance structures today. Schmitt referred specifically to two phenomena, namely, the economic interdependencies beyond state frontiers [an emerging '*Großraum* economy'] and the valueless rationality of technology-driven developments, which further the dictatorship of 'technicity' [*Technizität*].[51] He could have linked his pre-1933 writings with the *Großraum* theory when he designed it. But he did not – and had to let them remain as they were in view of the changed 'situation' in 1941. He also failed to consider a third alternative to international law, namely, its replacement by administrative law – even though here, too, Carl Schmitt had delivered pertinent contributions.

III.1. Economy

The theorising on private law and economic law during the Weimar era has received much less attention than the debates on state law [*Staatsrecht*] and constitutional law, although, despite being much less visible, private law jurisprudence is scarcely less interesting. The type of economic policy and law actually practised mirrored, as Knut-Wolfgang Nörr has argued in two monographs,[52] the 'organised economy' so characteristic of the German state economy. Nörr's notion recalls what the Bielefeld social historians described as nineteenth-century German 'organised capitalism',[53] a configuration which

[49] Schmitt, *Großraum*, n 17 above, at 305.

[50] Ibid, at 307.

[51] On this term, see JP McCormick, *Carl Schmitt's Critique of Liberalism. Against Politics as Technology* (Cambridge: CUP, 1997) 122, and Section IV.2 below.

[52] KW Nörr, Die Leiden des Privatrechts. Kartelle in Deutschland von der Holzstoffkartellentscheidung bis zum Gesetz gegen Wettbewerbsbeschränkungen (Tübingen: Mohr, 1994); KW Nörr, Die Republik der Wirtschaft. Teil I: Von der Besatzungszeit bis zur Großen Koalition (Tübingen: Mohr, 1999).

[53] See, eg, J Kocka, 'Organisierter Kapitalismus oder Staatsmonopolistischer Kapitalismus' in HA Winkler (ed), *Organisierter Kapitalismus: Voraussetzungen und Anfänge* (Göttingen: Vandenhoeck & Ruprecht, 1974) 19.

was to survive the end of the Monarchy.[54] The theoretical debate, however, was much richer, and the gamut of concepts between industrial society and economic democracy had – more or less powerful – backing in the political world.[55] The state-economy model, in which Nörr, in particular, is interested, is 'ordoliberalism', developed by such economists as Walter Eucken, Alexander Rüstow and Wilhelm Röpke, who were joined by the lawyer Franz Böhm at the end of the 1920s and in the early 1930s.[56] Both Carl Schmitt[57] and the ordoliberals advocated a strong state.[58] At the same time, Alfred Müller-Armack[59] and Carl Schmitt himself[60] showed their fascination with Mussolini's Fascism. For this – and other – reasons, Hermann Heller[61] characterised Schmitt's economic concepts as 'authoritarian liberalism'. This qualification applies to the common critique of a pluralism in which the conflict of interests determines the contents of state policy. Yet the 'order' of the economy that the ordoliberals hoped for differed from the ideas of Schmitt and his successors in one very important respect. Carl Schmitt had very clearly indicated in his talk of the 'strong state' and the 'healthy economy'[62] that he was advocating the primacy of politics over a politically obedient self-administration of the economy.[63] The primacy of the

[54] See J Bast, *Totalitärer Pluralismus*(Tübingen: Mohr, 1999) 200; P Manow, '"Modell Deutschland" as an inter-denominational Compromise', Centre for European Studies, Harvard University, *CES Working Paper*, Programme for the Study of Germany and Europe, No 003.

[55] G Brüggemeier, Entwicklung des Rechts im organisierten Kapitalismus, Band 1 (Frankfurt aM: Syndikat, 1977) 239; D Wielsch, Freiheit und Funktion. Zur Struktur- und Theoriegeschichte des Rechts der Wirtschaftsgesellschaft (Baden-Baden: Nomos, 2001) 103.

[56] R Wiethölter, 'Franz Böhm (1895–1977)' in B Diestelkamp and Michael Stolleis (eds), *Juristen an der Universität Frankfurt a.M.* (Baden-Baden: Nomos, 1989) 208, 215; D Haselbach, *Autoritärer Liberalismus und Soziale Marktwirtschaft. Gesellschaft und Politik im Ordoliberalismus* (Baden-Baden: Nomos, 1991); Manow, n 54 above.

[57] C Schmitt, 'Starker Staat und gesunde Wirtschaft. Ein Vortrag vor Wirtschaftsführern' (Lecture of 23 November 1932) in (1933) *Volk und Reich* 81, reprinted in Maschke, n 17 above, at 71; English translation: 'Strong State and Sound Economy: An Address to Business Leaders', Appendix to R Cristi, *Carl Schmitt and Authoritarian Liberalism* (Cardiff: University of Wales Press, 1988) 212.

[58] A Rüstow, 'Freie Wirtschaft – starker Staat' in F Boese (ed), 'Deutschland und die Weltkrise', 187 *Schriften des Vereins für Socialpolitik* (Munich: Duncker & Humblot, 1932) 62; F Böhm, *Wettbewerb und Monopolkampf* (Berlin: Carl Heymanns, 1933); F Böhm, *Die Ordnung der Wirtschaft als geschichtliche Aufgabe und rechtsschöpferische Leistung* (Stuttgart-Berlin: Kohlhammer, 1937); Haselbach, n 56 above, at 40; Wielsch, n 55 above, at 83; P Manow, 'Ordoliberalismus als ökonomische Ordnungstheologie' (2001) 29 *Leviathan* 179.

[59] A Müller-Armack, Entwicklungsgesetze des Kapitalismus. Ökonomische, geschichtstheoretische und soziologische Studien zur modernen Wirtschaftsverfassung (Berlin: Juncker & Dünnhaupt 1932); idem, Staatsidee und Wirtschaftsordnung im neuen Reich (Berlin: Juncker & Dünnhaupt, 1933).

[60] C Schmitt, 'Die Wendung zum totalen Staat' (1931) in idem, *Positionen und Begriffe im Kampf mit Weimar – Genf – Versailles, 1923–1939* (Berlin: Duncker & Humblot, 1988) 146.

[61] H Heller, 'Autoritärer Liberalismus' (1933) 44 *Die Neue Rundschau* 289; nowhere does Heller's essay mention the neoliberalism of the founding fathers of the Freiburg School. He is exclusively concerned with Carl Schmitt's 'Strong State' (n 57 above).

[62] N 60 above.

[63] See the analysis by I Maus, 'Existierten zwei Nationalsozialismen?' in idem, *Rechtstheorie und politische Theorie im Industriekapitalismus* (Munich: Fink, 1986) 83.

political over the economic, Ernst Forsthoff was to explain some years later, is a specific feature of the '*Führer* constitution'.[64] This primacy finds its expression in the 'plan', the 'specific action form of the *Führer* state … in the spheres of the economy and technology'. 'Order' and 'plan' are opposing concepts, even if both call for a 'strong state'.[65] And even with the pleas for this 'plan', interpretive caution is called for. Hans Freyer[66] to whom Forsthoff refers,[67] discusses the notion of 'plan' without National Socialist connotations.

Research on the implications of the primacy of the political in economic law after the *Machtergreifung* in 1933 is gradually intensifying.[68] However, on the question of how the economy of the *Großraum* might be legally structured, there is very little to be found – and maybe very little worth looking at. Werner Daitz, probably the best-known exponent of economic *Großraum* thinking,[69] is mentioned by Schmitt for the first time in a follow-up essay to the *Großraum* lecture of 1939.[70] This is difficult to understand, but, at the same time, illuminating: Daitz's writings document obedience to the regime and are of disastrous quality. This writer had first advocated a retreat from the world economy to a national economy, for the autarchy first of the national economy and then of the *Großraum* economy of the European 'family of peoples' as a whole.[71] More realistic contemporaries saw the *Großraum* economically as merely an emergency solution.[72] At any rate, Justus Wilhelm Hedemann, who was prominent in

[64] E Forsthoff, 'Führung und Planung' (1937) 7 *Deutsches Recht* 48.

[65] Specifically on the distinct positions of Franz Böhm, see Wiethölter, n 56 above, at 232. On the often cited contacts by the Reich Ministry for the Economy which, at the end of the regime, sought economic advice from exponents of ordoliberalism for an economic policy concept beyond classical liberalism and socialist planned economy, see L Herbst, *Der totale Krieg und die Ordnung der Wirtschaft* (Stuttgart: Deutsche Verlagsanstalt, 1982) 133 and 144; they are no proof to the contrary.

[66] H Freyer, *Herrschaft und Planung. Zwei Grundbegriffe der politischen Ethik* (Hamburg, 1933), reprinted in E Üner (ed), *Hans Freyer. Herrschaft, Planung und Technik. Aufsätze zur politischen Soziologie* (Weinheim: VCH, 1987) 17.

[67] 'Führung und Planung', n 64 above, at 48, fn 1.

[68] D Gosewinkel, 'Wirtschaftspolitische Rechtssetzung im Nationalsozialismus' (ms Frankfurt aM: Max Planck Institut für Europäische Rechtsgeschichte, 2000); W Seibel, 'Steuerung durch Recht im Nationalsozialismus?', Contribution to the Workshop 'Wirtschaftskontrolle und Recht im Nationalsozialismus – Zwischen Entrechtlichung und Modernisierung. Bilanz und Perspektiven der Forschung', Berlin-Brandenburgischen Akademie der Wissenschaften, Studiengruppe 'Das Europa der Diktaturen. Wirtschaftssteuerung und Recht', Blankensee, 14–16 June 2001; see, much earlier, G Brüggemeier, *Entwicklung des Rechts im organisierten Kapitalismus*, vol 2: *Vom Faschismus bis zur Gegenwart* (Frankfurt aM: Syndikat, 1979) 32, 69.

[69] See Salewski, 'Ideas of the National Socialist Government and Party', n 6 above, 37–178; Maschke, n 17 above, 364 and 465.

[70] C Schmitt, *Großraum und Völkerrecht* (1940), reprinted in Maschke, n 17 above, 234, at 237.

[71] W Daitz, *Der Weg zur Volkswirtschaft, Großraumwirtschaft und Großraumpolitik* (Dresden: Meinhold Verlagsgesellschaft, 1943); see Kletzin, *Europa aus Rasse und Raum*, n 2 above, 129 and 163.

[72] W Abelshauser, '"Mitteleuropa" und die deutsche Außenwirtschaftspolitik' in C Buchheim, M Hutter and H James (eds), *Zerrissene Zwischenkriegszeit. Wirtschaftshistorische Beiträge. Knut Borchardt zum 65. Geburtstag* (Baden-Baden: Nomos, 1994) 263.

German economic law long before 1933, and heavily involved in the *Akademie für Deutsches Recht*, in working out the new *Volksgesetzbuch* from 1939, took up the theme, in 1941 and 1943, in two essays which have received practically no attention.[73] He was looking for a leadership model for the economy, which would leave the economic actors and the citizens in the *Großraum* with some autonomy. The peoples [*Völkerschaften*] of Europe were perceived as the bases of law; self-administration, corporatist structures and planning were to complement each other – vagueness everywhere; but why and how could he seek clarification in what had become a war economy?[74]

III.2. Technicity

Carl Schmitt[75] had complemented his plea for the 'strong state' in which politics was to assert its priority over the economy with a polemic against all technocratic endeavours and promises to decide all questions of the polity by relying on technical and economic expertise, 'according to allegedly purely practical, purely technical and purely economic viewpoints'. In contrast with the US, where '*The Technocrats*' praised welfare and prosperity enhancing potential of technologically and economically underpinned expertise,[76] many of the conservative intellectuals who set the tone of the Weimar Republic saw the dominance of soulless technical machinery arriving, against which most cultural values could be mobilised, while it seemed hopeless to trust in the creative possibilities of Weimar democracy.[77]

[73] See H Mohnhaupt, 'Justus Wilhelm Hedemann als Rechtsdenker und Zivilrechtler vor und während der Epoche des Nationalsozialismus' in M Stolleis and D Simon (eds), *Rechtsgeschichte im Nationalsozialismus. Beiträge zur Geschichte einer Disziplin* (Tübingen: Mohr, 1989) 107, at 156, fn 259; Schmoeckel, n 20 above, at 224.

[74] On the 'scientific' tasks and activities of the German Institute for Foreign Studies, see R Eisfeld, *Ausgebürgert und doch angebräunt. Deutsche Politikwissenschaft 1920–1945* (Baden-Baden: Nomos, 1991), 152ff; Siebert, n 7 above; on the foreign trade continuities of *Großraum* ideas, see VR Berghahn, 'German Big Business and the Quest for a European Economic Empire in the Twentieth Century' in idem (ed), *Quest for Economic Empire: the European Strategies of German Business in the Twentieth Century* (Providence MA–Oxford: Berghahn Books, 1996) 1.

[75] N 57 above, at 73; the diagnosis of a turn towards the 'quantitatively' (but politically rather weak!) total state, also, Schmitt, 'Die Wendung', n 60 above; and idem,'Starker Staat', n 57 above.

[76] See C Radaelli, *Technocracy in the EU* (Harlow–New York: Longman, 1999), esp at 24; see, also, A Mohler, 'Der Weg der "Technokratie" von Amerika nach Frankreich' in H Barion, E-W Böckenförde, E Forsthoff and W Weber (eds), *Epirrhosis. Festgabe für Carl Schmitt*, vol 2 (Berlin: Duncker & Humblot, 1968) 579.

[77] T Vesting, Politische Einheitsbildung und technische Realisation. Über die Expansion der Technik und die Grenzen der Demokratie (Baden-Baden: Nomos, 1994) 9; N Stehr, Arbeit, Eigentum und Wissen. Zur Theorie von Wissensgesellschaften (Frankfurt aM: Suhrkamp, 1994) 278; McCormick, n 51 above, 31 and 83.

In his counter-revolutionary Barcelona manifesto,[78] Carl Schmitt had identified the Soviet Union as the institutional incarnation of a quasi-religious, soulless technicity.[79] Does this mean that the 'particularly strong' and 'qualitively total' state should lead not just the economy; should this state be able to ensure the primacy of the political over 'technicity', and thus accomplish what a powerless culture could not achieve? A frightening notion. Hans Freyer, who, with good reason, counted[80] among the conservative techno-pessimists who impressed, for instance, Ernst Forsthoff,[81] argued, in comfortingly Weberian terms, that technical formations become a reality only through the 'plan'; behind the plan stands 'political power'; power, however, pre-supposes 'rule' [*Herrschaft*]; but '*Herrschaft* is of lasting duration, because and in so far as it incorporates all … *Herrschaft* essentially seeks legitimacy, and its duration depends on the solidity of the legitimacy bases it finds ready-made or manages to create.'[82] It seems simply impossible to fit the positions of the conservative technology critique into the National Socialist domination fantasies.

III.3. Administration

Schmoekel[83] finds the most original contemporary elaboration of Schmitt's *Großraum* theory in what seems, at first sight, an inconspicuous article by Hans Peter Ipsen on the 'External administration of the Reich' [*Reichsaußenverwaltung*], with the explanatory subtitle: 'the German administration looks after [*sic*!] 145 million people outside the Reichfrontiers'.[84] This external administration, explained Ipsen, is 'concrete, objective, and functional' in its orientation. It presupposed the continued existence of 'country specific administrations', but claims unconditional supremacy. This idea, says Schmoekel,[85] is 'near genius' and, at the same time, has 'something downright

[78] C Schmitt, 'Das Zeitalter der Neutralisierungen und Entpolitsierungen' (1929), reprinted in idem, *Positionen und Begriffe im Kampf um Weimar – Genf – Versaillles 1923–1939* (Berlin: Duncker & Humblot, 1988) 120.

[79] Ibid, at 120: 'its vitality is strong enough to wield knowledge and technology as weapons; its courage for rationalism and the opposite … are overwhelming'.

[80] H Freyer, 'Zur Philosophie der Technik', reprinted in Üner (ed), *Hans Freyer*, n 66 above, 7 and 9.

[81] See M Vec, 'Aushöhlung des Staates? Selbst-Normierung im Staat der Industriegesellschaft als historisches Problem' (2000) 19 *Rechtshistorisches Journal* 517.

[82] H Freyer, n 66 above, 20, 28 and 38; see idem, 'Das Politische als Problem der Philosophie'(1935), reprinted in Üner (ed), *Hans Freyer*, n 66 above, 45; H Freyer, 'Beiträge zur Theorie der Herrschaft' (1940), reprinted in Üner (ed), ibid 65.

[83] *Großraumtheorie*, n 20 above, 225.

[84] HP Ipsen, 'Reichsaußenverwaltung' (1942) *Reichsverwaltungsblatt* 64ff, reprinted in HW Neulen, *Europa und das 3. Reich, Einigungsbestrebungen im deutschen Machtbereich 1939–1945* (Munich: Universitas, 1987) 111.

[85] *Großraumtheorie*, n 20 above, 226.

diabolical'. In fact, Ipsen's idea is to be differentiated from the rather dry classificatory exercises in the writings on the administrative practices in occupied Europe.[86] His concept precisely mirrored the *Reich*'s power claims. Ipsen retained a legal form while freeing rule from any legal constraint. And this was not just simply written down off the top of his head. In his 1937 Hamburg *Habilitation* thesis – in its comparative chapters scholarly and by the same token in its substance a depressing study – Ipsen had developed the preliminary concept.[87] This study dealt, as its subtitle announces, with 'judiciary free sovereign acts' [*justizlose Hoheitsakte*]. It offered, as a review of the study by no less than Ernst Rudolf Huber emphasised, an accurate 'internal interpretation of the essence' [*innere Wesensdeutung*] of those acts in distinguishing them from the familiar discretionary acts and establishing their 'complete freedom from judicial control'.[88] But Huber also discovers and defends another dimension of the argument. Ipsen is praised for basing himself – against Reinhard Höhn – on the continuing existence, in principle, of a control of the administration in the new state, which implies a protection of individual rights.[89] Yet higher than this latter principle is the genuine norm-setting power of the National Socialist government. This power is not derived from some legislative power, the government is the bearer of government power,[90] which embraces legislative power.[91]

This is unadulterated Schmittianism.[92] In his essay on 'Legality and Legitimacy', Schmitt had already proclaimed the end of the 'legislative state',

[86] D Majer, 'NS-Verwaltung im besetzten Europa' (1999) 90 *Verwaltungs-Archiv* 163.

[87] HP Ipsen, *Politik und Justiz. Das Problem der justizlosen Hoheitsakte* (Hamburg, Hanseatische Verlagsanstalt, 1937); on this book, see, also, n 92 below.

[88] ER Huber, '"Politik und Justiz": Zu Hans Peter Ipsens Schrift über das Problem der "justizlosen Hoheitsakte"' (1937/38) 98 *Zeitschrift für die gesamte Staatswissenschaft* 193, 195.

[89] Ibid.

[90] Ibid, at 196 (and suggesting the use of 'leadership power' [*Führungsgewalt*] as the more adequate term).

[91] N 87 above, at 180.

[92] Biographical remarks are in principle beyond the scope of this essay. The importance of Hans Peter Ipsen for European legal scholarship in Germany seems to warrant an exception. His *vita* and academic career illuminate the intellectual continuity/discontinuity *problématique* and Germany's 'reluctance to glance back in the mirror' (the 'Prologue' by M Stolleis to Joerges and Ghaleigh, *Darker Legacies*, n * above, 1) in an exemplary way. Ipsen, born in 1907 in Hamburg, was already a highly respected professor of public law when he focused on the new European Communities and became the *doyen* of European law in Germany: a successful supervisor of some 140 PhD students and no less then 7 *Habilitations*; for good reasons, an admired author of the first great 1,092-page textbook in German on European law (*Europäisches Gemeinschaftsrecht* (Tübingen: Mohr, 1972), of some 30 monographs and of some 150 articles, one of which [his 1964 Bensheim lecture on 'DasVerhältnis des Rechts der europäischen Gemeinschaften zum nationalen Recht' ('The Relationship between the Law of the European Communities and National Law'), published, *inter alia*, in *Aktuelle Fragen des europäischen Gemeinschaftsrechts, Europarechtliches Kolloquium*, Bensheim 1964, and in (1965) 2 *CML Rev* 397, suggested the '*Durchgriffswirkung*' (supremacy) of European law and is said to have been taken into consideration by the ECJ judges who attended the lecture and handed down, only 5 days later, on 15 July 1964, the seminal *Costa v ENEL* judgment (Case 6/64, ECR [1964] 1251); T Oppermann, 'Hans Peter Ipsen und das Europarecht' in Fachbereich Rechtswissenschaft der Universität Hamburg (ed), *Hans Peter Ipsen. 1907–1998* (Münster–Hamburg–London: Lit, 2002) 21, at 27 f; G Nicolaysen, 'Lebensbild Hans Peter Ipsen', ibid, 33, at 44 f.

a 'turn to the total state' with its inevitable trend towards the 'plan' (rather than, as a hundred years ago, to freedom). It was characteristic of the actual moment, Schmitt continued, that this turn presents itself as the establishment of

Ipsen was 25 years old when the Nazis seized power in 1933. Having published his *Dissertation* on *Widerruf gültiger Verwaltungsakte* in 1932, he handed in his *Habilitation* in 1936 and published it a year later (*Politik und Justiz. Das Problem der justizlosen Hoheitsakte*, n 87 above). In the same year, 1937, he was appointed *Dozent* [H Quaritsch, 'Hans Peter Ipsen zum Gedenken' (1998) 123 *Archiv des öffentlichen Rechts* 1, at 19: only in 1939] and joined the Nazi party on 1 May 1937 (according to a response by Ipsen, written in impeccable French, to a letter of 2 March 1960 from Professor Hames of the Faculté du Droit Comparé in Luxembourg; the letter – 'Prise de position au sujet de la lettre de la Faculté de Droit de l'Université Libre de Bruxelles du 27 Février 1960: mémoires, 12/11/1941–27/2/1960' HP Ipsen – Hambourg, 6/1960 – 22 p: dact – is being kept at the Studiecentrum Oorlog en hedendaagse Maatschappij, Wetstraat 155/2, B-1040 Brussel, België). He was appointed Professor in Hamburg on 9 February 1940. As Ipsen himself in the letter cited and G Nicolaysen ('Lebensbild Hans Peter Ipsen' in Fachbereich Rechtswissenschaft, ibid, 33, at 39) underlines, the local section of the National Socialist *Rechtswahrerbund* had resisted an earlier appointment. Still in 1940, the German Military Administration of Brussels appointed Ipsen Commissioner of the Colonial University of Antwerp and, subsequently, in May 1941, *Commissaire of the Université Libre de Bruxelles* – according to many reports of the German Military Administration, ... a Masonic, left-ist, anti-germanic institution. He was in charge when the University decided to close its doors rather than accept the appointment of 3 collaborators as professors. In 1945 Ipsen was dismissed from his professorial position by the military government of Hamburg, but soon, in December 1946, returned to his University position.

There is no mention of all this, not even of the subtitle of the *Habilitation*, in Rolf Stödter's *laudatio* in *Hamburg-Deutschland*-Europa. *Festschrift für Hans Peter Ipsen zum 70. Geburtstag* (Tübingen: Mohr, 1977) or in the (1998) 123 *Archiv des öffentlichen Rechts* memorial by Helmut Quaritsch. And indeed, an assessment of Ipsen's activities as a commissioner of the Free University of Brussels is not so easy. G Nicolaysen, 'Zu Leben und Werk' in Fachbereich Rechtswissenschaft (ed), ibid, 5, writes at 7 (my translation): 'When I applied for a position to work with Ipsen, he himself handed over to me in 1960 things that had been written on him, in Belgium and elsewhere ... Had I found anything compromising, I would not have accepted the position'. In his 'Lebensbild Hans Peter Ipsen', ibid, at 39 f. G Nicolaysen presents a more detailed defence of the activities in Belgium. The Belgium documents and publications, however, which Professor David Fraser from Sydney has made available to me, are not at all that favourable. In a publication for the Belgian Government Information Center in New York of 1947, 'Commissioner Ipsen of Hamburg University' is called 'a henchman of the Nazi party' ['The Universities under the Occupation', in J-A Goris (ed), *Belgium under Occupation* (Moretus Press); similarly in her assessment M-R Thielemans, 'Un commissaire allemand pour l'Université' in A Espy-Meyer, A Dierkens and F Scheelings (eds), 25.11.1941. *l'Université Libre de Bruxelles ferme ses portes* (Bruxelles: Archives de l'ULB, 1991), 25; see, also, H Liebrecht, *L'Université de Bruxelles et la guerre* (Brussels: La renaissance du livre, no year), esp at 35, 93]. In 1960, when Ipsen was invited to lecture in Luxembourg, a letter of Professor Hames of 2 March 1960 opined that 'cette nouvelle ... souleva une revolte'. In his response, Ipsen called the accusation that he was an ardent partisan of the Nazis 'absurd'.

This is a case of exemplary importance for two reasons. Our factual knowledge is imperfect. It could be improved, but, so I have been told by Sebastian Remus, *Dokumentar* for Military History in Freiburg i.Br., uncertainties are likely to remain. And even if we would find out more, how are we to assess Ipsen's political attitudes and his behaviour? What remains possible is to read what Ipsen has published. And then we see. His *Politik und Justiz* of 1937 is not just a comparative study. It is an analysis of the ideological and political background of the separation of powers ideas with a quite emphatic defence of Germany's New Order (esp at 200; see M Stolleis, *Geschichte des öffentlichen Rechts in Deutschland*, n 18 above, at 336–38). Among the acts that are to be removed from judicial Schutzpowers of review are (see his *Politik und Justiz* at 218): the 'Schutzhaftanordnung' (internment in a concentration camp); the 'Säuberung des Beamtentums' (cleansing of the Reich's civil service); the 'Reinigung der von der Deutschen Arbeitsfront beseitigten Gewerkschaften von politisch Unzuverlässigen' (cleansing of the trade unions). Nothing but a study in comparative 'law'? Ipsen clearly pays tribute to the political context that generated such ideas. Did he have to? Does it

the 'administrative state'.[93] This state, he added shortly before Hitler's seizure of power, was exposed to the influence of pluralist interests; it was out of this weakness that it penetrated ever more spheres of existence and hence became total in the 'quantitative' sense. This state was particularly strong, however, in that it used all new technical means to enhance its power.[94] Ernst Forsthoff seconded this:

> Under the Weimar constitution, the German state decayed because it became prey to social pluralism. This total state which has now become a reality cannot see the old executive power as sufficing. Now, alongside state officials, the *Berufsbeamtentum*, the 'commissar' enters in, not as a neutral but as a politically-motivated and decisive functionary, 'an exponent of political will'.[95] What applies internally no doubt has to apply all the more 'externally'.[96]

III.4. An Interim Observation

Carl Schmitt's *Großraum*, although loaded with state elements, remains internally empty. This discrepancy has its logic. The National Socialist vision of Europe, which sees a *Großraum* uniting racially-akin, fascist-led peoples from the North Cape to Sicily, and from Brittany to the Urals under German leadership, was not concerned with institutionalising any sort of economic, technical

make a difference that his study cites Jewish authors, as Nicolaysen emphasises (ibid, at 37)? At that point, our argument is again confronted with 'contextual' considerations: Ipsen could not, surely, be expected to give up his career. Perhaps, what he wrote can be read more benevolently and did not really reflect his inner beliefs anyway. Be that as it may, this much is sure: *Justiz und Politik* is a bad book. I am not aware of any theoretical and methodological standard which would provide us with a defence of the type of thinking presented in this *Habilitation*.

93 C Schmitt, *Legalität und Legitimität* (1932), cited from the reprint in idem, *Verfassungsrechtliche Aufsätze aus den Jahren 1924–1945. Materialien zu einer Verfassungslehre* (Berlin: Duncker & Humblot, 1973) 2nd edn, 265, 266; see the interpretation by JP McCormick, 'Identifying or Exploiting the Paradoxes of Constitutional Democracy? An Introduction to Carl Schmitt's *Legality and Legitimacy*' in C Schmitt, *Legality and Legitimacy* (Durham NC: Duke UP, 2004) xiii.

94 C Schmitt, 'Weiterentwicklung des totalen Staats in Deutschland', reprinted in idem, *Verfassungsrechtliche Aufsätze aus den Jahren 1924–1945*, n 93 above, 359, 361–65.

95 E Forsthoff, *Der totale Staat* (Hamburg: Hanseatische Verlagsanstalt, 1933) 28 and 36; see, also, E Forsthoff, 'Das neue Gesicht der Verwaltung und die Verwaltungsrechtswissenschaft' (1935) 5 *Deutsches Recht* 331; idem, 'Führung und Bürokratie – Einige grundsätzliche Erwägungen' (1935) 53 *Deutsches Adelsblatt* 1339.

96 For Forsthoff's further development after 1933, see E Forsthoff, 'Daseinsvorsorge als Aufgabe der modernen Verwaltung' in idem *Die Verwaltung als Leistungsträger* (Stuttgart-Berlin: Kohlhammer, 1938), partly reprinted in idem, *Rechtsfragen der leistenden Verwaltung* (Stuttgart: Kohlhammer, 1959) 23–34; Stolleis, *Geschichte, des öffentlichen Rechts in Deutschland*, vol 3, n 18 above, 352 f and 366; R Mehring, 'Epilogue. The Decline of Theory – Introduction' in Jacobson and Schlink (eds), *Weimar*, n 44 above, 313, 316 f; Pauly, n 9 above, 60, 70, 81 f and 98; on the continuity in Forsthoff's thinking, see V Neumann, 'Der harte Weg zum sanften Ziel. Ernst Forsthoffs Rechts- und Staatstheorie als Paradigma konservativer Technikkritik' in A Rossnagel (ed), *Recht und Tehnik im Spannungsfeld der Kernenergiekontroverse* (Opladen: Westdeutscher Verlag, 1984) 88; I Staff, 'Die Wahrung staatlicher Ordnung. Ein Beitrag zum technologischen Staat und seinen rechten Propheten Carl Schmitt und Ernst Forsthoff' (1987) 15 *Leviathan* 141, at 151; M Vec, 'Aushöhlung des Staates? Selbst-Normierung im Staat der Industriegesellschaft als historisches Problem' (2000) 19 *Rechtshistorisches Journal* 517.

or political rationality patterns. With the rupture that Schmitt's theory made with traditional international law, a second one went hand in hand: Schmitt was not capable of identifying, and his opponents did not even want to identify, the structures that would replace the autonomy which the sovereignty principle in international law had protected.

IV. THE RENEWAL OF THE FIRST LEGAL CULTURE IN THE INTEGRATION PROCESS

The European unification efforts that started with the 1950 Schuman Plan and led to the Treaty of Rome in 1957 meant a very deliberate overcoming of the racist imperialism of the Nazi regime. The situation differed radically from the one which existed after the First World War – both politically and academically. There had indeed, as Dreier notes, 'not been any noteworthy attempt at factual or legitimatory linkage back to the Third Reich, nor any substantive study of the further effects of National Socialist modes of thought in constitutional theory'.[97]

Nor were there any reservations, in principle, against the Basic Law's openness towards Europe. Instead, there were intensive debates about the legal nature of the European Economic Community, in which the representatives of *Staatsrecht* [constitutional law], of international law, of public international and of economic law took part.

IV.1. Focus

The histories of these discussions, which moved toward the twofold demarcation of the law of the European Economic Communities against international law, on the one hand, and *Staatsrecht* and constitutional law, on the other, thus establishing European law as an autonomous discipline, cannot, and need not, be retold in any detail here. The focus of the following section is on the continuities and discontinuities of legal concepts, on the necessity and difficulty to grasp a new situation conceptually, and, in so doing, to differentiate between discredited, undamaged and renewable elements of a complex legal heritage. The post-war situation of the young Federal Republic was very clear: democracy was to be established in the new polity. And, in addition, cooperation and trust were to be achieved with the former enemies (in the West). The German European law debate is marked by seeing the tensions between the integration process very early, on the one hand, and the political autonomy of the Member States, on the other, as a problem for the democracy that it had only just attained domestically, without on that account falling back into *völkisch* national nostalgias.

[97] Dreier, n 9 above, at 69.

Admittedly, this sort of openness towards Europe had, with a certain inevitability, or, at any rate, with striking historical 'logic', made the effort to mediate between democracy and integration in order to lead to the revival of the pre-democratic elements from Germany's 'first culture' in particular.

This was no easy task. As a reminder: all spheres of society – in the economy, technology, the administration – had been subjected to the leadership claim of National Socialist policy. This subjection was, after 1945, outdated in every conceivable sense. Yet the problems of the order of the economy, of the exposure of society to technological possibilities and necessities, and the difficulty of ensuring the political and social accountability of the administration did not resolve themselves with the disappearance of National Socialism. This was true domestically in the new republic (see below). And, paradoxically enough, it was the integration project in particular, which responded so convincingly to the militant past of the nation state, that was to give rise to new concerns about the legitimacy of European governance.

IV.2. Ordoliberalism, Organised Capitalism and the State of the Industrial Society

In his above-mentioned[98] studies on the recent history of private and economic law, Knut Wolfgang Nörr has described the history of the operation of the concepts of the 'organised economy' and the 'social market economy' under the Basic Law.[99] The so-called 'organised economy' – antitrust law was not to exist until 1958 – was the concept that (implicitly) prevailed in *Staatsrecht* and constitutional law: the inherited practices were, once again, tolerated or even promoted, this time by parliamentary majoritarian legislation, and hence understood as *ipso facto* constitutionally legitimate. In private law and economic law thinking, in contrast, ordoliberalism dominated, postulating that the ordinary legislator be bound by principles of a liberal, competitive market constitution.[100] Ordoliberalism became influential in practical political terms because – in contrast with its early form, which Hermann Heller had called 'authoritarian liberalism'[101] – it entered into an alliance with exponents of the new 'social market economy'.[102]

[98] N 52 above.

[99] *Die Republik der Wirtschaft*, n 52 above, 5.

[100] C Joerges, 'The Science of Private Law and the Nation-State' in F Snyder (ed), *The Europeanization of Law: The Legal Effects of European Integration* (Oxford: Hart Publishing, 2000) 47, at 51 (reprinted in pt II, ch 6 of this volume); see Nörr, *Die Republik der Wirtschaft*, n 52 above, at 58 and 81.

[101] N 61 above.

[102] See W Abelshauser, *Die Langen Fünfziger Jahre. Wirtschaft und Gesellschaft der Bundesrepublik Deutschland 1949–1966* (Düsseldorf: Schwan, 1987); Haselbach, n 56 above, at 117; Manow, n 54 above and n 58 above.

Carl Schmitt's gloomy vision of a 'strong state' and a 'healthy economy' had been left behind by each school of thought in its own way, without considerably irritating the praxis of politics with their theoretical queries and differences. The Federal Republic did both: it officiously cultivated ideas, conceptions and institutionalisations in the ordoliberal sense; at the same time, however, it displayed ideological indifference, in line with the mainstream view in public law, thus allowing legislative policy to come to terms with, or even re-establish, the patterns of the 'organised economy'. Nörr accordingly diagnoses

> a basic phenomenon in the history of the emergence of the Bonn Republic … [a] dual line, in economic policy and economic constitutional law [And] for the economic order that was to characterise the new State, we have even to talk about a dual *mise en scène*, two stagings of the same play that took no notice of one another.[103]

In Nörr's description, which concentrates on economic law, the position of Ernst Forsthoff is missing. It is interesting here not so much because of its importance for German administrative and constitutional law, but in the light of its transferability to the European context – and the continuity that marks Forsthoff's thinking. When, in 1933, Forsthoff welcomed 'the total state', it seemed to him, in all seriousness, a bulwark against the robberies of the 'societal pluralism' of the Weimar Republic.[104] This enthusiasm had already evaporated in the 1930s.[105] It is remarkable that Forsthoff, in his *Der Staat der Industriegesellschaft* [*The State of the Industrial Society*], referred to his early writings; and it was by no means post-war opportunism which motivated his characterisation of the control of the state by totalitarian political movements, a 'degeneration [*Entartung*] of the state'.[106] Even by 1938, Forsthoff had – quite in the style of conservative criticism of the 1920s[107] – in a seminal study which concentrated on the 'technicisation' of all relationships, found something which he complained of, yet also placed hopes in for taming the demon of the political: it was a consequence of 'industrial and technical development' and the associated 'mass forms of life' that 'modern man' could enhance his 'effective living area' and, at the same time, fall into new 'social need'.[108]

> The measures taken to meet appropriation needs, I call *Daseinsfürsorge* ['provision of subsistence'][109] existential security … The responsibility for meeting these appropriation needs, I call *Daseinsverantwortung* [individual responsibility for one's subsistence].[110]

[103] Nörr, *Die Republik der Wirtschaft*, n 52 above,84.
[104] Forsthoff, *Der totale Staat*, n 95 above, 28.
[105] Nn 95–96 above.
[106] E Forsthoff, Der Staat der Industriegesellschaft. Dargestellt am Beispiel der Bundesrepublik Deutschland (Munich: CH Beck, 1971) 53.
[107] N 95 above.
[108] Forsthoff, 'Daseinsvorsorge', n 96 above, 25, 32; see the analysis by Neumann, n 90 above.
[109] On the origin of this term, see Pauly, n 9 above, 98 and 114.
[110] 'Daseinsvorsorge', n 96 above, 26.

Forsthoff thus established existential security as a sort of fact of the matter of life, not as such up for disposal. Accordingly, in the post-war debate on the social state clause in Article 20 (1) of the Basic Law, he was able to classify social matters as belonging to an extra-constitutional realm, a factual sphere 'driven and determined to the utmost by social impulses'; it was these constraints which forced politics, legislation and the administration into supplementing the *Rechtsstaat* by material content, namely, the social state.[111]

The same type of argument, which guided his understanding of the social dimension of the modern state [*soziale Realisation*], he now used in his analyses of 'technical realisation' [*technische Realisation*]. Just as Carl Schmitt had demonised 'technicity' in his Barcelona lecture of 1929,[112] Forsthoff perceived a freedom-threatening potential inherent in the technical processes. The frontlines were still the same:[113] '[I]mmediately after taking power, Bolshevism had identified itself with technology', Forsthoff explained in an accompanying essay; but the 'free state, too, will have a partial identification with technology forced on it through the conditions of the technical process'.[114] All this had led to the point where 'technical and proper decisions' could often be taken only in ever-decreasing circles that possessed the necessary 'technical knowledge', while government and administration could no longer be controlled by the 'rule of law normative system'.[115] 'This is the situation that the politicians have not yet understood, and is beyond the horizon of contemporary legal thought that has shrunk down from *Staatsrechts*-science to *Rechtsstaats*-science operating inside its normative cage.'[116]

If such notions may have gone beyond the normative horizon of *Rechtsstaats*-science, Forsthoff was by no means alone here. We find similarly, for instance, in Helmut Schelsky:

> [P]olitical norms and laws are replaced by the objective regularities of the scientific and technical civilization ... which cannot be taken as political decisions and are not comprehensible as philosophical or ideological norms.[117]

[111] E Forsthoff, 'Begriff und Wesen des sozialen Rechtsstaats' (1954) 12 *Veröffentlichungen der Vereinigung der Deutschen Staatsrechtslehrer* 8, at 24, 29 and 31.

[112] N 78 above.

[113] Ibid, at 120.

[114] E Forsthoff, 'Technischer Prozess und politische Ordnung' (1969) 22 *Studium Generale* 849, at 852;WE Scheuerman, 'Unsolved Paradoxes: Conservative Political Thought in Adenauer's Germany' in JP McCormick (ed), *Mass Democracy and Industrial Technology. Political and Social Theory from Nietzsche to Habermas* (Durham NC–London: Duke UP, 2002) 221, at 228.

[115] N 106 above, 84, 105 and 158.

[116] Ibid, 46.

[117] H Schelsky, *Der Mensch in der wissenschaftlichen Zivilisation* (Cologne–Opladen: Westdeutscher Verlag, 1961) (reprinted in idem, *Auf der Suche nach Wirklichkeit. Gesammelte Aufsätze* (Düsseldorf: Diederichs, 1964), at 453.

In the middle of the so-called technocracy debate, the 'technicity' tradition was markedly prevalent.[118]

The technocracy debate did not concern itself with Europe. Forsthoff saw very well that 'the technical process' had burst the bounds of the state and was not to be controlled domestically. It was, then, 'not wrong' to think about the development of an 'international organisation', 'able to accompany the further course of the technical process as an effective guardian of humanity'.[119] Forsthoff did not reveal the source of these so unexpectedly sown hopes for humanity. He apparently took scarcely any account of the EEC; but the conceptual apparatus which he employed was, nonetheless, to become important in that new sphere.

IV.3. The Heritage of the German Tradition in Europe

In ordoliberalism and Forsthoff's theory of the industrial society, two concepts which promised to master the tensions between the democracy principle and the integration project were available. The ordoliberal school saw this very early. The freedoms guaranteed in the EEC treaty, the order of the national economies, the bans on discrimination and the competition rules, were understood as a common decision for an economic constitution that went to meet the ordoliberal concepts of the framework conditions for a market economy system (if only the many departures from that model were treated as mere exceptions, and a blind eye could be turned to the original sin of agricultural policy). And the very fact that Europe had started its integrationist path as a mere economic community lent plausibility to ordoliberal arguments: the Community acquired a legitimacy of its own by interpreting the economic-law provisions of the European Community as a law-based order committed to guaranteeing economic freedoms. This legitimacy was independent of the state's democratic constitutional institutions and thus placed limits upon the political powers of the Community.[120]

Yet, despite its orientation as an economic community, Europe fell within the disciplinary confines of public law. The concept of a supranational system of economic law that binds sovereign constitutional States was not exactly current in international law or *Staatsrecht* and constitutional law.[121] Nonetheless,

[118] For a famous contemporary critique, see J Habermas, 'Technik und Wissenschaft als "Ideologie"' in idem, *Technik und Wissenschaft als 'Ideologie'* (Frankfurt aM: Suhrkamp, 1968) 48.

[119] N 106 above, 169.

[120] Significant here is A Müller-Armack, 'Die Wirtschaftsordnung des Gemeinsamen Marktes' in idem, *Wirtschaftsordnung und Wirtschaftspolitik* (Freiburg: Rombach, 1966) 401; for a comprehensive account, see W Mussler, *Die Wirtschaftsverfassung der Europäischen Gemeinschaft im Wandel. Von Rom nach Masstricht* (Baden-Baden: Nomos, 1998) 94 ff and 113 ff.

[121] See C Joerges, 'Vorüberlegungen zu einer Theorie des Internationalen Wirtschaftsrechts' (1979) 43 *Rabels Zeitschrift für ausländisches und internationales Privatrecht* 6.

someone as close to Carl Schmitt as Joseph H Kaiser was able to take up the *maître-penseur*'s vague references to the triad of *Großraum* economy, technology and administration in order to categorise European public power in Forsthoff's sense as factually adequate and expedient, and entrust it to 'socially independent intelligence' [*einer sozial freischwebenden Intelligenz*].[122]

Similar statements can be found even earlier.[123] They were, however, deployed most fundamentally and systematically by Hans Peter Ipsen (first probably in 1964) in terming the (three) European communities 'purposive associations of functional integration' [*Zweckverbände funktionaler Integration*]. The concept 'purposive association' opened up Community law to tasks that had no place in an ordoliberal world – without exposing it, on that account, to democratic requirements. As a purposive association, Europe was to deal with questions of 'technical realisation', ie, with administrative tasks that could be – and had to be – conveyed to a supranational bureaucracy.[124]

How thoroughly thought-out the conception was can be seen in the very fact that Ipsen decisively differed from Forsthoff in his understanding of the Basic Law.[125] While wishing to root technocratic rationality in the EEC, at the same time he wanted to restrict its sphere of action: the Communities were to confine themselves to administering questions of 'knowledge', but leave truly 'political' questions to democratic and legitimated bodies.[126] With his theory of the purposive association, Ipsen rejected both further-reaching federal integration notions and earlier interpretations of the Community as a mere international organisation.[127] He saw Community law as a *tertium* between (federal) state law and international law, constituted by its 'objective tasks' and adequately legitimised by their solution.[128]

[122] JH Kaiser, 'Bewa hrung und Veränderung demokratischer und rechtsstaatlicher Verfassungsstruktur in den internationalen Gemeinscahften' (1966) 23 *Veröffentlichungen der Vereinigung der Deutschen Staatsrechtslehrer* 1, at 28 and 23.

[123] H Bülck, 'Zur Systematik der Europäischen Wirtschaftsgemeinschaften' (1959) 6 *Berichte der Deutschen Gesellschaft für Völkerrecht* 66, at 105 ff.

[124] Ipsen, *Europäisches Gemeinschaftsrecht*, n 92 above, 176.

[125] See, only, HP Ipsen, *Über das Grundgesetz* (Hamburg: 1950) reprinted in E Forsthoff (ed), *Rechtsstaatlichkeit und Sozialstaatlichkeit* (Darmstadt: Wissenschaftliche Buchgesellschaft, 1968) 16, on the one hand; Forsthoff, 'Begriff und Wesen des sozialen Rechtsstaats', n 111 above, 9 f, 28 and 32, on the other.

[126] *Europäisches Gemeinschaftsrecht*, n 92 above, 1045.

[127] Ipsen's famous 'Bensheim lecture', n 92 above, and idem, 'Der deutsche Jurist und das europäische Gemeinschaftsrecht' (1964) *Verhandlungen des 43. Deutschen Juristentages*, vol 2, pt L, 3 (Munich: CH Beck); idem, *Verfassungsperspektiven der Europäischen Gemeinschaften* (Berlin: de Gruyter, 1970).

[128] Ipsen, *Verfassungsperspektiven*, n 127 above, 8, and the interpretation by M Kaufmann, *Europäische Integration und Demokratieprinzip* (Baden-Baden: Nomos, 1997) 300 ff; see, also, M Bach, *Die Bürokratisierung Europas. Verwaltungseliten, Experten und politische Legitimation in Europa* (Frankfurt aM: Campus, 1999) 38.

IV.4. Concluding Remarks

Ordoliberalism and functionalism promised answers to the European legitimation dilemma which do without parliamentary democratic affirmation in the sense of the national constitutional state. Both conceptions had their *fundamentum in re*. They offered not just abstract legal doctrinal interpretations, but rationality criteria that could be institutionalised and applied in practice. Neither of these approaches needed to hide; on the contrary, in the total gamut of the contemporary debate, they represent exceptional achievements, not least because they faced the challenges inherent in the EEC's *Sonderweg* beyond international law and domestic legal systems. Both of them perceived and justified a new form of supranational governance that could not have been adequately legitimised by referring to the assent of the governments of the Member States alone even under the unanimity rule. Both positions have, also, to be sure, to see their limits. Here, the continuity with pre-democratic heritages of German legal culture is striking, but that, after all, is not very surprising. Ironically and fortunately, it is the successes of the European project that fundamentally challenge those traditions: Europe has developed in such a way that it needs a constitution that structures and legitimises its politics. If this constitution cannot copy those of nation-state democracies, this does not mean it has to content itself with inherited alternatives.

33

Working through 'Bitter Experiences' towards a Purified European Identity? A Critique of the Disregard for History in European Constitutional Theory and Practice*

INTRODUCTION: TWO INTER-DEPENDENT THESES

My contribution oscillates between two poles or aspirations. The first is to present reflections on the constitutionalisation process, which comprise both Europe's accomplishments and its performance in the light of a specific theoretical perspective, namely, the deliberative strand of theories of democracy. However, my objective in this respect is not to enrich this theoretical debate. Instead, I will focus on the transformation of theoretical deliberation into *legal* concepts, and suggest that conflict of laws would provide the proper legal form for the constitutionalisation of Europe. The second pole is complementary. Its main message is stated in the title: European Constitutionalism and the Convention both failed to pay proper regard to the weight of history when embarking on the adventure of writing a European Constitution. Neither the weight nor the differences of European historical experiences and memories have been taken into account. These experiences, especially in the twentieth century, were 'bitter', if not traumatic – albeit in different ways and to different degrees. In the case of Germany, the most appropriate term to capture its specific situation may be found in

* German Original ('Unitas in Pluralitate als Verfassungsauftrag: Plädoyer für einen "horizontalen Konstitutionalismus"' in C Joerges, M Mahlmann and UK Preuß (eds), *"Schmerzliche Erfahrungen" der Vergangenheit und der Prozess der Konstitutionalisierung Europas – Rechts-, Geschichts- und Politikwissenschaftliche Beiträge* (Wiesbaden: Verlag für Sozialwissenschaften, 2008) 26; translated by IL Fraser, EUI Florence.

Bernhard Schlink's '*Vergangenheitsschuld*'.[1] This notion is a construction with two components, which, through their conflation, exhibit a specific tension. The importance of the first element of the term – *Vergangenheit*, or the past – is simply obvious. Ideas about European unity are old. But the integration process that we are experiencing and studying was initiated after, and under the impact of, the Second World War. The remnants of this past have been engraved in the design of Europe, and thus remain 'somehow' present in the European Union (EU), even after, or especially because of, its enlargement. To put it even more strongly, we cannot understand what is happening in the EU, nor what we are doing and what we are achieving or failing to achieve, unless we bring to mind the meaning of institutional changes, legal commitments, and political processes and aspirations, within historical perspectives. It seems equally obvious, for a German at least, to qualify this past with the second component of Schlink's term, ie, first and foremost, with German guilt and the 'bitter experiences' related to it.[2] The conflation of the two components in Schlink's term produces a tension which the term '*Gedächtnispolitik*', the politics of memory, captures quite well.

My thesis that important links exist between the two poles of this essay – European constitutionalism and European historical experiences – is not just a reflection upon Europe's bellicose past and the Holocaust. Historical conflicts both between European nation states and within European societies are present in all important areas affected by the integration process. This essay will briefly address two of them, namely, the debate on Europe's 'social model' and European citizenship. Again, the message will be a critical one: European constitutionalism has not taken into account the weight of historical experiences in Europe's present and the weight of memory politics in contested political issues.

All of these references to history and the insistence that European constitutionalism should regain a historical consciousness should not be read as a

[1] B Schlink, *Vergangenheitsschuld und gegenwärtiges Recht* (Frankfurt aM: Suhrkamp, 2002); the essays in Schlink's collection deal mainly, but not exclusively, with the assessment of wrongdoing in criminal law proceedings in the past. But see, for the present context in particular, 'Die Gegenwart der Vergangenheit' ['The Presence of the Past'], ibid, at 145.

[2] I am referring neither to personal guilt, nor to the moral 'duty to remember', but to something factual which social psychology and trauma research will be able to decipher. Suffice it to quote from one of Habermas' pertinent essays: 'Aber liegt nicht seit jener moralischen Katastrophe, in abgeschwächter Weise, auf unserer aller Überleben der Fluch des bloßen Davongekommensein? Und begründet nicht die Zufälligkeit des unverdienten Entrinnens eine intersubjektive Haftung – eine Haftung für entstellte Lebenszusammenhänge, die das Glück oder auch die bloße Existenz der einer einzig un den Preis des vernichteten Glücks, des vorenthaltenen Lebens und des Leidens der anderen einräumen?' J Habermas, 'Geschichtsbewußtsein und nationale Identität: Die Westorientierung der Bundesrepublik' in idem, *Eine Art Schadensabwicklung* (Frankfurt aM: Suhrkamp, 1987) 162, at 164 [Habermas, at times, and especially when it comes to the German past, is writing very personally. Suffice it therefore to indicate that he is reflecting upon how the trauma of the Holocaust affects the self-consciousness of the later generations.]

purely negative critique. This critique also has a positive side. It may be best submitted as a bold and daring thesis: Europe should, by working through its past(s), renew and deepen its *acquis historique*; it may, in such processes, not only obtain or acquire a better understanding of topical and contested issues of 'the integration project', but also renew the legitimacy and even the dignity of the integration project as such.

I. THEORETICAL FRAMEWORK: HOW DO HISTORY AND LAW INTERACT?

It seems so obvious that the argument should not, and indeed does not, need any authoritative support. Nonetheless, I start with a well-known passage from Jürgen Habermas' contribution to the *Historikerstreit*:

> Our form of life is connected with that of our parents and grandparents through a web of familial, local, political, and intellectual traditions that is difficult to disentangle – that is, through a historical milieu that made us what and who we are today. None of us can escape this milieu, because our identities, both as individuals and as Germans, are indissolubly interwoven with it. This holds true from mimicry and physical gestures to language and into the capillary ramifications of one's intellectual stance ... we have to stand by our traditions, then, if we do not want to disavow ourselves ...[3]

This is the personal dimension. Its political complement was written out in the Habermas/Derrida manifesto published in the *Frankfurter Allgemeine Zeitung* of 31 May 2003:

> Contemporary Europe has been shaped by the experiences of the totalitarian regimes of the twentieth century and through the Holocaust – the persecution and annihilation of European Jews, in which the Nazi regime made the societies of the conquered countries complicit as well ...
>
> A bellicose past once entangled all European nations in bloody conflicts. They drew a conclusion from that military and spiritual mobilisation against one another: the imperative of developing new, supranational forms of co-operation after the Second World War.[4]

These statements will not provoke much opposition. But the constellations to which they refer have not had much impact on my profession. This may seem surprising, it may be uncomfortable and difficult to explain, but it is a fact.[5]

[3] J Habermas, 'On the Public Use of History' in idem, *The New Conservatism* (Cambridge MA: The MIT Press, 1990) 233.

[4] Cited from the translation in J Habermas and J Derrida, 'February 15, or What Binds Europeans Together: A Plea for a Common Foreign Policy, Beginning in the Core of Europe' (2003) 10 *Constellations* 291, at 296.

[5] See, for an instructive recent overview, T Keiser, 'Europeanization as a Challenge to Legal History' (2005) 6 *German Law Journal* 473, available at: www.germanlawjournal.com.

There is little explicit reflection by lawyers and legal historians on the shadows of the past in institutionalised Europe in legal history, not even in contemporary legal history.[6] This is not to say that legal historians are not ready to confront the law's 'darker legacy'. They may be accused of having avoided this topic for too long. But this avoidance has been over for some decades now, especially in Germany. It would, of course, be absurd to accuse them of ignoring European history altogether. Quite to the contrary, Thorsten Keiser recently observed that Europe has attracted much attention since the Treaty of Maastricht, and has, with the Convention process, become 'one of the most important reference points of legal historical research'.[7] The primary effort of pertinent studies in the fields of private law is, however, to reveal a common cultural heritage which, in the past, is said to have formed the basis of an *ius commune europaeum*, and which can now be revitalised in the search for legal unity. The equivalent in public law has been revealed by Felix Hanschmann.[8] Leading exponents of German constitutional thought, such as Josef Isensee[9] and Paul Kirchhof,[10]

[6] Such a statement requires qualification. There is a new sensitivity for the differences in the perception and evaluation of the integration project in the European '*demoi*-cracy'; see, in particular, J Lacrois and K Nicolaïdes (eds), *European Stories: Intellectual debates on Europe in National Contexts* (Oxford: OUP, 2010). Furthermore, there are, of course, important contributions to a historical interpretation of Europe in the legal literature on European integration. Suffice it to mention here JHH Weiler [from 'The Community System: The Dual Character of Supranationalism' (1981) 1 *Yearbook of European Law* 267 to *The Constitution of Europe: 'Do the New Clothes Have an Emperor' and Other Essays on European Integration* (Cambridge: CUP, 1999)]; M Kaufmann, *Europäische Integration und Demokratieprinzip* (Baden-Baden: Nomos, 1997); A von Bogdandy, 'A Bird's Eye View on the Science of European Law' (2000) 6 *ELJ* 208; A Somek, 'Constitutional Erinnerungsarbeit: Ambivalence and Translation' (2005) 6 *German Law Journal* 357, with references to his much more comprehensive work; U Haltern, *Europarecht und das Politische* Tübingen, Mohr/Siebeck, 2005); see also U Haltern, 'Europäische Verfassung und europäische Identiät' in R Elm (ed), *Europäische Identität: Paradigmen und Methodenfragen* (Baden-Baden: Nomos, 2002) 239, at 252–261. Haltern's contribution is the most systematic and comprehensive. It also reflects most explicitly on the linkages between theorising Europe, re-constructing it historiographically and determining the potential role of law as '*Sinnsprecher*' (instantiation). My reservations against his effort to understand law and integration in the light of the essence of the political will, reason and interest, which Haltern employs [see, also, his 'Pathos and Patina – The Failure and Promise of Constitutionalism in the European Imagination' (2003) 9 *ELJ* 14] would not enable me to address the law's darker legacy. In a nutshell, I am not troubled at all by a lack of the element of 'political will' in institutionalised Europe, but I am, instead, concerned with the complacency of constitutionalists. No rule is without exceptions, however; a notable one is C Closa, 'Dealing with the Past: Memory and European Integration', *New York, Jean Monnet Working Paper 01/11*, available at: www.JeanMonnetProgram.org.

[7] Keiser, n 5 above.

[8] F Hanschmann, '"A Community of History": A Problematic Concept and its Usage in Constitutional Law and Community Law' (2005) 6 *German Law Journal* 1129; German original, '"Geschichtsgemeinschaft": Ein problematischer Begriff und seine Verwendung im staats- und Europarecht' (2004) 5 *Rechtsgeschichte* 150.

[9] J Isensee, 'Abschied der Demokratie vom Demos' in D Schwab et al (eds), *Staat, Kirche, Wissenschaft in einer pluralistischen Gesellschaft.Festschrift für Paul Mikat* (Berlin: Duncker & Humbolt, 1989) 705.

[10] P Kirchhof, 'Europäische Einigung und der Verfassungsstaat der Bundesrepublik Deutschland' in J Isensee (ed), *Europa als politische Idee und als rechtliche Form* (Berlin: Duncker & Humblot, 1993) 63.

invoke a cultural communality of historical experience, which is now to become the bearer of a common polity upon the basis of which a united Europe can be, and indeed should be, constituted.

These latter positions contrast drastically with the theoretical assumptions which prevail in general historical research.[11] Not surprisingly, they are also much richer and differentiated. Historians began early[12] and continue to explore the integration process, including its institutionalisation in all its details. The intensity of the historical research into World War II, the Third Reich and the Holocaust is simply breathtaking. In addition, historical investigations which interpret the history of the integration process in the light or the shadow of European crises and failures are both available and meet with considerable interest.[13] And yet, concerns that are, indeed, very similar to my own personal uneasiness with contemporary legal history are being articulated.[14] Historians have not taken sufficient note of the diversity in Europe's historical memories, complains Konrad H Jarausch.[15] Not being a historian, I cite once more:

> Europe did possess a vague sense of cultural commonality before 1914, but that did almost disappear during the two world wars. The dominant languages such as Latin, French, and later English, and, in a regional sense also German, provided a communication medium for the educated élites. The social origin and intermarriage of the aristocracy or commercial bourgeoisie was another bond. The intensity of economic exchanges created a sense of togetherness. During imperialism, the issue of race also played a role by defining European simply as white. … The rise of nationalism, the fierce hostility of World War I, the destruction of the Central and East European Empires in the suburban Paris treaties of 1919, the breakdown of trade, the repetition of the War in 1939, etc, practically destroyed this sense of cohesion …
>
> After World War II, some residual feeling of cultural affinity grew from below and was promoted by specific sectors of the European population. The common suffering of war and oppression by the Nazis animated members of the resistance movements; the shared project of restoring cultural monuments and reviving high culture called for a degree of co-operation; moreover, the eclipse of European power led to a joint defensiveness against popularising cultural influences from America or ideological

[11] See the references in Hanschmann, n 8 above, especially fnn 47 et seq; see, also, B Stråth, 'Methodological and Substantive Remarks on Myth, Memory and History in the Construction of a European Community' (2005) 6 *German Law Journal* 255.

[12] See, in particular, W Lipgens, *A History of European Integration* (Oxford: Clarendon Press, 1982).

[13] See, for example, M Mazower, *Dark Continent: Europe's Twentieth Century* (London: Penguin, 1998).

[14] KH Jarausch, 'Zeitgeschichte zwischen Nation und Europa. Eine transnationale Herausforderung' (2012) *Historical Social Research*, Supplement 24, 313.

[15] 'Die Überwölbung eines Ensembles von disparaten Nationalgeschichten bleibt ebenso unbefriedigeng wie die teleologischen Anstrengung, das aufklärerische und liberal-demokratische Erbe Europas herauszustellen, oder das Bemühen, die gegenwärtigen Integrationsversuche in die Vergangenheit vor 1945 zurückzuprojizieren. Gerade weil Erkenntnisinteressen, Wertbezüge und europäischen Geschichte gänzlich unvermeidlich.' See, also, Stråth, n 11 above.

> subversion from the Soviet Union. But, in spite of similar social patterns ..., the nation-states were not so damaged that they did not make a come-back and culture remained organised on a national level ...
>
> Powerful factors have continued to limit the emergence of a European cultural identity.[16]

How to cope with cultural diversity and divergent historical memories: this seems to be the challenge that Europe is facing. Is it necessary to underline the importance of this point after enlargement? Not only did the accession countries from Central and Eastern Europe have their own national pasts, they also had other reasons for wishing to join the founding nations; last but not least, they were not involved in the writing of institutionalised Europe's '*acquis historique*'.[17]

Historians will respond to these challenges. We can even assume that, sooner or later, legal historians will listen and talk to their neighbouring discipline. At present, however, it is impossible to anticipate such developments. But it is all the more important to reflect, at the very least, on the methodological difficulties of an integration of Europe's pasts into our understanding of institutionalised Europe and European law. None other than Reinhard Koselleck dealt with this relationship between 'History, Law and Justice' some 20 years ago when addressing the German Legal Historians, albeit at a very general level.[18] Historians, Koselleck argues, have traditionally acted quite openly like judges in their accounts of history. Although they have become conscious of this role and sought to define their accounts more cautiously and subtly, they cannot avoid talking, explicitly or implicitly, about the justice or injustice of situations, changes or catastrophes.[19] There is a link between history, legal history and law. However, there is also a fundamental difference in the approaches of historians and legal historians. Inherent in the category of law is the *telos* of repeated application, which requires respect for formalism (Koselleck: 'the maximum of formalism') because the law has to ensure that its principles, procedures and rules all transcend the individual case. In their analyses of the preparation and adoption of legislative acts, the approaches of lawyers and historians are remarkably similar. However, when it comes to the study of the development of the enactment, the legal historian has to respect the law's *proprium*.[20]

This is all quite abstract, but it is, nevertheless, helpful, because it makes us aware of what is bound to happen once political processes end with a juridical

[16] KH Jarausch, 'A European Cultural Identity: Reality or Hope?', typescript Potsdam 2004 (on file with the author).

[17] See, on this latter point, F Larat, 'Present-ing the Past: Political Narratives on European History and the Justification of EU Integration' (2005) 6 *German Law Journal* 273.

[18] R Koselleck, 'Geschichte, Recht und Gerechtigkeit' in D Simon (ed), *Akten des 26. Deutschen Rechthistorikertages* (Frankfurt aM: Klostermann, 1987) 139, cited from the reprint in idem, *Zeitgeschichten. Studien zur Historik* (Frankfurt aM: Suhrkamp, 2000) 336.

[19] Ibid, 349.

[20] Ibid, 352.

act. It is not just that lawyers, as they did with the Draft Constitutional Treaty (DCT) in so many books, start to apply their methods of interpretation to the text that they received. They will also project their understanding of the meaning of the political sphere into their interpretations, and will bring their visions of the social functions of law and of its normative aspirations to bear. The case of the European Economic Community is particularly illustrative here. What, 'legal speaking', was new and promising in this Treaty? What kind of commitments had the signatories accepted? What kind of post-national legitimacy could the new entity claim? How could the rule of law in the European Community be strengthened? In his account of the European Community's *raison d'être*, Joseph Weiler has famously and convincingly underlined three rationales: Europe was about ensuring peace, promoting prosperity and overcoming discrimination on grounds of nationality.[21] These are all lessons that Europeans had learned from their pasts. The importance of both their 'juridification' in the Treaty and their subsequent implementation cannot be over-estimated. And yet, they are by no means sufficiently substantiated to document some comprehensive 'unity' or to exclude fundamental disagreements about the ends of the Community, about its legitimacy and its *finalité*. A comprehensive legal history informing us about the different national ways to write European law is still to be written. It is in Germany alone that we can identify at least three schools of thought, each of which promotes its own distinct vision in democratic positivism, functionalism and ordoliberalism.[22] This diversity would certainly become much richer through the inclusion of more legal traditions. And such an exercise could inform us about both the law's and the EU's capacity to live with pluralism and diversity.

II. *UNITAS IN PLURALITATE*

If legal scholarship has invested so little, what can we expect from Intergovernmental Conferences and even from the Convention? I am not aware of any analysis of the use of history and of memory politics in the Convention process.[23] Just one text element refers explicitly to the past, namely,

[21] JHH Weiler, 'Fin-de-siècle Europe: Do the New Clothes Have an Emperor' in idem, *The Constitution of Europe*, n 6 above, subtly commented on by Z Bankowski, 'The Journey of the European Ideal' in A Nortan and J Francis (eds), *A Europe of Neighbours? Religious Social Thought and the Reshaping of a Pluralist Europe* (Edinburgh: Centre for Theology and Public Issues, 1999) 149.

[22] See C Joerges, 'What is Left of the European Economic Constitution? A Melancholic Eulogy' (2005) 30 *ELR* 461. Even with national communities, the perceptions of what is noteworthy differ considerably. Ordo-liberalism, in my view, the intellectually most interesting and practically most influential German contribution to European law, is not part of the mindset of the general German European law scholarship.

[23] So much has been done – the review essay by Martin Große Hüttman, 'Das Experiment einer europäischen Verfassung' (2005) 28 *Integration* 262, presents six German language volumes – that I may easily have overlooked pertinent efforts.

the Preamble.[24] This was, in the original version of the Convention, a quite euphemistic document. But, at the very end of the whole process, in June 2004, the Intergovernmental Conference, following a Polish initiative, changed the Preamble quite considerably. The first two, somewhat ostentatious, passages were dropped, and the reference to 're-united Europe' was replaced by a 'Europe, re-united after bitter experiences'.

II.1. Constitutionalisation

One could have imagined a more substantiated reference. The 'bitter experiences' are simply copied from the Preamble to the Polish Constitution.[25] Poland, indeed, had particularly bitter experiences, and this notion will have very clear connotations. But what is their meaning in the ensemble of 27 Member States? More important, perhaps, and certainly painful, the formula can be read as comprising the suffering of European nations. Might it comprise German suffering? But why is there no mention of 'the persecution and extermination of the European Jews, in which the Nazi regime also involved the societies of the countries they had conquered'?[26] There is neither an official interpretation available, nor can one detect traces of discussions, let alone controversies, of Europe's 'bitter experiences'. This seems to be shaming enough. The intergovernmental silence may even be telling in a specifically political way. The revised Preamble seems to present what Germans call a *Verschlimmbesserung*: an improvement, in that it no longer just documents European pride, and a worsening, in that it documents self-pity, instead of shame and guilt. It continues to do what Tony Judt analyses so intriguingly and movingly in the Epilogue of his recent *Postwar* as a pan-European style of *Vergangenheitsbewältigung*.[27] It does what the Germans have done [and still do] for decades after the war, namely, to forget about their former citizens. It does what the Western Europeans have done, namely, to remember their liberation from the occupier, but to forget about their own involvement; and it does not liberate Eastern Europeans from the perverse interpretation of exterminative racism as a machination of capitalism. What a self-deception! We must not infer from the absence of the darkest side of our past in the official constitutional agenda that we have escaped from its shadows.

[24] For the text, see OJ C 310/2004, 1 of 16 December 2004, also available at: http://european-convention.eu.int. For an instructive analysis, see A von Bogdandy, 'Europäische Verfassung und europäische Identität' (2004) 59 *Juristen Zeitung* 53, especially at 55 ff; for a brief synopsis of the preambles to the different versions of the European Treaties, see Larat, n 17 above.

[25] Which reads: 'Mindful of the bitter experiences of the times when fundamental freedoms and human rights were violated in our Homeland …'

[26] Thus, Habermas and Derrida, n 4 above.

[27] T Judt, *Postwar: A History of Europe since 1945* (New York: Penguin, 2005) 803.

The real challenge, we concluded in our introductory observations, is the challenge of European diversity. How to accomplish 'unity in diversity' (*unitas in pluralitate*), the motto of the EU according to Article IV-1 of the DCT? Nicolaus Cusanus operated with his *coincidentia oppositorum* in a framework that too few Europeans understand. And, in the context of the Convention Process, we have certainly to ask how the Union's motto might be transformed into law? The answer submitted in the next section is this: through an understanding of European law as a new species of conflict of laws. This suggestion, it is submitted, is not only an appropriate response to the diversity of European pasts, but is also, as will be argued, the one most compatible with the state of the EU. It is a specifically *legal* conceptualisation which is, of course, not meant to replace theoretical and philosophical efforts to define the vocation of European integration.

In the presentation of my version of European constitutionalism, I have to refrain from any systematic appraisal of the plethora of suggestions that have been submitted during the last two decades (or previously). To prepare my own argument, it is sufficient to focus on just one learned sceptic, namely, Dieter Grimm, who has continuously and consistently defended the notion of constitutionalism against its transposition into Europe's post-national constellation. Pertinent suggestions, Grimm warns, are all at odds with the important functions which we are expecting the constitutions of democratic polities to serve. To cite from Grimm's lucid recent summary of his argument:[28]

> [The constitution] constitutes the public power of a society ...[29]
>
> People expect the constitution to unify their society as a polity ... The constitution is regarded as a guarantee of the fundamental consensus that is necessary for social cohesion.[30]

But here the law ends:

> Integration as a collective mental process cannot even be ordered by law.[31]

What cannot be guaranteed through constitutions within the nation state is unlikely to occur within the Union.[32] Here, an empirical observations comes in. The legitimacy of the EU, in the traditional Weberian sense, is eroding. What the proponents of the European constitution assume is that it will help to compensate for these failures and will foster social integration. This, however, is unlikely to happen; indeed, as we can say by now, this assumption has already proved to be erroneous.

[28] D Grimm, 'Integration by Constitution' (2005) 3 *International Journal of Constitutional Law* 193; for an update, see idem, 'The Achievement of Constitutionalism and its Prospects in a Changed World' in P Dobner and M Loughlin (eds), *The Twilight of Constitutionalism* (Oxford: OUP, 2010) 3.

[29] Grimm, 'Integration by Constitution', n 28 above, 194.

[30] Ibid, 194.

[31] Ibid, 196.

[32] Ibid, 197.

Grimm's argument insists both fairly and coherently on the specifics of constitutional law in democratic societies. He could have, following Giandomenico Majone's example,[33] pointed to 'Occam's razor' which prescribes 'not to introduce new terms unless they actually improve our understanding of the processes and phenomena under investigation' and *vice versa*: the Constitutional Treaty is, legally speaking, a treaty. It could not mutate through some *fiat* of the Convention. It did not transform into anything other than an intergovernmental act. There is no good reason, Grimm concludes, for any conceptual camouflage.

The argument is correct – and yet it remains somehow unconvincing. It is certainly important to remember that the 'juridification' of democracy was achieved in nation states, and that we must not equate transnational entities, including the EU, with states or fully-fledged federations. But this *caveat* does not tell us how to respond to post-national constellations. The quest for the constitutionalisation of the EU and for a cure to its 'democracy deficit' reflects the erosion of nation-state governance, the emergence of transnational governance – and the quest for its legitimation. To rephrase this concern, Grimm asks us to adhere to our inherited dichotomy of national constitutional law and international treaty law, assuming that the entrance into the post-national constellation is legally insignificant. Grimm, of course, does much to turn this assumption into a normatively and sociologically substantiated argument. What he fails to do, however, is to explore alternatives to the type of legitimacy that statal constitutional law provides, and to address the transnational deficiencies of that law. Europeanisation and globalisation may require precisely this.

II.2. 'Deliberative' Supranationalism

How do we find out? Since we seek to understand how constitutional law interacts with its societal environment, and in particular with Europeanisation and globalisation, it seems appropriate to consider how the closest neighbouring disciplines, especially integration research and international-relations theory, conceptualise these developments. Clearly, this is still too general a question, which does nothing but expose us to a rhapsody of approaches which pursue questions that the law does not pose, and which it is ultimately unable to answer. However, it is easy to see that we have a methodological problem in common, namely, the tensions between our categories and the changes of the context to which these categories refer explicitly or implicitly. Our core categories, in national constitutional law and in international law, just as in international-relations theory, all refer to the nation state as their basic unit. This dependence

[33] In his *Dilemmas of European Integration* (Oxford: OUP, 2005) 14.

has been called the 'misery of methodological nationalism' by Michael Zürn.[34] His diagnoses deal with the contextual conditions of political action:[35] the nation state, he argues, is no longer in a position to define its political priorities autonomously (as sovereign), but is, instead, forced to coordinate them transnationally. It is not only the members of nation states (national citizens) who must recognise their political action; states, too, have also become accountable to the transnational bodies in which their politics are subjected to evaluation. To be sure, national governments vehemently continue to defend their fiscal powers. 'Whilst resources remain at national level, the formulation of politics has been internationalised and recognition transnationalised.'[36]

Parallels with what we observe in the legal system are readily apparent. Like Zürn, we can argue that the entry of law into the post-national constellation is not at our – or the law's – disposition. We can observe how the law responds to this multi-dimensional disaggregation of statehood, and, in addition, become aware of the demands articulated at the transnational (European) level of politics, on the one hand, and at national and regional levels, on the other. We will then understand the pressure and requests for an adaptation of national law, and the honest and not so honest references to an institutionalised integration *telos*, etc.

This is, as Immanuel Kant famously and sarcastically observed,[37] the point at which lawyers tend to cease to rely on reason, and where they instead content themselves with authoritatively deciphering certified texts such as the Treaty and/or its interpretation by an institutionalised authority such as the European Court of Justice (ECJ). This may, to turn Kant's famous common saying[38] upside-down, be the way it operates in practice, but it does not suffice in theory. We cannot content ourselves with such self-perceptions or officious self-descriptions of the validity claims raised by institutionalised Europe. In addition, or even instead, we must ask ourselves whether these claims might 'deserve recognition'.[39] This type of critical reflection is inevitable simply because we know about the 'indeterminacy' of law and its inability to determine its own application.

[34] 'Politik in der postnationalen Konstellation. Über das Elend des methodologischen Nationalismus' in C Landfried (ed), *Politik in einer entgrenzten Welt. 21. wissenschaftlicher Kongreß der Deutschen Vereinigung für Politischen Wissenschaft* (Cologne: Verlag Wissenschaft und Politik, 2001) 181 ['The State in the Post-National Constellation – Societal Denationalisation and Multi-Level Governance', *ARENA Working Paper, 35/1999*, Oslo]. Similarly, U Beck, 'Beyond Methodological Nationalism. Towards a New Critical Theory with Cosmopolitan Intent' (2003) 10 *Constellations* 453 (their differences in the use of the term need not concern us here).

[35] Landfried (ed), *Politik in einer entgrenzten Welt*, n 34 above, at 188–191.

[36] My translation; ibid, 188.

[37] I Kant, 'The Contest of Faculties' in idem, *Political Writings*, 2nd edn, H Reiss ed (Cambridge: CUP, 1991).

[38] 'That may be all right in theory, but does not do in practice': I Kant, Werke in 10 Bänden – Band 9, *Schriften zur Anthropologie, Geschichtsphilosophie, Politik und Pädagogik. Zweiter Teil*, ed W Weischedel (Darmstadt: Wissenschaftliche Buchgesellschaft, 1971) 125.

[39] See J Habermas, 'Constitutional Democracy: A Paradoxical Union of Contradictory Principles?' (2001) 29 *Political Theory* 766.

What is true for legal decision-making holds equally true for the conceptual exercises that lawyers, especially German lawyers, call 'theories'. It is essential to understand that these exercises can rely neither exclusively on the authority of our given texts nor on the authority of social science. The insights, debates and approaches of political science cannot be translated literally into the language of the law and of legal discourses. Systems theory can provide us with the most elegant framework to substantiate this insight.[40] However, we do not need to subscribe to this framework. The law must discover for itself, with categories of its own, whether and, if so, how it can overcome 'the misery of methodological nationalism'.

Jürgen Neyer and I have submitted a response which we called 'deliberative' (as opposed to traditional or doctrinal) supranationalism – and continue to defend and elaborate this concept. In a nutshell,[41] we did not suggest that deliberation in transparent or opaque transnational bodies would constitute democratic transnational or European governance. Instead, we started 'from below', with the simple observation that no Member State of the EU can take decisions without causing 'extra-territorial' effects on its neighbours.[42] Provocatively put, perhaps, but brought to its logical conclusion, this, in effect, means that nationally organised constitutional states are becoming increasingly incapable of acting democratically. They cannot include all those who will be affected by their decisions in the electoral processes, and, *vice versa*, citizens cannot influence the behaviour of the political actors who are taking decisions on their behalf. It is, hence, only through a supranationally valid law that democratic governance can be accomplished. 'Deliberative' supranationalism seeks to identify principles and rules that serve precisely this end. It is a concept well-anchored in real, existing European law in doctrines such as

[40] See G Teubner, *Networks as Connected Contracts* (Oxford: Hart Publishing, 2011) 17 ff.

[41] For a re-statement on which the following remarks draw, see C Joerges, '"Deliberative Political Processes" Revisited: What have we Learnt about the Legitimacy of Supranational Decision-Making' (2006) 44 *JCMS* 779; idem, 'Rethinking European Law's Supremacy: A Plea for a Supranational Conflict of Laws' in B Kohler-Koch and B Rittberger (eds), *Debating the Democratic Legitimacy of the European Union* (Lanham MD: Rowman and Littlefield, 2007) 311; thereafter, for example, idem, 'Unity in Diversity as Europe's Vocation and Conflicts Law as Europe's Constitutional Form' in R Nickel and A Greppi (eds), *The Changing Role of Law in the Age of Supra- and Transnational Governance* (Baden-Baden: Nomos, 2014) 125 (reprinted in pt VI, ch 26 of this volume); Jürgen Neyer's latest restatement is *The Justification of Europe: A Political Theory of Supranational Integration* (Oxford: OUP, 2012). See, also, C Joerges and F Rödl, 'Reconceptualising the Constitution of Europe's Post-National Constellation – by Dint of Conflict of Laws' in I Lianos and O Odudu (eds), *Regulating Trade in Services in the EU and the WTO: Trust, Distrust and Economic Integration* (Cambridge: CUP, 2012) 762.

[42] This argument was first submitted in C Joerges, 'Taking the Law Seriously: On Political Science and the Role of Law in the Process of European Integration' (1996) 2 *ELJ* 105 (pt I, ch 2 in this volume), and then restated in idem, 'The Impact of European Integration on Private Law: Reductionist Perceptions, True Conflicts and a New Constitutionalist Perspective' (1997) 3 *ELJ* 378 (pt II, ch 7 in this volume).

the following: the Member States of the Union may not enforce their interests and/or their laws unboundedly; they are bound to respect European freedoms; they may not discriminate; they may only pursue 'legitimate' regulatory policies approved by the Community; they must coordinate in relation to the regulatory concerns that they may follow, and they must design their national regulatory provisions in the most Community-friendly way.

II.3. Europeanisation via Conflict of Laws Methodology

The primary function of these types of norms is coordinative. It represents a 'proceduralisation' of the category of law in the sense that Jürgen Habermas and others have defined this legal paradigm.[43] Deliberative supranationalism pleads for a proceduralised understanding of European law, for a 'law of law production' (Frank Michelman).[44] In order to illuminate its specific status, I have qualified European law as a new species of conflict of laws.[45] Conflict of laws seeks to identify the appropriate legal responses in multi-jurisdictional constellations. It is an old discipline which, in its 'modern' (post-1848) development, shares all the weaknesses of methodological nationalism. Its methodology, however, is rich and adaptable to 'vertical' conflicts between different levels of governance, as well as to the 'diagonal' conflicts which result from the assignment of different competences to different levels of governments in constellations which require the coordination or subordination of such partial competences.[46] It is, furthermore, an approach to the resolution of complex conflict-constellations, which is by no means appropriate only within international settings, but is likewise appropriate within national legal systems. It is an approach which reflects the continuous need for law production, and seeks to ensure the law's legitimacy through proceduralisation. It is precisely this need which is constitutive for the EU. To rephrase our initial thesis, the constitutionalisation of Europe should not seek to replace national constitutional law. Instead, it should be prepared to work continuously on Europe's '*unitas in pluralitate*'. This process can be characterised as a constitutional conflict of laws paradigm.

[43] See, as a brief summary, J Habermas, 'Paradigms of Law' in M Rosenfeld and A Arato (eds), *On Law and Democracy: Critical Exchanges* (Berkeley–Los Angeles CA: University of California Press, 1998) 13.

[44] FI Michelman, *Brennan and Democracy* (Princeton NJ: Princeton University Press, 1999) 34.

[45] N 41 above; see, previously, C Joerges, 'Transnationale "deliberative Demokratie" oder "deliberativer Supranationalismus"? Anmerkungen zur Konzeptualisierung legitimen Regierens jenseit des Nationalstaats bei R Schmaltz-Bruns' (2000) 7 *Zeitschrift für Internationale Beziehungen* 145; and idem, 'The Europeanization of Private Law as a Rationalisation Process and as a Contest of Disciplines – an Analysis of the Directive on Unfair Terms in Consumer Contracts' (1995) 3 *ERPL* 175.

[46] See, similarly, CU Schmid, 'Selective Harmonisation: Vertical, Horizontal and Diagonal Conflicts: Diagonal Competence Conflicts between European Competition Law and National regulation: A Conflict of Laws Reconstruction of the Dispute on Book Price Fixing' (2000) 8 *ERPL* 155.

It cannot be the objective of this essay to elaborate this version of supranationalism much further. Suffice it to re-state that deliberative supranationalism continues to do what conflict of laws has done during its long history, namely, to identify the rules and principles which frame multi-jurisdictional constellations. In the EU, it does this with much more strength and with orientations which form the fundamental achievements of the *acquis communautaire*: the Member States have, in principle, to recognise their laws mutually; however, they remain autonomous where domains and orientations which they regard as essential are concerned. The guarantee of this type of autonomy can be understood as an institutionalisation of tolerance in the trans-legal sense of this notion.[47] All this is not to say that the arguments, *critiques* and scepticism towards this vision of supranationalism do not deserve to be considered. What I understand to be the strength of the argument, namely, its perception of the democracy failure of constitutional states, also points to a practical weakness of the EU which the theory of deliberative supranationalism cannot cure.

III. EXEMPLARY ILLUSTRATIONS

Does all this have anything to do with Europe's *praxis*? Are all these matters merely for the Preamble, and not for the actual contents of a Constitutional Treaty? How compatible or dysfunctional are they when brought to bear on the mundane world of European affairs? My thesis is, of course, that Europe's pasts are present *in our daily business* and not just in debates about memorials for the European Jewry and/or the Roma and the Sinti, about surrender and/or liberation days, about resistance and/or collaboration, about genocide trials and the remuneration of forced labour, or about the true nationality of Albert Einstein. In order to substantiate my assertion, I could now go into a huge spectrum of topics – only to get lost there. It would, on the other hand, be carrying coals to Newcastle, and, at the same time, too abstract simply to insist that there are varieties of capitalism in Europe, that Scandinavian welfarism has always been distinct, that the history of antitrust in post-war Germany differs from that of Italy, that the French *planification* and *services publiques* are not identical with Germany's *Ordoliberalismus* and its *Daseinsvorsorge*. My argument is much stronger and more specific: it concerns the 'bitter experiences' to which European societies have responded individually, in concert or collectively, and my assertion is that it would be beneficial for Europe to reflect upon its working through its pasts. Two of the topics

[47] See R Forst, 'Toleration, Justice and Reason' in C McKinnon and D Castiglione (eds), *The Culture of Toleration in Diverse Socities: Reasonable Tolerance* (Manchester: Manchester University Press, 2003); J Habermas, 'Religion in der Öffentlichkeit. Kognitive Voraussetzungen für den "öffentlichen Vernunftgebrauch" religiöser und säkularer Bürger' in idem, *Zwischen Naturalismus und Religion* (Frankfurt aM: Suhrkamp, 2005) 119.

addressed explicitly and implicitly in our agenda seem particularly appropriate for exemplary discussions, namely, 'Social Europe' and 'European Identity and European Citizenship'. The advantage of this presence is that I can be very brief. Other topics would be equally important. One is the rule of law and of experiences with the de-formalisation of public governance. This may be too subtle. Another topic of high importance would be enlargement. But this seems too huge to be dealt with *en passant*.[48]

III.1. Social Europe and the Disregard for History in the Convention Process

I will not try to summarise the vast topical debates on '*L'Europa sociale*' here. Instead, I will address a neglected dimension of this debate, namely, the ambivalent legacy of 'the social' (the efforts to find a stable response to the social conflicts in capitalist societies) as a constitutional issue.

III.1.a. Rechtsstaat v Sozialstaat

The patterns of debate on social justice, democracy and the rule of law are enormously stable. It all starts – in the German memory – with Max Weber's warning that the intrusion of values of social justice into the legal system (the turn to substantive rationality) will threaten the law's formal rationality and the rule of law as such.[49] Or should we understand 'social justice' as an inherent promise of true democracy? Hermann Heller was probably the first to deliver a systematic constitutional theory in which a social model and the rule of law were synthesised, and the *soziale Rechtsstaat* presented as the best, or the only, conceivable democratic response to the tensions between the classes in capitalist societies.[50] Heller's defence of social democracy resonates famously in the commitments of Germany's Basic Law,[51] but was never uncontroversial. Two

[48] For a particularly thought-provoking starting-point, see T Judt, 'The Past is Another Country: Myth and Memory in Post-war Europe' in J-W Müller (ed), *Memory and Power in Post-war Europe: Studies on the Presence of the Past* (Cambridge: CUP, 2002) 157; in legal literature, see J Přibáň, 'European Union Constitution-Making, Political Identity and Central European Reflections' (2005) 11 *ELJ* 35; A Sajó, 'Legal Consequences of Past Collective Wrongdoing after Communism' (2005) 6 *German Law Journal* 425, all of them with rich references.

[49] M Weber, *Economy and Society* (Berkeley CA: University of California Press, 1978) 873 ff; on socialism, see his 'Socialism' in idem, *Political Writings* (Cambridge: CUP, 1994) 272 ff.

[50] See W Schluchter, Entscheidung für den sozialen Rechtsstaat: Hermann Heller und die staatstheoretische Diskussion in der Weimarer Republik, 2nd edn (Baden-Baden: Nomos, 1983); D Dyzenhaus, Legality and Legitimacy: Carl Schmitt, Hans Kelsen and Hermann Heller in Weimar (Oxford: OUP, 1997). Important texts by Heller have been made accessible by AJ Jacobsen and B Schlink (eds), Weimar: A Jurisprudence of Crisis (Berkeley–Los Angeles CA: University of California Press, 2000).

[51] Article 20 para 1: 'Die Bundesrepublik Deutschland ist ein demokratischer und sozialer Bundesstaat' ('The Federal Republic of Germany is a democratic and social federal state').

types of arguments are particularly important: in the neo-liberal and monetarist view, the quest for a 'social' democracy is economically irrational and risks destroying our freedoms. This second aspect was drastically articulated by von Hayek's characterisation of welfarism as a 'road to serfdom'.[52] The authoritarian and populist right never cared about the law's rationality. De-formalisation was inevitable, but should – and this was the fascist and national-socialist conclusion in the 1920s and 1930s – be compensated by strong political leadership representing *il movimento* or *das Volk* directly. This is no longer the vocabulary of modern populism. What remains a common *credo* of populist movements is their anti-modernism, their instrumentalisation of anxieties, their appeal to collective cultural or national – but always exclusionary – identities. How far away is our darker past? The issue that has just re-surfaced in the, at present, most intensively discussed book on the Third Reich in Germany, is Götz Aly's *Hitler's Volksstaat*.[53] Aly not only underlines how the Nazis cared about the welfare of their *Volksgenossen*, but also points to very uncomfortable continuities in social policies. This has become a subtext of the renewed debates on the compatibility of freedom and social justice, between the *Rechtsstaat* and the *Sozialstaat*.[54]

III.1.b. Social Europe in the Draft Constitutional Treaty

Hermann Heller's legacy was strong in post-war Germany. And Germany, in its search for a synthesis of a social model and the rule of law, did not choose a *Sonderweg*. The responsibility for ensuring welfare, balancing social inequalities and creating infrastructure for economic development has become a common feature of the European nation states. It is in this abstract sense that we can identify 'a European social model' as one of the four dimensions of 'a multi-function state that combines the Territorial State, the state that assures the Rule of Law, the Democratic State, and the Intervention State'.[55]

Given the strength of this tradition, it was predictable that the Convention, even though this was not originally foreseen, would have addressed this precarious dimension of the integration project. The ambition of the Convention to

[52] FA von Hayek, *The Road to Serfdom* (London: George Routledge and Sons, 1944).

[53] G Aly, *Hitler's Volksstaat. Raub, Rassenkrieg und nationaler Sozialismus* (Frankfurt aM: S Fischer, 2005). For a critical review, see, for example, M Sorer, available at: http://hsozkult.geschichtee.hu-berlin.de/rezensionen/2005-2-143, with many references. To mention Aly is not to acknowledge that statements like 'the defence of the *Sozialstaat* is a defence also of expropriation and robbery' would reflect the ambivalences of the social particularly well.

[54] Aly receives considerable attention for his continuity theses. On 11 August 2005, www.haaretz.com reproduced the report of the Deutsche Nachrichtenagentur on an infamous contribution of Oskar Lafontaine to the electoral campaign of Germany's new Left Party ['The state is obligated to prevent family fathers and women from becoming unemployed because of Fremdarbeiter (foreign workers) taking away their jobs by working for low wages'].

[55] S Leibfried and M Zürn, 'Reconfiguring the National Constellation' in eidem (eds), *Transformations of the State* (Cambridge: CUP, 2005) 1, at 8; for prominent historical confirmation, see Judt, n 27 above, 791 ff, and his *Ill Fares the Land* (New York: Penguin Press, 2010) 127 ff.

design a document of constitutional dignity left no choice. A refusal to enlarge the agenda would have damaged the political credibility of the whole endeavour. Working Group XI on Social Europe had a belated start, but worked all the more intensively.

This had an impact. Social Europe became a visible dimension of the DCT.[56] It mainly rests on three pillars: the commitment to a 'competitive social market economy',[57] the recognition of 'social rights'[58] to be implemented by the ECJ, and the introduction of 'soft law' techniques for the coordination of social policies.[59] It is, however, once again both remarkable and deplorable that all of these elements were introduced by political *fiat* and without much reflection on historical experience. Joschka Fischer and Jacques Villepin, to whom we owe the assignment of constitutional dignity to the concept of the 'social market economy', knew they were giving a political signal. But, apparently, not much more. Nobody seems to have explained that the '*soziale Marktwirtschaft*' was Germany's post-war historical compromise, supported by the Christian Democrats, the trade unions and both Christian Churches.[60] No one seems to have recalled the ambivalent past of this project. Nobody seemed to know or to care about the reasons which the German Constitutional Court had given for its rejection of the idea of a constitutionalisation of the market economy in its seminal *Investitionshilfe* judgment, handed down in 1954.[61] The standard response in the debates on the social dimension of the Convention to the openness and indeterminacy of the formula in the Constitutional Treaty was that all modern constitutions need to resort to programmatic commitments. Germany is then cited again as an exemplary case. The future *gestalt* of the *soziale Rechtsstaat* was, indeed, by no means clear at the time of the adoption of the Basic Law. However, as indicated, it was quite clear how the '*soziale Marktwirtschaft*' would try to give a specific content to the social commitments of the Basic Law, and it was apparent that this 'Third Way' met with broad political and societal support. The *Bundesverfassungsgericht* also found broad support for the view that the concrete design of Germany's social model should be left to the legislature and was not prescribed by the Basic Law.

Would such awareness have made a difference? It might, at least, have led some of the actors to proceed with more caution and to be more careful with

[56] N 24 above.

[57] Article 3 (3).

[58] See Title IV of the Draft Constitutional Treaty (n 24 above).

[59] See, especially, Article I-14 (4) of the DCT; the assignment of a competence 'to promote and coordinate the economic and employment policies of the Member States' has been repealed. Article I-11 (3) as amended on 22 June 2004.

[60] See M Glasman, *Unnecessary Suffering: Managing Market Utopia* (London: Verso, 1996) 96 ff; C Joerges and F Rödl, 'The "Social Market Economy" as Europe's Social Model?', *EUI Working Paper Law No 2004/8*, in L Magnusson and B Stråth (eds), *A European Social Citizenship? Preconditions for Future Policies in Historical Light* (Brussels: Lang, 2005) 125.

[61] *Bundedverfassungsgericht* in 5 *BVerfGE* 7 (1954). See, on the contemporary discussion in Germany, G Brüggemeier, *Entwicklung des Rechts im organisierten Kapitalismus*, vol 2 (Frankfurt aM: Syndikat, 1979) 269 ff.

their promises. The same holds true for two other pillars of 'social Europe'. What should make us trust in the capability of the ECJ to accomplish social progress through the powers that it has in the interpretation of the new social rights? Based upon what kind of evidence could the Convention's Working Group XI 'consider that the open method of co-ordination has proved to be a useful instrument in policy areas where no stronger co-ordination instrument exists', without taking note of the experience which we have had with the de-formalisation of social commitments?

III.1.c. Social Europe and the French Referendum

It was no longer possible to be more cautious in the presentations of 'social Europe' after the campaigns in France had got off the ground. It seemed that Pandora's box had been opened.[62]

There is hardly any doubt that the perceived dismantling of the French welfare state through the integration process, the portrayal of Europe as neo-liberal de-regulation machinery, and the anxieties that such portrayals of Europeanisation and globalisation provoked amongst the French had a substantial impact on their '*non*'. Political commentators and academic observers hold this view; solid opinion polls confirm their point.[63] The French referendum is certainly not so one-dimensional. Among the mixed motivations which seem to have guided the French, the disappointing insight that Europe could no longer be understood as just a *grande France* may have been as important as Joachim Schild assumes.[64] The attention this event attracted in the community of European constitutionalists is nevertheless disappointing.[65] What I seek to underline – and what the comments cited confirm, at least implicitly – is the presence of France's past, which manifests itself in the patterns of the debate. It seems to me unsurprising that the kind of European future which the DCT had so vaguely outlined, and which its proponents had so confidently proclaimed, could not cope with this past.

III.2. Identity and Citizenship

What does it mean to be a citizen in the EU? No other issue brings law and history in general, and law and 'bitter memories' specifically, so intimately together. Precisely for that reason the idea of a constitutional conflict of laws

[62] See D Della Porta and M Caiani, *Quale Europa? Europeizzazione, Identità e Conflitti* (Bologna: Il Mulino, 2006); J Schild, 'Ein Sieg der Angst – das gescheiterte französische Verfassungsreferendum' (2006) 28 *Integration* 187; especially enlightening for non-French observers, see also J-L Andreani, 'France solidaire et France libérale', *Le Monde*, 15 June 2006.

[63] For a detailed discussion, see Della Porta and Caiani, n 62 above.

[64] Schild, n 62 above, 199.

[65] See C Joerges, 'On the Disregard for History in the Convention Process' (2006) 12 *ELJ* 2.

deserves to be considered as a means to avoid the pitfalls which the concept of European citizenship entails.

It is difficult, even impossible, to avoid Habermas and the notion of constitutional patriotism when one enters this arena. As, in particular, Jan-Werner Müller has explained,[66] it was not Jürgen Habermas but Dolf Sternberger[67] who constructed this category. Habermas adopted *Verfassungspatriotismus*, transforming it into a cornerstone of his political theory in such a way that he could later, in 1991,[68] introduce the idea of constitutional patriotism into the European constitutional discourse. Does Habermas' constitutional patriotism abstract too rigidly from the social, political and cultural embeddedness of 'really existing' human beings, as has been argued so often? This *critique* is not valid. It is the great achievement of Sternberger and Habermas' constitutional patriotism that this is not a substantive concept of identity.[69] But it is, nevertheless, a concept which is embedded in a specific culture and *Lebenswelt*, designed to mirror Germany's transformation into a constitutional democracy.[70] Is it too 'thick' to become a European concept, or, if deprived of its German connotation, too 'thin' to represent Europe's *unitas*?[71]

Habermas later substantiated and modified his position. Constitutional patriotism, he explained, does not assume that citizens will identify with abstract constitutional principles. *Verfassungspatriotismus* is a conscious affirmation of political principles as citizens experience them in the context of their national histories.[72] He deepened this point in his discussion on the meaning of culture and of the, in his view, misconceived idea of guaranteeing cultures through collective rights: culture is of an intrinsic importance for our lifestyle;

[66] J-W Müller, *Constitutional Patriotism* (Princeton NJ: Princeton University Press, 2007) 15 ff.

[67] '"Verfassungspatriotismus." Rede bei der 25-Jahr-Feier der "Akademie für Politische Bildung" in Tutzing am 29.6.1982' in M-L Recker (ed), *Politische Reden 1945–1990*, (Frankfurt aM: Deutscher Klassiker Verlag, 1999) 702 ff.

[68] J Habermas, *Staatsbürgerschaft und nationale Identität* (St Gallen: Erkner, 1991). The short monograph was reprinted in idem, *Faktizität und Geltung* (Frankfurt aM: Suhrkamp, 1992), 632, trans, *Between Facts and Norms* (Cambridge MA: The MIT Press, 1998) 491.

[69] Habermas, n 68 above; see also J Habermas, *Die Zukunft der menschlichen Natur. Auf dem Weg zu einer liberalen Eugenik?* (Frankfurt aM: Suhrkamp, 2004) 124.

[70] On the 'militancy' and its credentials in this process, G Frankenberg, 'Der lernende Souverän' in idem, *Autorität und Integration. Zur Grammatik von Recht und Verfassung* (Frankfurt aM: Suhrkamp, 2003) 46; this example illustrates perfectly how problematical it would be to try to transmit social learning into another society – and how useful inter-societal observation and critique can be.

[71] See M Kumm, 'Thick Constitutional Patriotism and Political Liberalism: On the Role and Structure of European Legal History' (2005) 6 *German Law Journal* 319; M Mahlmann, 'Constitutional Identity and the Politics of Homogeneity' (2005) 6 *German Law Journal* 307. See, also, FC Mayer and J Palmowski, 'European Identities and the EU – The Ties that Bind the Peoples of Europe' (2004) 42 *JCMS* 573, with historical dimensions and a more cautious view than their title suggests.

[72] J Habermas, 'Vorpolitische Grundlagen des demokratischen Rechtsstaates?' in idem, *Zwischen Naturalismus und Religion*, n 47 above, 106, at 111.

the human mind (*Geist*) is culturally constituted[73] – and culture is perpetuated only through the acceptance of its addresses and the conviction that it is worthwhile maintaining this tradition.[74]

A European concept of citizenship which seeks to achieve a deepened integration through some form of intentional 'identity politics' would then be fundamentally misconceived. European citizens are not expected – by Habermas – to forget their histories and cultural traditions. They cannot escape from them, anyway, they should develop them further, and they should learn to live with this variety. Back in 1988, Habermas opined:

> By and large, national public spheres are still culturally isolated from one another ... In the future, however, a common *political* culture could differentiate itself from the various *national* cultures.[75]

This differentiation between a 'European-wide political culture' and many other cultural spheres which remain national resembles an exercise in conflict-of-laws methodology, inspired by systems theory and its notion of functional differentiation. It is a conceptually all-too-artificial and, sociologically speaking, unrealistic suggestion.[76] A conflict–of-laws approach would be much simpler: Let the differences persist, but subject these national communities to rules and principles which ensure mutual respect and coexistence. Do not create some élitist public space, but ensure that the national political cultures can observe and criticise each other.[77]

Notwithstanding its inclusion in the Treaty of Maastricht, the concept of European citizenship has remained a playing field mainly of political scientists and legal theorists. Lawyers trying to come to terms with Europeanisation processes in the fields which they examine have difficulties in transforming it

[73] 'Kulturelle Gleichbehandlung – und die Grenzen des postmodernen Liberalismus', ibid, 279, at 306.

[74] Ibid, 313. In his recent essay, 'Die Krise de Europäischen Union im Lichte der Konstitutionalisierung des Völkerrechts – Ein Essay zur Verfassung Europas' in J Habermas, *Zur Verfassung Europas: Ein Essay* (Frankfurt aM: Suhrkamp, 2011) 39, Habermas has moved to another construct, arguing that Europeans have a twofold citizenship as nationals and Europeans. It seems to me that he undervalues the intensity of the traditional ties of Europeans to their home polities. In this respect, Kalypso Nicolaïdes' notion of '*demoi*-cracy' seems more realistic and normatively attractive; see her essay, 'The Idea of European Demoi-cracy' in J Dickson and P Eleftheriadis (eds), *Philosophical Foundations of EU Law* (Oxford, OUP, 2012).

[75] J Habermas, 'Citizenship and National Identity', Appendix II to *Between Facts and Norms*, n 68 above, 507.

[76] See B Peters, 'Public Discourse, Identity, and the Problem of Democratic Legitimacy' in EO Eriksen (ed), *Making the European Polity: Reflexive Integration in the EU* (Abingdon: Routledge, 2005) 84.

[77] See K Eder's intensive work on the Europeanisation of public spheres, in particular 'Zur Transformation nationalstaatlicher Öffentlichkeit in Europa, Von der Sprachgemeinschaft zur issuespezifischen Kommunikationsgemeinschaft' (2000) 30 *Berliner Journal für Soziologie* 167; K Eder and C Kantner, 'Transnationale Resonanzstrukturen in Europa. Eine Kritik der Rede vom Öffentlichkeitsdefizit in Europa' in M Bach (ed), *Die Europäisierung nationaler Gesellschaften* (Wiesbaden: Westdeutscher Verlag, 2000) 306. See, also, H-J Trenz, 'Einführung: Auf der Suche nach einer europäischen Öffentlichkeit' in A Klein et al (eds), *Bürgerschaft, Öffentlichkeit und Demokratie in Europa* (Oplanden: Leske + Budrich, 2003) 161.

into legal concepts with a potential of structuring their inquiries. But it is at this level of concreteness that 'European citizenship' can deploy a great potential. It is a concept through which the inherited schism between the European 'market citizen' (Hans Peter Ipsen), who enjoys private autonomy in the great European economic space, and the un-Europeanised political citizen, who exercises his or her political autonomy under the umbrella of a constitutional state, can be gradually overcome. This potential has materialised in many fields. The most interesting example that I know of is from the not so mundane world of European company law, which I will not explore here.[78]

There are many more examples. They all could serve to illustrate in much detail how legal systems are re-constituting themselves in Europeanisation processes. This is by no means a linear and necessarily beneficial process. However, what is so important to underline, in my opinion, is that it is false to conceptualise European law as a ready-made or steadily growing *corpus juridicus* which will gradually replace national legal systems. What we have to develop is an analytical understanding of these processes. What we have to learn is how to organise and stabilise the balance of private and public autonomy in such a way that the European law of law production (*Recht-Fertigungs-Recht*) deserves recognition. But let me refrain from substantiating these visions here any further. What should have become plausible, however, is their potential to link law to history.

CONCLUDING REMARKS

The past – good or bad – is with us. Does it matter whether we make ourselves aware of it? We should try, especially in the cases of an unpleasant past, to learn! We may then even have a 'duty to remember'.[79] These answers seem so evident, even emotionally appealing. But appearances deceive. Until now, and indeed for the foreseeable future, Europeans will have to live with different, in many respects conflicting, historical memories – and there is no authority entrusted with deciding about such conflicts. It is all the more important to be aware that 'the glance in the mirror'[80] tends to have unsettling effects, both in one's own lifeworld and in the political sphere.

[78] But see C Joerges, 'The Challenges of Europeanization in the Realm of Private Law: A Plea for a New Legal Discipline' (2004) 14 *Duke Journal of Comparative and International Law* 149, at 173 ff; also available at: www.iue.it/PUB/law04-12.pdf. Fields such as anti-discrimination and labour law may appear more exciting. [Mechanisms of Europeanisation from below are instructively documented in the latter field by S Sciarra (ed), *Labour Law in the Courts: National Judges and the European Court of Justice* (Oxford: Hart Publishing, 2001).]

[79] P de Greiff, 'The Duty to Remember: The Dead Weight of the Past, or the Weight of the Dead of the Past?', typescript Princeton NJ, 2001 (on file with the author).

[80] M Stolleis, 'Reluctance to Glance in the Mirror: The Changing Face of German Jurisprudence after 1933 and Post-1945' in C Joerges and NS Ghaleigh (eds), *Darker Legacies of Law in Europe: The Shadow of National Socialism and Fascism over Europe and its Legal Traditions* (Oxford: Hart Publishing, 2003) 1.

There is hardly much room to choose. It may well be, as Armin von Bogdandy observes in his evaluation of the Preamble,[81] that negative connotations are unlikely to further identity-building. We can therefore argue against 'identity politics' altogether. We should not assume, however, that we can control the biases that insert themselves into narrative structures.[82] We can observe that this infiltration becomes consciously politicised, that it is simply impossible not to instrumentalise the past in general, and 'bitter experiences' in particular.

And it is all under way, Jan-Werner Müller observes in his essay.[83] The 'politics of regret', the exchanges regarding the recognition of guilt, the apologies by political leaders, the debates about memorials in schoolbooks, the painful self-interrogations in so many quarters about collaboration and involvement in the Holocaust. Is there a chance that these often painful processes and contestations will create a new sensitivity, that Europeans will learn something about themselves, from and for their neighbours, which will be beneficial for their Union? Could one even hope that the European project derives a new legitimacy out of these confrontations with the 'bitter experiences' in Europe's pasts? Jan-Werner Müller is sceptical and cautious. Mutual observation tends to provoke cross-border blame and to promote shame as governmental politics.[84]

Back to the Constitutional Treaty: Can Europeans really hope to 'forge a common destiny' while remaining 'proud of their own national identities and history' – as the Preamble suggests – if they fail to confront their pasts? 'Working through the past' is a European burden, and 'from the very beginning, the integration of Europe represents the remedy to centuries of imperialism, war and other kinds of inter-state conflict, and is shown as the only possible alternative to Europe's self-destruction and decay'.[85] This insight we may share. However, it will not suffice as an orientation when trying to come to terms with our pasts. Somewhat paradoxically, it is the Holocaust which Europeans seem to recognise as a point of negative communality. To cite *Postwar* again:

> The new Europe, bound together by the signs and symbols of its terrible past, is a remarkable accomplishment; but it remains forever mortgaged to that past. If Europeans are to maintain this vital link – if Europe's past is to continue to furnish Europe's present with admonitory meaning and moral purpose – then it will have to be *taught* afresh with each passing generation. The 'European Union' may be a response to history, but it can never be a substitute.[86]

[81] 'Europäische Verfassung und europäische Identität', n 24 above, 57.

[82] H White, *Metahistory: The Historical Imagination in Nineteenth-Century Europe* (Baltimore MD–London: Johns Hopkins University Press, 1973).

[83] Müller, *Constitutional Patriotism*, n 66 above, 93 ff.

[84] Ibid. See, also, JQ Whitman, 'What is Wrong with Inflicting Shame Sanctions?' (1998) 107 *Yale Law Journal* 1055, at 1088.

[85] Larat, n 17 above.

[86] Judt, n 27 above, 831.

34

Conclusion – Part VII

I. LOOKING BACK

WE NOTED THIS remark on the 'Darker Legacies' project in the introduction to this part of the book: 'You are damaging the dignity of the European project. This type of research should not be done at the EUI. Do it in Germany'.[1] Among the PhD researchers at the EUI, this critique had no lasting echo.[2] We have underlined the attention that the 'Darker Legacies' project attracted, and have also pointed to the continuation of the project at the EUI[3] and elsewhere.[4] At the time, we felt rehabilitated.

That once understandable feeling has, however, given way to renewed concerns. Already, at the beginning of the new century, Europe has witnessed a revival of anti-Semitism, which had seemed inconceivable given the impact of our 'darker past', the awareness of our 'guilt about the past' and the intense discussions of the pitfalls of memory politics. By now, however, a right-leaning form of populism has regained strength in new movements all over the Continent, and has even achieved governmental power. All of this should mean that, now more than ever, we must continue to remain aware of the 'bitter experiences' of the past, as, thanks to a Polish initiative, the preamble to the Draft Constitutional Treaty of 2004[5] requests. Our renewed concerns as European citizens are, *hélas*, shared well beyond the European borders.[6]

[1] See ch 30.

[2] See the report of PhD researcher, L di Preso, 'The Darker Legacies of Law in Europe: Remembering the dark past to write a brighter future' (2005/06) *EUI Review* 12, The text can be downloaded only via firefox at file:///C:/Users/c.joerges/Dropbox/35%20%20Darker%20Legacies%20Zeug/EUIRevWinter0506Web.pdf.

[3] See ch 30, nn 6–8.

[4] See C Joerges, M Mahlmann and UK Preuß, *'Schmerzliche Erfahrungen' der Vergangenheit und der Prozess der Konstitutionalisierung Europas: Rechts-, Geschichts- und Politikwissenschaftliche Beiträge* (Wiesbaden: Verlag für Sozialwissenschaften, 2008).

[5] Treaty establishing a Constitution for Europe as signed in Rome on 29 October 2004, [2004] OJ C310/1.

[6] See, eg, W Brown, *In the Ruins of Neoliberalism: The Rise of Antidemocratic Politics in the West* (New York: Columbia UP, 2019).

II. RELATED PUBLICATIONS

C Joerges, 'On the Context of German-American Debates on Sociological Jurisprudence and Legal Criticism: A History of Transatlantic Misunderstandings and Missed Opportunities' [1993] *European Yearbook in the Sociology of Law* 403.

C Joerges, 'History as Non- History: Divergencies and Time Lags between Friedrich Kessler and German Jurisprudence' (1994) 42 *American Journal of Comparative Law* 163.

*Epilogue: Europe's Crisis and Vocation**

THE ESSAYS GATHERED together in this volume trace the development of the integration project – and its *Begriffsgeschichte* (conceptual history) – since the epoch-marking fall of the Berlin Wall in 1989. European politics and the politics of European law cannot evade this history. Instead, it must be embraced and understood if politics and law are ever to master our contemporary problems and future challenges.

I.

These reconstructive endeavours are informed by jurisprudential approaches to the economy, the societal preconditions and frames for economic activity, as well as legal appreciation of the social importance and societal impacts of 'the economic'. This emphasis should not, however, detract in any way from the significance and lasting impact of the visions of the 'founding fathers' of the integration project. These visions, together with the ways in which they were idealised better,[1] surely belong to our integration DNA, just as do the 'painful experiences of the past' of which the Draft Constitutional Treaty of 2004 reminded us in its Preamble.[2] But, for all of that, the daily course of integration politics was determined in the final instance by the opening up of national economies, with all that this entailed in the wider social and political context. These changes in everyday life led to a constant, if never straightforward or crisis-free, trajectory of deepening integration. The impacts were felt ever more broadly and intensely within the societies of Member States. These were never uniform, however, either within individual societies or across the Member States as a whole. Conflict accordingly grew about the economic and social impacts of the integration process, but also, and increasingly so, about its legitimacy.

Such interdependences, and above all the significance and political embeddedness of the economy, were never a major feature within leading European law commentaries. Instead, as 'object and agent'[3] of the integration process,

* Translated by Michelle Everson, Birkbeck College, University of London.

[1] AS Milward, *The European Rescue of the Nation State*, 2nd edn (London–New York: Routledge, 2000) 318 ff.

[2] OJ [2004] C 310/1 of 16 December 2004.

[3] R Dehousse and JHH Weiler, 'The legal dimension' in W Wallace (ed), *The Dynamics of European Integration* (London: Pinter, 1990) 242, 243.

European law was deemed to be legitimate in and of itself. Many of the chapters in this volume take critical issue with this approach.[4] The most important exponent and cofounder of this hegemonic conception, JHH Weiler, himself knew far better. His first oath-breaking publication on the issue spoke of the 'dual character' of supranationalism: the functioning of the Community system – integration through law and its supranational claim to legitimacy – was dependent upon political support for the integration process of the Member States.[5] However, such views of the interplay between law and politics still fail to mention essential dimensions of the overall integration context. 'The economic' was sidestepped in the academic deliberations on the objectives and normative dignity of the integration project.[6] The one theoretical conception that was to take possession of this absence, or fill the economic gap, was the Ordoliberalism of German thought, with its vision of an Economic Constitution to accompany and legitimate the integration process.[7] Yet outside the ordoliberal school this approach found little resonance even in Germany's European law scholarship, and none whatsoever outside Germany.

II.

Contrary to a general disregard for the economic within academic writing on Europe, but also in stark contrast to Ordoliberalism's characterisation of the economic order as a constitutional order, my contributions in this volume emphasise the factual primacy of the economic within integration processes, as well as the normative imperative that integration must be democratically legitimated. The volume's reconstructions of the interdependence between economics, politics and law find their analytical mainstay in political science integration studies,[8] and further support in the studies of the economic sociologist Karl Polanyi,[9] who has greatly influenced my work for well over

[4] In particular, pt V, chs 21–23 and pt I, ch 3.

[5] See JHH Weiler's early seminal essay on 'The Community system: the dual character of supranationalism' (1981) 1 *Yearbook of European Law* 257; in his later reflection on these processes, Weiler applies Hirschman's dichotomy between 'exit' and 'voice' to the analysis of supranationalism and its limits: see JHH Weiler, 'The Transformation of Europe' (1991) 100 *Yale LJ* 2405, 2010 ff. This does not equate, however, with his having overcome his fixation with the behaviour of states.

[6] See, recently, N Walker, 'Where's the "E" in Constitution? A European Puzzle' in A Skordas, G Halmai and L Mardikian (eds), *Economic Constitutionalism in a Turbulent World* (Cheltenham: Edward Elgar, forthcoming); C Joerges, 'Economic Constitutionalism and "The Political" of "The Economic"' in G Grégoire and X Miny (eds), *The Idea of Economic Constitution in Europe. L'idée de Constitution économique en Europe* (Leiden: Brill, Legal History Library, forthcoming).

[7] See, in particular, pt V, ch 22.

[8] See, in particular, pt I, ch 2.

[9] Reference is made to his main work: K Polanyi, *The Great Transformation: The Political and Economic Origins of Our Time*, 2nd edn (Boston, MA: Beacon Press, 2001) (original English edn 1944).

a decade.[10] His theories have a striking relevance and descriptive power for all periods of the integration process. His core theses contain a comprehensive critique of the jurisprudential paradigm of 'integration through law'. Economic integration was not an evolutionary process. It was initiated in its beginning and continuously accompanied in its unfolding by political decisions. Quoting a famous passage from Karl Polanyi's *Great Transformation*, 'While *laissez-faire* economy was the product of deliberate State action, subsequent restrictions on *laissez-faire* started in a spontaneous way. Laissez-faire was planned; planning was not.'[11] 'In the beginning' of economic integration 'there was' the EEC Treaty and the 'constitutionalisation' of the treaties by the European Court of Justice.[12] It soon became apparent, however, that far more was needed in order to achieve economic integration. And it was here that the political in law came into its own: the 'General Programme of 28 May 1969 for the elimination of technical barriers to trade';[13] the line of case law on mutual recognition of Member State regulation,[14] initiated by the legendary *Cassis* Judgment of the ECJ of the 20 February 1979,[15] which was then built upon by the New Concept on technical harmonisation and standards;[16] the Delors Commission's White Paper on the Completion of the Internal Market;[17] and the move to majority voting with the Single European Act of 28 February 1986.[18] All of this was anything but an evolutionary process; it was, in the language of Polanyi, 'planned' – carefully planned and put into action step by step.

It would thus be very wrong to characterise the progress of integration as a one-dimensional evolutionary process that furthered more or less stringently the implementation of economic rationality criteria. Creation of the internal market was accompanied by pursuit of regulatory policies that responded to the problems created by the risk society and the 'politicisation and moralisation' of markets associated with it.[19] In this context, new – for Europe – fields of

[10] First, C Joerges and J Falke (eds), *Karl Polanyi, Globalisation and the Potential of Law in Transnational Markets* (Oxford: Hart Publishing, 2011); thereafter, eg, M Everson and C Joerges, 'Reconfiguring the Politics–Law Relationship in the Integration Project through Conflicts-Law Constitutionalism' (2012) 18 *ELJ* 644; C Joerges, 'How is a Closer Union Conceivable under Conditions of Ever More Socio-Economic and Political Diversity? Constitutionalising Europe's *Unitas in Pluralitate*?' (2018) 24 *ELJ* 257, reprinted in pt IV, ch 18 of this volume.

[11] Polanyi, *The Great Transformation*, n 9 above, 195.

[12] See the seminal narrative of Weiler, 'The Transformation of Europe', n 5 above, 1413 ff.

[13] Council Resolution of 28 May 1969, [1969] OJ C 76.

[14] Case 120/78 *Rewe-Zentral AG v Bundesmonopolverwaltung für Branntwein* [1979] ECR 649, Judgement of 20 February 1979 (Cassis de Dijon).

[15] See in more detail on the developments ch 2 (section C. 1) and ch 21 (section 2).

[16] [1969] OJ C136/1 of 4 June 1969.

[17] COM (85)310 final of 14 June 1985.

[18] [1987] OJ L169/1.

[19] N Stehr, C Henning, B Weiler, *The Moralization of the Markets* (Piscataway, NJ: Transaction Publishers, 2011).

regulatory politics speedily developed.[20] These policy fields are full of political decisions, because the weighing up of economic rationality and the demands of labour, environmental and consumer protection cannot be measured against given fixed economic criteria.

III.

Whereas the weakness in orthodox European legal thought and doctrine is to be found in its fascination with state actions, a comparable failing in ordoliberal thought might be argued to be its obsession with autonomous market processes. Using terminology taken from the economic sociologist, Karl Polanyi, the particular weakness in this approach results from the resilience of the three 'fictitious commodities' – land (nature), labour and money – all of them goods that are not 'made for the market', against their marketisation, that is, their treatment within the market conceptualisation of economy and society *as if* they were normal market goods. Polanyi argues that the commodification of 'fictitious' goods is a normative error that will provoke social opposition to this form of discipline.[21]

Polanyi's observations and prophecies are separated from the signing of the Rome Treaties by 13 years. Nevertheless, they have retained explanatory power. The original machinery of the EEC Treaty foresaw that the so-called 'fictitious commodities' were a matter for the Member States, so that their respective 'social embeddedness' within each national realm would continue to be respected. The process of integration, however, was to be characterised by an ever more expansive interpretation of the 'limits of EU competences',[22] in particular in the form of 'market-building' strategies. The most spectacular example is the CJEU case law postulating the hierarchical precedence of the economic freedoms of the European Treaty above national collective labour law, which is strongly criticised in chapter 16.

In Polanyi's analysis, commodification processes are bound to provoke counter-movements.[23] And all ordoliberal reservations notwithstanding, commodification processes were captured within the evolution of European consumer, environmental and labour law protection policies. Social and labour policy as a whole, however, remained weak.[24]

[20] The works of Giandomenico Majone are pathbreaking. In his understanding, EU regulatory policies should concern consumer safety, safety at work policies and environmental protection policies; Europe is not, however, legitimated to implement distributive policies in order to achieve social justice; see the discussion in pt I, ch 2, section C 2 and in pt V, ch 21, section III.1.

[21] See, eg, in *The Great Transformation*, n 9 above, esp 12 ff, plus the analysis of A Ebner, 'Marketization: Theoretical Reflections Building on the Perspectives of Polanyi and Habermas' (2015) 27 *Review of Political Economy* 369.

[22] See E Steindorff, *Grenzen der EG-Kompetenzen* (Heidelberg: Verlag Recht und Wirtschaft, 1990), which criticised the lax treatment of the division of competences norms in the Treaty.

[23] See reference in *The Great Transformation*, n 9 above, esp 64 ff on the 'self-protection of society'.

[24] See pt V ch 21 of this volume on the one hand, and pt IV, ch 17 on the other hand.

IV.

Money is the third of Polanyi's fictitious commodities. The expectation and dream that the establishment of economic and monetary union by the 1992 Maastricht Treaty would complete the project of creation of an ordoliberal-flavour European Economic Constitution were nevertheless comprehensively disappointed by the long years of financial and sovereign debt crisis. The contributions in Part V of this volume are instead witness to a dilemma that is a long way away from finding a solution: Economic and Monetary Policy (Title VIII, Maastricht Treaty) is committed to the goal of 'monetary stability'. The European Central Bank (ECB) pursues this goal in concord with the 'Central Banks of the Member States, whose currency is the Euro', in full independence from the political process (Article 282 TFEU). Transposition of this goal into practice has made the ECB Europe's 'overmighty citizen'.[25]

The national economies of the Eurozone have yet to grow together and coalesce into an optimal currency area. The markets with which the ECB deals have no pre-ordained organisational model; meanwhile, the Member States have yet to relinquish their fiscal and economic policy competences. Above all, the Member States have been subject, some more and some less rigidly, to a discipline of austerity politics in the name of monetary and stability and the stability of the financial system as a whole – 'some more and some less', since the political economies of the Member States continue to diverge, and in some cases the differences are only deepening. The conclusion is surely paradoxical: the political autonomy of the Member States is strictly controlled, yet fiscal overseers are afforded a practically unlimited degree of discretion or room for supervisory manoeuvre.[26] We are often given to believe in academic studies that the politics of austerity that is deployed to defend monetary stability has been bequeathed to us by Ordoliberalism. Yet such assertions fail to recognise the anchoring of the ordoliberal tradition in the rule of law and the critique of managerial politics. What is correct is the fact that the founders of this tradition were critics of the pluralism that was characteristic of democracy in the Weimar Republic and sought to discipline it by means of their 'Economic Constitution'. One of the core prescriptions of the leaders of this tradition within the Federal Republic, however, was an additional demand for an economic policy amenable to being bound by legal and constitutional norms.[27] The authoritarian

[25] P Tucker, *Unelected Power: The Quest for Legitimacy in Central Banking and the Regulatory State* (Princeton, NJ–Oxford: Princeton University Press, 2018) 525 ff.

[26] See commentary on the judgments of the CJEU in Case C-370/12 *Pringle*, EU:C:2012:756 and Case C-62/14 *Gauweiler*, EU:C:2015:400 in pt V ch 23; as well as C Joerges and M Weimer, 'A Crisis of Executive Managerialism in the EU: No Alternative?' in G de Búrca, C Kilpatrick and J Scott (eds), *Critical Perspectives on Global Governance, Liber Amicorum David M Trubek* (Oxford: Hart Publishing, 2014) 295.

[27] E-J Mestmäcker, 'Power, Law and Economic Constitution' (1973) 11 *The German Economic Review* 177, 187.

economic management of European crisis politics has parted company from such forms of anchoring within law and the constitution. A further constitutive characteristic of ordoliberal economic policy is respect for the prescription of 'the discovery process of competition'. When the head of the ECB declares that 'the bank will do whatever it takes to preserve the Euro',[28] this suggests that the market process of discovery will be supplanted by its decisions. There is nothing ordoliberal in this construction.

This speaks to a second theme of this volume. The project to establish a transnational Economic Constitution was the most ambitious of those pursued by a policy of integration that sought to free itself from the model of the democratic constitutional state. That too much has been asked of the law within this project is not simply a problem for Ordoliberalism; the integration through law movement has similarly been overwhelmed, albeit in a different manner. Ironically, this paradigm is a victim of the very success of the integration project. The aims and achievement of integration have all too often and ever more explicitly exhausted the famed legitimation model of the 'Community method'. The deepening of integration itself created ever more tasks that had to be addressed in the integration process. The creativity of the architects of the process, their determination in stepping up to overcome these challenges, is remarkable. We need only to recall the New Approach to harmonisation and standards and the development of so-called social regulation.[29] The essay reproduced in chapter 12 on comitology in the European foodstuffs sector reports upon this impressive synthesis of facing functional challenges and preserving normative demands in a functioning transnational framework. The committee structures for foodstuffs analysed in this piece were nevertheless not to become paradigmatic examples within the developing integration process. Instead, the debate was dominated for many years by the so-called 'New Modes of Governance' called into being by the Prodi Commission's White Paper on European governance of 2001.[30] The White Paper responded with an extraordinary degree of innovation to the mismatch between EU competences as laid down in the then European Treaty (EC) on the one hand, and the regulatory challenges posed by deepening integration on the other. The most spectacular amongst the innovations that sought to overcome the bottlenecks in the Community Method was the 'Open Method of Coordination' (OMC) established following a suggestion by the European Council meeting in Lisbon in the year 2000. The OMC was supposed to spring into action in the social policy sphere and to ameliorate the social deficit within the integration project. This fact explains the strong attraction, even affection, felt for the OMC in progressive political circles and European disciplines: goal setting by

[28] Verbatim at www.ecb.europa.eu/press/key/date/2012/html/sp120726.en.html.

[29] See references above in n 18.

[30] European Commission, *European Governance. A White Paper*, COM(2001) 428 final of 25 July 2001.

means of *benchmarks*, *multilateral surveillance* of participants, *peer review* of achieved goals and identification of *best practices* – this matrix was to be understood as *democratic experimentalism* or a *directly deliberative polyarchy*, and was ascribed the power to legitimate governing.[31] The leading lights behind this theorising did not feel the need to reassess their approach in the light of European policies to combat crisis. They continued to misapprehend the enormous power the EU's functional constitution 'behind a dense fog of linguistic obfuscation'[32] and to underestimate the 'lure of technocracy' in European governance.[33]

V.

With this, we return to the diagnoses made and conclusions drawn in Section I above. Financial and sovereign debt crises have not only impacted on economy and society, 'the European social and economic', but have also taken their toll on the law. Any more comprehensive study would only give us an even darker picture of the current state of European integration and its future prospects than that presented here. The manifold crisis scenarios with which Europe and its citizens are confronted share one thing – they all play their part within a complex of uncertainties. It is far from surprising that the social sciences have no new paradigms to offer, or that our political environment is peppered with conspiracy theories, or that constitutional theory has taken refuge in narratives[34] and imaginaries.[35] This mode of dealing with uncertainty is far from irrational. But we must find forms for and fora within which discussions of these visions can take place. This would be true to the motto of the Constitutional Treaty, 'United in Diversity'; this would also be true to the vision of European Constitution founded within the notion of the conflict of laws and its democracy-enhancing potential.

[31] See ch 13 nn 43 and 75.

[32] T Isiksel, *Europe's Functional Constitution* (Oxford: OUP, 2016) 10.

[33] See J Habermas, *The Lure of Technocracy* (Cambridge: Polity, 2015).

[34] D Innerarity et al (eds), *A New Narrative for a New Europe* (London–New York: Rowman & Littlefield, 2018).

[35] M Loughlin, 'The Constitutional Imagination' (2015) 78 *MLR* 1; J Komarek, 'European Constitutional Imaginaries: Utopias, Ideologies and the Other', *University of Copenhagen Faculty of Law Research Paper No 2020-88*, available at https://papers.ssrn.com/sol3/papers.cfm?abstract_id=3477160.

Index

agencies:
comitology, as an alternative to, 177–79, 202–3, 212–13, 216, 316–18, 456, 508–9
European agencies, 316–18, 400, 443
regulatory networks, 312, 318–19, 320
ratings agencies, 273
***Alpine Investments* case,** 93–94
Amsterdam Treaty, 203–4, 225, 417
authoritarian managerialism, 274–75, 389, 391
autonomy:
autonomy of science v authority of experts, 157–58
budgetary autonomy of member states, 38, 40, 376
collaboration v political autonomy, 33, 77–78, 208, 276, 358–59, 370, 433–34, 463, 513–14, 552–53, 579, 587
consumer protection, 67–68
autonomy and liability, 68
interdependence, tensions with, 502–4
respect for national autonomy, 50–51, 90–91, 121, 190–91, 400, 493–94
regulatory autonomy of member states, 28–30, 84, 144, 157, 174, 187–88, 239–40, 462–63, 498

bail-outs:
no bail-out clause, 273, 371, 378–79, 380
rescue package for Greece, 373–75
bank guarantees, 95–96
Basic Law:
constitutional complaints, 374
eternity clause, 125, 222–23, 375–76
Forsthoff, 408–9, 554–55, 557
Forsthoff-Abendroth debate, 227, 409
Ipsen, 407–8, 557
legitimacy of private law, 125
monetary policy, 21
ordo-liberalism, 553–54
Rechtsstaat v Sozialstaat, 573–74
right to bargain collectively, 431
soziale Rechtsstaat, 44, 359, 407–9, 554–55, 575–76
technocratic rationality, 407–9
block exemptions, 89
Böhm, Franz:
economic ordo-liberalism, 118, 251, 286, 328, 409–11, 545
Bonn Republic, *see* **West Germany**
Brussels Convention, 236–37, 435
budgetary autonomy of member states, 376
OMT programme, 38, 40
***Bürgerliches Gesetzbuch* (BGB; German Civil Code),** 87–88, 95, 124
***Bundesverfassungsgericht (BVerfG)* (Federal Constitutional Court):**
constitutional guardianship, 372–73
crisis management, 368–69
economic integration, 24, 40, 44–45, 356–57
constitutional value of economic integration, 20–22
Investitionshilfe judgment, 575
Maastricht judgement, 20–22, 24, 32–33, 325, 334, 337–42, 374, 376
national reserves, 222–23
OMT programme, 44–45
compatibility of budgetary autonomy principle, 40

capitalism:
capitalist market economies, 268–69, 488–89
class conflicts, 573–74
organised capitalism, 544–45, 553
varieties of, 107–8, 112, 120–21, 269–70, 273–74, 391–92, 491–93, 505
agrarian capitalism, 403
high-speed capitalism, 346, 349
laissez-faire, 269, 279, 328–29, 331, 441, 449–50, 452–53, 477, 488–89, 585
***Cassis de Dijon* case,** 26, 105, 139–41, 164, 187, 314, 426–28
conflicts law, 462–63, 468–69
mutual recognition obligation, 201, 202, 313, 335
technical harmonisation and standards, 201, 202, 305
CETA, *see* **EU–Canada Comprehensive Economic and Trade Agreement**

Charter of Fundamental Rights of the European Union, 234–35, 280
choice of law:
implementation of EU law, 17
institutional dimensions, 450–52
cold calling, 93–94
collective action:
ECJ recognition of right to take collective action, 237–41, 265
Albany judgment, 238
Laval judgment, 243–44, 246, 429
Rüffert judgment, 429–30
Viking judgment, 237–41, 246
collective bargaining agreements, 242–43, 358–59, 429–30, 430–31
comitology, 30–31, 130–31, 161–63, 166, 170
agencies as an alternative to, 177–79, 202–3, 212–13, 216, 316–18, 456, 508–9
constructivism, 181–82
decision-making, quality of, 169–70
deliberative supranationalism, 183–84, 190
constitutionalism beyond nation-state, 184–86
economic implications, 187–88
social regulation, 186–87
development, 163–64
food sector, 164–66
economic implications
distributional concerns, 167
European administrative law, development of, 173–74
intergovernmentalist bargaining v centralised rule-making, 174–76
evaluation of, 170–71
institutional conflicts, 171–73
European administrative law, development of, 171–76
legal perspective, 171–76
political science perspective, 176–83
functional supranationalism, 179–81, 190
governance, 200
institutional conflicts, 171–73
intergovernmentalism
agency structures, 177–79
centralised rule-making, relationship with, 174–76
national v supranational interests, 167–68
origins, 163
research findings, 168–69
risk regulation, 166–67, 188–90
community, Europe as, 252–53, 261–62, 411–12
constitutional complacency, 421
Community Charter of the Fundamental Social Rights of Workers, 280
Community method of rule-making, 131, 343–44, 416–17, 588–89
alternatives to, 131, 199–200
comitology, 200
independent agencies, 202–3
mutual recognition, 201–2
OMC, 203–4
technical harmonisation and standards, 202
Union method compared, 368, 369–72
company law, 50, 68, 347, 579
comparative law, 58–60
competition law, 260–61, 296, 300, 302–3, 335
block exemptions, 89
collective action, 238
economic policy, as, 297–98
franchising agreements, 87–88
ordo-liberal concerns, 419–20
resale price maintenance, prohibition of, 88
standardisation bodies, 469–70
supremacy of EU law, 89–90, 296–97
compatibility, relationship with, 90–91
territorial restrictions, 88
uniform applications, 89
vertical restraints, 88–89
complaints:
complaints procedures
appropriateness, 154–55
constitutional complaint (*Verfassungsbeschwerde*), 37, 374, 375
inadmissibility of, 38–39
judicial review, 152, 154–55
politicisation of social regulation, 146, 148
see also individual cases
conflict of laws:
constitutional form, as, 231–34
Europeanisation by, 571–72
methodological nationalism of, 448–52
supranational conflict-of-laws, 204–5, 209–10, 231–34
deliberative supranationalism, 205–9, 232–33
interpretation of governance practices, 208–9
'unity in diversity', 205–8
see also conflicts law

conflicts law, 399–401, 421–22
alternatives to
judicial restraint v judicial activism, 432–34
Sweden (social democratic *Sonderweg*), 432
conflicts law constitutionalism, 109–10
constitutionalising transnational governance, 231–34, 471–73
global administration law, 478–81
para-legal regimes, 481–82
reinterpretation of WTO law, 473–78
democratic legitimacy, 515–16
convergence and reconstruction, 423–24
internal differentiation, 424–25
multi-level governance, 424–25
law and democracy, 422
proceduralising constitutionalism, 425–26
supranationality of, 422–23
diagonal conflicts, *see* diagonal conflicts
ECJ, critical assessment of, 444–45
environmental issues, 434–35
Land Oberösterreich v ČEZ, 435–40
EU law as, 458–59
diagonal constitutionalisation, 468–71
horizontal constitutionalisation, 462–65
multi-level governance, 459–61
methodological nationalism, 459–61
three-dimensional conflicts law, 461–65
vertical constitutionalisation, 465–68
Europe as community compared, 434
Europeanisation by, 571–72
horizontal conflicts, *see* horizontal conflicts
intra-state conflicts law, 456–58
methodological nationalism
private international law, 448–450
para-legal regimes, 468–71, 481–82
political administration, 465–68
post-interventionalism, 441–42
proceduralising constitutionalism, 425–26
second order conflicts law, 478–80
social Europe, 262–65
supranationalism, 204–5, 209–10, 231–34, 422–23
deliberative supranationalism, 205–9, 232–33
interpretation of governance practices, 208–9
'unity in diversity', 205–8
three-dimensional conflicts law, 424–25, 440–41, 442–44, 446–48, 461–65
transnational trade governance, 504–5
EU–Canada CETA, 512–14
Europeanisation, 505–9
globalisation, 509–12
WTO, 473–78
vertical conflicts, *see* vertical conflicts
welfare and social policies and principles, 262–65
WTO law as, 473
genetically modified organisms dispute, 475–77
hormones in livestock dispute, 474–75
regulatory prudence, 477–78
constitutional complaint (*Verfassungsbeschwerde*):
non-treaty changes to primary EU law, 37, 38, 374, 375
OMT controversy, 37, 38
constitutional guardianship, 372–73
ESM Treaty, 375–77
fiscal compact, 375–77
Pringle case, 377–80
rescue package for Greece, 373–75
constitutionalisation process, 352–53
constitutionalism:
comitology
deliberative supranationalism, 184–86
conflicts law constitutionalism, 109–10
deliberative supranationalism
comitology, 184–86
national constitutionalism, relationship with, 79–80
private law constitutionalism, 81–82
economic constitutionalism, 20–22, 272–73, 322–26
authoritarian liberalism, 329–31
constitutionalisation process, 352–53
decoupling, 331–34
erosion of, 325
meaning, 326–29
ordo-liberalism, 331–34
social market economy, 329
see also economic constitution
Europeanisation of private law, 65–66, 82
analysis of European regulation, 82–83
neglecting European law, 67–69
normative national private law, 71–75
public/private distinction, 82–83
supremacy of European economic law, 69–71

horizontal constitutionalism, 234
transnational governance, 471–73
global administration law, 478–81
para-legal regimes, 481–82
reinterpretation of WTO law, 473–78
consumer protection law, 50, 52, 67–68, 76, 139–40, 146–47, 288, 304, 494
door-step selling, 96
GB-Inno-BM case, 92–93
minimum standards, 61
regulatory competition, 313–15
see also scientific expertise
contract law:
cooling-off periods, 95–96
diagonal conflicts, 88–90
fairness, 88–89
franchising agreements, 87–88
national autonomy, 90–91, 300, 508
cooling-off periods, 95–96
crisis law, 43–44
economic cultures, 120
economic governance
new modes and mechanisms, 116–17
economic policy, 115–16
EMU crisis, 114–18, 356–57
'law', concept of, 114–15
Maastricht Treaty, 115
monetary policy, 115
OMT, 117
private law, impact on, 118–19
SGP, 115–16
six-pack regulation, 116

***Dassonville* case,** 139–40
decoupling of social and economic spheres, 222, 226–27, 228–29, 231, 235, 238, 245–46, 331–34, 342
deformalisation of governance, 131
deliberative democratic theory, 77–78, 99
deliberative supranationalism, 78–79
national constitutionalism, relationship with, 79–80
disintegrative implications of Europeanisation of private law, 72–75, 83–84
negative integration of European private law, 85
positive integration of European private law
disintegrative implications of, 72–75, 83–84
private law constitutionalism, 81–82
transnational governance, 80–81
governance structures, 84–85
legal principles, 84–85
deliberative supranationalism, 112, 130, 183–84, 190, 233, 513, 568–70, 571–72
comitology, 183–84
constitutionalism beyond nation-state, 184–86
economic implications, 187–90
social regulation, 186–87
conflict-of-laws, 205–9, 232–33
juridification of governance practices, 208–9
national constitutionalism, relationship with, 78–80, 99
unity in diversity, 205–8
Delors Commission:
Completion of the Internal Market, 26, 61–62, 102, 199, 229–30, 259–60, 310, 313, 334, 335, 419, 465, 585
democratic deficit, 109, 323
EU, 21–22, 63, 130, 205–6, 277, 389–92
international law, 458–59
member states, 206–7, 233, 392–93, 400, 461
democratic legitimacy, 38, 41–42, 120, 131, 184–86, 249–50, 481–82
conflicts law, 421–22
convergence and reconstruction, 423–24
internal differentiation, 424–25
multi-level governance, 424–25
law and democracy, 422
proceduralising constitutionalism, 425–26
supranationality of, 422–23
enumerated powers principle, 274
internal market rationality, conflict with, 116–17
conflicts law constitutionalism, 109–10
economic sociology, 106–8, 324
legal responses, 108–13
mutual responsiveness, 110–13
Rodrik, 491
social deficit, 226
social regulation, 137–38
trade liberalisation, tensions with, 494, 512–14, 516
transnational governance, 516
see also rule of law
denationalised governance, 31–32, 194
national private law, defence of, 71–72
social regulation, 137–38, 159–60

diagonal conflicts, 35, 507–9, 571
contract law, 88–90
EU legitimacy, 424–25, 441, 442–43, 460–61, 468–71
monetary, fiscal and economic policy, 363–64
private law, 88–89, 110, 113, 115
social policy, 222
Viking judgment, 239
direct effect, 78, 102, 236, 294, 326
disintegrative implications of Europeanisation of private law, 72–75, 83–84
doorstep selling, 95–96
Draft Constitutional Treaty, 120, 125, 325, 350–52, 401, 414
duty to remember, 535, 560–61, 579
see also Vergangenheitsschuld (guilt about the past)

Economic and Monetary Union (EMU):
competence conflicts, 34–37
crisis
juridification of monetary union, 362–65
erosion of monetary union, 365–66
reactions and crisis summits, 366–69
community v union, 369–72
constitutional guardianship, 372–81
economic constitutionalism, 20–22, 272–73, 322–26
authoritarian liberalism, 329–31
constitutionalisation process, 352–53
crisis, 354–57, 380–81
community v union, 369–72
compatibility with social issues, 358–59
constitutional guardianship, 372–81
ESM Treaty, 375–77
fiscal compact, 375–77
juridification of monetary union, 362–65
planned economy v market economy, 359–60
Polanyi's economic sociology, 360–61
Pringle case, 377–80
rescue package for Greece, 373–75
Weber's *Nationalstaat*, 357–58, 402–4, 412
decoupling, 331–34
erosion of, 325
meaning, 326–29
ordo-liberalism, 331–34, 335–36
objections to Maastricht, 337–38
social market economy, 329
'economic' as an economic sociology concept, 267–68
economy as polity, 268–69
place of politics, 269
capitalism and market economies, 269–70
ideational and cultural dimensions, 270–71, 324
legal scholarship, 285–86
economic freedoms, 50, 97, 285–86, 291–92, 333, 355–56, 410, 427–28, 556
autonomy of member states, 440, 462, 586
denationalised governance structures, 179–60
economic regulation, balancing, 92–93, 227–28
free movement of goods, 93
labour protection, balancing, 7–8, 222–23, 235–36, 245–46
Laval judgment, 241–44, 430–31
Viking judgment, 236–41, 264
social policies, tensions with, 222–23, 245–46, 490–91
supremacy of, 69–71, 433–34, 439, 586
supranationalism and, 79–80, 103, 185–86
economic integration, 584–86
BVerfG's criticisms, 20
constitutional value of economic integration, 20–22
Europeanisation, 24–25
denationalised governance, 31–32
rationalisation processes, 30–31
single market programme, 25–30
regulative functions of economic law, 23
intervention, 24
see also economic constitutionalism
economic policy:
diagonal conflicts, 363–64
governance, 35
TFEU, 35, 115–16, 272, 364
economic rationality, 60–61, 227–28, 409–11
economic constitution, 331–34, 335–36
objections to Maastricht, 337–38
institutionalised economic rationality, 250–51, 259–61
integration through law
de facto alliance, 103–4
see also ordo-liberalism
embedded liberalism, 256–58, 359, 414–16, 487, 504
Ruggie, 101, 221, 387, 489–90, 493–94
emergency powers, *see* **politics of emergency powers**

environmental protections, 434–35
Land Oberösterreich v ČEZ, 435–40
equivalent effect principle, 139–40
eternity clause, 125, 222–23, 375–76
EU–Canada Comprehensive Economic and Trade Agreement (CETA), 488, 495–96
investor-state dispute settlement, 500–2
regulatory cooperation and governance, 496–500, 512–14
right to regulate, 496–500
Eucken, Walter:
economic ordo-liberalism, 251, 269–70, 328, 409–11, 545
Europe as community, 252–53, 261–62, 411–12
constitutional complacency, 421
European Central Bank (ECB):
Gauweiler case, 39–43
OMT programme
competence of ECB, 39–43
European Constitution referendums:
France (2005), 405, 576
Ireland (2008), 405
Netherlands (2005), 405
European corporatism, 315–16
regulatory networks, 319–20
European Court of Justice (ECJ):
conflicts law mandate, 444–45
technical questions/scientific expertise, 132–34, 138
Community commitments in law-making, 150–56
Community competencies, 145–49
regulatory competencies, relationship with, 138–45
see also individual cases
European Financial Stability Facility (EFSF), 38, 40, 367, 380
European Pillar of Social Rights, 280–81
European social model, 7–8, 101, 221–24, 353, 362, 390–91, 574–75
European Stability Mechanism (ESM), 38, 40–43, 367–68, 373, 375–77
Pringle case, 377–81
European System of Central Banks (ESCB), 41–42
Europeanisation as an alternative to conflicts law, 505–9, 571–72, 576, 578–79
Europeanisation of economic law, 32–33
denationalised governance, 31–32
European corporatism, 315–16
regulative functions, 22–25
regulatory patterns, 24–25
single market programme, 25–31
Europeanisation of private law, 61–64, 100–2
constitutionalist dimensions, 65–66, 82
analysis of European regulation, 82–83
neglecting European law, 67–69
normative national private law, 71–75
public/private distinction, 82–83
supremacy of European economic law, 69–71
disintegrative implications of, 72–75, 83–84
instrumentalisation, 104
integration origins, 49–50
integration through law
'one size fits all' approach, 102–4
internal market rationality, 104–6
transdisciplinary elements, 91–92
judicial standards, 95–98
rights of market citizens, 92–93
soft regulation, 93–94
transnational governance structures, 91
Europeanisation of social regulation, 129, 135–36
comitology, *see* comitology
cooperation, 136
integration through de-legalisation, 193–94, 211–16
supranational conflict-of-laws, 204–10
mutual recognition, 137
standardisation organisations, 137
'ever-closer union', 100, 114–15, 266, 285, 325, 334, 355
excessive deficit procedure, 339–41, 367–68

Federal Constitutional Court, *see* ***Bundesverfassungsgericht***
financial crisis:
crisis law, 114–18
economic cultures, 120
private law, impact on, 118–19
fiscal compact, 370–71, 373, 375–77, 391
food standards and regulation, 7, 130, 175, 211–14, 307, 499
agencies, 212–14
comitology system, 161–62, 164–66, 200, 211–12, 400, 513, 588
genetically modified organisms, 475–76
hormones in livestock farming, 145–47, 472, 474–75
precautionary principle, 475–76
regulatory prudence, 477, 510

risk regulation, 166–67
scientific expertise, 140–43
Scientific Committee for Foodstuffs, 179–80
vitamins, 148
formative period of integration, 11–12, 248–49
Europe as community, 252–53
European Social Model, 227–29, 266
institutionalised economic rationality, 250–53
private law, 100–1
technocratic administration, 249–50
Forsthoff, Ernst:
technocratic administration, 407–9, 546, 548, 551, 554–56, 556–57
forum shopping, 236–37
franchising agreements, 87–88
free movement of capital, 25, 289
free movement of goods, 25, 26, 92–93, 108, 135–36, 240–41, 305, 314, 462, 472
free movement of labour, 25, 222–23
see also Laval judgment; *Viking* judgment
freedom of services, 25, 94, 239, 242, 313, 429
functional integration, 15–16, 22, 292–94, 295, 331, 557

Gauweiler and others v Deutscher Bundestag:
OMT programme, 37–45
***GB-INNO-BM* case,** 92–93
General Agreement on Tariffs and Trade (GATT), 489–90, 493–94
genetically modified organisms dispute:
WTO law, 475–77, 477–78
German legal culture and thought, 534–48
European integration process, during, 552–53
democracy v integration, 556–57
ordo-liberalism v functionalism, 556–58
ordo-liberalism, 553–54
organised capitalism, 554–56
technocracy, 556
'first' legal culture, 525
integration process, during, 552–58
post-war return to, 529–33
Großraum theory, 538–39, 551–52
administration, 548–49
controversies, 540–43
core ideas, 539–40
Europe as a *Großraum*, 534
Großraum economy, 544–47
technicity, 547–48
Ipsen, 530–33
post-war legal culture
1968 unrest, 526–28
theoretical basis of private law, 529–30
third *Reich*, 524–26
global administrative law, 478–80, 509–12
governance, 194–96
economic governance
crisis law, 116–17
deformalisation of governance, 131
deliberative democratic theory, 77–78, 99
deliberative supranationalism, 78–80
national constitutionalism, 79–80
denationalised governance, 31–32
national private law, defence of, 71–72
social regulation, 137–38, 159–60
'European level of governance', 197–98, 199–200
comitology, 177–208
independent agencies, 202–3
mutual recognition principle, 201–2
open method of coordination, 203–4
private transnationalism, 202
technical harmonisation and standards, 202
integration through de-legalisation, 193–94, 211–16
supranational conflict-of-laws, 204–10
multi-level governance, 98–99
deliberative democratic theory, 77–80, 99
deliberative supranationalism, 78–80
national constitutionalism, 79–80
integration through law, 75–77
social regulation, 156–59
proceduralisation of law, 198
social regulation, 156
authority of experts, 157–58
practical difficulties, 158–59
transnational governance, 80–81
governance structures, 84–85
legal principles, 84–85
***Großraum* theory,** 538–39, 551–52
administration, 548–49
controversies, 540–43
core ideas, 539–40
Großraum economy, 544–47
Europe as a *Großraum*, 534
technicity, 547–48

Habermas, Jürgen:
'deserve recognition' formula, 42, 195, 198, 388, 464, 470, 479, 509

economic constitution in crisis, 43, 387–89
historical context of law, 523, 561–62
theory of law, 105–6, 123–24, 195, 198, 381–82, 387–89, 422, 427, 455–56, 506
constitutional patriotism, 577–78
external effects principle, 277–78
proceduralisation of law, 571
social functions of law, 105–6, 123–24, 195, 234, 246, 247, 454
Streeck, controversies with, 123–24, 270, 353

Hall, Peter A.:
capitalism, varieties of, 107, 269, 490, 491–93

harmonisation policy, 24, 26, 164, 287–88, 303–5, 308–9, 315
internal market policy
social regulation, 307–8
standardisation programme, 306–7

history, *see* **law and history, interaction between; *Vergangenheitsschuld* (guilt about the past)**

horizontal conflicts, 35, 90, 115, 443, 460–61
Land Oberösterreich v ČEZ, 435–37
WTO law, 507–9, 510

horizontal constitutionalism, 46, 234, 462–65

horizontal cooperation:
supremacy of EU law, 28

hormones in livestock farming, 145–47, 472, 474–75
precautionary principle, 475–76
regulatory prudence, 477, 510

identity and citizenship:
law and history, interaction between, 573, 576–79

independent agencies, 202–3, 317

institutionalised economic rationality, 229–30, 250–52, 259–61, 325–26, 335–36, 363, 419–20

integration in practice, 296, 302–3, 310–12
competition policy, 296
economic policy, as, 297–99
integration as de-regulation, 299–301
jurisdiction and supremacy, 296–97
harmonisation policy, 303–5, 308–9
internal market policy, 307–8
social regulation, 307–8
standardisation programme, 306–7

integration theories, 290–91, 295, 302, 309–10, 318–19, 406
analytical integration theory, 77–78
decision-making processes, 294–95
Europe as community, 252–53, 411–12
institutionalised economic rationality, 250–52
legal structures, 294–95
neoliberal economic order (*Ordnungspolitik*), 291–92
non-functionalism, 17–18
ordo-liberalism, 409–11
special purpose associations of functional integration, communities as, 17–18, 292–94, 295, 557
technocratic administration, 249–50, 407–9

integration through law, 11–12, 13–16, 50, 228, 355
crisis law, replacement with, 114–15, 361–62
end of, 25–26
free movement, 221
free trade, 202, 221
law in political science, 16
EU law, implementation of, 17
neo-functionalism, 17–18
rational choice theory, 18–20
multi-level governance, 75–77
neoliberal economic order (*Ordnungspolitik*), 356, 588
new conflicts of law, 209–10
'one size fits all', 102–4, 109, 113
Polanyi, 360–62, 584–85
trade barriers, removal of, 202
Weiler, 584

internal market policies:
erosion of, 337
intensity of, 61–62, 104
conflicts and tensions, 105–6
internal market rationality, 104–6
interpretation of, 335–36
mutual responsiveness, 110–13
single market programme, 25–27
see also integration through law; internal market rationality

internal market rationality:
democratic legitimacy, conflict with
conflicts law constitutionalism, 109–10
economic sociology, 106–8
legal responses, 108–13
mutual responsiveness, 110–13
social policy, 229–31

international relations theory, 15–16, 18–20, 194, 221–22, 446, 449, 515, 568–69
investor-state dispute settlement, 500–2
Ipsen, Hans Peter, 530–33
special purpose associations of functional integration, 17–18, 292–94, 295, 557
technocratic administration, 22, 30, 211, 249–50, 302, 318, 386–67, 407–9, 548–51

judicial restraint, 38, 98, 154–55, 432–33
judicial review, 40, 133, 152–53, 154–55, 156, 158, 367

labour protection:
economic freedoms, balancing, 7–8, 222–23, 235–36, 245–46
Laval judgment, 241–44, 430–31
Viking judgment, 236–41, 264
***Laval* judgment,** 241–46, 429
dissenting opinions, 430–31
law and history, interaction between, 561–65
identity and citizenship, 576–79
social Europe
draft Constitutional Treaty, in, 574–76
French referendum, 576
Rechtstaat v Sozialstaat, 573–74
law as governance, 454–55
law as regulation, 441, 452–54
legal certainty, 589
judicial standards, 95
regulatory competencies and scientific expertise, 143–44, 157
legal conceptualisations of the foundational period, 248–49
accomplishments
turning away from European conflicts, 253–54
community, Europe as, 252–53
institutionalised economic rationality, 250–51
legal historical evaluation of, 256–58
short-comings
social poverty, 254–56
technocratic administration, 249–50
legal culture and thought, *see* **German legal culture and though**
legitimacy of EU decision-making processes:
Europeanisation of private law, 63–64
Europeanisation of social regulation, 137–38

Lisbon Treaty, 225, 234–35, 241, 258, 261, 280, 361–62, 409–10, 417–18, 431, 531
Bundesverfassungsgericht, 444
Ireland referendum, 405
no bail-out clause, 273
Protocol 27, 261, 420

Maastricht Treaty, 5
Bundesverfassungsgericht, 20–22, 24, 32–33, 325, 334, 337–42, 374, 376
"ever-closer union", 100, 114–15, 266, 285, 325, 334, 355
treaty design, 271–72
economic constitutionalism, 272–73
public authority interventions, 273–74
majority voting, 25–26, 139, 145, 168, 189, 261, 263, 405, 421, 468, 585
market integration, 7, 24, 31–33
comitology, 164–66, 200
consumer protection, 91–92
EEC Treaty, 70, 291–92
European corporatism, 319–20
Europeanisation of private law, 61–64, 91–92, 98–99
defencing normative private law, 71–75
neglecting EU law, 67–69
rights of market citizens, 92–93
standard-setting, 95–98
supervision of regulatory policies, 93–94
supremacy of EU law, 69–71
legislative activism, 27
private law, tensions with, 49–51, 55–57, 120–22
Europeanisation of private law, 61–64
regulatory policy, tensions with
regulatory autonomy of member states, 28–30
regulatory competition, 319
regulatory networks, 320
social regulation and new harmonisation policies, 303–9
mega-regional trade agreements, 487–88
autonomy
interdependence, tensions with, 502–4
conflicts law
autonomy v interdependence, 502–4
investor-state dispute settlement, 500–2
regulatory governance, 496–500
conflicts-law constitutionalism, 504–5
Europeanisation, 505–9
globalisation, 509–12

EU–Canada Comprehensive Economic and Trade Agreement, 488, 495–96
investor-state dispute settlement, 500–2
regulatory cooperation and governance, 496–500, 512–14
right to regulate, 496–500
move towards, 495–96, 514
investor-state dispute settlement, 500–2
regulatory governance, 496–500
Transatlantic Trade and Investment Partnership, 488, 495–96
investor-state dispute settlement, 500–2
regulatory cooperation and governance, 496–500
***Meroni* doctrine,** 40, 172–73
minimum standards of justice, 96, 242–43
monetary policy, 34–35
exclusive competence of EU, 35–36
supranationalisation of, 21–22
see also European Monetary Union; Outright Monetary Transaction programme
multi-level governance, 98–99
deliberative democratic theory, 77–78, 99
deliberative supranationalism, 78–80
national constitutionalism, 79–80
integration through law, 75–77
social regulation, 156
autonomy of science v authority of experts, 157–58
practical difficulties, 158–59
mutual recognition principle, 137, 201–2, 313, 335
mutual responsiveness:
social legitimacy in internal market, 110–11
external effects, 111–12
social deficit, 112–13

nation state:
private law, relationship with, 52–55
private law's self-justifications
common European legal culture, 52–53
natural law, 52–53, 57
rational law, 52–53
scientific nature of private law systems, 52–53, 62–63
supra-national law, relationship with, 53, 62–64
German private law, 53
anti-formalism commitment to social justice, 54
legal formalism, 54
Nazi legacy, 54–55
nation statehood:
abandonment of, 55–56, 405–7
community, Europe as, 411–12
historical indeterminacy, 414–16
omission of social dimension, 412–14
ordo-liberalism, 409–11
technocratic administration, 407–9
Weber's value criterion, 56–57, 412
European integration
economic dependencies, 55–56
economic policies, 55–56
Europeanisation of private law, 55–57
sovereignty, erosion of, 55
Weber, 357–58, 402–4
value criterion of economic policy, 56–57, 412
national private law, defence of, 71–72
cultural diversity, 74–75
disintegration objection, 72–75
legitimacy and validity of European private law, 72–73
national reserves:
eternity clause, 222–23
'nature of things', 152
negative integration, 3–4, 85, 113, 135–37, 222, 225, 235, 246, 362
neoclassical economic theory, 16
neofunctionalism, 16, 17–18
neoliberalism, 16, 70–71, 90, 302–3, 410, 501–2, 576
neoliberal economic order (*Ordnungspolitik*), 70, 90, 251–52, 291–92, 295, 351, 356, 363, 411
no-bailout clause, 273, 371, 378–79, 380

'one size fits all' approach, 102–4, 109–10, 113, 116–17, 274, 277, 504
democratic deficit of EU, 389–92
democratic deficit of member states, 392–93
open method of coordination (OMC), 203–4, 345–46
democratic experimentalism, 346–49
origins and development, 342–44
output legitimacy, 344–45
reflexive law, 349–50
soft governance, 349–50
ordo-liberalism, 60–61, 227–28, 409–11
economic constitution, 331–34, 335–36
objections to Maastricht, 337–38
ordo-liberal concerns, 419–20

integration through law
de facto alliance, 103–4
see also economic rationality
Outright Monetary Transaction (OMT) **programme,** 36–37
compatibility with EU law, 38
competence of ECB, 39–43
no alternative, 44–45
power of German courts to adjudicate, 38–39
social injustice, 43–44
Verfassungsbeschwerde (constitutional complaint), 37

para-legal regimes, 468–71, 481–82
Polanyi's economic sociology, 360–61, 483–86, 586
social embeddedness, 488–89
politicisation of markets, 217–18
politics of emergency powers, 6
authoritarian managerialism, 274–75
financial crisis, 118, 354–57, 365–66, 384–85
populism, rise of, 8, 223–24, 278–79, 389, 416, 573–74, 581
post-formalism, impact of, 50
posted workers:
Laval judgment, 242–44, 429, 431, 432
law reform, 244, 281
pre-emption doctrine, 102, 110, 147–48
price stability, 21–22, 39, 41, 42, 280, 338, 341, 354, 363–65, 366, 375–76, 380
***Pringle v Ireland*,** 37, 377–80
private international law, *see* **conflict of laws; conflicts law**
private law, 100–2
denationalisation of scholarship, 57–60
comparative law, 58–60
private international law, 57–58
Europeanisation of, 61–64
see also Europeanisation of private law
German private law, 53
anti-formalism commitment to social justice, 54
legal formalism, 54
Nazi legacy, 54–55
integration through law, *see* integration through law
multi-level governance, 75–77
nation state law, relationship with, 52–55
national private law, defence of, 71–72
cultural diversity, 74–75
disintegration objection, 72–75
legitimacy and validity of European private law, 72–73
self-justifications
common European legal culture, 52–53
natural law, 52–53, 57
rational law, 52–53
scientific nature of private law systems, 52–53, 62–63
supra-national law, relationship with, 53
see also consumer protection law
'private-law society' (***Privatrechtsgesellschaft*):**
Europeanisation of, 60–61
private transnationalism, 98, 202, 215–16, 469
privatisation of regulation, 443–44
product liability law, 50, 61, 469–70
prohibition of monetary financing:
OMT programme's compatibility with, 38, 40
***Pronuptia* case,** 87–88
proportionality principle, 140, 143–44, 146, 150, 153–54, 157, 201–2, 208, 236, 238–39, 424, 430–31, 510
proprietary medical products, 148

rational choice theory, 18–20, 177
rationalisation processes, 98, 151–52, 404
economic rationalisation, 252–53, 411–12, 466
comitology, 30–31
horizontal cooperation, 30
internal market rationality, 104–6
technical bureaucratic regime, 30
reasonableness principle, 96
regulatory reasonableness, 135, 149, 153–54, 160, 494
regulatory autonomy of member states, 28–30, 144, 174, 187–88, 239–40, 462–63
conflict with ECB, 34–35
scientific uncertainties, 157
soft regulation, 93–94
regulatory competencies and scientific expertise of ECJ, 138–39
ECJ's supremacy over national legislatures
obligation to consider scientific evidence, 140–42
supervision of member states, 139–40, 144–45
regulatory competition, 313–15
regulatory networks, 319
regulatory failures, 335, 453–4
'regulatory politics', 287–88
approaches to, 289–91
legal stability, conditions for, 289

market freedoms, 289
origins, 289
resale price maintenance, prohibition of, 88
respect for national autonomy, 50–51, 399–400, 493–94
right to strike:
Laval judgment, 241–46
Viking judgment, 236–41, 245–46
risk assessments, 188–90, 495–96
hormones in livestock, 474
legitimacy of, 159–60
politicisation of, 149
scientific uncertainties, 134, 142, 147, 158–59
social acceptability of risks, 166–67, 177
SPS measures, 476–77
Rodrik, Dani:
social policies and economic freedoms, tensions between, 490–91
Rome Treaty, 60, 100–1, 285, 552
social deficit, 221, 256–57, 280–81, 414–15, 416
***Rüffert* judgment,** 429–30
dissenting opinions, 430–31
Ruggie, John G.:
embedded liberalism, 101, 221, 387, 489–90, 493–94
rule of law, 35–36, 41–42, 274–75
conflicts law approach, 441–43, 455, 477
economic constitution, 323–25, 348–49, 380–81, 385–87, 389–90
ESM, 377
law-bound and law-legitimated rule (*Herrschaft*), 195, 548
private law and integration, 116–17
social deficit, 226
social regulation, 193–94, 408–9, 529, 574–76
Rechtsstaat v Sozialstaat, 573–74
technicity and, 555
see also democratic legitimacy

Sanitary and Phytosanitary Measures (SPS) Agreement, 472–79, 494, 511
Scharpf, Fritz, 222, 228–29, 255, 275, 324, 333, 359, 366, 413, 417, 463–64, 492
Schlink, Bernhard, 521–22, 559–60
see also Vergangenheitsschuld (guilt about the past)
Schmitt, Carl, 527
economic constitution in crisis, 382–87
Großraum theory, 537–39, 551–52, 554
administration, 548–51
controversies, 540–43
core ideas, 539–40
Europe as a *Großraum*, 534
Großraum economy, 544–47
technicity, 547–48, 555
scientific expertise, 132–34
hormones in livestock farming, 145–47
integration of experts into decision-making, 155–56
inter-institutional conflicts, 149
reasonableness of regulatory policies, 149
role of science, 149
legal systems, 134–35
proprietary medical products, 148
regulatory decision-making, 134–35
regulatory competencies, relationship to, 138–39
consideration of scientific evidence by national legislatures, 140–42
constitutive importance of supervision of member states, 144–45
legal certainty, 143–44
scientific uncertainties, 142–43
supervision of member states, 139–40, 144–45
social regulation by ECJ, 132–34, 138
Community commitments in law-making, 150–56
Community competencies, 145–49
regulatory competencies, relationship with, 138–45
scientific nature of private law systems, 52–53, 62–63
services of general interest, 50, 241
Single European Act, 26, 61–62, 102, 104, 139, 163, 248, 405, 468–69, 585
single market programme, 25–27
horizontal cooperation, 28
market integration
legislative activism, 27
regulatory autonomy of member states, 28–30
primacy of EU law, 28
six-pack, 116, 275, 367, 385
social deficit of integration, 225–26, 226–27, 323–24, 413–14, 416–17
democratic legitimacy, 226
identity and citizenship, 576–79
mutual responsiveness, 112–13
Rome Treaty, 221, 256–57, 280–81, 414–15, 416

Vergangenheitsschuld (guilt about the past), 236, 521–22, 559–61
draft Constitutional Treaty, in, 574–76
French referendum, 576
Rechtstaat v Sozialstaat, 573–74
social embeddedness theory, 229, 231, 334, 391, 394–95
Polanyi, 112–13, 123–24, 483, 488–89, 586
Ruggie, 489–90, 494
see also embedded liberalism
Streeck, 124
social dimensions of private law, 50–51
fragility of, 416–17
identity and citizenship, 576–79
omission of, 413–14
Vergangenheitsschuld (guilt about the past)
draft Constitutional Treaty, in, 574–76
French referendum, 576
Rechtstaat v Sozialstaat, 573–74
social market economy, 234–35, 325, 329
see also Lisbon Treaty
social policies, 221–22, 225–26, 234–35
conflicts-of-law, 231–34
economic freedoms, tensions with, 222–23, 245–46
Rodrik, 490–91
exclusion from integrationalist objectives, 226–27
Laval judgment, 241–46
social market economy, 234–35, 325
social rights, recognition of, 234–35
Viking judgment, 236–41, 245–46
social regulation, 129
comitology, *see* comitology
Community commitments in law-making, 150
consideration of scientific evidence, 150
precautionary principle, 150
pre-emptive effects, 150
rationalisation processes, 150–51
Community competencies, 145
politicisation of social regulation, 145–47
protectionism, 145–47
secondary law, 147–49
ECJ's scientific expertise, 132–34, 138
Community commitments in law-making, 150–56
Community competencies, 145–49
regulatory competencies, relationship with, 138–45
Europeanisation, 135–36
cooperation, 136
mutual recognition, 137
standardisation organisations, 137
hormones in livestock farming, 145–47
integration through de-legalisation, 193–94, 211–16
supranational conflict-of-laws, 204–10
inter-institutional conflicts, 149
reasonableness of regulatory policies, 149
role of science, 149
judicial review
differentiating approach, 152–53
multi-level governance, 156
autonomy of science v authority of experts, 157–58
practical difficulties, 158–59
proceduralisation, 154–55
proportionality principle, 153–54
proprietary medical products, 148
reasonableness principle, 153–54
regulatory competencies and scientific expertise, 138–39
consideration of scientific evidence by national legislatures, 140–42
constitutive importance of supervision of member states, 144–45
legal certainty, 143–44
scientific uncertainties, 142–43
supervision of member states, 139–40, 144–45
see also consumer protection law; environmental protection; food safety; labour regulation
social sciences and legal systems, 15
Soskice, David:
capitalism, varieties of, 107, 269, 492–93
special purpose associations of functional integration, communities as, 17–18, 292–94, 295, 557
Stability and Growth Pact (SGP), 35, 114, 115–16, 118, 272, 339–41
state aid, 335
Sreeck, Wolfgang:
Debate with Habermas, 123–24, 353
Varieties of Capitalism, 107, 492
substitution of national private law by European law:
consumer protection, 67–68
autonomy and liability, 68
private ordering, 68
self-responsibility v paternalism, 68

institutional hesitancy, 67
social function, erosion of, 68–69
supervision of member states:
para-legal regimes, 468–71
regulatory competencies and scientific expertise, 139–40, 144–45
supranationalism theory:
Weiler, 227–28
supremacy of EU law, 102
competition law, 89–90, 296–97
supremacy v compatibility, 90–91
economic freedoms, 69–71, 433–34, 439, 586
economic law, 69–71
horizontal cooperation, 28

Technical Barriers to Trade (TBT) Agreement, 472, 479, 494, 511
technical harmonisation and standards, 137, 202, 215, 305, 315, 585
technical questions, *see* **scientific expertise**
technocratic governance, 217–18, 249–50, 258–59, 407–9, 418–19, 513
territorial restrictions:
competition law, 88
Transatlantic Trade and Investment Partnership (TTIP), 488, 495–96
investor-state dispute settlement, 500–2
regulatory cooperation and governance, 496–500
treaty freedoms, 96–97
free movement of capital, 25, 289
free movement of goods, 25, 26, 92–93, 108, 135–36, 240–41, 305, 314, 462, 472
free movement of labour, 25, 222–23
see also Laval judgment; *Viking* judgment
freedom of services, 25, 94, 239, 242, 313, 429
individual v organisational freedoms, 98
Treaty on European Union (TEU):
co-decision procedure, 172
democracy and rule of law, 370
precautionary principle, 475
simplified revision procedure, 367, 380
social market economy, 250
Treaty on Stability, Coordination and Governance (TSCG), 367–68, 385
Treaty on the Functioning of the EU (TFEU):
ECB independence, 587
economic policy, 35, 115–16, 272, 364
environmental protection, 457–58
ESM, 377–80
financial assistance, 365–66, 367
Greece, 374
free movement of goods, 462
labour rights, 257, 415
posted workers, 264
monetary policy, 35, 39, 41, 115–16, 364
OMT programme, 38, 40
precautionary principle, 475
social protection, 431
stability mechanism, 365–66, 367
two-pack, 275, 367–68, 385

uniform application:
competition law, 89
reasonableness principle, 96
'united in diversity', 120–21, 125, 266–67, 275–76, 278–79, 401–2, 565–66
collaboration v political autonomy, 276
conflict of laws methodology, 571–72
constitutionalisation, 566–67
deliberative supranationalism, 568–71
democratic deficit of EU, 389–92
democratic deficit of member states, 392–93
external effects principle, 277–78
globalisation paradox, 276
inter-democracy, 277

***Verfassungsbeschwerde* (constitutional complaint):**
non-treaty changes to primary EU law, 37, 38, 374, 375
OMT controversy, 37, 38
vertical conflicts, 460, 507–9, 571
vertical restraints:
competition law, 88–89, 508
***Viking* judgment,** 236–41, 245–46, 428–29
dissenting opinions, 430–31

Weiler, Joseph H.H.:
constitutional complacency, 421
Europe as community, 411–12, 421
integration through law, 584
supranationalism theory, 227–28
waste imports, 150–51
Weber, Max:
inaugural lecture, 402–4
Nationalstaat, 357–58, 402–4, 412
value criterion, 56–57, 412
***White Paper on Completion of the Internal Market*,** 26, 61–62, 102, 199, 229–30, 259–60, 310, 313, 334, 335, 419, 465, 585
***White Paper on Governance*,** 131, 193, 199, 217, 588

World Trade Organization, 446, 471–73
reinterpretation of WTO law as conflicts law, 473
genetically modified organisms dispute, 475–77
hormones in livestock, 474–75
regulatory prudence, 477–78

Zweigert, Konrad:
comparative law, 58

www.ingramcontent.com/pod-product-compliance
Ingram Content Group UK Ltd.
Pitfield, Milton Keynes, MK11 3LW, UK
UKHW020224290926
15470UKWH00001B/368

9 781509 926954